THE

MAGIC STAFF

Andrew Jackson Davis

THE

MAGIC STAFF;

AN

AUTOBIOGRAPHY

OF

ANDREW JACKSON DAVIS.

"Though I walk through the valley of the shadow of death, I will fear no evil; for thou art with me; thy rod and THY STAFF, they comfort me."—HEBREW POET.

BOSTON:

COLBY & RICH,

BANNER OF LIGHT PUBLISHING HOUSE,

No. 9 BOSWORTH STREET.

This facsimile reprint published by
SNU PUBLICATIONS

First published in 1857 by Colby & Rich, Boston, U.S.A.

This facsimile reprint published by
SNU PUBLICATIONS
Redwoods
Stansted Hall
Stansted Mountfitchet
Essex   CM24 8UD

ISBN 0 902036 13 0

Reprinted in England by Booksprint

CONTENTS.

6 CONTENTS.

CONTENTS. 7

8 CONTENTS.

INITIAL CONSIDERATIONS.

BY THE AUTHOR'S COMPANION

IN commencing an Introductory Section to this AUTOBIOGRA-
I HY, it occurs to me that several inquiries, relative to the object
sought, will arise in the minds of many who may peruse the present volume. Some of these inquiries I will briefly state, in order
to assist the reader, by my succeeding responses, into the pleasurable path of satisfactory biographical research :—

1. *Why should this Autobiography be indited, instead of such
philosophical matter as has hitherto claimed the Author's attention ?*

It is in the attractive garb of narration that many most important truths have been promulgated throughout society. But we
have no need of precedent. The Author of this work has been
induced to place it before the world by the conscientious conviction that in no way could the psychological principles which it
embodies be so effectually impressed on the thoughtful spirit, as
in connection with and illustrated by the incidents of a life. . The
philosophical volumes, already among the things that are, give
detached fragments of Mr. DAVIS's extraordinary experience;
but still, the skeptical "How?" comes ever up from the restless
soul of the invincible logician. As an instance of this, I will refer

to a communication from James Barnaby, of Ohio, to one of the Boston papers, in which he says of A. J. DAVIS:—

"*None* BUT HIMSELF *can ever know that he has not learned from books, or other known sources,* the scientific facts and technical terms found in his writings, as any one of good intellect could learn all this without the knowledge of others.

"Here, then, is the evil. To admit these extraordinary claims is to admit Mr. Davis to be in possession of means of obtaining knowledge of the laws of Nature and of man vastly superior to those of others. The evil effects of such admissions are so numerous and apparent as not to need pointing out. Mental and spiritual tyranny have always sustained themselves by similar pretensions. The particular lack of discrimination to which I referred in the beginning of this article is shown in the fact that ' The Liberator,' and other reformatory journals, have not pointed out more clearly these dangers, and discouraged the course of things that has tended to produce them.

"It will be said, however, that if these claims in behalf of the superior powers of Mr. Davis are true, we need not fear any evil consequences as a result of receiving them as such. But are they true? Some of them, you seem to think, are established beyond dispute. Of course, I shall not attempt to prove by testimony that Mr. Davis does not possess this faculty of ' interior sight,' or the other wonderful faculties attributed to him. Neither can I admit these claims. The things to be established are opposed to the consciousness, reason, judgment, and experience, of myself and of mankind generally: hence, the testimony which sustains them must be stronger than their own inherent impossibility ; and, to my mind, no testimony has been or can be adduced that is not, at least, as liable to be false as the claims are to be true."

The above extract is but a fair specimen of the abounding skepticism which obtains among various classes, relative to the life and writings of Mr. Davis, and the grand subjective laws which underlie his development. Hence, the demand seems imperative that, for the advantage and advancement of both **physics and meta-**physics, this work should be sent forth on the current of the world's literature.

2. *Why does Mr. Davis write his own history — and that, too, while so young?*

> " We live in deeds, not years ; in thoughts, not breaths ;
> In feelings, not in figures on a dial.
> We should count time by heart-throbs.   He most lives
> Who thinks most — feels the noblest — acts the best."

In this light, the life of Mr. Davis has been long.   During a half-score of years, he vibrated from one extreme in external life to the utmost verge of the other ; while, interiorly, he swept through a vast, rich field of doubt-dispelling investigation.   By this process he has been educated.   Since his powers were awakened by the aid of human magnetism, he has been to a School of which Nature is the teacher ; and, with " attentive and believing faculties," has toiled for the priceless dower of Wisdom.   In every sense he has been a tireless student, differing from the ordinary methods only by going directly to the *essence* of things ; thus gleaning from the very heart of the Universe, so to speak, that knowledge which others get, at second-hand, from books.   Hence, his education is now just as available, at all hours, as that of any other well-trained intellect ; and it is only when some new and intricate subject presents itself for investigation, that he needs to abstract his mind and enter the still more illuminated " Superior State."   It is plain to be seen, then, that his present *ordinary state*, in which he writes this Autobiography, is vastly " superior" to that former dependent condition in which he dictated " Nature's Divine Revelations."

That Mr. Davis should write his own history seems advisable from the circumstances of the case.   His experience belongs to the world, inasmuch as it reveals many subtile and most important phases in the constitution of mind ; and also points to a time when soul will be less under the sway of sense, and less dependent on external appliances for expansion and progression.   At the same time, he alone can relate accurately the events of his own life, and give a faithful transcript of what would otherwise be for ever obscured by misapprehension and consequent misrepresentation. Besides, many a contemporary actor in this life-drama can now be appealed to, as a living presence, for evidence concerning these simple and straightforward *memoranda*. Nor will such an appeal be deemed at all difficult, when it is known that the whole primary psychological development of "The Poughkeepsie Seer" took place within ninety miles of the city of New York! Indeed, many testimonials, from those well acquainted with his early history, might be added to those already published;* but I will select only the following, which was addressed to me by a well-known citizen :—

DEAR MADAM: This brief notice of my friend, your honored husband, is most respectfully dedicated to your kind care and keeping, as a testimonial of regard for merited worth.

In 1843, Professor Grimes, a lecturer on Phrenology and Mesmerism, came to Poughkeepsie, New York, and raised considerable interest among the people upon those subjects. His lectures and experiments were largely attended by all classes, and almost everybody began to mesmerize each other. Among others, Mr. William Levingston, a tailor, succeeded pretty well as a manipulator, and many submitted to his experiments.

A. J. Davis was then a youth of about sixteen years, living next door to where I was employed, with Ira Armstrong, as an apprentice to the shoemaking business. Said Davis, with other boys, called on Mr. Levingston to be magnetized, as it was then termed. He proved susceptible to its influence, was put at once into the clairvoyant state, and began to see through his forehead, without the use of his natural eyes; which phenomenon caused much surprise to all who saw or heard of it, and many were anxious to learn about the strange manifestation. I became much interested in the subject, and sought for all the information possible for me to get. I talked with Samuel Davis, Levingston Armstrong, &c., and learned what they were able to give concern

* See Introduction to "Nature's Divine Revelations."

ing the origin, disposition, education, and character, of Jackson. 1 became satisfied that he was poor in purse, honest, amiable, and honorable. His education at that time consisted of reading, writing, and ciphering, and only rudimental in these. I found, by conversing with him, that he had read but very little, and did not possess any general information. He was a light-hearted, well-disposed youth. In answer as to what books he had read, he said, " I have only read a book called 'The Three Spaniards,'" which I suppose was a romantic tale, as I have not seen it. I was fully satisfied that his schooling had been very limited. He had no time, then, nor for many years after, to apply himself to books, and, from all that I can learn, has not done so to this day. His knowledge, now displayed, has been mainly gained in the clairvoyant state.

His newly-developed powers took a medical turn ; and, after a few weeks of experimenting, to satisfy the curiosity of himself and his friends, he commenced practising as a clairvoyant physician, Levingston being his magnetizer. Armstrong gave him up to follow his new calling. He continued in and about Poughkeepsie for a year or two, taking a tour out occasionally, and again returning to see his old patients and friends. His descriptions of various ailments, both mental and physical, as well as his prescriptions for cure, were truly wonderful and astonishing to all who knew him. Educated doctors would admit that his anatomical descriptions were correct, and that his remedies were curious and philosophical, displaying a knowledge of things of which he knew nothing when in his normal condition. At that time he had no power to remember what transpired in his clairvoyant state, while in his natural condition ; but he has since attained that power, as well as that of self-magnetization. He does not therefore now need a manipulator. His experiences are still quite as astonishing to himself as to others, as he informed me not long since.

While living in Poughkeepsie with Mr. Levingston, and continuing to follow the healing art, Jackson received an impression, in his interior state, that he would be the instrument of communicating a work to the world — "Nature's Divine Revelations" — which work was dictated in word and sentiment, and written down from his lips, by William Fishbough. This volume contained philosophy and sentiments not in the mind of Fishbough, *as he himself informed me*, but contrary to his cherished views. Having read the work, I can decidedly pronounce it next to a miracle for Davis to perform at the time it was published.

Ira Armstrong told me that he often had impressions that Jackson would attain some distinguished position in the world, but did not dream it would take the direction it has. He was a practical utilitarian of the Dr. Franklin school, and never doubted the success of any one who had a trade, and a disposition to follow it with patience and economy. He was a man of candor and philanthropy. His present address is Huntington, Indiana.

I have taken an interest in clairvoyance, as developed in the career of Jackson; and, being personally acquainted with him, I have traced his progressive steps, and read most of his works up to the present time. Having doubts upon the immortality of the soul, I hoped to be convinced through that source, and have often conversed with him upon the subject. He has ever told me, since he became developed to a communion with spirits, that to himself it was knowledge — not faith; for, in his interior state, he both saw and conversed with the disembodied. I have no doubt of his sincerity, nor of its reality to him; but, as I am low in the organ of marvellousness, and constitutionally an honest skeptic, I do not, up to this time, feel clear upon the immortal existence of our race. But I am still investigating all alleged sources of information, with the view of finding the " pearl of great price."

Let this be as it may, however, I can truly say that I consider A. J. Davis as one of the marvels of the age, and his " Harmonial Philosophy" as one of the purest and most reasonable systems of religion extant. It professes to teach the *gospel*, as inspired by " Father-God and Mother-Nature," and is fully worthy of such an origin. Designed, in the " good time coming," of which it is the prompter and forerunner, to establish harmony, justice, and happiness in the earth, and fit our race for blissful abodes in any future life that may await them, I bid it " God speed," and recommend it and its author to the favorable consideration of the world.

Hoping that I may one day realize the truth of his sublime anticipations and exalted theories, I hereby subscribe myself the candid friend and rational admirer of the life and writings of Andrew Jackson Davis.

JAMES FLAGLER.

156 BROADWAY NEW YORK, *February* 17, 1856.

3. *Why does Mr. Davis, in writing this history, portray events so minutely, and especially those of his juvenile days?*

Though many of these events are related in humorous style, and with a particularity that may seem trivial; still, it should be remembered that nothing is unimportant which tends to build up the immortal structure of Soul; and no language is irrelevant that helps to picture the consecutive stages of its advancement. That I am not alone in this estimate, may be seen by the following suggestive quotation from a paragraph in the New Orleans Picayune:—

"The world is made up of trifles. The grand movements of great events, and the changes of empires, are founded in causes, very generally, which would be pronounced trifles by the world. Yes, 'trifles light as air' have led to some of the most important discoveries we have. The fall of an apple gave Newton the clue to gravitation; the rising up of the lid of a tea-kettle gave us our railroads, steamboats, ocean-steamers, and a thousand other things —not to speak of the press—that, combined, put the world centuries ahead in the mysteries of the universe and the purposes of God. To the observation of a flower dimly pictured on a stone, we owe the philosophical researches in chemistry and light which ultimately gave us the daguerreotype. . . . . .

"The foundation of the Roman empire was a cunning trick in an individual combat, or duel. American liberty and thirty-one glorious states arose from a strong cup of tea made by the Bostonians in 1775. A little piece of magnetized steel led to the discovery of a New World. The erection of a sawmill in California changed the currency of the world. The crossing of a little stream of water speedily subverted the liberties of Rome, and gave the name of Brutus immortality. From a little acorn the grand American forests have sprung:—

> ' A pebble in the streamlet scant
> Has changed the course of many a river;
> A dew'*:op* on the baby plant
> Has warped the giant oak for ever!'

It is impossible to enumerate, especially in a newspaper article, the almost numberless 'trifles' that have produced numberless great events, and made numberless radical changes in the history and destiny of the world. Suffice it to say that 'trifles' are not to be scoffed at. The world may learn great, and true, and valuable lessons from these same 'trifles.' The fable of the lion who was released from his prison by a little mouse, was written by a great man. Upon a less foundation than this there have been erected deathless poetry, wonderful tragedies, and many noble novels. Hold nothing in contempt: nothing contemptible ever came from the hands of the Almighty. The worlds which the microscope has revealed to us in the drop of water, are as wonderful and mysterious as the bright and beautiful worlds brought to our eyes by the telescope. The loathsome caterpillar, which we long to crush beneath our feet, will one day be a beautiful creature, with rainbows for wings. The little pool of dirty water into which we have stepped will be woven into a bright and beautifully-embroidered veil, by the miraculous sun, for the face of the queen who trails her robe of light among the countless stars !"

4. *How can the Author state with certainty the circumstances of his earliest life?*

His father, Samuel Davis, and his eldest sister, Eliza P. Williams, are still living, and have a vivid remembrance of the varied domestic scenes through which their rugged pathway has led. Hence, they have freely furnished particulars concerning all the events which transpired previous to the hour when their juvenile relative awaked into conscious memory.

5. *Why does he give the exact language of his vernal associates?*

Should our Author round out and grammaticize those chaotic passages of conversation, which show his own early mental defects no less than those of his illiterate companions, it would be a departure from that *strict fidelity to truth* which characterizes this work, as well as every previous action of his life. As it is, these faithfully-reported colloquies show how far he was removed from all advantages, such as refined and educated parents, brothers, sisters, and playmates, are likely to bring to the opening faculties of childhood. Nor was the misfortune of such a beginning counteracted by any subsequent polish of the schools.

But, to the true child of Nature, time and circumstance are not. He has his own awakening, in the still regions of Thought—over which there is the flutter of no wing—through which there is the rushing of no tide. On and on, over the swift pathway of suns, is then his flight, till his feet press the centre of Universes, and all around him stretches off the surging sea of Life!

6. *What is the moral bearing of this Autobiography?*

To the young, its mission is evidently of great importance. While it holds their attention by the charm of anecdote, it will teach them lessons of virtue, which any number of moral harangues, however finished and elaborate, might fail to impress on their untaught faculties. The child-nature will inevitably be encouraged, by perusing these pages, to avoid duplicity, anger, dishonesty, profanity, and intemperance; and to cultivate gentleness, kindness, hopefulness, purity, and integrity.

To parents and guardians, it will be as a living mentor, aiding them to comprehend how tenderly the young mind should be treated, how carefully and judiciously trained, in order that seeds of virtue, harmony, and progression, may be early sown. In this regard, the humble pair who gave immortal being to the writer of these memoirs might be referred to as worthy of imitation by many of far greater pretensions and intelligence. Untutored in all that pertains to polite society, poverty-haunted and contemned, they still watched carefully the daily conduct of their son, and kindly, though promptly and thoroughly, corrected every act that seemed to lean toward *moral delinquency.*

To all classes, the story of such a life will be a well-spring of hope. The experiences of the "Harmonial Philosopher," thus far, are sufficient in themselves to prove the blessed truth of im mortality, and the possibility of intercommunion with the happy dwellers in our radiant Spirit-Home. Nor is this all. The diverse situations, the temptations, the trials, the discouragements, and the triumphs, that have marked his past career, are a study, the pursuit of which will awaken courage and inspire aspiration in the souls of the most despised and desponding. That he has reached a state of beautiful existence, where his affections are warm and beaming, his intellect clear and comprehensive, his soul pure, serene, devotional, and steadfast, and his heart ever filled with a "joy unspeakable and full of glory," by the dewy freshness of Wisdom's precious gifts — that he has reached this glorious eminence, in spite of organizational faults and discouraging conditions — is a fact in human development full of promise, even to the lowliest and loneliest child of God!

MARY F. DAVIS.

NEW YORK, *April*, 1857.

THE

MAGIC STAFF.

CHAPTER I.

THE USE OF AUTOBIOGRAPHY.

" Tell me not in mournful numbers,
' Life is but an empty dream !'
For the soul is dead that slumbers,
And things are not what they seem."

IT seems to me that nothing less than the Divine Intelligence
can comprehend the infinite possibilities and the eternal destinies
that slumber in the forthcoming germ of a human being. Nothing can be of more importance, to such a being, than Existence ;
all else, as time ultimately demonstrates, is secondary and subser-
vient. The beginning and the end of all human endeavor is, TO
EXIST. The arts, and sciences, and machinations, by which men
subsist, are as transient as the passing clouds — as ephemeral as
the shadows of earth-born dreams.

And yet, without these transient arts and time-serving inven-
tions, human *existence* would be impossible. Indeed, the foundation of existence is laid in the art of subsistence, and no two relations were ever more inseparable. Nay, more, without the myriad

items which on review we find strung on the rosary of the flowing years; without the manifold imperceptible and unrecordable attentions bestowed by mother and father, by brother and sister, by the friendly neighbor, and " the stranger within thy gates" — without these, there could be no preservation of body, no awakening of love, no increase of knowledge, no satisfaction with life, no — EXISTENCE.

Hence it is, that, despite themselves, and apparently in direct violation of broader aspirations, mankind devour with an instinctive relish whatever is supposed to be truly autobiographical. If a person seriously report himself in some periodical, even though an utter stranger, the world will receive the news with an appetite insatiable. The realm of subsistence is the realm of biography. For example, every adult reads with grateful pleasure of the discovery of America; but when the private story of the *Discoverer* is told, then behold how all classes, and all ages, of both sexes, imbibe the biographical revealments !

The history of the world is interesting; that of a person is fascinating. There is always *something* in a stranger's experience which no mortal can divulge save the stranger himself. The illiterate confessions of a human being about to be hanged, are unspeakably more thrilling and impressive if told by himself than by another, even if that other be his spiritual adviser, and an adept in the art of narration. This instinct for autobiography is implanted in the nature of all men; but, when left to seek gratification unguided by Wisdom, it rapidly degenerates into deformity, and exhibits imperfections the most repulsive. Pernicious talebearing and extemporaneous gossip disturb an otherwise peaceful community. The sanctuary of private life is ruthlessly entered by a gang of headlong biographical investigators; and the individual character is tarred and feathered, if not lynched, by an infuriated mob of reputable newspaper-scribblers or unscrupulous pamphleteers. All this is deplored, both in private and in public, by true men and noble women.

Again : it may and does sometimes happen that the principal events of individual experience are wrapped in mystery and uncertainty, or may be distorted by the flitting shadows of appearances and uncontradicted reports. Now, should a person thus misinterpreted pass along without taking his own life, why, then he is liable to be unexpectedly assaulted, and perhaps murdered, by some supposed friend or unknown foe. Hence it follows, as by a logical necessity, that if individual life has in it developments of any practical value to mankind — if it contains any fresh lessons of encouragement and instruction, and is at the same time involved in falsehood or mystery — then it most manifestly becomes a work of justice and mercy for the said person not to retire at death *intestate*, but to bequeath to all whom it may concern a straightforward and conscientious autobiography — a plain rendering of the voyage of life — a confession of the inner Heart.

Man is born near the base of a hill — in a valley full of shadows ; but, once out of the cradle, he begins to climb. He forthwith struggles and pants, impelled by the hidden force of destiny, to attain the summit. With an eye upon the sunny future, but knowing not the pathway, he tugs, and frets, and tumbles, at every turn. The mists of the valley may envelop him, the dreary waste of poverty and disease may stretch away between the hill and him, his path may pass even through the solitudes of the dismal swamp ; yet, undaunted, and led by unseen guardians, he pushes boldly forward, and gains triumphantly the height of his first ambition : when, lo ! he finds himself in a valley still, or — which is the same thing, but more suggestive — at the base of an eminence yet higher and more irresistibly attractive.

I make these symbolic affirmations, because the journey of my own life has been from the common level of birth to the summit of a commanding hill. The first position reached, I saw a vale before me ; and, beyond this, a yet higher hill for my feet to climb In due time and trial, this greater eminence was also safely reached , and, strange to relate, I found myself at the foot of still another elevation, which was yet more mountainous and more difficult of ascent. Yet my way was plainly pointed out and shown me; and so, amid impediments apparently insurmountable, I pursued the rugged mission.

The broad magnificence of the scene, from the fertile summit of this majestic mountain, far transcended every previous picture or experience. For a while I dwelt contented on this gorgeous mountain-home — from which I could see the errors, and wanderings, and mists, and tempests, and significance, of every vale below, through which I had passed. It was like standing on a solid rock by the seaside, away from turmoil and danger, beholding ships as they rise and fall and struggle with the storm. For thus it was that, far down the hills, and everywhere in the vales below, I could see my fellow-men, too proud to be taught, jumping from gorge to cliff, and marring their personal welfare at every step, vainly striving to reach the Highest and the Best by methods impossible to prove advantageous.

At length, however, I was moved to turn my face in the direction of my pilgrimage; and, lo! contrary to my expectations, I saw that the high elevation, on which I had made my home, was but the basis of still another mountain, more stupendous and distant than any over which I had found my way. There was a work to do on this higher place; and, as I will hereafter show, that work was accomplished.

Between this last elevation and another mountain, which is yet scarcely visible in the extreme distance before me, is an intervening vale. In this valley I am now temporarily residing, just as I have spent weeks and months in other valleys behind me; and my occupation, while thus tarrying, is to write this Autobiography. This will be the first public writing, except the ordinary work of answering correspondents, that I ever did while sojourning in a vale. But this is not to be wondered at, because this valley is higher up — is more elevated and commanding — than the highest peak of the second mountain; thus giving me normal abilities better than I then possessed, even after a thorough magnetization. To relate what hannened to me in the many and various regions which I have from time to time explored, both while in the valleys and on the mountains, and to give the *rationale* of the providential precision with which my feet have been made to step from one mental position to another, will be the sole end and purpose of this volume. Be patient, then, dear reader, and judge not till thou hast travelled with me through the successive chapters of my life.

CHAPTER II.

THE LOCAL HABITATION.

IN vain might the inquisitive antiquarian read through Humboldt's scientific observations of natural scenery; in vain study the travels and discoveries of the world-renowned Peter Parley; in vain dream through the poetic descriptions of Bayard Taylor, the cosmopolite, whose wandering footsteps on oriental lands are sought by hundreds who choose travelling through books to encountering perils by sea and land; in vain peruse any history—to become acquainted with the existence of a certain isolated, unpainted, unfinished dwelling, in which was enacted the first scene in the life-drama which is about to be delineated. You need not marvel at this omission on the part of ubiquitous historians, because there was nothing about this human habitation worthy of the least remark, save the conspicuous humility of its structure and immediate surroundings. It was built about the year 1824, in Blooming-Grove, Orange county, in the state of New York; and was owned in part by a half-weaver and half-shoemaker, but wholly honest man, who, in common with his wife, had amassed considerable of that property, both real and personal, which is most easily acquired by the married poor, under the specific titles of Eliza, Jane, Sylvanus, Amanda, and Julia Ann.

The husband had attained the summit of forty-five years. Poverty had left its traces upon him. All the days of his youth were replete with self-supporting endeavors. As soon as the sun of

BIRTH PLACE OF A. J. DAVIS

S.W. OTT N.Y.

boyhood had arisen upon him, he was bound out as an apprentice to learn the art of weaving with the hand-loom : and while the web of his private life was being woven by external circumstances, he acquired the rare accomplishment, without books or school-teachers, of weaving linen fabrics, cotton and woollen cloths, and rag-carpetings. In subsequent years, on discovering that he could not support a family by the loom alone, he set himself to learn the trade of repairing dilapidated boots and shoes—an art which, aided by his native talent to invent and persevere, soon expanded into larger dimensions. In a word, he graduated from the primary condition of " cobbler" to the more productive and reputable position of journeyman shoemaker. As he divided his time between the loom and the bench, with an occasional variation in the way of farming for a few days now and then, we shall mark him as the half-weaver and half-shoemaker of this history.

The wife, upon whose form the weary weight of thirty-three years had left its mark, was equally destitute of education, her only dowry being a frail body, animated by a spirit which ever appeared like a stranger in a strange land. Her inward nature was simple and childlike. The heavy chains of inevitable poverty, which her husband could and did wear with only ordinary fretting, on the contrary had the effect, combined with his intemperance, to cut deep channels in the very substance of her soul. She had many excellent endowments, however, which, in moments of great trial, shone beautifully forth. Of these traits we shall have occasion to speak in subsequent pages. In regard to their children it may be remarked, *en passant*, that the imperishable parts of little Jane and Amanda had flown from the shadows of Earth. There was a melancholy vacancy in the family group, and there were two more elevations in the churchyard, to remind the bereft that they had been.

The country in all that region, at the time of which we write, was just becoming obedient to the spirit of civilization. Standing in the door of the poor man's home, or looking from either window of blistered glass, a rough and rugged landscape would rest upon the vision. And yet industrious farmers had cut and cleared away the manifold hinderances to their progress; and instead of unproductive stones and fields of useless undergrowth, you might behold in many directions apple-orchards, and well-fenced tracts of land, covered with a fair quality of grass and grains. The work of refinement and extermination, however, was still unfin-ished. Besides other evidences of a semi-civilization in that re-gion which could be mentioned, were an abundance of venomous reptiles known as "pilot-snakes," or copperheads, whose sociable propensities became at times a source of no little annoyance. We are told by an eye-witness that these loathsome creatures would crawl against the basement-lights and look fearlessly in, sometimes entering the humble dwelling, as if to welcome the impoverished family to that part of the world, with a special desire to exchange hospitalities.

It was near the close of a sultry day, August 11, 1826, when the half-weaver and half-shoemaker received the intelligence that another item of property had been added to his estate. The at-tendant physician, after due examination of the title, &c., declared it to be free and unencumbered.

"You don't say so!" exclaimed the exultant cordwainer, who had just returned, with unsteady step, from the nearest vil-lage.

"Yes I do, sir," said the doctor; "and what is more, your baby, sir, is a fine-looking boy."

"A boy, eh?" soliloquized the enriched man — "that's good! — that's just what I wanted — that's the best luck yet!" Over-come by the congratulations of nurse and doctor, and with his head swimming in a river of parental delight, he seated himself to collect his scattered thoughts. But rest and sobriety were impossible. In fact, if the sad truth must be told, the effect of the intoxicating draught was already upon his brain. Thus con-ditioned, he went reeling and dancing to the sick-couch, to take a survey of the plump little parcel of poor man's riches ; which, as already said, had been so recently added to his previous good fortune. After feasting his eyes to his heart's content, and satisfying himself fully that it was not all a dream, he bethought to ask the prostrate woman concerning her situation.

CHAPTER III.

THE NAME.

"Many have died in their misery,
And left their thought untold."

THE breathing of mountain-verdure and the sweet fragrance
of harvest-fields, added to the music that floated in from the purling streamlet below the sloping eminence on which the house was
built, had the effect to revive the mother from the sinking weakness consequent upon her accouchment. But the exhalations of
a whiskey-breath, which now passed like a pestilential miasm over
her, summoned a return of those despairing moods with which for
years she had been only too familiar.

"I do wish you would keep sober," she sadly said, "and get
things in the house to do with."

"Oh, never you fret and worry about me; I guess I can keep
the family out of the county-house a while longer," returned the
still jolly father.

The presence of the nurse and a neighbor served only to increase the mother's mortification. She looked up into his face as
he bent over her, and, with one of those expressions which can
only arise from fear, grief, and despondency, she said:—

"Now, do try to keep steady! Don't stand here. Go away —
away!"

The nurse now offered her some scanty refreshment; and, from
sheer exhaustion, she closed her large, dark eyes in slumber.

By this time the children, who for some to them unaccountable reason had been sent to visit a neighbor, hearing that the doctor had left a baby for mother, came rushing in like so many young colts. Eliza, the eldest, who possessed the not uncommon virtue (which treads hard upon the heels of a vice) of being particularly amiable only when everything went to please her, demanded an immediate sight of the new-comer. The cheerful nurse held the baby up for exhibition. But it was a boy, and for that reason received a provoked slap from Eliza, who in a moment was ready to quarrel with the doctor and everybody else.

" Don't let me see you do that again !" said the awakened mother, as she pressed the darling yet closer to her loving heart; " what do you mean by that — say ?"

" Oh, pshaw !" exclaimed the wilful daughter ; " why didn't the plaguy old doctor bring mother a little gal? I won't have a boy 'bout me ! — can't do nothin' with such a young 'un. I want a baby-gal to dress up and play with — so, there !" Saying this, she walked sulkily out, leaving the less excitable and less disappointed brother and sister to look, and think, and indulge their childish curiosity, on the new things that had come to pass.

At this time, as is usual for months previous to presidential elections in the United States, there was more or less discussion concerning the merits, and especially the *demerits*, of the antagonistic candidates. There was a certain major-general, well known for the decisive victory he gained over the English at New Orleans in 1815, which terminated the war. This notoriety was still more extended, with which his popularity kept even pace, in consequence of the invincibility of his will to quell the Creek tribe of Indians. The gallantry of his exploits, and the success which ever crowned his efforts on the battle-field, secured the gratitude and admiration of every true democratic inhabitant of America: in part expression of which, the party bearing that name brought him forward as a candidate for the highest honor possible to bestow in a country so republican.

" Hillo, there ! I say, you, hillo ! What's turned up ? How's the woman by this time ? And how's the baby ? Come, let's know !"

Uncle Thomas Maffet, from whom this abrupt salutation pro‹ ceeded, at first acted as if determined to remain seated in his wagon, with which he had just arrived from the village, freighted with a plough and other implements used in the art of agriculture. Friendship and cordial good-humor generally, beamed forth from his countenance, giving even a stranger to believe that any such determination was to him quite impossible. And so it proved. Not waiting to be invited, out he jumped, and, laughing with that heartiness which is so natural to nutritive temperaments, he entered the poor man's habitation.

" Well, neighbor Davis, when did the thing happen ?" asked the farmer, as he bent over the rough-hewn cradle of domestic manufacture, and turned off the coverlet that concealed the baby from his view.

" Four days ago," replied the cordwainer. " What d'ye think of the little lapstone ?"

" Four days old, eh ?" and Uncle Maffet tried to get the infant into his arms. But those days were without temperance lecturers. Farmers considered it next to impossible to work at mowing and reaping, during the hottest days, without some sort of stimulating beverage to keep body and soul decently together. So thought the present visitor, at least, as his trembling hand and unsteady eye too clearly testified.

" Take the child," said the sick woman, addressing the nurse " I'm afraid Uncle Thomas will let him fall."

The baby was returned to the rustic cradle, and the still unreconciled Eliza — which disposition she contrived to make manifest by sundry emphatic twitches and jerks of the rocker — was told to keep the child from crying. Meantime, the two men struck up a political talk, and went through the usual agreements and contradictions regarding the merits and demerits of the popular candidates

"Who d'you vote for, next election, neighbor Davis?" inquired the farmer.

"I'm Old Hickory, up to the hub!" replied the cordwainer, who prided himself on being right up and down on matters of opinion.

"Ditto," returned the good-natured Thomas. "Now, I'll tell you what, neighbor—if you want to please me to-day, you'll let me name that 'are boy of yourn."

"Oh, I don't care who names him—what d'you say, mother?" said the father, addressing his wife, who was still extremely debilitated.

"Don't let the child fall, or get hurt—that's the most I care about," she replied; which was taken as equivalent to a verbal consent.

"Enough said!" exclaimed the laughing Thomas; "now let's kiss the nurse!"

On hearing this, the excitable and irreconcilable Eliza sprang to her feet and ran like a wild fox into the field, to tell the children who were at play. The whole thing was done in the twinkling of an eye.

"Uncle Thomas Maffet is come, and is goin' to name the baby. Come quick!"

Whereupon, Julia Ann tried to get hold of Sylvanus's hand, and Sylvanus grasped after Eliza's, but missed it, and tumbled headlong into the entangling grass; then Eliza, who had by this time almost reached the house, catching the sound of the cry for help, went bounding back to jerk Sylvanus along; when, as bad luck would have it, Julia Ann discovered that she had lost her sun-bonnet, and couldn't go without it; whereupon Eliza, whose nominal business it was to take care of the younger members, flew round here and there through the grass in wildest haste, and, not finding the article, had the additional misfortune to lose her patience; then, sans bonnet and sans patience, back they scampered under a full head of explosive curiosity, which as a motive

force is next to steam; each running and tumbling against the
other alternately, and by divers indescribable mistakes impeding
one another's progress, until the juvenile trio stood side by side,
nearly out of breath, looking at the farmer as he contrived to balance himself sufficiently to give the mother confidence in his
ability to hold the baby as safely as anybody else.

With his usual mental agility, the half-weaver and half-shoemaker mounted the high summit of parental excitement, and
shared in the momentary harmony of blended interests, to which
the maternal bosom was far from being insensible. A large glass
of brandy was placed in the farmer's left hand, while on the right
arm rested the infant candidate. The faithful old nurse stood
very near, however, to catch the baby, should it fall from the intoxicated embrace. This amiable assistant was not a little relieved when informed that "kissing the nurse" meant drinking
the brandy, and nothing more.

"Attention, company!" said the inebriated Thomas. "The
first thing I want to know is, whether you'll call this 'ere boy just
what I say." Affirmative exclamations leaped from every mouth.
" Well, then," he continued, "remember this : I'm a-goin' to vote
for ' Old Hickory,' the hero of New Orleans — the greatest man
a-livin' in the world ; and I want this 'ere boy to bear that 'are
great man's name — ANDREW JACKSON! And now, neighbor
Davis, keep in mind my words — I ain't so boozy as you seem to
think. I know what I'm a-sayin' — and (hic) I say (hic) that
are great man's name (hic) hasn't reached further than will the
influence of this 'ere son of yourn ! He'll grow up a young (hic)
' Hickory' — mind that ; and you'll never be sorry (hic) that he
was born !"

Nothing could be more evident than that the good Uncle Thomas
had waxed more patriotic, and more pathetic, and more prophetic,
than he at first intended, or supposed himself capable of ; and
instead of the laughing mouth and dizzy eye, there fell upon him
the spell of a serious and religious temper, which seemed to sober

his brain, and open a new place in his heart? It was a beautiful scene! No magic art ever wrought a change so quick and thorough. A breathless hush, like that of death, spread through the room — which stillness nothing broke, save the heavings of the farmer's breast. He seemed to blend his destiny with that of the whole world; and, while sobbing like the infant in his arms, he invoked "the blessing of Heaven" to rest upon them all. Uncle Maffet, almost entirely sobered, then hurriedly departed homeward; and, although an apparently healthy man, he was, but a few days subsequently, placed beneath the soil. The baby's sad mother believed, for years afterward, that the jovial neighbor was made solemn by a providential vision of his own funeral.

CHAPTER IV.

THE VENDUE AND DEPARTURE.

NONE but the poor can fully understand the multitudinous perplexities which crowd themselves into their struggles for daily subsistence.   The catalogue of items that stand between the family and
what is called "respectable circumstances," are well nigh beyond
computation.   Discouragements stare the impoverished household
directly in the face, at nearly every turn in the path of life.

So, at least, thought the man whose unpainted and incomplete
homestead was not yet paid for, and whose various other exertions to establish himself had met with many unbearable defeats.
For two whole years after the birth of the last-named child, the
half-weaver and half-shoemaker, with now and then the terrible
exception of intemperance, steadily combated the host of petty
obstacles which ever arise in the poor man's presence ; but without success.   The self-conscious, non-adaptation of his wife to
the warfare consequent upon the rearing of a family, combined
with the frequent lack of patient and indulgent affection, which
her nature silently craved as the foundation-element of her every
thought and effort, had the effect to generate painful misunder-
standings, and discouragements innumerable.   On such occasions
the excitable husband would do the principal amount of talking
and fault-finding, while the wife, naturally deficient in the usual
ease of expression wherewith to contend and explain, would sink
right down into a state of depression the most piteous to behold.

During these two years there happened nothing of any note to the individual child whose biography we are now recording: but to another member of the family an important change had occurred; the chronology of which is written on a blank leaf, between the Old and New Testaments. There happened a curious incident, in connection with that " change," which we will here digress sufficiently to relate.

The children were out playing upon the hillside, bounding hither and thither with a freedom quite spontaneous, when Sylvanus seemed to be suddenly transfixed with a visual wonder.

" Eliza !" he presently exclaimed, " come quick — d'you see that ?"

" See what ?" she hastily inquired.

" That 'are light yonder !"

" No, you foolish feller, I do n't see nothin' !" returned she.

" Then you 're real blind," said he, somewhat provoked, " can't you see that 'are round white light moving right along over the grass yonder, toward the woods ?"

" No, nor you nuther !" replied Eliza.

Then little Julia Ann tried and strained her bright blue eyes, but all to no purpose ; whereupon Sylvanus, actuated by a medley of motives, in which alarm and disappointment acted the principal parts, ran straight home " to tell mother all about it."

When the mother heard the boy's hasty account of what he had just seen, she affected no interest in it whatever, and with her accustomed quietness of tone, bade him return to his play among the children. And yet, to one familiar with the woman's mental peculiarities, there were certain lines on her countenance which betokened an inward grief. When asked by Eliza, " what ailed her," she sadly replied :—

" Sylvanus will soon leave us."

But her reputation in her husband's mind for being a believer in dreams, and for putting confidence in signs, and omens, and superstitions, caused him to eject an unsympathetic " Poh !" at everything of the kind. The day soon arrived, however, when the skeptical father might have been seen sorrowfully preparing a *coffin*, to hold all that was mortal of his son Sylvanus. Whenever his opinion of this circumstance was subsequently sought, the cordwainer would reply, with ill-suppressed impatience, " Poh, nonsense ; the light hadn't nothing to do with his death !" Notwithstanding, however, this habitual rejection of whatever appeared extraordinary ; notwithstanding even the common vice of intemperance to which he was addicted, it should be here noticed, that this man's disposition was neither profane, uncharitable, nor irreligious. On the contrary, he seemed ever ready to condemn penuriousness and dishonesty, as well as every expression of religious disbelief.

To return : believing it to be impossible to support the family, and also to pay for the humble dwelling in which this history begins, the desponding cordwainer packed up his " kit" (or tools) and gave public notice that he meant to migrate to some other section of the Empire state. No man ever possessed a stronger or more resolute propensity, when once he fairly got the notion, to sacrifice at auction every household god, and try his luck elsewhere. And, perhaps, there never was a feminine nature more fond of a fixed and settled " home," than that of his companion ; and, perhaps, also, no person's disposition was ever more perplexed and injured by the frequent recurrence of such violent breaking up of every local affection, than hers.

" Don't be in a hurry, father," she imploringly exclaimed one day — as her husband avowed his resolution to make " a clean sweep" of the pig, hens, house, and furniture — " don't be so impatient to be off. We've had trouble enough already. A rolling stone, you know, never gathers no moss."

" My mind's made up," he sternly and quickly replied, " and I'm determined to be away from this."

" Next season may be better for us," continued she encouragingly ; " it's hard to pack up, you know, and it's so painful to move away among utter strangers."

" I won't be in debt," returned the honest half-weaver and half-shoemaker, " I 'll be bound if I 'll stay here — hanging by the eye lids, as I am — no! not I — I 'll sell and quit."

The certainty of having a vendue, and of selling everything at a sacrifice, broke with a melancholy force upon the domesticated nature of the wife. It was another wound to her inhabitative heart; and opened afresh many sores in the inner memory which had not yet healed up. " Change, change, nothing but change," she sighed — " Oh, when shall we rest?" And she went on with a weary step, doing up the housework.

But the disheartened cordwainer, having resolved, as he said, " to pull up stakes and leave," continued to defend himself and fortify his positions on the question of an auction and departure. Taking his wife's words to signify a proposition to postpone proceedings, the bare intimation of which, to his temperament, was a quick cause of impatience and irritation — he began combating the evils of procrastination, in the following definite style :—

" If there's anything I hate, it's this dilly-dallying along, and this putting things off. What's the use? Nothing ventured nothing had. When I see anything to do, I want *to do it* — and not be for ever doing nothing. There hain't work enough for me on the bench, nor at the loom nuther; and the farm-work is good only a short spell right in haying and harvest — so there's no let up — I 'm determined to go! You need n't fret about it. We 'll sell out — make a clean breast of everything — pay all we can, and seek our fortune among strangers."

There was a quick, keen, resolute twinkle in his brown eyes, as he spoke; which was too well known to the worn and fragile woman; for her only reply was a long-drawn, sad sigh, as if her heart was loaded with a full consciousness of the impending trial.

Now in regard to procrastination, there is surely much to be thought. Half the minor troubles of the domestic world may be referred, with justice, to this cause alone. The indolent habit of postponing the work of to-day until to-morrow, is next to a vice, if, indeed, it be not, strictly speaking, *a crime* against the soul's happiness and prosperity. Persons who gracefully put off, from day to day, the performance of duties which belong to *the time* when they are first seen to be duties, are usually considered as being afflicted with only an amiable human weakness. But the truth is, that no weakness ever came nearer merging into a heinous moral deformity, and producing a vast multitude of misfortunes, than this same procrastination! Hundreds of families suffer domestic annoyances, of which — but for this indolent habit of postponement — they would never have the least practical knowledge. A quick and reliable sense of justice is seldom found in that mind which shirks the trial of the hour, and pleads the necessity of procrastination.

But the difficulty in this instance was, an ungovernable impatience under the restraints and drawbacks of poverty. If the conscientious shoemaker had been endowed, like his wife, with a spirit less fond of domestic adventure, and more of a disposition to work right straight through a mountain of difficulties, like some men, there would have been greater unity and more social satisfaction in the isolated habitation. There is, without doubt, much wisdom in procrastination, under circumstances when the thing to be done properly belongs to some future day; but only the truly wise can safely and successfully practise it. Idleness is ever more to be feared and shunned than energy and action. The wife possessed a spirit of meekness and quiet, unqualified by any really positive element of character; which frequently caused her to submit and be defeated even by an ordinary trial; while the husband, ever ambitious to be " up and doing," and with no submissive will, would urge her into positions the most distressing, because foreign to her organization. Destitute of the commonest education, and, therefore, without a charitable solution of human weaknesses, each sadly misunderstood and painfully afflicted the other — she, by feeling and saying disheartening things; he, by disregarding her most tender and predominating sensibilities.

We stop to notice these peculiarities, in order that the reasonable reader may the better comprehend the parentage and social
condition of the subject of this biography. It may be added in
this place, that this radical or temperamental incompatibility —
the barrier to conjugal peace and unity which Nature had unmistakably erected between husband and wife — came out with life-
like manifestations in the mental characteristics of Eliza, and, in
fact, with more or less distinctness, in each of the subsequent
offspring. Hence, in this case, as in every other of like nature,
each child was born with certain hereditary disadvantages of
body and disposition ; which, to modify and control, required a
labor of many years ; besides making the summit of " personal
harmony" of no easy attainment, even after its outlines became
visible in the far distance, and it was recognised as being within
the reach of human effort.

" Well, I can't help it then !" the mother at length resumed,
with a complaining sigh, " we'll all go to rack and ruin ; and
where we'll go next the mercy only knows. When will the
vendue be ?"

The half-weaver and half-shoemaker turned his eyes from the
" stone on his lap and the strap on his knee," and replied in a tone
somewhat subdued and mirthful :—

" Don't know, eh ! Why you just said ' we'll go to rack and
ruin.' Day after to-morrow, at ten o'clock, forenoon, the trump-
ery will all be sold under the hammer. 'Tis hard, I know,
mother ; but — who cares ?" This tenderness and mirth were
ominous — indeed, they were a certain proof — that the bottle imp
had perched himself on the throne of the unbalanced brain.

The noted day at last arrived, and the housekeeping articles,
of little value, were sold one by one, and carried away to homes
and families more permanent and happy. The wilful Eliza
concealed some knives and forks, and smuggled them away with
a few revered keepsakes — thus retaining, contrary to her father's
expressed wishes, the basis of a future home. But nothing

of importance was rescued from the ravages of the auction-sales, save the bedding material, which was put straight into a baggage-wagon for immediate emigration. Eliza was running and jumping about with Julia Ann, regardless of the sufferings endured by the bewildered mother; while the father, full of fictitious courage and alcoholic hopes, lent a hand to every one who asked, and cheerfully laughed at his own calamity. Presently, the word came—"All aboard!"—meaning, all in the travelling wagon—and, in a few minutes, you might have seen the depressed mother, with the boy-baby in her lap, the two daughters stowed in between the bundles of bedding, and the half-weaver and half-shoemaker in front with the thirsty driver—all, pioneer-like, except in unity of purpose, going, without compass or rudder, on a reckless voyage of domestic discovery.

The thousand and one little hardships and shipwrecks which the impoverished family experienced, between the Blooming Grove house and the less agreeable tenement of John Myers, in Staatsburgh, New York, we will not stop to delineate. Suffice it to say, that the wanderers eventually terminated their journeyings in a spot yet more isolated than the one they had deserted—a place where the writer's first impressions of existence took their rise—and where, therefore, the biographical character of preceding chapters becomes transformed into sober autobiography and history incidental.

CHAPTER V.

MY FIRST MEMORIES.

" When at eve I sit alone,
Thinking on the past and gone —
While the clock, with drowsy finger,
Marks how long the minutes linger —
And the embers, dimly burning,
Tell of life to dust returning —
Then my lonely chair around,
With a quiet, mournful sound
With a murmur soft and low,
Come the Ghosts of Long Ago!"

WHEN the Soul makes its first record on the ledger-leaf of Memory, it then merges from the mystic vale of babyhood into a definite and self-conscious being. Individuality and memory are, therefore, inseparable in autobiography. The semi-unfounded tales of contemporaries may thenceforward be revised and corrected by the individual himself. Without egotism, then, the personal pronoun " I " may be hereafter used. Henceforth whatever might appear uncertain in history, becomes, by this direct testimony, translated and actualized to the reader as being next in value to positive knowledge.

Three years and a few weeks had glided away ere Memory received the news that, without and beyond itself, there existed an objective world. This was in the autumn of 1829. By means of intro-and-retro-spection, the original scene is easily revived and made manifest. I was in the open air, with my face toward

a small, weather-beaten, lonely house, but which, to my inexperienced mind, looked like a very spacious and wonderful superstructure. Whether I had ever been in it or not, I could not
remember. Towering trees environed the strange domicil; and
a road, the use of which I could form no conception, stretched
away through the dreamy depths of the encircling wilderness.

"What is them high things called?" I soliloquized, viewing the
erect and wavy trees so very far above my head. "And what's
that called?" I asked, pointing my finger toward the dilapidated
tenement, the dimensions of which seemed so great.

But, quicker than thought, there flashed athwart my nature a
dreadful feeling of lonely and helpless desolation; and awaking,
as it were, from a dream of fright and anxiety, I screamed *a
word*, the sound of which I had till then no knowledge of my
power to make — *Mother! mother!* Like the fabulous Robinson
Crusoe, while a lone wanderer on the island of Juan Fernandez,
I started in surprise at the cry with which my own voice broke
the deep silence. And yet, as I can now well remember, there
was something in the term "Mother" which seemed familiar and
full of blessed significance. Like a magic wand, it appeared to
open a narrow pathway through some well-known landscape: and
this path presently ultimated in certain definite enclosures — perhaps, reproducing an idea of the rooms in the rural dwelling
already described as my birthplace.

"What is 'Mother'?" I could not tell. Whether it had form,
size, and dimensions, or was the absence of these, I could not
decide. Two sensations I knew: my personal littleness, made
more appalling by the contrast of the great trees and immense
house before me; and *my desolate state*, more terrifying because I
could see nothing like myself in any direction. When I screamed
"Mother!" I evidently appreciated the fact that I was soliciting,
imploring, demanding, the presence of *something* which could
make me feel warm, safe, satisfied, and happy — something of
which I was a part, a lesser portion — without which I would be

cold, hungry, thirsty, and miserable. But, strange as it may appear, it is true nevertheless, that I could not or did not form the least conception of the objective appearance of that indefinite something which I called " Mother," and which I fully realized to be somehow related to my safety and existence. This fact I now regard as being rich in value to all metaphysicians.

I think no little boy ever cried, " Mother!" longer or louder than did I. A host of indescribable terrors crept through my mind. The tall trees were swaying to and fro by means of a force or agency which, I had a vague idea, possessed the attribute of motion. " Will it hurt me?" was my instant query. Away down yonder, looking into the forest, I saw darkness. " Do bugaboos live there?" I thought; and, louder and quicker yet, I called for the warmth, protection, and sympathy, of my mother. As I cried, there came from among the trees behind me a familiar voice, singing a semi-unmeaning song, which was then very common in the plebeian homes about us. I listened :—

> ' This poor man came in from his plough,
>   Dando, dando!
> This poor man came in from his plough,
>   Clam an' a clish and a cling go!
> This poor man came in from his plough,
> And asked his wife, ' Is breakfast ready now?'
>   Sing, clam blarum glere arum,
>   And a cling go !"

My infant mind readily caught the song as my blessed mother sung it — for I knew as by instinct that she it was whose voice I heard - - and I feel justified in recording the eccentric words, as a tribute to the *first impression* which her spirit made upon the memory of mine. My loneliness, as might be imagined, was quickly dissipated; for, with her arms full of brush, to make the fire burn for supper, up she came ; and, cheerfully bidding me to follow her, we entered the house, wherein my father sat, making shoes. This was the first of my memory thereof; and also of my sisters, as they invited me to go out and play with them.

On comparing my primary reminiscence (in awaking thus suddenly to a consciousness of a world without) with that of others, I find very few, if any, whose mental history reports a similar circumstance. Still, I do not doubt but there are many who, if they could but distinctly recall the time and place when memory began first to gather impressions from the outward world, might corroborate my experience and bear me company. Most people marvel and look skeptical when I declare and describe this initial event of my own biography; and this plainly enough assures me that I am not reporting an experience which is regarded as common to my fellow-men. Can I cause my doubting friend to comprehend the fact? I will make the attempt.

During infancy, the inmost spirit of man is slumbering in the cerebral substance, like an ungerminated seed in the earth's bosom. The child-brain is not yet impregnated with the immortal principle. The seed of the future being lies embedded therein. As with germs in the soil, so it is with the gradual growth and upspringing expansion of the mental energies. As a sequence of this progressive germination of the mental seed, from its enveloping womb which is situated in the centre of the brain, the outer fibres of the different organs, for the first few months of existence, do not receive the indwelling spirit, without which *reflection* and *memory* are quite impossible. According to this philosophy, you perceive that the spiritual forces expand from the central germ, till they fill, and thrill, and saturate with appropriate energies, the myriad minute vessels and nerves which, together with the cerebral embroidery, constitute what in these days are termed phrenological organs. It is owing to the absence of the spiritual forces — to a defective circulation of the imperishable principle through the fine extremities of these organs — that some persons complain of an incapacity to *reflect* and *reason* easily; and yet more especially do such deplore the *unfaithfulness of their memory*, even when the records of that organ are most in requisition. On the foregoing theory, it is plain to be seen that, should a person possess a spiritual nature of slow growth, united to a temperament which is nowise *untrue*, but definite and positive alike in the rejection as in the reception of impressions (as mine is), it follows that the period preceding the taking on of a *memory* might be lengthened out many months beyond the time commonly supposed ; and that when the awakening at length comes, so vivid an impression might be made as that no subsequent events could ever obliterate it. I know it is hard to remember *exactly* when you began to memorize common impressions ; but could each one do so, I think all would be amply satisfied with the above explanation of my individual experience.

CHAPTER VI.

MY FIRST TEMPTATION.

LEAVING philosophy to other volumes, I proceed with my record.

The occupation in which I saw my father engaged, day after day, considerably excited my curiosity. It was so funny to see him cut both soft and hard leathery substances into different forms and sizes; and still more, to watch him as he wet them, and hammered them, and fixed them firmly, with cunning little nails, on a piece of wood, fashioned after a big foot; and next to notice the diligence and regularity with which he made holes, with a sharp pointed instrument; and then to witness the quick, unerring exchange of bristles by which he pulled a waxed thread in opposite directions; and, finally, to look at the veins suddenly swelling on his forehead, and to hear his invariable and characteristic " Ugh !" as with a long, strong pull (which concluded in a jerk), he seemed to satisfy his mind that the thing was done for good. There appeared to be an amusement in all this, in which I longed to participate. But the fun of it began rapidly to disappear one morning when I caught the impression that—from some cause which I did not comprehend—my father felt compelled to keep doing so, even while he wished to be absent from home.

My sister Eliza had the charge and direction of me most of the time; that is, I found that I was forced to obey whenever alone with her, and this frequently happened. On one occasion, she ordered me in a whisper to go into a sort of cellar, which was built in the side of a small hill just in the edge of the woods, and bring her my apron full of apples, which I would find there. Like children in general, I was fond of such fruit, and so proposed to go and bring them immediately.

" Don't tell nobody I sent you," said she, in a quick undertone; " I 'll knock the daylights out of you if you do !"

Hearing this terrible threat, coupled with the injunction of secrecy, I trembled with a strange apprehension. It seemed to me that I was about to do something which I should not do. This seeming was entirely new; that is, I did not recollect ever doing any such thing before. And yet, I would presume to write myself as being neither more nor less prone to good deeds than many other boys. But here was an innocent moment when I felt halftempted and half-forced to commit an undefinable evil act. Thus confused and agitated, I asked —

" Ain't them apples yourn ?"

" No, you little goose, you !" she snappishly replied, " them's John Myers's apples; so mind, don't let him see you go nor come !"

" I guess I can't go at all," said I, attempting to run by her into the house; " I 'm so afraid he 'll see me."

" No you do n't nuther !" exclaimed she angrily, as she caught me and turned my face toward the cellar, with a whirling force that made me feel and fear her physical superiority; " now you go, as I tell you, or I 'll pound you — see if I do n't !"

Children, I think, are all natural democrats. Moral obligations, fine distinctions, or rules of right and wrong, are without influence on very young minds. Thus, not quite understanding what wrong there could be in going for what I wanted — nor yet perceiving what moral difference there existed between apples in our cellar under the house and apples in John Myers's cellar under the hill — off I started, pushed open the unlocked door, and filled my apron with that fruit which tempted the fabled Eve.

Returning with more apples than I could keep from rolling out
of my uplifted garments, I had the fresh fright of beholding their
owner looking right at me from the road. What to do I did not
know; but, though the fruit dropped at every step, I kept running
to get home. The owner hailed me; but 't was no use. Fleeter
and faster still I bounded over the rough ground, until I reached
the house. Forgetting all my sister's threats of punishment, I
sprang toward my mother, buried my face in her lap, and wept at
the top of my voice a full confession! She heard me through,
told me to dry my eyes, and never to do so again; and then, to
my great satisfaction, she went out to "settle" with Eliza for sending me on such a wicked errand. What happened to my sister,
during that settlement, I will not pause to chronicle; but, instead,
will enter my solemn protest against any similar temptation being
placed before the human spirit. For, although at the time, it
seemed like a harmless and playful enterprise, yet there was a
poison lurking beneath, which, had I fully imbibed it, might have
debilitated my moral organism through every subsequent year.

My mother, being fond of solitude, often sought gratification by
rambling in the wild, woody environments. One day, toward
evening, we all remarked "how long a time" she had been absent;
but consoled one another with the saying, "She'll be back before
sundown." At length, however, the beautiful sun rolled down
behind the dense forest, touching as it went the loftiest and the
fairest leaves with hues inimitable. But where was the lone woman? The mystical drapery of night fell round about the world;
the cheer and chirp of daylight creatures were no longer heard;
and as we children stood tremblingly on the edge of the dark
distance, we fancied that we did hear a sound of wailing coming
from the woods, blending with the sad, low moan of the grandly-
swaying wilderness. Every moment became more and more
painful. We looked and called, and called and looked, till choked
•and blinded with fright and tears. "Mother's lost!" I cried, and
ran to get father out in search. 'T was quickly done. He did

not fear the darkness, neither the spirit of night in the forest, but went boldly into it. Anon, in the midst of our listenings, we heard the sound of voices ; and, ere we fully recognised tLem, our parents stood before us ! The pleasure of that meeting was the first positive joy recorded in the life-book of my memory.

Our family did not sojourn long in this isolated tenement. My father returned one night, and said : " Well, I 've found another hut ; so, let 's be off this week." To this sudden proposal my mother complainingly demurred ; and then I witnessed, for the first time in the life of my memory, a prolonged, loquacious struggle between them — the effect of which still lingers, as the most shocking impression ever made upon my infantile mind. Well enough do I remember, after getting under the clothes in the trundle-bed that night, of thinking thus : " I wonder whether the Big Good Man up in the sky seen that ! If he did, what does he think about it ?" While meditating thus, I was seized with *a strange terror ;* and, as the most natural thing, I screamed " Mother !" with all my vocal power.

" What is the matter, Jackson ?" she quickly and kindly asked.

" I do n't know," I cried ; " I 'm 'fraid to go to sleep. D' you think I 'll wake up again, if I go to sleep ? '

" O yes, my son — nothing 'll hurt you." And so I tried to believe. But 't was impossible. What troubled me I knew not, except a terrifying apprehensiveness that I should not open my eyes again if I slept, and the dreaded loneliness of an endless sleep. It reminded me of what I felt when our mother was *lost* in the forest. Therefore I begged to get in bed with my parents, for there only could I feel safe in slumber.

" Do n't humor that boy so !" said my father sternly ; 't ain't nothin' but worms ailin' him."

Now, though a very little child, I felt that I *knew better ;* and so, for the first time, I found my mind rejecting my own father's judgment. Here was individual sovereignty in a trundle-bed. But this unexpected development of an opinion, in positive oppo-

si'ion to my worthy and venerable progenitor, served only to add
more strength to my indescribable terror. Having no knowledge
of words wherewith to dispute my father's worm-theory, I cried
and continued to cry, until, perhaps to get rid of me, I was taken
by mutual consent into the protective embrace of the sympathizing
mother — wherein, feeling a blissful security out of harm's way,
I soon forgot all trouble in a slumber too sound for dreams.

On reflection, I have since concluded that my awakening spirit,
young and untutored as it was, had receiv ' on this occasion some
vaguely intuitive conception of Deity and Death.   An idea of the
" Big Good Man" had never been imparted to me by any person
that I could remember; neither had I ever witnessed such a
shocking event as " going to sleep and not waking again," which
formed the groundwork of my childish apprehensions.   Therefore
I put this down as an interesting psychological fact, impairing the
doctrine that denies to the soul an innate organic knowledge of
corresponding outward realities.

CHAPTER VII.

A CHANGE OF SCENE.

" He lived not in himself, but did become
Portion of that around him.'

PATERNAL authority being greatly in the ascendant, our family sorrowfully bundled together the housekeeping material; and two days subsequent to my father's announcement, we were once more on our way to a strange habitation. Walking and riding by turns, on a rather hard and lonely road which led through a large tract of woodland, we at length reached another isolated tenement, of extremely limited dimensions. It was situated in the same town, Staatsburg, not far from Rhinebeck, on the farm of a good-natured Dutchman by the name of Bart Cropsey, whose years were rolling him down the afternoon of rudimental existence.

South of this incommodious dwelling you could see the fields and distant farmhouse of the nearest neighbor; while on the north there was next to no prospect whatever; only an indistinct wagon track (a cheering sign that human beings had been there before us) leading far away around a hilly, stony section of the old man's real estate. Toward the east, and but a few rods from our door, there was, as nearly as I can remember, a chain of irregular acclivities. These were overlaid with a coating of soil too sterile to yield anything abundantly, save tons of gravel and countless splinters from the slate strata above. Looking westward the eye would very naturally and pleasurably rest upon a swift-running stream, that skirted the timber-land just beyond it, and which continued its musical pilgrimage downward through the verdant fields that made our southern prospect almost beautiful.

When arrived, there transpired a succession of those hurly-burly events so common at such movings. Everything to do, and nobody ready to do it; yet each busy doing something with all available strength and speed. The house was divided into two compartments—had what an extravagant imagination might term, " a reception room," and " an attic chamber." The first was as extensive as the walls of the foundation, and occupied all the lower story; while the second, accessible only by climbing up a flight of rickety stairs, had remained without lath and plaster, or other finishings, from the first day of its erection.

But the half-weaver and half-shoemaker indicated no sorrow of heart. His hand was quick to get the bedstead corded up, the straw ticking on, the washtub (with a few tea things and crockery wares in it) pushed into the old cupboard which was already occupied by such natives as rats, mice, and spiders. The children were not less industrious. They helped to unload the wagon, and prepare the reception room for the best arrangement of our limited stock. But my mother looked sad and weary. Her eye was filled with an expression of insight. There was a something of distance in the air of abstraction which pervaded her. I record this fact, because, although she may have appeared thus interior a thousand times before, this is the first time when my attention became arrested and fixed by it. Her mind seemed far from the immediate scene.

Nothing of importance transpired worth recording, for several weeks. My father worked diligently on the shoe-bench every day; and, excepting sundry frettings and fault-findings, all went on very well.

One day I overheard some suppressed conversation, from which I gathered that my sister Eliza might get married. What that meant I could form no idea; it was something, I noticed, which mother did not like. I ventured to ask the reason, but was told by father to "mind my business," or he'd "take the strap to me!" But my mind would work. I was not long concluding that getting "married" meant going from home to live with a stranger. So believing, I thought that mother was right and father was wrong — because she complained and objected to the marriage, while father objected to her complainings and useless interference. And now I began to be reminded of something I witnessed while we lived in John Myers' tenement. More than once I had remarked a strange young man who came through the woods to our house, and laughed and talked with Eliza just as if they had always been acquainted. And I remembered, also, how they made molasses candy and sugar, once, from maple sap; and gave me some if I would run away with Julia Ann and play.

My sympathies were with my mother on this subject. And, therefore, though but four years old, and habited in a short woollen frock, I coaxed her out doors, beyond my father's hearing, to ask these questions: "Mother, will I ever be as big as father? Then you won't let me be married — will you?" If my memory serves me right she returned me no answer; but went into the house with more merriment and laughter than I had ever heard from her on any previous occasion. This conduct had the effect to leave me void of satisfaction. "How curious," thought I, "to weep at Eliza's marriage and then laugh at mine!" But the sight of a stranger coming through the twilight of the evening, dissipated my thinking, and made me once more a portion of that around me.

CHAPTER VIII.

THE DUTCHMAN'S GHOST.

AT this time my mind began to take an interest in the varied changes and hues of human faces. As yet but few persons
had made a place for themselves in my memory. Before this
date I do not recollect seeing more than four individuals, besides
our family triangle. I do not say "family circle" because, for the
most part, my parents were stationed at opposite points, while the
children (my eldest sister, Eliza, more especially) stood, as by a
logical necessity, at the third point; thus forming, by a kind of
spontaneous geometry, a complete three-cornered family alliance;
out of which a circle was never more than foreshadowed and
indicated as a bare possibility, in certain hours of domestic
spheroidal communion.

The existence of this condition could not fail to impress me
painfully. My infant tongue was, perhaps, never moved with
words of rebuke which I thought were many times deserved,
but this can not be recorded of my mouth; for, whenever I
thought that mother was troubled by father's moods, I could not
restrain a propensity to cry loudly and lustily, and thus restore
them to comparative unity by means of my counter-irritation.

Uncle Bart Cropsey's hired man seemed very fond of visiting
at our house. Through the deepening twilight we frequently saw
him coming down the indistinct wagon-track toward our habitation.
But he made his visits too early and late, as well as too frequent,

to please even the generous Dutchman. Therefore, after numerous remonstrances, "Dave" (as he was called) made up his mind
to go home earlier. But what he termed "earlier" was to me
very late indeed. Often and often I strained my eyes to keep
awake during his stay, but sleep would steal over me at length,
and the next morning's sun would sometimes shine ere the deep
slumber of childhood was again broken. It will be remembered
that our "reception room" contained our kitchen, our bedchamber,
our shoemaker's shop, &c., &c. ; and 't was for this reason that, whenever visitors were there, it became a rather delicate matter for any
member of the family to undress and retire for the night. Hence
we all rejoiced, when Uncle Bart entered his positive protest
against Dave's long nocturnal visitations. But our joy was ere
lone greatly diminished, by his apparent forgetfulness of the old
man's injunction. Indeed, in a few days his visits commenced as
early and terminated as late as ever.

One black and dreary night which I well remember, the jour-
neyman-farmer left us later than usual. The autumnal wind
whistled round about the old house, "and music made of melancholy sort." There was a moon in the sky, but 't was almost
totally obscured by the threatening clouds. If there had been
shutters on our windows, swinging and slamming on their rusty
hinges, it would, without doubt, have augmented yet more the
doleful melody of the storm and darkness.

"Ain't you afraid to go home, Dave?" asked my father.

"No, not I!" he courageously returned; "I've walked through
the woods in more 'n one dark night! So, good-night, all!"

"There! he's gone at last," said Eliza; "now, let's go to bed."
The motion was seconded by all hands, and, in a few minutes, we
were all under cover, except father who, as he said, had "a shoe
to finish." We were just on the verge of sleep when there came
a loud knocking on the outside of the window, accompanied with—
"Hallo! hallo! I say, Mr. Davis, come out quick!"

The only light in the room was made by the wick of father's

exhausted tallow candle, flickering on a stick's end before him; but which, owing to a false move of his hand, was immediately extinguished, leaving the panic-struck family in poor plight to render assistance. Nothing daunted, however, father opened the outer door, and demanded :—

" What's the matter ?"

There stood poor Dave quaking and trembling with fright, scarcely able to utter a sentence, but presently he stammered out :—

" I've seen a thundering spook — or — a — something white !"

" Where d' you see it ?"

" By the big oak tree, up in the corner of the woods, where the little slab bridge is !"

" What does it look like ?"

" Like a thundering great man, dressed in grave-clothes ! Can't you go with me till I get past the thundering thing, Mr. Davis?"

" Well, I 'll see," said father. " Let's hunt up a lantern. I guess we 've got one."

While father was preparing to go with Dave, we all declared that we could n't and would n't stay alone ; and acting under the speed of fright, the four of us (mother, Eliza, Julia Ann, and myself) got quickly dressed and ready to turn out in the gloomy darkness. It was all alarmingly new to me. I had not heard of a "thundering spook" before, and felt no little curiosity to see one. Perhaps I was also very much frightened ; if so, 'twas more than balanced by the novelty of the object about to be seen ; and hence, keeping tight hold of my mother's hand, on I trotted " in the footsteps of our illustrious predecessors," father and the farmer.

" What's a spook, mother ?" I pantingly asked while running rapidly by her side.

" Oh, 't ain't nothin' to hurt us," she replied, " 't is somethin' that means somethin', if one knows how to take it right."

Not satisfied with this explanation, I inquired :—

" How does it look ?"

" Hush — hark — keep still — hold yer tongue — can't you,"

vociferated Eliza; " a body can't hear nothin' for your everlastin' clackin'."

But lowering my voice, I continued to interrogate : " Mother, what did Dave mean by a *thundering* spook ?"

" Oh, never mind. Dave's a wicked man. I'll tell you to-morrow."

By this time, as the slackened pace of the vanguard indicated, our party had nearly reached the point of interest. Father made a voluntary declaration of skepticism and heroic fearlessness. Whereupon Dave, being inspired with fresh courage, drew up a verbal resolution to the effect, that " he wouldn't run now, even if left alone. Didn't care for the 'thundering thing' when he first got a glimpse of it. Came back after us merely out of good nature, to have some fun." And, so declaring, the ploughman struck up a bold, courageous, don't-care-ative whistle; which, to tell the truth, made but very little impression on the rude blasts of wind that came roaring through the woods in the direction of the open country.

But as if 't were designed, at this frightful and momentous crisis, out popped the great, round-faced moon from behind its cloudy curtain ; and, wonderful to behold ! just by the dilapidated bridge, right against the great oak-tree, there stood, towering up in the darkness, a monstrous form — enveloped in a snow-white sheet, with a hat on its head, and its apparent arms flying and flapping frantically in the howling tempest.

" Good gracious !" exclaimed Dave — " D'you see that ?"

As he said this, he stepped back so quick against us, that three fourths of our party were thrown violently to the ground. This accident took immediate effect, in giving each the terrible impression of having been struck by the ghostly monster ; and, accelerated by the motive force of this horrid thought, our mutual retreat resembled the flight of John Gilpin. As for me, I must confess that my opinion was expressed by an unbroken yell of agonizing fear, poetically termed " weeping," which added not a little to the awful condition of the fleeing quartette, headed by the more than ever affrighted Dave.

"Stop! Hold on!" cried father, who was just in our rear — "What you running away for? Come back! Let's ask the spook what it wants there."

Obediently we halted. The elder heads planned a battle, and then all cautiously returned. When within hailing distance, my father shouted : " Hallo, there — what's wanted?"

We were silent a moment, which seemed a great while, but no answer came.

" Hallo, I say! Who are you? What d'you want?"

Autumnal blasts, full of strange sounds, gave back the only response. Father's candle, too, was nearly out in his lantern; and the fitful moon kept up a constant dodging in and out of the heavy folds of the storm-king's drapery. Hence our prospect was fast becoming very dark and doubtful. But my father's intrepid conduct, on this occasion, inspired me with a particular respect for him.

"Poh! nonsense! If you don't answer me I'll knock your brains out with this 'ere stone," said he impatiently, picking up a big pebble.

And sure enough! To our great consternation, away flew his missile, and down came the ghostly hat! Obeying orders we didn't " budge a yard;" but witnessed, with rapidly increasing courage, the bombardment and demolition of the White Spook. And I believe the reader's disappointment will not be more provoking than was ours, when I record that some mischievous individual, knowing that Dave frequented our house and returned that way late every night, *had wrapped up a bundle of straw in an old sheet*, with Uncle Bart Cropsey's broad-brimmed hat to indicate where a head might have been.

Our party returned home in fine spirits, and slept undisturbed the remainder of the night. 'Tis my belief that the experience and discovery of that memorable hour has had an unmistakably wholesome effect upon my organ of *marvellousness,* which is said, by phrenologists, to exert only a very moderate and secondary influence on my mental organization. Methinks Providence could not have better prepared my mind for investigating and discrimi nating between genuine spiritual personages and fallacious appari tions than by this midnight encounter with the phantom-man of straw.

> " Thus, when I am all alone,
> Dreaming o'er the past and gone,
> All around me, sad and slow,
> Come the Ghosts of Long Ago."

CHAPTER IX.

IN WHICH I MAKE MORE DISCOVERIES.

IN due course of time there was established something like a
family circle of harmony concerning the impending marriage of
my eldest sister; the result of which was a cheerful preparation
of sundry sandwiches, cracked walnuts, and a few small pies, the
crust being shortened, or more properly lengthened and toughened,
with what father called "white-oak splits." I looked upon the
whole proceeding with a curiosity common to children. I helped
place the wooden chairs in a row on either side of our "recep-
tion-room," and wondered where all the people would come from
to occupy them.

At length the neighbors one by one arrived, and the seats, including father's shoe-bench and the two beds, were literally covered with visitors. I was too much astonished and intimidated to
speak or cry; and so, having acquired the habit, I yielded to it—
that is, as often defined by father, I " clung to my mother's apron-
string," and wouldn't let go—but followed her out doors after
wood and water, down cellar after the molasses-jug, up stairs after
a pair of newly-darned stockings; and thus, round and round the
ten-by-twelve tenement, I pursued her, as if to relinquish my hold
was to be hopelessly wrecked and cast away among utter strangers! One of the women brought with her a little girl, who attracted my attention, because hers was the first human form I had
ever seen more diminutive than my own. She wore frocks, and so
did I—a fact which my mind regarded as being very curious.

Presently a well-dressed man entered, who acted as if he knew everything. As he advanced, the people got off the beds, and, together with the others there, stood up without speaking. My sister came down the rickety stairway from the attic chamber aforesaid, all dressed and beautified as I had never seen her previously. Then up stepped the young man, with whom I was now well acquainted, who, taking Eliza's hand, stood with her in a most solemn mood directly before the man who seemed to know everything as well as the name of it. He opened his mouth, and spoke some of the longest, hardest, biggest, strangest words I had ever heard. Whereupon my mother began to weep; then my sister wept; then Julia Ann cried outright; and last, as well as least, I brought up the rear with a regular burst of uncontrollable lamentation. What I was crying about I did not know; but mother cried, and that was enough. However, the wedding was soon ended, the sandwiches were quickly consumed, the walnut-shells delivered up their meats, and father's bottle of strong drink was passed from one man's mouth to another; when the company began to depart, each wishing our folks "long life and much joy."

The impression of that event was very unpleasant. It exerted a sad influence upon me, like that of sickness, or fault-finding; which made me importune my mother, over and over again, never to let me get married.

Weeks hurried by, and ere long we stood on the margin of another year. The curtain that hung between our house and the world — which folded in obscurity the private afflictions of our family — I will not roll up. That which concerned my psycho- logical progress is alone relevant in this autobiography Hence, . pass on to the advent of Santa Claus!

Hearing of his name and near approach — that he brought good gifts for good children — that no one could see him as he crept down the chimney, and filled suspended stockings with sweet treasures — I resolved to be very good (that is, not cry or follow

nother), and then see what would come as my compensation.
T'was the last day of bleak December, when mother said :—

"Come, Jackson—you run out and draw your sled about, and
)lay till I call you."

"What for, mother?"

"Oh, 'cause I want you to go."

"Sha'n't I get froze in the snow?"

"No, no—you go, now—I'll call, when I want you."

Now, this was so new—asking me to do what she had frequently prevented me from doing without any reason as I sometimes thought—that it excited my imagination. Hence I persisted in questioning her :—

"What for, mother—what for?"

"Oh, never mind ; go, as I tell you : and when I call, you shall
have a warm cookie."

"Why, mother—what for? Mother—say, tell me, won't you?"

But father, hearing me teaze the already half-overcome woman,
rapidly described a semicircle on his shoe-bench, and sternly said :

"Don't humor that boy so! Make him mind, or crack his
head!—Jackson, you sir! do as your mother bids, or I'll take
the strap to you, quicker!"

Of late years the American world has heard something of what
Albert Brisbane calls "attractive industry," in contradistinction
to painful and unrequited toil as suffered by the masses ; but I
venture to say that no embryo man (between four and five years
of age) ever more realized the beauty of "attractive playing," and
the distressing constraint of repulsive amusement, than I did immediately on the conclusion of my father's great speech on that
occasion. Amusement, when disagreeable, is repulsive labor; as
labor, when adapted to one's genius, is attractive amusement. But
at this moment, delay was dangerous to my personal welfare ; the
paternal weapon lay curled up by the lapstone and hammer ; and
thus, victimized and dejected, forth I went to ride down hill on
ice and snow.

Up the eastern acclivity I drew my sled. But instead of coast-
ing, I concerned myself with fishing for the reasons of the maternal anxiety to get me out doors. " Could Santa Claus have asked
them to send me out ?" soliloquized I ; " and who is he ?" Glim-
merings of the possibility of the existence of such a being seemed
to flicker and twinkle on the horizon of my awakening intellect
And yet, the attribute of his *invisibility*—of his power to descend
the chimney, and put palpable things in my stocking, without exposing himself to mortal vision — this was a statement very hard
for me fully to believe, although it came from my worthy, loving,
revered mother, and challenged my confidence. " She's so big,
and so old, too," thought I, " why, of course she knows." And
straightway I believed *all* I had been told concerning the invisible
friend of good children. " But," methought, " how strange that a
being so pure should get into and shuffle down a dirty, sooty chimney to the very fireplace, amid the embers and ashes there !"
Still thinking to myself, I said : " Good Santa Claus must go very
fast, and that's why no one can see him." Whereupon I made
several snowballs, and hurled them into the air with all my force,
to experiment upon rendering objects invisible by the swiftness
of their flight. But I obtained very little satisfaction from this
exertion ; and so, resolving to sleep that night with one eye wide
open, I tried to amuse myself paradoxically—that is, by tugging
and laboring to gain the hill-top, in order to purchase the short-
lived pleasure of sliding and tumbling head over heels into the
snowbank below.

At length the married Eliza called, and said I might come in
and warm myself. Accordingly, I went in, but saw nothing unusual, except a few fresh-cooked doughnuts ; from which I received some reward for remaining out so long, agreeably to maternal request and paternal command.

Night hastened on ; and how glad was I to get into the trundle-
bed ! Next morning, early as I might awake, I was destined to
find presents in my stocking ! Mother hung a pair of clean hose

against the sooty jam, just at the end of the great back-log; all of which proceeding I witnessed by her permission.

"Now, Jackson, be a good boy, and go to sleep," said she soothingly, "and you'll see what'll come of it."

Doubtless, like most juveniles under corresponding circumstances, I was remarkably obliging, and got straight into bed. Once or twice previous to her retiring, my eye met hers peering under the corner of the blanket, evidently to see if I had my lashes closed in sleep. This had the effect to make slumber still more difficult.

Steadily, through a hollow fold in the bedquilt, I fixed one eye on a right line with the suspended stockings, and looked, with no ordinary anxiety, till our folks all found their pillows for the night. Presently I heard each inmate breathing heavily as in sound repose, save my mother, who, after a while, crept stealthily from her bed to the cupboard, thence to the pendent hose; and then, through the moonlight in the room, I saw her put something in each stocking, and hasten back to her resting-place over mine.

It was perhaps an hour subsequent to this scene ere I managed to obtain sleep. When "Nature's sweet restorer" at length came over me, I dreamed that Santa Claus, dressed in a suit of black, found his way down our chimney, with his every pocket filled with beautiful gifts. And in my dream I thought I got up, took hold of his outermost gown, pulled it off, and lo! there stood *my mother*, smiling benevolently, through one of her most winning and tender expressions.

"Happy New Year!" shouted Julia Ann, so close to my ear, that I started, fully awake, and sprang after the woollen receptacles which still hung against the chimney-corner. Filled to the very top! Santa Claus had not forgotten me! And I hastened back between the warm sheets to discover what was given. Out came a small roll of candy; out came four doughnuts, tasting just like those of the previous day, only shaped and fashioned after an old man, a cat, a cow, and a little boy; out came three butternuts.

six chestnuts, and a very big potato; and, to conclude, out came father's shoe-strap — the veritable stirrup of this industrious disci ple of St. Crispin — a gentle admonition from Santa Claus that 1 "must mind my Ps and Qs." Vibrating between faith and doubt, and tasting alternately of both fear and joy, I hopped up, and, for the first time, got into a pair of undeveloped pantaloons.

"Mother, didn't you put them things in my stockings?" I asked, looking directly into her eyes. My dream was realized at once. A benevolent smile pervaded her countenance, as she answered — "Yes, Jackson, I put in everything but the potato and strap."

This confession was quite satisfactory, and I felt that I loved her for giving me so much pleasure.

But, deeper than the joy of that New-Year's day, there was made upon my mind an impression of incorrigible skepticism. Nothing could have been more pertinent and salutary. Simple as that event was, it tended greatly to strengthen my already awakened proclivity to rigid investigation. A vigilant incredulity regarding the existence of *invisible personages* was, by this Luman solution of the mysterious Santa Claus, made very easy of subsequent development.

CHAPTER X.

OTHER SCENES IN THIS DRAMA.

ONE day I overheard some conversation between my mother and an aged woman, who had called to make a visit, concerning the premonitory signs of death in a neighborhood.

" How cur'us it is," said mother, " that a body what's born with a veil over their face can tell sich things! There's my Jackson —he was born with a veil over his face: may be he'll be one o that 'are sort."

" Du tell!" exclaimed the nervous, excitable listener; " is that so? Why, I want to know!"

" Yes!" replied mother, with a deep sigh, and almost stifled with a sudden gush of painful emotion. " Yes — I remember well," she continued; " and when I looked at the baby, with the veil over his hull face, then ses I to myself, ses I, ' He's born to see trouble, or — somethin' else — I don't know what!'"

But, returning to the subject of seeing signs of death in rural districts, mother related, by way of illustration, how, on a certain moonlight evening years before, she beheld a man solemnly walking, with his arms folded across his breast, as if meditating on a theme of the saddest and gravest import.

" Who was he?" interrupted the old lady.

" Ah! that's what I can't say," returned my mother. " But I tried to find out. I went to the winder fust; and then, as he appeared like near, I opened the front door quick, to ask him tc

come in. Not a single soul did I see there! Well, I thought
't was queer 'nough ; and so 't was. But next night, same time,
I seen the same person ag'in, a-walkin' sad like, jest as he did
afore : 'and now,' thinks me, 'I knows who 't is.' But I didn't,
after all."

" Du tell !" exclaimed the visitor. " You couldn't say, eh, who
't was there, walkin' so ?"

" No, I couldn't. But I know'd that it meant a death in our
neighborhood. And so it proved. For, a few days afterwards,
'Squire ————, who loved to smell the snuff of a taller-candle so
much, died very sudden with consumption.'

" Why, I want to know !" ejaculated the amazed woman ; " du
tell, now ! Was it true that he liked the smell of candle-smoke ?"

" Yes, he did," replied mother ; " and, what's more, I've allus
noticed that short-lived folks allus liked the candle-snuff as a
somethin' to breathe."

That night was rife with trouble for me. When my industrious father planted his stick on the floor, surmounted with a candle,
I seated myself close by, to ascertain whether I had any fondness
for such an odor. Horrible ! I did love, as I supposed, to smell
the feathery vapor that went curling up from the burning wick !
'T was enough ! Although the evening had but just dawned, I
asked permission to retire, because I was afraid I might get sick
if I remained up as long as usual. The favor being granted, I
went to bed with tears trembling on my eyelids. My thoughts
dwelt on going to sleep and awaking not again. How insupportable ! Overcome at last with sheer fright I cried outright, and
begged mother to tell me —

" Do I like to smell candle-wick ? Say, mother, say — do I
like to smell the snuff of it ? Will I die, mother if I do ? Say,
will I die ?"

Father caught the burden of my lamentation, and laughed loud
enough to drown the sound of my voice. But this method of consoling me did neither allay my fears nor reduce the strength of

my mental weakness ; and I persisted in soliciting aid and instruction from mother. She gave me rest, but no satisfaction ; and I could not get over the fear of immediate death for many days afterward. In the meantime my father would alternate between threats to use his strap upon me, and the assertion that I was " troubled with worms," and should take " a teaspoonful of brimstone and molasses every morning."

The reader will now hasten with me over the uninteresting details of many weeks, and halt to consider another item of more vital importance.

Poverty, with its hideous train, dwelt in our habitation. I do not mean that vice and crime were with us, as the usual sequences of poverty ; but that sickness, and depression, and scoldings, and frettings, and humiliations of many kinds, were constant visitors at our home. Oft and again I have seen my mother busy baking the last handful of Indian meal in our possession — without meat, or potatoes, or the flour of other grains — and, wonderingly, I have heard her ask my father where and when he would get more provender to keep the family from starvation. Sometimes I would inquire if everybody, in all houses, had the same trouble to get food and raiment. To such questionings my father would impatiently and sternly reply :—

"No, hang it! the poor man gets poorer, and the rich man richer : that's the way with the world."

Thus conditioned were we, when one chilly spring day receded on her purple car, spreading a mystic twilight wide o'er hill and plain, and ushered in the star-gemmed night which, like a royal pall, was thrown upon the bosom of the still Earth. Of course, these natural beauties and changes I did not in my childhood perceive. But, instead, I saw tears, sorrowings, and many anxious looks. We had no food! Neither had we been feasting recently. But, having lived poorly for days, each felt that intensely fearful desire to eat which only the really famishing can ever fully comprehend. My mother said she believed that " Providence would provide for us."

" Well, I believe so too," returned the half-weaver and half-shoemaker, but wholly honest man, as he whacked a piece of sole-leather for the reparation of a neighbor's boot; " but," he contin- ued, " it seems to me that Providence always depends more upon us than we depend on Providence."

" Why, how queer you talk !" said my mother, whose face now began to light up with hope as the morning brightens the face of Nature ; and she added : " I don't think no harm will befall us jest yet; as old 'Squire ———, who's now dead and gone, used to say :—

> ' The Lord my pasture shall prepare,
> And feed me with a shepherd's care.' "

Now, as the logical reader might easily imagine, all this serious conversation about " Providence," and being fed by a Lordly " Shepherd," seemed to me very much in keeping with the story of good old invisible Santa Claus, or like the great white spook made out of straw. And hence, though only in my fifth year, I could not help believing more in the providence and protection of my honored progenitors on whom I realized a sweet dependency.

At this moment we were mutually attracted to the door by the sound of tramping horses and the rumbling of an approaching wagon.

" What can bring anybody this way at such an hour?" exclaimed my father ; " who can it be ?"

" Hallo, there !" shouted a voice from the wagon; " our folks wants to get Mrs. Davis to come and help do our washing to- morrow."

" Who are you ?" asked Eliza.

" Why, don't you know? We're just from John Radcliffe's fishing-grounds—just going home with the team."

" Oh, goodness save us !" said my mother hopefully ; " let 's get some fish for supper. I know'd that Providence would provide."

"Yes! yes!" said father; "let's ask for a shad, or a dozen her ring. Eliza, go out to the wagon, and see what he's got."

'T was no sooner said than done. Out she ran, followed by Julia Ann and myself, to get something for supper. But great indeed was our disappointment when the driver declared that every herring and every shad had been sent down the Hudson to New York; that he had n't anything aboard, save the nets and a few bunches of shad-eggs scattered here and there through the meshes. Mother said, "That 'll do." But father exhibited considerable dissatisfaction, yet agreed that "shad-eggs would taste better than nothing;" while I did not realize any preference whatever. The difference in the quality of shad and shad-eggs was unknown to me. All I wanted was something to eat. And the family sharing in this feeling, the fire was forthwith kindled, and the providential eggs were soon snapping and cracking in the frying-pan.

"What you got to eat with them?" inquired the inspirited cordwainer.

"Nothing," replied my mother.

"Nothing!" echoed he — "nothing! Why, what the dogs will be done? Who can eat shad-eggs and nothing else, I'd like to know?"

But the fact was that there could not be found in that tenement a bit of bread of any description, nor any substance resembling a vegetable, except a few decayed turnips in the attic chamber — or, more strictly speaking, in the unfinished garret up the rickety stairway. Hence the marine provender had to be served up that night alone, without a second article of diet. Fortunately, we were not members of any vegetarian society. On the contrary, each one was free to devour as many shoals of embryological shad as his or her appetite seemed to demand. Therefore we all ate, and thus satisfied, for a time, the painful longings of hunger. This time was brief. A thirst came on — a horrid, crazy, sickening thirst — which water allayed but for a moment.

"There, I thought so!" groaned the impatient and again disheartened cordwainer. "Just as I thought. Fish will swim twice!"

Hearing this, I hastened to my mother's side to ask what father meant by fish swimming twice; for, besides the thirst I felt, there were other unsatisfactory symptoms down my throat, which made me fear that the eggs were possibly hatched, and that little finny flukes might be sprawling and wiggling about inside! Mother explained, however, that fish usually make one drink after eating. Receiving this explanation, I felt mentally quieted; but, gastronomically, the case was quite otherwise.

Father got very sick, and disgorged freely; then Julia Ann's turn came, and out belched the most of her supper; whereupon Eliza, with ill-suppressed disappointment, projected her head and her last meal simultaneously out of the window; and then, to complete the *shadowy* trials of that memorable night, mother and I groaned and vomited, and vomited and groaned, till each particular egg was cast upon that solid foundation which, according to the oriental story, was so satisfactory to the ejected Jonah.

Oh, the sickness of that dreary night! Fatigued with the combined labor of supporting hunger, and the more recent trial of expelling the so-called providential food, we each at last found nutrition in the depths of dreamless slumber. But the following morning brought healing in its wings; for, ere the family again awoke to a knowledge of their destitution, our father, now fully aroused from the apathy of despair, had procured meat and meal sufficient to give us all a good and grateful breakfast.

CHAPTER XI.

SUNSHINE AND CLOUDS.

"Life's but a walking shadow; a poor player,
That struts and frets his hour upon the stage,
And then is heard no more."

ALCOHOL is an accursed tyrant! His ruthless tyranny is terrible. His victims strew the earth's bosom. Their groans rend the air. The stench of their corruption fills innumerable homes with the seedlings of death!

My organ of memory, though usually prompt in the performance of its functions, does not report the precise cause of our extreme indigence; but, starting from my knowledge of father's occasional intemperate habits, I infer that Rum played the leading character on the boards of our domestic theatre. Nevertheless, as I now view the scene backward through the gloomy vista, I seem gratefully to see the paternal hand plying the awl industriously for the laudable maintenance of our impoverished household. Hence, I have no disposition to cast the imputation of neglect, or of wilful unkindness, upon the being from whom, according to the laws of marriage and reproduction, I received, in part, the priceless boon of an eternal individuality of existence.

The lowest plane of depression, in the affairs of our pantry and hearthstone, was reached at the close of the last chapter; therefore, the next turn of the wheel of fortune carried us higher in the scale of subsistence and external life.

Death is a phenomenon of the world; to which, as yet, I was almost a total stranger. Neither in man, nor beast, nor bird, had I seen the process. But by the advent of meat on our table, as well as by other common indications, my mind became, as I supposed, familiarized with the fact that living creatures ceased to exist. I was mistaken as to the extent of my familiarity, however, as the following circumstance will clearly show :—

In order to frighten and banish the members of numerous nocturnal *rat*ification meetings, that were held in different apartments of our isolated dwelling, our folks procured of some neighbor a fine purring kitten which in due time developed into ample *cat*egorical proportions; and, obedient to the design of its being, presented us, one fine morning, with almost half a peck of very diminutive cats, *sans* eyes, but chuck full of interest to me. I busied myself supplying their supposed wants, by feeding the feline fountain with full saucers of skimmed milk, and thus made their growth a subject of daily concern.

By inquiry, I came to know that nine days were required to mature their visual apparatus; and that then each individual kitten would open its own eyes, and take an interest in things external. For this event I patiently waited. But my father insisted upon a destruction of the whole cat family — alleging, as a sufficient reason, that " one set of hungry mouths was all he could manage to feed." And yet, notwithstanding the terrible threatenings and deeds of cruelty of which the cordwainer was ofttimes verbally guilty, he had not the hardness of heart to destroy that inoffensive cat's numerous children. This gave me confidence in father's real goodness; over which mother, Julia Ann, and I, made ourselves quite merry.

As bad luck would have it, however, there came to our house a disagreeable looking old man, with overhanging brow, disfigured by shaggy locks of uncombed hair, a wide mouth, and a voice like the growling of some angry animal. I was surprised when father hailed him as an old acquaintance. In the course of his stay, the kittens were alluded to, and, much to my con:ternation, their immediate destruction was planned and agreed to; in pursuance whereof, the helpless, sightless, guiltless, and crying little creatures were seized by the merciless visitor; and, contrary to my wordless but pantomimic entreaties, out he went with them (myself closely following), when, one by one, he whirled and twisted them by the neck and cast them unfeelingly away into the rushing stream! Vividly do I recall my horrible prejudice toward that man. In fact, that one circumstance was so shocking that it gave me *my first fear of a fellow-being:* and, as a sequence, a dread of meeting certain looking individuals has not even to this day passed entirely out of my mind.

Horrid thoughts of death infested me for many days and nights succeeding this scene; but my mother's gentle hand and kindly tones soothed me at length, and thus prepared me for another event.

Although I had frequently asked to go and play at neighbor Cookingham's house, which was located perhaps a mile south of ours, yet I was uniformly denied; till, near the close a warm spring day, mother said she wished me to go over there and stay with the juveniles all that night. This sudden change in my affairs and habits I could not comprehend. But obedient to the unaccountable, yet welcome dictate, away we peregrinated, trudging along through thick and thin, till the desired threshold was beneath our feet. When once within the strange and, to me, wonderful abode, the striped carpets and painted chairs, the brass andirons on the hearth, the window curtains and beautiful bedquilts, the wheat bread and sweet butter — all made my visit a complete holiday. I was in a museum; and wondered why our house wasn't made just as attractive and comfortable.

On the subsequent morning, after a good breakfast of what they termed spon and milk, I was led home; across the two saplings which formed a sort of temporary (short cut) foot-bridge, over the rushing stream, between our house and the woods. Entering through the door-way, I noticed a change, that is, Eliza's bed was utterly hid by a canopy of old quilts. Next, I heard a groan behind the enclosure; but, ere my tongue forged a word, mother said :—

"Come in, Jackson — Eliza's got sick."

Father's occupation was also changed. He was busy sawing a board into several pieces; which he soon nailed together, and formed a small box. In reply to my interrogatories he would authoritatively bid me to "stand out of his way and not busy myself about what didn't concern me."

But my curiosity was up, and I persisted in maintaining the position of "spectator." The box completed, it received a lining of brown paper; and then — what do you think? — why, father went behind the suspended quilts, brought out a very, very little baby which was motionless and cold in death, and then laid it down in the rough and ready coffin! Contrary to his emphatic remonstrances, I examined that human being in miniature; with what emotions I know not, save those of extreme simplistic wonderment. Silently, I watched his every movement. Placing a cloth over the inanimate babe, down he pressed it; then nailed a thick cover on, and so closed out the world.

With spade in hand, and the box under his arm, forth he went into the southern potato patch — which, poetically speaking, was our garden — and, halting beneath an apple-tree, began digging a deep hole. On this initial occasion my father was undertaker, hearse, and sexton; while I, without appreciating the solemn fact, was at once the funeral train and the only mourner. The grave was dug, and got ready; in the shape of a big iron kettle. And then the sexton, still silent as myself, deposited the coffin, and returned the earth whence it came. Unspeaking yet, he went to the house with quicker step; and when I followed, I found him at his accustomed and more congenial employment.

CHAPTER XII.

WHICH I ASK MANY QUESTIONS.

"Do not muse at me, my most worthy friends;
I have a strange infirmity, which is nothing
To those that know me."

AN important and novel region of human life was now partly exposed to my view; and true to the impulses of the organ of causality, I could not help going for a thorough exploration. Accordingly on returning from the funeral, I ran straight to the maternal fountain for light and knowledge.

"Where d' you get that 'are baby, mother?"

"Oh, do n't bother me; I'm very busy now." And she hastened behind the quilt canopy, with a bowl of nourishment for Eliza.

"What made Eliza get sick?" I asked as mother emerged from the concealment—"say, mother, say—what made her so sick?"

There was, evidently, "other fish to fry" than answering my questions; for, though an expression of sadness filled her eyes, away she flew, here and there, doing all sorts of things with the greatest despatch; and so I had as much as I could do to keep up, and "get in a word edgewise" now and then.

"Say, mother—won't you? Where did you get that 'are baby?"

After numerous evasions and prevarications, which served only to stimulate my already much-excited inquisitiveness, she replied :

" Why, the doctor brought it ?"

" The doctor !" thought I. " Who's the doctor? I hain't seen no nothin' like a doctor !" But quickly gathering my recollection, I asked :—

" W~s that 'are man what know'd so much—what spoke such great, long, hard words when Eliza got married—was he the doctor ?"

" Why don't you crack that dummy's pate ?" vociferated a voice from the hidden bed. " If I had hold of him, I'd shake his day-lights out if he didn't stop ! *That* I would !"

Although emanating from a weakened and prostrate individual, whose form was wholly obscured, yet I was not at a moment's loss to know who originated the awful but characteristic threat. There was in that exclamation a *something* so irritating and so self-evidently unnecessary as applied to me, that I felt nettled and combative ; and hence, readily remembering Dave's big word when frightened by the ghost, I tartly returned :—

" I guess you hain't so *thundering* sick as you make b'lieve."

But contrary to my anticipation, if I had any, this emphatic retort greatly disturbed the equanimity of my mother. At the same time it had a marvellous effect on the muscular fibres of my father's right arm. His hand grasped the ever-present strap, with which he struck at me ; but missed his aim—an accidental result, for which I am even at this late day very, very grateful. Be-cause, as I thought at the time, I did not deserve to be punished ; and if, in spite of this private moral conviction, my father had hurt my budding self-respect by brutal blows upon my person, I tremble to think of the germs of hatreds and cruelties which might have been then implanted, to ripen at some subsequent period, into fearful deeds of violence toward domestic animals, and, perhaps, even against my fellow-men.

No ! Explosive as were the promises of punishment made by this paternal veteran, and hasty as were his gesticulations in the direction of their immediate fulfilment ; yet, as the gentle angel of memory joyfully testifies, he invariably preserved my infantile mind from the life-long injuries and maddening mortifications, which are likely always to result from a *forcible* correction of the errors and wrongs of childhood!

In the mere pronunciation of the word "thundering," I could not perceive the least harm. In fact, as I thought when first I heard it used by Dave, it seemed the very best name for anything greatly disagreeable. Therefore, the evil of the speech being unknown to me, I esteemed my father's anger as a great discount on the excellency of his judgment. Consequently, as the genius of nature infallibly dictates to the young, I hastened to my mother for unbounded sympathy and protection.

"Don't scare the boy's life out," said she to her husband "He didn't know no better."

"Yes! I'll warrant it," he returned snappishly, "you'll spile that young one, and bring him to the gallus. Don't humor him If you do, my word for't, you'll rue the day you begun it."

The good woman sighed heavily, and continued in mute silence the discharge of her household duties; while the excited cord wainer, though repairing the sole of a neighbor's shoe, continued at an inverse ratio to *impair* the soul of his domestic happiness In short, there was developed a fearful dispute between husband and wife — the "bone of contention" being me, and only me!

But as time brings flowers to earth, so brought it comparative peace to the family triangle; and I, once more rescued from the danger of castigation, revived the subject of my curiosity. Pursuing my affectionate apologist out doors, I asked:—

"Mother, now tell me — where did the doctor get that 'are baby?"

"What makes you ask?"

"'Cause I wants one to play with: only I don't want a dead baby though."

She smiled benignly upon me, and said:—

"You must be still and wait, child, till Uncle Bart comes over to our house; then ask him, and see what he'll say."

This gentle advice was sufficient. The subject was never broached again, till the venerable Dutchman, who owned the tenement we occupied, arrived one day to hoe the corn and examine the sprouting potatoes in the garden. He was uniformly very social and jovial; and we, children, having been told to use either the prefix " Mr." or " Uncle" when addressing those mother called "grown-up people," preferred the latter expletive for our patronizing friend.

" Vell, mine leetle poy," said he to me, as I followed him to the lower end of the lot, " how ish de sic voman?"

" Eliza's got well now," I replied; busily plotting meanwhile as to how I could open up the interesting subject which had been referred to him by my mother. But his next question assisted me.

" Vell, vat ish dat place under de tre yonder?" he asked, pointing to the unturfed mound made by the baby's grave.

" Why, don't you know, Uncle Bart?" I inquired; "that's where father buried the little dead baby, that the doctor brought for our folks."

" Vy, ish dat so, mi poy?" asked the good-natured Hollander, as he busily removed the weeds with his hoe. " Vy dat was vari padt, inteat."

" Yes! 'twas so," responded I mournfully. " But I wants a live baby of my own to play with. Can't you tell me where the doctor got it, Uncle Bart?"

" Ha! ha! ha!" heartily laughed the jolly man. " Vot! you vont life pape?"

" Yes, Uncle Bart, I does," said I, blushing. " I wants a live one, too."

" Vel den, pe a coot poy, and I vil tel vare de doctor cot it."

With much enthusiasm I promised to be good; and he thus continued :—

" In de fust plash de doct pounds de holler tre, den puts hish ear tc de tre; an if de chile ish widin an wake, den he hears dim cry for sum milch; den he saws te tre down, an taks te pape to hish own housh; den he sel te leetle cretur to de fust sic voman vot vonts dim."

Wondrous revelation! Astounded by the grand sweep of the venerable Dutchman's superior intelligence on the origin of "leetle papes," I became, contrary to my reputed character, very reverent and well nigh worshipful. The simplicity, sincerity, and willingness, with which Uncle Bart instructed me in the art of procuring a live baby, as a pet to play with, encouraged me to make him a *chum* for the time being; and I was consequently emboldened to question him still further on other subjects of interest to my young mind. The entire baldness of his head had often greatly excited my childish curiosity, and now I asked:—

"Say, Uncle Bart, say — what's the reason you hain't got no hair on?"

At this the old man's face flashed out and gathered up into multitudinous comical wrinkles, the result of mirth restrained, and he replied:—

"Nix kom ahraus, mi poy! How vari punny! Vot you vonts to kno dat fur, eh? He! he!—vel—ha! ha!—ef yu ish coot to say nothing ven axed, den I vil tel hows de ting vus kom to happen."

This mysterious introduction to the forthcoming information exalted my anxiety a degree higher; and rendered any delay of the sequel so hard to bear, that I cheerfully promised to preserve secrecy. Conditions complied with, the bald-headed and broad-faced Hollander supported himself against the hoe-handle; and laughing and sober by turns, as near as I can remember, he thus proceeded:—

"Vel, ef I mus tel yu, mi poy, I vil. Mine frow had pen vonting von printle kow. Vel, I goes an finds de vari ting vot she vonted. Te man taks mi tollars an I taks te printle kow. Mi frow wus vari pleast, inteat, mit to cretur—'cause he give town a pig pail ful of milch. Put von morning apout noon, jist ash mi frow wus making te pot boil fur spon and milch for supper mi headt *itcht* an *itcht* lik te vari tifel ; an mi frow sed te donder ing printle kow's tamt lish hat cot sprinkled mit mi pig mesh of hair. Vel, dey voldent pe combed out—no tamt a pit of it— put dey eat and eat and grubbed avay till de hair wus all gone !''

The deferential emotions which moved me toward Uncle Bart, previous to this narration, rapidly subsided, as he concluded it, into a horrid repugnance to continuing longer in his presence. With mingled feelings of alarm and loathing I listened to the last sentence, and then fled precipitately houseward—to make, despite my promise of secrecy, a full report (as I did in the apple case) of the old man's disagreeable story. I did so ; and, with apprehensive tears and shuddering whimpers, besought my mother to save my head from a like calamity. She quieted me, as usual, and gave me the most satisfactory assurances, that Uncle Bart had only told me what he did *in fun*. But somehow, through several subsequent years, I could not get over a fear of having my own hair destroyed in a manner equally disgusting and horrible.

The sport of this verminly narrative gratified my father and sisters considerably. They seemed to think the joke a fine feather in the old man's cap : while I, being naturally disposed to confide implicitly in the wisdom and authority of those advanced in years, received a shock from which I did not soon fully recover. And, therefore, I hereby put in my individual protest against that ruinous laxity of moral principle, on the part of aged persons, which permits them to talk to children as if they were idiots or imbeciles in matters of truth. 'Tis my belief that more than one child may be found, in every community, whose ordinary propensities are privately regarded in self-estimation, as better authority than the decisions of older minds ; all as a sequence, to the flippant and disrespectful manner in which the delicate confidence of infantile intellects has been too frequently neglected, repulsed, or abused.

CHAPTER XIII

IN WHICH I GO BABY-HUNTING.

" Can such things be,
And overcome us like a summer's cloud,
Without our special wonder ?"

THERE is doubtless a marked difference in the original suscep-
tibility of imagination in different persons, as of any other mental
possession ; but, if I write the exact truth of myself, I must confess
that the finely-drawn lights and shades of external Nature had next
to no effect whatever upon my juvenescent sensibilities.

Only this do I remember—that, taking counsel with myself
alone, I set out one bright day on the very romantic mission of
hunting up a live baby. Previous to my departure, I crammed
my pockets with round stones of various sizes, as a means of
rousing the sleeping innocents which, according to the Dutchman's
serious account, were to be found only in the dark concealment of
hollow trees.

An imaginative and sentimental mind could easily picture to
itself the delicate beauties of objective creation, which, poetically
speaking, broke lovingly and lavishly upon the eye from every
point of human observation. The glorious monarch of heaven,
the mighty sun, shone resplendent between the horizon and the
meridian. There was a transparent, crystalline brilliancy in the
air, giving to each object a sharpness of outline, and inspiring the
human senses with an intense realization of existence. I presume

that the feathery songsters warbled their melodies in each tree; and I suppose, also, that the music of many dancing streamlets was conveyed to my ear. Wild, melodious, and free, doubtless, came every note from the song of the circumscribed world in which I then lived.

But of all this, and many other enchanting realities surrounding me, I had not the least appreciation. This fact in my own psychological history predisposes me to the belief that certain idealistic writers, when describing the myriad beautiful romances and dreams of juvenility and adolescence, indulge in a poetic license of no ordinary magnitude. The blooming Eden of childhood is known only to the full-grown, healthy man; that is, 'tis a pure maturity alone which can truly appreciate the good, the romantic, and the beautiful.

The plain truth is, without any poetical embellishment, that my hunting-expedition was mentally planned to come off in the great woods, across the stream, just west of our rustic residence. The nearest way to this woodland was by the foot-bridge already described as being composed of a couple of limber saplings reaching across from bank to bank. When once I got my feet upon it, the poles vibrated and dashed so rapidly up and down in the rushing tide, that I came very near being precipitated headlong into the swollen current. This at first terrified me much; but, throwing overboard some of my ballast, I reached the opposite bank without accident.

Having gained the field of discovery, in high hopes of success, I commenced my novel peregrinations. As I picked my way through the brush and quagmires, I thought thus: "Suppose I should wake up more babies than *one*, what shall I do? 'Twould make me sick to leave them crying in the woods; but 'twould make me sicker to see that grim, ugly old man wring their heads off as he killed the kittens!"

With the mental conclusion to step along lightly, and pound the trees as carefully as possible, I religiously approached a lofty rock oak, which I regarded as large enough to be "hollow;" and then and there I inaugurated the quickening or awakening process. I knocked and listened, and listened and knocked, and then I whispered, and presently shouted aloud; but without hearing the infantile "cry," which I was tremulously prepared to hear as my reward. Then I tried my experiment on other trees, and finally upon various *logs* which lay scattered here and there through the forest; but nothing save my own sobs of disappointment and whimperings of fatigue broke upon the listening ear.

Disheartened, I began to retrace my steps. 'Tis said by some that childhood is the happiest period of life, because it is esteemed to be *freest* from the vexations, and onerous cares, and possible disappointments, of weighty responsibility. But, so far as my own experience goes, I verily believe that no man was ever made to feel more humiliated or saddened by the misfortunes of speculation and commerce, than I, as a child, felt as a consequence of my failure of success on this particular expedition. Fancy me, dear reader, returning to the home of my early memories *childless*, and without any adequate compensation!

Of course, I was of necessity thoughtful. "Now," said I mentally, "that 'are plaguy old Uncle Bart has been foolin' me ag'in; I don't b'lieve nothin' what he ses no more!" My simplistic confidence in the goodness and reliability of gray hairs began to decline. Superannuated wisdom, though crowned with a bald cranium, and leaning on a most useful instrument of agriculture, seemed next to foolishness.

Thus thinking and concluding, I trudged on to the brink of the swift waters. The stream appeared considerably more swollen and more rapid than before, for a heavy rain of a previous day had greatly enlarged the tributary streamlets through the upper country.

To walk the shaking foot-bridge, made of insecure saplings, was beyond my pedestrian skill. So, down I got on "all fours"—a quadruped form of locomotion by and through which the human

.nfant is developed into a permanent biped—and, cautiously creeping, I made some headway toward the opposite shore. But the
rushing waters, splashing and dashing on every side, added to the
rapid undulations of the elastic poles beneath me, proved too great
a trial for my strength.

"Mother! mother!" cried I. But the distance was too great
for my voice to be heard. "Come! help!—I can't stir!" I
screamed, as, with every nerve, I strained to retain my hoid. No
aid came. A dreadful dizziness seized my head, which seemed to
make everything whirl and buzz with a frightful celerity. Another moment, and the springing poles seemed to fly from under me,
throwing me with violent force into the roaring torrent! In my
agony I grasped the horizontal saplings—now above me—when
the speeding tide, at the moment, carried my head beneath and
projected my feet into the air! I tried to shout and vociferate for
assistance; but the foaming water ran down my throat and painfully closed out my breath! Although the sun was now at the
zenith, yet do I remember how dark the world suddenly appeared;
and I recollect, also, *as I lost all fear,* how the twinkling stars
came out in the bending heavens, causing me so gently to think
of sleep. They soothed me, like my mother's eyes, and I slept!

Parents, guardians, superintendents of public schools! "Come,
and let us reason together." Let me ask you—"Should little
children be taught to disrespect and insult their more matured
and more experienced protectors and associates?"

You may think yourselves very expert in evading your child's
questions on delicate subjects; you can invent momentary subter-
fuges; you can gracefully and stealthily prevaricate; you can
manifest your superior discretion through a squeamish denial of
what you know; you may be too delicate to tell the truth, but not
too delicate to construct a festooned refuge of cunning little "white
lies," just suited to your child's undeveloped capacity and inexpe-
rience; you may treat your juvenile pet as if it had not *a memory*

that, one day, will rise up to rebuke and charge you with deception
your amiable prudery; your silly denial of the ever-beautiful facts
of maternity; your profane shirking of what underlies the origin of
man—all, too plainly declare that your delicacy is spurious, that
your veracity is mixed with deception, that your refinement is un
civil, that your capacity is not adequate to the comprehension and
rearing of the young!

But how many parents there are, good and intelligent, who really do not know what to reply when questioned by children.
Such inquire, " What shall we say?"   In reply, I will refer to the
case described in preceding pages.   Let us suppose that the boy's
mother, instead of answering, " The doctor brought the baby," had
simply replied: " The doctor knows more than I do about it.
When you see him, perhaps he will tell you what he knows.   If
he does not, the reason will be that you are now too young to understand him."

With such a reply in his mind, the little inquisitive urchin
would rest satisfied for the time being; and, on making the discovery at some future day, and recalling what his mother said, he
could not withhold either his admiration for her truthfulness or respect for her refinement.   And so with the venerable Dutchman.
Instead of filling the youngster's brain with ridiculous imaginings,
suppose he had said: " Vel, mi leetle poy, dar ish many tings dat
shildren can't do mid dar han's, as yu vel know; an' so dar ish
many tings dat shildren can't understand mid dar heads.   Now,
pe a coot poy, and, ven yu ish pigger, and ven yu can vork as
pig peeples vorks, den yu shall know jest' how te doct' bro't de
pape to yourn housh."

Now, it seems to me that the most limited understanding can
at once perceive the moral benefit of such counsel.   The subject
of this history would nave been, by those few words of truth,
rescued from the fast-flowing waters; and saved not less from
many bad impressions concerning the foolishness and falsehood of
persons advanced in years.

CHAPTER XIV.

THE CURTAIN AGAIN RISES.

"To-morrow, and to-morrow, and to-morrow,
Creeps in this petty pace from day to day,
To the last syllable of recorded time."

GLIDING along over a dead level of commonplace experiences, of several weeks' duration, the reader may behold, in the year 1832, the exodus of the cordwainer's family — bound for another tenement, in the town of Hyde Park, Dutchess county, New York — himself, meanwhile, hopeful and jovial under the despotic enchantment of the infernal wizard Alcohol.

There was now, as on occasions of similar trial, an expression of deep dejection upon the countenance of his wife. In her large eyes there was a look of Extreme Distance; as if beholding a vision of some other, fairer, holier, higher state of existence. Mournful indeed was the sigh with which she openly announced the fact that, at certain moments, o'er the past her thoughts were sadly roaming. Her dissatisfied expressions too plainly told (to those who could read them) that she felt herself a stranger in a strange land — a dove, set forth from the Ark of Life, finding not where to rest the sole of her foot in safety. If, at such moments of inward retrospection, her thoughts had been truly rendered into symbolic language, they might have reminded one of the " Deserted Village :"—

"Sunk are thy bowers in shapeless ruin all,
  And the long grass o'ertops the mouldering wall ;
And trembling, shrinking from the spoiler's hand,
  Far, far away, thy children leave the land !"

For thus, when viewed as a whole on the background of hei
deeper life, appeared the many homes she had been compelled tc
desert, in obedience to the fiat of her restless husband.   In justifi
cation whereof he would in substance say :—

"Nothing ventured, nothing had.   What's the use o' staying
here, with my nose to the grindstone ?   Make or break — that's
my way !"   And thus organizationally impelled, he treated his
wife's constitutional yearnings and spiritual lingerings as the childish ebullitions of a childish intellect.   Was that right in him ?
Was that wrong in her ?   Where shall the praise terminate ?
Where shall the blame begin ?   Who can infallibly judge them ?
Who will answer ?   Away o'er the mountains of rudimental existence, methinks I hear the responsive echo, " Who ?"

As the loaded wagon rolled along on the highway toward the
house already indicated, the desponding woman was by an urchin
thus addressed :—

" Mother, tell me once more — how did I come to breathe ?"

" Why, child, 't was so ordered that you wasn't to leave us
then."

" Who ordered it, mother ?"

" 'T was Providence, Jackson.   It was so to be.   It couldn't be
no different.   You wasn't a-goin' for to die so young.   That's the
reason, bub."

" Say, mother, say," continued I, " hain't that 'are Prov'dence
somethin' like that 'are Santa Claus what you told me ?"

At this, the unsophisticated and reverential woman shuddered,
as if alarmed, but replied :—

" Oh, don't talk no more like that, Jackson !   Providence, you
must know, is the Maker of the hull world — the source cf every
blessin' ; and 't ain't good to talk so about Providence."

" Well, I won't no more," I replied, blushing with a regretfu' feeling that I had unintentionally wounded her spirit; "but, I'd like to hear you tell, mother, how I was made to live again."

In her own provincial and unpretending dialect, she proceeded:
"Somehow or ruther, it so happened that Eliza and Henry (her husband) was a-standin' by the well-curb a-talkin', when, all to once, she looked down at the big creek, and, seein' somethin' curious pokin' up by the poles, she tells Henry to go see what 't was. So down the hill he goes, and, when he got near enough, he screams, 'Why, as I live, it's Jackson's feet!' Then Eliza knocked at the winder, and yelled to me and father, and ses— 'Make haste! our bub's got drownded in the brook!' We both jumped all to once, and didn't stop for nothin', but run out jest as Henry was a-bringin' you up to the house. Oh, how the water dripped off o' your clothes! You was as wet, bub, as a drownded rat. Father sed, 'I guess he ain't dead.' But we'd heerd that *rollin'* was good to bring drownded folks to life ag'in. So we rolled and tumbled you, over and over, on the hard floor but you didn't show no signs of breathin' or livin' at all. But I know'd Providence wouldn't take you from us so young. Henry went and got an old barrel, and father rolled you face downwards on it very quick, and shook you at the same time. Oh, how glad I was to see the water begin to pour out of your mouth! You was very sick, and threw up as much as a gallon of water; then you groaned, and I know'd you would get well. We wrapped you up in warm flannel, and covered you all over with thick bedclothes. And by night you was able to set up and talk — don't you remember *that*, Jackson?"

"Oh, yes, I remember *that*, mother," I responded; "but why didn't Prov'dence keep me from fallin in the creek?"

"'Cause," she replied, "'t ain't his way. He lets folks go on jest as they pleases, till they gets in trouble; then, if he likes 'em, he helps 'em out; but, if he doesn't like 'em, then he lets 'em get out hap-hazard, or any way they can."

At this moment, the inebriated cordwainer came running back

to us from the forward wagon — with his dark eyes dancing a horn pipe, while his shaky legs seemed ludicrously endeavoring to perform that function which is characteristic only of the sober-minded — to announce that yon house, whose chimney-top was just visible across the fields, was to be our next habitation. The ride thither was brief. Without detailing the fusion and confusion incidental thereto, I will just record the agreeable fact that, ere the ebony drapery of Night clothed the fairy, frosted landscape o'er, we were pretty well fitted in and reconciled to our new quarters.

We were really pleased with and proud of our exchange. Instead of a crumbling rookery, we found ourselves in a comfortable cottage, situated in the midst of apple, peach, and plum trees, and not more than two rods from the public road. How rejoiced we were! Julia Ann and I expressed our enthusiastic delight in various fantastic ways; and when we got into the trundle-bed that night, I remember exclaiming aloud: "Hain't father real good, mother? He's helped us out of a bad place — jest like that 'are Prov'dence what you told me."

CHAPTER XV.

IN WHICH ARE SIGNS OF SECOND-SIGHT.

"I fear, too early; for my mind misgives,
    Some consequence, yet hanging in the stars."

OUR industrious and thriving landlord, Hiram Marshall, was our very best friend. He cheerfully provided my father with sufficient field labor to pay the rent, to buy a young cow, and otherwise to advance the private fortunes of our domestic triangle.

One warm afternoon in mid-summer, the farmer called at our house for a drink of cold water; and while there he remarked to mother, that he had just spent two whole hours in searching for an ox-chain, but without success. As he spoke, I observed an air of dreamy *abstraction* sweep athwart her mild face; and, contrary to her habit, she appeared not to hear anything he was relating. Presently, however, she recovered from her involuntary revery, and said: "I guess 't ain't lost, Mr. Marshall."

"Guess what ain't lost," he replied, "the ox-chain?"

"Yes! that's what I mean. It's jest where you left it your own self."

"You're mistaken—good woman," said he, smiling with incredulity. "The last time I had it, I was drawing stone in my upper lot yonder; and, as I've looked that field all over, I'm sure it ain't there."

"Yes, 't is, though," returned she with unshaken confidence, "you'll find it jest where you left it—agin the big stump, in the north corner of the lot—now, see if you don't."

Actuated by the simplicity and definiteness of her direction, off he went to the specified spot. When next we saw him, he acknowledged that the chain was just where she said, but declared he couldn't imagine how it happened, unless mother "was a witch."

Aided by the refinement and delicacies which have resulted from years of subsequent discipline and culture, I can look back upon the sensuous experiences of my youth, and allow myself to fancy, as many individuals do, that the poetic and the beautiful in external nature made a legitimate impression upon the canvass of imagination and memory. Doubtless it is true, that some very young children, born of certain parents, do have, like Lucretia and Margaret Davidson, an early perception of the beautiful; but, as already said, if I write exactly of my own reminiscences, I am constrained to acknowledge the realization of no romance, no fascination, no spiritual delight, in anything connected with early life. On the contrary, I remember that I valued trees, in hot weather, for their fruit and their shade; in winter months, for the fire-wood they made after being laboriously sawed and split. Stones existed, to build fences with; grass, for cows to eat; water, for all to drink; the sun, to keep us warm; the rain, to make vegetation grow; the snow, that children might ride down hill; the ice, to slide and play upon; thunder and lightning, because (as I thought when mother was frightened) something had got loose in the clouds, and might fall like a great rock on somebody's head; and thus, throughout the entire programme of my juvenile experiences, I valued all objects and sensations — my parents and sisters included — in proportion as they administered to the desires and gratifications of my bodily needs and sensibilities.

But now, facing the past, and looking with eyes measurably trained to detect the delicate and the super-terrestrial in the commonest things, I know that there was great *opulence* in the poorest blade of grass beneath our window; *music*, in the patter ings of the rain upon the cottage-roof; *pictures*, in the furlongs of landscape visible from our door; *angels*, as much in clouds and darkness as in sunshine; *poetry*, in summer's and winter's myriad lights and shades; and a divine *substance*, in the dark and dreary depths of every shadow! But, alas! not knowing of the existence of these imperishable riches — which were as much ours as that of any other family in the world — we felt ourselves frequently and painfully embarrassed. Our oppressors were — Ignorance, Intemperance, Poverty, Discord. These terrible despots seldom exerted their power at once; but, like so many demons in the poor man's path, took turns in tormenting and chafing us.

One day my mother had upon her that look of Distance, which I began to dread, as the certain precursor or omen of domestic evil. At different times, while engaged at her housework, she appeared like one lost in the vision of some far-off scene. With her great eyes wide open, she would look abstractedly against the wall — or *through it* as it were — into the vacuity of a remote and unknown space; at which, more than ever before, I felt disconcerted and terrified; and, all unconscious of any filial disrespect, I tried to make her act social and natural, by pulling at her dress, and by passing my hand rapidly to and fro, between her eyes and the direction in which their vision seemed to set. But all this, I noticed, had next to no effect. When recovered from her dreamy and dreary revery, she gently rebuked me: "Don't do so, bub! do n't you know no better than that?"

Generally speaking, almost every healthy boy at my age would have been out-of-doors flying a kite, or at some other amusement usual to the all-glorious month of October. But, to this sport-loving season of childhood, my history is a uniform and positive exception. Instead of gathering walnuts or grapes in the woods — rather than climbing trees for favorite fruits — I chose to dwell with the lone woman: "hanging," as my father sneeringly said, "to my mother's apron-string." She was not alone in any social

understanding of the term, for every member of the family was a
constant inmate of that house, except Eliza, who had gone to live
elsewhere with her husband.   But, to me, she ever appeared to
have an undercurrent of private life, with which there was min-
gling the affection of no congenial spirit.   Not a creature was there
to understand her; no soul to sympathize with and help her on
her incomprehensible pilgrimage.   It was a vague conviction of her
loneliness, doubtless, added to the natural selfishness of my dependent nature, desirous to be cared for and indulged, which
caused me to make her my particular associate and confidant.
After she had passed through another day's uncertainty and
absent-mindedness, imparting that dreaded and wandering expression to her eyes, I asked :—

   " Say, mother, what makes you act so queer all the time ?"

   My question, so unexpectedly and pointedly put, evidently dis
turbed her, because she replied: " Oh, 't ain't nothin' to nobody
but me."   This rejoinder was neither new nor satisfactory ; and
hence I started out on another track, and said :—

   " Hain't we better off than what we was in Bart Cropsey's
house ?   Hain't father more soberer and steadier than what he
was in that 'are old shanty?   He's a workin' on the farm every
day, hain't he, mother?   And hain't our cow e'ne most paid for ?
Say, mother, what's the matter of you ?"

   To all this juvenile review of the improvement in our existing
circumstances, over those of previous months within my recollection, she despairingly replied :—

   " Oh, 't ain't no use a talkin', child.   There's more trouble a
comin' !   'T is man's lot !   It's so ordered to be ; an' can't be no
different I'm 'fraid."

   " What trouble, mother, what's a goin' to happen next ?"

   " None but Providence knows," said she gloomily, " but I have
seen the signs."

   " What signs ?   What was it that you seen ?   Tell me, mother,
I won't tell father — nor nobody else."

I've been feelin' jest as I felt when lost in John Myers's woods," she replied; "I've seen the new moon over my left shoulder lately; and last night, when washin' the supper things, I dropt a fork on the floor, tine foremost; and then, in the middle of the night, I dreamt one of my bad dreams, about crossing muddy water and combin' my hair with a coarse comb, when my hair come out in bunches : and besides, I seen some dark shadders out in the road four or five times, within a couple of days; so I know well enough, as I allus knows, that there's trouble for this 'ere poor family."

To this recital I listened with childish wonderment, mingled with considerable agitation. I knew not how to utter a word of comfort. Indeed, in writing this history I have, as I fear, reported my mother's as well as my own speech as being more direct and less uncouth and bungling than it was in fact. At this day, with my present knowledge of the English language, I recall the tautological talking, the rustic chatting, the ungrammatical conversations of our family, with unfeigned surprise and subdued amusement.

Thus brought up, or rather *pushed* up, I did not know words enough wherewith to convey what little sympathy my limited capacity allowed me to experience for my mother in her psychological trials. But I began to feel a need of confidence in the protective watchfulness of the Good Big Man in the sky; and that night, with considerable enthusiasm and emphasis, I repeated many times this supplication : " Say, kind Prov'dence, you won't let nothin' happen to our folks; will you?"

CHAPTER XVI.

MY TEMPTATION TO BE PROFANE.

A spirit not my own wrenched me within ;
And I have spoken words I fear and hate."

THE harvestings and corn-cuttings over for that season, my
father, agreeably to his established custom, went about in search
of shoemaking, as a means of supporting his family through the
fall and winter months. Success crowned his exertions at length,
and he took his seat on the throne of St. Crispin with all the regal
majesty and self-satisfaction at his command.

One genial autumnal day, as this industrious artisan was departing — with the results of his labor, for the wholesale and retail
shop, located in some distant village beyond the hills, whence the
work had been procured — he pleasantly accosted me, and said ·
" Look here, Jackson, if you 'll bring brush all day from the
woods, to kindle fires with, I 'll fetch you a jewsharp."

Now this notorious musical instrument was the greatest and
most extraordinary human invention, to yield melody, that had
ever come within the range of my natural vision. It possessed,
to my imagination, untold charms, and embodied the greatest advantages. What made the harp seem peculiarly attractive was,
the idea of playing and getting pleasure out of it with one's mouth
—just as gratification was got out of cherries, strawberries, apples,
peaches, and other delicious eatables. As a natural consequence,
then, I cheerfully ratified the spontaneous bargain ; and, taking

only time enough to acquaint mother with the promise and conditions of its fulfilment, I straightway went to my day's labor.

If the reader knows anything about gathering brush all day in the woods — especially while too young and too weak to pull and draw the best pieces from clinging brambles and entwining briers — then will I be understood when I describe it as one of the most vexatious of occupations. There is much work, but little show. I tugged away for hours. Toward night I got very tired — very nervous with anxiety — and a piece of bread and butter. But at last I actually accumulated what I proudly regarded as a great pile of kindling-wood and brush near the garden-gate. My object in stacking the evidence of my industry there was, to overcome father's mind at first sight with the conviction that the jewsharp was fully earned and honestly deserved. To this belief I had already brought my mother, by getting her to come out to see for herself the unmistakeable triumphs of my toil.

Thus satisfied, I stationed myself against the outside doorpost, to catch the first glimpse of the absent progenitor, whose return was every moment expected. Anon, through the lengthening shadows of the approaching twilight, I beheld with joy the well-known man, staggering along laden with a great package of leather, to manufacture into boots and shoes during the next two weeks. Self-control being now absolutely out of the question, I ran to meet and welcome him, and so get my musical remuneration in advance. He bade me wait till we reached the house. As he passed the garden-gate, and saw the brush-heap there, my ears tingled with delight when he said, "Why, you've been very smart!" But who can express my disappointment, when he declared that he had entirely *forgotten* to bring me the jewsharp! What a revulsion of feeling! A wealthy landholder, hearing that all his property had been swallowed by an earthquake, could not have felt worse. My sudden bankruptcy, for a boy's mind, was just as hard to bear, as a man's misfortune is hard for a man's capacity. I was both sad and angry. I was honestly and stoutly

enraged against my father for his negligence. Half-suffocated
with the contending emotions of disappointment and rage, I determined to go out by the wood-pile, *and swear an awful oath!* 1
saw no other plan to get relief—no other way to do the subject
justice. This resolution took immediate effect. Thither I deliberately proceeded; and concentrating, at one burning focus, all
the ugly words I could recall at the moment, I actually and knowingly swore: "*I'll be dod darn to dod darnation if that hain't too
thunderin' dam bad, any how !*"

Twilight had died away into darkness, in which I stood alone
and enveloped. Serenely shone the evening stars. Not a breath
of air moved the foliage in the garden; not a sound could I hear
from the apple-orchard; not a sigh of sadness from the woods
whence the brush had been so laboriously obtained. Still, very
still, too still, was all the world—within the reach of my physical
senses—at the moment when I so wilfully disturbed the scene
with my terrible profanity.

Hark! What's *that?* In an instant after I had vented my
rage, there passed into mine ear an exclamation, heavy laden
with that mysterious condemnation which penetrated me to the
very core of my being—" WHY, JACKSON !"

'T was my mother's voice—or I thought it was—and in a moment my frame quivered and shook with fear. Darkness fell
round about me with a sudden and alarming density. The very
air seemed undulated and convulsed, as by the throes of some
offended deity. A swift wind seemingly circumgyrated and
buzzed close to my head, and, as I imagined, lifted my cap and
replaced it several times.

" *Why, Jackson !*" Once only heard I these plain words; but
they thrilled me with an unaccountable horror. They unmistakea-
bly conveyed, and awakened in me toward myself, *astonishment,
rebuke, grief, commiseration!* " O pshaw! what's the use bein
'fraid of mother?" soliloquized I; " she can't blame me, no how.'
This thought refreshed my courage; and though still uncontrolla-

bly agitated, into the house I went, and poutingly exclaimed "Don't care if you did hear me swear. 'Twas too bad, any how!"

Fortunately, the maternal ear alone heard my spontaneous confession. The fatigued man, having walked far and imbibed much, was almost asleep by the fire; while Julia Ann, ever kind and ever active, was busy with preparations for the evening meal. The good woman looked very sad and much troubled, which caused me to regret still more my profanity.

Supper being over, and the sleeping-hour arrived, she said: "Now, Jackson, me and you must talk. What I wants to know is, be you becomin' a bad boy? Be I to be disappointed in everything in my life? Is you a-goin' to act jest like other folks's bad children, an' bring sorrow to your poor mother everlastin'ly?"

Her desponding discourse greatly intensified my sufferings, and made the tears come, with words of self-justification: "Don't you think 'twas too bad? War'n't father to blame for not gittin' the jewsharp?"

"Oh, 'tain't no use talkin' that 'are way," replied she peevishly; "everybody does wrong sometimes. An' if you're wicked 'cause other folks is bad, then there's no use for to live no more. Now tell me jest what you said out doors there."

Sobbingly and regretfully I repeated, *ad literatim*, the string of wicked words, and asked, "Didn't you hear me?"

"Mercy save us!" she exclaimed. "No, I didn't hear you; and I'm thankful I didn't. Providence know'd I couldn't bear to hear my boy speak such bad words."

This answer astonished me greatly. "Then, who called me?" said I. "Who hollered so loud, and said, 'Why, Jackson'? I tho't 'twas you; but bein' so dark, I couldn't see. Must be 'twas Julia Ann."

"No, 'twasn't nuther," returned my quietly-listening sister. "This is the fust I've heard of your swearin'—an' I hope to mercy 'twill be the last."

"Now I know why I seen them shadders in the road," sighed my mother. "'T was so ordered to be, an' can't be no different, I'm 'fraid. That 'are voice, child, makes me think of what the Bible ses about Cain bein' hurried on from one bad thing to another, until he killed his brother. Then *he heer'd a voice* cryin' from the blood on the ground, an' from the clouds over his head, sayin', 'Where's your brother Abel?' O dear me," continued she gloomily, "I'm 'fraid there's trouble a-comin'. Providence has been *a-callin' you* to be good, an' you don't mind a word he ses!"

Perhaps the thoughtful reader — remembering the chidings of a parent who employed *kindness* as the only rod of correction — can imagine the painful, heart-broken, inexpressible *regret* which the foregoing conversation engendered in my young and sympathetic spirit. But the most painful trial was yet in store for me.

As the last word was complainingly uttered, the good woman arose and procured an old book — with one leather cover, but without pictures — which I had seen father peruse many times, on sabbath-days, when he never worked. She laid the dusty volume open on her lap, and began rumaging it in quest of something to read. At first, this manœuvring rather interested me, because 't was almost new — my mother being next to no reader at all.

"This 'ere book is the Bible, Jackson," said she; "the book of kind Providence. In this 'ere Bible is a sayin' about what'll become of bad folks. I want you to hear all about that 'are."

Finding the right verses, she began *spelling* the words in order to read of the horrid fate of wicked people. But the uneducated woman could make no headway with the sacred orthography. Accordingly, she quietly closed the revered volume, and, trusting to her defective memory, said :—

"Providence is good to them that's good. But he's jest as merciful as he's promised to be, to all them that's ugly and wicked. He ses that the good people shall be happy with him everlastin'ly. And he ses next, that them what lies, and steals, and *swears*, shall be sent headlong into a dretful big lake of b'ilin'-hot brimstone, where there's nothin' but a-weepin', an' a-wailin', an' a foamin' at the mouth, an' a-'nashin' of teeth, an' a-frettin' to get out, an' a-wantin' to drink dretfully, an' a-prayin' everlastin'ly tc die! But there's no comfort — no rest — no sleepin' — no water to drink — no friend to help — and, NO NOTHIN'!"

Overcome with the accumulated horrors of the soul-sickening revelation, I could listen no longer. "Do let me go to bed!" I cried. "I won't swear no more, never." My request was granted. But no sooner had I got under the bedclothes, than mother began to coax and insist that I should repeat after her the well-known juvenile prayer commencing with —

"Now I lay me down to sleep."

The third line — "If I should die before I wake" — revived all my original fear of death. Nothing seemed more risky than slumber. Silently I lay awake. I fancied that my breathing was becoming every moment more and more short and difficult. All doubt fled, and I supposed I knew that I was surely dying! With great pulmonary exertion I screamed for immediate help. But I had the misfortune to suddenly awaken my father from his deep sleep of fatigue, who impatiently exclaimed: "Why didn't you give that 'are boy some brimstone and molasses, to physic his blood? He'll never git red of them plaguy worms if you don't!"

This absurd and repulsive diagnosis of my psychological complaint, had the effect to neutralize and dissipate the "hypo" of my imagination — a result which acted so beneficially, that respiration became as healthy as ever, and every symptom indicated a speedy convalescence. Of course, the aroused sire did not know that I had just swallowed an immense quantity of "b'ilin'-hot brimstone," to purge my spirit of blasphemous inclinations. Slumber soothed me tenderly after a while, however; but, ere the next morning's sun shone upon me, I was a victim of disease in the form of fever-and-ague

Memorable, indeed, was the terrible lesson of that night! So deep and so impressive was it, *that never, from that date to this hour, have I been conscious of uttering a profane word.* And in the depth of my soul do I desire that every young mind could be made to feel, in some manner equally impressive and salutary, the uselessness of anger and the vulgarity of the language which expresses it.

CHAPTER XVII.

MY MOTHER'S DREAM.

As music's Goddess taketh down her lute,
Touches the silver cords of dulcet sound,
And sets the summer melodies to words;
So from the Spirit Land an Angel comes,
And, when profoundest slumber folds us fast,
Wakens our highest faculties of soul
Into serenest contemplation.

A SEVERE headache, accompanied with symptoms of chilliness and thirst, caused me to awake earlier than usual on the morning that succeeded the trials chronicled in the last chapter. Looking about, I saw the still anxious mother sitting close up 'neath the projecting mantlepiece, drawing consolation from her pipe.

As the narcotic vapor floated out leisurely upon her breath — escaping with the smoke of bits of the memorable brush now burning in the ample fireplace — methought, " Oh, how I'd like to use a pipe and tobacco! Why not? Old folks does — big folks who allus knows what's good — then why not I?" Self-interrogating thus, and dreaming o'er the advantages of doing just what my seniors do, I asked :—

" Can't I have one of your old pipes, mother? I want to smoke as well as you. Father chaws terbacker, you know; but I doesn't like the taste ; only smokin' like you is what I wants."

" Mercy on us !" she exclaimed, " what'll you want next?"

" I don't know," I replied, " I want to be good, mother, an'

I'm goin' to foller you, an' do jest as you does; then I know I ll be what you allus wants of me."

At these words her countenance betokened grief. But knocking the ashes from her pipe, and refilling it to the brim with the narcotizing and seductive weed, she persuasively and soothingly said: " Don't 'spose, bub, that I'm good. I tries to be so allus, and want you to be better than me, an' so you mustn't smoke, never."

" My head aches so, mother, I doesn't know what to do. I guess smokin' would make me feel better. If 'tain't good to smoke, what makes you smoke?"

" Why, bub, didn't I tell you once? Two years afore you was born, when we lived in the Jarseys, I had the dropsy dretfully. No doctor couldn't do me no good; an' I come near to the brink of my grave; when an old woman happened in. Ses she to me, ses she, 'I know what'll cure you.' Ses I to her, ses I, ' What is it?' Then ses she, ' You must throw the water off o' your stummic by smokin' terbacker.' I follered her remidee an' I got well agin. But somehow or ruther, I can't leave off the pipe now; if I does, I feels bad at my stummic, an' I can't do nothin' about the house, which you knows I must keep a doin'."

This brief and unartistic history of how she formed the habit, took from me all desire ever to follow my mother's example. Indeed, so tractable was my nature when thus appealed to, that neither the pipe nor anything resembling it (except once a bit of lighted ratan) ever got between my lips. And I am very thankful.

On every alternate day for two weeks, I shook with the ague and sweltered with the fever; but, owing to some medical preparation which I do not recall, the symptoms subsided and convalescence set in! To cheer and strengthen me, mother proposed that I should accompany her to the village on a trading expedition.

These pedestrian excursions, almost more than any other

custom among the lowly, indicate the ignorance of the North American peasantry. There is, perhaps, intelligence enough among this class in the exchange of country produce for house-keeping articles, dry goods, groceries, &c. ; but, intimately asso-ciated with such families as ours represented, there is ever to bo seen a deplorable lack of that knowledge which finds economy no task or hinderance to happiness. For instance : my mother, obe-dient to her own habits and the husband's commandments, would save dozens of hens' eggs and make rolls of sweet butter, (from our brindle cow's milk,) and exchange them for such useless, injurious, and expensive sub-tances as, *Young Hyson tea, burnt coffee, plug tobacco, and tobacco fine-cut for smoking !* While in other things — rice, sugar, molasses, calico, newspapers, books, pictures, &c. — we lived on the extremest edge of want.

Returning from the scene of traffic in the afternoon of this chilly autumn day, with what our folks termed " necessaries" for the family, I was threatened with a revival of the dreaded fever and ague. So severe were the aching and chilliness that pervaded me, that mother seated herself and pillowed my head upon her lap. In order to divert my attention from the distressing symp-toms, she said :—

" Now if you 'll cheer up and be a little man, I 'll tell you a dream what I had once."

I promised to try and not cry till we reached home, and asked : " When did you dream it, mother ?"

" When I got lost in John Myers's woods," she replied. " Don't you remember ?"

I answered in the affirmative ; whereupon, in her own untutored style, she continued in substance as follows :—

" Well, as I was a walkin' an' a lookin' for kindlin' wood, a thin shadder fell over my eyes. I tuk up my apron an' tried to wipe it out. I could n't do it, though. And pretty quick I forgot every-thing, an' did n't recollect nor know nothin no more. Then I

dreamt I lived on the side of a high mountain; alone by myself
an' away from every livin' cretur.

"But a strange man kept a walkin' an a walkin' toward me.
When he got up close to me, I ses to him, ses I, 'What do you
want o' me, mister?' Then ses he to me, ses he, 'You hain't fit
to be a livin' all stark alone on this 'ere high mountain.' 'Oh,
yes I be too,' ses I to him. 'No you hain't nuther,' ses he to me,
'an' I won't have it so.' Then ses I, 'You clear out an' let me
alone; you're a strange man to me, an' I do n't want nothin' to do
with strangers.'

"But somehow or ruther, he made me foller him down into the
hollar, at the foot of the mountain, where the grass was green, an'
the blummies a bloomin'. 'Now,' ses he to me, ses he, 'good
woman, I'm a goin' to show you a sight what you never seen
afore,' 'Well,' ses I to him, ses I, 'let's see you do it.' I kinder
tho't I was sassy to an utter stranger; but I looked an' seen jest
what he p'inted at."

"What d' you see, mother?" interrupted I with the greatest
interest, and quite forgetful of my weariness and pain — "what
d' you see?"

"Why, I'll tell you, bnb. I look'd an' I seen a somethin'—
which I did n't see, a kind o' strong hand out o' sight — lift a big
white sheet up in the middle of the field. Under it there stood
anuther man whose face, somehow or ruther, I seem'd to know
very well. Then, as I look'd, I seen three men a comin' from
different corners of the country. They kept a walkin', nearer
an' nearer, to the man what was under the sheet. Bimeby, they
got to him. The first put in the middle man's hand a bundle
of pens, to the number of a dozen. The second put a jug of
very black ink in his t' other hand. The third opened a big package of very white paper an' laid it right at his feet."

"Why, mother!" cried I in the height of childish excitement,
"did n't you wake up an' stop dreamin'?"

"No," she replied, "I didn't wake up till I heer'd father a callin' my name."

"Didn't you see no more?" I asked, my health nearly restored.

"Oh, yes!" she continued, "I seen the three men stand still. An' the man took a pen an' dipt it in the ink an' writ over a hull lot o' paper. Then he took anuther pen an' done the self-same thing; an' so on, first one an' then t'other till the pens was all used up an' there was n't no ink nor no paper that was hisen.

"Jest at this 'ere instant there came up a whirlwind an' scattered the paper, what was writ on, all over the hull country, some one way an' some a nuther. An' I was kinder scared when I seed the hull dozen pens turn into a dozen full-grow'd men, drest in pretty white an' blue clothes. Each man went to work, without no orders to work, an' collected the scattered sheets o' paper. When they put a leaf o' paper down it turned right into white wheat bread; an' the ink flow'd right off jest like oil, an' turned into somethin' what looked like port wine, which the men pour'd into stone pots all round there.

"Now I tho't that there was a goin' to be a famine, or a war, or a somethin', I did n't know nothin' what. For the hull country was full of folks. The strangers kept a comin' up, closer an' closer, to where the dozen men stood; the one man standin' bolt upright in the middle of the hull tribe. The folks what kept comin' was so many, that I could n't see nothin' o' the ground nor nothin' t' other side. It look'd jest like a river—an' like human bein's a swimmin', with their faces jest out o' the water. But up they come, an' ses they to the dozen men, ses they: 'We be all hungry an' we be dry: won't you give us somethin' to eat an' somethin' to drink; say good folks, won't you?' An' then the dozen ses to the hull, ses they—'Yes! we'll do it in kindness to you all.' Then they all falls to an' eats an' drinks. jest like hungry wolves. An' while the hull world was eatin', an' a drinkin', an' a laughin', an' a dancin' for joy, I heer'd father hollerin' an' screamin' after

me to come hum.   An so I woke up an' found 't was dark, an']
lost in them 'are pokerish woods !"

Imperceptible as the fall of dew was the displacement of my
physical uneasiness by the fascination of her just-related dream.
" Mother !" exclaimed I, as we proceeded homeward, " what
makes folks dream ?"

" Ah, that 'are's what I can 't say," returned she ; " but I allus
believes that 'tis Providence what does it for them he loves."

" Does Prov'dence make you see the new moon over your left
shoulder ? or makes a fork fall tine foremost ? or makes you see
them shadders in the road ?"

" No, child," replied she, " them 's bad omens — bad signs — of
bad things what's a goin' to happen to them what sees."

" Mother !" I still persisted, " you told me once all about good
old Santa Claus, what nobody could n't see — an' you sed once that
the doctor brought the dead baby to our house — an' I found out
that 't was n't jest so ; now does n't you think that that 'are white
spook what Dave seen, an' the bad shadders in the road, an' the
Prov'dence what makes you dream, be all jest alike — one jest like
t' other ?"

The good woman was at once silent and sad.   My questions evidently perplexed and non-plussed her mind.   She walked gloomily
on and on, making no reply, till we reached home.   Before going
to sleep that night, however, I coaxed her with all my might to
tell me once again that curious story ; which, as a reminiscence
of my early years, lingers like an angel's song of glad tidings.

CHAPTER XVIII.

SIGNS, AND THE THINGS SIGNIFIED.

" Reason can not know
What sense can neither feel nor thought conceive
There is delusion in the world — and wo.
And fear, and pain."

IGNORANCE is man's strongest enemy ; and the cause of his greatest misfortunes. Besides the main trials this unblushing Monster tyrannically imposes upon his countless victims, he is the commander-in-chief of an innumerable host of minor forces ; with which, at any time, he can attack the citadel of individual happiness, and take the defenceless inmates into months and years of diabolical captivity.

The term " superstition" was the first word employed by the converted Roman Pagans to signify what moderns mean by the phrase " Religion" that is, to *stand above* the world, to put one's trust in whatsoever is supernatural, to doubt the known and rely confidingly upon the incomprehensible. But in the philosophical progress of recent centuries, the original meaning of the term has been changed to convey an idea of idle fancies, or a belief in the existence of imaginary personages, as ghosts, witches, imps, &c., who, by the superstitious are supposed to exert more or less influence on the character and destiny of human beings.

Now what is quite singular, and therefore remarkable, is, that Religion or superstition or a belief in whatsoever is divine and celestial and eternally steadfast, and a faith in omens and signs and changeful wonders — require the same class of mental faculties; which goes to establish the universally conceded fact, that the possession of knowledge makes all the difference there is between the religious opinions of the inhabitants of North America and those of the people of Lapland or the Sandwich Islands. It proves that every ordinary mind is superstitious unless it be refined and exalted by education. And the private mental history of hundreds serve to fix the fact, that, in sailing from the continent of Superstition to the harbor of true Religion, there is a strait (or narrow strip of water) that may be called Skepticism; in which the person is beset by tempestial gales from the shores of both hemispheres, but feels none of that beautiful repose which either form of faith sometimes so graciously bestows upon its faithful follower.

My cherished mother was one of those very few persons who never doubt the incomprehensible. Her native faith was supported by irresistible evidence. She never saw the new moon over her left shoulder, never began anything on Friday, never dreamt about crossing muddy water or combing her hair, and never saw certain shadows in the distance, but the circumstance was in due time succeeded by some sort of domestic trouble; between which affliction and the signs, the believing woman never could detect the slightest discrepancy. Although the husband would refuse all credence, with his ejaculatory and significant "Poh!" yet she never swerved a hair's breadth in her own belief.

From my present knowledge of spiritual things I am led to conclude, on retrospection, that my mother's ignorance of the subjective causes of several of her experiences, not only rendered her incapable of discriminating between the real and the imaginary, but also greatly increased her unhappiness and despondency. She was compelled by organization to "borrow trouble;" but although a righteous neighbor she would not, because she could not, return it. This was her omnipresent misfortune, as it is everybody's who remains in ignorance of psychological principles. She had real clairvoyance, and, as I think, real spirit intercourse. But not being able to distinguish between fact and fancy, her life became a meandering stream of trial, sadness, and nervous apprehensive‑ness. In order to show how the maternal faith was established by what was to her " irresistible evidence," I will proceed to chronicle a chapter of accidents and family misfortunes.

CHAPTER XIX.

A CHAPTER OF ACCIDENTS.

SHORTLY after the trading-excursion mentioned in foregoing pages, there happened a serious accident. It occurred thus: Our landlord's hired man was conveying husked corn from the field to the barn. Besides the oxen and cart, he was using the great lumber-wagon, the pole of which he had lashed to the two-wheeled conveyance, in order to transport a double load each time. On one of his trips he halted with both vehicles in the public road adjacent to our house.

"Here's a chance to play ride horseback!" cried I. Unnoticed by the workman, I bestrode the wagon-pole behind the cart, and, with gleeful impatience, waited for the driver to exclaim, "Haw buck, gee bright—go 'long!" The gladsome moment came; the oxen pulled the cart; this jerked the pole; and I, losing my balance, fell into the loaded wagon's track. I screamed. Hearing which, the driver stopped the team suddenly, with the front wheel directly upon my waist! He started and stopped them again, with the back wheel resting its dead weight upon me, just as before! Another revolution forward released me; but I was taken to the house as one upon the verge of death. Hours subsequently, being restored to the use of my faculties, I asked my mother if I would die; when she replied: "No, child, 'tain't so ordered. Providence is good to them what loves him. But you was hurt jest where I seen them black shadders." Thus fixing in her mind, and clinching there, the reliability of her painful presentiments.

This severe accident left me such reminders as a weak back, a soreness in the sternum-bone, a stiffness in the intercostal muscles, and a very sensitive stomach. A debilitated digestive system is still in my possession. The weakness and frailty that lingered through my breast ofttimes made an hour's sitting on the shoe-bench next to torture. But my energetic and wilful father, though never cruel in a physical way, would stoutly reject the explanation of my uneasiness, and say : " You 're a *lazy feller* — that 's the reason. You 'll never earn your salt. What to do with such a young 'un I do n't know !"

Although that accident, at the time of it, was a seeming evil, it turned out, as every other has or will, to be a " universal good." How so ? Obviously, it unfitted me for being a useful disciple of St. Crispin ; it made exposure to sun-heat unbearable — as I suffered from indigestion, which produced biliousness and headache — and so rendered the usually healthy employment of agriculture repulsive and impossible ; and, lastly, it curtailed my desire to eat heartily of any heavy substances. This was undoubtedly advantageous. Every domestic as well as public physiologist is well acquainted with the fact, that abstemiousness in diet has much to do in developing the intellectual faculties.

Declaring this opinion, on one occasion, to a person who was extremely anxious to become clairvoyant, he asked : " Would you then advise me to get run over by a wagon loaded with corn ?" To which I replied : " If you would not voluntarily throw yourself beneath the Juggernaut of your own physical appetites, and thus stultify the spiritual within you, the accident which I now celebrate as embodying a good, would appear to you as a personal misfortune of no small importance. If, then, you wish to be clear-headed, *do n't get run over* — especially not, by your own habitual intemperance and over-eating."

Succeeding this bodily injury, I shivered through many weeks with fever-and-ague. But, getting well again, I was induced to accompany Reuben Kipps (a Quaker neighbor's son) to a distant school. Here, as I now vaguely recollect, I imbibed no lessons of instruction. I wondered greatly where all the children came from, who they belonged to, and where they were going after school was dismissed. I think I went two or three weeks, with several intervals of remaining at home; and got — among other things — a scolding, a black mark, a bad cold, and a penny primer full of pictures! This inaptitude for acquiring my letters, or even a good name for trying to, was another source of trouble to my solicitous mother, and fulfilled to a fraction one of her *bad dreams!*

It was now midwinter. About this time my father, returning one evening from the village with his package of work, was seized with a kind of paralysis which caused him to fall in the snow, unable to rise or to make himself heard, while (as he relates) his mind was clear and conscious of his perishing condition. The poor man lay there all that night, wallowing and struggling in the snowbank, while our house was a scene of painful watching and piteous lamentation. The neighbors brought him to us on the following morning, almost frozen. For a poor family, this was another great trouble. We all depended upon his daily toil for our subsistence, and he was for many days quite disqualified to make any exertion. And mother, as usual, said "'t was jest what she expected from her *bad dreams!*"

Not long after this we received intelligence that sister Eliza was left alone, penniless and nearly starving; that her young husband, Henry, had deserted both her and his infant son, and departed to regions unknown; and, as a matter of course, that my father must get his suffering daughter and grandchild, and bring them under his own roof for maintenance. This was accordingly done, much to our general disadvantage; but it served to bring true one of my mother's *bad dreams!*

Chills-and-fever again invaded my young and debilitated body.

" Do n't dare to ask me that again," said he with stout severity, " or I 'll thrash you within an inch of your life !"

My mother heard this trial, with a countenance expressive of anguish ; but, for some private reason, she did not interfere. Disconsolate indeed was the maternal bosom. There was a humid ether between her eyes and mine. Something told me that she felt an inexpressible despair in the fear that I—her only son —was already on the highway to certain destruction. Hence, she could not conscientiously protect me ; her words did not come to excuse my deed ; and doubtless her mind recognised the justice of father's summary proceedings. Doffing his begrimed leather-apron, and donning his coat and hat, he said :—

" Now, you sir ! keep that 'are iron in your hand, and go with me."

He walked very fast, and uttered many hard things. He said that I was " idle, good-for-nothin', and mischievous !" But I did not altogether feel the truth of his epithets ; therefore I could not respond " Amen." Thus I was hurried on back to the very tool-box whence the toy was purloined, and there the honest cord-wainer compelled me to leave it ; making me promise, on penalty of great punishment, that I would ' never again take what did n't belong to me."

'Twas a mortifying ordeal. But that night I felt very happy and contented. My father's method sank deep in my moral organism ; and *I do not know that I have ever violated the promise he then forced me to make !* A course less prompt, less energetic, less impressive, might have engendered dangerous carelessness about matters of conscience. And who knows but that little circumstance, with the rigorous way I was treated, has saved me from those vices and crimes which so disfigure the biography of many intrinsically noble natures ? A world of deformity and mis-direction is open to every young mind ; and a parent, it seems to me, can not be *too prompt* in wisely checking a child's departure from the strait road of individual righteousness.

CHAPTER XX.

THE GAMBLER'S FIERY FATE.

———— " I recall
My thoughts, and bid you look upon the night."

CERTAINLY I would not be deemed guilty of filial irreverence
if I should say that, upon the railroad of our domestic experience,
the restless and impetuous cordwainer was the only reliable locomotive. He would put on the steam, blow his whistle, and admonish all hands to clear the track ! On a short run, with a moderate load, he was a fine engine, and gave satisfaction to every
passenger, till he began to let off steam — a proceeding which
would have seemed normal and congenial enough, had it not been
accompanied with an inconvenient amount of blinding smoke and
burning cinders.

In the spring of 1835, he got us all on the train, with the baggage and furniture, and landed us at another *dépôt*. If the reader
is curious to know where it is, he can see it when he takes a drive
from Hyde Park to Pine Plains. When passing the ample homestead and out-buildings of Hiram Marshall, just look directly
south, and observe a crumbling structure situated about six furlongs from the public road. That is the very place where our
triangle, with the implements for scanty housekeeping, was deposited by the mutable force aforesaid. Our conditions and comforts
were distinctly on the decline. We found ourselves minus several
items of property, especially our young and valuable cow. Why

this move was made I can not remember. But I think it was done to bring father into closer proximity with his various pursuits, and to enable my mother to perform more days of remunerative labor in the neighbors' kitchens.

In this sequestered and dilapidated dwelling my father erected a weaver's loom. 'T was quite a spectacle! When rainy weather drove him from off the farm, he would repair or manufacture shoes; and, when destitute of this employment, he would mount the loom, set the warp, and put in the filling, with enviable artistic success. In the branch called "quilling" I was occasionally of considerable assistance. But I was of more service to him, as he thought, in the faithful discharge of certain commissions. I refer to repeated errands, the burden whereof was *a jug of cider!* If one neighbor declined selling me a gallon to intoxicate my father, my orders were to go on till I obtained the desired quantity. It is with no little regret that I find these errands pictured on the canvass of Memory. I trust the reader will be strong to save anybody's child from such memories; for the heavenly angels can not always stand between the young and those influences which contaminate. It was fortunate for me, however, that my taste was in no instance tempted by the inebriating beverage.

The philanthropic heart that throbbed in my mother's bosom, together with her mysterious faculty to foretell the future, made her a favorite among the rural inhabitants. They appeared to enjoy a visit to our humble dwelling. Parties of unmarried persons would sometimes call and depart with expressions of delight. By the active help of such, we had a jolly "apple cut" one night, which concluded with a rustic dance. On another occasion, there was what mother called a "quiltin'-party" in our house, which was succeeded by several novel amusements — such as fortune-telling, blind-man's buff, guessing riddles, playing the fiddle, telling anecdotes, and card-playing. But on the occasion of each of these assemblies, I remarked my mother's reservation. When she looked into the teacup, to tell some one's fortune, she invariably treated the operation as mere sport. And yet, being accustomed to her expressions, I could at times discern that look of Distance —a blankness and introspectiveness of vision— which made even her most ordinary verbal statements replete with an interest quite undefinable.

In this connection I will relate an impressive circumstance. The card-playing entertainment became gradually attractive to me, although I did not participate in the game. But those who did take sides seemed to be so full of wit and joy, that I was induced to believe there must be something funny and bewitching lurking in the constitution of the pack which none but the players could comprehend and enjoy. To test the validity of this thought, I one day went about among the young men of the neighborhood, and, on my own private responsibility, invited them to a card-party at our house that very night.

Many accepted the invitation, and arrived at the appointed hour. My parents were astonished at the large assembly. The visitors said, " Your boy asked us to come and play cards here." Accordingly, the pictured folios were brought out, and the party were permitted to enjoy themselves just as if the invitation had emanated from headquarters. But I thought I saw that there was a recollection of a bad dream going on in my mother's brain, and that its fulfilment was near at hand. At length the young people departed, and we all retired. A cloud hung between the sad woman and my disturbed spirit. That night I prayed many, many times, in the silence of my heart, for immediate pardon and better luck. Finally, I slept. When I awoke next morning, the afflicted mother was smoking her pipe by the fire on the hearth. As soon as I got dressed, she approached me and said :—

" Now, me an' you must settle. What did you ask all them folks to come here for ?"

" 'Cause I wanted to see 'em play."

" What did you get by them playin'?"

" Nothin', but to see 'em play high, low, jack, and the **game.**" returned I with painful confusion.

" What's in *that* to you?"

" Nothin', only I want to see 'em when they saves their *Jack!*'

" Oh, *that's* it, is it?" she returned.

" Yes, mother, 'tain't nothin' else," said I.

" Well, I'll tell you how I'm a-goin' to save *my* Jack?" replied she calmly. In her right hand I observed the well-known pack of cards. " Now look," she continued; " I'll let you see what's sure to happen to them what loves to play cards." While speaking thus, she laid the package directly in the midst of the fire! Holding my hand firmly, and riveting my attention upon the rapidly-consuming symbols, she exclaimed :—

" See that! In that burning pile is picters of many grandees! There's the king an' queen o' spades, an' there's the king an' queen o' clubs, an' there's the king an' queen o' diamonds, an' there's the king an' queen o' hearts — an' there's the ace-spot, an' there's the dretful JACK! Now, child, save 'em if you can!"

There was a majestic dignity in the woman's manner, and a deep and magic strength in the meaning of her words, that startled me and went like lightning through my being. I trembled in every nerve. I was sick at heart — very, very sick! But as she had commanded me to *save the jack*, I was forced to reply:—

" Mother, I can't! 'tis burnt almost out o' sight."

" Oh, it is, is it?" said she triumphantly; " then see in *that* jack what'll become of every man what lives by gamblin'! The good Providence can't do him no good: so the Evil One takes and puts him in the fire of destruction."

It would require a more skilful pen than mine to portray the overwhelming horror of that conflagration to my young mind! I was lost to the obvious fact that only pieces of pictured paper were being consumed. As the flames leaped up and danced around the cards, it seemed to me that great men and beautiful women were actually going through the gambler's fiery ordeal. "Mother," I exclaimed, "don't scold so — I won't never play cards — I won't never do so no more !"

Twenty-one years, full of temptation, have rolled by since that morning, with its remarkable lesson. My perception of the Divine government — of how the good are rewarded and the evil punished — differs greatly from the plan suggested by the maternal companion of my early life. Yet I think that, essentially considered, she had a true knowledge of the inevitable mental sufferings and heartburnings of that misdirected class called gamblers. And it is with profound gratitude that I can retrace, one by one, my footsteps — contemplate my pathway up the mountains of the past — and see no instance when the pledge I made in that isolated dwelling has been broken.

CHAPTER XXI.

IN WHICH I GO TO SCHOOL.

"And then the whining school-boy, with his satchel,
And shining morning face, creeping like snail
Unwillingly to school."

ABOUT one mile east of Hyde Park village is a small cluster of dwellings, called Union Corners — that is to say, a wheelwright's shop, a blacksmith's shop, a contracted grocery, and a spacious groggery termed a "tavern," (by the imaginative a hotel,) for the accommodation and destruction of both wayfaring men and those who live within its deleterious atmosphere. Directly opposite this baneful resort, there stood (perhaps yet stands) a tenement of most unwholesome dimensions; with but two rooms, the first occupying the whole body of the structure, the second being quite as large, right overhead, but just under the rafters, and accessible by what might be termed a flight of ladder-stairs. Not a shade tree or shrub was there to shut out the cheerless and ominous prospect of that publican's house. Neither did there exist the slightest obstruction to a free communication. Only space to the extent of six yards, and time to the amount of ninety seconds, served to draw a line of distinction between the inmates of the house and the interior of the groggery.

Well, reader, while the spring spirit of 1836 was vivifying the ample fields of Dutchess county, we were moving into that narrow and dangerous dwelling. Within the light of the front window you might have seen my father practising his predominating profession. And in that contracted place, too, you could not fail to observe the sorrowing woman ; binding shoes, mending clothes, and performing other labors without respite, for which by nature she was far less adapted than many merely physical ladies who adorn wealthy and fashionable homes.

I was now in my tenth year; the first decade in an eternal life ! Had you seen me, you might have said — " I take this youngster to be somewhere in his seventh year." Deficient in almost every expression of bodily strength, as also in that energy of countenance which betokens a teachable intellect, I was at first regarded by our new acquaintances as a very good boy to have nothing to do with.

Thanks to my parents, I was now sent to school. The teacher was a middle-aged lady, and very kind to the children. But with all her kindness and exertions, I could not be made to recollect and comprehend at the same time the letters and unity of the alphabet. At length, however, her place was occupied by a masculine teacher by the name of De Witt. He put me through the A-B-C department with inconceivable speed — so rapid, indeed, that, when I came out at the bottom letter, I invariably lost nearly all memory of the preceding sounds and connections. But I went forward, nevertheless, and got triumphantly into my a-b, abs. Shortly, however, this responsible teacher of the district-school was superseded by a religious-minded man, named Lacy.

Under this gentleman's austere training and vigilant supervision, I progressed into spelling words of two syllables ; but so badly and clumsily, that my perpendicular position at the foot of the class became a fixed fact! The great Napoleon never had a sentinel who stood his ground and guarded his outposts more faithfully. My fundamental position, as logicians say, was well taken ; nor do I remember that I had the misfortune to be displaced more than three or four times, and then only for a few minutes. But this teacher was quite gentle and patient with me, withal, and concluded to set me at the multiplication table. He wished to make me believe, through my understanding, that *that table* was laden with sumptuous articles for the juvenile intellect. He did n't convince me at all! Writing lessons came next. But the cramping of my thumb-joint, in order to hold the quill just as the other scholars did, had the effect to postpone my penmanship to a period remote and indefinite.

Acting, as I supposed, on the master's suggestion, my father invested forty cents in a Pictorial Geography, authorized by the renowned Peter Parley. That unpretending volume captivated my eyes ; and, perhaps, also, instructed my mind. The frontispiece is in itself a charm to children. There is a comfortably furnished room, a cheerful fire crackling on the hearth, an elderly and fatherly gentleman reposing in an old armchair, his disabled foot resting on a more common one, with a company of story-loving juveniles crowding around, to induce the cosmopolite veteran to relate another travelling adventure — and, then, just below is the sentence, making one wish to be there also — "Take care there! take care, boys! if you run against my toe, I'll not tell you another story!" The author employs the story-teller's phraseology, and presents his ideas in a pictorial way, almost irresistible to childhood and youth. By some means I was induced to memorize the few lines :—

> "The world is round, and like a ball
> Seems swinging in the air ;
> A sky extends around it all,
> And stars are shining there."

But I could not make myself recollect the remainder. In fact, my mother's memory and mine closely resembled each other. Neither could fix a recollection of words, dates, or names, so as to reproduce and use them properly and exactly. Map lessons, therefore, were almost utterly out of the question ; as well as the names of various towns, villages, and cities. The map of the world looked to me something like *a cobweb* into which the bookmaker had dumped here and there a mess of words, too hard to be

either spelled or spoken ; and hence, notwithstanding the captiva-
ting influence of the pictures and images of houses and of strange
people, I could not make any headway with my geographical
studies.

But here let me say that Peter Parley's (Mr. Goodrich's) geography for children *is the only school-book I ever valued, cherished,
or studied.* I value it now, as I did not then, because it throws
the attractions of imagination around the facts of the world, and
imparts pleasure and instruction at once to the unfolding faculties.
I have preserved that book as the only charm of the hours I spent
in school. My eyes have looked the pictures almost out of sight.
The beautiful dresses of the English, French, Scotch, &c., are
worn almost threadbare. That book is my pyramid. The contents thereof, like so many embalmed mummies, serve as a link
of connection between that year and this!

Among the numerous scholars at the district-school, of either
sex, I was never quite at ease. The boys were rough and harsh
to play with, and seemed most happy when quarrelling; while
the girls inspired me with an unconquerable shyness, a painful
and embarrassing timidity. The result was that I found myself
entirely without any agreeable associate. Several of the boys
called me " gumpy;" a few girls called me " sleepy-head;" the
former teacher called me " blockhead;" and my eldest sister
called me " dummy." These epithets tended to increase the characteristics in me which suggested them; and so I grew no wiser
or happier among those of my own years and circumstances.

The code of honor among boys of a certain stamp is very remarkable. I will give an instance. One afternoon, just subsequent to the dismissal of the school, my father wished me to take
a package of work to his boss in Hyde-Park. Procuring a very
gentle old horse, belonging to the venerable and generous Isaac
Stoughtenburgh, I mounted and set out on the errand. It was
about twilight when I arrived at the proper destination. The

return work not being quite prepared, I was obliged to remain outside near the store longer than I wished; for, to tell the truth, I had never been so far from home before without ample protection. My only fear was the quarrelsome village-boys! I had no combative propensities of my own to gratify, no ambitious inclinations toward physical prowess, and I trembled to think of the cruelties that rowdyistic characters sometimes practise upon helpless urchins. 'T was getting dark very fast. As I expected, the village-boys like so many young barbarians gathered around, as I stood on the sidewalk, to teaze and insult me.

"Who be you, sonny?" asked one tauntingly. "Where d' you live when you 're to hum?" shouted another. "What's your daddy's name?" said a third, as he run violently against me, and knocked my cap into a mud-puddle.

I answered them just as well as I could; making no show of resentment, as I felt none; only a shrinking timidity which they made fun of. I besought them not to injure me as I had n't in jured them, and did n't mean to; at which they set up a mortifying hoot, and called me by names too vulgar to reiterate. They stepped on my toes, twitched my hat off many times, and otherwise indicated their savage desire to get me angry and resentful.

At this moment of trial, I distinctly heard what sounded like my mother's voice calling me by name, as if she was seeing my peril from the upper window of some building! It strengthened and encouraged me to be very calm with my persecutors. A little resentment on my part, a show of rage and fight, would have been to them sufficient justification for striking me. But I thought thus: "If I should do what these boys do, I should be ashamed and afraid to go home to my mother." Thus thinking I did not feel revengeful, nor even unkind, toward my tormentors. And yet, contrary to the non-resistant doctrine that the peaceful soul is safe, one of the tantalizing band, more hasty and unprincipled than the rest, jumped against and knocked me down; and then, for no reason except that I was "a country pumpkin," and in the village alone, he struck me many times with great violence, causing a hemorrhage at my nose and several sore places in my face and breast!

But my interior bosom was not bruised, and the face of my spirit was still radiant with kindness, at which I was myself greatly astonished. I wept to be sure; but 't was for bodily suffering only. I told my mother all about it. She gave me an abundance of her approving smiles; and my wounds were soon healed. But there is a sequel to this apparently irrelevant incident, developing an important moral principle, to be unfolded in a future chapter.

CHAPTER XXII.

MY FATHER AND ALCOHOL PART COMPANY.

*" Strength is born
In the deep silence of long-suffering hearts."*

A RUM-SELLER may be just as honorable and philanthropic as a rum-drinker.   Twenty-one years ago, and even now in some unreformed places, the man whose daily occupation produced drinkers, paupers, gamblers, and victims for the prisons and the gallows, was considered by professing Christians and the masculine community in general, as being quite as respectably employed as other merchants and men of business.   For example : I never heard any complaint about my father's intemperance, and the means by which it was induced, outside of our contracted domicil. Inside, the misery thereof was replete with the most painful concomitants.

Look at the temptation !   Leaning leisurely against the tavern window, with seductive smile and crowned with beads, was a red-faced chap — called Brandy !   Next to him sat a loaferish, grinning, imbecile, watery-looking individual — with a very pale and sickly countenance — called Gin !   Beyond the red-faced and bloated brandy decanter, you could see a lazy, filthy, swiney vagabond — too indolent to shine by candle-light and ashamed to open his fiendish eyes before honest people — called Whiskey !   And be- sides these ruffians, there were other and lesser scoundrels who caused husbands to forget their wives, fathers to neglect their

children, brothers to insult their sisters, men to trample on the
priceless innocence of virgin women — yes, good reader, a detach-
ment of the alcoholic band of incendiaries who produce misfortunes beyond the power of words to describe, could be seen at all
hours of every day in the window of the commodious tavern just
opposite the cordwainer's hovel

'T was first of January. The snow was deep; the weather
extremely cold. Now and then two affectionate neighbors met,
wished each other " Happy New-Year," and subsided into the
bar-room to ratify the wish.

Obtaining permission, I slung my unmated skates across my
arm and sallied forth to find a strip of smooth ice. I enjoyed the
sport for awhile, but the intense cold caused me soon to return.
Passing the door of a debauched but friendly old dram-drinker,
whom father well knew, I thought I would just step in and wish
him happy new-year. I entered and did so. He was alone,
dozing by a hot stove. He asked me to be seated.

Presently the intoxicated man went to the closet, mixed some
molasses with brandy, and, after drinking a portion himself, offered
me the remainder. I tasted; and its sweetness refreshed and
charmed my palate ! Our folks could n't afford to let me have
anything so sweet ! And so I made the most of that New-Year's
luxury ; of which the gray-headed and unscrupulous drunkard
gave me every few minutes. I became remarkably social and
loquacious. My present memory and judgment assure me that
I talked like an unconscionable fool. My words, which indicated
nothing, I laughed at heartily ! What was worse, I did not realize
that I was intoxicated. But when I arose to go home, then, alas !
I knew too well my deplorable condition.

The room spun like a top ! Stove, chairs, tables, doors, windows, the old man, and all, reeled and rolled horizontally around
me like so many millstones. I made a plunge for the street door ;
but it eluded my hand, and shot off to the other side of the apart-

ment. Now the floor began to wave up and down, bending like thin ice beneath my feet! What was to be done? The besotted old man was unable to aid me. In his recumbent position by the stove he had long since become incognizant of the mutations of surrounding circumstances. He was not favorable to rotation in office, while I became an anxious seeker for a permanent footing in society.

A lucky thought struck me: to spring upon the door-latch next time it came around! As the room revolved — bringing the specific door within my grasp — I caught it with energy. Wasn't I glad? To reel and stagger through the narrow passage, and to plunge into a great snowbank outside, was comparatively an easy task. But to arise and go to my mother, *that* I could not do! Only two things remained within my power: to groan and gasp in my frosty bed — weeping at my own calamity — and to shout feebly, " Oh, I'm so drunk! so drunk! so drunk!" I was suffering, perishing, and willing to die! Oh, the horrid mortification of that New-Year's day! My driveling lamentations — going up as they did on the clear air — finally brought me timely assistance; and I was forthwith carried home in a condition well nigh bestraught and insensible. The brandy and molasses — " black strap" — flowed out of my mouth, and, at first, gave my mother the impression that I had ruptured a blood-vessel while skating. But the well-known " odor" gave ample testimony as to the nature of my wound. Oh, how dangerous that wound!

Dear reader! do you vote in favor of distilleries? Do you put in office men who treat and traffic with the ruffian-monster, Alcohol? Do you believe in granting a license to your neighbor? Will you put one man's pecuniary interest at deadly strife with the health, prosperity, and happiness of hundreds of families? Are you a friend of riots? Do you wish to increase the number of fatal accidents? Do you desire to build a railroad and run an express train from every man's door to asylums, poor-houses, prisons, gambling dens, and the scaffold? Do you cry " Down

with virtue, up with vice! down with happiness, up with misery?"

Do you work to diminish the comforts, demolish the characters,
destroy the health, and shorten the lives of the people about you?
Do you mean to sow the seeds of sorrow in the blood of myriads
of children yet unborn? If not, then vote for a Harmonial government. If not, then work for the Era of Harmony on the
Earth. Will you do so? We shall see; for no individual act,
however private, is lost to the vast FUTURE!

Gladly and gratefully do I record the fact, that the demon-
serpent, Alcohol, never got me fixed within its deadly embrace,
save in this one instance; when the seductive hospitality of an
inebriated old man was added to the larger freedom and unguarded
liberty of a New-Year's day. Twenty years have elapsed since
that disgusting experience, but this fiendish foe of man has not
found the least refuge in my affection or judgment. And I verily
believe that my prophetic mother perceived that it would not; for
she manifested less anxiety and grief at this circumstance than
at either of those trials already chronicled.

Shortly after this, my quiet and tender sister Julia Ann, returned home very ill. Her melancholy face was discolored with
jaundice; and her deep-sunken eyes betokened a vital and mortal
disease. Poor girl! How I pity her through the sympathy of
memory! There she lay stretched on the bed of death, so very
feverish and sensitive in every nerve; in the midst of all the
housekeeping turmoil, and the hammering of the shoemaker,
within that one contracted and inadequate room. A physician
was summoned, and her disease was treated, probably, with the
usual skill; but no power on earth could keep her from soaring
to the "House not built with hands," in which there are neither
rich nor poor, but *plenty* for all God's children!

One night, as my mother sat watching by the bedside of the
departing girl, I was made quite sad by observing in her eyes that

ominous vacant stare — that look of Distance — which I had long regarded as the forerunner of domestic misfortune. The suffering patient asked for something, but the maternal ear did not catch the sound thereof. This demonstrated the depth of her revery; which continued unbroken for several minutes. When again she aroused to aid the sick girl, there was a calm resignation in her face, but in each eye there trembled a tear of sorrow. Retiring to the back window, and gazing out upon the frozen earth, she wept aloud. This expression of grief I did not comprehend, and asked:—

" What makes you cry so, mother ?"

" Julia Ann is going to leave us, afore long," she replied.

" How do you know that 'are ?" said I. " What makes you think so ?"

" 'Cause," answered she, " I seen the little white lamb."

" What white lamb was it, mother ?"

" The same heavenly messenger what Julia Ann seen at Peter De Garmo's upper winder."

" When d' you see it ?"

" To-night, jest after dark ; when father went out to the tavern."

" Why, mother !" I exclaimed ; " did it really and truly come in this 'ere room ?"

" Yes, child, it slipped in when father went out."

" What did the lamb do then ?"

" Why, I seen it walk on all-fours to the poor girl's bedside ; an' then it took hold of the quilts by its mouth, an' pulled them very gentle. " There !" ejaculated she, looking blankly at the door, as father entered — " there ! the pretty lamb is gone away, an' I 'm real 'fraid 't will take Julia Ann along."

" What d' you see ?" asked my father impatiently.

" Oh, 't ain't nothin' to nobody but me," she replied ; and tearfully did that anxious, yet resigned, woman proceed to nurse and console the dying daughter.

" Don't be a frettin'," said father. " Don't fret about what can't be helped. What can't be cured must be endured you know. As for me I'm ready for anything what's likely to happen."

A few days subsequent to this conversation we followed the deserted body to the burying-ground. My parents and sister Eliza wept excessively at times; but, though I lamented to part with my relative, I could not shed tears. They said my grief was too deep for weeping. But the fact was, that joy overbalanced sorrow in my heart. A voice told me that my sister's present situation was to be envied and sought rather than grieved over; and I longed to tell our folks that, while I dreaded the dying process, I felt mysteriously drawn to the life which came afterward.

But the graveyard was a terror! Those ghostly white marble posts and slabs, and the solemn sound of the bell which rung the knell of my sister's departure, conjured up unwholesome imaginations. And when the sexton threw a few shovels of pebbles and cold earth upon the deposited coffin, there came back a sound so hollow, so subterraneous, so sepulchral, and heart-broken, that my very soul was harrowed up to the most doleful and repulsive ideas of death. After this, I feared to go without company through a churchyard at night. In fact, I could not conquer a disagreeable apprehensiveness whenever I slept alone in a dark room — a painful timidity — which lingered upon me until that glorious day which inaugurated the Era of my spiritual illumination.

How well do I remember the dark and stormy night when the rum-drinkers, at the tavern across the road, brutally pushed my father into our front-door in a state of beastly intoxication. He was more absolutely in the enemy's power than I ever saw him before. I will not stop to portray the desolation that his condition spread through the garden of my mother's heart. How every hope seemed crushed! How every struggling prayer seemed to be sent back unanswered upon its fountain source!

How every faintly-cherished expectation of "a better day" was crowned with the cypress wreath of death and disappointment! No! I will not present a picture of despair so appalling! Do you not see that we needed the power of some efficient Reformer? Verily, we needed the friendship and aid of a man whose mission was——

> "To grapple with the fell destroyer—
> The Lethe draught that brutifies the soul;
> To banish from our home the peace-annoyer,
> And on our hearthstone dash the fatal bowl."

But I am about to record one of the most glorious examples of individual reformation. After this dreadful night my father never tasted alcohol again! The resolution to be "a temperance man," was taken and kept in the calm silence of his own heart! With the enemy full in view, with tempting associates all around him, and through weary months of deadly and desperate struggle with the foes in his own nature, he gained this noble victory! For nearly forty years previous to this he was intoxicated frequently; and very much so about once a week while at Union Corners. Hence, toward the end of the next week my mother expected to witness another scene of desolation. But neither that drama, nor any part of it, was ever again enacted!

There is hope, then, for the drunkard's wife! The calm, pure heavens are peopled with hosts of strong powers whose great sympathetic hearts beat, through all the intervening space, responsive to our every soul-born prayer for purification and righteousness. And, believe me—every such prayer is some day wisely answered.

CHAPTER XXIII.

INITIAL EXPERIENCES IN HYDE PARK.

One of Belden Delamater's unpainted tenant-houses is (or was) situated on the post-road that leads the traveller directly through the village of Hyde Park, either toward New York or Albany. On the north, in close proximity, was Mr. Parker's blacksmith-shop. On the south was a much larger wood-frame residence, a rod further back from the highway — the families of the two houses drawing water from the same well. Into the former habitation we moved in the spring of 1837 — my father having secured permanent work in the journeyman department of John Hinchman's boot and shoe manufactory.

I was now in my eleventh year. So far as the development of either body or mind was concerned, however, I was considerably behind most boys four or five years younger. Timid, sensitive prone to solitary rambles, and meditative at times, I was quite disinclined to seek the companionship of village-boys, or to participate in their rough-and-tumble sports. In view of this seeming apathy and worthlessness, I do not treasure up any unkindness toward my energetic and working father because of his frequent exclamation —

"You ain't worth your salt!"

To which my maternal protector and ready advocate would reply :—

"Don't scold the boy! What can you expect of a child?"

"A *child!* Poh! Before I got to that 'are boy's age, I was bound out for my victuals and clothes," the father would rejoin, "and I don't see that he's any better than I was. I won't bear it. He's old enough to help support himself.—You sir!" he continued, addressing himself to me, "keep a sharp lookout for somebody who wants a boy."

Accordingly I went in quest of employment, and succeeded in procuring a situation with our landlord. He owned a large flour and plaster mill in the village, and wanted "a boy to tend hopper." Seated by the horizontal grinding-stones, my business was to see that the grain fell steadily from the containing-box above into the revolving pulverizers below. This monotonous occupation required not the least exercise of intellect, and scarcely none of my muscular system, save the right arm, and that too leisurely to keep one from dreaming and absent-mindedness.

Although not more distant than an hour's walk from my mother's side, yet I could not resist the enervating melancholy of "homesickness." When I went to my sleeping-place in the land lord's garret, and got under the buffalo-skin for the night, my thoughts would fly to the dearest object I knew on earth—my mother! And now, somnambulism—more commonly called sleep-walking—began to show itself in my nightly exercises. A thousand shadowy forms of wheels and revolving upright shafts would cover the entire surface of my brain. Besides those mill-works which I had seen during the day, I could perceive and comprehend the operation of new structures. Complete machines for splitting shingles, for grinding grains, for pulverizing plaster-stones, for sawing and planing boards, for doing the drudging kitchen-work usually imposed upon woman—these and several other very novel representations of mechanical improvements would weave themselves into the substance of my daily experiences—all brought together, and yet never confounded, during the silence of the bend-ing and brooding night.

The exceeding vividness and unfailing recurrence of these "dreams," together with my almost irresistible propensity to tramp about and actualize them during hours properly devoted to slumber and recuperation, soon fatigued and discouraged me; and hence, without asking permission to depart, I one day hastened homeward. On entering, my father, being at dinner, eyed me for a moment, and said —

"What sent you home?"

Not knowing how to explain, I replied, "'Cause, I couldn't stay no longer."

"What the dogs is the reason you couldn't?"

"'Cause the plaster-mill hurts me — an' the flour gets me a-dreamin' — an' I'm 'fraid to sleep up garret," replied I, much disquieted and alarmed — fearing he would send me back without judgment or mercy. But, fortunate as ever, mother came to my justification and rescue, and said: "Oh, what can you expect of a child? How d'you know but the boy tells the truth? Let him stay home to-day, at tener rate; for to-morrow we'll know more about it." And thus I was permanently prevented from becoming a professional and practical miller.

For weeks subsequent to this first absence from the parental presence, I tried to whittle out some of the mechanisms that had painted themselves upon my imagination, but without success. Father would persist in the declaration that I "hadn't gumption enough to make a whistle," and many times avowed his belief that my main trait was "laziness," combined with a fondness for play. Nevertheless, the tireless vigils of my somnambulic faculty kept me at various midnight employments. Without artificial light, I would move about the little bedroom, never making a misstep, and use the penknife with entire success. These nocturnal exercises I did not remember on the subsequent morning; but I can now recall them, and make the record as if I was outwardly conscious at the time. My contrivances, however, were so sneered and jeered at by my father, that I kept them out of his sight; and finally abandoned them altogether, as being utterly worthless even as curious toys for children.

About this time I formed the acquaintance of a notorious village boy named " Bill," who was the terror of nearly every other youngster in that community. He was an apprentice to a wheelwright, whose manufactory was located a few rods south of our house. Like other folks's boys, I went into the wagon-making department for shavings to kindle fires. I had long dreaded the great risk of an encounter with this belligerent apprentice. At last he spied me, hastily filling my basket with the desired kindlings. The boss being out, he fearlessly yelled :—

" Hey, there, you d—n turkey-buzzard ! who sent you here ? Tell me, you blunderin' lummix, or I 'll give you a touch under the fifth rib !"

With the greatest difficulty I replied, " Our folks."

" Who 's our folks ?" he vigorously demanded. " Tell me, you lumberin' young cuss, or I 'll hide you !"

As well as I could, I told him who my parents were, and said coaxingly : " Please, do n't hurt me ! I won't come here no more, if you do n't want me to."

" Oh, go to thunder !" said he, smiling contemptuously, " and come back when you want more shavings. I would n't lick you ! You 're too big a coward — too much of a spoony — altogether !"

But when again I entered the shop, and found him alone, he was remarkably docile and inclined to ask me questions. He was my senior by some five years ; and I looked upon him, through the strong colors of his pugnacious reputation, as being a person to fear and shun under all circumstances. His body was firmly and powerfully proportioned. His features were rather large, and somewhat irregular ; but his eyes, though black and commanding, softened his entire countenance by the genial smile which they had the power to diffuse over its every lineament. In short, notwithstanding the fearful reports of this boy's fighting propensities, I could not help accepting him as my only out-door companion.

Shortly after the commencement of our acquaintance, I introduced him to my parents and sister; and, contrary to my expectations, he was also quite agreeable to them.

Subsequent to my first interview with this combative fellow, I never heard him utter a word of profanity, or propose a fight in the street. Of course, I was not his constant associate. But I did not hear any more reports of his quarrelsome enterprises. What could have wrought this change in his conduct? I know not. But this I believe, that he had the foundation of a good man under his outward characteristics. The timber sufficient to the erection of a moral temple was within him rough hewn, and his nature awaited the period when the true superstructure could be commenced.

One warm summery day, while rambling together in Dr. Hoosack's beautiful park just north of the village, he said:—

"Let 's take a seat here — right under this 'ere shady tree — for I want to tell you somethin'."

Seating ourselves, he began: "There 's one thing in my memory that troubles me more than all else what I ever did."

"What is that, Bill?" I asked.

"Why, hang it! the thing 's foolish enough, like a bushel of other things I 've done, but I can 't get over it somehow." After a brief silence he continued: "And I never seen nobody I could tell it to before you come to live in Hyde Park."

"Well, Bill, you can tell me anything, you know: I wcn't leak it out, never." (And yet, dear reader, here I am letting it all out into your confidence.)

"Well, 't ain't nothin' worth a-mentionin'," said he; "but it is, though, or I would n't be a-thinkin' about it so."

"Oh, go on, Bill," said I; "do n't stop ag'in."

He proceeded: "About this time last year, I was mean enough to kick, an' cuff, an' lick a country-feller who had n't done nothin' to us village-boys; an' I 'll be blamed if I hain't felt more sorrier an' more madder at myself since than ever before."

" Why, Bill!" exclaimed I, concealing my actual emotions, "did you really hurt him?"

" Yes, and bad enough, too!"

" Did n't you know who the boy was?" I asked.

"No! 'Twas dark almost afore I heer'd the muss down the street. When I got on the ground, I could n't see his face hardly; but I pounded him like sixty, you'd better b'lieve."

" Well, Bill," said I, "you need n't fret no more about that 'are: for *I am the boy* what you hurt, but I do n't owe you no ill will!"

" You!" shouted he with great surprise; "you that 'are boy what I licked so like thun—"

" Do n't swear, Bill! Yes, I 'm that 'are same country-feller. But what makes you so sorry about it, Bill?"

" Well, now—ha! ha! By the powers of mud, if *that* hain't the most funniest thing yit! Why, the reason I did n't feel right about the thing was, because you did n't get mad an' try to strike back! If you 'd only done somethin' like that, I 'd felt all right. But you did n't; an' what 's more, you did n't act as if you felt mad at me at all—on'y cried an' took on hard 'cause you was hurt like thun— sixty."

" Never mention it, Bill," said I affectionately; "I do n't feel hurt any now, you know—so what 's the use?"

" Well," said he, rising to return to the village, " I hav' n't hit but two fellers under the fifth rib since that 'are night, an' then 'cause I could n't be dared more 'n once to do it. Now see here," continued he, " I 'll jest take odd spells out of my own time in the shop, an' make you a real first-rate peeler of a sled for next winter."

Earnestly I assured him that he owed me nothing, but that the sled would be a rich present to possess. His promise was soon redeemed, and I kept for several years that carefully-constructed pledge of lasting friendship. And thus, dear reader, in the practice of self-control and non-resistance, we behold the ultimate development of an impressive and salutary moral. Had I returned blow for blow, or even indicated a disposition to violently oppose my antagonist, would he have been so deeply rebuked? Would a painful regret have lodged and wrestled in his soul? I think not. The beautiful lesson of this story reminds me of the poet's forcible assertion :—

> " If men, instead of nursing pride,
>   Would learn to hate it and abhor it ;
>   *If more relied*
>   *On Love to guide —*
>   **The** world would be the better **for it !"**

CHAPTER XXIV.

A CURIOUS CASE OF WITCHCRAFT.

> " Our superstitions twine
> Each with the next, until a line
> They weave, that through each varied stage
> Runs on from infancy to age,
> Linking the spring with summer weather,
> And chaining youth and years together."

THE banishment of alcohol from our house was soon followed by substantial evidences of domestic prosperity. One step toward comfort and luxury was the purchasing of enough rag-carpeting to cover half of our main floor; another was, a new two-dollar shawl and a beautiful calico dress for mother; another, a warm cap and a pair of satinet pants for me; but the best of all was, the procuring of and paying for a fine-looking cow, whose snow-white stream of daily benefaction flowed with great ease and uniform abundance. My mother seemed to place a great deal of natural affection upon this valuable creature, and felt a genuine pride in preparing marketable butter and selling the extra milk which was thus obtained.

For many weeks everything in this respect went on swimmingly, except one slight circumstance which grieved my mother, and caused her to dream out one of those warnings of impending trouble. That circumstance was: the manifest jealousy of our next neighbors, from whose well we drew all our pure and sparkling water. These neighbors also owned a cow, less beautiful and less fountainous than ours; and they, too, made butter for the market, and sold morning's milk to some of the inhabitants. But *our* butter was the sweetest, and *our* milk was the creamiest, and, as a matter of course, *our* customers were most numerous, and *our* stocking-foot purse received the most frequent accessions of filthy lucre. Both cows were pastured in the same meadow; and it was ofttimes my business and pleasure to drive them — that is, our own noble animal, and our neighbor's merely ordinary " crittur"—to and from the field every morning and night. But the green-eyed monster, jealousy, soon generated a bitter and unspeaking antagonism; and, as one result, the opposition cow was soon driven to and fro by a member of the opposition family.

Things continued in this unsatisfactory state for some four weeks; during which no woman ever suffered more from *vaccination* than did my well-disposed and inoffensive mother. " She could n't help it, if our cow was the handsomest! Neither were the inmates of our house to blame if our cow did yield the most milk and produce the best butter!" In short, we were entirely innocent—do n't-you think so, dear reader?

Conditions, however, became every day more complicated and critical. In fact, a real crisis soon happened in our cow-pen, which served to bring my mother's dream almost true! One evening our unfailing quadruped would not give down a drop of milk! Mother tried every inducement. She climbed over the fence, pulled an armful of beautiful clover, and put it before the domesticated creature, but not a particle of gratitude was exhibited in the milky way. All further effort was postponed for the space of an hour; then resumed, but without success; and, lastly, was abandoned. At the usual hour on the morrow our friendly customers came; but the answer was, " Our cow won't give down no milk." So I drove her to the pasture as before, where she remained till brought home at night; when the same ominous fact was repeated. Not a drop of the sweet beverage could be obtained! Meanwhile, the opposition family got plenty of milk (*such as it was!*) from the opposition cow, and we had the mortification of seeing our patrons go and purchase it. On the succeeding morning the milking operation again proved a failure; and from the evening's exertions my mother returned with a like defeat.

Different persons presented different theories to account for this. One said the cow had the horn distemper; another, that a snake had imbibed the milk during the day; another, that she had swallowed her cud; another, that she had a wolf in her tail; another, that there was a spasmodic contraction in the muscles of the udder. But each individual hypothesis was triumphantly exploded by each speculator successively making his own examination and applying his experimental remedy. The creature's horns were pronounced all right. The snake theory could not stand in view of the fact, that from day unto day her *bag* was greatly swollen and painfully distended with an abundance of its undischarged secretion. The cud explanation was acknowledged worthless when her mouth revealed its presence there. The man who egotistically retailed the latter end doctrine was permanently shut up, on finding grounds for believing that the creature's well-formed caudal terminus was perfectly sound and useful; and, finally, the muscular contraction postulate was just as completely refuted by mechanically depressing the animal's back, with a simultaneous attempt at milking.

Not the least progress was made toward a satisfactory solution of the case. But there was one person whose fixed opinion remained unexpressed. That person was my mother. Her confidence in the supernatural, as I have heretofore said, had never been impaired or disturbed. Superstition seemed an inevitable concomitant of her genuine spiritual experiences. The ticking of a harmless insect on the bedroom ceiling, the howling of some nervous dog at midnight, the running through the house of a strange black cat, the striking of a clock weeks after it had ceased to record time, the sudden cracking of a looking-glass — any unusual sound or unexplained sight — were signs of approaching changes and calamities in the affairs of our household. And, strange to tell, several just such mysterious things had been occurring through the summer months in our little domicil! In a word, my mother was a believer in charms, obsession, witchcraft, and sorcery. She admitted the alleged possibilities of the Black Art. The power of some persons to prevent cream turning into butter in a neighbor's churn, or to cause the transformation of the shape of one living thing into that of another, she did not doubt; and yet she seldom made these things subjects of conversation. Among my early recollections I can find but just one of her stories, concerning curious old women —

> " Who roamed the country far and near,
>   Bewitched the children of the peasants ;
> Dried up the cows and lamed the deer,
>   And sucked the eggs and killed the pheasants."

Four mornings and four evenings did my mother, aided by various experimentors, try to obtain milk from our gentle and beautiful cow. Then, without qualification, she exclaimed —

" That are poor cretur *is possessed!*"

" What d' you mean, mother?" I asked.

" I mean," she replied, lowering her voice to a distinct whisper " that our poor cow is under a spell."

" Poh!" ejaculated father, who had just returned from the shop, " I don't believe no such stuff as that!"

Nothing daunted, however, my mother rallied to the encounter with home skepticism, somewhat as Bunyan's Christian did in the great valley where Apollyon straddled over the whole breadth of the way, and replied — " Nothin' else can make that poor thing act as she does."

" Act how?" asked father.

" Come out and see for yourself," she confidently answered, at the same time leading the way with milk-pail in hand. We all followed, and saw with amazement, that as soon as mother tried to milk her, the afflicted animal, quiet before, was seized with a

singular frenzy which rapidly induced a fantastic witch-dance
Yes, incredulous reader! I testify only of that which I actually
witnessed. The poor beast literally lifted her feet quickly up and
down, with a swaying motion, as if impelled by some demoniac
musician invisible, while her eyes seemed like balls of fire that
might almost inflame and burn her to death. And what made
the case stronger and yet more aggravating, was this: as we
turned to go into the house our eyes caught the gaze of our opposition neighbors! It really seemed that they looked amused, and
even jeeringly triumphant, at the cow's pranks and our mutual
misfortune.

Mother's opinion (or belief) became forthwith infectious. We
each shared her suspicions as to who it was that had laid an infernal spell on the innocent animal. In the midst of the family
deliberations, however, I asked if witches were not like Santa
Clauses and such ghosts as Dave saw; but my interrogatory
made no impression on the excited mother, whose anxiety about
"losing the poor thing" was every minute growing more and more
insupportable.

After a semi-serious deliberation, it was unanimously resolved
that father should go after *a seventh son.* He did so; and at
length the witchmaster came. His solemn examination of the
cow's condition was brief and mysterious. He first felt of the
creature's nose, then punched her side with his thumb, and,
lastly, which was quite logical, he twisted her tail a little, and
then said—"What ails this crittur is more than I can say tonight."

His test-prescription, however, and his directions for the dis-
enchantment of the field in which the beast had been pastured, I
distinctly remember. They were so remarkable that, under the
circumstances, I think the record of them will be pardonable:
"Watch and catch about a pint of the animal's urine — put it in
an iron pan, with nine sharp sewing-needles — and, while boiling
it, see who comes to your door. Meantime, you must take some

hair from the cow's ears, forehead, and tail — bore a hole in some tree in the meadow — put the hair into it, and seal it up."

Saying this, the mysterious seventh son — with a truly remarkable combination of physical proportions and wizard-like features — departed, promising to return on the following morn.

Father straightway disposed of the pasture business; and then, with all commendable vigilance, we took turns in waiting for the primary ingredient of that wonderful prescription. When obtained, the pan was carefully placed over the previously prepared fire. That fire seemed determined to do its duty. It was not confined within a black, prison-like, idiotic stove (as most stoves are), neither did it arise from some subterraneous heating apparatus (which suggests an idea of how Infernal regions may be kept at a high temperature) ; no, indeed! that fire burned briskly and beautifully in the proper place on the old-fashioned hearth, and threw its glowing light honestly out upon our awe-struck countenances. "A wood fire," said Cornelius Agrippa, "doth drive away dark spirits." Whether this assertion be true or false we did not know at the time, as neither had ever heard of the saying; but there did seem to be an intelligence in the prompt behavior of *that fire*, which imparted a sort of courage and confidence to each member of our domestic triangle.

At this critical juncture, I will not stop to paint the horrifying thoughts awakened during that dread incantation! We were half-jovial and half-terrified. The magician's prescription was, doubtless, being administered through the air to somebody! But who could it be? There the great conjurer's testing-fluid was — bubbling, and simmering, and spirting, before our marvelling eyes! It was a dreaded and irresistible summons — far more certain than if served by an officer of justice. Yes, in *that pan* we beheld the master and magic spell that was to do one of two things : either break and remove the subtler and weaker charm on our cow, or bring the malicious witch (or wizard) in person to our very door! If the latter, whence would come the sorceress?

And how would she travel? Perhaps, 't was a hideous monster —some dark, ghostly, demoniac being — who,

> " O'er bog, o'er steep, through straignt, rough, dense, or rare,
> With head, hands, wings, or feet, pursues his way,
> And swims, or sinks, or wades, or creeps, or flies."

What would happen, or how, was as yet all a speculative mys. tery. But the boiling and bubbling continued. Now and then a needle (there were nine in the pan) would come upon the liquid —would whirl and float on some bewitched bubble for a moment —and, then, down it would plunge into the sedimentary deposite beneath. Was that strange? Mother remarked it first; and then we each watched for another needle.

" Hark !" exclaimed Eliza, " what 's that a-knocking ?"

We listened, and distinctly heard some gentle tapping at our kitchen-door. " Who'll go and open it ?" asked Eliza: " that's the question !" The night had become very dark, and our employment made that darkness visible. Ever and anon while boiling the fluid, our cow would tramp about and bellow in the yard, close to the house ! Yes, dear reader, we had the disenchanting prescription over the fire, when we heard that knocking at the door. How, then, could we receive a visiter? But the seventh son had said, " See who'll come to your door." In order, then, to obey directions some one must go and see who stood without! Didn't that require some courage?

Well, the stout-hearted cordwainer was not to be frightened " at such nonsense," and forth he proceeded to welcome the stranger in. What next? Nothing to alarm us; only an elderly lady, a recent boarder of the family who owned the opposition cow ; and nothing more.

" What d' you wish ?" asked my father good-naturedly.

" Only to borrow a teaspoonful of salt," she tremulously replied; " I'll return it to-morrow."

Oh, to be sure," returned mother, with characteristic promptness to accommodate a neighbor ; and, well nigh forgetting all her

suspicions, she placed the salt in the old woman s cup, and smi
lingly said — " You may have it, an' welcome."

By this time the incantation was over ! The marvellous liquid
had evaporated ; and the nine needles, having good eyes, looked
just as sharp as ever. Therefore, without further experiment or
controversy, we retired for the night, sorrowing for the distress of
our domestic favorite ; but laughing also at the ridiculousness of
the bare idea that the harmless and uniformly well-behaved old
lady was the witch we sought to exorcise. And yet, it was so
very strange !

Shortly after our breakfast next morning, the disenchanter
entered, and interrogated : " What did you do ?"

" Jest as you sed, an' told me," replied mother. " But nothin'
happened."

" Did n't anybody call during the boiling operation ?" inquired
the seventh son.

Mother then informed him of the ordinary circumstance, to
which he hastily replied : " You should n't have given her the
salt."

Who can imagine our confusion — almost consternation — when
the man thus reprimanded my mother for her indiscretion. " Mercy save us !" she exclaimed, thinking, no doubt, that she had unconsciously put the long end of the lever into the hands of our
opposition neighbors. They again had the advantage and we
were the victims !

Mother took the pail, and went out to try the milking experiment once more. There came a small stream of milk, but a less
gleam of hope ; for the lacteal excretions were disgustingly mixed
with blood and mucus.

Ascertaining that the salt had been given to the old woman, the
conjurer, planting himself on the dignity of his reputation, grimly
preceded my mother into the yard, and instituted a more careful
examination of the animal's real condition ; while I occupied
myself, at this investigation, in observing the changes in his fea

tures. His face was this moment ridiculously solemn; next it was gathered up into knotty wrinkles; then every muscle seemed to be puckered up on one side and elongated on the other; but, finally, with a voice made low and coarse by the absence of true intelligence, he said: "This 'ere cow of yourn is diseased; and my 'pinion is, you might as well fat her for the market."

"Diseased!" exclaimed mother, "*where* is the poor thing diseased?"

"This crittur has the horn-distemper," replied the man, "an' a wolf in her tail. No mistake, marm — that's just what ails her."

"What! both disorders at once," muttered my father incredulously. "I doubt that any how."

"I'll satisfy you," confidently replied the wizard, "if you'll jest let me bore her horn and cut her tail."

This more rational test agreed to, the gimlet and knife were furnished; and the cow-doctor (before a witch-finder) soon demonstrated the accuracy of his recent affirmations. Therefore, as the kindest act now possible, the suffering animal was soon despatched by the unerring blow of an experienced arm.

Thus we see how much trouble a little scientific knowledge, applied at the first, would have saved this humble family: as it would, no doubt, hundreds of others, who are now beclouded and well-nigh demented by common superstitions. The fantastic movements of the distressed beast, with these two previously-undiscovered diseases upon her, were entirely natural; as were also the peculiar coincidences which we construed into events of supernatural significance.

The unwholesome effect of this case of superstition did not pass away for several months. I remember how mortified my mother felt — how ashamed and penitent we all were — over the silliness and injustice of the imputation. The proceedings of that night of incantation we managed to keep very private. Indeed, the whole experience we sought to bury in the tomb of oblivion. But the opposition neighbors with the opposition cow did not become wholly *disenchanted* of a tendency to antagonism, until the resident clergyman (of the Dutch Reformed Church) was called in to exert the magic of his influence upon them. The closing up of that valuable fountain of rich milk and sweet butter, was a serious loss to a struggling family; but, thanks to the *temperate* cordwainer, we soon possessed another cow, and still other evidences of domestic prosperity.

CHAPTER XXV.

OTHER EPISODES IN THIS HISTORY.

ABOUT this time an Israelitish merchant visited our village, with the avowed intention of opening there a "branch store" of dry goods, groceries, and a general assortment of useful articles — ranging, with nicely-shaded gradations, from a case of jews-harps to a bale of brocade silks, from a toy wheelbarrow to glass and china ware the most beautiful. Having nothing to do, (which was the only thing I could work at without bungling,) I endeavored to make myself as useful as possible in assisting the clerk to open and dispose of his goods in the building which had been secured by the merchant. This agreeable gentleman liking my voluntary performance, engaged me for a few shillings per week to remain with and help the young man, to whom the business had been intrusted.

While unpacking, arranging, and classifying the goods, I was pronounced a satisfactory subordinate and co-laborer. But when the people began to ask the price of certain articles, then it was that I tumbled from my lofty position down to the common level of those whose education had been neglected. My computing faculties were obtuse in the extreme. I could n't figure up even a short catalogue of prices. And my incapacity became still more apparent when fractions of dollars had to be deducted from or multiplied into a customer's bill. Neither could I give the correct name to any unusual description of merchandise. Add to this a conspicuous lack of vivacity and gracefulness — nay, an awkward and clumsy habit of saying and doing things—and you may readily anticipate my discharge from that establishment. Before I left, however, my mind was freed of an unavoidable prejudice which I had unconsciously imbibed against the Jews. While the store was being arranged for business, I would many times hear, when going to and fro for my meals, such reproachful speeches as: "A Jew'll cheat you out o' your eyes!" "The Israelites is under the cuss of God." "I would n't trust a Jew with brickbats," &c., &c. Nevertheless, during several weeks of constant observation and familiarity with this Jewish clerk, I never heard the slightest suggestion of cheating, nor did I ever receive any directions from him to give a purchaser wrong impressions of the real quality or true price of any saleable article. But I can not record as good a testimony in favor of several of those who jeered and scoffed at the gentlemanly Hebrew merchant.

"What to do with that boy, I do n't know!" said father, frowning with impatience, as I related to mother why the storekeeper would n't keep me.

"Why, the boy wants more schoolin'," replied my mother encouragingly. "He can't never keep no place in no store if he can't say his figures, you know." This reasoning was sound, and, in harmony therewith, I was sent to school. When the pleasant teacher, a lady, asked my age, I replied, "In my twelfth year." To her question about how long I had attended any school, I said, "Only a few weeks at Union Corners." When she wished to know precisely where I stood in my studies, I responded, "At the foot of the spellin' class." She desired to ascertain what I had learned, and I answered—"In the spellin'-book I got to 'baker,' an' in the g'ography all the way thro' every picture." Whereupon she gave me a lesson in the English Reader, which, after two days' hard spelling, I did commit to her satisfaction. Subsequently, I was placed at minor studies and made some permanent progress up the hill of useful knowledge.

By the spring of 1838, I had gone through the lesser portions of the multiplication table, but I invariably encountered difficult obstructions whenever I reached "nine times nine." In ciphering I waded through all the problems of simple and compound addition In spelling words of not more than three syllables I had consid :rable vexation and trouble. In writing I made some visible advancement. I could and did describe hooks and trammels after the teacher's examples. In the orthography class there were about a dozen children, considerably younger and smaller than I; yet I must confess that, during the most of the time, I came within ten or eleven of standing triumphantly at their head! When the days of absence are deducted, I think the amount of my schooling there did not, altogether, exceed six weeks.

Gloomily I left school, without any promotion consonant with my years. Not a laurel wreath could be seen upon my fevered brow. The fetters of inwrought ignorance seemed to bind my soul to the earth. The foot of a great mountain appeared to rest upon my youthful neck. My desolated head was covered with the cap of no climax. The car of Time sped by, conveying onward my jolly school-mates, and left me crying at the Blockhead Station. The bright scholars seemed to embrace each golden opportunity without blushing; while I, willing to buckle on the armor of a conqueror, always neglected the spur of the moment. The wings of the morning never shook out a quill for my chirographical benefit. Neither did my scholarship sail in the winds of adversity like the crafts of other boys. And so I was desponding.

In the early springtime of that year I felt the symptoms of a hepatic and gastric disease. A bilious fever centred and burned upon my forehead, and my stomach rejected all forms of nutrition. I grew rapidly very sick, which was a sad misfortune; but another was soon added, that is, an allopathic physician. For several days and nights what little of substantial Nature there was in me fought bravely and without cessation. In spite of leech and lancet, however, in spite of subtile poisons and murderous calomel, I won the battle and felt myself victorious!

But my previously impaired frame was yet more shaken and disabled. It bore marks of violence. My arm was weakened with a wound from the enemy's lance. The beautiful present which I had received from the hand of Mother-Nature — a set of pure and pearly teeth — was colored, and cracked, and opened to the march of General Decay, whose chief officer is called Tooth-ache, and whose trials in Court-Martial are conducted by Judge Turnkey and the lesser tools of torture. My tongue silently lay in the midst of carnage — nearly slain on the battle-plain — full of gashes and bleeding pores made by the spear and pike of that valiant Knight of the Cross, known throughout the world as Sir Calomel. My hands were worn away and palsied; my knees kept up the strife by smiting each other on the least exertion; my feet would not obey their head and master; but, amid all, my innermost spirit was stronger than before.

"Your son must not drink cold water, ma'am," said the visiting physician to my solicitous mother. "His case is a very critical one. The least cold taken at this stage of salivation, ma'am, will endanger his life."

The careful reader is already aware of my lively dread of dying. The thought of ceasing to breathe — of closing my eyes for ever — of being put in a coffin — of that confinement in the ground — was inexpressibly horrible. And yet, notwithstanding this awful dread added to the physician's emphatic warning, I seemed to hear something whispering. "*You—may—drink—the sweet—water—of—maple—trees.*" At first I thought it was but a fever dream; the suggestions of my burning thirst; a hint from the liquid fire that coursed wildly through my veins. But 't was twice whispered between mid-day and evening. The breathing thereof was refreshingly welcome. And I could not longer re-strain myself. The voice was like imagination's — very low, clear sweet, dreamy, influential. Hesitating no more, I told mother every word of my supposed dream — and insisted that, early in the next morning's dawn, I must drink the sap of sugar-maple. She believed with me, cherished my request, and obtained from the tapped trees a pailful of their drippings. Freely and fearlessly — yea, in perfect faith — I drank of the cooling water! What followed this draught? A substantial convalescence; and, in a few weeks, physical health and hopefulness.

Shortly after the conclusion of this illness, I obtained a situation in the household of W. W. Woodworth, a lawyer of acknowledged abilities and extensive reputation. He was, I believe, widely respected for the refinement and democracy of his hospitality; and not less for his manly bearing and legal skill whenever his talents were called into public action. He ascended from the position of private counsellor-at-law to that of judge, and was afterward elected to a seat in the National Congress.

This humane gentleman, knowing that our family was in somewhat straitened circumstances, interested himself in our behalf and assigned to me the responsible position of porter at his residence. I tried to serve him with faithfulness and integrity. But my inaptitude and constitutional clumsiness — each finger being as stiff as a thumb, and each foot as awkward as that of a clodhopper — soon made me an unpopular candidate for that honorable profession.

These personal disqualifications, however, did not impair the lawyer's friendship. He was an agent for the aristocratic family and widow of Dr. Hossack; by which means I was removed from his house to their great farm north of the village. My principal employment while there was that of a shepherd — or watcher and keeper of about seventy head of cattle, that grazed upon the beautiful park, environing the horticultural gardens and the magnificent mansion of the widow.

Could the space be spared, I would here digress sufficiently to paint the gorgeous scenery that lies upon the spectator's eye while viewing the Hudson from the heights just west of the lady's attractive country residence. It is diversified and beautiful in every direction. My imagination can now luxuriate in the charms of that well-remembered pastoral experience; but, while passing through it, I enjoyed nothing worth recording—save the sight of my punctual mother wading every morning through the surging and dewy grass, with a tin-pail containing my breakfast, and the encouraging words that ever and anon flowed from her heart's deep fountain into mine.

All the nabobs and aristocratic families that lived in such princely magnificence along the romantic banks of the Hudson, "worshipped" in the Episcopal church, of which the Rev. Mr. Sherwood was the esteemed and established pastor. Judge Woodworth's family bowed before that altar; and I, being in his employ, went to the same manger for religious nutriment. A very devout, proper, discreet, even-mannered lady, manifested genuine interest in my sabbath exercises. She gave me a lesson to memorize, and lent me a Sunday-school book embellished with many pictures. By dint of swerveless perseverance, I perfectly committed, as I supposed, the catechismal answers; and, on the next sabbath, presented myself at the proper place, in a proper state of mind, to deliver them in a proper manner, to the proper lady.

"Who made you?" asked the devout and precise lady.

"God," I replied—inwardly delighted that I had not forgotten my Maker's Christian name.

"Who redeemed you?" she softly and sweetly asked.

The meaning of the word "redeemed" dwelt rather vaguely in my brain, and caused me for a moment to forget the printed answer; but, quickly gathering my thoughts into form, I replied—"Christ." How glad I was that she did not question me as to the precise time when my redemption happened! If she had, I felt sure that my memory would have failed me.

"Who sanctified you?" she then inquired.

"The Holy Ghost," I promptly answered.

"What do you believe?"

"I b'lieve," said I—flushing with a sudden fear that my memory would not hold out to the end—"I b'lieve—in—God, the Father, Almighty Maker of heaven and earth; and—in—Jesus Christ, his only Son our Lord, who was conceived by the Holy *Ghost*, born of the—of the—born of the—of—"

"Do you not remember your lesson?" inquired the teacher, with a withering expression of chiding and surprise.

"No, ma'am," said I, "I hain't got a good mem'ry."

She thought a moment, and then asked: "Did you know every word of it before you came here?"

"Oh, yes, ma'am," I replied; "'t was all in my mind afore to-day. But when I come to that 'are word 'Ghost,' I kinder lost myself a-thinkin' about somethin' else what happened afore this."

"Or *what* did that blessed word remind you?" she asked, with a look of overtaxed forbearance.

"Oh, nothin' much, ma'am," I responded with trepidation, blushing to my very temples. "But," I stammeringly continued, "that 'are word made me think of a *straw* ghost what a feller named Dave once seen up in Staatsburgh. Yes, ma'am—that's jest what I was a-thinkin'! I forgot the lesson—'cause I got to wonderin' whether one ghost meant anything like t'other."

Hearing this, the dignified and sanctimonious teacher bit her lips—having hard work to choke down the profane laugh that kept rising out of her bosom; but presently, collecting all her wonted circumspection and gravity, she gave me one of the severest of rebukes for my irreverent treatment of sacred subjects. In that reprimand, however, I regarded her as totally misapprehending the nature and magnitude of my difficulty; and therefore the only effect of the reproof or admonition was, to turn my religious inclinations or prejudices toward the Dutch Reformed church of which my serious and spiritually-minded mother had recently become a member and practical advocate.

During all that autumn I cheerfully accompanied my parents every Sunday morning to the village-church. There was here less exclusiveness. As to practical piety, however, I could discern no difference between the supporters of the two institutions. But the spectral shadow of that meetinghouse rests upon my memory yet! The steeple rose high and saintly. The reverberations of the tolling bell went tremblingly through the still sabbath air, or vibrated with moral accents on the night-winds, that went away to sigh in village-homes, and then die among the distant hills. In the graveyard there I could see a mound, marked by two rough stone slabs, reminding me that Julia Ann's face once smiled on mine. Oft and again have I seen my mother saddened by words from the preacher's lips, and homeward take her dreary way, with thoughts on awful subjects rolling—" damnation and the dead !"

Out of pure filial sympathy, I began to believe all the minister said on Sunday. To be sure, I did not comprehend scarcely any portion of his teachings; but that there was something awful in being alive, and still more in being *dead*, I was distressingly certain. Many a night I have huddled myself into a constrained and painful heap, after going to bed—fearing that something might happen to our family before morning. Regularly, however, I attended that Reformed Dutch church; studied out lessons in its catechism; and, with characteristic freedom, talked right out what I thought. The eternal attributes with which the Calvinists dressed up their God, became measurably familiar to my understanding. The doctrine of election and reprobation was one day ably explained to the Sunday-school class of which I had been rather a silent member. I listened with anxiety, mingled with confusion. On a subsequent occasion, an elderly gentleman, who was seriously devoted to the propagation of the essential doctrines, delivered a brief exposition on the momentous subject of " elec-

tion." At my particular request, he repeated his theory of God's
ways to mankind. My head could not receive the profound explanation. The other children affirmed that they understood and
believed it all, and, as usual, gave me the jeering and tantalizing
elbow-hint that I was *non compos mentis.* I thought I could understand just as much of theology as the rest, but they seemed to
entertain a different opinion. The silver-haired teacher, however,
though somewhat inclined to their estimate of me, earnestly com-
pounded, expounded, and pounded the sacred theme, until I be·
came confounded, and at length found myself believing less than
ever. Taking courage one day, I thus interrogated :—

"Uncle Isaac, you told me that God *is Love*—didn't you?"

"Yes, my child," he smilingly replied, "I did."

"And did n't you say that God *is wise* too?"

"Certainly, my little son," said the old man; "God has both
Love and Wisdom. And just as much of the one as of the
other!"

"Well, you say I must be very good, and love and obey my
parents, else God will send me to hell for ever?"

"Yes, the Scriptures plainly teach that."

"Now, Uncle Isaac," said I, "let me tell you why I can't get
that 'are belief into my head like Bill, an' Joe, an' Tommy."

"Well, tell me, child," said the venerable teacher.

"It seems to me," said I, "that if God is *all-wise* he know'd
before I was born whether I would go to hell or heaven."

"Why, y-e-s," interrupted the old man with solicitude, "but
he — you know — he — God, in his great wisdom and gracious
mercy, has — you know — opened a strait and narrow way for all
to be — for *most* all — for a few — to be saved if they will but enter in thereat."

"But that are hain't what I'm wanting to know, Uncle Isaac,"
I replied. "What I want to know is this 'ere: Could a God of
Love, knowing for certain that I would be miserable after death
bring me into existence? Yes, Uncle Isaac, that's what I want

to know.   I keep a-thinkin' in my brain that a God of Love and Wisdom is TOO GOOD to create anybody to suffer in hell for ever."

"Oh, my child!" exclaimed the teacher, apparently much astonished and alarmed.   "You mustn't talk so to those who have read the Scriptures.   The ways of God, my son, are past finding out.   Men's hearts are naturally depraved, you know; their reason is carnal and surely delusive.   The Evil One tempts men — tempts you I fear — to have such thoughts and doubts about the ways of God."

This startling admonition was substantially the last lesson I ever received at a Sunday school.   I was deeply impressed with the awfulness of my impudent controversy with a man whose emblems of wisdom floated, like a snowy screen, round about his matured brow.   Straightway I went and told my mother all. Her mind was not constituted for the examination of doctrinal questions.   But the holy genius of pure religion dwelt in the sanctuary of her heart — teaching her that Goodness is the only happiness, that Virtue is the only key to unlock the emerald gates that open upon the gardens of Paradise — and thus, in this my first of theological troubles, she could lend me no aid, but, instead, sought to wash away the stumbling-blocks by a flood of tears.

Soon after this, being nearly half-way up the first mountain of my life, I experienced a sudden and brilliant development of somnambulism.   It showered a clear radiance over the entire bed in which I lay, and as I then thought, made an external representation of light like the Aurora Borealis.   But I now know that the effulgence was strictly a spiritual exercise of my own perceptive faculties.

While passing through this anti-sleep experience, which then continued nightly for some three weeks, I persistently sought the repose of solitude during each day.   This I could do only by means of pretexts of various kinds ; such as getting permission to hunt in the woods, or to fish for herring by the river-side.   So attractive to me were these solitary rambles that, much to my mother's discomfort, I sometimes lingered whole nights by the water's edge, listening to the ceaseless moaning of the regurgitating waves. Physicians, I believe, usually consider "sleep-walking" a disease. But my experience was based invariably upon the healthiest conditions. And, besides, I was not what might strictly be called a sleep-walker. My mind was more self-possessed and intelligent at such times than during the day; and my eyes (whether open or shut I know not) could see things about me with far greater accuracy. In short, I had to go through a certain sleeping process in order to become as bright and quick-witted as other boys of my age. In one of these nocturnal crises, I arose eight nights in succession, and painted upon a small canvass (which I had previously prepared, without knowing at the time why I did it) a beautifully diversified landscape which, subsequent to completion, I recognised as a view of the *Garden of Eden* which had been impressed upon my mind at the Episcopal sabbath-school.

Remembering nothing more in my history for several months — of any psychological interest to the reader — I will close this chapter and begin the next with a different experience.

CHAPTER XXVI.

IN WHICH I HEAR STRANGE MUSIC.

My parents had become acquainted with two industrious men, who were exemplary professors of both agriculture and religion; and, being of a practical turn, they never failed, to my best knowledge and belief, in the discharge of duties commonly allotted to days called sacred and secular. At this time, (the spring of 1838,) these friends were associated in culturing the vast fields which, as heretofore said, were known for many leagues around as "the Hossacks' Farms." It was ascertained that these farmers wanted a strong and active boy to perform the lesser labors consequent upon tillage. Therefore, unable to store my mind with the primary accomplishments of a public school, my father concluded that, excepting the "strong and active," I could otherwise well enough fill the proffered situation. After due deliberation, the husbandmen agreed upon the question of victuals and clothes; and, a few days subsequently, you might have seen me dropping corn or hoeing my own row — tugging, and sweating, and fretting, with an intense headache, to keep up with the somewhat companionable group of skilful workmen.

I became quite handy with the hoe, and so had a day's work marked out for me. One extremely warm day, however, when I chanced to be left alone at my appointed task, in the middle of a twenty-acre cornfield, my attention was arrested by the sound of sweet, low, and plaintive music. It seemed to emanate from the airy space above me, and had a pathos like the sighing of autumnal winds. Being far away from trees and human habitations, its source was unaccountable. Unlike anything I had ever before heard, it appeared to be breathing in the very fibres of my brain —yea, through the substance of my inner being and throbbing heart—awakening there the tenderest emotions, and filling my juvenile mind with loving sympathies toward the unknown human world. Previous to this moment I had entertained no enlarged affection for strangers. The idea of loving anybody not loved by my immediate relatives, or of disliking persons who were openly recognised as the friends of our humble little household, never appeared to me before this as being other than unnatural and blameworthy. Indeed, my sympathies and antipathies, like those of uneducated youth generally, were bounded by the selfish affinities of the family group. But, now, there was born in me an inexpressible yearning to know and love everything human. I seemed to be lifted, as by a miracle, above the mists of selfishness. While I listened, confounded and transfixed with joy and wonderment combined, I seemed distinctly to hear, floating down upon the glistening solar ray, as it were, and indescribably blending with the Æolian strains of the mysterious melody, these words: " *You —may—desire—to—travel.*"

Breathless and exhausted with increased amazement, I stood leaning on the handle of my hoe, by which I kept my trembling form from falling, nervously hearkening—oh, how intensely!—. for whatever else might reach me through the dreamy music of the abounding air. But, ere I knew it, the oppressive silence of the immense field was upon me, and only familiar objects in the surrounding distance reflected themselves upon my wondering gaze. For three or four days afterward the enchantment lingered upon me. I would involuntarily halt near the charmed spot, all forgetful of my work, and devote myself to wishing for another strain of atmospheric harmony so delightful.

The shrill toot of the dinner-horn went bounding over the extensive plantation, summoning the various laborers to their accustomed nooning, myself among the number. The associated farmers, as already said, were tilling the land on shares. Hence their respective families lived in opposite apartments of the same spacious farmhouse; and, to make expenses equal, divided the time between such of the workmen as engaged themselves by the month, with board included. On this plan, I ate during the first three days of each week with one of the joint-stock employers, and the remainder with the other — always going home on Saturday night, and returning Monday morning.

The younger of the two farmers was an awfully — and, as I thought, a miserably — religious man. There was a thoughtfulness and solemnity in the expression of his eye, a prayer-like tone even in his most ordinary vocal exercises, and a kind of churchyard precision in the measured tread of his feet, which invariably exerted an unwholesome restraint. Besides, it tended to produce and confirm a disagreeable apprehension that the cheerless obligations of "Sunday" had become, by some tremendous accident, flatted down and crushed into the meshes of the secular fabric — giving all to feel that "religion is the chief concern of mortals here below." But he was, withal, a just man, and, in his own way, uniformly kind to me. And yet, when I ate at his table, notwithstanding the blest food, my appetite was somehow impaired. My teeth would masticate well enough, but, when I came to swallow, the provender would stick and tarry by the wayside. In short, toward the end of the second day my head would ache, and my stomach report indigestion. The senior agriculturist, on the other hand, although conscientious and equally strict in his attendance at public worship, was very far less rigid, and presented a more human and approachable aspect to all who dwelt with him.

Some four days subsequent to the event recorded on a preceding page, I was eating at the table of the gravest of the two farmers. After thanking Heaven for bestowing the meat, pota toes, and turnips, that lay smoking before us, and invoking a continuance of the Divine blessing, the farmer fixed his eye inquiringly upon mine, and I felt that something would be soon said for my specific edification.

" Did you hoe one row across the field this forenoon ?" he asked.

" Not quite," I replied, with a choking, lumpy sensation in my throat, as if the small boiled potato then in my mouth had gone down before it was sent.

A brief silence reigned however, during which my thoughts flew back to the field to estimate how much work I had really done; but, instead, I could only think of the delightful sounds and mysterious whisperings of that music so unaccountable.

" We can't hire boys to idle away their time," he at length solemnly remarked, " or to stand looking at crows flying over cornfields."

On hearing this, the aforesaid lump in my throat suddenly extended itself downward, and produced a feeling in my stomach as if I had unexpectedly swallowed one half of everything on my plate. My embarrassment was painful. Never did any boy more wish for a few words wherewith to explain and get excused; but I venture to say there never was a boy more impoverished in a knowledge of the simplest forms of language.

I walked out, and seated myself on the grass in the garden. " Can it be," thought I, " that he saw me standing when I should have been at work? He spoke about crows! I didn't see them. Besides, I don't believe *any* bird could make all I heer'd." But a doubt was evidently started in my mind as to whether I was not deceived by some person, or in a sort of dream; and, wishing to be considered as smart and useful as other boys, I resolved that, should I be again left alone at my task, never to squander away that time which justly belonged to my esteemed employers. And, indeed, I was not without certain unpleasant misgivings lest the report of my idleness should reach my father, and result in casting me, as before, on his protection and industry.

We will now pass over an interval of several months. In the winter of 1839, it was parentally decided that I should attend the district school. But my memory reports no progress even in the commonest branches of education. The teacher put the same questions concerning where I stood in spelling, reading, writing, ciphering, &c., and my responses were as heretofore recorded—-that is, *in statu quo*, at the caudal extremity of the several classes thus distinguished and denominated. Nominally, I got the credit of going some two months; but, in fact, sixteen days would probably cover the whole extent of my attendance. I had an inwrought repugnance to the compulsiveness of studying a book. In order to avoid the hateful constraint, I procured little jobs and errands to occupy the most of my time, and thus furnish me with a good excuse for non-appearance at the institution of learning.

Early in the spring I had the good fortune to obtain more employment on the Hossacks' farms. One day, while clearing some new ground for a crop of buckwheat, methought I heard that marvellous music again! I was fortunately alone at my work, and could devote myself to giving audience. When first I listened, no extraordinary sound reached my nervously-intensified ear. Anon, however, the pure and bird-like melody floated dreamily through the heavens! And again all was silent.

In order to fix that Æolian harmony in my recollection, I tried to imitate some of its properties — to reproduce a few of those tremulously-delicious sounds which had previously so utterly charmed me, by preponderating the emotions of astonishment and admiration. To my great delight, I could and did imitate certain notes by a sort of ventriloquism — of which, till then, I had no knowledge. This peculiar, purling symphony — a breathing through the epiglottis and pharyngeal passages — I have since ofttimes produced in the presence of familiar friends.

Ever since the mortifying case of witchcraft and superstition at our house, I had concealed from my parents the most of my individual experience. Dreams and omens frightened or saddened my good mother unnecessarily, as I thought: and hence I withheld a relation of my musical enchantment in the cornfield. Oft and again, however, I have when alone inaudibly asked myself: "What did it mean? And those insinuating words, 'You—may—desire—to—travel!' what did they mean? Was that a voice from kind Prov'dence, or was I jest then a-dreamin' as mother does?" And again: "Was that a permission, or a prophecy? Which word does the sentence turn upon? If upon 'may,' then it is a permission. If upon 'travel,' then it is a prophecy. How perplexingly vague! How dreamlike and mysterious!"

Thus, after imitating the celestial notes, I mentally questioned the blue space above me. But no answer was returned. Resuming my work at length, with the conclusion that I had only been imagining music, I heard, apparently near my ear, the same well-remembered voice (like my mother's), whispering, "To—Poughkeep-sie." With the celerity of thought the whole matter flashed intelligibly before me. "What!" I exclaimed, "then I may desire to travel to Poughkeepsie?" I waited for a reply, but none descended. From that hour, however, I yearned to have our domestic interests removed to the mysteriously-specified locality.

As might be expected, this new experience — added to and explaining the preceding — lent irresistible enchantment to the idea of travelling. I began to recall the pictures in Peter Parley's juvenile geography — to realize, through them, the wonders and advantages of large villages and populous cities. My organ of inhabitiveness was evidently subordinated by the locomotive power of other faculties. I regretted to be the cause of suggesting a change so expensive to a poor family. But I did suggest it nevertheless. After a while, I induced my father to think of it; and, finally, I persuaded my mother to agree to the movement also, if it could be accomplished with but a moderate outlay of labor and means. My main expressed reason was, that I had become tired of the village-boys, &c. At last, father and I walked to beautiful Poughkeepsie. He found an opportunity for steady work at Mr.

John M. Cable's manufacturing establishment. Next we discovered the locality of three rooms, all vacant and to let, in the immense tenant-house of Mr. Thomas Simpson. And so, in the
early autumn of that year (1839), our family moved to what, by
virtue of adoption, I have frequently and affectionately termed my
native village.

And now, as new characters may soon have the unsolicited
pleasure of appearing in this drama, I will just remark that my
sister Eliza, having again united herself in wedlock to the heart
of her choice, was left behind, and in all probability will not reap·
pear until near the close of this Autobiography.

CHAPTER XXVII.

MY LANCASTERIAN EDUCATION.

PERHAPS no member of the Society of Friends was ever more friendly to youth than Joseph Lancaster, of England. Through many parts of Albion's isle he travelled and delivered eloquent orations on education, to which the noble, wealthy, and fashionable, listened with the strongest and cheapest evidences of approbation. His benevolent exertions were followed by severe personal embarrassments. Patronage of the rich was not accompanied with sufficient money; and the philanthropist fled to the "land of the free" for relief and substantial co-operation. But America did not at once assist the enthusiastic Quaker — whose deepest heart throbbed with profoundest aphorisms for the youth of the world — and so, having been accidentally and fatally injured in the great metropolis, his spirit ascended to a land where mutual methods of instruction are universally received and set in harmonious operation.

In Church street, Poughkeepsie, there stood a large, utilitarian-looking building, where about four hundred children were daily sent to school. The plan of teaching was professedly Lancasterian — that is, a regularly-graduated descending scale of monitors and admonitors — beginning with the principal, Mr. Howe, and terminating with the personal presence and intellectual exercises of the writer.

The truth is, that my father, after several weeks of unsuccessful effort to make me of use to him in his art, bade me attend the

Lancaster school, "to keep me out of mischief." Obediently I
went, reported myself at the desk, and, like Oliver Twist, wanted
to know what was coming next. After one day's hard drilling,
the "head and front" of the institution pronounced me "behind"
in spelling, reading, writing, and arithmetic. The intelligent
teacher, therefore, put me under the supervision of boys younger
than myself, but who were greatly more advanced in the several
branches above specified. And I too, though a pupil, was likewise
promoted to the honorable and flattering distinction of monitor.

But this promotion did not occur immediately. No, indeed!
The honor was conferred only after many days of pupilage—
when the superintendent had determined, by virtue of observation
and tests, just the situation to which my genius was adapted.
Where was that? What particular group in the vast assemblage
of classes was I qualified to teach? I had attended school, as you
know, at Union Corners and in Hyde Park: to what point of exaltation, then, had my mind attained? Reader, I will tell you.
Mr. Howe placed me as monitor over the A-B-C class! A mis-
cellaneous band composed of above twenty snarly-haired, bad-
odored, dirty-faced, ragged-dressed, comic-acting, squinting, lisp-
ing, broad-mouthed, linkum-slyly, and yet somewhat promising
urchins, surrounded and looked upon me as their respected teacher.
My memory was well trained to the required mission. My eye
could discern any alphabetical character at a glance. The lettered
cards hung in front of my heterogeneous class. With simultaneous pronunciation of each letter by the pupils, I taught them the
rudiments of the English language—yea, of all external book-
knowledge! Oh, how proud I was then—how proud I am now
—with my work on the plan of Joseph Lancaster! But I would
have passed it over in silence, had I not promised to write a truthful history. During the ten weeks of my attendance there I
made no advancement save in writing and ciphering. My attention was apparently stultified whenever the larger studies were
placed before me; and hence, excepting several new games at

marbles and ball-playing, I left school without learning scarcely anything

Before leaving this section of my pilgrimage, however, I will reaffirm that while at school I was not put to the study of history, grammar, geometry, nor any of the intermediate branches of science. The fine arts — geography, astronomy, drawing, music, dancing — were strictly withheld. And who will indite the volumes of my gratitude? The schoolbooks did not prejudice my mind, for their really useful teachings I could not receive. In the presence of my playmates, in the higher departments, I was intellectually a dwarf. This backwardness and dullness sometimes grieved me, but a few skips in the open air would restore my usual contentment.

This was the last of my schooling. Added to the several weeks before, it made little more than five months — the whole amount of my attendance at places of instruction. With the most limited appreciation of the elements and uses of books and education, I returned to my parents; and never, from that day to this hour, have I ever attempted to study any book treating upon grammatic, historic, scientific, or philosophical subjects. The reason why I have not will fully appear in future chapters. Since that memorable winter I have allowed myself several times to ask " whether the spirit of Joseph Lancaster ever looked down upon the numerous classes that were then being educated according to that system of mutual instruction, which he, while a dweller of earth, had so earnestly promulgated on both sides of the Altantic?" To this question I have as yet received no answer; perhaps, because the reply hath no value of wide-spread importance.

CHAPTER XXVIII.

THE UPS AND DOWNS OF LIFE.

> " If his call
> Be but our gathering to that distant land
> For whose sweet waters we have pined with thirst,
> Why should not its prophetic sense be borne
> Into the heart's deep stillness, with a breath
> Of summer winds — a voice of melody,
> Solemn, yet lovely ?"

BENEATH the ripple of mirth I ever realized a calm flow of serious thought. While bubbling and bounding along through the ordinary channels of subsistence, I could feel the motion of a deep fountain of existence which I had no words to reveal. There were within no volcanic, eruptive, explosive forces that yearned for vent and expression. On the contrary, the mystic current that set through my soul was like the deep, calm, ebbless flow of some baptismal river. Gentle beings, bowed down with sickness and sorrow, walked spectre-like upon its banks. Their tears dropped upon the soil, and beautiful flowers sprung up. I could laugh, and sing, and dance, (in my own way,) but, ever and anon, my soul was conscious of the tremendous profundity of existence.

Such were my mental realizations immediately subsequent to leaving the Lancaster school. Mother said to father, who was complaining because I could n't sit still on the bench: " Do n't find fault all the time. He 's nothin' but a child yit."

" A child !" returned the cordwainer satirically. " Let me tell you he ain't worth his salt. He's old enough to earn his victuals and clothes. He's got to do it too."

'Twas now the full spring-time of 1840. Sunbeams were liberated from their frosty imprisonments. Ice-bound streamlets were unmanacled by the solar ray, and fled away through the meadows dancing for joy. The sublimest epic of North American waters, the noble Hudson, was again chanting its melodious song. And commerce, too, the mighty river of human traffic and subsistence, began to roll its tides through the beautiful village.

But my soul was bound, hand and foot, in the prison of doubt and depression. "Why did we move from Hyde-Park?" I asked myself one day, as my feet were listlessly taking me down Main street. "*There* I was of some use. I hain't of no use here. My breast pains me so that I can't sit bending over the shoe on my lap. And my mind hain't on it nuther! Father don't like me for it — mother is unhappy about it — and I'm real sorry that I can't learn somethin' and be somethin' useful."

At this moment a solid-looking and out-spoken individual, standing on the sidewalk, accosted me and said: "See here, sleepy youngster, help that young man unload his potatoes," pointing to a farmer in the street, who had evidently sold his stock of country produce to the speaker. "Carry the bags down there," he continued, indicating a basement-grocery to the right, "and count 'em too. Come! be astir — keep your eyes open — don't miscount 'em, mind that."

Notwithstanding the salutation that emanated from this stranger, all commanding and unexpected as it was, it did not fully counteract the depth and extent of my abstraction. Doubtless I hesitated and acted as if disinclined, until I heard the voice like my mother's: "Jackson, do it." Instantly I was awake and ready to serve the basement-grocer. I did so, and continued till 'twas time to go home for my evening meal, when the merchant said: "Come back to-morrow. I'm not young now, nor in good health; so a boy is what I want for a while."

My delight was great. Entering home with a bound, I told mother all that had happened, and received her counsel to return next morning. Thus was commenced the basis of my usefulness in a retail grocery. The proprietor was Nicholas Lawrence. Under all circumstances he gave me his confidence, made me his clerk and companion during business hours, and remunerated me to my satisfaction. My calculating faculties were so deficient, however, that he had to make out the bills; but, fortunately, 1 could write well enough to keep a correct day-book record of business transactions. But from day to day the merchant's health failed. Disease crept through his frame like an assassin. The periods of his absence from the store, to get bodily rest and relief, became more and more frequent and protracted. And so, being excessively fatigued one day with the cares of the little property, he said: "Why don't your father buy this small stock, and put you in it? You'll make a good grocer, I'll bet: tell the old man to think of it."

The mere idea of my father purchasing a grocery for me was extremely preposterous. The stock was not worth more than three hundred and fifty dollars; but my respected progenitor hadn't a dollar over paying his weekly bills on Saturday night; so what could he do toward a purchase? And besides, the energetic cordwainer did not fancy the idea of forced publicity. "Poh!" exclaimed he, "jest think of my name on a sign-board over the door — '*Samuel Davis, Grocer*' — without a dollar in my pocket to keep the plaguy concern in operation!"

Mother's countenance shone with a mild radiance. The suggestion seemed to inspire her with hope. She sympathized in every exertion I made to escape the constrained posture consequent upon aiding my father at home. An opportunity to place me in congenial employment, therefore, was seized upon and cherished by her as a providential opening. Hence, in opposition to the sterner partner of her life, she replied: "'T ain't so dretful impossible as you think. I'm willing to live right down in the basement where the grocery is — so save the rent — and tend the store when Jackson is gone out to buy things."

Father thought about the matter, talked it over, rejected the proposition, laid it on the table, put it to vote, suggested emendations, kicked the plan sky-high, waited for it to come down, laughed at the enterprise, believed it would work, knocked mother's counsel into flinders, gathered up the fragments, concluded to go it — and, wouldn't postpone a day! He disliked to be doing things by the halves. So down street he went, and told Mr. Lawrence that, although he hadn't any money, he had plenty of industry and honesty, and would pay for the stock by degrees. (ten dollars every Saturday night,) and, if that was satisfactory, he would take possession of the whole concern immediately. The proposal was accepted. And at the end of the second day we were living in the dark, damp, gloomy basement.

The details of my experience in that subterraneous place are of no public importance. Perhaps, however, in passing, I might remark upon my own deficiency as a merchant. Owing to the fact that we had no extra capital to work upon, our limited stock, without feet, soon got low and ran out. Father obtained credit for some seventy dollars' worth of saleable articles; but when the day arrived to pay that bill, we were hopelessly bankrupt. The news of our insolvency was whispered through the interstices of trade, and our creditor, J. O. Van Anden, authorized the sheriff to close up our baseless enterprise in the basement, whereupon we moved back again into Mr. Simpson's tenant-house.

But there was one circumstance which greatly depressed us all — the rapid decline of mother's health. Her exertions to maintain our position — to bolster up father's fretful courage, to sustain the trembling and tumbling business — impaired and exposed her feeble constitution to the invasion of a distressing disease. She was very ill. This heavy misfortune, added to the weight of pecuniary enthralments, almost crushed my father's spirit. He grew impatient a.id irascible, and compelled me, regardless of the lameness and pain in my breast, to assist him on the bench.

In a short time, it was difficult to obtain sufficient employment. Hence our circumstances were becoming oppressive and embarrassing. The entanglements of poverty hemmed us in on every side. But to warm and sustain us there was the sunshine of our honest purpose. Lower and lower still sunk the clouds of misfortune. Soon it was hard to obtain the commonest necessaries of daily subsistence. The disabled and patiently-suffering woman, worn and wan, needed attentions which she did not receive, and palliatives, too, which we had not the power to bestow. The philanthropic physician gave no encouraging word concerning her restoration. The horrid agonies of neuralgia swept through her shattered fabric. A chronic inflammatory rheumatism lurked about her head and neck, and, like a deadly enemy, dealt fatal blows at every exposure of its victim. And—but no, I will not dwell upon harrowing scenes of human suffering long past.

In our straitened and desperate condition, my father wrote a begging letter to the pastor of the Cannon street presbyterian church; of which my mother was a member in good standing, (morally speaking,) and where we periodically went for our religious refreshment and instruction. The venerable minister responded in person. He delicately inquired into our private circumstances. With becoming regret, he assured us that pecuniary aid was not in the line of his congregation, but gave father two dollars out of his own pocket! The pastor was himself poor, and so his charity fell like angel's tears upon our hearts. But the assistance was too circumscribed; it did not cover our needs for twenty-four hours. On the following morning, in accordance with a silent resolve, I ascended "College Hill" to beg for cold victuals.

Did you ever behold that glorious eminence, dear reader? and the classic structure with which the elevation is crowned? If not, and your means will sustain the trip, I commend you to visit them. There are distant mountains which reflect themselves upon the surveying eye, and a broad expanse of farming landscape to the south and east. The beautiful scene from this summit is almost worthy of Eliza Cook's melodious lines:—

> " There are forests, there are mountains,
> There are meadows, there are rills,
> Forming everlasting fountains
> In the bosom of the hills.
> * * * *
> There are golden acres bending
> In the light of harvest rays,
> There are garland branches blending
> With the breath of June's sweet days;
> There are pasture grasses blowing
> In the dewy moorland shade,
> There are herds of cattle lowing
> In the midst of bloom and blade."

This imposing mount, with its temple of knowledge, had awakened my reverence. Its advantages to youth, contrasted with those of the Lancaster school, seemed unspeakably superior. But I was invariably glad that my path did not lead through a college. This singular gladness came, as I supposed, from my dread of studying books.

Toward the attractive edifice I now bent my reluctant steps, urged on by the necessities of a destitute family. When arrived, I rang the bell, which summoned an elegantly-dressed gentleman to the door. As well as I could I made the humiliating object of my visit known; whereupon his previously graceful manners and amiable smile subsided into a stiff attitude and gruff denial. I returned with a full heart but empty pail. Before reaching home, however, a thought struck me like lightning. The surprise and force thereof made me tremble and reel for a moment; but my mind retained the proportions of this sentence: "*A—little—leaven —leaveneth—the—whole—lump.*" Now the meaning of the word " leaven" was doubtful, but it made me think of yeast; such as our folks had used for bread, &c. And this suggestion was succeeded by the self-instituted query: " Suppose I peddle yeast every day — could n't I earn a loaf of bread and a pound of meat?   Yes! I 'll do it !''   Accordingly, without reporting where I had been or whither I was going with my tin-pail, I coaxed twelve cents out of father's almost exhausted exchequer, and started o..' in great haste for M. Vasser & Co.'s immense brewery by the river.   Investing my entire capital in the frothy substance, and thanking the clerk for adding a little ale to increase the quantity, I proceeded on my novel pilgrimage to people's kitchens and housekeepers.

"Have some yeast to-day?'' I asked.

"Some what?'' returned a certain colored cook.

"Some yeast, for raisin' bread an' buckwheat cakes.''

"Oh, sartainly I does!   Give us two cents' worth.   It's kinder new business ain't it?   I likes the commadation of it though. When 'll you come agin?''

I made my appointment there, and thus also at many other residences ; and, before the sundown of that day, I disposed of my entire stock, and had laid the foundation for a wider extent of custom.

On examining my cash account, I found a profit of twenty-five cents.   Carefully preserving my capital for the next morning's operations, I invested the day's proceeds in one loaf of bread, one pound of meat, and a little fruit, to cheer the appetite of my suffering and sinking mother.   That was a glorious night for me ! To find that I could earn money enough to purchase *food* for us all gave me a perfect inward jubilee of joy and gratitude, though I signified it by no boisterous outward demonstration.   For several successive weeks I continued to be a pedlar of yeast, utterly alone and well-nigh in tatters ; but my efforts glittered with bits of that magic metal which rules the proudest worldling.   In my business perambulations, I met face to face with persons who, then austere and unapproachable, are now gentle and hospitable in the extreme !   Verily, the ups and downs of human life, like the flowings and ebbings of a mighty river, work out many mar-

vellous transpositions. Let the supercilious man check his pride,
therefore; and let the child of sorrow forsake his grief.

Near the close of a chilly day, February 2, 1841, when I was
about to open the back-yard gate which separated our door from
the public street, something like *a black veil* suddenly dropped
over my face, shutting out every object and enveloping me in
utter darkness. I groped and fumbled my way along like a blind
boy, as if in a dark night, while the sun was yet shining in the
west. My consciousness was much the same as when under the
somnambulic trance; but, unlike that condition, my closed eyes
now could discern nothing, and my unguided feet stumbled
against unperceived obstacles.

In this place, however, I should chronicle my reflections while
wending my way homeward, from that day's unprosperous ped-
dling of yeast. "Why did I want to move from Hyde-Park?"
thought I. "Why did I coax father and mother to make the
change? There, we had n't such trouble to obtain work. There,
we had a cow and none of this sickness. There, mother seemed
more contented and father less irritable. Now, everything is
changed. Sadness, sickness, sorrow, hunger, dwell with us now.
Oh, why did I want to come here? I'm 'fraid that 't was owing
to that 'are cornfield dreamin'. Well, one thing is sure, I won't
do nothing *blind* ag'in." This resolution was formed and fixed
just as I had reached the garden-gate. But now, lo! I was
made blind in open day!

Anon, while I was without feeling for the gate-latch, all space
seemed to be instantly filled with a golden radiance! The world
was transformed! Winter snows and icy barriers had melted and
glided away; warm breezes played with glowing sunbeams; fruit-
trees were blossoming in the garden before me; bright birds sent
out their melodious songs upon the perfumed air; new and beautiful flowers decorated the margins of many paths that led to a
gorgeous palace which stood where the tenant-house was just a

few moments previous; a celestial bloom and an immortal loveli
ness shone forth everywhere; and I heard what, as on other
occasions, sounded like my mother's voice calling as from an unseen window of the palatial superstructure—" *Come here, child.
I—want—to—show—you—my—new—house !*"

Without an emotion of astonishment or haste, (at which I am
even now astonished,) I opened the begemmed gate before me,
which gave out music from its very hinges, and then I walked
calmly through the pure air, between the spraying fountains, beneath the waving gleeful trees, amid the diversified bloom and
unwasting glory, until I gained the gilded door of my mother's
high and holy home!

A moment I hesitated, thinking " how shall I act if she's got
visitors ?"   The thought departed, and, rustic-like, I knocked
loudly against the bespangled and over-arched door.   No answer !
While waiting for admission, I turned to review the magnificent
habitation.   With thought's own speed, I recalled the many miserable houses we had occupied.   The contrast made *this* lovelier
than all else my mind had ever imagined.   My bosom swelled
with ineffable pride—then with a gladness—which made me
shout and dance.   I think my joy was very fantastic and boisterous; for, in the midst thereof, the stately door swung open, and a familiar Hibernian neighbor raised her forefinger ominously, and said:

" Jist wait a bit.   It's yer own poor mother that's a dyin' !
Yer a bould lad to be killin' her, swate heart, wid yer noise.   It's
a power o' sad news for ye.   Shure an' dyin's no play.   Go in
softly — put yer pail snoogly away up-stairs — thin go an' spake
a bit to yer mother."

All this solemn talk seemed extremely ridiculous !   Could n't
I see?   Did n't I know better?   The hall before me was spacious,
the walls glittered with golden embellishments, the stairs to which
she pointed were radiant with flowery carpetings, and was n't I
the proud son of the healthy and happy mother who owned the
palace ?

I had as I thought evidence enough that the sympathetic lady of Erin was simply checking my mirth, so that the joy of our new home might break more calmly on my mind. And so I would n't be restrained. Laughing aloud at her foolish words of caution, I bounded by her through the enamelled doorway. In an instant the resplendent vision vanished! *The black veil* was again before me! It fell — and, lo! the ill-furnished room — the darkened bed — the emaciated woman — alas! I stood in the midst of poverty and death! Who can portray my feelings? The doctor whispered — " She 's dying !''

Again the matronly Hibernian, in a subdued tone, addressed me : " Oh, lad! it 's the Bible ye should be reading. 'T would sarve yer swate mother now. Poor sowl! she 's laving the world, and if ye wants to be prayin' for her pace, this is the time. The could world is yer own after this. So quit yer singin' an' yer dancin', lad. She 'll be a lang way off soon, an' ye 'll know it whin she 's dead, mind ye that."

But I could not weep. I did not even feel sad. In fact, I was filled with a certain tameless enthusiasm at which I greatly marvelled. In spite of my father's woful dejection, and my sister's abundant tears, I was overflowing with gladness! I wanted to exclaim: " Hain't this 'ere good? What a great house we have! Mother! hain't you a queen in a beautiful palace?" I did not speak, however, but gazed only with a wild joy nestling in my heart. " Hain't this feeling wicked?" soliloquized I. The answering thought said — " No, you ca n't help it." And such, indeed, was the truth. In that peculiar and extraordinary state of mind, (for which I had no explanation aside from dreaming,) I witnessed the death of the confidential companion of my early years ; the name of whose relation my tongue first engraved upon the tablet of memory — my ever-strange — ever-prophetic — ever-cherished — Mother !

The natural spring of that year was but the covering of a spiritual spring for me. Not that our circumstances were improved, not that my body was any stronger or more manly, but a stouter and nobler heart beat within my bosom. Intellectually and to all appearance, I was yet very dull, uninteresting, and clumsy. But spiritually, (*i. e.*, in my soul's heart,) I was almost born again. My spirit had no tears for the sepulchral urn! The ashes of the dead contained the germs of life. The sealed eyes, the faded smile, the pallid lips, the dew of death — what were these to me? Signs and symbols of a new creation! Celestial perfection, beyond all speech, was set like a diadem on the brow of Nature. I was present at the coronation of the unknown! After the funeral of my mother, and when all the members of the lamenting family were hushed for the night, I remember that I many times repeated: "I thank you, kind Prov'dence, I thank you for taking her out of trouble; and, kind Prov'dence, I pray you won't forget the rest of our folks never!"

CHAPTER XXIX.

A LESSON OF SELF-DEPENDENCE.

SOON after the impressive event last chronicled, my father rented part of a dwelling on Mansion square — belonging to and mostly occupied by the family of Jonathan Clark, of the Society of Friends — into which we moved, and where we assiduously labored.

From our side-door could be seen the collegiate superstructure, with its calm front and imposing columns, like a signet of intelligence set on the brow of the hill. Its supposed wondrous lore frightened and repelled me far away. I reverenced, and feared, and shunned it. My well-remembered visit thither, too, and the classic elegance of that rocking-charity which I witnessed, made me believe that we were wide as the poles asunder.

Recent trials had considerably dispirited my worthy progenitor, which, taken in connection with his growing disinclination to visit the shoe-merchants even to secure either labor or its needful reward, threw the responsibility of both on me. In addition to this, I had the commission of procuring nearly all the commodities of daily doing and corporeal subsistence. And steadily as I could, in the midst of father's increased fretfulness, I co-operated with him in those branches known to practical cordwainers as "closing uppers" and "in-seaming" women's grain-leather buskins. In fact, many and weighty responsibilities rested on my shoulders. The pressure thereof caused each particular joint to settle more firmly

in its native socket.   And I began to feel the existence of capa·
bilities which, till now, had slumbered in the folds of my being.

During this season, I obtained from Mr. Wilson's "circulating
library" in the village, a number of books of narrative and adventure to amuse my father.   He seemed to read them with pleasure
and profit, and one day said : "Why don't you try to read something?   You'd better stop moping about, like a sleepy-head, and
learn your letters."   Now I knew my letters, and could read tol-
erably well ; hence, I did not relish his satire upon my characteristic stupidity.   But I attempted to follow his counsel.   After
searching the lengthy catalogue through, I resolved to take out a
book entitled "The Three Spaniards."   To the spelling and reading of these three Spaniards I devoted my spare time for several
weeks ; and then I gladly returned the volume, the extravagant
and ghastly absurdities of which I had almost wholly forgotten.

The influence of what I then considered a beautiful dream, on
the eve of my mother's death, had now subsided.   The outlines
thereof lingered in my memory still ; but even such parts as were
not effaced, merely dwelt among the tombs of buried hopes.   Like
the departed one, my spirit ofttimes wore an expression of sadness,
for which I could neither realize nor vocalize a reason.   One day,
however, while walking in one of those depressive moods, I distinctly heard my name pronounced (as it were from the large tree
then near me), and these words : "*Eat—plenty—of—bread—and
—molasses.*"   This circumstance roused, while the words amused
me ; and I hopped and skipped along with lively merriment.
"Hain't I a real dreamer?" said I mentally ; "why, I can make
myself believe that I hear a voice !   How funny !"   But, strange
to relate, from that day forward into the extreme autumn, I had
an appetite for no other food ; and this I consumed with such unfeigned relish, that my father could not restrain his propensity to
fret, criticise, scold, and exclaim with irritation : "Look at that
'are boy ! see him soak up that molasses !   He'll eat us out of
house and home !"   But, thirty-four months subsequently, I had

acquired sufficient wisdom to comprehend the utility of that exclu sively *sweet* and simple nourishment. My sanguineous system was greatly purified thereby ; and my nervous forces were equalized to some extent, and refined in their normal operations.

Near the close of this year I obtained a clerkship in the boot and shoe store of Simon Bierbaur, a temperate and industrious German, who more than once made the paradoxical declaration that he " did n't want to make nothing — only a comfortable living, an' lay up a leetle." Previous to this, however, I held for a brief period the position of assistant with Charlie Roe, an extremely quiet man, who kept an extremely quiet refectory in the basement of the courthouse, which was seldom visited except by extremely quiet customers.

My situation with the paradoxical German was but the stepping-stone to my acquaintance and engagement with Mr. Ira Armstrong. And, inasmuch as my path for the ensuing two years lies directly through the business affairs and domestic relations of the last-named individual, I will now, without hesitation, let down the curtain that has been for so many years rolled up, exposing my father's personal peculiarities and private circumstances to the gaze and criticism of the unknown public.

CHAPTER XXX.

MY LIFE WITH IRA ARMSTRONG.

IRA ARMSTRONG was a boot and shoe merchant, and a manu facturer also, to some extent, in the most business portion of Main street. (The reader will of course bear in mind that these latter records take their rise in the village of Poughkeepsie.) His physical form was composed of excellent materials, capable of enduring much labor; while his mind was self-possessed, thoughtful, and devotional. Constitutionally, or by nature, he was a strict political economist and utilitarian; spiritually, or by heart, he was a steadfast friend and private benefactor of human kind.

How I rejoiced, in the spring of 1842, when we entered upon a mutual agreement of good-will! He gradually intrusted to me the general conduct of the retail trade. In due time he carefully instructed me to make records in the day-book, to put them into the ledger, to keep the cash-account, to deposite money in the bank, to calculate for and take up notes, &c.; all of which I was only too glad to accomplish faithfully, as an expression of the gratitude his kindness awakened in my bruised and jaded spirit. Whenever a customer asked for credit, or wished a reduction of price, I was usually inclined to grant it; because I could not but recall periods in my own life when a little "faith and charity" would seemingly have saved our family from months of discouragement and suffering. Mr. Armstrong, however, detecting this disposition one day, admonishingly but kindly said:—

"Jackson, I fear you place too much confidence in strangers. Honesty is not a universal trait. It takes a business man to find *that* out."

"Folks don't mean to cheat, do they?" I asked.

"Perhaps not," he replied. "But some of them are very slow in paying up; while others shirk their bills, and never settle them at all."

"Then I'm *real* sorry," said I regretfully; "for I have trusted Mrs. ——— with a pair of red children's shoes, and your neighbor ——— with a pair of pegged coarse men's boots."

I supposed that, without doubt, I should get a short chapter of disapprobation and mercantile discipline from the utilitarian boss then at work on the bench; but instead, I heard him laugh with a critical expression, and exclaim: "Red children, eh? and pegged coarse men, eh? Did you ever see any red children, or pegged coarse men?" But seeing that Edwin, the eldest apprentice, was freely enjoying the "rig" at my expense, he sobered right down, and gravely continued: "If you wish to speak or write correctly, Jackson, you should say 'children's *red shoes*' and 'men's *coarse pegged boots*.'"

Referring again to the credit system which I had involuntarily adopted and granted to customers, I said: "I'll not trust nobody no more, unless you know it, that's certain. Scarcely had I terminated my promise, however, when the religious-minded business man sought refuge from the mutations of time, in singing, as well as he could :—

> "I would not live alway,
>   I ask not to stay,
> Where storm after storm
>   Rises dark o'er the way!"

But the chilling suggestion that I "placed too much confidence in strangers," occupied my mind to the exclusion of the criticisms on my grammatic blunders. And the result was twofold: I forgot what I was thinking about. and also how to speak and write correctly as I was told. Therefore, some months subsequently, when Mr. Armstrong conferred upon me the honor and responsibility of composing and mailing an order to a wholesale dealer in the great metropolis, I wrote nearly as follows :—

"POUGHKEEPSIE *June* 1843

"D Daniels & Co—dear sir Mr Armstrong wants me to write to you to send to him 2 doz red morrocco childrens shoes 1 case of fine mens calf boots 1 case do of coarse stoga mens shoes and 1 do of pegged mens cowhide boots

"and oblige &c"

With this chirographic and mercantile accomplishment I was quite proud—especially when the stock arrived precisely in accordance with my employer's verbal specifications—and would have remained innocently so till this day, doubtless, had the firm not communicated my ridiculous transpositions to the esteemed utilitarian, who thereupon gave me one of his critical but good-natured looks, and another *hint* about "red morocco children" and "coarse stoga men."

Under Mr. Armstrong's benevolent administration was inaugurated the first opportunity in my life of jingling money to the amount of fifty cents on the 4th of July.   Listen, Young America! According to family records in an American bible, I was over fifteen years old, an American by both parentage and nativity, without an American education, in a useful American business, with a chequered and uninterpreted American history at my back, an unknown and uninterrogated American future in the distance, going out in America after one o'clock, P. M., with the first half of an American dollar in my pocket, to celebrate the anniversary of American Independence!   Powder and pride, fire-crackers and baker's biscuit, friendship and peanuts, headache and spruce-beer, formed the basis of my patriotic enjoyment.   Doubtless I acted just like a country-village boy transplanted into the soil of a future city.   While the cannon boomed from the hill-top, and the fireworks showered the air with innumerable stars, and my money held out, I was in the height of patriotic enthusiasm, and cherished a feverish regard for the possession of American independence. And now I feel inclined to ask the reader whether most of what men term patriotic celebrations of American liberty are not precisely like my thoughtless excitement on that glorious Fourth?

By Mr. Armstrong's family I was accepted more as a member than an apprentice; and I have treasured up many kind words as golden apples dropped from the tree of Life. Although then a member of the Methodist church, and the devout pronouncer of thanks over each meal, yet I never remember that Mr. Armstrong asked me to attend public worship. Hence, being allowed the freedom of the house and the yard, the children would frequently unite with and aid me in trying to sing Washingtonian temperance songs. One Sunday, while singing—

> "Where are the friends that to me were so dear,
> Long, long ago?" &c. —

there happened a pleasing mystical circumstance, of which I was the sole recipient. When we sung the words "In their graves laid low," I heard the word "No!" distinctly and emphatically shouted in my ear.

"Don't do that, Russell," said I to the eldest son.

"Do what?" he inquired, with a look of surprise.

"Don't holler 'No!' when 'tain't in the song," I pleadingly exclaimed.

"I didn't," he quickly replied; "and I didn't hear it neither."

The younger children, Austin and Freddy, also denied any participation. So we proceeded with our singing. But whenever we sung the affirmation that our friends are "in their graves laid low," I would hear the negative "No!" as clear and positive as any word pronounced by ourselves! At the time, I could not comprehend it. My belief (if I had any) was, that my dearest and most loved relatives were mouldering in the grave; that death was an escape from trouble—a kind of sleep; that their souls would be awakened one day, and rewarded or punished according to deeds done in the body. This, or something like it. was the belief of all the gray-headed men and wise-looking women I ever knew. My mother seemed to think somewhat so. The esteemed Mr. Armstrong, too, held to this doctrine, as I supposed. So, also, the learned men at the academy. And, more impressively tremendous than all, so believed (as I was told) the elegantly-dressed and classic gentleman who presided over and directed the mental destiny of rich men's sons on the revered College hill! Hence I could not imagine the voice to be anything but what I had heard in years previous—a self-imposed dream!

In these chronological statements, I desire to introduce such recitals and events as bear directly on the psychological objects and aims of this volume. The story of my life is not based in fables. It is all a sober and solid reality, and is interesting only when and where it differs from common manifestations. And yet, no reader can truly comprehend the bearing of extraordinary experiences unless they are seen to rest upon and mix familiarly with the ordinary occurrences and daily transactions of human existence.

Mr. Armstrong's nominal attachment to and apparently unwavering belief in the cardinal doctrines of the Methodist denomination was a sufficient inducement to cause me seriously to attend such meetings, and to put forth an honest endeavor to be recognised as a Christian by him and others enshrined in my confidence.

Occasionally, but without divulging the full extent of my wishes, I would obtain permission to attend evening prayer-meetings; also the probationers' class of inquiry and mutual encouragement; and, lastly, I sought aid from listening to Sunday expositions of the sacred text. And in the spring of 1843, I think, I was somewhat excited Zionward by a revival in the Methodist church. Whenever business and Providence permitted, I presented myself among the anxious seekers, and in silence prayed that the Divine Spirit (or anything else holy) might propel or lead me to the altar

This process of self-indoctrination or voluntary seeking for and willingness to accept of grace, I kept up privately for several successive nights. But it was almost fruitless, at which I felt no little consternation. What alarmed me most was, the more I desired the further I receded from conversion. On one occasion, a thin-bodied journeyman shoemaker, with a high and remarkably narrow forehead, but who had the religious excitement very severe, whispered to me :—

" May I call you my brother in Christ Jesus ?"

" Yes," I obligingly replied, " you may if you want to."

" How do you feel, brother ?" he confidentially inquired.

" Got a pain in my breast," I fraternally responded ; " but 't ain't nothin' new. I 'm used to it."

The excited and sympathetic convert groaned in behalf of my aching breast, as I supposed, and said : " My bowels yearns for you, my brother — my bowels yearns !"

Now, being deficient in a knowledge of the scriptural phraseology, and equally stupid in the organal department of imagination, I made the characteristic blunder of taking the convert's metaphoric words *literally ;* and so, with unfeignedly pathetic tones, I replied : " B'en eatin' somethin' what do n't agree with you, I s'pose. Better take some catnep-tea when goin' to bed. It s good, b'lieve, for stomic-ache."

Hearing this, he gave me a very extraordinary look, and subsided into the midst of a shouting group of brothers and sisters across the aisle. What had happened I could not imagine. The abruptness of his retirement from my side, and the half-angry expression of his countenance, made the whole talk about being " my brother in Christ" seem extremely foolish and absurd, if not absolutely hypocritical and wicked. This little circumstance greatly diminished my ardor ; and therefore, in a few minutes, I cautiously slipped out of the meeting, and bent my steps, at full gallop, toward Mr. Armstrong's suburban residence.

Good, honest Edward Southwick, a tanner and currier at the Lower Landing, was in the habit of calling upon and chatting with my esteemed employer. On one particular occasion I overheard a conversation in substance as follows : —

"At the last election there was plenty of 'hard-cider' talk, but next to nothing on the rights of the slave."

"True," Edward replied; "still, I live in hopes."

"The folly, tyranny, and injustice of the system," resumed the utilitarian, "will be acknowledged some day, no doubt, but not by unprincipled politicians either North or South."

"Peace, and justice, and truth, the people are slow to see," suggested the moderate tanner.

"But," interrupted Ira, "the national government is made to sustain a system opposed to the entire interests of the North. When the people once see *that*, a change will then come through the influence of the Northern abolition vote."

The two friends continued their conversation, until others arrived who changed the topic. I mention this slight event because it was *the first time in my life* when I came to a knowledge of the existence of slavery in the United States! I had a great many questions to ask about it. When told that there were millions of men, and women, and children, with no pretended disqualification for liberty save ignorance and a black skin, who at that moment were dwelling in hopeless bondage; kept, as the farmers keep oxen and horses, to perform heavy toil; deprived of personal freedom, and bought and sold like beasts — when I heard all this, my heart throbbed with mingled emotions of surprise, sympathy, and unutterable alarm. "Jest think of it!" thought I; "s'pose I'd b'en born black down South, with my ignorance, why, I'd b'en somebody's slave!" The mere idea *chilled* me to the core. It made me crouch, and fold my arms in silent consternation. "How strange that my mother never told me about these slaves! How curious that I never heer'd the ministers preach about 'em!"

Thus I thought, and was greatly troubled. But a few weeks

of labor served to bedim the impression, and soon I lived on, nearly as before, without a conscious prejudice. In this connection, however, I will express my charity for those uneducated and sluggish individuals who come into being and go beyond the grave destitute of a conscience on the question of human rights. When thinking of such, I remember myself—that I was sixteen years old even before I heard definitely of chattel-slavery, and had attained the summit of twenty-two years ere I possessed an abiding conscience against it.

CHAPTER XXXI.

THE DAWNING OF LIGHT.

"The dawn flowed forth, and from its purple fountains
    I drank those hopes which make the spirit quail."

ONE day I had a brief but useful conversation with Mr. Armstrong concerning the exercise of conscience in all business transactions. As nearly as I can recollect, he said: "Honesty is the best policy, and no man will succeed without it."

"Yes," returned I; "but what must I do in a case like this: John ——— brought in a pair of customer's shoes yesterday, with the upper cut and pasted down so it need n't be seen, but I know it's cut and that it won't wear as long as sound leather. Now, shall I *tell* the customer or keep still?"

"Ah!" ejaculated he, evidently disturbed, "did John cut the upper bad?"

"Yes, *real* deep," said I, "most through."

"Let me see."

I produced the morocco buskins. After a moment's inspection, he said—"That won't do—ca n't have such work as *that!* Put them among the sale-work, and send out another pair to the binders."

"Must I allus tell a customer everything I know about shoes?" I inquired.

"Make a point never to sell bad work," he replied; and then continued—"Do you know what Robert Burns has written upon honesty?"

I answered, that " I did n't know nothing about that 'are gentleman." Whereupon he proceeded to quote, as with a hearty relish, the poet's words :—

> " To catch dame Fortune's golden smile,
>   Assiduous wait upon her;
> And gather gear by every wile
>   That's justified by honor;
> Not for to hide it in a hedge,
>   Not for a train-attendant;
> But for the glorious privilege
>   Of being *independent.*"

In accordance with the *animus* of this extract, I have frequently heard my employer, when orally addressing the throne of Grace, quote the very reasonable words of Agur's petition: " Give me neither poverty nor riches: feed me with food convenient for me; lest I be full, and deny thee; or poor, and take the name of my God in vain."

Shortly after this excellent lesson, concerning the use and exercise of strict candor and principle in mercantile pursuits, an itinerant revival minister entered the store; and seeing me engaged and alone behind the counter, he inquired — " Well, Brother Davis, how do you feel ?"

" Very well, sir," said I, cheerfully.

" No, no, my young friend — I have reference to your religious welfare."

Now, thought I, here's a chance to be candid in business. So, suppressing as much as I could my arising confusion, I replied — ' I do n't know, sir. Some how or ruther I ca n't get converted as easy as the rest."

" Do you feel sorry for your sins ?" he asked with a searching look. " Do you feel that your soul is sinful and hateful before God ?"

It seemed impossible to answer. But I was resolved to be honest in business — " for the glorious privilege of being independent." Hastily as possible, therefore, I mentally reviewed my childhood, my boyhood, and my youth. First, I thought of the apples taken from John Myers' cellar; next I shuddered at my terrible oath when father forgot the jew's-harp; then, I recalled the article purloined from Willet Marshall's tool-box; then, the card-playing party which I invited on my own responsibility; and, lastly, I reproduced the dismal scene of my intoxication. These were the missteps of my life which I regretted. Nevertheless, I did n't feel "sinful and hateful before God," and therefore replied:—

"No, sir, I do n't feel that I 'm very wicked; only sorry for some things, which I won't never do again."

"This is the time, young friend, for you to get religion," returned the clergyman gravely. "Have you sought to make peace with your God?"

"To make peace with my God!" soliloquized I, greatly bemuddled — "Why, *I hain't never had no disturbance with him in all my life.*" But in my embarrassment, I managed to stammer out, "No, sir!"

"Well," continued he, with increased surprise, emphasis, and reprehension, in his tone, "do n't you *fear* to meet your God?"

"No, sir," said I, (still determined to exercise honesty in business,) "I ain't afraid to meet my God."

"Oh, unconverted youth!" exclaimed the pastor with a deep groan, and a censorious and withering expression. "*I fear the day of grace is past! I fear you will be lost for ever!*" Thus saying, he turned and left me.

Oh, reader, can you imagine my thoughts, as he closed this atrocious sentence? The love of my young nature was chilled into the coldest hate, and suggestions horrible occupied my soul! For a moment I feared no one — dreaded nothing! Neither did I love anything — life, myself, man, earth, heaven, nor God! "A long life," thought I, with novel sensations of desperation — "a long life is before me — why not turn *vagabond* or *pirate* at once? If I live a pure and blameless life, damnation will be my destiny; and if I should be desperately wicked, it could in the end make no difference; for if it be true, as this man says, that the day of grace *is* past, I am eternally lost — lost in hell — where, as mother told me, 'there's nothin' but a-weepin' an' a-wailin' an' a-gnashin' of teeth!'" I paused a moment, and a beautiful tranquillity succeeded my agitation. A soft breathing passed over my face, and I heard in a voice like the gently whispering summer breeze — "*Be—calm! The—pastor—is wrong; you—shall—see!*"

'T was perhaps two days after this, when a resident pastor (of a persecuted denomination) placed in my hand two pennies, to pay for a pair of shoe-strings which I had sold to him many weeks previous, at which time he chanced to be without the amount. "Well, what of that?" say you. Nothing remarkably important, dear reader; only this, that my mind was impressed with a contrast which in memory is vivid still. I had let customary acquaintances have shoe-strings, and other small articles, before — leaders at Methodist meetings, and young men gifted in oral prayer — who said they would pay for them some time. But such never did pay, however, except in three solitary instances. Yet this man, round about whose religious convictions the prejudices of the people surged like an overwhelming flood, with outstretched hand, presented to me the forgotten sum, and said, with an honest smile beaming from his mild blue eyes — "Owe no man anything, but love."

From the little fountain swells the ocean-tide. In like manner, this small transaction had the effect to establish a sweet and lasting friendship between our two souls — besides bringing to light the fact that there existed some people who did not believe in a God of implacable wrath! Their novel and unpopular conception of a Deity of love seemed more congenial and desirable to my better nature; still, even that never satisfied my soul like the whole-hearted and straight-forward friendship of the persecuted clergyman. Sometimes, during my intimate acquaintance and intercourse with Rev. A. R. Bartlett, (for this was the name of my friend,) I would get the loan of books for others who wished to read, but who did not sufficiently know the pastor to borrow for themselves. My own time was too much occupied for reading, even if I had realized any inclination to do so. And I could not interiorly accept my friend's theology, because it implied a personal knowledge of language, and a love of biblical criticism, which I could not bring to the examination; and yet, owing solely to the attractive influence of pure friendship, I allowed myself one day to be openly recognised as a brother in the Faith! Mr. Bartlett was a practical preacher — too much so to be popular with his own people. His lessons were quite straight-forward and comprehensible. But when some controversial dignitary of the denomination arrived, and occupied the desk, then would come all sorts of outlandish and to me meaningless words — "*sheol*," "*Hades*," "*aionion*," "*gehenna*," "*apo-aionos*," "*le-oulom*," &c., used to explain or refute popular ideas of hell, darkness, generation, everlasting, &c., as set forth by scriptural writers who teach unmistakably the doctrine of future rewards and post-mortem punishments. Noticing one of those *long* words in a newspaper one day, I asked my utilitarian Director, "how he would speak it?" He replied: "When I see a word that *looks hard*, I give it a *hard name* and let it go."

In short, I got no relief from the deep-seated and painful apprehension that the Bible did teach just what my mother had declared; and, therefore, in spite of large words and learned discourses, I feared that the most of mankind would be severely dealt with after death for sins committed before that event. Indeed, so horrid and gloomy were my contemplations one night, in view of the possibility of dying, and going to a pit of inextinguishable fire, that I leaped from my bed, dressed myself, and was about to ask permission to sit by the kitchen-stove till morning, when I heard the voice — soothing and loving like my mother's —repeating in minor tones: "*Be—calm! Jackson. The—*

pastor—is—wrong ; you—shall—see !" The promise of this unseen and unknown annunciator—that I should in due time see
the clergyman's doctrinal error—tranquillized my troubled heart.
" Dream or no dream," thought I, devotionally, " I 'm. real thankful to kind Prov'dence for it anyhow !"

The villagers became about this time greatly excited by reports
of certain mesmeric miracles then being performed by an itinerant
expositor of Phrenological science.   Flaming announcements were
made through show-bills headed, " Mesmerism"—a word entirely
novel to me—which stated that " Professor Grimes" would continue to exhibit his wonderful experiments at the Village-Hall,
&c.   Almost everybody laughed at the stranger's pretensions,
yet all wished to test the matter by personal trial.   The excitement spread like an epidemic.   And, among many others, I also
was seriously attacked with a desire to be conveyed into the mysterious slumber.

But Mr. Armstrong looked very dubious and skeptical about
the utility of the professor's exhibition of magnetic buffoonery.
He did not, however, refuse to grant me part of one afternoon in
which to place myself under the magician's power.   Accordingly,
Edwin and I proceeded down to " Hatch's Hotel," where, in a
quiet room up-stairs, we joined some fifteen young men who, like
ourselves, had arrived to present themselves as willing subjects of
the new mystery.

The party were seated in systematic order, each facing the intelligent and somewhat egotistic operator, and thus we remained
nearly two hours.   At length it became almost impossible, at
least for me, to resist a natural sleep; but a vigilant curiosity, to
know which of our group would receive the enchantment, still
served to keep my mind on the alert.   The professor went
through a series of motions—resembling the " presto change"
of legerdemain performers — and then imperiously said : *" You
ca n't open your eyes !"* He was mistaken.   I did open my eyes

with perfect ease. Whereupon he passed to the next subject, then to the next, and so on, to the end of the line, without particularly affecting any. I make this statement in order to correct the subsequent unqualified assertions of Mr. Grimes, " that he was *the first to magnetize me*, and to reject me as a subject for experimentation ; because," as he alleged — even in my own hearing — " he recognised a clairvoyant propensity in my mental organism, which would not serve his public purposes."

A few days after this — about the 1st December, 1843 — William Levingston called at our store. During a recital of many magnetic marvels he had himself performed, both at home and abroad, he addressed himself to me and said : " Have you ever been mesmerized ?" In reply, I informed him of the unsuccessful experiment upon me by Mr. Grimes. Then he said : " Come to my house to-night. I 'll try you, if you don't object, and Edwin too." There was no reason for declining, and I therefore accepted his invitation.

Before relating what happened on that memorable night, however, I wish to call attention to the fact, that having no confidence in the alleged phenomena of mesmerism, I was actuated simply by what seemed to be the suggestion of the moment — just like others whose curiosity had become superficially excited. Furthermore, as a foundation on which rationally to rest the extraordinary results of Mr. Levingston's manipulations, I will give a summary of my mental peculiarities and physical condition at the time.

First, mentally : I had a love of truth ; a reverence for knowledge ; a somewhat cheerful disposition ; a deficient imagination ; an unbelief (or ignorance) concerning the existence of ghosts, &c. ; an unconquerable dread of death ; a still greater dread of encountering what might exist beyond the grave ; a vague, apprehensive faith in the Bible doctrine of eternal misery ; a tendency to spontaneous somnambulism ; an ear for what I then called imaginary voices ; a memory defective as to dates ; a mind nearly barren of ordinary education; a heart very sympathetic in cases of trial and suffering; and, lastly, I was disposed to meditation and the freedom of solitude.

Second, physically: my body was imperfectly developed; my breast was narrow; my spine was short and weak; my stomach was very sensitive; in my blood flowed the subtle poison of my father's alcohol; my muscular fabric was unsound and inefficient; my nervous system was highly impressible and injured by the parental use of tobacco; my face was pale and marked by a prominent nose; my reverted eyes were almost black, and slightly near-sighted; my head was small in circumference, with a retreating forehead; my hair was jet black, and fell awkwardly over my brow; my hands bore decided marks of my trade; and, lastly, my whole appearance was calculated to inspire strangers with but little interest in my existence.

CHAPTER XXXII.

IN WHICH I YIELD TO THE MYSTIC POWER.

"From the nerves at each pulsation,
From the mystery of sleep —
Comes a lesson, a monition,
Whose significance is deep."

PERHAPS the reader may have never witnessed the magnetic operation. At all events, I will venture a few descriptive sentences. Situated in close relation to the one who intends to produce the physical sleep, the subject is compelled, (in order that the state may be properly induced,) to sit in an easy position — entirely quiet — with mind free alike from external intrusions and internal desires. The subject's thoughts should be calmly concentrated; to accelerate the accomplishment of the end. At length he will become wholly passive, while the operator is active. Care should be taken to exclude all unfavorable circumstances that might render the operation either tedious or unsuccessful. In due time he will know the result — flowing from such reciprocal exchange of sympathy and sensation. The following account embodies the result of the first operation under which I placed myself at the residence of Mr. William Levingston: (see the first diagram, p. 205.)

I felt the operator's chilly hand pass and repass my brow, the chamber of thought. The living blood which had flowed undisturbed through my youthful form during its brief existence seemed well-nigh arrested. The ten thousand avenues of sensation were

No. 1.	No. 2.	No. 3.	No. 4.
The Ordinary State.	**The Psychological State.**	**The Somnambulic State.**	**The Superior Condition.**
SEPARATE PERSONAL SPHERES.	PARTIAL BLENDING OF SPHERES.	COMPLETE BLENDING OF SPHERES.	MENTAL SPHERES SEPARATED.
The above represents the operator and subject beginning the magnetic process.	The above condition is favorable to sympathetic and transitional phenomena.	The above state brings out excursional, examining, and medical clairvoyance.	The above state leads to independent clairvoyance and intuitional wisdom.

illuminated as with the livid flames of electric fire.   Anon, all was
intensely dark within.   Dreadful and strange feelings passed over
my body and through my brain.   My emotions were painful.
As the reader knows, I had horrid convictions of what the world
terms DEATH.   " Oh, mother !" thought I with terror, " can this be
the period of my physical dissolution ?"   My heart continued to
perform its office ; but its beatings were less frequent.   I felt the
different senses that connect the mind with the outer world gradually closing.   " Alas !" methought despairingly, " are they closing for ever ?"   Thus, my senses yielded imperceptibly to the
subduing power.   I could no longer hear the busy and active
world without, nor feel the touch of any object, living or dead.
" No longer," thought I, " can I behold the system of nature.
The fragrant fields are gone ; never more to be the scenes of
happy contemplation."

Thoughts essentially like these flashed rapidly through my awe-
struck mind.   " What am I to do ?"   I queried silently.   " To
resist the sensations is to resist the effect anticipated.   And yet,
to remain in this condition much longer will result, perhaps, in
closing out for ever the beauties of the material universe."

But the counter and skeptical query now occurred, " whether
all this was any more than the illusion of the imagination ?"
" Certainly, I *think* I feel strange ; but do I actually *know* that
my sensations are real ?"   Thus questioned I myself—without
making the least exertion to satisfy my judgment.   I sat almost
breathless a few seconds longer—encouraging a hope that the
experiment might not succeed ; and yet, paradoxical as it may
seem, I was actually assisting to produce it.   " I am alive yet."
thought I over-joyed, " for I hear the operator inquire the hour—
I hear him respond seemingly to something said by another—
but I do not hear any other person speak !   Ain't this exceeding
strange ?" (See the second diagram, p. 205.)

Another silence occurred, longer than before, during which I
endeavored to analyze my feelings.   The enchantment had pene-

trated the innumerable recesses of my whole structure. Shortly, I heard a voice — low, distant, strange, unpleasant — from the human world, calling me back to earth which I was mentally leaving. This sound troubled me. "It is true, then," thought I sadly, "that my sense of hearing — along whose delicate halls has reverberated the pleasurable music accompanying the sacred voice of pure affection and friendship — is closed! Closed to seal the reality of an eternal silence? Can this be so?" continued I silently. No, indeed! The moment has arrived. I will submit no longer to this dangerous and dreadful experiment. Never shall my marvel-seeking and dreamy mind again lead me into such fearful perils! Yes! I will speak and protest against this dreadful operation."

But oh, how frightful! My tongue seemed instantly to be enlarged and clung violently to the roof of my mouth. My cheeks seemed extremely swollen and my lips were joined as if by death — apparently to move no more. Another resolution passed through my brain, and instantly I obeyed its suggestion. I made a desperate effort to change my position — particularly to disengage my hands — but (horrible beyond description!) my feet, my hands, my whole body, were entirely beyond the control of volition. I could no longer claim the proprietorship over my own person. All was lost — it seemed — irretrievably lost. I felt convinced that external life was for me no more. What could I do? True, I could exercise my mental faculties to the highest degree — could reason with a startling clearness — but I could not hear, see, feel, speak, or move! I had no means of ascertaining my true physical or mental situation. I queried and reasoned within myself thus: "I have a body, a tangible body — I reside in the *form* — but is it my natural or spiritual body? Is it adapted to the outer-world, or to the post-mortem life? Where am I? Oh, I am so lonely! Alas, if *this* be *Death!*" A natural consciousness, however, pervaded and reassured my mind. Preconceived or *innate* ideas were evolved from my inmost sensibilities. What surprised me more than anything else was the gushing forth of novel and brilliant thoughts — extending apparently over the vast landscape of some unknown world of indescribable beauty — comprehending more than it is possible for me even now to relate. These conceptions — as I am now fully persuaded — were an influx of many interior and immortal truths. (See " Philosophy of Question and Answers," in the Penetralia.)

Presently, all was dark as before ! This moment demanded an absolute decision. Death seemed an inevitable consequence of my helpless situation. Every moment I approached nearer and nearer to a mysteriously dark valley ! Perverseness and resistance filled me with strength, but even this strength impelled me onward. Again and again I retreated in mind. But every wave of thought wafted me nearer and nearer the fearful vale of inconceivable darkness ! Now was the time for a powerful exertion. Resistance was necessary — or else I should be lost in the impenetrable gloom ! But I advanced nearer and nearer still. In thought, I leaped back suddenly, and lo ! I stood on the margin of the ocean of Eternal Night ! The warmth of my whole person was exchanged for death-like coldness. Horrid thoughts of disorganization continued to distress me. I was filled with terror. The darkness grew more dark and appalling. I was seized suddenly with an unearthly shudder, and — terrible to relate — I found myself whirling in that blackened gloom with an inconceivable velocity ! I seemed to be revolving in a spiral path, with a wide sweep at first, and then smaller ; so that every revolution, on my descending flight, contracted the circle of my movement. And thus, dear reader — down, down, I sank — till immersed in that dreaded ocean of darkness, the mountain waves of which grasped me within their mighty folds, and I sank to the lowest depths of forgetfulness ! (See the third diagram, p. 205.)

This psychological event makes a bold and ineffaceable mark on the first mountain of my pilgrimage — the mountain of USE.

Looking back upon that magnetic experiment, with its precious results, I am filled with speechless gratitude. Immutable, indeed, are those powers which manifest themselves throughout Nature! Nothing can possibly occur opposed to the highest well-being of the innumerable worlds intrusted to their exclusive and eternal control. After years of study, I am compelled so to believe. Explicit evidences have been presented to my mind. All minds, I know, are not equally susceptible to these impressions. Nevertheless, the evidences can not be doubted by those who practise the privilege of observation. That my own conviction rests upon a substantial basis the reader will be prepared to admit, when I relate the mysterious restoration of my lifeless body and distracted mind to the enjoyment of external existence. The story is very short:—

I awoke to physical consciousness, mentally revolving in a circuitous form. The darkness continued (with my ascending movement) to increase and expand, till I gained the margin that bounded the ocean of the dreaded oblivion, whose restless waves conveyed me to the longed-for state of thought and wakefulness. My senses, the windows of the soul, were again opened; light broke in upon my dimmed vision; sound vibrated through the labyrinths of my ear; sensation flashed over my whole frame; and I moved, shouted, and opened my eyes. But how joyfully surprised! I was in precisely the same position as when I first seated myself for the experiment. Many acquaintances were sitting near and around me, with countenances beaming with pleasure and astonishment. For a moment, however, I felt dissatisfied. I could remember nothing, except my mental sufferings; and somehow, in my bewilderment, I did not feel quite certain that I had not died. I could not realize that I had, in reality, returned from the dark "valley of the shadow of death." But a few penetrating glances about the room. and upon the familiar faces of those around, convinced me; whereupon I arose, as if from the gloom of the grave, and with strength renewed

greeted the amazed and delighted witnesses. (During this ex
perience, I did not reach the fourth state represented by the mag
netic diagram.)

"What's the matter?" I asked with unfeigned anxiety. "What
brought these folks here? What have I been about?"

"I sent for them," replied the operator, "to see you perform."

"Perform!" said I, perfectly oblivious of the significance of his
words.

"Yes, perform!" returned he with a triumphant smile. "You're
a queer youth, to be sure ; but I know what your Power is called."

"What is it?" I inquired.

"Chancey Hare Townsend calls it ' Clairvoyance,'" replied the
operator. "I've read his book on ' Facts in Mesmerism,' wherein
he describes cases of seeing, blindfolded, just as you have done
to-night to perfection."

"What's been done?" I again asked. "Tell me all about it."

"Why, after a little, you read from your forehead the large
letters on a newspaper; told the time by our watches, &c.; besides, you described where some of us are diseased; all to our
perfect satisfaction."

Well do I remember my reflections that night, while walking to
Mr. Armstrong's suburban home. Translated into my present
use of words, these were my queries and meditations: "What
is this power? This magic spell? This wizardly operation?
What was that which so benumbed my flesh? Which shut out
the world? Which caused me to die a dreaded death? Which
brought me back to life again? How strange, that so much time
should have unconsciously elapsed! An unremembered period —
a blank in my mental history — yielding a harvest so mysterious!
Can this be prophetic power? Is it like the witchcraft of the
ancients? Can it be a dream? An imaginary display? Is it
mental hallucination? Am I a victim of satanic incantation?
Nay! there is a something deeper than thought, which assures me
that this is an important and beautiful truth. And I remember

too, the sweet, familiar voice, softly breathing through the air: "*Be—calm! You—shall—see.*"

That night, as the reader might imagine, I could not sleep. Next morning early, I related all that had happened. On the face of the utilitarian there was a scrutinizing look of incredulity. He did not dispute it, however, neither did he deny me the solicited time (though he had often told me that "time is money") for further magnetic experimentation. During business hours, nevertheless, I was punctually in my place—discharging the several duties consequent on my calling. But there was a mystery hanging over my path—a spell on my soul—a higher calling from the pinnacle of some unknown mountain—which impelled me, every evening, into Mr. Levingston's parlor in order to test and demonstrate what the new power could accomplish. 'T was a mental struggle, dear reader—a laborious and continuous ascent—a weird and wild experiment for both my body and soul. It was a region of life unexplored—an ocean without a shore. Yea, I was literally "going it blind;" not flippantly and carelessly; but with apprehensions inexpressible.

By thus subjecting myself periodically to the magnetic process, I excited the curiosity of the surface population; and the marvel-loving would flock around my chair, and contend for chances to get individual tests. Like the poet of "the lonely shore," it seemed that when this mysterious sleep first passed from my quivering frame, "I awoke and found myself famous." My popularity, however, was far from being co-extensive with my notoriety. The latter, without the former as a shield, made me a target at which certain "college boys" projected snow-balls and hoots, while sundry older heads—professional men and the fashionables—discharged the cold-hearted hot-shot of ignorant condemnation. In a word, I was universally the object of private scandal and public ridicule.

Almost every night, however, our experiments were successfully continued. At each session some new truth or interesting wonder

would make its appearance; and by verbal report its influence
became scattered far and wide over the community.   But the
heart of the monster, Ignorance, was quickly touched; and the
prejudice of gloomy religionists began to be aroused.   Individuals
of various denominations arose in rebellion against the developments; and, in their blind zeal, protested against further proceedings in the operator's parlor.   As the surprise and persecution
of the inhabitants increased, so were my apprehension and anxiety
magnified.   Ever and anon, I prayed to be informed whence came
this power? whether I should continue to exercise it? and what
constituted its true nature and purpose? Know, then, gentle
reader, that the events which I have related, and the emotions I
have portrayed, comprise all the actual recollection and knowledge
then in my possession concerning this marvellous illumination

CHAPTER XXXIII.

MY FIRST FLIGHT THROUGH SPACE.

" O backward-looking son of Time !
The new is old, the old is new —
The cycle of a change sublime
Still sweeping through !"

In order to bring the progressive steps of this mystery properly before the mind, I will now detail the impressions that I received on first viewing clairvoyantly the surface of the globe. (The philosophy of this mode of interior observation is explained in the third volume of "The Great Harmonia.")

By placing myself in sympathetic relations to the operator — by turning my thoughts inwardly, and shutting out the fleeting disturbances and interruptions of the outer world — I passed readily into the third magnetic condition. This particular event occurred, I think, on the eve of the first of January, 1844. At that time, (and during the four subsequent years,) I could not recall to my mind, when out of this condition, anything which I had seen or said while in it. But now the vast scene breaks upon my memory, in all the vividness and beauty with which it was originally invested; and I can view and investigate — with far more certainty and with deeper satisfaction — the same fields n connection with still higher planes of existence and thought.

Before I seated myself, facing the operator, I observed a few individuals in the room ; as usual, they were after tests and wonders; but I had, at the time, but little idea of having anything resembling a successful experiment. I knew as yet but very little of the nature of magnetism; had not learned anything definitely of the wonderful phenomenon of clairvoyance; did not, in fact, entertain a clear conception of any such condition. Nevertheless, the mystic magnetic state was completely induced in less than thirty minutes. As usual, my mind was rendered incapable of controlling the slightest muscle, or of realizing any definite sensation, except a kind of waving fluctuation, between what seemed to me to be either decided action or inertia. This was a very strange feeling, but not at all unpleasant. In a few minutes, however, all this mental commotion subsided; and then I passed into the most delightful state of interior tranquillity. Not a discordant sensation rolled across my spirit. I was completely "born again" — being in the spirit. My thoughts were of the most peaceful character. My whole nature was beautifully expanded. I thought of the joys of friendship! of the unutterable pleasures of universal love! of the sweetness and happiness of united souls! And yet, strange to say, I experienced no unusual heart-emotion, which one might suppose would be a natural consequence of themes so pleasurable.

Notwithstanding the fact that my mind was exalted and meditating in this manner, I perceived as yet not the least ray of light in any direction. Therefore, I concluded that I was physically in a deep sleep, mentally engaged in a peaceful revery, and nothing more.

But this conclusion had no sooner settled among my thoughts, as a probability, than I observed an intense blackness before me — apparently extending hundreds of miles into space, and enveloping the earth. This reminded me of my first night's experiment. Gradually, however, this midnight mass of darkness lifted and disappeared; and, as gradually, my perception was awakened and enlarged. All things in our room — together with the individuals in it — were surprisingly illuminated. Each human body was glowing with many colors, more or less brilliant and magnetical. The figure of each person was enveloped in a light atmosphere which emanated from it. The same emanation extended up the arms, and pervaded the entire body. The nails had one sphere of light surrounding them, the hair another, the ears another, and the eyes still another; the head was very luminous—the emanations, taken in combination, spreading out into the air from four inches to as many feet. (The reader will see this illustrated in the diagrams, by the oval line around each person.)

The utter novelty of this view overwhelmed my mind with astonishment and admiration. I could not comprehend it. Again I felt confounded, and could not feel perfectly certain that I was living on earth. It seemed that the whole earth, with all of its inhabitants, had been suddenly translated into some Elysium. I knew then of no language which could describe my perceptions: hence, I did not yield the slightest exclamation, nor attempt an utterance; but continued to observe, as one in solitude, with a feeling of unutterable joy and holy reverence. A few moments more, dear reader, and I not only beheld the exteriors of the individuals in that room—clothed with light as it were—but I also as easily perceived their interiors, and then, too, the hidden sources of those luminous magnetical emanations. In my natural or ordinary state, remember, I had never seen the organs of the human viscera; but now I could see all the organs and their functions—the liver, the spleen, the heart, the lungs, the brain—all with the greatest possible ease. The whole body was transparent as a sheet of glass! It was invested with a strange, rich, spiritual beauty. It looked illuminated as a city. Every separate organ had several *centres* of light, besides being enveloped by a general sphere peculiar to itself. And I did not see the physical organ only, but its form, aspect, and color also, simply by observing the peculiar emanations surrounding it. For example: I saw the heart—surrounded by one general combination of living colors—with special points of illumination interspersed. The auricles and ventricles, together with their orifices, gave out distinct *flames* of light; and the pericardium was a garment of magnetic life, sur rounding and protecting the heart while in the performance of its functions. The pulmonary or respitorial department was also illu minated with beautiful flames, but of different magnitude and color. The various air-chambers seemed like so many chemical laboratories. The fire in them wrought instantaneous chemical *changes* in the blood that flowed through the contiguous membranes; and the great sympathetic nerve, whose roots extend throughout the lower viscera, and whose topmost branches are lost in the superior strata of the sensorium, appeared like a column of life, interwoven and super-blended with a soft and silvery fire!

The brain was likewise very luminous with prismatic colors. Every organ of the cerebellum and cerebrum emitted a light peculiar to itself. I could easily discern the form and size of the organ by the shape and intensity of its emanations. This view, I well remember, excited in me much admiration. But I was so deeply in the magnetic condition, and so impoverished in language, that I neither manifested any delight nor described a particle of anything which I then beheld. In some portions of the smaller brain I saw gray emanations, and in other portions lower and darker shades of this color—in many and various degrees of distinctness—down to a sombre and almost black flame.

On the other hand, in the higher portions of the larger or superior brain, I saw flames which looked like the breath of diamonds. At first I did not understand the cause of these beautiful breathings; but soon *I discovered them to be the thoughts of the individuals concerning the strange phenomena then manifested in my own condition.* Still I continued my observations. The superior organs of the cerebrum pulsated with a soft, radiant fire; but it did not look like any fire or flame that I had seen on earth. In truth, the brain seemed like a crown of spiritual brightness—decorated with shining crescents and flaming jewels. Here I will parenthetically remark, that what is thus natural to the human brain in this its first stage of existence, is preserved and indescribably improved in the Spirit-Land to which we all are surely tending. Each brain seemed different — different in the degrees, modifications, and combinations of the flames and colors — but very, very beautiful! From the brain I saw the diversified currents of life or magnetic fire, as they flowed through the system. The bones appeared very dark or brown; the muscles emitted in general a red light; the nerves gave out a soft, golden flame; the venous blood a dark, purple light; the arterial blood a bright, livid sheet of fire, which constantly reminded me of the electric phenomena of the clouds. Verily, gentle friend, I saw every ligament, and tendon, and cartilaginous and membranous structure, each illuminated with different sheets and magnetic centres of living light, which indicated and set forth beautifully the presence of the spiritual principle.

Thus I saw not only the real physical structures themselves, but also their indwelling essences and vitalic elements. Another thing was very remarkable: I knew the individuals had garments upon them, *because I could see an element of vitality, more or less distinct, in every fibre of clothing upon their persons!* Just as you would look, by an act of volition, from the blisters in a pane of glass, through it, at the objects and scenes beyond, so could I discern, and that, too, without a conscious effort, the whole mystery and beauty of the human economy — and enjoy that festive illumination which the ten thousand flames of the golden candles of life imparted to every avenue, pillar, chamber, window, and dome, of the human temple!

But the sphere of my vision now began to widen. I could see the life of nature in the atoms of the chairs, tables, &c.; I could see them with far more satisfaction - as regards their use, structure, locality — than I ever remembered to have known in my ordinary state. Next, I could distinctly perceive the walls of the house. At first, they seemed very dark and opaque; but soon became brighter, and then *transparent;* and, presently, I could see the walls of the adjoining dwelling. These also immediately became light, and vanished—melting like clouds before my advancing vision. I could now see the objects, the furniture, and persons, in the adjoining house, as easily as those in the room where I was situated.

At this moment I heard the voice of the operator. He inquired "if I could hear him speak plainly." I replied in the affirmative. He then asked concerning my feelings, and "whether I could discern anything." On replying affirmatively, he desired me to convince some persons that were present, by "reading the title of a book, with the lids closed, behind four or five other books." Having tightly secured my bodily eyes with handkerchiefs, he then placed the books on a horizontal line with my forehead, and I saw and read the title without the slightest hesitation. This test and many experiments of the kind were tried, and repeated; and the demonstration of vision, independent of the physical organs of sense, was clear and unquestionable.

At length, feeling somewhat exhausted, I resigned myself to a deeper sleep which seemed to be stealing over my outer form. Presently, my former perceptions returned with greater power. The village was now instantly subjected to my vision. It was now as easy for me to see the people moving about their respective houses as in the open thoroughfares, and it was also as easy to see their most interior selves as the external lights and shades of their physical bodies.

'Twas the first of January, remember—cold, bright, cloudless, frosty, beautiful! A piercing wintry wind swept o'er the earth, chilling and freezing as it went; but my perceptions waved on— the village with its inhabitants melted away before me, and my enjoyment was greater and fresher than ever I experienced in the glow and beauty of May or June.

By a process of *inter-penetration*, as I now term it, I was placed *en rapport* with Nature! The spirit of Nature and my spirit had instantly and for the first time formed—what seemed to me to be

— a kind of psychological or sympathetic acquaintance — the foundation of a high and eternal communion. Her spacious cabinet was thrown open to me, and it seemed that I was the sole visitor at Nature's fair — a royal banquet!

The properties and essences of plants were distinctly visible. Every fibre of the wild flower, or atom of the mountain-violet, was radiant with its own peculiar life. The capillary ramifications of the streamlet-mosses — the fine nerves of the cicuta-plant, of the lady's-slipper, and of flowering vines — all were laid open to my vision. I saw the living elements and essences flow and play through these simple forms of matter; and in the same manner I saw the many and various trees of the forests, fields, and hills, all filled with life and vitality of different hues and degrees of refinement. It seemed that I could see *the locality, properties, qualities, uses, and essences, of every form and species* of wild vegetation, that had an existence anywhere in the earth's constitution. The living, vivid beauty and overawing sublimity of this vision I can not even now describe; although, as the reader will see, I have since frequently contemplated scenes far more beautiful and ineffable.

But my perceptions still flowed on! The broad surface of the earth, for many hundred miles before the sweep of my vision — describing nearly a semicircle — became transparent as the purest water. The deep alluvial and diluvial depositions were distinguishable from the deeper stratifications of stone and earth, by the comparative and superior brilliancy of the ingredients of the former. Earth gave off one particular color, stones another, and minerals still another. When first I discerned a bed of minerals — it was a vein of iron-ore — I remember how I started and shivered with a sensation of fright. *It seemed that the earth was on fire!* The instantaneous elimination of electricity, from the entire mass, gave the appearance of a deep-seated furnace under the earth. And my agitation was not lessened by perceiving that *these rivers of mineral fire* ran under the ocean for hundreds of miles, and yet were not diminished in a single flame — yea, could not be extinguished!

Innumerable beds of *zinc, copper, silver, limestone,* and *gold,* next arrested my attention; and each, like the different organs in the human body, gave off diverse kinds of luminous atmospheres. All these breathing emanations were more or less bright, variegated, and beautiful. Everything had a glory of its own! Crystalline bodies emitted soft, brilliant, azure and crimson emanations. The various salts in the sea sparkled like living gems; sea-plants extended their broad arms, filled with hydrogenous life, and embraced the joy of existence; the deep valleys and dim-lit ravines, through which old ocean unceasingly flows, were peopled with countless minute animals — all permeated and pulsating with the spirit of Nature; while the sides of ocean-mountains — far, far beneath the high pathway of travel and human commerce — seemed literally studded with emeralds, diamonds, gold, silver, pearls, and sparkling gems, beyond computation. Oh, the ocean is a magnificent cabinet of beauty and wealth immense; and, by virtue of more recent investigations, I am impressed to say that man shall yet possess it!

Be patient, friendly reader, for I have yet other scenes to relate. I now looked abroad upon the fields of dry land, and saw the various species of animals that tread the earth. The external anatomy and the internal physiology of the animal kingdom were alike open to my inspection. An instinctive perception of comparative or relative anatomy filled my mind in an instant. The why and the wherefore of the vertebrated and avertebrated, of the crustaceous and molluscan divisions of the animal world, flowed very pleasantly into my understanding; and I saw the brains, the viscera, and the complete anatomy, of animals that were (at that moment) sleeping or prowling about in the forests of the Eastern hemisphere, *hundreds and even thousands of miles from the room in which I was making these observations!*

It must not be expected that I shall detail a three-hundredth part of the particulars of my *first* introduction to an intuitional perception of Nature.   At best, I can but give you a rude outline, for words do not answer the purpose: they seem to me like stone prisons in which too often we coercively incarcerate our highest thoughts.

In this mystic vision, gentle reader, I saw everything just as you will — with the penetrating senses of the spirit — after you pass away from the visible body at physical death.   It was very, very beautiful to see everything clothed with an atmosphere!   Every little grain of salt or sand; every minute plant, flower, and herb; every tendril of the loftiest trees — their largest and minutest leaves; the weighty mineral and ponderous animal forms, existing in the broad fields before me — each and all were clothed with a dark, or brown, or gray, or red, blue, green, yellow, or white atmosphere — divided and subdivided into an almost infinite variety of degrees of intensity, brilliancy, and refinement.   And — mark the fact! — in each mineral, vegetable, and animal, I SAW SOMETHING OF MAN!   In truth, the whole system of creation seemed to me like *the fragments of future human beings!*   In the beaver I saw, in embryo, one faculty of the human mind; in the fox, another; in the wolf, another; in the horse, another; in the lion, another: yea, verily, throughout the vast concentric circles of mineral, vegetable, and animal life, I could discern certain relationships to, and embryological indications of, Man!   Had I then possessed my present instinct of language, I would have exclaimed, in the language of the poet-psalmist:—

> " Herbs gladly cure our flesh, because they
> Find their acquaintance there
> *   *   *   *   *   *   *
> *All things unto our flesh are kind.*"

Understood in this sense, candid reader, how instructive and approriate was Peter's vision — related in the tenth chapter of Acts — in which he saw a great white sheet let down from heaven, containing all manner of four-footed beasts, creeping things, &c and was told to slay and eat! All this was saying simply thus " Peter, thou needest not feel too exclusive, too partial, too aristo cratic, too high-minded, and lifted above the meanest of thy fellow men, nor yet above the little worm that crawls beneath thy feet ; for, behold, thou art related to every four-footed beast and creep· ing thing that the Lord hath made : acknowledge, therefore, thy universal relatio ships and concentring sympathies, and be kind and lenient henceforth to everything that lives."   Now, since that memorable night, I have met with too many who need Peter's lesson.   They, like him, shrink from this new method of tracing out their genesis or ancestral derivation ; and such say, " We are not used to eating unclean things."   But the time is fast approach· ing, I believe, when mankind will feel their oneness with Nature and its God — to the total annihilation of all narrow-mindedness and empty superficiality.

In my glorious vision, I well remember how I gazed at the little plants in the fields — and saw, lovingly encircling each one, an atmosphere of life peculiar to itself. This ′golden and hazy emanation — encircling some species of vegetation — was appa rently from four inches to eight feet in diameter. Some animals gave off a sombre sphere three or four feet thick, and beyond this a very dark, thin air — as many feet more — which shaded off into the surrounding space. In all this, the Law of Sympathy wa·' very distinctly visible. (See third volume of " The Great Har monia.")   I saw that everything in Nature was arranged and sit uated in accordance with this universal law ; and, by it, that all true sympathetic relationships are established and reciprocally maintained. The relative positions of mineral bodies in the bosom cf the earth ; the situation of trees, vegetation, animals, and human beings ; yea, the relative positions of the sun and stars, even — were manifestly conducted by this infinite sympathy. I saw the different crystalline bodies of the earth act upon each other, and, intermediately, upon the solid substances to which they were attached — by means of a generous commingling of their magnetic emanations. I saw the flowers exhale their odors, with which perfume they clothed themselves, and then formed attachments with neighboring flowers — by breathing out upon them, according to a spontaneous blending of spheres, the sweet breath of their life. There was not a dew-drop, chambered in the petals of the rose, that did not glitter with a living essence — prophetic of coming animation! I saw currents of electricity flowing from a mineral bed in one portion of the earth, to its kindred (but positive) neighbor in another department of the same hemisphere. And I saw the little flames, arising from the essences of plants and trees, leap upward into flowing currents which were instantly absorbed and wafted away to more foreign and proper destinations.

No, no, language can not describe this scene! Sufficient to say, that all Nature was radiant with countless lights, with atmospheres, with colors, with breathings, and with emanations — all throbbing and pulsating with an indestructible life-essence — which seemed just ready to graduate and leap up into the human constitution! Everything apparently emulated to be Man! But I could no longer endure the exquisite happiness — I felt incapable of maintaining a quiet feeling — my emotions had become so deep and unutterable!

I now yearned for a companion, for association. For a moment I realized painfully that I was viewing all this magnificence alone! This thought made me feel isolated also, and incapable of retaining my recollection. Whereupon I began to think yearningly of the village — of the room in which I had taken a seat for the magnetic experiment — of the individuals whom I had seen in the room — of the operator, too — and, immediately, my vision began to diminish and contract. The distant continents, oceans, fields, hills, forests — all gradually faded and disappeared. The effulgent lights were left far behind! Now, I could discern, as before, the interior condition of those in the room, and the face of the operator also, who now said: "Come, come, Jackson, you've been

very still! Can you see anything—have you anything to say?"
I made an effort to describe what I have been writing in this
chapter. I remember how I struggled for a few words; but, as I
was about to relinquish all attempts thereat, I involuntarily exclaimed, in a low and tremulous voice, "How beautiful!"

I heard my own accents, and never did I stronger realize the
total inexpressiveness and impotency of human language! At
that time I said and beheld no more. In a few moments I felt
the hand of the operator passing over my head. Soon I returned
to my ordinary state, with not a single vestige—of what I had
seen—alive in my external memory. Therefore, all that I have
herein related is a revival of the impressions that were then made
upon my mind.

CHAPTER XXXIV.

THE SUMMIT OF THE FIRST MOUNTAIN

"A wonderful stream is the river of Time,
    As it runs through the realm of tears,
With a faultless rhythm, and a musical rhyme.
And a broader sweep, and a surge sublime,
    And blends with the ocean of years."

THE honorable and gentlemanly operator — having a conscientious and benevolent spirit — continued to invite the people to come and witness our nightly demonstrations.   Freely and indiscriminately were these invitations extended; without fear of defeat or hope of reward.   Nothing was done in secret.   During the day we each pursued our different and ever-to-be-respected occupations; and neither had, at this period, the remotest idea of ever devoting a business-hour to these mystical proceedings.

Internally, as the reader is now perfectly aware, there had dawned upon me a clearer, brighter, truer, higher world; but, externally, with the whole shut out and unremembered, I remained dull-headed, mystified, and apprehensive.   Officious acquaintances were at hand with words of advice or opprobrium.   One said — " 'T will make you sick;" another — " You 'll get crazy;" another — " You 're a fool to be so bamboozled every night;" another — " You 're a humbug — a cheat — an impostor;" and thus subjected to the buffetings of an opinionated community, my daily life was far from cheer and repose.   But —

"Like the current of the ocean,
        Man is urged by unseen powers;"

a fact, fully set forth and demonstrated in this portion of my pilgrimage.   An uncomprehended sympathetic influence, like the
air of heaven, now floated daily upon everything I touched.
Shortly it seemed to unsettle and weaken my attachment for Mr.
Armstrong, and to define and strengthen a secret wish to live
within the circle of Mr. Levingston's delicate fascination.   Final
ly, the unknown attraction predominated over my business obligations to the former; and as the fish leaps joyously into its native
element, so plunged I with delight into the bewildering magnetic
Elysium!   I did this, prudent reader, with no expectation of im
proving my then present condition or future prospects.   Mr. Levingston did not offer me any pecuniary inducements; only said
" he would like me in his family," and nothing more.   In short,
like the bird that seeks its congenial clime, or the planet that rolls
as with extatic pleasure round its celestial sire, *so followed I my
indefinable attractions*.   Whereupon the prudentialist sighed, the
skeptic scoffed, the religionist groaned, the merchant shook his
doubtful head, the familiar friend regretted, the boys hooted, and,
last, but not least, the street-politician (perforce of habit) pronounced it *a trick* to make money.   Not that I had to encounter
these conflicting and obstructing influences all at once; but they
descended by slow degrees — like a cold, sleety, drizzling, fitful,
haily *storm,* of several weeks duration.   This spontaneous change,
this magnetic union with the operator, took place about the first
of March.

Symbolically speaking, I was now within a few steps of the top
of the first mountain that stood between my cradle and the Future!
The last few furlongs had been passed over only by virtue of continuous private struggling and resistless obedience to the hidden
law that then stirred my nature.   But just before I gained the
psychical summit, there occurred *an event,* more remarkable and
important than anything else I had previously experienced.   And

although the details thereof have been previously published, yet the object of this volume can not be well accomplished, it seems to me, unless the main features of that initiatory vision are made to reappear in this connection; and, aided by my present addi tional recollections and increased knowledge, I am fortunately enabled to render that experience with more brevity and less mystery.

'T was a chilly, fitful, disagreeable evening — March 6, 1844 — when Mr. Levingston and I proceeded to No. 24 Garden street. Already I had indicated considerable power to inspect, while in clairvoyance, the condition of persons diseased. To make such an examination was the object of our visit on this occasion. On our arrival, few words were exchanged previous to the inductive process, during which I experienced my usual mental transforma- tion, with an additional glow of intense excitement and sense of novelty, like that which characterized my first attempt. The en- gagement being fulfilled, the operator endeavored to relieve me of the mysterious Sympathy. But, for a long time, it seemed im- possible. Again and again he made the attempt, but without suc- cess. Anon, however, I felt returning life streaming through my flesh, causing me to feel natural, and free from the subtle influence to which I had been subjected.

After conversing a few moments with those present, I felt a painful prejudice to their several spheres. Yielding, I descended to the street. I now imagined that my system retained a portion of the imparted influence. This was confirmed by a sudden and paralyzing illumination in the region of the intellectuals. I stood transfixed! On leaving the room, my intention was to return home; and, not feeling quite well, immediately to retire. But now confused, I leaned against the street-gate, seemingly at the mercy and disposal of some power superhuman. While standing thus, a desire sprang up within me to visit Rev. A. R. Bartlett, for whom, as the reader knows, I had formed a strong attachment. This suggestion I speedily obeyed. I advanced to his door:

wildly rang the bell; was ushered into the sitting-room; a seat was furnished near the window. My mind was painfully distracted. The clergyman entered, and warmly welcomed me. Bunglingly and hurriedly I offered many apologies for my intrusion at that late hour. Naturally enough he wondered what could be the real cause and object of my sudden appearance. He fraternally urged me to pass the night with him. This I was impressed to decline. And so without giving or receiving any satisfaction as to the cause or intention of my visit, I rather abruptly departed. I proceeded to Mr. Levingston's home in Main street. I entered the front-door, passed through the hall, and ascended two flights of stairs to my bed. With extreme agitation, of both body and mind, I laid me down. My thoughts were few and fleeting. My physical system yielded, and I sank into an unconscious slumber.

How long I slept I knew not, but I was fully awakened by a sensation of brisk fanning over my face. I opened my eyes, but could see nothing. I concluded that I had been dreaming, and attempted to sleep again. Presently, however, amid the stillness of my room, I heard these words: "*Arise! dress—thyself—and —follow—me.*" It seemed as if my loved mother had once more spoken, but with a voice of far more energy and imperiousness. I obeyed. Indeed, I could not help it. Nothing was now done awkwardly or tardily. I was dressed in a minute, and out in the street. My feet clung to nothing. There was no friction. They were like wings, and I fled with a fleetness indescribable. My exuberant joy was extatic. The unseen power (which I thought might be what mother called "kind Providence") conducted me to the sidewalk, corner of Mill and Hamilton streets, where there were, at this time, no dwellings. My mind was instantly sobered. "What can this mean?" I mentally queried. "What a change! The heavenly archway is exceedingly glorious and beautiful! The many stars stationed throughout the vast labyrinth shine with an immortal effulgence — to guide the traveller onward and upward to the city of eternal joy! And here stand I alone—unseen by any save the Eye of the Eternal Being, and unheard by any except the Ear that hears the silent echoing of all human thoughts!* Yes! I am clad in my usual garments, and am contemplating the most high and sublime of subjects!"

Thus, dear reader, I was meditating, not knowing by what power I came thither, or the length of time that had elapsed since I retired. Nevertheless, I felt great calmness, and yet I could not suppress feelings of curiosity relative to my marvellous ability to contemplate and reason. But I was fully prepared for a vision.

A strange sound now vibrated on my ear. I looked, and lo, I beheld, with admiration, a shadowy congregation of clean and beautiful sheep! The flock was large, and their condition poor. Their bodies, however, were perfectly *white ;* and they manifested great gentleness of disposition. Shortly, I was impressed with the following interpretation; which I now apprehend as true, and giving the *use* of the symbolic scene :—

" The sheep corresponded to the vast brotherhood of mankind. Their beautiful external whiteness corresponded to the innate purity and goodness of all, indicating that all are capable of material refinement and spiritual elevation. The poverty of their bodies corresponded to the wretched physical condition of the earth's inhabitants. Their social affections are disunited; they are opposed to each other's highest *good* and happiness; and their spiritual sympathies are misdirected. Yea, the whole human race represents a flock of sheep, whose shepherd is the Universal Father !"

These truths flowed into my unfolded mind as freely as rain falls from heaven to earth. I recognised their use and importance. But I continued my meditation. The sheep remained at peace as when I first saw them. But now, as I comprehended the meaning intended, they began to change their position—seem-

* At this time, I had no belief in the existence of individual spirits

ingly desiring some *fold* wherein they might rest undisturbed
Being greatly confused, they proceeded to pass along the street
in such a way as would have shown (had they been men) that
their judgments were *weak* or impaired, and that they were thus
incapable of choosing the proper and righteous path which would
have led them to that goal which all seemed to be seeking.

At the next moment I beheld a shepherd. His sudden and
spiritual appearance surprised me not; and I approached him as a
divine friend. I saw that he was much perplexed, yet fully determined (though inefficient) to urge the sheep hence where peace
and harmony reigned. He had great elegance of form, and was
plainly and usefully attired. He presented an air — of unassu-
ming and stately dignity — to be admired in any being. His
countenance, and sky-blue eyes, indicated purity. His whole
appearance was that of a kind and gentle being — endowed with
physical and spiritual perfection. On my approach he spake not,
but expressed in simple language (by the illumination of his countenance) the desires of his soul. He needed sympathy and assistance. The sheep were in ignorance and confusion which he had
labored to overcome. They required gentle but regular discipline.
To his request I immediately acceded. By a powerful exertion,·
we succeeded in establishing order among them — to which they
mutually adhered — whereupon, as if substantial beings, they and
their delighted shepherd naturally proceeded down the street.
Their uniform motions seemed to melt into one harmonious movement, till they faded and vanished amid surrounding objects that
formed the distant scene.

With impressive solemnity, and illumined by a rosy light, the
whole scene came and passed away. Upheld by the unseen
power, I was tranquil throughout the amazing representation.
The following significance of its closing part was also made distinctly manifest: " The beautiful shepherd corresponded to a great
and noble reformer, whose spirit breathed '*peace on earth and
good will to men :*' whose exalted wisdom comprehended the

many physical and spiritual requirements of the human race whose grand system of moral government transcended all others conceived since intelligence pervaded the bosom of Nature. The state of painful confusion into which the sheep were thrown, corresponded to the confused condition of the theologic world — to the conflicts between truth and error, reason and theology, reality and imagination, theory and practice — and, lastly, to the intense anxiety of each person who desires, but can not believe in, immortal life. The request that so benignly beamed forth from his fair countenance denoted that I, like all men, am called to perform a moral part in life's sacred drama." So I am compelled to report: first, because the instruction, intended by the beautiful representation, flowed into my mind irresistibly, and regardless of my own thoughts at the moment; and, second, because my personal transportation to that portion of the village was produced and governed by a power superior to myself.

But the scene now changed. I stood almost free from thought; the blood chilled in my exposed body; my head and chest were painfully congested; I was surrounded with a death-like darkness, and became almost insensible. I struggled and gasped for breath; but the effort failed. Life had almost fled. All was cold, dark, deathly. I made a feeble effort to escape that lonely death, and then fell unconsciously to the ground.

Anon I was awakened, and caused to run as before with bounding fleetness. I was conducted many, many miles over a new road. At length, I turned toward the frozen river Hudson, which I crossed, and hastened up the hills as if on a hunting excursion. My natural powers were so exhausted at this crisis, that I was rendered unconscious of life or existence; and had not my body been resupplied with life and energy, I could not have changed my position. But, after a good rest, a sweet and gentle sensation aroused and renewed me. I moved, and rejoiced. I stretched forth my hand, and felt the vivifying atmosphere. I could also hear: and I opened my eyes. In a few minutes my sight was quite clear, and I glanced over the scene   I was under a psychologic influence, and saw common things in a new light.   Yet I was nearly stupified with wonder.   I was in a reclining position, elevated about seven feet from the ground.   The mass on which I rested was composed of underwood and youthful trees - - neatly and closely interwoven one with another — forming a well-proportioned structure, which I fancied resembled an artificial *altar*. On either side was a barren, craggy, stupendous mountain.   I was thus situated in a deep and apparently inaccessible valley.   The towering acclivities were covered with ice and snow ; and through this hard coating protruded large, ill-shaped rocks, between whose interstices were decayed trees.   I observed, however, that the valley was terminated by the mountain acclivity about ten rods to the west, there being an apparent opening leading to the left, around the mountain's base.

> "In the west was a gleam of glory,
> Fading over the mountain hoary."

On turning eastward; I beheld the river at a seeming distance of four miles.   On the opposite side of the river, I observed ill-fashioned and dilapidated dwellings, desolate and abrupt hills, and forests dark and gloomy, which strangely reminded me of my sad mother.

The heavens were now shrouded as if mourning a world's death. Sorrow filled their bosom with bursting convulsions.   Like smothered groans of universal agony, the thunders rolled forth far and wide with terrific violence.   The electric fire illumined the vast concave.   Light and darkness followed each other in instantaneous succession.   Oh, it was a horrid vision !   I never can forget how, as the rain descended, the heavens *seemed* to weep, and groan, and sigh, and laugh ; and how I, alone, did sympathize with them, and pray for power to still their troubled elements. Terrible, indeed, to my psychologized spirit, seemed my exposed condition.   The rain fell in torrents, and the fleeting elements (while warring among themselves) seemed to menace my destruc tion   An awful and impressive solemnity pervaded the whole. Upon the framework of a natural scene there was painted a spiritual lesson of instruction. From the psychologic representation I learned submission and elevation ; and, from the quickness of the lightning, and the terrific positiveness of the thunder, I confessed that "the Lord God omnipotent reigneth." I beheld my own insignificance, and meanwhile, in common with all mankind, I beheld an unspeakable importance in the fact of existence. I learned also to revere, obey, and depend upon that Power which directs and controls the universe.

> " Every thought was a holy prayer;
> Every sigh was enchanted air;
> Every word was a tone of heaven,
> But in love to the earthly given."

The sun seemed about two and a half hours high when the storm ceased and the sky was clear of clouds. As the representations which had suggested my reflections had passed, I began pondering on the change in my locality. Where I was I could not imagine. The place was strange ; I had never seen it until then ; and I felt assured, from past experience, that, if I had travelled far, I should have been fatigued ; but I was not. Obedient to my guide, I had laid on the brush-heap (*altar*) during the shower, and was thoroughly wet. Feeling free now, I desired to dry my garments, and to learn, if possible, what portion of the earth I was in. Accordingly, I arose and descended to the ground. While leaning against the pile, (on which I had lain,) I felt a dull, sleepy sensation, which was instantly followed by a reaction, and I became unusually clairvoyant.

All things seemed remarkably romantic and beautiful. But an indefinite sound now reached my ears. I listened. Presently, I heard the same several times rapidly repeated — whereupon I turned, and beheld (by means of psychologic impression) one of the strangest sights imaginable. A flock of sheep in a state of indescribable confusion. They were running in every possible direction. Some were making exertions to ascend the *hill-side*. I saw them leap against the glazed mountain, from which they rebounded and came down, with dreadful force, upon the stony basis. Others were striving to pass the place I occupied. But they were ignorant, and could not proceed; neither could they obtain a substantial foothold. The mountains were too high. The frozen earth was too unpropitious, and the passage too well guarded. At this moment, through the opening at the base of the mountain, appeared their shepherd. He advanced toward me with a slow but firm step.

These visionary sheep corresponded to those I had seen in Poughkeepsie, at night; and the shepherd resembled the beautiful one I there saw, in every particular. I stepped forward to meet him, and, without speaking, to observe as before the indications of his countenance. I read his wishes. He solicited help in his work of gathering the strange and scattered flock. At first, the creatures made a strong resistance. But, seeing the positiveness of our intentions, they yielded submissively. We gathered and guided them into the path leading around the mountain's base.

A new peace now seemed to characterize their condition. Both sheep and shepherd were, for the first time, inseparably united. Eternal principles of Right had accomplished their salvation. The sheep departed, like evening shadows, with their gentle shepherd, up the valley through the opening. And it seemed that —

> "Angels moved in the space enchanted,
> 'Twixt the sky and the valley haunted."

Overjoyed, I returned to my resting-place, and, leaning against its side, drew my garments more closely around me, and sank into deep meditation. Presently, I beheld a man approaching deliberately — apparently absorbed in thought. He was a person of diminutive stature, yet had a beautiful structure. His fine symmetry, beauty, and elegance of deportment, cap tivated my attention. He appeared advanced in years, and was attired in a style corresponding nearly to that of the Friends. His hair was of a silvery white, floating in shadowy locks over his brow, and hanging gracefully about his neck and shoulders. His face was full and expressive. His moral and intellectual developments were prominent. He was a spiritual being.

In his hand I perceived a clear white *scroll*. Its edges sparkled with gilding of the finest quality; and the care with which he preserved its beauty, excited in me the deepest respect. When I would have advanced to meet him, he raised his hand, and gently intimated that I must remain perfectly tranquil. A most heavenly radiation played upon his countenance. He elevated the scroll to his lips — affectionately imprinted upon it a pure and holy kiss — then handed it to me, to open and read. I was not now awkward and clumsy. With delicacy and precision, therefore, I unfolded it. It contained *writing* in characters which I had never before seen; but I could translate them without hesitation. The language was clear and comprehensive. The form of expression was simple, but powerful. It contained a world of beautiful meaning. It read thus:—

> "As they were, so they are;
> As they are, so they will be!"

Beneath was the following interrogatory: "*Now do you believe it?*" I felt its convincing power, and bowed assent. Observing which, the messenger handed me a singular pencil, (for I had none,) with which I signified my conviction and signed my name. This being done, he received the scroll with a gentle bow, rolled it together, pressed it to his lips, then turned and departed as he came — slowly, firmly, deliberately. I followed him with my clairvoyant eyes, till his form vanished around the base of that stupendous mountain.

"How unaccountable," exclaimed I, "that a stranger should

come, obtain my signature, and depart, without uttering one word vocally, and yet so eloquent!" Mighty truths now gushed up from the depths of my spirit, and I was impressed with the following correspondence :—

"The scroll-bearer represented a reformer, who (while on earth) had shed light upon life and immortality. The white *scroll* represented the purity of his mission. The contents of the scroll represented the grand consummation, viz., 'Peace on Earth.' Thus :—

" '*As they were ;*' As the sheep were (when first I saw them) in a state of universal confusion, wretched, having no knowledge of their true interests, or of that wisdom, which would lead them to happiness. '*So they are ;*' So *mankind* are — in the same disorganized condition, ignorant, superstitious, skeptical, bigoted, fanatical, intolerant.

" '*As they are ;*' As the sheep *are* — united for ever, striving for one purpose, pressing forward to one grand and glorious end, which is *Happiness.* '*So they*' (mankind) '*will be.*' That is united in like manner. From all unnecessary evil free! from personal misdirection and suffering; from ignorance and depravity; from pride and sectarian intolerance — Free! There shall be a new heaven and a new earth wherein dwelleth righteousness. As the sheep were united, so all men shall be joined into one Brotherhood."

The interrogatory, "*Now do you believe it ?*" was addressed to my youthful judgment, after it had been so unrighteously impressed by traditional theology. And those initiatory representations were necessary, that I might apprehend the vicissitudes of my future life, and bear them with wisdom and patience. The question appealed to my then impressible judgment, whether I would believe the instruction I had received in preference to my previous religious opinions. My faculties were now restored to their ordinary state, and I stood once more free from everything but fatigue and embarrassment. I commenced descending the valley, to discover, if possible, my geographical situation. I was now in my natural state. Presently, I observed a man attired in a farmer's dress, carrying a spade on his shoulder, walking leisurely in an opposite direction. I hastened to him, and inquired, in an anxious manner:—

"Sir, will you tell me the name of this place? where I can get some food? and how far it is to Poughkeepsie?"

He smiled, and gave me an inquisitive look: "This 'ere place," said he, "is Catskill, and them is the Catskill mountains; perhaps, you may get somethin' to eat at the inn. You asked me about Poughkeepsie. Well, I s'pose it is about forty miles from t' other side the river."

Acting upon this information, I recrossed the river, and then rested in a reclining posture on the railing of a ferry-boat. And now *sleep* came upon me imperceptibly again, as I lay reflecting on the scenes through which I had passed. I was startled when I became sensible of a return of those mystical feelings which precede the closing of the senses and illumining of the internal principle. As they came on, my body yielded, as I was willing it should; external life again vanished, as if for ever, and I was once more a being of the interior.

Soon, however, I arose and fled along the road like a reindeer. Many, many miles I ran; and then I slept again.

How long I remained asleep I know not; but, as in previous instances, I at length felt returning life streaming through my system, and my spirit was restored to a high degree of animation. I opened my eyes, and, wonderful to relate, I was seated upon a marble grave-stone about eighteen inches from the ground! The melancholy sanctuary in which I found myself, was enclosed by a huge stone wall, surmounted by a top-railing, similar to farmers' ordinary fences. The enclosure was in the form of a triangle, and, I think, occupied about one acre and a half of smooth land. I counted eleven whole grave-stones standing, five broken, and several scattered upon the ground. A dense wood concealed the surrounding country from my view; and I was thus sequestered in a solitary place, for a purpose of which I had not the least knowledge. Nevertheless, without fear, I resolved to continue in the same position as when I awoke to consciousness, and await any suggestions that might flow from within or without.

At this instant I experienced a breathing sensation, unlike any other, upon the front and side of my head, in the region of the organ of ideality. Its increasing attraction caused me to turn in the direction whence it proceeded, and I beheld a man of ordinary stature but of a spiritual appearance. He approached, and, without speaking, turned to the right near me, and furnished himself with a similar seat. As by instinct, I observed that he was a lover of Nature and of truth—had a constant thirst for knowledge—and was endowed with strong powers of investigation. His quick natural perception, sustained by his highly-cultivated faculties of intuition and reflection, presented a combination of intellectual powers seldom witnessed. He was a being whom I felt constrained to love—for love was prompted by his superior wisdom. I felt quiet and happy. And it is a truth, that I conversed with him, and he with me, for a long period, and that too, by a mutual *influx* and reflux of thought! His discourse was substantially on this wise:—

"I lived," said he, "on the earth, in the form, among the inhabitants thereof, for a length of time determined by my obedience to Natural Law. From youth, I imbibed the impressions made upon my mind by my parents, the religious world, and philosophy. But artificial education served more to retard my mental progress than as an auxiliary to useful advancement. I discarded, early, these unfavorable influences, and commenced interrogating and communing with Nature and her productions—within the circumference of my vision and mental capacity—whereby I became acquainted with truths of deeper importance and of greater magnitude. It was demonstrated to me that all the diversified external forms in this, as in other universes, are unfolded by virtue of an element or spiritual principle, contained in each, which is their life, or Soul; and this essence, by *men*, is called God; also, that the *external* corresponds to the inner or productive principle; that *forms* are determined, as perfect or imperfect, by the specific character of their prompting soul, which actuates them to *life* and development.

" By this I learned that the gross matter and minerals of our earth are formed and governed and sustained by a law — *an inherent principle* — which also operates in higher worlds of material organization. And as this principle, in various modifications, ascended in the order of nature, higher and more perfect forms were unfolded — being actuated and perfected by inner life, to which the outer existence corresponded. These forms," he continued, " I understood constituted the vegetable kingdom. From this established basis, I perceived those Laws breathing forth the animal kingdom; and, in their next stage of ascension, developing, sustaining, and perfecting man! And all this came to me (as it will come to you) by discovering and meditating upon corresponding truths, dwelling within, about, and above me.

" In my analytical investigations, also, I discovered a threefold or triune Power in every compound — three essential parts to every established organization — which is absolutely necessary to all things, in order that they may be perfectly organized.

" This knowledge led me to reflect upon the many physical violations, occurring every hour, among the inhabitants of the earth — and impressed me that these frequent transgressions of laws sustaining the human form, called for some effectual remedy to relieve the diseases caused thereby. Accordingly I founded a system upon these principles and considerations, which may be called a ' medical system of the trinity.' In this system I maintain the proposition that every particle in the human body possesses a close affinity to particular particles below in the subordinate kingdoms — and that these latter particles, if properly associated and applied, would cure any affected portion or organ of the human frame.

" To establish this theory, I labored diligently ; and now I have the satisfaction of knowing that my system was a germ enlivened by interior truth ; whereby new and more truthful systems were developed, to bless the earth's inhabitants ! Now I love truth because it begets wisdom ; for my love has become wisdom ; and my wisdom substantial knowledge !" His spiritual countenance, as he closed these sayings, brightened with a delightful and beautiful smile !

Astonished at his learned discourse — and my mind being filled with thought concerning his revelations, the like of which I had never before heard — I individualized a thought which he instantly perceived, and answered.

Mentally I inquired, " Can I become acquainted with you, kind stranger, and with your system, too, by appropriate means within your power and pleasure to afford ?"

"Ah ! 't is for this, that you sit in my presence," said he, inclining to the right, and raising in his hand an elegant cane, which, till then, I had not seen in his possession. " Here is a full synopsis of my system and practice," he continued, turning to me, " and I desire that this you should comprehend ; and in understanding its fundamental principles, you will gently and justly apply its teachings to the good of your brethren, mankind !"

Thus saying, he touched a singular spring at the top, and the cane mechanically parted into three longitudinal strips or pieces. A strong rod ran through the centre, graduated to accord with the cane's shape. This rod was very straight and beautiful, having the appearance of highly-polished silver. The parts were neatly adjusted one to another, and when arranged on the rod, formed a staff far exceeding in beauty any I had ever beheld. I saw that the pieces remained whole when disengaged from the rod. These he took in his hand, and unfolded them piece by piece, until they completely separated. The smaller pieces now assumed the diamond form, especially when closely observed.

" Here," said he, " on these little blocks," presenting them to me, "is the name of every disease with which the human race is afflicted."

I saw, felt, and read the name of each and every disease, with most of which I was entirely unacquainted; and, as I read, I returned them to him, one by one, in the original order.

Now, elevating his person (which seemed less earthly than my body) he discoursed thus: "In the inside of these blocks you will find a composition which, when applied, will palliate or remove the disease named upon its exterior. Of this compound make you a quantity suggested at the time you examine the diseased individual, and sufficiently strong to be well adapted."* He restored the pieces to their respective places, and quickly joined the cane, so that I could not see any possible means to disunite its parts again.

"Take this," said he, handing the cane to me, "and preserve the charge devotionally; for it is a work of a lifetime, demanding equal attention, reflection, and application." I received the precious gift with ineffable delight and gratification.

"Moreover," he continued, "that you may behold the complete correspondence between this system and Nature, I will explain the cane's signification. The pieces, when disunited in the manner observed, correspond to those principles dwelling and operating in the natural organization; and the blocks to the various individuals that constitute the human race. The disease specified on the outside of each block, corresponds to the truth that disease tends to affect only the bodies of men, and not their living, interior principle. The composition on the inside of each block corresponds to the truth that everything's exterior is determined precisely by the interior, creative, and moving principle; to the truth, also, that *the spirit is* the creating, developing, perfecting, expanding, beautifying, organizing, healing, eternal essence in the possession of every being.

---

* This system of medical treatment is developed in " The Great Harmonia," vol. i.

"The rod that runs through the cane, and connects its parts together, corresponds to the principle of divine truth running through and sustaining this system, as well as all the vast creations both in this and higher spheres. And the rod being in the interior, signifies that the great law of truth is the interior of all things, and especially in the soul of all things—dwelling there imperceptible to outer sense, yet known to be existing from the regular manifestations of a united and complicated Universe!

"Inward searching after truth will lead to, and disclose, the great and important realities so delicately typified by this Staff—for it is an accumulation of interior and external evidences, assisted by the promptings of Nature, and sanctioned and consummated by the consciousness of truth dwelling in the soul."

Thus ended his eloquent interpretation. His countenance became illuminated with ecstatic delight, and his thoughts entered my spirit and were responded to, without even once having the senses audibly addressed.

A sweet and gentle sensation now passed warmly over my left breast, face, and head. It seemed to proceed from something human immediately behind me. Impressed thus, I turned and beheld a man of an appearance very different from the one beside me. His anatomy was of wise proportions; he possessed perfect symmetry of cerebral structure, and was seemingly about six feet in stature. His head particularly attracted my attention, for I had never beheld such an harmonious combination of moral and intellectual developments. The cerebrum indicated a most vigorous and gigantic intellect—as also an exalted power of conception, great ease of expression—and a high degree of spirituality. He drew near, and reclined against the stone the first speaker was occupying, and spake in this wise:—

"By permission long granted me by the divine mercy of the Lord, to visit this and other earths, I am enabled to instruct thee, as it is becoming me to do, concerning things pertaining to thy interior life, and exterior sphere of thought and usefulness. Thy spirit is now untrammeled — has experienced a joyful resurrection from the artifices of the social world without; therefore thou hast become an appropriate vessel for the influx and perception of truth and wisdom. Spiritually, thou hast left the world where men reside; but physically, thou art there with them still. Thy mission hath been shown thee. Great is the Universe wherein thou shalt labor and do whatsoever thy most *interior* understanding shall conceive to be good, and true, and profitable.

" I will be near thee in thy stewardship — pointing to the right path. The things thou shalt bring forth will surprise and confound those of the land who are considered deeply versed in science and metaphysics.

" Obstructions of various kinds will affect thy external life; but they will tend more fully to expand thy interior being. Press on thy way: and love only those things tending to truth and wisdom.

" By thee will a new light appear; it shall be new because it will brighten and purify that already in being, and reflect intellectually upon that heretofore conceived; and it will establish that which has been, and still is supposed to be the wildest hallucination, viz., The law and 'kingdom of heaven' on earth — Peace on earth and good will to men.

" In due time these things will be made manifest through thee, and to others, while residing in the form. By others they will be comprehended and believed, and at the end of a little season they will be generally acknowledged, their beauty and importance appreciated; and they will be loved, and proclaimed in practice.

" At a time not far distant, I will instruct thee concerning the opening of thy interior understanding, and the laws to be observed to render thee qualified to commune with the interior realities of all subordinate and elevated things. This phenomenon when openly manifested, will testify of those divine spiritual truths, not as yet comprehended by those who admire Nature merely for the delights thereof, and by those imprisoned souls everywhere, who believe nothing beyond the sphere of their bodily senses. See to the *promptings* of thy living spirit. In a just season thy great labor will commence, which, when consummated, will elevate the human race to a high degree of harmony.

"For the present I communicate no more. But now I repeat, love wisdom, which is food and light to the internal: and wisdom secureth health; and health procureth happiness. And thus strengthened, enlightened, and purified, thou wilt find it *congeniat* to seek and thirst after interior and beautiful truths."

Thus ended the last speaker's prophetic admonitions; and, as he closed the above sentence, I saw a smile of joy (and even ecstacy) pass over his countenance which seemed sweet and heavenly—coming, as did his thoughts, with a kind of spontaneous ease.

I felt directly impelled by some influence to arise, and, with my staff, depart. This impulse I immediately obeyed. I went to the fence, placed my foot upon the wall-side, and raised my body to its top. On endeavoring to surmount the railing, however, my clothing became entangled, and I experienced a sense of irritation approximating to *intense anger*, because of the obstruction. This was unusual, for I had not had such feelings for many years— indeed I can scarcely remember ever being so angry, except when my father forgot the jewsharp. I was thus exasperated at the rail which, being split at the end, had caught my coat. I knew that my actions and gestures were clownish and awkward—that my manners betrayed the fact, that I had not mingled with polite society—which greatly wounded my pride and excited impatience and mortification. Meanwhile the strangers were observing my feelings and movements with apparent complacency. On seeing this, I requested the one who had given me the cane, to hold it till I gained the opposite side of the fence. He courteously advanced and received the cane from my trembling hand. Being thus free, I grasped the rail at the open portion, and tore it completely in twain. Having vented my rage, I descended to the ground and desired the staff. At this, the person who had last spoken drew near, and gently spake thus :—

"Keep well the instruction given thee; moreover, learn to be wise and gentle; and add to gentleness, love; and to love, wisdom; and wisdom, being pure, begets illumination, and illumination, happiness. And, as it was given me to say, in a due season thou shalt return, and then this staff shall be thine; *but thou must first learn not to be under any circumstances depressed, nor by any influences elated :* for these are the extremes of an unguarded impulse, in minds not strong with pure wisdom.

"From this learn meekness and humiliation," he continued, "and sustain these by a proper dignity in thy natural living. Receive this thy first and sufficient lesson, and by its light lead others to seek the pathway leading to Wisdom and the Tree of Righteousness—whose fruit shall be delicious to the hungering, but untasted except they nourish the seed and cause the tree to spring up within them—which will for ever reflect a refreshing shade over the spirit within and the world without."

Thus he closed. As I stood and listened, gratitude swelled my soul into volumes of thankfulness, that the magic cane was sacrificed for such valuable instruction; while, at the same time, I felt assured that the beautiful and comprehensive Staff would ultimately be mine, and that, too, because I should be worthy of its possession.

Being on the outer side of the wall, I could now see their bodies no more, for the fence rose too high, and the ground where I stood was lower than within the yard; and whether they remained within the yard, or vanished to other portions of the world, I did not discover.

CHAPTER XXXV

AN ENTIRE CHANGE OF PROGRAMME.

" There 's a divinity that shapes our ends,
    Rough-hew them how we will."

' You 're a queer youth, to be sure," said the operator, laugh‧
ing. " I suppose, now, you 'll tell us where you 've been since last
night !"

" Tell where I 've been ?" echoed I dreamily.

" Yes, that 's what we want to know," he replied, evidently ap
preciating my abstraction.

Collecting at length my bewildered and wandering senses, I
replied : " I 've been on a long journey, and seen many curious
sights. But," continued I, still confused, " I can 't make out what
it all means."

The reader need scarcely be told, in this connection, that I had
reached the operator's home, soon after the interview described at
the close of the last chapter. But what happened, in the interval
between that circumstance and the above conversation, yet remains
to be chronicled.

Immediately upon leaving the graveyard, I passed unexpectedly
into spontaneous clairvoyance ; and, wishing to know my where-
abouts, I directed my perceptions here and there over various
roads and localities until I fixed upon Poughkeepsie. So real or
literal was my vision of natural objects along the way, that I supposed myself journeying, and marvelled that drivers and travellers

did not recognise me! And it was long before I learned that I
had confounded the flight of my vision with the act of ordinary
walking — the knowledge of which fact greatly relieved the circumstance of its mystery. Ascertaining thus the bearing of the
distant village, and forming a judgment as to the most direct route
thither, I again became normal, and commenced the journey. And
yet, I remember of being conscious and feeling natural only at
intervals, as I walked on the road Poughkeepsieward.

As I approached home, my mind became exceedingly disconcerted by sensations similar to those usually experienced when
waking from my magnetic condition. I perfectly recollect meeting several acquaintances, each of whom manifested surprise on
seeing me. I spoke to no person. On reaching Mr. Levingston's
house, I passed directly through the hall; at the termination of
which, I suddenly lost the most of my memory concerning my
recent visions. This bewildered me for a moment, but soon on I
passed through the adjoining room, up the stairs, into the dining-
apartment, where the family were engaged in eating. Oh, wasn't
I hungry!

I threw off my coat and hat, and seated myself at the table.
Doubtless the family were somewhat astonished at my unceremonious and ravenous actions, and still more so at my unconversable
state. They began questioning me in reference to my mysterious
disappearance; but they subsequently informed me that I made
no reply; that I ate a hearty dinner; and that, when done, I proceeded to wash myself at the further end of the room.

Such a meal was certainly well calculated to make me feel natural. Yes, I now felt a return of normal sensibility. As the
strange influence which had held me for so many hours receded,
I saw a brilliant light — it flashed — and again all was darkness.
But now another flash, and another, came, and I was completely
freed from the abnormal condition. And yet I was absolutely
frightened! The fact that I remembered entering the front door,
and then lost all consciousness till that moment, when I found my

self standing in the presence of the family, with a napkin in my
hand, appeared so unaccountable, that, for a moment, the familiar
friends about me looked like strangers, and I seemed subsiding
into blank nothingness.

Just then I was aroused by the cheery words with which this
chapter begins; and still pursuing the theme, Mr. Levingston
kindly inquired:—

"Well, Jackson, can't you tell us something about it?"

"How long have I been gone?" I hastily questioned.

"Since last night," replied the operator. "At one time this
forenoon we were on the point of searching the town for you; but
it was suggested by some one that the power which caused your
disappearance would preserve and restore you, and so we concluded to postpone giving the alarm."

During the afternoon of that day, I was able to recall the general impression which the graveyard strangers had left upon my
mind. The smaller of the two men I knew was called GALEN, a
physician of considerable renown; and the more beautiful one was
once known as SWEDENBORG, a Swedish philosopher and theologian; but, up to that time, I had never heard anything of the
names or works of these persons, by means of either books or
reports, and so I began already to entertain troublesome misgivings as to the reality of my experience.

In the evening I was magnetized as usual. As usual, also, there
were present plenty of large-eyed and open-mouthed seekers for signs
and wonders. One had brought his pugnacious friend, who wished
to be convinced by having me, while thoroughly blindfolded, tell the
time by the watch then in his pocket. Another had at last induced his
skeptical and contrary wife to come and satisfy herself by getting
me to look within and tell what articles of food she had taken for
supper. Another had at length prevailed upon her stoical and
sneering husband to come and get a test by having me read the
titlepage of the book that he had carefully stowed away under the
linings of his great-coat for that purpose. Besides these, there

was a group of the sick, and sore, and suffering — persons who not only *wanted* to be convinced, but actually *needed* what they wanted — a true report of their condition, and a knowledge of the most direct means of restoration.

Thus the "wants" and the "needs" of the villagers encompassed me like a hedge-fence. But I was now very still, and very insensible to all demands and environments. My spirit, all unseen by the insensate crowd, was passing through an important crisis. An entire change of programme was about to be made! My clairvoyant powers were on the eve of a glorious graduation. With the speed of the whirlwind I surveyed every nook and corner of my immediate future. A grand joy pervaded my soul — for I saw that there was a sublime USE even in the exercise of clairvoyance — a substantial benefit to sore, and lame, and blind Humanity! O the happiness, the ecstatic bliss, of that world-wide view! There was a lofty grandeur in the philanthropic emotions with which I felt inspired and strengthened. There was a new benefit in existence. My happiness consisted in the certainty that I was to bestow health, to snatch from death the suffering infant, to guide the blind man into light, to sound the voice of healing in the ear of the deaf, to be a support when disease oppressed my neighbor, and a staff of strength to the sick who stepped in the path that lay before me. And yet, friendly reader, I was not lifted up with self-importance. The blessed work that I saw to do, instead of exciting my self-esteem, almost oppressed and overcame my soul. My gratitude was very deep; the responsibility would be weighty, and my life was to become a sober reality.

The prolonged silence, or rather my incommunicativeness, induced the operator to ask, " Can you see anything to-night, Jackson ?"

"Oh, yes !" I ejaculated with enthusiastic emotion, " I have some new directions to give. I now see the good of my late visions."

" Well," said he, " I am ready."

"In the first place, then," proceeded I, "we must make a change."

"A change!" exclaimed the operator, somewhat startled — fearing perhaps that I was about to leave him — for his heart was already set upon the daily practice of throwing me into clairvoyance.

"Yes, 'tis good that we should," I replied; "and to-night is the time to begin."

"Well!" sighed he with true submission.

"First, then, I see 'tis good," said I, "to spend no more time upon wonder-seekers; because, even when satisfied, they do not advance the truth of this science; neither do they continue to be believers, but, either from sheer intellectual indolence or actual lack of judgment, they return night after night for a repetition of old tests, or else want different evidences. All time spent to gratify such, is immorally squandered."

"How, then, shall we convince the unbelieving?" inquired the operator.

"By doing good," I enthusiastically replied; "by examining and prescribing for the sick."

"Must your powers be confined exclusively to the sick?" he asked, with a little show of disappointment.

"Yes, after this," I replied; and then proceeded to give ample directions. Our future time was to be systematically employed. Certain hours were to be devoted to diseased applicants. I was to remain in the clairvoyant state only just so long (two hours and a half) at each sitting; the magnetic process was to be conducted thus and so; and our time was to be rewarded by the charge of a moderate fee to those only who were in easy circumstances.

What further happened that night I will not stop to record. The reader is now made acquainted with the disposition of my time, and the direction of my clairvoyant faculty. But it should be borne in mind, meanwhile, that no knowledge, of either the great uses and benefits which I saw, or of the rules and regulations by which we were to be guided, was brought out into my natural state. Hence, when not clairvoyant, my mind was not without an indefinable apprehensiveness — a secret feeling, a fear perhaps — that my soul was the involuntary *dupe* of some mischievous magician, the victim of some baneful and irresistible enchantment. These dreamy misgivings were frequently roused by the slight intimations and dark insinuations of certain meddlesome persons; and yet, whenever I let down the line and sounded the depths of my soul, I found no unhappiness there, nor even a wish to restore my former relations with the ever-esteemed Mr. Armstrong.

In justice to the operator, it should be related that, as a merchant-tailor, he stood among the first and foremost, and consequently had a large proportion of the public patronage. His business was abundant and profitable. Notwithstanding this, however, his love of humanity was so pure, and his spirit so conscientious, that, encouraged by the adoptive heart and energetic mind of his wife, he abandoned his profession, and devoted himself to obeying the rules which I had presented. He did this, incredulous reader, with the bald prospect of unbounded persecution and of continued pecuniary loss.

Shortly after my vision of the sheep and shepherd, the compound mystery of which had become nearly gossiped out, I called upon the utilitarian, or rather, in a thoughtless mood, I found myself wandering into his store; whereupon he said:—

"I hear strange stories about you, Jackson: some say you're half-crazy."

"Crazy!" I exclaimed, with unfeigned uneasiness.

"People will talk, you know," said he. "How long do you think of continuing as you are?"

"What — to be magnetized?"

"Yes — that's what I mean."

"I don't know," said I; "perhaps all next summer."

"Do you mean to let mesmerism step in between us," he

asked, "and put a damper on your fair prospects as a business man?"

"I don't know," answered I gloomily; "it seems just now that my clairvoyance is useful to sick folks."

"Indeed!" exclaimed he; "do you make cures?"

"Folks say so," I replied.

"Yes, I've heard so too; but do your patients really get well?"

"Several persons declare that I have cured 'em," returned I; "but we've got new rules now, and may cure more."

"Well, success to you, Jackson," he responded good-naturedly. "If you're really a prodigy in that line, I suppose I must spare you a while longer; but mark! don't be wheedled out of your share of the remuneration."

And this, for many months, was the last conversation between Mr. Armstrong and his truant apprentice.

In this place I feel moved to record several remarkable occurrences that transpired both before and after the startling events of the memorable 7th of March. The incidents to which I now refer were evolved during my medical examinations.

Permit me, kind reader, to premise somewhat by alluding to the fact that, through clairvoyant inspection, I soon ascertained Disease to be a want of equilibrium in the circulation of the vitalic principle. Of this there was uniformly presented one of two evidences—either an *excess* in some particular organ or locality, or else a *deficiency*. The results of the former I soon learned, as by instinct, to term *acute* or inflammatory, of the latter, *chronic* or slow and surreptitious diseases; each form requiring very different treatment from the other. And, what was equally remarkable and beautiful, while in my clairvoyant condition I seemed to be a sort of *connecting link* between the patient's disease and its exact counterpart (or remedy) in the constitution of external Nature! For each visceral or organic deficiency and need in man (which may be the basis of disease), I instantly perceived a corresponding agent of gratification or restitution.   Even so to his every functional, nervous, or muscular necessity or demand (which may also become a disease), I could discover an appropriate and adequate supply.   The existence of this supply, this agent, this remedy for disease, I first felt as by an instinctive sympathy; and then, in nearly every instance, I would proceed to exercise my power of vision to see in what field, or book, or drug-store, the required article was located or described.   In this silent and mysterious manner—that is, by looking through space directly into Nature's laboratory, or else into medical establishments—I easily acquired the common (and even the *Greek* and *Latin*) names of various medicines, and also of many parts of the human structure—its anatomy, its physiology, its neurology, &c.; all of which greatly astounded the people, and myself not less when not clairvoyant—for then I had to rely solely upon hearsay and gossip.   The secret, then, of my prescribing successfully was, the bringing together of specific medicines to supply a physiological demand, or to equalize the unbalanced vitalic principle.   And yet, what is not a little strange and paradoxical, during the first years of my medical experience I could not give a satisfactory solution of my own method.   In fact, I did not comprehend the extent and import of my own perceptions—no, not even when most exalted in my mental illumination.   The reason was, that I had not yet reached that superior condition which is represented by the fourth of the diagrams describing magnetical progression.

Having made this prefatory digression, I will now proceed to relate a few illustrative incidents :—

One night, while at Mr. Bartlett's residence, he requested me to go (in spirit) and examine some person in the vicinity of Utica, New York.   As was customary in such experiments, the operator resigned ms seat to the soliciting party, who, taking my hand, asked, " Will you go with me to see a friend ?"

On this occasion my clairvoyant condition was good, so I replied in the affirmative, and waited further suggestions. At this hour I can remember how plainly I could then read his mind. He knew the direct road to travel, and the house where his friend resided, and hence could readily pronounce and decide upon the correctness or inaccuracy of my observations. Printed distinctly in his mind, like the lines on a map, I saw the highway leading from Utica to the house in question; and had I been disposed, I know that, from such a picture alone, I might have satisfactorily described the externals of the route and the habitation in which the patient was at the time. But suppose I had relied upon his mind and recollections for my impressions or knowledge of the localities, then how would I have obtained the next branch of information — the exact condition of the diseased individual — of which he had no accurate knowledge?

The case was clear. Independent vision, alone, was my only reliance. So off I started! Over hill and over vale I sped — flying like thought from county to county — till I located the neighborhood. Orally I described a house here, a barn there, a church yonder, &c., all of which Mr. Bartlett recognised in the main as correct. When arrived at a certain residence, I slowly described it and the appearance of its inmates, especially the symptoms of a sick person there. This description did not quite satisfy Mr. Bartlett. It seemed at best but partially correct, and somehow to be blended with the personal appearance and symptoms of another friend of his in that region. But I persisted that I could find no other sick person in the neighborhood; and after a few more descriptive remarks, which were also unsatisfactory, I yielded to the attractions of my body and returned like lightning to its welcoming embrace.

Now, investigating reader, here are two points to remember for further explanation: one is, that I supposed that I actually travelled with my spirit's entire personality through the space, and yet I could all the time hear and converse with the clergyman;

the other is, that, in relying exclusively and resolutely upon my own powers of clairvoyant discrimination, I ran off the track, so to speak, and, like a boy delighted and bewildered with the perfect panorama of new sights, I overlooked the true object of my search in my impulsive sympathy for another suffering person in a remote corner of the county. But this experience seemed to be sandwiched or interposed between a long catalogue of excursional tests the most convincing. I record it, therefore, for the benefit of the impartial psychologist who loves to search out metaphysical laws.

A very different fact comes next in order. One day a countryman took the chair for an examination. My vision was clear, and, after a few moments' inspection, I discovered his disorder to be deafness. With the internal structure of the ear I had already become familiar; and, being a connecting link between the empire of want and the world of supply, I easily felt out the remedy. This was very remarkable. The singular character of his deafness (the thickening of the lining membrane, &c.), called for the magnetic moisture of the rat!

"Of the rat!" exclaimed the astonished operator, as I suggested the strange remedy. "How can it be done?"

"The patient must place the warm skins of the rats over and back of each ear, every night," said I, "for a certain length of time, and then let me see him again."

The countryman was at first greatly discomposed by this fantastic prescription, but finally resolved to have traps set in every house and barn in his rural district, besides offering a reward for a certain number of live rats delivered at his home. The premium soon brought him dozens of the fated creatures, with the hot, humid skins of which (immediately after killing) he ratified the eccentric prescription. And I subsequently heard that, contrary to all belief, the disagreeable remedy wrought his much-desired restoration.

One cold night, while I was examining some patients, a citizen entered in great haste, and requested immediate attention.

" I don't believe much in't," said he, " but I want relief."

He took the chair, and instantly I detected a monstrous *felon* — not in his heart, but on one of his hands — which was growing rapidly worse, inflaming the entire arm, exciting the whole nervous fabric, and threatening him with the agonies of lockjaw. Away, away, flowed and spread my sympathies over the fields of creation — feeling, feeling, feeling, with an exquisitely intensified sensibility — for the nature and name of the most appropriate and expeditious remedy.

" Oh, yes !" exclaimed I, " that's it — that's just the thing."

" What, Jackson ?"

" This," said I : " get a live frog, take his skin right off, and bind it on the diseased parts."

" Are you certain," inquired the anxious and agonized patient, " that I can save my finger ?"

" Yes, quite certain," I replied ; " only do what I have directed."

But where to get the frog — that was the next question. The inexorable Frost-King still carried the keys of streams and springs dangling from his royal girdle. The ice was thick over every cavernous retreat in which the frog-family takes up its winter residence, and hence the prospect of obtaining the remedy was densely beclouded and disheartening. And yet, as if directed by some ever-seeing and controlling intelligence, the suffering man betook himself to a certain spring below the village, where, lo and behold ! a frog had providentially just hopped out, and was hastily and impiously scrabbling back again, when he was caught, instantly killed, and his electrical skin bound upon the incorrigible felon. The cooling effect upon the inflamed hand was delightful. And I was afterward told that the cure was perfect.

One more illustration may be given. A patronizing and semi believing individual, belonging to the wealthy classes, opened the

way for our admission into an aristocratic family. The respectable head of the establishment, an elderly gentleman, was afflicted
with deafness. Aside from the amusement which the party sought
flippantly to extract out of clairvoyance, they seriously desired
that an examination should be made of the old man's diseased
ears, with especial reference to their restoration. After looking
into them a moment, I exclaimed —

"He's too old!"

"What's that?" asked the operator.

"He's too old to get well," returned I. "Besides, there's a
thick incrustation along the passages leading from the ear to the
throat. There's some ossification, too."

"Hey?" shouted the patient. "What's all that.

The operator in a loud voice explained. To which the thoughtful old gentleman very reasonably replied: "I have long since
abandoned all hope of having my hearing entirely restored. All
I ask is, relief, relief — that's what I seek."

"Do you understand him, Jackson?" asked the operator.

"Yes," replied I; "and I will now see what there is for him."

Away I floated through the wild-woods and far over the extensive fields, and presently returned with —

"Good! I've found the true agent of relief."

"What is it?" — "What is it?" shouted half the party. "Why,
it'll be the boy's fortune if he makes a cure!"

"Yes, what is it, Jackson?" inquired the animated magnetizer.

"He must get," I replied, "he must catch thirty-two weasels."

"Hey?" screamed the deafened patient — who had heard just
enough to be shocked and alarmed — "catch what?"

"Thirty-two weasels," I repeated, and then continued: "take
off their hind legs at the middle joint, and boil out *that oil* which
Nature has deposited in the feet and the parts adjacent thereto;
and this preparation, being an oleaginous and penetrative liquid,
must be dropped (one drop at a time) in each ear, twice a day,
till the whole is gone — when you will be nearly cured!"

" Reediculous !" exclaimed a feminine member, almost over-whelmed with a flood of silk and satin upon her refined person; " perfectly reediculous ! And how disgusting, too ! Bah ! wea-sels' feet ! But — I wonder if he can tell what ails me ?"

" Wait a little, madam," the operator politely suggested, " till I ask a few questions. Jackson," he continued, " do you really mean to prescribe weasels' oil for this gentleman's deafness ?"

" Yes," said I, " there's nothing else so sure to help him."

" Nothing else !" muttered the half-disgusted patient, " then I'll remain as I am."

After two or three more examinations we departed, leaving the elderly gentleman more prejudiced than we found him. But to you, considerate reader, I can whisper some good reasons to support that singular prescription. They are these : There was just pen-etrative oil enough in the specified number of weasels to make *relief* certain; and besides, these creatures' feet contain an oily secretion, soft and searching, unlike that of any other living thing, and much better for the purpose contemplated than that of any known tree, herb, or other American vegetable. All this I fully comprehended in my clairvoyance at the time, but I uttered no word in self-justification.

The skeptical villagers soon set the weasel-story into successful locomotion. It travelled like the " something black as a crow," until the whole gossiping side of the community was overrun with imaginary weasels; which excitement, however, ultimately sub-sided into a profound belief that Mr. Levingston was " a humbug," and that I voluntarily helped him for a moderate salary.

About this time, too, there was circulated a horrifying story, purporting to emanate from my clairvoyant state, that on a certain day all the northwestern portion of the village would sink — be swallowed up by the prodigious mouth of a hungering and thirst-ing earthquake — and that all the inhabitants thereof, especially disbelievers, would disappear down the same yawning chasm, and

never be heard of more! But the monstrosity of this wholly un
truthful report ere long put the extinguisher upon it.

Another, however, soon followed. It was this: that the well-
water everywhere in the village had suddenly imbibed from the
earth a deadly poison, which could be separated from the fluid
only by straining the water through *red* flannel. Believers went
straightway and purchased the crimsoned substance. One merchant affirmed that, in one day, he sold a great number of yards
of *red* flannel expressly for strainers! But the skeptics laughed,
used the well-water without filtering, and didn't feel the first
symptom of being poisoned. Hence they "knew 'twas all a
humbug," and wondered how people could be so deceived.

But, sick of these silly slanders, I turn once more to you, fraternal reader, to whisper a word of explanation. It was true, I did discover some unwholesome properties in a tumbler of water brought
from the operator's well, and I did admonish the family not to
drink or cook with it unless it was properly filtered. My suggestions were followed. A piece of red flannel was employed for the
purpose, without attaching any importance to the color; and from
this trifling circumstance alone flowed a big river of scandalous
rumors detrimental to clairvoyance.

CHAPTER XXXVI.

"I see the light, and I hear the sound;
   I'll sail on the flood of the tempest dark,
With the calm within and the light around
   Which makes night day."

In stillness deep and deepening I pursued my lonely way.
Outwardly the spirit of spring was rife with beauty, glee, and
glory. The sky was all blushes, the earth was bespangled with
budding flowers, and the sun smiled down upon the habitations of
men. But I, though a mere youth, did not share in the cheer and
chime of the season. Solitary and sad walked I down toward the
valley — which separated Mount Use from Mount Justice — and
there was dwelling there no familiar heart to calm and comfort.
The azure concave of heaven was too cold and too far off; the rose-
mingled skies of the upper realm gave me no solace, no message of
peace; the holy glistening stars of night looked kindly down, but
from too lofty places; the beauteous birds laughed and chirped and
twittered with far too much levity; the greetings and gabblings
of the young men and acquaintances were too thoughtless and
insincere — in short, I was not in accord with anything without or
within, save this: a prayer to know my doom, to have the doubt,
and gloom, and agony of my young soul, either dispelled or fixed
as the penalty of my unresisted enchantment.

The subjective effects of my initiatory vision began to be fully
realized. Remembering nothing when awake, of what I had

..n or said in my mystic slumber, I was deprived of nearly every rational source of strength. Had I retained but a thousandth part of the truth, the beauty, the sublimity, the consistency, or the prospective usefulness which I saw and comprehended while in clairvoyance, there could have been no drear, no gloom, no empty-mindedness, such as I now painfully experienced, but my pilgrimage would have led away through fields of golden light and normal understanding.

One effect of the sheep-and-shepherd vision was, the cleansing of my brain of what little information I had absorbed from contact with my mother and the world. In my mind I felt as if some practical *housecleaner* had hoed, and scraped, and scrubbed, and swept everything out! Whatever of intellectual furniture — of thought, of opinion, of belief, of doubt, of proclivity — I had before was utterly gone! Hence my soul felt not only extremely *small*, but that what little space I had in it was empty — unoccupied, but very clean and white, like the "rose just washed by the shower," as in the juvenile ditty delineated. No mind ever felt more destitute of sense. The surface of no idle river ever looked more idiotically calm. No book was ever more deficient in thought-substance. No sheet of cream-laid paper was ever more blank, unscribbled, or unblemished. Such was the first psychical or subjective effect of that marvellous vision — a result which became more and more definite in my inner consciousness as the weeks rolled away.

Another effect of that experience — the outlines of which had by this time faded and vanished out of memory — was, a panic-like conviction that I had *lost or forgotten something*, without which I could not get along on the path of life! This singular oblivion hung like a pearly but impervious night-veil between my feeling and the fact out of which it sprung and to which it pointed. Dreamily, drearily, wearily, walked I down toward the valley that skirted the future mountain. Now and then, it is true, a shadowy hope lit up the empty cells of my understanding. "But I guess

I do n't know nothing," thought I; "and that are 's jest what I b'lieve too." After trying to reason a moment I added: "No! there 's one thing I b'lieve — that folks is right when they ses I 'm makin' a fool o' myself. But I won't though! I 'll go right straight back to Ira Armstrong's, and let this 'ere confounded sleepy business go to grass."

My spiritual depression was rapidly becoming unbearable. Impatience, and almost anger, disturbed my interior nature; and, not knowing *what I had lost or forgotten*, if anything, I concealed my condition from the operator. One night, on being freed from the magnetic power, I ran up-stairs, flung myself down by the bedside, and burst out into the following supplication :—

"Oh, kind Providence who art in Heaven, I thank thee that I live; but, as I now feel, I do n't know whether I 'm right or wrong. Oh, kind Providence, let me know what I have *lost or forgotten!*" At this moment I seemed to remember, vaguely, that I had lost a walking-stick — a sort of cane — which some kind stranger had given me weeks previous, but I could not recall the circumstance, and so my haunted soul was once more filled with silence and gloom. Then I continued: "Oh, good Providence, of whom my mother used to tell me, I will be very much obliged if you will show me what is right."

There was a quick flash of light! Alarmed, I glanced around the room. Nothing but a faint star-light relieved the intense darkness. Again I bowed my head and again the dazzling flash! I looked, and beheld an oblique line of light — *an exact image of the cane shown and given me by Galen!* Instantly my memory returned! I perfectly knew the beautiful gift, and reached forth my hand to receive it. 'T was gone! Darkness was again there, and, in my mind, a feeling of unsuppressed displeasure.

Time passed — perhaps half an hour — ere I ventured again to supplicate: "Forgive my hastiness, my momentary anger, kind Providence; but do grant, I pray thee, that I may get and keep that beautiful cane!"

Another flash of golden light shot through the abounding darkness, and, looking up, I beheld a strange, transparent sheet of whiteness, on which was painted glowing words that seemed to burn and beam and brighten amid the silent air. I was not frightened, but charmed! Calmly I read the radiant words:—

"Behold!

HERE IS THY MAGIC STAFF:

UNDER ALL CIRCUMSTANCES KEEP AN EVEN MIND.

Take it, Try it, Walk with it,

Talk with it, Lean on it, Believe on it,

For ever."

Over and over again read I those glowing, glittering, transplendent words of wondrous significance. But a doubt seized me, and I asked: "Is that longest sentence my Magic Staff—'*Under all circumstances keep an even mind*'—is that my cane, which I thought I had lost or forgotten?" In a twinkling the sheet of whiteness vanished, and in its place was beautifully beaming forth the reply—"YES." 'T was enough! My soul swelled with thanksgivings! "The Magic Staff, then, is no fiction," I joyfully thought; "the secret is to take it, try it, walk with it, talk with it, lean on it, believe on it, for ever." Yes, friendly reader, I seized this mental cane—the magic staff—and ran down-stairs, went out in the open air, walked the streets, returned to my bed, lay down with it by my side, arose with it in the morn, ate breakfast with it, examined the sick with it, leaned on it whenever things went wrong, believed on it at all times, and thus trudged I along down toward the intervening valley.

There happened about this time, in the midsummer of 1844, an event of trifling importance; but I will relate it on the conviction that no other circumstance can so well illustrate my mental *status*, physical temperament, and deficient education.

In accordance with the established programme, our medical examinations occurred at regular intervals during the day. Between these sessions I usually occupied my spare time in walking or visiting some friendly neighbor. One day, during my absence, a young lady, an acquaintance of the operator's family, left a bouquet and her compliments for me! On my return both were presented. The beautiful flowers I enjoyed very well, but what to do with the "compliments" I did n't know. At length, however, I concluded 't was all right, and so let the affair pass without further attention.

But two days afterward I received more flowers and more compliments; and what was yet more shocking, a cunning little note, concealed in the bouquet, asking me to take a walk *with her* that very afternoon! "Now," thought I, "now 's the time to lean on my Staff." The invitation was very modest, and very prettily worded, but I could n't think of accepting it! Consequently I hastened up-stairs, penciled off a brief note of excuse, delivered it in person, and returned just as fast as I could. How glad I was that she did n't see me at the door!

Another bunch of garden roses, interspersed with geranium leaves, was next day left on the mantlepiece for me, with more verbal compliments, and another note embodying a similar invitation! My blushing suddenly attracted a visiter's attention, who, being an acquaintance, said: "Davis, you 're the greenest chap I ever saw!"

"Why so?" I asked.

"Why, there 's a pretty girl in love with you," said he, "and you 're so verdant you do n't know it."

"In love with me!" exclaimed I, astonished and confused. "What businesss has she to get in love with me, I 'd like to know?"

"Why," replied he laughing, "she thinks you 're a fine, smart, good-looking young fellow."

"Well," said I earnestly, "she must be made to know that I

wants nothin' to do with gettin' in love, nor I won't nuther."
Here I leaned firmly on my Staff and mentally continued; "Why,
I ca'n't think of marrying! If there's anything I do n't want to
do it's *that*. Why, I've coaxed mother more'n twenty times
never to let me get married. I do n't like the girls — they act so
foolish, and giggle, and simper, and sly-about so — I ca'n't like 'em
any how!"

That night, however, brought me another sweet epistolary
appeal from the fair one — calling me unfeeling and unsocial —
gently requesting me not to sleep myself to death — advising me
to attend church and get religion — and, lastly, urging me to visit
her at my earliest convenient opportunity. And, in order to wind
the chain of affection still more closely around my heart, she concluded with a few very original lines about joy, love, hearts,
friendship, bees, hot weather, sweet briers, honeysuckles, trailing
willows, &c., &c., all of which I read and studied over several
times. Finally I tried very hard to indite an answer to the best
of my poetic ability. Persistently I scribbled and scrawled away,
and, 't was only after I began to ache with fatigue in almost every
joint, that I succeeded in composing the following extraordinary
reply :—

" dear miss ——

"I got your pretty letter
and read it every word
Your poetry makes me better
i feel just like A bird.

"But my heart hain't reddy
to go beyund my keeping
And my feelins is too heddy
and my business is a sleeping.

"So i hope youl excuse me
For not going a walking
and i trust you won't abuse me
if I stop our futer talking."

After this poetic effusion, which is literally transcribed, I had
no further trouble from that side of human nature.

But my Staff was of the greatest benefit; in truth, it was my invisible palladium — my two-edged weapon of defence. Every day would bring to light some fresh business embarrassment, or some new and difficult test of clairvoyance, or some groundless but perplexing story of injuries wrought by our practice, and so on to the end of the chapter; but, amid all, my Staff was my private strength, my rod of support, my unbending consolation.

One day we were visited by a grim-visaged money-digger — a believer in fortune-telling, signs, omens, &c., who insisted in using clairvoyance for his material benefit. But, on this occasion, as when assailed by other and similar temptations, I relied solely upon my Magic Staff, and my escape under all these circumstances was sure and speedy. There was within me an unconquerable repugnance to all Yankee speculatism and money-getting operations generally. My unutterable dread of them — I will not say hatred — repelled me from every one who dug for, grasped at, or clutched after, " the root of all evil." In this particular I was quite the opposite, in fact, from many who solicited my services. At times, however, I had more agreeable visitors, who, notwithstanding, sought for information quite as much out of harmony with our programme. From many instances of this latter sort, I will cull one which (preserving in part the phraseology of a friend to whom I related it) may interest the psychological investigator.

A fine-looking, portly, well-dressed, old English gentleman came a number of times to Poughkeepsie, and wished me to look clairvoyantly at something regarding which he was seeking information; but for a considerable length of time we had so many calls on our medical attention, and so many engagements with the sick, that I found it impossible to gratify him.

One day, however, just as I was coming out of the mystic condition, the same gentleman, who called himself Dr. Maryatt, entered our apartment. As on other visits, he had brought an egg-shaped white crystal, into which he requested me to look, and tell him what I saw. "The observation," said he, "should be made in a dark room." Accordingly, I took the crystal into the garret, which was the darkest place in the house, and sat down with it at the head of the stairs; and, though I looked at it intensely for some time, I saw nothing. Presently, however, shadows seemed passing off like the clearing up of clouds from a landscape, and then the crystal began to brighten up beautifully. Soon after, it became so very bright that I was alarmed, and went precipitately down.

Dr. Maryatt, however, assured me that no danger would occur; so I went back, and renewed my observations. The same changes which I had first observed again took place, and, when the light began to soften, I perceived a landscape. It was a side-hill, rising out of a ploughed field, and there were several trees. Two men were standing under the trees, one of them in the common English dress, and the other in a sailor's garb. Having seen this, I felt considerably agitated, and again went down.

The dignified doctor said it was very satisfactory. But he asked me to go once more, and look at the right of the hill-side. Presently, I did so; and soon found a stone-house developing itself in that direction, emerging, as it were, from the clouds in that portion of the crystal. Next I saw what was in the house, and then described people and furniture. One more observation, and I discovered a paper under one of the roof-plates. As it looked brighter than anything else, I thought it must be important. It was covered with dust and spiders' webs, and seemed to have been long neglected, if not absolutely forgotten, by the inmates of the house.

On making this report, the doctor expressed great satisfaction, saying, "that was the very thing which he wanted;" but he asked me "to go back again, and see if I could discover what the paper was." Then I went again, and reported that it was "a deed." But just at that moment I saw a copy of the instrument burned under the trees.

It seemed to me that the man who had burned the copy of the

deed was a distant heir, but had no fraudulent intention in doing so Plain enough I could see that he was dressed in the old English style, and was more than six feet high. He had thought the family-heirs resided in Germany. The Maryatt family, then living in the house, did not know the value of the paper, and that was the reason it came to be thrown away and destroyed so carelessly. All these points, as seen and explained by myself, proved perfectly correct.

The foregoing account explains the fact, known to many, that some temperaments, by looking on or into a stone, mirror, or crystal, have the power of seeing certain representations connected with the inquirer, and thus of describing the past, or foretelling the future, which is commonly known as fortune-telling; and notwithstanding the probability that many gipsey-like persons, who pretend to these occult arts, are impostors; yet there are multitudes of facts which clearly and incontrovertibly prove that some individuals really do possess this gift.

But when I made the examination, I had never heard of anything of this kind. In fact, for some four or five years, this circumstance seemed to me unaccountable on any principle of prevision with which I was acquainted. At length, however, I resolved to examine the *cause* of my vision in the crystal. And then, for the first time, it occurred to me that my gazing into it, with so much characteristic earnestness, had induced, temporarily, the state of conscious clairvoyance, which had enabled me first to see the landscape, house, paper, &c., and then, by simple concentration of thought, produced a miniature reflection of them in the glass before me. Since then, I have met several persons, especially very light or very black-haired females — who are most susceptible — who, by virtue of long and concentrated gazing at an object, glide, without going into sleep, into a state of conscious clairvoyance, which, in the early chapters of this volume, I have denominated spontaneous somnambulism.

In regard to the origin and history of the magic crystal, I have ascertained but little; indeed, I have felt no interest in it, and the foregoing was my first and last experiment; but I, somehow, entertain an impression that it, or something corresponding thereto was invented by a physician of Scotland more than a century ago

"The magic crystal," says Dr. Gregory, "is generally a round or oval-shaped piece of clear glass. Several exist, and one is now in my hands, which were made long ago, and used for the purpose of divination, as in the case of the crystal of Dr. Dee. It is said that Dr. Dee's crystal is still extant, and, according to some, it was a polished mass of jet; but it does not appear that the nature of the substance is of much importance, or rather, it would appear that Dr. Dee had a globe of glass or of rock-crystal, and also a magic mirror, probably the piece of jet alluded to. The essential point is that persons who gaze earnestly on the crystal, often see the figures of absent persons, nay, as in ordinary clairvoyance, of such as are unknown to them. The crystal of which I speak, is of the size and shape of a large turkey's egg, and was sold some years since, by a dealer in curiosities, as an old magic crystal, with a paper containing certain mystical and magical rules for its use."

Having told all I know concerning the crystal, and of the philosophy of the vision which I saw in that of Dr. Maryatt, I will take my staff and continue my walk toward the bottom of the valley.

CHAPTER XXXVII

SPECIAL PROVIDENCES.

> "A traveller through a dusty road
>   Strewed acorns on the lea —
> And one took root, and sprouted up,
>   And grew into a tree."

WITH the advent and bestowal of the Magic Staff came a light-hearted exuberance of feeling, closely approximating to a flippant levity, which, at times, I was not a little ashamed to exhibit. A thoughtless species of juvenile sport, bordering upon that of the clown or buffoon, seemed to bubble fantastically forth, even on solemn and religious occasions, causing me involuntarily to laugh and manifest innocent merriment quite unbecoming to one of my age and respectable surroundings. And yet, strange as it may seem, all this joviality, though natural and spontaneous, was invariably superficial, and never touched that mysterious sub-current of noiseless energy which ever flowed through my spiritual constitution.

One day I was abruptly accosted and severely treated by a ministerial-looking stranger, who affirmed that my occupation was not only "wicked," but that my daily doings and momentary thoughts were being recorded in heaven.

"In heaven!" ejaculated I — "recorded in heaven! What do they want of my doings and thoughts up there?"

"Punishment, young man," he warmly replied; "to award punishment for the bad deeds done in the body."

" Well," said I mirthfully, " the writer of all my language during my medical examinations must have a great mess of hard words to spell out."

" The eternal God of heaven will not be mocked, sir !" he replied, with manifest indignation ; " and, sir, be warned—take heed to your steps—before it's too late !" And his eyes flashed with what farmers would call heat-lightning.

Fortunately the Magic Staff was in my possession, and so I asked : " Does God punish a feller for doing wrong when he thinks he's doing right ?"

" God, sir, has nothing to do with what *you* think—remember that, young man !" replied the loquacious and dogmatic stranger. " His rewards and his punishments are based on his own system of government—not on yours, sir, nor on mortal man's—and you 'll find it out when it's too late, or I 'm mistaken !"

" His own system of government," soliloquized I, with a sudden abstraction, " I wonder what that means—his own system of government !"

In a moment I forgot the presence of the pompous stranger, and, under a trance-like pavilion of emotion, I hastened up-stairs and quickly passed into the somnambulic condition. This relapse was a positive refreshment. It carried me back to my Hyde Park nocturnal experiences, and caused me once again to enjoy that brilliant auroral lucidity of imagination and intellect in which I had painted so beautifully the garden of Eden.

My interior judgment and intuitions were bright and clear as the cloudless sky of the upper realm ; my melodious thoughts flew hither and thither like flocks of carrier-doves ; and hence I was made ready for the examination and appreciation of some profound subject.

" The government of God," exclaimed I ; " that's the question !" And so it was ! Reverently, and with every emotion stilled like the hush of evening, I besought some knowledge of the system of Divine rewards and punishments. What I saw I will not here relate. But next day, vaguely recalling the outlines of my systematic meditations, I wrote them down. While engaged in this employment, my door was opened, and in stepped my confidential friend A. R. Bartlett, who, seeing me pen in hand and cap on head, said jocosely: "Ah! you're quite a good-looking student. What's your subject?"

"The government of God," said I gravely.

"Indeed!" returned he. "That's a good subject. Got any thing written on it?"

"Yes, Brother Bartlett," I answered, "I have a few pages which I'd like to read to you."

"That's good," said he, smiling at my uncommon thoughtfulness. "Read away; I want much to hear it."

So I read over what I had remembered and written; to which he replied: "That's very good. The subject is important, and you have treated it well, very well. Why, Brother Davis, if you keep on in that way, you'll become a good thinker."

But, three days subsequently, I verily believe that I could neither recollect nor connect twenty words of what I had read to my friend; and had I not recorded them at the time, I think my mind would have obtained but little benefit from that hour of intuitional illumination.

In order to give the reader some idea of my moderate ambition —to show that, while, in my natural state, I felt no anticipations nor aspirations after fame—I will record the following little circumstance :—

I purchased a two-dollar accordeon. The inconsiderate enemies of clairvoyant revealments have asserted that my spare time was devoted to the studying of books. But I think the unfriendly neighbors who, day after day, heard the *drawling discordances* of my accordeon, would be willing to take a solemn oath to the contrary! The fact was, that, without the use of notes, but aided solely by my uncultivated love of musical accords, I meant to learn to perform on the instrument. What for? Candidly this I knew of my extreme poverty; of my very deficient education, of my dependent condition, without a trade or other reliable means of support; and I was not certain that my clairvoyance might not fail me any day, or I be so unfortunate as to lose my eyesight, or my hearing, or my limbs, by some unforeseen accident or disease · and hence, as a precautionary measure, I concluded to employ my spare hours, between the magnetic sessions, in perfecting myself on the accordeon. "Who knows," thought I mournfully, "but I may be obliged some time to depend on this instrument for a few crusts of bread? Who knows but I may become a blind accordeon-player in the streets of some unknown city? Who knows but in years to come I may be compelled to repeat those plaintive words I heard at school:—

> "'Pity the sorrows of a poor old man,
> Whose trembling limbs have borne him to your door,
> Whose days are dwindled to the shortest span :
> Oh, give relief, and Heaven will bless your store!'"

The wizard-mystery that still hung over my daily occupation, and the occasional feeling of uncertainty as to its continuance and actual value, served to dampen that aspiration which is natural to youth; and, but for my strong Staff, I think my dreamy and unambitious mind would have led me back to resume the trade of Ira Armstrong.

"Day unto day uttereth speech, and night unto night showeth knowledge." Like imperceptibly was woven a golden weft of sympathetic interest which brought me numerous intelligent admirers — persons of high and low degree, who valued my rare gift, and extolled in unmeasured terms the good I was doing — yet, spiritually, I remained unmoved and stoically dispassionate. No pride inflamed my spirit; no vanity; no ambition for distinction; no love of power; no desire for wealth; no aspiration to know the secrets of cloister, school, or college; no sensations of vaunting self-importance, ever disturbed the unseen current of my soul. On the contrary, from hour to hour, from day to day, from week to week, I lived and travelled on — even without in any manner realizing that I was taking a single progressive step — toward the very bottom of the psychological valley.

Now I puffed and blowed (or played) on my asthmatic accordeon; and then my young flesh would become benumbed by the operator, and my spirit examine the present or absent sick. Awakened, out I would go to get a breath of fresh air; and then return to the instrument with which I might one day possibly earn a livelihood. Thus for months dwelt I in the psychical valley — where a gray haze pervaded and bedimmed every intellectual object, giving a neutral and doubtful appearance to my immediate future — and yet, I was even then at the base of another mountain, still invisible, but toward the summit of which I was steadily and unconsciously wending my way.

Several patients were undergoing examination when a gentleman entered as an invited observer. This was Rev. Gibson Smith — then occupying my friend Bartlett's former position in the pulpit — a very decided skeptic concerning the professions of clairvoyance. An interest was soon awakened in him, however, almost amounting to conviction; and, being somewhat diseased, he requested an examination of his own condition. This was given, and he said: "That's perfectly satisfactory."

This man was possessed of a positive, decided, up-and-down, uncompromising, mental organization, which he wished me to examine and report. I did so, while blindfolded and clairvoyant, and he said: "The truth is irresistible, and I'm compelled to believe it."

Having got along thus far in the new faith, he said: "That there is something in Mesmerism I can not doubt. When the animal heat is withdrawn from flies, toads, serpents, bears, &c., why of course they go to sleep, and sleep all winter too, and wake up all right in the spring. Now," said he, addressing himself to me, " can you tell me what's the difference?"

At this interrogatory my mind became wonderfully lucid, and I promised to give him three or four lectures on the subject. Now this announcement was a new thing. The operator was greatly astonished, while I, privately seeing a benefit therein, was not less delighted.

"But," continued the skeptical gentleman, still addressing himself to me, "while I admit Mesmerism and this thought-reading power of yours, I do n't believe that your mind can travel with any more accuracy than mine does in dreams."

"You do n't, eh!" exclaimed the sanguine operator; "then just try him! Ask him to visit any distant locality, and you 'll get satisfied."

"Well, I will," said the honest investigator. "Jackson, I want you to go some five hundred miles — to New Portland, Maine — and give me a description of the house and family of Mr. ——, who resides in that place."

Obedient to his request, off I sped as the light darts through space, and, within the brief period of ten minutes, returned with a perfect daguerreotype of the premises and occupants!

"That 's true! That 's a fact! That 's just so! No mistake!" were the successive sentences of affirmation and surprise which broke from the now fully converted witness.

"When shall I come for the lectures?" said he. The appointment was made. The operator now restored me to normal consciousness, and told me that I had given notice to lecture. 'T was all unintelligible. That I should attempt anything of the sort now seemed to be the height of absurdity — so completely *unlike* were my two conditions.

At the hour fixed upon, however, the new convert punctually arrived, with paper and pencil, to take down the words which I might utter. All the illuminations and emotions and events and conversations and visions of my clairvoyant history — as will be hereafter explained — are now the unpurchasable property of my every day or external memory, from which repository I can at any time draw data and circumstances as from a well-spring of diligently acquired knowledge. Therefore, as if 't were yesterday, I remember my sudden mental elevation when I began to deliver the promised lectures to the interested amanuensis. Oh, how much I thought I could comprehend! Nature had come so to say, within the circle of my personal understanding. My uprising intuitions were like so many educated and communicating angels. My expanded reason was like the ocean that rolls over the earth, and images forth, meanwhile, the changing phenomena of the bending firmament. But my extravagant exclamations and enthusiastic professions at that moment I will not repeat, because the curious reader may find the record thereof, with my corrections, on page 210, Vol. III., of the "Great Harmonia." Neither will I make further reference to Gibson Smith's testimony, for that, also, may be found, as penned by himself, in Vol. II. of the same series, commencing on the fourteenth page.

"What name will you give to the lectures?" asked the recorder, after I had completed them. "Your explanation of human magnetism *is nearly all new to me*, and I'd like to know what you'd call this novel science?"

Easily as water runs down hill did the appropriate title glide into my mind; and I replied, "Clairmativeness."

"Clair — what?" inquired the operator.

The word was duly repeated, and recorded, and published to the world. But I now wish to correct its orthography. The thought in my mind was this: *the clear production of clairvoyance* — and the term should have been "Clairlativeness," as defined on page 153, in one of my recent volumes, entitled, "The Present Age and Inner Life."

The new mountain was looming up in the distance, dear reader; and, all unconscious of my advancement, I was hourly climbing up its rugged slopes. The imperfect lectures on *clairlativeness* were but steps — seeds scattered along the road — acorns strewed on the lea — but they helped to accelerate and perfect the psychological pilgrimage. But one seed bore a rose — one acorn only produced an oak — dwarfed, yet good and useful of its kind. That is to say, those fragmentary words and imperfect explanations of magnetism and clairvoyance were wrought into a brace of popular discourses. And Mr. Smith, taking it to be his duty to deliver them, went firmly forth.

The operator and I must accompany him. 'T was a new and painful trial for me, the presenting of myself, blushing with timidity and reservation, before a strange and heterogeneous audience; to be put into my mystic slumber amid an impatient and boisterous assembly; and subjected to the pin-prickings, the finger pinchings, the forcep-nippings, and the other physical tortures devised by committees of medical skeptics. Although I had explained the laws of my own mental state, yet was I as ignorant of them as a Hottentot, and knew not what mischief might befall me in presence of the people. Amid all, however, there was in my possession an agent of strength — the Magic Staff — on which I confidingly relied, and by which I was never for a moment betrayed.

The persecuted trio — the lecturer, the operator, and myself — set out for Albany, New York. This side-hill city was the Sebastopol of conservatism. Its chronic indifference to every new discovery — to anything out of the usual routine of mercantile trade or theological tradition — rendered the advent of our allied forces not only an emphatic failure, but also inconveniently expensive. In our dilemma I was thrown into clairvoyance. Advice was freely given: to depart next morning for Danbury, Connecticut. Unmurmuringly we sped away over the Housatonic railroad, toward the specified destination. This was my first ride behind the steam-horse. What I thought about *the speed* I will not stop to indite. The recently-fallen snow was deep along the track, and beautiful Danbury was reached only after a tedious journey. Arrived, the lecturer's bills were posted, proclaiming the novel subject, "Clairmativeness;" and promising the public that experiments would be exhibited.

Night hastened on, the hall was filled to its utmost capacity, and I was seated upon the platform. Oh, that I could have been left to the gratification of my love of solitude! As it was, however, I could but long for the refuge or panoply of my mystic slumber. The usual sleep was readily induced, the excursional tests of clairvoyance were tried, the committee announced their satisfaction, and then followed the restitution of my normal state. Wasn't I glad 'twas over? And didn't I hasten from the hall? At our next lecture and exhibition I was again placed upon the stand; to be tested with reference to the fact of physical insensibility. Among the diagnosticating group, which was selected *viva-voce* by the audience, was a certain officious disciple of Esculapius. His skepticism had provided him with various instruments of torture, some of which he used upon my person, but without disturbing the serenity of my individual consciousness. In fact, I was removed far beyond nervous pain or bodily suffering—so profoundly thorough was my magnetic disenthralment. On preparing for bed that night, a small piece of flesh fell out of my pantaloons, having been instrumentally pinched from the inside of my right limb; and yet, when this cruel experiment was made, I was totally unconscious of the laceration. In justice to the sympathy of the people, it should be related that the doctor, who had committed this unwarrantable outrage, was ere long christened "Pinchers!" The town-boys, imbibing the spirit of the general disapprobation, on seeing him, hooted "Pinchers!" And subsequently, as I was told, the persecution became so intolerably *pinching*, that the professional gentleman left for parts unknown. But, though his extreme test was uncalled for, and the injury he inflicted might have been serious and lasting, yet I cherished none of that hostility manifested toward him by the inhabitants.

The sick came from all directions. Poor, diseased humanity—

aching, groaning, limping, coughing, dying! Our rooms were filled to excess all through the day, and my external life was mainly spent in the unconscious slumber.

About this time Mr. Smith perceived that his services were no longer in demand. The people wanted physical, not intellectual assistance : therefore he turned back to discharge his professional duties. But the Poughkeepsie branch of the sect to which he was then administering, (the Universalists,) being in quest of respectability and popularity, refused to extend as cordially as before the right hand of fellowship. This gave him an opportunity to revise the curious lectures, and prepare them for publication. Perhaps the reader may have seen that strange and really suggestive pamphlet — a fugitive and mongrel production — containing a strong infusion of the editor's own mind — with the fourth and last lecture reported word for word from my clairvoyant utterances — the whole entitled " Clairmativeness, or Human Magnetism, with an Appendix, by Rev. Gibson Smith," who must have been a morally fearless man, a lover of truth and liberty, else the public would never have heard of my simple words, uttered as they quietly were under the protective retirement of the operator's parlor.

Our long list of patients, in both Poughkeepsie and Danbury, caused us to divide our time between the two places — occasionally visiting Bridgeport and contiguous localities — during all of which I continued, externally, to be the same reserved and ignorant youth ; but, silently relying upon my Staff, I walked steadily up the high and rugged mountain. On our first visit at Bridgeport, where many sick were added to our list, I formed the acquaintance of a certain character who will ere long appear in this psychologic drama, but for whom I did not at the time realize any special attachment, as prophetic of the peculiar relations which were soon to subsist between us.

Nothing happened of any psychical interest to the reader until May, 1845, at which time I was sorely assailed by an ardent be liever in Special Providences and the second coming of Christ. The religious encounter came off near the Episcopal cemetery, whither I was leisurely walking for recreation and retirement. The sectarist began by sarcastically pitying me in my perilous entanglements.

"In your benighted and unsanctified condition," said he, "you're at all times in danger of death and the judgment."

"Ain't you in danger of death and the judgment as well as me?" I asked.

"Assuredly I am," he warmly replied, "but I'm one of those who believe on the Lord Jesus Christ."

"Well," said I, "are you safe on that account?"

Disregarding my question, and bristling up with combative zeal, he plunged into a long profession of faith, in substance as follows: "I believe, sir, in Holy Writ, which says that there is to be a second coming of the Messiah. I was taught in my youth to read the Bible, sir, and to believe in a superintending Providence."

"So was I; my mother taught me to believe in an overruling Providence," said I promptly. "And, what's more, I believe that I've heard *the voice* of Providence a good many times since I was a boy."

"No, sir! no, sir! that can't be," interposed he with energetic emphasis; "'twas the devil more likely! Why, sir, the Bible and Jesus Christ both denounce the business you follow. Do you know, sir, what the Bible says?—that the Jews were the chosen people of God?"

"Yes, I know that well enough," replied I, with a strong desire to proceed with my ramble unmolested.

"Oh, you do, eh?" he sharply returned; "then, sir, let me tell you that the Jews were led out of the wilderness to the promised land, but, while on the journey, it was their duty to overcome and exterminate the inhabitants of that country."

"What good did all that do?" I asked.

"What good, sir?" exclaimed he, with rapidly-increasing warmth,

"I'll tell you, sir! The extermination of the heathen, sir, was a providential way of promoting the cause of Christianity and civilization."

"Is the act of murder an evil?" I asked.

"Certainly, 't is wrong to destroy human life."

"Then," said I, "does God do evil that good may come?" As I spoke, I felt a flash of mental illumination which momentarily excited my intellectual organs, and I continued: "Doesn't God inculcate a different doctrine?"

"Aha!" said he, with a contemptuous sneer, "I thought you didn't know anything unless you're asleep. But I'll expose you!"

"Please answer my question," quietly solicited I.

"Oh yes, sir, I will. The government of God is in his own hands. He can change it when he adjudges necessary, and none can stay his hand. Thus, when he wills so to do, he strikes wicked men down in the street; sends bitter, biting frosts to destroy the fruit of ungodly farmers; fills the land with lice and locusts; makes wars on disobedient races of men; stops the sun in its course; turns the heavens into an oven of consuming fire; and unconverted souls he sends into everlasting misery."

"Are you very sure?" I inquired.

"Holy Writ," he answered, "is God's own word, sir; and that says that he has done so in all ages of the world. And now, sir, I believe that the end of all things is near, even at the very door; and my counsel to such as you, sir, is this: Give up your sleepy occupation, go back to your former business, keep the sabbath-day, and prepare for the awful conflagration."

"What conflagration?" I asked, with great astonishment.

"Why, sir, the end of the world—the second coming of the Messiah—the end of all things, as foretold in Holy Writ!"

"Oh, yes, I understand you now," said I, "and I will promise to think of it."

"Will you?" replied he, mellowing down into a beseeching

mood: " will you think of it?   Do so, my friend, do so — without
delay — and may the Lord of heaven help you !"

During all this conversation I depended on the strength of my
Staff, and it bent not; neither did I fear that it would break under
even a much greater pressure.   But when the nervous and zeal-
ous preacher passed on his way, and I had gained the still retreat
of the burying-ground — through the sequestered paths whereof I
walked in deepest meditation — then the Staff was well-nigh neg
lected, and my mental affliction became exceedingly intense.

For many subsequent days my mind was painfully exercised on
the solemn subject which the severe and persistent sectarist had
forced upon my attention.   The world-wide interesting problem,
*Whether there had been, or were now, supernatural interpositions
among men, for the purpose of changing, reversing, or regulating
human affairs and designs,* was agitating my spirit almost continually ; and I well remember the circumstances which attended its
final examination and settlement.   And let me here express —
which I can not but feel — the wish that every inquiring mind
could be enriched with a similar revelation.   I know, to the depths
of my soul, that it would emancipate the individual from the slavery
of ignorance, superstition, and bigotry.

It was the last day of the beautiful month of June when I received an authoritative impression, from the interior life, to ascend
the summit of a high but familiar mountain.   My native village
(by adoption) was visible at a distance on the opposite side of the
river.   This mountain was my usual retreat; nothing was there
to disturb — but all outer things, the solitude, the stillness only
broken by the song of birds, and the scenery, were conducive to
spiritual development, elevation, and vision.   Upon this mount,
and at this time, my spirit, in its accustomed manner, was enabled
to subdue and subordinate the body to itself, and my interior principles of perception were opened, and were permitted their easy
and natural exercise.

The problem rested upon me with the weight of a mountain

But what I then and there witnessed I will not here repeat. The reader can find it entire in my pamphlet entitled " The Philosophy of Special Providences." Strange as it may seem to thee, dispassionate reader, yet it is true that, for five days after that vision, I was a believer — an ignorant, miserable, inconsolable believer — in a Divine Providence of changeful and fantastic manœuvres and manifestations. My unreasoning conviction was so entire, that I would not have been surprised to hear the thundering blasts of that awful trumpet which was to awake millions to everlasting happiness, and many more millions to everlasting misery! And I trembled lest I had from earliest youth been made the dupe of some destroying angel; lest *that mysterious voice* which had so frequently soothed my troubled spirit, was but the trick of some unseen evil genius — the prince of darkness, concerning whose existence I had heard so much. And yet, amid all this mental commotion, the Magic Staff was my support!

At length, as I was walking in the pathless meadows near the village, I resolved to address a prayer to "kind Providence," and invoke his aid in my tribulation. I did so, and that too may be found in the pamphlet heretofore specified. Immediately upon concluding my earnest petition, I experienced, throughout my entire system, the evidences of coming vision. As soon as my clairvoyance was perfect, there came unto me a glorious presence — an ultra-terrestrial being — very beautiful and tender-looking — *whose voice was the same that I had heard in moments of trial since my boyhood!* 'Twas like my mother's — only sweeter and more musical. What a divine revelation! Quick and luminous as the lightning's flash was the talismanic gleam that cleaved the overhanging shadows of my past pilgrimage. The whole of my preceding history was opened up and explained. I had not been dreaming — the voice was no imagination — the personage was no baseless fabrication — no! no! no! Half-overcome with an exalted joy, I still leaned on my Staff, and listened to the angel-voice and celestial wisdom of my glorious Guide. His sublime

utterances I have written out in the above-named publication
Hence, in this book, I will but reiterate the fact that my spirit
was lifted triumphantly out of all doubt on the subject of Special
Providences.

As I pursued my walk homeward, my heart was filled with
happiness and contentment.   The night had come on, and it was
dark to the physical eyes.   But the sunlight of an Infinite and
Eternal Day shone brightly through the now-unfolded portions of
my immortal soul; and, by that Light which knows no darkness,
I had learned not to *fear* but to LOVE the Supreme Principle!

But, alas! the feebleness of my young body and the unmatured
faculties of my mind deprived me of the blessed memory when not
in clairvoyance — so impenetrable was the curtain of forgetfulness
that hung between my two conditions.   And hence, though I felt
a peaceful tranquillity in reference to the exciting topic, yet I
could not give, in my daily walk, a single reason for the faith
within me!

CHAPTER XXXVIII.

STRUGGLE FOR THE SECOND EMINENCE.

> "Ah ! to the stranger-soul when first it peeps
> From its new tenement, and looks abroad
> For happiness and sympathy, how stern
> And desolate a tract is this wide world !"

THE beautiful naturalness of events about to be written, can be appreciated only by reviewing a few weeks and thus obtaining the advantage of a background. The charm of a landscape, for example, depends chiefly on the relative position of the spectator. The enchantment of distance is never to be rejected. No intelligent artist ever walks into the depths of a wilderness to see a forest, nor puts he his head under "the sad sea wave" to behold the grandeur of an ocean scene. In like manner, the intelligent reader who would perceive consistency and beauty in this psychological history, should withdraw occasionally from the vicinity of its items and survey the whole surface with the eye of a generalizing mind.

Previous to the experiences chronicled at the end of the last chapter—during one of our professional visits at Bridgeport, Connecticut—I distinctly foresaw, while in a lucid condition, a new and higher psychical programme. The mysterious burthen of a forthcoming employment I had vaguely anticipated and announced some months prior to this date, (May, 1845,) but owing to my now greater mental advancement and comprehensiveness of vision, I could contemplate the new territory, calmly, like some aged man well acquainted with the labyrinthine paths of human enterprise.

My prevision related to a series of extraordinary revelations, which I would ere long be prepared to dictate for the present and future benefit of mankind. These novel disclosures were to be in part replies to hundreds of questions put to me by convalescing patients and investigating minds, from the very beginning of my mystical experience. Some of these interrogatories were curious, entertaining, and important. An intellectual patient, for example, having been satisfactorily examined, would beg the privilege of asking such verbal or mental questions as these :—

" Can you tell me what constitutes the soul ?" or, " Is man's spirit immortal ?" or " Is man a free agent ?" " Is God a person, or an essence ?" " What is life ?" " How did the earth become populated ?" " What is the main purpose of man's creation ?" " Is the Bible all true, or in part only ?" " If man lives hereafter, where is the locality to which he goes on leaving the body ?" " Was Jesus Christ the Son of God, or God himself ?" " Can you tell me what is meant by the word hell ?" " Is there a literal place of suffering ?" " Is the devil a person or a principle ?" " What do you understand by the term Holy Ghost ?" &c., &c. And to all such queries my invariable answer was — " Be patient ! I shall some day know just how to give your mind ample satisfaction. When that time arrives, as it surely will, then I shall dictate a Book, which will contain my answers to your interrogatories. Be patient ! I can not examine anything but diseases yet."

Thus from day to day, through all the time I spent with Mr. Levingston, did I repel every attempt to divert my mind from the original programme. In short, if the exact truth be told, I had not yet reached the perfectly independent state. (See the diagram of the different stages of magnetism, p. 205.) My general condition was considerably mixed ; and my mind was but partially liberated. This fact I did not know till the first of July following at which time it began to dawn upon my understanding.

This dawning was characterized by certain conspicuous evidences or premonitions. One indication was, the intermittent nature of my clairvoyant vision — accompanied with a partial suspension of my original capacity to endure the trance. The period of my magnetic sleep was consequently shortened or variable; and the feeling and lucidity of my mind partook largely of the approaching change.

These unmistakable irregularities or fluctuations privately disturbed the semi-habitual equanimity of my spirit. I grew sad and dissatisfied, without any obvious reason, and this reacted upon the operator. One day he asked me " to explain the cause of my restlessness or discontent."

"I can't tell," said I with undisguised emotion. "Perhaps your magnetism is n't good for me any more."

"Ah!" exclaimed he sorrowfully, "I thought 't would be so."

"That what would be so?" I asked.

"Why, that some of these new acquaintances would prejudice your mind against me. Yes, I see how it is. They wish to get you under their influence."

Now I am free to confess that this unqualified avowal surprised and disconcerted me; and, but for my Magic Staff, I think I should have walked angrily out of his presence. It was a reflection upon my unshaken friendship for him, and so I replied. "No, sir! you are entirely mistaken. It is true that I have been offered large sums to leave Poughkeepsie and go westward, but none of our friends or acquaintances have ever tried to break up our relation."

"I 'm very glad to hear it," said he; "for it would be a pity to do anything to prevent the delivery of *that Book* you have so often promised."

To this I made no reply; but looked downcast and thoughtful. Seeing which he proposed to give me a larger proportion of our insignificant income, and so forestall all pecuniary temptation which he suspected might be presented by others.

Appreciating his generosity and kindness, and knowing that our average income for months together did not exceed what he used to make at his calling in half the time, I strove to be cheerful once more and to act wholly contented. All went on harmoniously for a short time, save the peculiar variations in my clairvoyant powers, preceded by a heavy magnetic slumber, and occasionally terminating with severe headaches which the operator could neither remove nor mitigate as formerly. These symptoms were for the most part my own private property. To me they were extremely ominous! The shadow of a coming event darkened my horizon. What the future had in store for me I could not discern. Therefore, though walking with and leaning on my Staff, my spirit was painfully disturbed.

In this connection, dear reader, I wish to introduce a new character. Nay! be not shocked. He's quite gentle and won't bite. His name was Richard; but, for short, I called him " Dick;" and the chief companion of my daily walks was he. In form and weight he was remarkably small and light; but, instinctively, he was the biggest and most knowing dog in the village. My fondness for the exclusive society of this little Dick was undisguised. His head-and-tail manifestations of dogmatic delight — on my every return from a professional tour — were strictly honest and gratifying in the extreme.

I introduce him at this juncture, because that *morceau* of the Spirit of Nature which animated his little body, *did certainly perceive the presence of invisible beings* — and that, too, sometimes in advance of my own far more exalted impressibility! And this impulsive and unreasoning animal performed a valuable deed for me at this crisis in my mental affairs, which I shall presently proceed to relate. Allow me parenthetically to remark that, since the advent of the circumstance about to be recorded, I have observed that three breeds of the canine species are particularly susceptible at times to the presence of disembodied personages. The first, is the unadulterated mastiff or house-dog; the second, a cross between the spaniel and the bull-dog; the last, a second remove from the common cur and a fourth from the pointer or bird-dog.

On the particular occasion to which allusion is now made, I was rambling and meditating in a distant field. My spirit was bowed down by the pressure of some unknown responsibility. Hence I walked like one fatigued with the baggage and burden attendant on a long and lonely pilgrimage. The only visible companion of this solitary ramble was my little Dick. His blithesome gambols in the open fields — his gay and graceful springs and bounds for the feathery songsters — could not now divert me. My spirit was prayerful. I lifted up my voice toward heaven for instruction. But no sacred sound reached my ear, and I was about to retrace my steps; when little Dick attracted my attention by divers demonstrations of uneasiness. He doggedly refused to return with me homeward. On the contrary, he whined and snuffed the air, looked frantically upward, howled most piteously, and otherwise pantomimically signified his instinctive conviction that the atmosphere contained something for me. Methought the unreasoning animal was momentarily crazed by his enthusiastic labor to catch the little birds; and so believing, I whistled to him and proceeded a few rods apparently unmindful of his singularly frantic beseechings.

But no! he would not be persuaded; and overcome at length by curiosity and a love of gratifying my pretty favorite, I resisted no longer, but followed to a sequestered spot whither the affectionate creature invited me. "Well, Dick," said I sportively, "what's going on here?" In reply he exhibited his usual testimonials of delight, and went dancing about as if his litttle heart was perfectly happy.

At this moment I felt the presence of my invisible benefactor. This sudden explanation was sufficient, and being at once abstracted, I listened to these musically spoken works: " *Seek—the—mountain! At—four—o'clock. Delay—* not. *A—vision—will—be—shown—thee.*" Breathlessly I waited for one more beautiful word, from the being whose voice was so like my beloved mother's. But all remained still as a July noon, and I departed homeward.

Before the appointed hour I crossed the Hudson, *via* ferryboat, and was waiting in my familiar seat—upon the beautiful Mount—nearly due west of the Poughkeepsie Main-street landing. Gradually I passed into a high clairvoyant exaltation, when lo! there stood my glorious Guide like an angel of light!

"Thou art cast down and sorely troubled," said he soothingly "wouldst thou know the reason?"

"Yes," I replied, "I am oppressed. But I know not why."

" Then, if thou wouldst know wherefore thy spirit is cast down, gaze yonder." Here he pointed above the horizon into the depth of open space, and continued: " In a moment will I picture forth thy past and thy future."

As he spoke, I beheld the vacant space suddenly occupied with a most natural and romantic scene. There was before me in the distance a castle-looking structure, reared in the body of a great mountain. The side of the edifice toward me seemed to have been hewn down and removed, giving a free and natural view of its interior parts and arrangements.

"Behold!" said he affectionately. " That represents the externals of thy mental history."

"Indeed!" exclaimed I. " How cold and desolate! But I can not understand the picture."

"Then," replied he, " direct thy vision into the first and lowest apartment."

I did as he bade me, and lo! I beheld an exact counter-likeness of myself. It represented me in somnambulism. I was walking about in the dark—seeing machinery, painting the garden of Eden, &c.—while my expression was that of simple boyhood.

In this basement story there were several windows, but they looked upon the solid rock, and admitted no light.

"Yes," said I much amused and animated, "that's just exactly true!"

"Then," said he, "direct thy vision into the next and higher apartment."

On lifting my psychological vision to the second story, I saw another perfect representation of my own personality. There I saw myself in the attitude of listening as if to words from unseen speakers. Thus was I reminded of what I had heard in the Hyde-Park cornfield, &c.; and again did I express myself delighted with the perfect pictorial representation. Also, I remarked that the windows of this higher department opened against the blank walls of the mountain, and admitted no ray of natural light.

"Yes," said I, "that's just the state my mind was in during all that period."

"Then," replied he, "direct thy vision into the third and still higher apartment."

Most gladly did I obey his direction. And this view was a great relief. There I saw myself seated before Mr. Levingston, and, though my eyes were closely bandaged, they could discern sunlight streaming through and vivifying the spacious room. Now, the windows opened directly upon wide crevices in the mountain fastness; and the silvery light which poured in through those openings made them seem like loopholes leading the sou out into a broad and sunny landscape.

"The picture is perfect!" shouted I with enthusiasm and grati tude. "Yes! that's just the way of my mind." But while speaking these words of recognition, I felt a sudden sadness — a desire for a vaster range of prospect. Then I said: "Oh, kind Guide! can you tell me why I can not see more of the exquisite landscape beyond?"

"Wouldst thou have a larger vision of this stone-bound house of thine?"

"Oh! yes, yes!" exclaimed I, "that's what I would have next."

"Then," said he, "direct thy vision upward into the last and nighest apartment that thou canst for a season behold."

I looked and again saw myself impersonated. But now I was seated before a man whom I immediately recognised as the recently-formed acquaintance of Bridgeport, Connecticut. Still my bodily eyes were bandaged, but the room was filled with light! It was far, very far above every mountain projection; and the windows, looking out from the circular apartment, opened upon a scene the most effulgent and magnificent!

"What a desirable change!" I fervently ejaculated. "What a delightful prospect! But I fear that can never be!" and, feeling momentarily depressed, I dropped my head, and the vision vanished.

"Why dost thou doubt?" he sweetly inquired.

"Oh, kind Guide!" I replied sorrowfully, "because my present relation is wound round about with very strong ties of sympathy. It is firmly fixed in Mr. Levingston's affections. Besides, if I should withdraw from him, and take another magnetizer before giving the Book, methinks our few and valuable friends would not understand it, and I fear the validity and correctness of my future clairvoyance would everywhere be disputed and denied."

"Fearful, indeed, is thy youthful mind," replied the Guide. "Tell me, if thou canst, which of two human attributes is the highest and the best — Sympathy? or Justice?

This interrogatory made me think long and profoundly, as I supposed, but my soul could not answer it, and I said — "Your question, kind Guide, is too deep for my mind."

Hearing which he smiled benignly and said — "Tell me, if thou canst, which of two conditions of physical matter is most useful and admirable — trees and no ship? or a ship made of trees?"

In a breath I replied: "A ship is most useful and admirable."

"Ah!" he said with the same sweet and tender smile, "thou art a quick scholar. But again; tell me, if thou canst, which of two vessels is the safest in a storm — A ship given to the capri cious winds? or a ship given to the mind of man?"

The utter simplicity of this question excited my mirth and I laughed outright; but looking upon the calm countenance of the Guide, I stilled myself, and replied: "The safest ship is that which is given to the mind of man."

"Verily!" exclaimed he, "thou art getting thy lesson well. Keep it in thy remembrance from day to day. And tell me, if thou canst, which of two human attributes is the most admirable, the safest, the highest, and the best — Sympathy? or Justice?"

As he spoke these words my mind comprehended the meaning and I answered: "Pardon me, O Guide, for not seeing your lesson sooner. The highest and the safest is JUSTICE, and I will remember it."

"That," said he, "is the name of the mountain from the summit of which thy first teachings shall emanate."

Overwhelmed with an appalling sense of a painful labor — that of withdrawing from my kind and clinging operator — I bent forward and looked dejectedly on the earth. In a few minutes I raised my head again to ask another question. But, alas! my beautiful Guide had disappeared. Whereupon, realizing that I was additionally enriched by some golden drops from Wisdom's fountain, and that Justice had been newly enthroned in its own realm within my soul's territory, I relapsed into my common state, and returned to the operator's residence, with a heart full of joy wholly inexpressible.

CHAPTER XXXIX

THE MOUNTAIN OF JUSTICE.

"Ever the truth comes uppermo-t,
   And ever is justice done."

BEFORE retiring that night, only six hours af er the foregoing lesson on the upland height, my memory was unable to recall the particulars of what had transpired. " 'T is too bad," thought I, " to have a useful dream— to discern a beautiful truth —and not have wit enough to remember it." And on the following morning I had well-nigh forgotten the precise reason that led to the circumstance of my crossing the Hudson. Nevertheless, there was a newborn and beautiful strength within— an energy and fearlessness in my organ of justice — which caused me to think of doing whatsoever my conscience might eventually dictate. The seed of change had been secretly planted, and it would grow; the tide of a new river had just set through my being, and it would flow; another sun was designed to brighten my mental world, and it would rise; the Magic Staff had been fixed in the mountain, and the banner of " justice" would be unfurled; and so, although still too feeble-minded to carry in memory the immense wealth of my private providential experiences, there was a certain unintermitting consciousness that gave me a strong heart and a steady will.

Shortly after this we departed on one of our professional trips to Bridgeport. But I did not forget to take my Staff. In conversation with a resident-physician, some of whose patients I had previously examined, I asked, " Can you tell what ails me ?"

" What ails you ?" said he, with evident surprise that I could feel bodily uneasiness like the rest of mankind.

" Yes," said I, " there's something wrong about my state. Whether it's physical or mental I know not."

" Are you not able to examine yourself while in clairvoyance ?" he inquired. " Seems to me you can. ' Physician, heal thyself,' as the good book says."

" No," I answered. " I can't discern my own state of health as I can that of others. 'T would be like lifting one's-self by his ears."

" Does your power of clairvoyance ever seem like fading out ?" he asked.

" I think it has of late," said I. " And that's what makes me feel so unhappy, I guess."

" Does Mr. Levingston's power over you decrease ?"

" No, I think not ; but he can't carry me any higher in clairvoyance ; perhaps, he may not hold me where I am now. I sometimes feel so."

" Indeed !" exclaimed the physician. " If there's anything desirable in this world, it is your power. Why, my dear sir, I'm indebted to you for a faith which I would not exchange for anything I know of."

" Well," said I, " if I go on as I am, my clairvoyant candle will soon be snuffed out. But there's a *change* of some sort at hand."

" Ah !" responded he, " do you think of changing operators ?"

" Not that I know of," said I, gloomily. " But I'm certain there's going to be something different, though I don't know what it is."

" I suppose," returned he, " that you can see who the right person is, if you should have to get a new magnetizer. For myself

I'm free to say that nothing would afford me more gratificatior than practising medicine by the aid of your prescriptions."

"Well, what's before me I can't foretell," I replied. "But should you be *the man* to magnetize me, I shall surely present myself at the proper time."

And thus ended our candid conversation. But from day to day my spiritual discernment faltered and flickered; which fact conduced greatly to the reinstatement of the drooping depression that had weighed me down during the few weeks preceding. Finding it next to impossible to advance with the examination of patients, we (Mr. Levingston and I) departed rather precipitously from Bridgeport, to fulfill our corresponding engagements in Danbury, whither we arrived the same afternoon.

'Twas now about the nineteenth anniversary of my birth-day. The rich and pearly hours dripped their ripeness into harvest-field and meadow. The gracefully twining vines and upspringing affluence of the soil, the soft breathing of garden-flowers, and the musical chorus of delicately-formed insects, imparted manifold pleasures to the susceptible imagination; but such pleasures were not the guests of my bosom; and the congratulation of friends upon the recurrence of my birthday, so grateful always to him who values his existence, fell like dead flowers upon my oppressed and bewildered spirit. Decision of character I had recently acquired; but what to decide upon? *that* was the question. One moment, judging from my contending sensations, I feared the incoming of a protracted illness — the next, I didn't know but duty called me back to Ira Armstrong's. Now, my affections leaned toward the Bridgeport physician — then, they nestled clingingly in the operator's kindly heart. At length, I sought my tower of defence, Solitude. Leaning on my Magic Staff, I interrogated the bending heavens for instruction.

Long and patiently waited I for a few words of comfort. None came. 'Twas a calm and lovely hour, however, and I lingered far from my fellow-men. I watched the effulgent sunbeams as

one by one, they formed the holy temple of the Day. I heard
the wild bee sing its song of labor; and marked the beauteous
robin as it bestowed kindly offices on its young; but these joyous
creatures had no message of wisdom for me. Mine was the poet's
sad song:—

> " I feel like one who treads alone
>   Some banquet-hall deserted ; ·
> Whose lights are fled, whose garlands dead,
>   And all but he departed."

But relief was at hand. In the midst of my meditations a
change came over my spirit. My nature appeared to spring, as
by an instantaneous growth, into unfettered and self-reliant manhood. The cable-like chain of locked arms and fraternal hearts
that bound me to Mr. Levingston, seemed suddenly broken! The
magical spell with which he unintentionally drew me from Ira
Armstrong, was wholly neutralized and dissipated. The luxurious freedom of individual ownership rushed over me like a flood
of heavenly joy. My soul was strong, and free, and wholly my
own. What a marvellous liberation!

On returning to our boarding-place, through the thickening
twilight, I met the operator, who, with a look of unusual anxiety
and impatience, said : " You 're a truant youth, and no mistake.
Several patients have been waiting all day for you. Now they 're
gone. Where have you been so long?"

The glorious news of my unexpected emancipation I did not
reveal; but, planting myself firmly on self-justice, I told him that
my condition demanded a suspension of his magnetism. And then
I intimated that we had better refuse all applications for the present. To this he stoutly objected, as I anticipated he would; but
I as stoutly insisted, and so the matter terminated.

Next morning I was no longer wandering in the fog of doubt.
The horizon of my individual rights and duties was luminous as
with spiritual sunshine; and I walked once more like a being of
independent life and understanding. My very life-blood and

nerve-auric principle had been saturated with magnetism for nearly two years — making me the mere "subject" of another's will — but now my will and my individuality were wholly distinct and self-controlled. But I was still a youth, and too weak to go forward alone. Presently, therefore, I realized a drawing toward the Bridgeport physician. This influence soon became very powerful. And as the needle points to the pole, so followed I this positive attraction. 'T was obedience to a like impulse which, in the first instance, separated me from Ira Armstrong; and now, with the additional luxury of a conscience, I yielded to the same law, and thus permanently severed my relation with William Levingston.

The Bridgeport physician, Dr. S. S. Lyon, received me very fraternally; and when I told him that he was chosen, he manifested unfeigned gratitude. This man's physiognomy was peculiarly marked. The profile outline of his head was pleasingly regular. But his face indicated a mixed temperament — a cross between Aristotle, the philosopher, and a Jersey deacon — being no reliable index to his excellent interior character. He was moderately social, very regardful of others' feelings, fond of children, honorable in his dealings, humane, exceedingly strong in his friendships, orderly in his life, and naturally religious. But the retreating eye, the overhanging brow, the thoughtful cast of his entire face, rendered him to many a closed and sealed book.

Now for another sacrifice. My new operator had, by severe and continuous effort, established himself in business. Those who believed in the virtue of botanic remedies, and knew of the doctor's uniform success, employed him, and his gradually increasing remuneration was equal to, if not greater, than the income likely to accrue from my clairvoyant examinations. But the conviction of duty was upon him. Hence, in obedience to my interior directions, he relinquished his practice; and, together, we proceeded to that immense commercial dépôt of the United States, known as

New York city. Here, as I had previously announced while illuminated, the lectures were to be delivered. His influence was refreshing and liberating. Distinctly, while in the magnetic state, did I perceive the pathway; but as usual, when in the ordinary condition, my mind was limited and benighted.

In the commencement a programme was given, that I should only examine diseases for a certain number of weeks; and then, all things having been got ready, I would begin the long-promised discourses.

Let the reader now glide with me over ten weeks — during which I slept from four to six hours per day — and halt at our private boarding-house, No. 92 Green street, in the great city. It was near the middle of November, 1845. And now, if the psychological investigator wishes to read a very extraordinary illustration of what I term "Missionary Mediumship," which came suddenly upon me at this time, he can turn to page 181 of my work, entitled, "Present Age and Inner Life." There is a romantic and instructive matter hidden within that wonderful experience, which in some future day may be given to the public.

A few days after this, while in clairvoyance, I scanned the immense foreground of my forth-coming work. Of this my recollection at the present time is very perfect. But what I saw in that comprehensive contemplation, belongs properly to the next chapter. The motive for the appointment of witnesses is sufficiently obvious. The motive for selecting the particular person who was chosen as a scribe, may not be equally apparent; and hence, as I can recall the circumstance and the reasons, I will proceed to divulge them.

In reviewing and reflecting upon our prospectus for the ensuing two years, which I could do from my state of mental exaltation — just as a man on a mountain can see more of the country than when in the valley below — I foresaw the necessity of having a scribe who could comprehend the general drift of the lectures, and who, being possessed of a lively conscience, would voluntarily

defend our proceedings from the aspersions of prejudiced and un
scrupulous journalists. In order to find such a man, I looked far
and wide over the population of this country, but saw no one
whose mental qualifications and external circumstances were
alike favorable, save Rev. William Fishbough, of New Haven,
Connecticut. This gentleman I had previously seen in my normal state. But prior to this interior survey of his qualifications,
I had not discovered the slightest tenure of relation between him
and the work about to be commenced. In accordance with my
selection, the doctor wrote Mr. Fishbough, who, notwithstanding
a combination of external impediments, cheerfully accepted the
nomination, and presented himself an hour before the time fixed
upon for the delivery of the first lecture.

My impressions of the scribe's interior character were these:
that his mind was thought-loving, truth-loving, man-loving, God-
loving, Heaven-loving, humility-loving, and moderately ambitious
of personal success and distinction. It seemed to me that he was
careful, cautious, critical, and conscientious; and that in any
laudable literary enterprise his endowments were obtainable and
in the main available. The maternal nature predominated in
him, as I read his organization; and hence I judged that, whatever be his intellectual beliefs, his affections would, in the issue,
invariably overrule them, and thus establish his destiny in the
human universe. Perceiving these traits, and discerning the
favorableness of his outer circumstances, taken in connection with
the peculiar nature and demands of our immediate future, I counselled the soliciting of his aid, which, as already stated, was readily
and cheerfully rendered.

It may be difficult for the reader to keep in remembrance the
vast contrast between my mind illuminated and unilluminated.
The time dividing the two conditions was not longer than " the
step" which is said to separate the sublime from the ridiculous.
Twenty strokes of the doctor's hands would change and promote

me from an ignorant youth to the high elevation of the profound philosopher. Or five minutes devoted to the reverse manipulations, would bring me from the exalted throne of Jupiter down to the common level of an untaught and unremarked dweller of Manhattan isle. If the reader can bear in mind this fact, he will not marvel that, previous to the commencement of my lectures, I fled to my mountain opposite Poughkeepsie for consolation and further enlightenment.

Sadness was upon me once more. Because I could not feel positive, at all times, that my steps were truly and safely taken. It is true, my Staff saved and supported me on many occasions. But I was again beset with doubts on the question of Special Providences; and with fears that I was in some manner duped and led astray. In this over-anxious and distressed mood I stepped on one of the North river steamers, and, reaching once more the consecrated mount, I poured out my soul in a flood of beseeching interrogatories concerning the perplexing subjects by which I was overwhelmed.

My spontaneous illumination, the harmonious exaltation of my faculties, was unusually sweet, and the welcome discoveries of my soul's trackless sweep were graphically grand. Intellectually, I gazed upon the immutable principles that regulate the universe. How easily and gratefully did I drink in these never-to-be-forgotten truths of temporal and eternal existence! But the result of my philosophical examinations, on that occasion, I have already published, in that portion of the pamphlet on "Special Providences," entitled, "The Argument." Hence I will not record it in this volume. The inestimable details of those metaphysical reflections were, as usual, locked up in the treasury of my clairvoyant memory. On returning New-York-ward, however, feeling calm and prepared for the lectures, I kept mentally saying. "Thanks! thanks! thanks!" and nothing more. But now 1 know that the grand effect of that last contemplation was stamped indelibly upon the inner folds of my soul-substance Surely there are · special providences. There are invisible guardian powers. 'Twas by and through their aid, added to my own exertions and the unfailing Staff, that I attained the top of the Mountain of Justice; from which psychical summit, as my Guide informed me, the sublime revelations of Nature were ere long to emanate.

CHAPTER XL.

THE PRINCIPLES OF NATURE.

"I remember the time, ye sun and stars,
    When ye raised my soul from its mortal bars,
    And bore it through heaven in your golden cars!"

HAVING accompanied me thus far, and seen the many and various changes and scenes through which I have passed since birth, methinks the reader will not now turn back. Nay, for a curtain, which has long deprived the spectator of a novel representation, is about to be rolled up.

The locality was No. 92 Greene street, a few doors north of Spring, on the well-known isle of Manhattan. The *dramatis personæ*, or those who sustained the principal distinctive characters in these private theatricals, were Dr. Lyon, Mr. Fishbough, and the writer. The auditorium was occupied with three witnesses, the most prominent and educated of whom was the amiable and quiescent Dr. T. Lea Smith. His gentle mind was suffering with his body at the time; but, besides being my patient, he was a sincere investigator of truth, and a semi-believer in clairvoyance. The novel piece announced to be performed in part on the occasion was entitled "Lectures by A. J. Davis, the Clairvoyant." But it should be kept in remembrance that this announcement was not made public. Only a few persons were privately notified, and invited to witne s the enactment. For the object was not notoriety and money; but, on the contrary, as noiselessly and steadily as dew descends and grass grows, was prosecuted the mutual aim to gain admission into the ever-sacred temple of Truth! Therefore the terms "farce," "comedy," "jugglery," &c. — subsequently used with such evidently malicious intent, by some of the New York journalists, to characterize and caricature that performance — were grossly and ridiculously inapplicable.

If you possess an impressible faculty of imagination, dear reader, now is the time to exercise it legitimately. 'T is by means of this organ alone that you may shut your eyes and recall the features of an absent friend, or enjoy, while sitting by your fireside, the charms of a remembered landscape, or mingle with the peculiarities of some locality and event in the world which your eyes have never seen. Fancy to yourself a small room, furnished with articles convenient for a couple of itinerant gentlemen-boarders, without a library or other evidences of intellectual tastes and pursuits. Picture to yourself a grave-visaged man in the act of manipulating a pale-faced and thin-bodied youth. Also, at the right of this twain, behold a mild-eyed and broad-browed individual, seated in front of a table, on which lie the usual conveniences for writing. And, on either side, fancy three men half-fascinated with the ever-charming process of magnetization. The pleasure of silence is mutually realized. All is still as the sun. And now, as the youth is about to take the principal character, suppose you gaze into his cranium.

In the first place, let us take an inventory of his intellectual stock, and check down each article at its marketable valuation. The circumference of his head is unusually small. If "size is the measure of power," then this youth's mental capacity is unusually limited. His lungs are weak and unexpanded. If "the mind is invigorated in proportion to the capacity of the chest," then this youth's mind must be feeble and circumscribed in its operations. He had not dwelt in the midst of refining influences. If "circumstances mould the character," then this youth's manners must be ungentle and awkward. He has not read a book save one, and that on a very unimportant subject; he knows nothing of grammar or the rules of language; neither has he associated with literary or scientific persons. If "'t is education forms the common mind," then is this youth's intellectual stock too meagre for the literary market.

But see! The grave-visaged operator ties a handkerchief about the youth's uneducated head — closing the world yet more out, and leaving him to his own psychical changes and transformations. Do not turn away your gaze, dear reader, for the mental crisis has just arrived. Behold! the inner folds of his intellectual organs begin to tremble and expand like opening flowers. They emit a soft atmospheric ether, which rapidly saturates the air of the room, and ascends, like the water-spout at sea, toward the heavens. What a delicate column of light! See it arise! — above the house, above the highest steeple, above the loftiest mountain, above the pale moon, above the holy stars, above the reach of telescope, above — away — higher — beyond all elevation, save that of the true soul's aspirations!

Unnatural!" you exclaim. Nay, not so, most worthy friend. Allow me to substitute the term "extraordinary." Surely you do not mean to assert the ascension of life to be *unnatural!* Why, just look into yon field where the oak arises above the soil, above the reach of grass, above the power of prowling brutes, above the freezing depth of wintry snows, above the destroying floods of spring, above the ambition of plebeian forest-trees, above — beyond — higher — than the heads of conceited priests, kings, popes, or emperors! Yea, all life looketh heavenward; and, once disentangled, behold how it hasteneth thither!

Yes! can you not see that radiant shaft of spiral light reaching all the way from the sleeping youth's uneducated head to a Focus of Thought beyond the stars? There! do you see that? An answering shaft descends! His benumbed hands do quiver with a new sensation, and the muscles of his face do vibrate and tremble with the inflowing power.

"Impossible!" Nay, nay, not impossible, dear reader. Why if you will but behold a corresponding exhibition, but one far, very far inferior, then will I show you a well-known phenomenon of the northern seas. Fix your gaze upon the Arctic ocean. Behold the water whirling with a frightful gyration. Now see the ascending column of water forming a junction with the spirally-descending column from the cloud-region above the ocean. See the vortex of foam beneath! See that tremendous marine prodigy—wonderful and impossible to landsmen, but certain and dangerous to the mariner who ploughs with his ship the northern seas. Beholding this distant object, and believing in its actuality, can you doubt your own eyes and your reason when looking upon the head of that magnetized youth? So close at home, too! Have you forgotten the locality? Why, it was in the very centre of New York—I had almost said of civilization—in the nineteenth century!

"Hark! what's that?" inquired the grave-faced operator. The mild-eyed and broad-browed scribe listened. The witnesses were still as pall-bearers.

"This night," replied the youth, with reverent and measured intonations, "I reach my superior condition." (The reader can understand this language by reviewing the magnetic diagrams. The writer attained the fourth stage *for the first time permanently* on the 28th of November, 1845.)

"Can you give the lecture to-night?" asked the doctor who had magnetized the youth.

"To the great centre of intelligence—to the positive sphere of thought—to that Focus which treasures up all the knowledge of human worlds," said the youth calmly—"to the spiritual Sun of the spiritual sphere—I go to receive my information."

"Does he wish to have that written down?" whispered the vigilant scribe.

The doctor repeated the question, and the youth replied, "No, not that." But after a pause he said, "Now I am ready."

The scribe set his chirographical hand in order, and the doctor — who, according to previous direction, was to pronounce aloud after the low-spoken youth, to make sure that each word was correctly heard and written — being also ready, the clairvoyant slowly and without excitement began :—

"Reason is a principle belonging to man alone." This sentence being written, he continued : "The office of the mind is to investigate, search, and explore, the Principles of Nature, and trace physical manifestations in their many and varied ramifications." When those words were duly recorded, the youth — the *same* youth, remember, whose mental stock we have carefully inventoried — proceeded : "Thought, in its proper nature, is uncontrolled. It is free to investigate, and rise into lofty aspirations. The only hope for the amelioration of the world is free thought and unrestricted inquiry. And anything which opposes or tends to obstruct this sublime and lofty principle, is wrong."

Thus, with the occurrence and recurrence of short intervals of extreme abstraction between paragraphs, the first lecture was delivered. And when the youth returned to his ordinary state, all memory of his knowledge had vanished, and he was once more an ignorant and uninteresting person. What was uttered on that and subsequent nights, in the precise manner and style described, the reader can find in the First Part of my volume entitled "Nature's Divine Revelations."

"Incomprehensible!" methinks I hear you incredulously exclaim. Nay, nay, be not so hasty in thy rejection. Here! lean on the Magic Staff awhile, and let me talk to thee, to thine inmost reason, of this rare exhibition. Put aside thy pride and thy learning for a brief period at least, and open the child-part of thy being to this old truth, newly delineated in our quiet room on Greene street. Will you not be calm and philosophical? How skeptical thou art! Is that a proof of thy *strength* of intellect? O conceited intellect! Dost thou not know that my mother *believed too much*, because her intellect was uncultivated? And dost thou not know, also, that thou *believest too little*, because of the same fact — that thy intellect is yet in its infancy?

Well, the marvellous drama was performed. The uneducated youth sustained the principal character, viz., that of a thoroughly-educated philosopher. His part was well conceived, and personated to the entire satisfaction of the audience. And at this moment, after the lapse of many intervening years, his most interior reminiscences occupy my soul. Therefore, I am the most reliable witness, and feel no reluctance in divulging the secret workings of my mind on that and subsequent sessions.

The new and different operator, Dr. Lyon, completely disenthralled my mind from the disturbances of the nervous system. I was therefore more mental, more spiritual, and less physical, than on any previous occasion. Like a biennial plant, my soul flowered out, and presented that rare fruit which had been so long anticipated. Accordingly, added to my clairvoyance, there unrolled from within the Superior Condition.

" What's the difference ?" The difference is the same as between sight *without understanding* and sight crowned with the latter unspeakable advantage and improvement. For example : you *look* at a piece of gold ore or at a pound of gypsum. This sight, without a full understanding of the chemical constituents of what you see, corresponds to clairvoyance. But suppose you both *look at* and *chemically analyze* the ore or gypsum, then you illustrate both clair-voyance and clair-science, or, in other words, interior perception in combination with intellectual understanding, which is the superior condition. Hence it follows that one who is a clairvoyant merely is more or less liable to err and mistake the locality, properties, nature, and relation, of whatever he may thus perceive; while, on the other hand, he who is both clear-seeing and clear-knowing — or who possesses at once the double blessing of *clairvoyance* and *clairscience* — is liable to err only in three directions, viz., in quantities, times, and magnitudes. Both conditions, therefore, are capable of being eternally improved.

Entering upon the superior condition on that never-to-be-forgotten night, my mind at first seemed to expand all over the isle of Manhattan. Watching and intellectually analyzing as this novel feeling crept on, I discovered that it was not a bodily but an intuitional awakening and soaring which so beautifully identified my individual consciousness with that of all human kind. Nor was this all. My instincts identified me *equally* with the animal creation, and thence with the essences and laws of plants and vegetation; and thus I felt like a *conscious mirror*, if I may so say, on which were reflected and in which were focalized the principles and properties of the System of Nature!

This conscious reception and subjective focalization of absolute *reflections* made me affirm — " To the great centre of intelligence — to the positive sphere of thought," &c., " I go for information." The idea here embodied is correct, but the form of expression is ambiguous. It is liable to give the reader a false impression — that I went, mentally, to the spirit-world for each paragraph I uttered; whereas my intellectual " impressions" were wholly derived from a contact of my exalted intuitions with the *ultimate essences of external substances.*

If this be true, then what did I mean by my affirmed rising " above the stars"? Simply the ascension of my intuitions, the flight and expansion of my superior sensibilities, which, in every human being, are infallible so far as they are enabled to reach out into the empire and laws of life. " Are you not mistaken?" say you. Nay, friend. Let me convince you that I am not by asking and answering a few familiar questions: What is the greatest geometrician? The greatest is that creature which has never studied books — the honey-bee. What is the greatest architect? The unscholastic beaver. What is the sweetest musician? The untrained bird of song. Who is the truest lover of God? The untutored Indian. What knows the art of love better than did Ovid? The unsophisticated heart. Who appreciates the value of childhood better than any philosopher? The unpretending

mother.   Who understands the science of dietetics better than
any physiologist?   The hungry laborer   Now allow yourself to
imagine, for a moment, the simultaneous *liberation*, and *expansion*,
and *exaltation*, of these implanted, infallible teachers.   That was
my experience, and nothing more.   Through the disenthrallment
of these inherent intuitions—*which are the only reliable philosophers in the universe*—I received my knowledge.   Yea, I obtained my "impressions" from the ultimates or spiritualized essences of objective Nature.

What do I mean by "ultimates"?   By ultimates I mean the
products of primates.   For illustration: you hold in your hand a
peach.   What is that peach?   An ultimate!   An ultimate of
what?   (Ah! now you become an incipient Interior Philosopher.)
The peach is an ultimate of a flower.   Whence the flower?   From
a bud.   Whence the bud?   From a twig.   Whence the twig?
From a branch.   Whence the branch?   From a body.   Whence
the body?   From a seed.   Whence the seed?   From spiritual
forces.   Whence spiritual forces?   From the Divine Fountain.
Whence the Divine Fountain?   Most exalted question!   It will
consume an eternal life to yield the correct answer.

Or, take another illustration.   My intuitions arise above New
York, and I realize the presence of a certain impalpable ether.
Whence the ether?   From boiling water.   Whence the water?
From earth-bound gases.   Whence the gases?   From the vitalic
forces of the earth.   Whence the earth?   From the sun.   Whence
the sun?   From another sun.   Whence that sun?   From a sun
still greater and more remote.   Whence that remoter sun?   From
a sun yet more inconceivable.   Whence that still vaster sun?
From the central Sun of the Univercœlum.

Or, take a different example.   My intuitions ascend like a light
column of ether toward the upper realm, and I come in contact
with an atmosphere of Thought!   Whence that atmosphere?
From a congregation of professors, students, and guests, at Union
college.   Why that congregation?   It is commencement-day.

What's the subject of the present speaker? The relation of Christianity to Civilization. Whence Christianity? From the teachings of a person named Christ. Whence that person? Now, in asking myself this historical question while mentally exalted, my intuitions become centred upon the myriad-form 'racks of human history. Presently I strike the right vein. Then, true as the earth to the sun, I glide swiftly "down the enormous grooves of Time"—hailing the intervening Centuries as I pass—till I fix upon the exact events which preceded and characterized the birth and life of the individual under examination. In like manner, every other question—scientific, ethical, psychical, poetical, prophetic, literary, &c., with which I come into intuitional *rapport*—is subjectable to my voluntary investigation. And thus, from the ultimate of any matter—which invariably contains the exact minutiæ and summary of its genesis, biography, incidents, properties, nature, and relations, as well as the certain indices of its future destinations—I receive my "impressions." Whether I obtain them correctly or otherwise is a question which in part remains to be decided by my individual industry and love of truth while thus intuitionally exalted. I say "in part," because a certain proportion of such experience can be truly explained only by reference to the propitiousness of organization and hereditary inclinations. Thus I become to some extent individually responsible for my "impressions;" and in the reception and impartation of them (for my perception and use of language are also intuitional) I can greatly progress, or cease altogether, as my moral *status* and will may incline me.

In all this, then, you perceive the inestimable utility of the Magic Staff. And, in view of the foregoing reliable explanation, how glaring becomes the misapprehension of those who advertise my lectures as "given through the *mediumship* of A. J. Davis"—as if my mind (while in the superior condition) were an insensible, unintelligent, and passive substance, or *spout*, through which disembodied personages express or promulgate their own specific opinions! This is an egregious error — a most unwholesome mis-representation. The special influence and guardianship of spirit-ual beings are interpolated, so to speak, into the independently-written chapters of individual existence. Such is an immutable law of humanity. And thus, amid the trials of life and the changes of death, the consolation is, not that we have been playing the part of insensate automatons under incessant inspirations from spirits, but that we are self-existent and responsible beings; and that, aided now and then by these providential agents, we have at last climbed to the summit of that rudimental mountain which enables us to step upon the less rugged acclivities of a yet higher and more happy world

CHAPTER XLI.

THE SORROWS OF NEW YORK.

THE city of New York, the metropolis of America, is a magnificent dépôt. The various nations and savage tribes of the earth dwell, through certain self-appointed representatives of more or less accuracy and distinction, within the city limits. And the nervous and muscular speed with which everybody walks, and the locomotive anxiety depicted on every pedestrian's countenance, serve to give a countryman the impression that each is hastening to take the next train of cars, steamer, or flying-machine, bound for California, Oregon, Minnesota, Kansas, or Perdition.

Doubtless, most young men of my age would have revelled in the multitudinous sensuous elegancies that shine in one unbroken line on either side of Broadway from the Battery to Union Park. Examples of the wares and works of all civilized races may be seen on exhibition in the palatial store-windows, and so tastefully classified and charmingly displayed, too, that the spectator must be dull indeed who does not imagine himself a visitor in an endless museum, or at the World's Fair, which is to close with a week's carnival and a military parade of the most gorgeous and magnificent character. To these countless attractive sights and seductive external influences I was not insensible. But the horrible personations of vagrancy and distress which I daily saw — appealing as they did to my constitutional sensitiveness and disposition to

sympathize with the suffering—eclipsed all the glories and neu
tralized many of the temporary pleasures of my city life.

The streets were covered with snow, the wind was piercing,
yet the sun shone effulgently upon the Isle, and I was walking
leisurely for purposes of bodily health.   But could I feel happy?
Perhaps the first sight was a weeping child, barefooted and destitute of warm garments.   The next was a distressed woman, with
a sick husband at their miserable tenement, and several diseased
children, suffering equally for food and raiment.   And so on to
the end of my walk.   The forlorn look, the despairing tone, the
heart-rending solicitation for money and assistance, would sink
into and move the depths of my heart ; and impelled thus to the
exercise of pity and charity, I would nervously bestow upon the
lone child, the mendicant mother, or the decrepit old man, whatever sum I could spare, and then hasten on my way—oppressed
with the sad reflection, that the few pennies I had given were as
flies to a famishing lion, or as drops of water to a drove of thirst-
ing cattle.

But the Magic Staff many times gave me tranquillity.   What
little money I had obtained by examinations, was at length ex-
pended on supposed genuine objects of charity, but I remarked
that those objects became no less numerous nor more happy.   This
painful discovery led to another—less painful but very absurd—
that I was trying to fill a "bottomless pit;" and this led me, while
in clairvoyance, to examine the causes and cure of Poverty in
New York.   The results of that probing were at least of great
personal service.   You will find a faithful record thereof by turning
to page 105, volume second, of "The Great Harmonia."   After
that singular investigation I suffered much less from impulsive
sympathy with the apparent sorrows of the street ; but, relying
more upon the wisdom of associative efforts for the poor, I
resisted many daily appeals, and devoted the surplus of my scanty
income to the current necessities of my only remaining and pov-
erty-stricken sister.

A few days prior to the commencement of the Second Part of the Revelations, the first section of which volume I was almost every night engaged in delivering, the scribe wrote and presented a communication to the "New York Tribune," entitled "Remarkable Phenomena," which the fearless editor of that daily journal accepted and published. The article sketched out in general terms the progress then being made with our private lectures, and remarked briefly upon the complete and harmonious character of the truths already revealed. Before my magnetic session on the morning succeeding the appearance of the article, several new characters introduced themselves upon our boards. We were now located at No. 24 Vesey street. One gruff old man I particularly remember. Having read the communication, he wished to make specific and *exact* inquiries concerning the subject of the lectures. When fully informed he asked: "Can't you read me a few paragraphs?"

The circumspect and accommodating scribe, with his characteristic deliberation, read aloud portions of a recent discourse. The elderly visitor listened with strict attention. The selections contained a string of strange, long, hard, obscure phrases — such as "palætiological sciences," "zoological formations," "morphological theories," &c. — which greatly befogged the auditor's judgment, and, I may add, my own not less when not mentally exalted.

Becoming suddenly overwhelmed with the new phraseology, the half-provoked listener exclaimed: "Hold! Let me ask, does that first big word have reference to the palate?"

"No, sir," replied the scribe respectfully. "It is, perhaps, a new coinage. The clairvoyant says he uses it to signify those sciences formerly established, from which different theories and speculations may be evolved."

"Humph!" growled the crusty visitor. "Take my advice, sir, and leave *that* word out." Then he continued: "What's morphological mean?"

The mild scribe again replied: "This term is another new

word, I think, which the clairvoyant employs to designate irregular forms of matter, or a succession of heterogeneous developments, during the different epochs that mark the geological formation of the globe."

The befogged old man looked still more rigid. And planting his eyes firmly on those of the scribe, he said: "What's *the use* of all that unknown language? Use words, sir, that people can understand, sir. That's what's wanted."

"If explanatory notes be appended to the obscure parts," said the patient scribe, "then will not the new words be comprehended by the reader?"

But at this moment the doctor notified me that the hour for my medical examinations had arrived. Whereupon the austere old man arose abruptly to depart. I conducted him to the outer door, where he sharply said: "Are *you* the chap that uses those big words?" Receiving an affirmative reply, he continued: "Then, young man, take my advice."

I was silent. His address amused me, however, and I waited for the advice.

"Burn that lecture I heard read this morning," said he with a scowling look and a croaking voice, "and then write something that folks can understand." Saying which he shuffled away, smiting the pavement with his cane as he went — as if to make the insensate stones applaud the profound counsel he had just uttered for my individual benefit.

In the afternoon of that day we received a visit from a very different type of humanity. His inquiries and attentions were of the most intelligent, direct, and amiable character. But we did not know, till he was about to take his departure, that our agreeable guest was Professor Bush, the able philologist and theologian. This circumstance did me good. It taught me to believe that, notwithstanding the unpopular nature of our magnetic proceedings, there was at least one worthy person who *dared* to examine for himself.

Shortly after this pleasant visitation, another gentleman arrived on a similar errand. His remarkable face bore traces of feminine mental characteristics; but upon his spacious brow there sparkled the gems of rare endowments. In his critical eye, however, I observed an ominous shadow! Thinking to myself, I said: "This person's talent immolates his genius." At length he informed us that his name was "Edgar A. Poe." During an interior conversation, I recollect of assuring him that, though he had poetically imagined the whole of his published article upon the answers of a clairvoyant, the main ideas conveyed by it concerning "ultimates" were strictly and philosophically true. At the close of this interview he departed, and never came again.

The evening for the delivery of the first lecture of the Second Part, at length arrived. My present recollection of that night's "impressions" is extremely vivid. Already I had searched and explored the principal departments of the great temple of Organized Nature. My mind had become measurably familiar with the fundamental laws of composition, crystalization, segregation, disintegration, refinement, the correspondence between things visible and invisible, the origin and uses of animal and human organizations, &c., &c.; and consequently, owing solely to the progressive unfolding and invigoration of my own powers of comprehension, I was intellectually prepared to trace out the grand laws which underlie the very foundation of the present universe.

In harmony with the method set forth in the last chapter, I soared out into the boundless sea of existing life; and then traced, link by link, every successive stage of planetary growth, until I reached and solved the primeval condition.

Having arrived, by the intuitional railroad, at the Central Dépôt of the universe, and viewing the facts and principles that were both involved and evolved, I was moved to break the silence with these startling words: "In the beginning, the Univercœlum was one boundless, undefinable, and unimaginable ocean of Liquid Fire.

"What was that word?" asked the intensely-interested scribe, referring to the newly-coined term "Univercœlum."

Now it is not a little remarkable that, while I instinctively knew the roots and orthography of this novel phrase, I could not give it the correct pronunciation. Therefore I carefully spelled it, letter by letter, to make the scribe's writing a matter of certainty.

This word being fixed, I proceeded: "The most vigorous and ambitious imagination is not capable of forming an adequate conception of the height, and depth, and length, and breadth thereof. *There was one vast ocean of liquid Substance!* This was the original condition of Matter."

THE SUN OF THE UNIVERSE.

The diagram is designed to illustrate what I then beheld. Now let the reader imagine a Sun large enough to fill all space, the

Centre of which is the residence of that Omnipotent Mind called the "Sensorium," and the white circle or belt near the Centre as an inconceivably vast Spirit World, populated with spiritualizea personages who were once men and women, and then he will entertain a faint but *correct* outline of the stupendous spectacle which I beheld just before delivering the above brief sentences. Thus, I continued and completed the discourse, and then, night after night, proceeded with my wonderful visions and strange utterances; which, having been so fully and ably reported, I will not stop to reiterate.

CHAPTER XLII.

SEVERAL NEW STARS.

THE Magic Staff supported and saved me on many occasions of severe trial; and what should not be overlooked is, the more I used it the greater was my contentment. Throughout a protracted and distressing illness, which, about this time, almost shattered my exhausted frame, this Staff was the invisible magic wand that summoned to my bedside not only loving friends from this world, but heavenly and strengthening influences from skies too pure for physical eyes to gaze upon. "Take it and try it," dear reader: the result is sure as destiny.

My clairvoyant examinations of the sick every morning—our only source of pecuniary income—were imperceptibly becoming less frequent and profitable. Not that applications from the diseased world were less numerous, but the lectures monopolized and consumed a large proportion of my cerebral strength. Out of the limited proceeds we had, first, to defray our own current individual expenses; and, second, to liquidate certain definite obligations to the scribe for pencilling down and copying off the lectures. His weekly remuneration we made as generous as possible — knowing that, while thus engaged, he could not receive much, if any, aid from his former profession and brethren.

Finding it necessary we removed temporarily into cheaply furnished rooms in Canal street, where, as I now remember, my soul seemed more than ever conversant with the stellar universe. The sublime events of that era are brilliantly painted on my memory. Intuitionally, or by virtue of the superior condition, I became intellectually identified with what scientific minds had discovered in astronomy. In a few hours I found, to my astonishment, that the progressive history of scientific discoveries, is traceable in the mental *atmosphere* of the planet; just as in the *fragrance* of a rose, you may find *atoms* representing its particular genesis, historic incidents, respective qualities, &c.; the original sources of which are still concealed within its external or physical constitution. In these more sensuous sources the chemist finds the qualities of the rose, just as scholars read books and papers to acquire a knowledge of astronomy. Of all this externalism I was independent. Neither was I compelled to report according to my clairvoyance merely. But when my intuitions were disentangled and inspired, then I could *feel* and *see* and *know* what the Earth's mental atmosphere contained.

Soaring back thus through the long vista of bygone centuries, I observed men, beneath the mild climate and upon the level plains of Chaldea, examining and classifying the heavenly bodies. Thence I traced the astrological observations to the natural scholars of the valley of the Nile. Thence to the still more advanced wise men among the Egyptians. Thence to what is now called Central America. Thence backward to the Chaldeans again, from whom the ancient Indians and Chinese obtained their data; out of which I witnessed the stellar developments of Eratosthenes; and thence, nearer and nearer home, the works of Galileo, Newton, Kepler, La Place, Herschel, &c., till I reached the results of the last telescopic observation. And what is remarkable, as I now remember, when describing the facts and phenomena of our own particular solar system, I did not feel the impulse to vary from the information generally received by living astronomers. During all that period I was but uttering, in my own language, a summary of existing astronomical knowledge. Hence I did not conceive it to be necessary to use clairvoyance, *as I should have done*, to ver ify my intuitional apprehensions of the astronomic history. Had I surmised for a moment that astronomers *had not seen all the bodies there were to be discovered in our immediate band of planets,* it seems to me now that I should not have failed to detect and report the community of asteroids which the telescope has since revealed. In fact, when I proceeded to consider the scenery and inhabitants of the planets, the exercise of independent clairvoyance became straightway indispensable. And, besides, when I interiorly found (several months before the report reached America) that Le Verrier had *inferred* the existence of more distant planets, but that he did not yet know for certain that his surmises were correct, then, moved solely by the motive to criticise or confirm the inference, I arose out of the historic sphere, and, investigating independently, discovered " the lone pilgrim of immensity" ere the news of M. Galla's final demonstration was known in this country.

One day, while in my common state, I heard one of the witnesses, in the course of a conversation, remark: " How like the ' Vestiges of Creation' some of his teachings are !"

" In certain principles and propositions," returned the scribe, " I think there is a resemblance."

" Seems to me," said the other, " that several of his late lectures are very much the same. Though I must confess I have never read the book; only a few extracts in a newspaper some time since."

This conversation excited my curiosity. And so next morning, as we were walking down Broadway, I said: " Doctor, do you think it would hurt my lectures if I should read the ' Vestiges of Creation ?' "

" Why do you wish to read it ?" he inquired.

I informed him of my curiosity to find out for myself, whether I was lecturing upon similar ideas, as one witness had affirmed. To which he said: " I have no fear that you will carry any outward memory into your clairvoyant state."

"Then," said I, "let's buy a book and see." Acting upon the suggestion we entered a store and made the purchase. "It seems very funny, doctor," said I, "for me to own a book."

As soon as we got back to our rooms, I seated myself, opened the volume, and tried to read a few sentences. But the hard words bothered me exceedingly. So slowly did I read that I could not keep the connection of the ideas. Thus I was struggling down the first page, when the scribe asked me a question; to which I made no reply, but perseveringly continued my efforts to master the difficult phrases.

"Don't speak to me, Brother Fishbough," said I, as he repeated the question, "for I'm busy reading."

"Oh, yes!" exclaimed he, mirthfully, "you're concocting something for your next lecture."

Although I knew that he was but quoting the expressed suspicions of skeptics, and meant nothing serious by the remark, yet it acted upon me as a valuable suggestion to throw the book aside. I did so immediately, and never again attempted its perusal. Subsequently, I destroyed it with other valueless articles of luggage. But, two years afterward, I examined the work by clairvoyance. And I can truly affirm that its doctrines resemble those I then taught about as closely as broad-brimmed Philadelphia resembles locomotive New York. That is to say, both localities are populated by human beings, and are regulated by municipal jurisdiction; yet, in almost every distinguishing characteristic, they are two very different cities. So with the "Revelations" and the leading doctrines of the "Vestiges of Creation." The fundamental laws of nature are presented in a somewhat similar manner in both books, but the specific deductions from them are strikingly at variance—a fact which is a sufficient confirmation of the statement that my mind was independent of the last-named volume.

Shortly after this the scribe moved his family to New York; and the doctor and I were accepted as his boarders. It was in the spring-time of 1846. How many blessed memories date from that consecrated dwelling! Did you ever pass that way, dear reader? It was just like the other buildings on either side; and no stranger could know that the glories of the spirit spheres were photographed in one of the upper rooms. No! I can never forget it. 'Twas at No. 252 Spring Street, close to Hudson. But it seemed to me ofttimes that the inhabitants of distant orbs were our most familiar neighbors.

Staff in hand I was steadily travelling over Mount Justice. As I entered the examination-room one morning, to take my chair for the usual magnetic process, I observed, among the patients, two middle-aged ladies, one of whom seemed to express great curiosity and some amusement at my personal appearance. This from strangers was not particularly new, however, and so I passed without thought into my clairvoyance.

One of the ladies then took the patient's seat, and requested an examination. But, quick as thought, there sounded in my ear these words: " *Read—the—Book—of—Life!*"

'Twas the voice of my invisible guide! But the lady did not hear it, neither the operator, nor any other person there. I alone perceived the meaning, and I alone looked into the lady's private history. In ten brief minutes, during which I uttered not a word, I read her biography from the natal-day to that hour. Revealing nothing, the doctor at length asked: "Jackson, will you examine this lady's physical system?"

Perceiving it to be wisdom not to speak of what I saw, I proceeded with my examination. Then I fixed upon another day on which to speak certain strange words unto her soul. Promptly, and even before the hour, she came. This time I had to utter a sentence which none should hear save herself. It pertained to her present plans for future happiness. All left the room, therefore, save the doctor, and I proceeded: " No — that is wrong, you must not go!"

These few words, ambiguous to the operator, shook the lady's heart. It trembled with strong emotion, and poured forth a flood of tears, as the fountain overflows in spring-time. She knew that her life-book lay open to my vision. But the doctor's presence seemed to annoy her. She wished to speak with me in private. She ventured the request. But this would have been a violation of the laws governing the magnetic sleep, and so the reply was a denial. Her proud soul rebelled. But quieting her expression, she asked: "*Parlez-vous Français?*"

"No," said I, "but I understand it." And I continued, "Are you prepared for my words?"

"*Oui, Monsieur,*" said she, earnestly, "*je suis!*"

Whereupon I mentally recounted the many disadvantages of her contemplated expatriation. She was about to leave her country, and on the soil of a southern clime, near the city of Rio Janeiro, find a place to spend her days. Distinctly I saw she would not go, and hence I said: "There are circumstances which will make the prosecution of your plans impossible."

"Circumstances!" sobbed she with violent emotion. "How can that be? My plans are all completed, and the vessel is to sail week after next."

"I see that you can not go," said I, firmly.

"Can not!" she ejaculated. "Are you able to see beyond the hour? Can you," she vehemently asked—"can you discern my future?"

"Not much of it," I answered. "But I have read your past— I understand your present—I know you will not leave North America."

"*Mon Dieu!*" said she, with a tone of despair. "Thy will not mine be done." And she wept abundantly.

Several days subsequently she came again. As I entered the apartment, she took from her finger a beautiful ring which she gave me; and when she departed, as she said "never to return," she also gave me the hankerchief still wet with her tears, as tokens of the gratitude she felt toward me. What I had said, while in clairvoyance, to awaken these expressions of regard, I could not then recall; but now, these interior conversations are familiar as household words.

"Are you a-goin' away?" I inquired, being again in my normal state.

"Yes, my young friend," said she sadly, "I'm about to sail for Buenos Ayres."

"Do you know any folks a-living there?" I kindly asked.

"If God so wills," said she devotionally; "I shall take a friend with me, who knows the American minister at Rio Janeiro."

Thus saying, she departed from my presence. But ere the lapse of three weeks, the letter-carrier brought for me the following:—

"BOSTON, ——, 1846.

"MY DEAR YOUNG FRIEND: It is with surprise that I find myself still in the United States. The vessel in which I was to have sailed has left this port without me! Indeed, as you so truthfully foretold, several circumstances over which I could exert no mastery, have prevented the contemplated departure—the most beautiful one being a thrilling dream which the spirit of my deceased father impressed upon my dear sister ——, who came from New York to relate it to me. This timely dream has perhaps saved me from a perilous situation. . . . . .

"It appears now that I may again have the pleasure of seeing you in your wonderful trance. May I come soon? You told me 'all things which I ever did.' If I may soon see you, while in your elevated condition, please address me. . . . . .

"My God! thy will not mine be done!

"Sincerely and gratefully, your friend,

"—— ——."

The reader should keep in remembrance that, since my first extraordinary introduction to the clairvoyant region, I had regulated all my outward movements by laws and suggestions interiorly obtained. Such was my habit at the time of which I am now writing, and such, with swerveless purpose, has been my method up to the present moment. Furthermore, from the first magnetic operation to the day of my unconditional emancipation — of which glorious event the reader shall in due time receive reliable intelligence — I was compelled to rely wholly upon the probity and frankness of the operator for a statement of directions thus evolved for my benefit external. Hence, not being able during my dependent experience to remember my own interior counsels, I was exposed more or less to imposition; but, on reviewing the items and incidents of my past connection with either operator, I can not recall an instance of unfaithfulness to words clairvoyantly imparted.

On the reception of the above letter, I at once requested to have my interior judgment passed upon it, previous to mailing a reply. Consequently, when next in clairvoyance, the lady's written question was submitted.

Again did I penetrate and unravel the history of her sad wanderings up and down the earth, both in Europe and America; and again, but more minutely than before, did I trace out the unbroken procession of circumstances that eventually would blend her interests with the lectures then being delivered. And I also beheld, in the indefinite future, more than I may now relate. Of what I then and thus saw, nothing was communicated to the confidence of the doctor. But instead: that he must tell me, when awakened, to answer the lady's interrogatory adversely — to the effect that, in my wisdom, I saw that she should not again visit me in person, but that I would at any time cheerfully prescribe in her absence for her physical indispositions.

Having returned to my outer state, the grave-visaged operator candidly reiterated the above decision, and I hastened to mail my answer :—

"New York, 1846.

"Esteemed Lady: In reply to your real kind letter. I am directed to say that it is not wisdom for you to visit me again. I can't tell why — only I write what Dr. Lyon says I said to him in my sleep, and I dare not disobey. He says, that I am willing to tell what ails you when sick, and send you prescriptions by letter."

[Here my forehead began to grow warm, as if exposed to a July sun. A flash of light almost blinded my eyes. Knowing what was coming — spontaneous illumination — I waited till it was quite perfected, when I looked once again into the lady's past and future. It was a repetition of the previous vision. Becoming eloquent in the midst of it I thus proceeded :—]

" Beautiful and wonderful indeed, dear lady, was the holy providence that led you into my presence ! Your soul is beloved by innumerable unseen hearts. There is a regenerating music sounding for you in the other life. My conscientious operator, a valuable man in the present work, does not know what I now perceive in your behalf — that I may meet you in the future. When or where I do not see. And I trust you will never urge, before that period, another personal interview. Be assured, dear lady, that I shall be ever in readiness to administer medical aid to you in the manner above described.

" The God of eternal destinies, the great Positive Mind, keeps your feet in the right path ! Believe on Him. Then His ministering spirits will watch over and guard you night and day !

" Pardon my familiar language and accept the best wishes of
                    " Your friend,   " A. J. DAVIS."·

The conscious clairvoyant excitement subsided, as the last sentence was indited, and I was directly my ordinary self again. Resolving to conceal from the doctor both my half-remembered vision and the contents of the letter, (which I think was the first well-expressed epistle I ever penned,) I hastened away to the postoffice ; where I found another communication from the strange lady, and thus began a long and uninterrupted correspondence between us, through which I poured forth a half-inspired account of the novel truths which were being set forth in my evening lectures.

A few weeks after this, while in the midst of one of my lectures, I heard the well-known gentle voice, like my mother's, saying " Seek—the—mountain. A—person—will—meet—thee—there "

What was going to take place I could not divine. (The reader will remember that "the mountain" is situated opposite Poughkeepsie.) Possessing a true knowledge of my own ordinary condition, I requested the operator not to communicate the impending event to me when awake—inasmuch as I would be impressed when the right day should arrive, and thus be saved al previous mental excitement.

Accordingly on the 11th of June, without the slightest external anticipation, I heard the voice once more: "*Thy—memory—is—yet—weak! Seek—the—mountain. Do—not—delay.*"

It was extremely necessary that my Magic Staff should support me now, for I had completed arrangements for an excursion to an entirely opposite locality. But I kept calm, suppressed my disappointment, and took passage by the steamboat without procrastination.

Among several gentlemanly-dressed persons in the promenade saloon, there was one who unfortunately "knew me by sight," while the rest, to whom I was reluctantly introduced, pretended to "know me by reputation;" and thus I was directly hemmed in by a band of captious interrogators.

"I've read in a newspaper," said one, "that you are ignorant when not magnetized. Is that so?"

"Yes, sir," I replied. "That's the fact."

"Is it true," asked another, "that you can see into folks?"

"I think I can," said I. "Three years' experience is at my back to prove it."

At this moment a ministerial-looking person advanced and said: "Pray, sir, is it true that you teach infidelity?"

"No, sir. I teach *fidelity* to the laws of God." As I uttered these words, there flashed over my mind a partial illumination. The dark color in my eyes must have suddenly deepened, for the gentleman seemed to think me angry.

"Pray, sir, don't get provoked," said he. "I simply wish, sir to ask a few questions."

"I'm not provoked," rejoined I. "Your questions may be too deep; and I can only promise that I will *try* to answer them."

"That's candid. Pray, then, young man, tell me—what do you think of the Bible?"

"I hav'n't lectured on the Bible yet," I replied. "So I do n't know what I think."

"Well, do you keep the sabbath-day holy?"

"I hope so," said I quietly.

"Do you believe," continued he, "that God made the earth in six days?"

"No, sir—I do not."

"Indeed! And yet you do n't teach infidelity, eh?"

"No, sir," I replied, "I'm no infidel. Why do you ask about the six days of creation?"

"Oh, I only wanted to know," said he, "on what ground you keep the seventh day."

Leaning on my Staff and being illuminated, I replied: "The word 'sabbath' is from the Hebrew *shebang* or *yom shaba*, meaning the seventh day. The meaning of the root of the word is 'age' or a period of *rest*, and it was originally applied to men, the ancient sages especially, who periodically assembled for purposes of teaching, worship, and the offering of sacrifices. The particular day on which these sages met was determined in round numbers by the obvious periods of the lunar changes. The moon's revolutions were naturally divisible into four periods of seven days each, and every seventh day in this division was called the *rest day*, or the sabbath, as established by the Chaldean and Egyptian astronomers."

"Ho, ho!" exclaimed the supposed parson, "you are not so much of a fool as the papers report. Go on, pray—it's most excellent—do go on, sir."

Still intuitionally exalted, I continued: "The Jews themselves were regulated by the lunar periods, in all their religious and secular institutions and public meetings. In fact, the religious beliefs, forms, ceremonials, and sacrifices of that period were almost all derived from the Oriental Magi, the Egyptian astronomers, and other erudite sages of the East. Such is the origin of the modern sabbath. This I know," said I, "and therefore I realize none of that sabbath-day sanctity which is so universally exhibited by certain credulous clergymen and their devotional supporters."

"There!" exclaimed he triumphantly, "who'll say this young man is ignorant after this? Pray, sir, where did you attend college?"

"I hav'n't attended any college," I replied, "and what I have just said to you is new to me!"

"Humbug!" said he sarcastically. "You can't get that down my throat."

"I do n't wish to," said I. The illumination here declined; and I was about to retire from the company, when another stranger asked: "Are you able to tell what lottery ticket will draw a prize on a certain day?"

"My mind," I replied, "takes no pleasure in such matters."

"Well, won't you tell me if I give you half the sum received?"

"No, sir," was my reply, "I would not interiorly look at such a matter any more than I would live by highway robbery."

The gameful-looking man started as if he thought I meant something personal, and said in an under tone: "See here, young man! You'll not see the next wharf if you insult me."

Hearing this angry threat I immediately withdrew, and remained in a more retired part of the floating palace, till I heard the welcome announcement—"Passengers for Poughkeepsie!"

CHAPTER XLIII

THE SPIRITUAL SPHERES.

" For me, if I forget the darling theme,
  Be my tongue mute, my fancy paint no more,
  And, dead to joy, my heart forget to beat!"

A WONDERFUL, twofold daily life was mine! I was living a double existence. The mystic line of demarkation, separating my common from my superior condition, was still sharply and strongly drawn.

Few even of my personal friends could fully realize that my soul was the centre from which states so widely and startlingly *different* were evolved and manifested. A trifling boy this moment, a sedate man the next; now a mirthful simpleton, then an intellectual prodigy; a denizen of the external world ten minutes ago, now a traveller and spectator in higher realms of the Infinite. Although these mental conditions remained for the most part marvellously distinct, dissimilar, and independent, each of the other, yet there was meanwhile silently going on a personal change or apotheosis — an elevation of my natural condition so as to meet and interblend with the condition superior — of which none but myself could consciously receive the intimations and indubitable evidences.

My hasty trip to Poughkeepsie began to look rather wild and useless. I had already spent the most of three days in making friendly calls and writing to the lady-correspondent. Loitering along beneath the shady trees of Cannon street, and doubting the wisdom of my being there, I heard: " *Seek—the—mountain. A —person—desires—thy—presence—there. Do—not—delay.*"

In obedience to this well-known guardian voice, I hastened at full speed toward the ferry; but ere I reached it, my mind occasionally wandered, or fluctuated between the two states, which caused the original motive to become so weak and uncertain, that I hesitated and lingered listlessly on the way.

In a short time, however, the primary impulse was recommunicated, and then I passed directly into the superior state. Thus I crossed the river. In the mountain-retirement, in that sacred retreat, I met and saluted a noble personage. It was the gifted Swede—the author of " Arcana Celestia"—the Prophet-Seer of the intellectual North. In this place I will republish the following letter which, by SWEDENBORG's particular request, I mailed on the following morning to Professor GEORGE BUSH:—

" POUGHKEEPSIE, *June* 16, 1846.

" DEAR SIR : Yesterday morning, after eating breakfast at No. 49 Washington street, where my friend Mrs. Lapham lives, I went down to the bookstore, to get some paper to write to ————. After buying it, I visited several persons about the street, staying only a few minutes at each place. Soon I had a desire to go down to the river; what caused it I don't know. But went down; called on one or two friends on the way.

" I soon lost all knowledge where I was, recollect of being about the river somewhere, and also ascending a hill. I am conscious of meeting the same person that I had seen in the graveyard in Hyde Park. I also remember conversing with him, and taking out my pencil and writing all the thoughts given me. I remember him leaving me suddenly, and I came out the state. I was surprised to find myself wet with rain, the paper on my lap, and dry—and being in the mountain opposite Poughkeepsie, about 4 miles, where I had been before, 2 years ago.

" I came directly home, it was 6 o'clock in the evening, I was wet and muddy, and very hungry. The paper had *not* been wet. The very moment I came into the natural state, I *felt* you should

have the paper immediately. I do not understand the meaning,
nor the letters *A. C.* and them *figures.* It appears now that I
know it then, but can't recollect what it was. As I felt impressed
so strongly to send it to you, I do so, for it must be right.

" The friends here can tell about it. I am at Mrs. Lapham's,
49 Washington street. If you can tell me about the meaning,
please write me at the above *No.* I copy the writing exactly
from the paper, as written by me then.

" Yours, &c.   " A. J. DAVIS."

The reader can not fail to perceive that the foregoing communication was written by one unacquainted with the rules of gram·
mar and the usual school-taught elegancies of epistolary composition. It is a genuine illustration, I think, of the difference between
the interior and the external condition, as manifested by one and
the same individual. A report of what Swedenborg so beautifully
and breathingly communicated at that time would be irrelevant in
this volume. He quoted certain postulates from one of his published works, and gave several numerical references to corresponding expressions contained in other volumes — all of which Professor Bush ably commented upon and fearlessly issued in his valuable
treatise upon " Mesmer and Swedenborg." Of the precise object
of that interview, however, I have not yet acquired a definite idea.

During the hottest of the summer season, I remained away
from New York, and dwelt in the midst of human hospitalities.
Nothing occurred of any importance during my absence, save the
following impressive instance of special providence :—

A widow lady, with whom I was acquainted, was mourning for
her only son, who, in an angry and discontented mood, had left
her to embark for the high seas. Just in the midst of her deep
affliction I chanced to make her a friendly call.

While relating to me the cause of her sorrows, her feelings
overpowered her, and she retired with heart-broken sobs to an
adjoining room. Soon I heard her voice in prayer. To the
great Father she poured out her agonized feelings in behalf of her
wandering child. I desired to see what would be the result of

her earnest supplications; and, feeling almost immediately the power of clairvoyant insight, I directed my vision to her apartment.

I at once saw a soft ethereal light playing just above her head, and inducing action in the organs of hope and veneration as well as in several other contiguous departments of her brain. From this light a narrow line of silvery whiteness extended upward somewhat obliquely until it reached a point some twenty miles, I think, above the earth's surface. I traced this delicate thread of light to its terminating point, and there beheld *a radiant spirit*, who was controlling this beautiful phenomenon. From him another brilliant line, forming an angle with the former, stretched off earthward until it reached the distant city to which the youth had fled, and at length impinged upon and penetrated the very substance of his brain.

The effect was marvellous. His affectional and moral organs were aroused. And there were awakened in his nature such feelings of repentance and desires to return to his widowed and cruelly-forsaken mother, that before another day had closed he was again in her presence, fully resolved to lead a better life. Her joy was deep, and her gratitude to the God whom she believed had answered her prayer was unbounded. Of that sacred vision I told her not a word. But full well did I know that when the Spirit-Land should become her home, it would be a still sublimer joy to learn that her long-lost *companion* was the hearer of her anguished petition, and the savior of their darling son!

On returning to the progressive metropolis, I was prepared to proceed with the revelations of Nature. One evening I was a silent listener to a conversation of some importance. Several skeptical guests were controverting the idea, expressed by the deliberate scribe, that "while in the abnormal state my mind received the influx of the science understood in the spiritual spheres."

"There is something so peculiar and wonderful in animal magnetism," said one of the guests, "and the whole subject is wrapped up in so much uncertainty, that it first becomes necessary to examine into the laws of sympathy between mind and mind."

"What do you mean by the laws of sympathy?" asked a witness.

"Why, just this," replied the doubter: "how do I know but Davis gets his lectures out of Mr. Fishbough's head?"

"That would be very flattering," interrupted the scribe with a modest smile. "Brother Davis, while in his superior state, displays a power of analysis and generalization perfectly unparalleled and absolutely overwhelming, and no man possessed of such abilities would ever wish to conceal them. No; I know there are ideas in these discourses which were never in my mind; and as for Dr. Lyon, why, he can speak for himself."

"Yes," said the doctor, "I feel that I am not yet acquainted with half the ideas which the clairvoyant has expressed in my presence."

"Oh, I don't doubt," returned the visitor, "but that mesmerism enhances Mr. Davis's own reflective faculties—a fact which may help explain how he gets at his ideas and reasonings."

"That theory will not cover the ground," the scribe replied.

"Why not?" he asked. "I am willing to concede that he can remember and reason far better when magnetized than he can commonly: this, added to his sympathetic relation to and absorption from your minds, will explain the whole matter better than Professor Bush's plan and yours. And—"

"Allow me to remark," interposed the scribe, "that your hypothesis is defec—"

"Wait till I get out what I was going to say," said the guest hurriedly, "and that is this: The theology of the work is inclined toward Universalism, of which you are an intelligent preacher. Now, don't he get *that* from association with *you* and others of like faith?"

"As to the theological doctrines of his lectures I can not exactly say," replied the scribe, "because he has not yet come to that part of his revelations."

The conversation continued a little while longer, but it was not satisfactory to the disbeliever's mind.

The reader is now invited to listen to another brief parley — occurring posterior to the foregoing, and in another place. The location was in the inside of a carriage-repository down Broadway. One of the disputants was Harvey R. Haight, a proprietor; the other our considerate scribe, with whom the reader is supposed to be now well acquainted. The auditors were the operator and myself. The subject under discussion was the theological bearing of my clairvoyant lectures. Mr. Haight, a positive-spoken man, vigorously said :—

"No, sir! He can not support the Bible as a divine book."

"Why not?" asked the scribe. "My opinion is, that the Bible *will be* fully sustained."

"No, sir!" replied Mr. Haight, "I tell you no, sir—not if I understand his leading principles. He can't do it, sir, and still be consistent with himself."

"Yes he can, though," returned the scribe confidently. "His principles lead directly and legitimately that way; and I am sure, from what has already been delivered, that the lectures will endorse the Scriptures as given of God."

Shortly after this, however, the revelations progressed to the theological part. Immediately subsequent to the delivery of the first discourse on "The Origin of Mythological Theology," I well remember how wofully sad was that expression which pervaded the scribe's usually placid countenance. He labored with a heart full of disappointment. The divine origin of the Bible, its superterrestrial derivation and value, was an idea which involved his sentiments and religious experience. His attachment to that belief was affectionate more than intellectual. Reason he had employed from the first, doubtless, as a porter to wait upon his sentiments of veneration and worship.

For two whole weeks he was mourning the loss of the darling idea of his affectionate mind—during which he was extremely taciturn and wrapped in laborious thought. But one morning, which I distinctly recollect, he came tripping cheerfully into the examination-room, saying: "Good! I have found my way out! My mind is free! I have solved the difficulty, and I am now at rest." But his liberation was not absolute. Instead of possessing *intellectual* affections—which alone can fully grasp and steadfastly love the principles of an interior philosophy—he possessed, on the contrary, an *affectional* intellect, and hence could not completely centrifugate or throw off his educational convictions. That this statement is true, the sequel will clearly show. But the value of the foregoing to the reader consists in its enunciation of the fact that my impressions of the origin of the Bible, and my ideas on religious questions generally, were by no means obtained from my associates.

As my lectures on theology progressed, one witness after another began to withdraw; so that, out of some eight or ten who were often present, only two or three continued to the end. While in clairvoyance, this openly-expressed subsidence of their friendship did not disturb me; but, ordinarily, I felt many times like one forsaken and banished. Hence, I was of necessity compelled to walk and talk with, and lean upon, my Magic Staff.

Among others, Professor Bush began to exhibit lukewarmness, and to intimate that my "moral affinities *might* be such as to lay the foundation for a mixture of truth and falsity on the grand doctrines of Christianity." On one occasion, at a later day, I remember that the ingenuous professor avowed his belief that, while my "gift," as he termed it, "was evidently managed and overruled by a certain providential intelligence which subordinated it to some important use," yet, "in respect to its treatment of the Bible and several of its cardinal doctrines, the book would be an absolute enormity." In view of these words, how unsound appears the oft-repeated suspicion that my mind was in sympathetic *rap-*

port with that of Professor Bush, the fixed and talented Swedenborgian!

My intuitions were daily becoming more and more exalted And when the biblical discourses terminated, I was prepared to form a yet closer relation with the upper spheres. By virtue of the gradual elevation and expansion of those divinely-inspired Philosophers — the Intuitions — I discovered that the Second Sphere of the present order of the Universe *is an Encyclopædia or infallible Compendium of the history of all pre-existent universes.* And not only this, but that tl e present knowledge possessed by the inhabitants of higher spirit-spheres is freely showered down upon the soil of the Second Sphere; and also that such knowledge is obtainable by means of that clairvoyant perception and intuitional sympathy which I was enabled voluntarily to put in operation while in the superior condition.

The diagram (page 340) illustrates my discoveries. Let the reader imagine that he is looking upon the plane of an immense sphere divided through the centre, like an apple cut in two halves; imagine that the dark margin is an inconceivably vast ocean of unorganized matter, in a state of fire-mist or elemental nebulæ — between which and the outer or *first circle* of suns and planets, there are innumerable incipient bodies, or baby-suns and baby-planets, commonly called " comets;" then imagine that " our sun," and " our earth," and " our planets," make one of the groups of the outer circle at the right hand, near the bottom of the diagram; next imagine, when looking upward at night, that your eyes can only see " our own circle of suns and planets," called the " milky way," (or fixed stars and constellations,) and that you can not penetrate, even with the best telescope, into the region of the third planetary circle, which is more interior, geographically speaking, than the " Second Sphere," or Spirit-Land, to which we are all tending; then imagine that the centre is the seat of Intelligence, the fountain of all Love and Wisdom, and the most perfect ATTRACTION in the stupendous organization of matter and mind; next

DIAGRAM OF THE SPIRITUAL SPHERES.

imagine that *that* DIVINE SUN gives off emanations of life and light
which saturate and energize the whole system of the Universe,
and that while it attracts spirit it equally repels matter—not that
the latter is repulsive and the former agreeable, but because such
is the immutable law whereby rare entities and dense substances
are governed with an unerring government; then imagine, in harmony with this law, that human spirits at death, *feeling the Divine
Attraction*, leave the earth and go to the Second Sphere—that,
after the lapse of many centuries, they are progressed sufficiently
to ascend, without the dying process, into the "Third Sphere," or
still more interior Spirit-Land; and again imagine that the *Central Attraction*, being unchangeably in the ascendant, continues to
draw lovingly and tenderly until the spirits of all men reach the

" Sixth Sphere," which is the closest possible approach to the Spiritual Sun of the Univercœlum — that stupendous system which, from eternity to eternity, has rolled upon its immense axis just like the earth; and now, all spirits being personally safe near the Centre or residence of Father-God, imagine that the entire organization of Mother-Nature undergoes a process of universal renovation, and enjoys, so to speak, a season of rest from the offices of reproduction or child-bearing—during which the suns and planets, from centre to circumference, dissolve and mingle into one indefinable Ocean of liquid matter and moving forces; then imagine that out of this Ocean there once more roll forth new circles of suns and planets, which in due time begin to do *right over and over again* the same thing, only better — that is, produce minerals, vegetables, animals, and human beings; and, lastly, imagine that the " Second Sphere" of this new order is higher and more attractive than the " Sixth Sphere" of a previous order, and that, as a sequence, the entire spiritual population of the old Universe emigrate, like birds of passage, to the more pleasant latitude and genial climate which characterize the " Second Sphere" of the new Universe—and thus that no truly human spirit ever loses its identity in the lapse of eternally-rolling ages: imagine all this, dear reader, and you will entertain *a rude outline*, merely, of the magnificent scene which, in 1846, broke upon my intuitionally-prepared understanding.

There are certain scientific objections, I am well aware, which may seem utterly to invalidate these declarations of the Harmonial Philosophy; but if I live on earth long enough to write a book on Universal Astronomy, *as the fruits of my more recent and more accurate investigations*, I think those objections will vanish and appear no more for ever.

Upon the conclusion of my lectures concerning the Spiritual Spheres, I began to realize that I was travelling toward the psychical valley which separated Mount Justice from Mount Power

Fortunately, what the future had in store for me I did not discern. My Staff never failed me in these mystical journeyings, however as I walked down toward the unknown plain in the shadowy distance.

One day I heard a visitor, with a nervous determination of under-tone, exclaim: "When that Book is published, I shall lock up the Bible in the drawer under the desk, put the key in my pocket, and preach the angel-utterances of the New Philosophy!"

"That resolve is rather too sudden," thought I. For I knew that he had not heard my lectures, save in a few isolated instances, and hence could not exercise a reliable judgment upon their value to mankind.

"The world must be awakened!" he continued. "Religious organizations are trembling and tottering with age. Decay is certain! Shining and speaking through these lectures is the mighty spirit of a struggling Humanity. The spirit of Divine Love is misrepresented and crucified by modern churches of pride and power!"

He emphasized almost every word, as he spoke it, with a firmly-clenched fist; his whole frame shook; his eye was oracularly luminous; and he appeared as I had seen him on several previous occasions when before the assembled public. The extreme brilliancy of his eloquence, and the dazzlingly high-colored character of his most ordinary declamations, caused my spirit to shrink back as one would shut his eyes against the intrusion of too much light. The flood-tide of his philanthropic enthusiasm had arisen so suddenly, and so far above what was very high-water mark to my moderate mind, that I stepped instinctively aside, lest the ebb should drive me out into the open sea. The splendid pendulum had swung like lightning to one extreme, and I tried to keep out of that space through which it would as swiftly vibrate in the opposite direction. But I was destined to pass through a brief experience with this talented and vivacious person; and, as he was distinguished for the preaching of brilliant sermons and the writing of eloquent poetry, I shall introduce him to the reader as "the Poet" of this psychological drama.

The Third Part of the Revelations, entitled "A Voice to Mankind," was proceeded with and completed. And as the closing paragraphs were enunciated, I distinctly realized a well-known prophetic mental depression; not like that which succeeds excitement, but 'twas an instinctive perception of *a change* in my circumstances. The nature of that impending change, however, was at this time almost wholly beyond my discernment.

Soon after the completion of the lectures, I delivered "An Address to the World," and then proceeded to bequeath the entire work, and all moneys that might accrue from the sales thereof, equally to the scribe and the operator.

On returning to my natural state, the beloved twain (and a witness) informed me of the bequeathment. My depression for a moment was severe. For I had not accumulated a dollar out of years of clairvoyant diligence, and what were to be my future resources I could not imagine, because I had for weeks felt a distinct, secret conviction that my magnetic career was about to terminate. Sadly I walked to the window; but in a moment I heard the blessed words: "*Fear—not! There—are—treasures—in—an—angel's—hand.*"

'Twas the familiar voice of my venerated Guide! Instantly, therefore, I surrendered myself in joy to celebrating the unexpected circumstance. In consideration of the time I had consumed in delivering the lectures, however, the delighted brothers presented me their joint note for one thousand dollars. This promised ample compensation I did not solicit. But thinking that thus meant my Guide, I fraternally accepted the note which was so cordially and generously bestowed.

CHAPTER XLIV.

EVENTS OF THE VALLEY.

NEAR the last of March of this year, 1847, I announced, while in clairvoyance, that the doctor should not continue his magnetism after a specified date. Also, that he must not receive patients who were too much diseased to be healed by virtue of one single examination and prescription.

He acted upon these rules, and all went on harmoniously. From day to day I could distinctly realize a temporary decline of my clairvoyance. During this short period, however, we received as usual many letters, containing locks of hair and small sums of money, from diseased persons soliciting immediate medical aid. The monetary contents of these letters, save in a few instances where our rule would apply to the patient, were punctually returned.

One day the doctor received a letter, containing the requisite lock of hair and the ordinary fee, and purporting to be written by a Mrs. Brickett. This professed lady affected great illness, and, appealing to our common humanity, sought the aid of my clairvoyance. She described her symptoms, and did not ask for more than relief.

As usual, the doctor submitted the case to my clairvoyant judgment. Feeling the hair, it led me first to a healthy person, then to no person at all; whereupon I asked for "the letter," as a medium of sympathy between myself and the sufferer. This did not serve me. But still taking it for granted that the *statements* in the letter were *true*, and therefore neglecting to examine the author's mind for the real motives which prompted the communication, I yielded at once to my desire to relieve the suffering depicted by the words before me, and started off independently in search of the sick person. I gazed here and there in the neighborhood of the specified locality, some four hundred miles away, and soon discovered a female diseased with consumption. She could be considerably helped — perhaps nearly cured by the one prescription — hence I proceeded to specify the syrup. The description and recipe were accordingly sent, and we retained the customary remuneration.

Let the reader judge of my surprise and the doctor's indignation, when the news reached us that the letter was a tissue of falsehoods — that the whole was a "pious fraud" — the unscrupulous fabrication of a professional priest, who was preaching Christianity and publishing a saintly sheet, called "The Gospel Banner," somewhere in the state of Maine! The *appearances* in this affair were wholly against clairvoyance. The *facts* themselves, however, were our best friends. But the unprincipled trick of this minister — with his external and malicious interpretation of the circumstances — was heralded all over the country. And plenty of people can be found, doubtless, who are still deceived by the influence of this priest — just as the world has been blinded by similar characters for eighteen hundred years!

The next question was — "how to get means to publish so large a volume?" The lectures were to be stereotyped, and presented to mankind in a good suit of clothes. That is, the mechanical arrangement and execution were to be measurably consistent with the supposed intrinsic value of the revelations. The scribe and operator, however, like myself, were not liberated from the trammels of a deficient purse. Whence, then, the means to carry forward the blessed Reform?

This question troubled me for several successive days and nights, until I heard: " *Write—to—thy—Spirit—Sister !*"

'T was enough. I wrote a full statement of our external circumstances to the lady with whom I was in correspondence. I stated to her in plain words the necessity for money to prosecute the glorious Reformation. She was then sojourning in New York. I sent the letter by the morning's mail; and ere the sable curtains of night fell o'er the world, a French hand-maid inquired at our door for "Monsieur Davis." She placed in my hand a letter, in which occurred the following sentence :—

"Thanks! my Spirit Brother—my only earthly friend— thanks! many, many, thanks! Gladly would I *do everything* to help the work of your life. But I am only able, under the existing state of my pecuniary affairs, to let Messrs. Lyon and Fishbough have the sum of one thousand dollars. I will take their note and preserve it for your future benefit."

The reader may imagine the deep gratitude of my soul. Having received this amount, the partners obtained, elsewhere, an additional loan of five hundred dollars and thus secured the material power to progress with their work.

The second magnetic crisis in my life had at length arrived. The operator's influence became more and more unfavorable to my clairvoyant exercise. A sort of stultification and numbness pervaded and blunted my faculties. 'T was a repetition of the old experience on a new degree of consciousness.

Of all this I secretly knew just enough to believe that my operator could not understand it; and thus, for the sake of entire tranquillity, I concealed the prophetic intimations that I sometimes felt, of our approaching magnetic separation. When last magnetized by him—on the 10th of April, 1847—I remember that I did not feel quite certain about the future. And perhaps, while in the valley of this uncertainty, I might have left upon his mind the impression tha I would continue to be "his subject" through the coming years. Be this as it may, I soon left the city for beautiful Poughkeepsie; where I began to realize the possibilities of an independent existence!

A fortnight after reaching the "banks and braes" of my beloved Hudson — on the 16th of May — I realized yet more of that sublime revolution which had been going on within. The bodily fatigue and prostration consequent upon my New York labors were being rapidly displaced by a beautiful vigorousness and liberty of spirit. The interior signs of the psychical change, were many; and my present individual illumination was quietly inaugurated.

Oh, that flowery day! It shines in my memory like the holy star of destiny. A widowed female friend, at whose house I then boarded, was afflicted with a cancerous disease. It acted principally upon the membranes of her stomach. Her physical distress weighed upon my sympathetic heart; and, earnestly *desiring* to aid her, I passed into my superior condition. (See "Great Harmonia," vol. i., p. 204.) 'Twas a great novelty! I had entered the somnambulic and clairvoyant states many times, as the reader knows, without the help of an operator; but to consciously attain to the *highest* mental eminence, independently and in the secrets of my own closet, was like a rainbow of promise spanning the firmament of my soul.

My sight darted through intermediate substances — two walls and a floor — and I saw her disease and the appropriate means of relief. My superior powers were never better; and they were not at the beck of a third party! "Great God!" exclaimed I. "My soul is crushed with tons of gratitude. Oh, let me use my soul's endowments as gifts from Thee, and I promise that I will never, never, dishonor Thee by a misdirection of them!"

Everything was done for the aged woman's relief. But the Laws of Nature left a summons at her door. The breath of a spiritual spring entered her nostrils. The body kept wasting

slowly away, but the spirit grew stronger in its might and aspirations. One day she said :—

"Jackson, my friend, can you not cure me?"

"I fear not," said I with much emotion; "your disease is mighti-
er than your body."

She gazed calmly and intelligently into my eyes for a moment,
and then said : "That's good news, Jackson — very good news —
do n't you think so?"

"The news is not bad," replied I. "To me there are glad
tidings in death."

"Then would n't it be best for all mankind to die at once?"

"Death is good," said I, "only where it is not sought."

"Is it wrong for me to desire death?" she inquired.

"No," said I, "it is not wrong after you have done all you could
to get well."

"What do you mean?" she inquired, looking somewhat alarmed
and confused.

"I mean," said I, "that we should live in this body as long as
we possibly can."

"Well," replied she with energy, "suppose I should neglect to
take a medicine that might cure me, and I should die in consequence, would this be a misfortune to my soul in the other world?"

"I perceive," said I, "that they only are entirely happy after
death, who feel that their life on earth and departure from it were
strictly in harmony with the righteous Principles of Nature."

Her mind seemed to wander a little, as I spoke, and she said:
"Just put another quilt over me. I'm very chilly. Has the
weather changed?"

The summer weather was exceedingly warm, and so I supposed
the chilliness to be a symptom of her gradually approaching release. But I covered her with more blankets, and then asked:
"Did you hear my last remark?"

"To be sure I did," said she, cheerfully ; "and now let me ask
— do you think I have done all I could to keep alive?"

A DEATH SCENE.

"Yes," said I. "As far as I can see, you have done youɪ whole duty."

"Then death is most welcome!" exclaimed the liberal-minded and spiritually-aspiring woman; "but take that weight off my feet."

There was no unusual pressure upon the feet of the dying, save the body weighing down the spirit; and, thus perceiving, I called the members of the family to her bedside, and retired to the privacy of my own room. The superior condition was immediately upon me. And 1 witnessed and comprehended the minutest particular of that spiritual translation. The spectacle was impressively and supremely holy. Oh, most beauteous process! Oh, most sublime beatitude! But I will at once restrain my pen, and refer the reader, for a full and truthful description of that death-scene, to page 163, Vol. I., of the "Great Harmonia." The artist has attempted to picture that ineffably glorious transformation — "Death" — which will be experienced by all mankind as the years roll onward.

The reader is supposed to know, by this time, the leading traits of my mental organization. Perhaps the strongest element was an almost irresistible impulse to respond to demands made upon me from all sides of humanity — ofttimes in direct violation of the law of self-justice and self-preservation. On the reception of a stranger's letter, appealing for relief from some trial or disease, my disposition was immediately to return a humane and beneficial answer. This unrestrained proclivity, as the sequel will show, exposed me to much imposition and suffering. Yet I have no desire that my nature should be less disposed to universal goodwill, nor would I intimate that the exercise of selfishness is right or conducive to happiness.

My unsought fame as a seer of hidden things, and the great scarcity, at that time, of similarly-endowed persons, brought me scores upon scores of letters. If thɪ task of spelling and reading

these epistles was arduous, as it was, how shall I describe the
toiling that was necessary to answer them? From one correspondent's letter I extract the following:—

"New York, 1847.

"MY DEAR SIR: I take the liberty of addressing you, though
a stranger, to get some information on a business-matter of the
utmost importance.

"To-morrow, I expect to fail! The vortex of bankruptcy is
whirling through my brain! I am a young merchant, sir; my
hopes and ambition have been high; my father has advanced
me large sums, sir; and I have invested largely in stocks, to
my utter ruin, unless you, by means of your supernatural powers
of insight, will tell me how I may recover these losses by invest-
ments which will prove immensely and speedily profitable.

"I could myself receive this misfortune and die a beggar, or
terminate existence by suicide, sir, were it not that I have a darling young wife and an infant son, who look to me for sympathy
and support.

"For God's sake, sir, help me if possible — with the greatest
despatch — and enclose your bill for services. Yours, &c."

My reply was that I could not relieve him from pecuniary embarrassments — that my mind was absorbed in questions of universal import — that suicide would not help him out of trouble,
but only increase it — and that, by working perseveringly for an
honorable position in the world, he would receive the assistance
of merchants who knew him.

Twenty days subsequently the post brought me another letter
from the same person, in which he said:—

"All is lost! I am a ruined man! — all because I relied upon
your *pretended power* to tell what will happen. In your letter to
me, you say positively that 'I would receive the assistance of merchants who knew me' Not a word of it has come true! No, sir
— not a word — and never will!"

And thus did the half-crazed man misconstrue my counsel.
Next, I would read over a package of perhaps fifty letters from

persons half-sick or half-dead with various diseases. And then there would come a request of this kind:—

"Philadelphia, Pa.

"Dear Friend: I suppose the claims of disordered humanity upon thy time and patience are numerous, but thee is able to do good as few are, and thee is willing, I am told, to use thy power in a case of humanity like mine. My youngest son is lost or dead we fear. He left home a few months ago to visit a relative in the country, and has not been heard from since. Now, my dear friend, if thee can find him, thee will greatly relieve the broken hearts of his distressed parents. With great respect, &c."

Almost every day the post would bring me letters containing questions like the following:—

"Will my present connection with Mr. —— involve me in more pecuniary losses?"

"Can you tell me the name of the bank where I can negotiate a loan on the securities in my possession?"

"Shall I pass through the present crisis and sustain my credit?"

"If I should come to your village, can I see you in reference to my present shipments?" &c., &c.

Some time previous to the date of these letters, while living in the psychical valley, I was a guest at a merchant's mansion. Serenely shone the sun upon the rich man's ornamental possessions. Warm hearts beat within the hallowed precincts of that home, and the endearments of friendship added tenfold to the attractions of the merchant's hospitality. Fancy me, dear reader, walking in the garden arm in arm with the proprietor, who asked: "Can you enter clairvoyance now without the doctor's help?"

"Yes," I replied, my *will* can induce the superior condition when I desire it."

"Do you suppose, said he, "that you have the power to tell, for instance, the state of the flour-market at any given time, if you desire to do so?"

"Yes," said I. "If I should *desire* to see the flour-market, I could understand all about it in thirty minutes."

"How would you get at it?" he inquired.

"First," I replied, "I would examine the condition of the crops now in the ground; then the amount of flour held in check by speculators; then calculate about storms, to ascertain how much wheat would be probably damaged; and lastly, from these data, I would purchase flour for a certain amount, and hold it till the highest price was offered."

"That would require considerable calculation," said the merchant. "But why don't you do it, if you *can*?"

"Because," was my reply, "I can not *will* to do it."

"Why not?" he asked.

"Because I can not desire it," I answered. "The *reason* is, that I believe all speculation to be both an injustice and a fraud which greatly afflicts the working-classes."

"Perhaps, that is true," he argumentatively replied; "but somebody will speculate in flour — the thing will be done — money will be made — and wouldn't it be better and more in accordance with wisdom for a liberal man to make it than a merely selfish speculator who wouldn't help on Reform?"

"No," said I; "all speculation is wrong, no matter who goes into it; and the money, thus obtained, is seldom of any value to the world."

"Your reasoning, I must confess, is rather muddy to my mind," said the merchant. "Now suppose the crop prospect was so and so, and suppose the flour-market is thus and thus, and you could get so many barrels at such a price, what would you do?"

"If I were a merchant," said I, "and the market and conditions and opportunities were as you describe, I should lay in a good stock of flour."

The foregoing is in substance a correct report of that conversation. Of the results thereof I had no thought whatever, as I harbored no suspicion of evil. But ere the sun of that day went down, my *unilluminated* words were taken as a standard of action! Subsequently, on hearing the effects of my friend's impulsive movements, I felt surprised and grieved; but, actuated by benevolent impulses, I withheld all expression of my regrets and disapprobation. But others afterward seized upon the unexplained circumstance, and I received volleys of misrepresentations from the enemy's battlements.

The reader will bear in remembrance, while glancing over these few "wants" from the world, that I had been the recipient of similar demands since 1844. Then, however, I had the protection of an operator. And, besides, the appeals now made were far more numerous and trying to my sensitive nature—because I was sojourning *in the mental valley*, between Mount Justice and Mount Power, in a sort of transition which exposed me to trials unknown to the citizens of the world. One more illustration from the wide-spreading thicket of my correspondence will suffice:

"A. J. DAVIS, Esq.: Pardon a stranger in writing to you upon so delicate a matter as that of a domestic quarrel. I will not intrude upon your time by writing apologetic words, but will come to the difficulty under which I suffer. The circumstances are these: Some ten months since, I courted a young lady with the intention of making her my wife. But one day we had the misfortune to disagree upon a trifling matter, at which she took great offence, and I find it impossible to conciliate her by any means in my power. . . . .

"If you can inform me as to what will bring about the state of affection and confidence that existed a few weeks since, you will greatly oblige, &c."

Besides these, there came unto me letters of every conceivable shade of scientific, historical, and philosophical inquiry—never imparting a particle of information, but asking innumerable questions about all sorts of out-of-the-way and never-to-be-thought-of subjects. And thus, dear reader, lived I in the valley. What could serve me, in my lowly habitation, save the Angel World and my Magic Staff?

Receiving, at length, an invitation from an acquaintance in Vermont, to visit and take a carriage-ride with him all the way from Bennington to Burlington, I fled from the presence of my wearying anxieties and rested three whole weeks.

CHAPTER XLV.

MISSIONARIES IN THE FIELD.

" They wrought with sad sincerity,
  Themselves from God they could not free,
  They builded wiser than they knew,
  The conscious stone to beauty grew.''

THE balmy breezes of the great Green mountains had fanned much feverish fatigue out of my flesh, and I departed from the presence of my Vermont friend with a blessed repose in my spirit. There was a certain promise to be fulfilled — that on my return, I would halt in Troy, New York, and call upon my new acquaintance, the poet. I did so. His refined and free expressions of regard were to me refreshing and pleasurable. There was now less impetuous excitement in his manner. He said: " The mission on which I am about to depart, Brother Davis, is one of great importance."

" What have you resolved to do, Brother Harris ?" I inquired.

" Having privately withdrawn from the Universalist denomination," said he with deep energy, " I am now preparing a course of lectures to deliver on my western tour."

" Have you made out the plan of your trip ?" I asked.

" I shall need your impressions, Brother Davis, on the best course for me to pursue," said he with much emotion. " I shall consider myself in due wisdom, as acting under your guidance." Saying this he relapsed into a child-like quietness for a little space, and then continued: " I expect much labor, much hardship and even persecution; but I hope that my will and love and wisdom will be strengthened and guided—so I shall meet all discouragements with fortitude, all insults with magnanimity, and labor with the serene and patient courage, which, in so good and divine a cause, must at last insure success."

" Has Brother Fishbough got the Revelations published yet ?" I asked—for as I had just returned from the journey, I had not ascertained the facts.

" No," he replied; " the Book is expected here about the first of August. I am anxiously waiting to see it out. Have you seen the pretended review in the ' Troy Whig' ?"

I answered that I had not. " Then," said he, " let me read you my rejoinder."

I thanked him for his kindness, and procuring his manuscript, he read an exceedingly candid and dignified reply to the " falsehoods" of the journalist. In that article he ably maintained *three* propositions, as follows :—

" 1. The book originated as is claimed, because the characters of Dr. Lyon, the operator, Mr. Fishbough, the scribe, and Mr. Davis, are above reproach ; and their known proved reputation as honest men procludes the possibility of deception.

" 2. Neither Messrs. Lyon or Fishbough, any or all of the witnesses, nor Mr. Davis himself, in the normal state, was capable of producing the work, or had opportunity to do so without detection if capable.

" 3. The evidence of hundreds of eye-witnesses attest the reality of Mr. Davis' spiritual powers, and proves him to have capacities equal to the production of the work."

In addition to the foregoing the poet had inserted the following " In March last, he [Mr. Davis] stated that a further development of his powers would soon occur. This has taken place. He is now able, without being magnetized, to make full use of his spiritual powers—to heal the sick—to foretell future events—to see the most distant occurrences—to solve the most abstruse questions in psychology—and to declaim for hours with the eloquence of an angel, in defence and exposition of the principles he has revealed."

There was a divine glow in the poet's eye as he read, and I listened with painfully pleasurable emotions. His manner, more than his words, interested me. "What do you think of it?" he tenderly asked.

"The positions are essentially true," said I. "But I fear, Brother Harris, that your journeyings will overtax your powers of endurance."

"Much will depend on the promptness of your impressions," he tremulously replied, "and I trust the importance of my mission will induce you to write me from time to time, giving me interior guidance. All things show my mission to be divine, and I will go on life or death."

At length I departed for Poughkeepsie. While sailing down the Hudson, I recalled the foregoing interview, and tried to penetrate its results. But, alas! I was living in the valley. The mists and fogs that had chilled me before, many times during similar periods, were once again upon my faculties. My intuitions would not rise upward. 'Twas well. The lowly plain was a period of rest, and, knowing this, 't was wrong in me to repine.

And yet, though I leaned upon my Staff I was deeply troubled. Have you not had many beclouded days and trying weeks, dear reader—when your circumstances compelled the exercise of wisdom, and yet you could not see your way clear enough to act wisely? At least, such was my state, with some effulgent exceptions, for weeks succeeding my conversation with the poet-missionary.

Walking the steamer's deck, and recalling the unsought responsibility that had just been conferred upon me, I thought: "Well, I suppose that I must take it. And yet, it seems to me that the Principles of my Book teach a different course. Each man is an

individual.   Each person must reverence and obey the dictates
of his own Reason.   When a man's soul is self-harmonized, the
spirit-world is revealed to him.   Man is a microcosm, in other
words; and all things are contained in himself.   A man plenarily
inspired, then, is one who has access to all Truth and all Wisdom.
Well, now, suppose I counsel Brother Harris?   That will be
right, because I may aid him to become plenarily inspired, and
thus his own centre of strength.   Very well, then, I'll do all I
can to help him.   He seems to love universal Reform, to be
religiously sincere, to feel heroic devotion to duty, and he is very
talented.   All this is good and desirable; and yet I shrink from
his impulsiveness."

Thus ended my meditations on that matter.   But there was
another thing that troubled me: his positive exaggeration of my
personal abilities.   "Why, I don't pretend to foretell future
events," thought I, "only so far as they lie in the track of fixed
principles.   And again, I can not 'declaim for hours with the
eloquence of an angel.'   The fact is, people complain that I don't
talk enough, and that, when I do talk, I bungle words together so,
that I am often unintelligible to them."

Thus meditating, I began to feel alarmed.   "That won't never
do," I mentally exclaimed.   "Brother Harris will speak of me
in his lectures, without qualification, as being 'an angel' and all
that, when I am nothing of the kind any more than he is."   My
thoughts began to succeed each other with tumultuous speed, but
excusing Benevolence soon checked and quieted them; and I
thus soliloquized—"Oh, never mind.   Brother Harris is a poet.
That's the way with poets.   They don't tell things just as they
appear to common people.   It's all right for him—and I guess
I'll let it pass, and not think nor worry any more about so trifling
and manifest a matter."

We will now glide over a few uneventful days.   The next scene
opens at the scribe's residence, in Williamsburgh, Long Island.

'T is the twenty-first anniversary of my birthday; the **eleventh of** August, 1847.   The title of the piece to be performed is, "**Men and** means to edit and publish a Reform paper in New York." The curtain rises; and the play begins.

The particulars of the drama, as evolved during a few hours, need not be rehearsed in this volume.   Suffice it to say, that the prominent parts were well sustained by the able and candid artists. Nay, 'twas not an artificial performance, dear reader, for there was a *sad sincerity* streaming through every heart.   Each man's duty was to stretch forth his honest arm, and help turn the tide of human existence into better and higher channels.   The world was clad in blackened robes woven upon the loom of Ignorance and Superstition; and these men met to construct a factory for the weaving of garments of whiteness and immortality.

'Twas resolved to begin a journal by an harmonious association of labor, capital, and talent.   Several one-hundred-dollar shares were at once purchased by individuals in the audience.   And after many good speeches, one asked: "What shall the paper be called?"

Various captions were suggested.   At length an auditor remarked that "the new word in Brother Davis' book would be unexceptionably excellent."

"The Univercœlum," repeated the chairman, "Yes — a very good name, indeed."

"Who shall be the principal editor?" was the next inquiry.

"Why, of course the brother who originally proposed the publication," said one.   "He is just the best man for that position in our ranks."

"Yes, Brother Brittan," said the conscientious and deliberate scribe, "you are *the* man."

The designated gentleman gracefully expressed his heartfelt acknowledgments, and then said: "Permit me, brethren, to suggest an additional title.   My reasons for offering it will be sufficiently obvious.   Below the leading appellation, I would have the supplementary expression, "And Spiritual Philosopher"—with this motto: " The things which are seen are temporal; but the things which are not seen are eternal."

The appointed editor is a new character in this drama, and should therefore be introduced to the consideration of the reader. Prior to the present occasion, I had many times been a guest at his residence. The fraternal sympathies and kindly hospitalities of his family were unsparingly bestowed upon me — for which I was then and am now deeply and cordially grateful. Many times, too, have I gazed into his mental structure, and delighted my spirit-eyes with the landscapes, symbols, figures, archetypes, and images, that cluster and glow and stretch far away, scene beyond scene, in the region of his vivacious Ideality. And during his illnesses, also, I have looked into and prescribed for his physical organism. He was my friend. In his eye, there was a look of love; in his smile, a token of confiding affection. His ruling traits were: a love of Liberality, a love of Beauty, a love of public Esteem, a love of Truth. He became the editor of "The Univercœlum," and will ere long again appear in this history.

The missionaries were now in the field. The reader will bear in mind that I had not summoned them into it, though I cheerfully became their coadjutor. There was the operator, the scribe, the poet, the editor, and myself. We stood side by side on the stage of life, our spirit-arms about each other's neck, while the turbulent billows of the disunited world rolled on before us. Besides ourselves, there were others there who declared their intention to write articles for the Reform paper. The play was soon over for that day, however, and the curtain dropped amid what the imaginative would term, " thunders of applause."

My absence from Poughkeepsie was of brief duration. While returning thither, my mind was filled with unintelligible misgivings. A publication was to be started in advance of public demand, without the required complement of twelve editors, and before a sufficient capital had been accumulated. Methought I saw, in the little distance, a cloud full of rain. The water descended in torrents, the paper was dissolved into shapeless fragments, and its editors were drifting on a sea of discord. "Oh, dear!" exclaimed I in much agitation, "Shall I never get over this dreaming?" But a moment's thought restored me to quiet, when I heard the blessed voice "*To—the—Mountain! Do—not—fear!*" Hearing these words, I leaned firmly on my Staff and felt perfect faith.

Soon after this an acquaintance reported to me a conversation, between himself and my former operator, substantially as follows :—

"Have you seen Mr. Davis's large volume?"

"No," returned Mr. Levingston, "I hav'n't."

"Are you not very curious to see what the clairvoyant has been saying since he left you?"

"No," said he, moodily. "I do n't expect much from *that* book."

"Ah, indeed! You astonish me. Tell me, pray, why do n't you expect much from his book?"

"Because I do n't believe that he's been in the high clairvoyant state since those men enticed him away from me."

"You do n't?"

"No," said he, "I do n't."

"Why, can it be possible that you believe that?"

"Yes, that's my opinion," replied the operator. "If Jackson had remained with me, and had continued to let me magnetize him, he might have given a book worth reading."

"But some of the papers say that his Revelations are very interesting."

"Oh, that may be," he responded. "Jackson might have said a few smart things, now and then, while under Doctor Lyon's influence, but he has n't delivered the lectures he would have given, if he had continued to be magnetized by his first operator. I'm quite certain of *that*."

"Then you do n't wish to see the great Book?"

" No, I feel next to no interest in it — though I expect to read it when I get time."

When the substance of the foregoing conversation became known to my New York and Bridgeport friends, they smiled contemptuously, as if the former operator had not exercised his common sense. His stand-point was esteemed to be extremely preposterous. And so it was. But ere long the tables were turned; and, then, a position precisely identical with this absurd one of Mr. Levingston in regard to the Revelations, became *altogether reasonable* and convenient for others to assume with reference to my subsequent volumes. In this particular, the sequel will be extremely novel and valuable to the reader.

While the Revelations were being stereotyped in America, a suggestion arose concerning their speedy publication in England. The grave-faced operator submitted to me a catalogue of grave questions on this point; after due interior consideration of which, I answered favorably to the interest of the publication. 'T was not mammon, dear reader, that prompted the new partners to send the book to our Motherland across the blue Atlantic; but, on the contrary, they were actuated by a genuine desire to maintain and exert their mutual and sacred guardianship over the spread of its sublime principles.

But whence the means? I will tell you. Through a letter, I presented their plans and wishes to my Spirit Sister — the lady correspondent — whose face I had not seen since my first impression that we should not meet. Her reply was prompt and characteristic :—

" MINE OWN BROTHER! — My soul's best, truest friend — dear as thou art to me, yet dearer is the work of thy life, and I would do everything to aid thee in it. But my means are not abundant, dearest brother, and I regret that I can not do more. Out of what I have, however, I will cheerfully lend twelve hundred dollars to Messrs. Lyon and Fishbough, to be appropriated (as you say) in defraying the expenses consequent upon the publication of the Book in England. But, my best friend, let me add that you receive the profits coming from its sale there, to pay your current travelling and boarding expenses, until you receive back the entire sum, for which I will take their joint note. Will this do? Do not deny me, my own best brother. I wish to be of some use to the world. I would serve thee! "Thy Spirit-Sister ———."

Therefore, in addition to the previous loan, and two hundred and fifty dollars subsequently bestowed with which to help sustain the Univercœlum, a still greater sum was now offered by the generous lady to aid in the dissemination of this blessed Reform.

Mr. Joseph H. Cunningham, an intelligent disciple of both St. Crispin and progressive thought, agreed to take the duplicate plates of the book to his native land. The results of his mission thither were satisfactory. But prior to his departure—during a visit at his residence below Poughkeepsie—I had a most wonderful and useful vision. It concerned the past, present, and future, of the human race. Viewed merely as a generalization of historical truth, and as a systematic statement of what appeared to be focalized upon the air before me in the brief space of twenty minutes, it is as much superior to the "Revelations" as these are higher than the philosophy of the schools. But ere I present this vision to the reader, I must, to avoid anachronisms, relate what occurred soon after the meeting at Williamsburgh.

Feeling dubious as to my future course with reference to the operator, and dreading the approaching danger of being made *the supernatural centre* of a semi-philosophical and eventually superstitious propagandism, I hastened away to my mountain sanctuary for instruction. Quiet and holy as the lull of twilight was that dreamy state which preceded my superior condition.

My Guide was there! He pillowed my spirit on his beating bosom, and said: "The bounty of Heaven hath given me wisdom for thee, my son."

"Thanks, kind Guide," said I, as the aroma of his pure presence floated into my soul. "I am very thankful."

On my uttering these words he withdrew a few yards, and replied with gentle firmness: "Why callest thou me 'Guide'? Thy guide is within thee!"

"Oh, say not so!" I exclaimed with great agitation—"do not leave me! My every day's life hangs upon your truth and overruling providence!"

"Oh, man!" said he, "art thou still an ignorant youth?"

"No, no, I do not mean to be a helpless child," replied I; "but my heart recalls your words, without which I had many times gone astray."

"Dost thou lead the seer as one who is sightless?" he inquired.

"No," said I, "'tis only the blind who require a guide."

"Art thou a seer?" he asked; "or one who merely gropes his way through the galleries of long-departed experience?"

"The past is not my guide," said I. "When I wish to take a step, I look upon the ground before me, lest I should stumble."

"'Tis even so, my son," said he, with kindly tone. "Thus shouldst thou see from thine own central sight, the palest beam of light o'er thy pathway. And I will come only when thou hast done all thou canst, and yet requirest sight and power."

"Do you mean," I inquired, "that I can penetrate the future for myself unaided?"

"Each man," he answered, "like the Earth and the Sun, is a centre; the more true the man, the more true his revolutions. Tell me, my son, hast thou travelled over the Mountain of Use and also of Justice?"

"Yes, I feel that I have," was my reply.

"Then art thou not able to be *useful* and *just* without my words?"

"Yes," I replied, "I feel that I can do whatsoever appears to my own conscience to be useful and just."

"'Tis well! Do thus! Nothing more is required of any living soul!"

He now retired a few paces further, and continued: "As before, I will picture to thee thy works and ways. Behold!"

Looking in the direction indicated, I instantly beheld a reproduction of the impressive scene once before witnessed — the mountain, a castle-like structure within it, the four successive stories, and a representation of the four stages of my own career. "Yes," said I, "'tis true, very true. These are my boyhood scenes, the mysterious voices of my youth, the operations of Mr. Levingston, and my work with Dr. Lyon. Yes, it is all true. But what is next to be done? My soul yearns to see the future."

"Then," said he, "direct thy vision higher!"

To my astonishment, on looking upward, I saw another story in the structure, more brilliant and beautiful than all the lower ones combined. It seemed to be made of crystal, through which golden and purple sunlight perpetually streamed. And in the centre of the room, I saw myself seated by a table busily writing. The table was glowing, the apartment shone like a sun, and my whole head seemed to be illuminated. Below, I recognised my friend, the doctor, and others who knew *nothing* of that upper room. And, looking once again to make my vision sure, I saw a pleasantly-furnished room, leading from the one in which I was writing, dimly lighted from a mundane source, and seated in an easy chair, *the strange lady* with whom I was in correspondence!

"Oh, tell me," exclaimed I, "do you mean to foreshadow a personal interview with my Spirit Sister?"

The vision vanished. But my Guide stood in the foreground, with a smile glowing like a sunbeam on his heavenly face, and I asked: "What is the work for me next to do?"

And he replied: "The bounty of heaven giveth me wisdom. See! The road before thee guideth the traveller, through midnight mists, all the way up the Mountain of Power into plains and valleys beyond. Hold thy Staff firmly, then, for the enemies of progress are many and mighty. Thus saying, he disappeared and I returned to outward life.

Wending my way homeward, I pondered on all that had passed —for my memory was no more suspended—and the reader can easily anticipate my resolutions.   They were: that I would henceforth live an independent life, be my own centre of sight, my own inditer of impressions, be responsible for my own mistakes, distribute the generosities of my own soul, help on the work of human progress as *one* among *many*, be the leader of no party, the friend of no useless compromise, and thus walk over the mountains and through the valleys of my individual pilgrimage.

Reaching my boarding-house, I hastened to my room, and lo! — between that moment and the end of the ensuing hour — *the past was all merged into my outward recollection!*   The mystic Past—that had been to me as a dream—was all mine!   My memory could now revert to *each minutest particular* of my every clairvoyant vision.   No more contradiction!   A double and twisted existence no more!   The abounding wealth of my experience was no longer locked in another's bank.   No man could now hold the key with which to go in and out of my soul at pleasure — leaving me, as an outward being, a lone wanderer and destitute of common understanding.   " No, no!" exclaimed my joyful heart, " henceforth, I shall walk the surface of God's earth, not proudly, but a companion at once to the lowly clod-hopper and the educated academician.   Oh, I am wholly awake!   The sable curtain of mystery —so long hanging between my outer and inner world — is rent in twain and for ever banished!   The secrets of a clairvoyant life are before me, and no man can wrest them from my reason and memory!"   *There came a natural feeling into my flesh, on the harmonious blending of these previously separate memories.*   Not that the superior condition was drawn down to the level of my common life, but my common life was elevated to the very threshold of the superior condition.   After that memorable and gracious hour —as I said in my first article to the Univercœlum — I could voluntarily enter the " superior condition," investigate truths, see for myself, draw my own conclusions, and retain a perfect recollection of the whole experience.

In all this, then, you may behold *a prophecy* of what Father-God and Mother-Nature have in reserve for every son and daughter of humanity. Not that all men will pass through the mystical ordeal of magnetization; but the immutable laws of mind will sooner or later, waft each soul into "the superior condition"—when, as with the bee and the angel, the only and sufficient guide to good and truth will be that totality of Divine life in the soul, which I celebrate under the name of "INTUITION."

CHAPTER XLVI.

VISION OF PERPETUAL PEACE.

ALTHOUGH several eventful years have wafted my barque far from the place wherein I beheld the substance of this chapter, yet do I recall each little incident and circumstance of the occasion as if 't were yesterday. " Each soft remembrance springs like blossoms in the heart."

Breakfast over, and the sabbath morning partly spent, Mr. Cunningham said : " Come, let's all walk to church this forenoon. The music is usually very good."

The two daughters at once consented, and I, being a guest, cheerfully acceded to the proposition. Never was sabbath sun more bright, nor Sunday scenes more beautiful. The walk was short—just over the bridge, and up to the Episcopal sanctuary on the hillside, in Channingville, Dutchess county.

I entered a cushioned pew with the family. The organist extemporized a prelude, the choir sung its solemn chants, the devout clergyman went through divers prefatory exercises, and I tried to get interested. One of the audience handed me a prayer-book. I appreciated his benevolent intentions, but 't was a decided impediment to my devotions. Not being used to books of any sort, I had a double temptation — that is, to appear to read, and yet not to do anything of the kind.

At length, the solemn minister began his solemn discourse to a solemn congregation. He said nothing that met my mind during the fore part of his sermon; but when perhaps within a few inches of the end, he exclaimed: " Who thinks of man's redemption? Who can tell when Jehovah's words were first delivered to erring nations ?"

Those questions interested my mind at once. "Yes," methought, " I would like to know when the first minister began to preach. In fact, I would like to see the very first form of religious belief—and what sort of people they were who believed the first theology."

As I meditated, I looked and beheld a faint light before me— causing the altar, the pulpit, the minister, and the church, to melt, and fade, and vanish away.

My intuitions were liberated and blended with clairvoyance; the superior condition was perfectly produced; and, though in the midst of people, no one knew the workings of my soul. The material confinements of the local sanctuary did not restrain me; neither did the presence of minds form the least part of my individual consciousness.

" What was the first theology ?" I mentally inquired. Knowing that I possessed the power to answer my own question, away I looked through cloudy skies and stormy centuries, along Stygian shores and over oceans of buried men, until I fixed upon the primeval conditions of human existence. This was SAVAGEISM. The theology of that stage was Fetichism. Then I gazed upon the turbulent billow of human history rolling toward me, and that was BARBARISM. The theology of that stage was Polytheism. Then I looked upon the next nearest billow of mankind's past, which was PATRIARCHALISM. The theology of that stage was Pantheism.

Fixing this in memory, I looked at the mountainous wave of the present, called CIVILISM. The theology of this stage is Dualism.

" Now," said I thoughtfully, " why not see what's next to flow out of this era? What will be the future of the race ?" Seeing

the fixedness of principles, I could readily produce an exact mental picture of the approaching destiny of mankind. It would be
REPUBLICANISM. The theology of that condition will be Mono-
theism.

The grandeur of this view made me shiver with delight. "But,"
methought, "why not look into other departments of history?
Why not cleave the darkness of the past?" And immediately I
began the labor. My penetrations were voluntary and profound.
"Now," said I inwardly, "let me first look at the complexion of
the races in the different *Social States*, then at their Architecture,
then at their Commerce, then at their Language, then at their
Science, &c., &c.—each in its order—until I get a history of the
whole past; and, from the immutable laws that regulate human
existence, let me read the wondrous scroll of Destiny!" And,
urged by these my own interrogatories, dear reader, I labored
upon the dead past, the living present, and the unborn future,
until I actually elaborated and focalized a chart of history and
prophecy. It seemed to me at the time—owing to my large and
projective organ of individuality—that the chart was pictured in
the air. But I am positive that it was the systematic action of
my own intuitions and clairvoyant discernment.

"Have you been dozing?" whispered one of the young ladies
near me, as I relapsed gently back into my outward state.

"No," replied I. "My mind has been wide awake."

The minister was just closing the morning services. By calculation, I made out an *interior exercise* of not more than twenty
minutes' duration!

Of this extraordinary vision I said nothing that day. Next
morning I hastened to Poughkeepsie, and began transcribing from
the pages of memory. I wrote it out methodically, just as I had
fixed the form in my mind, without referring to the dictionary or
any historical work. Therefore, I present it as one of the triumphs
of the superior condition. But, in order to bring this picture intelligibly before the reader's mind, I will insert a few explanations:

INTRODUCTIVE EXPLANATIONS.— On the succeeding two pages, as the reader will perceive, there are two Formulas. These constitute the firm foundation of that which I term " A Vision of Perpetual Peace." The Chart, in other words, is based upon an Intuitional (or self-evident) Theory of the DIVINE MIND, the Structure of the Universe, and the Elements of the Human Mind. The philosophy is this: that Man possesses, to a finite degree, the attributes of the Infinite; that Man is a microcosm or universe in miniature; therefore, that all arts, sciences, philosophies, theologies, &c., have their seat or germ in the living Human Soul. This explains the value of the two Formulas.

Next, as to the eight pages succeeding. The reader will observe, on turning to the first page following the second Formula, that Human History is divided into Five Ages — 1. Savageism. 2. Barbarism. 3. Patriarchalism. 4. Civilism. 5. Republicanism. These Five Ages are as a Key, put in the reader's hand, whereby to unlock the treasures of the Past, the Present, and the Future, on this globe. Keep in mind that these Five Ages run transversely all the way through the eight pages which embrace the Chart, and that the Captions of the sixteen longitudinal (or up-and-down) columns are indicative of the different *phases* of the Race at the period specified by the Age on the left side of the first page. For example: suppose you wish to see what description of houses were built in the Age of Barbarism. First look for the caption " Architecture;" then look directly beneath into the second line, and there you will find the word " Pyramidalism." Now, then, to ascertain what this word means, see the explanation in smaller type below, (to which you are referred by the corresponding figure 2,) and you there read, " Sacred piles, altars, monuments, &c." Thus you may find the condition of Art, or Music, or Theology, and so forth.

This brief guide to the Chart will, I trust, make it useful to the world. Indeed, as it seems to me, almost any person may grasp the generalization.

FATHER-GOD.	MOTHER-NATURE.	NUPTIAL-LAW.
CAUSE { Love, Will, Wisdom.	EFFECT { Substance, Aggregation, Universe.	END { Association, Progression, Development.

THE above is the fundamental formula. 1. FATHER-GOD is the CAUSE — the invisibly-active and immutably-energizing Principle. 2. MOTHER-NATURE is the EFFECT — the receptive and reproductive Principle. 3. NUPTIAL-LAW is the END — the marriage Code and conjugating Principle. This Formula may be stated in a different phraseology, thus: Father-God is an organized and intelligent Being; a Spirit in the central Brain of the Universe. Mother-Nature is an exact counterpart; the organic system or Bride of God. Nuptial-Law is the code of conjugal action; which leads to the propagation of all forms of life and intelligence.

Father-God's first, innate, involuntary, central Desire is the projection and multiplication of Himself. The type of Himself, on the summit of creation, is Man. In order to unfold this type, to gratify this constitutional Desire, the Universe is filled with instrumentalities innumerable. And inasmuch as *perfection* is the aim of Father-God and Mother-Nature, the complete fulfilment of their Desire will consist in the harmonious development of inherent qualities which characterize Mankind. Such is the primary proposition of the Harmonial Philosophy.

SPIRIT.	BODY.	DESIRE.
CAUSE $\left\{\begin{array}{l}\text{Motion,}\\\text{Sensation,}\\\text{Intelligence.}\end{array}\right.$	EFFECT $\left\{\begin{array}{l}\text{Mineral,}\\\text{Vegetable,}\\\text{Animal.}\end{array}\right.$	END $\left\{\begin{array}{l}\text{Parentalism,}\\\text{Immortality,}\\\text{Happiness.}\end{array}\right.$

THE above Formula is but a reproduction of the preceding one: in an ulterior and infinitely less degree of development. 1. SPIRIT is the CAUSE — the active and imperishable Principle. 2. BODY is the EFFECT — the receptive and reproductive Principle. 3. DESIRE is the END — the motive and actuating Principle. This Formula may also be stated in different words, thus: the perfect human spirit is a miniature of Father-God; the perfect human body is a miniature of Mother-Nature; and human *Desire* is the *Cause* of all human action. Whence desires? Desire springs from the innate properties of the Spirit. What is the highest form of desire? The highest development of Desire (or Love) is Wisdom. The masculine elements of Father-God and the feminine properties of Mother-Nature meet and appear (to a very limited extent) in the Man's constitution; out of which they unroll progressively, and from which they bloom with an immortal beauty, in spheres beyond the stars. Such is the secondary proposition of the Harmonial Philosophy.

INFANCY

ADOLESCENCE

VIRILITY

MANHOOD

MATURITY

1. SOCIAL STATE.	2. ARCHITECTURE.
1. SAVAGISM.	1. Cavernism.
2. BARBARISM.	2. Pyramidalism.
3. PATRIARCHISM.	3. Palatialism.
4. CIVILISM.	4. Domesticism.
5. REPUBLICANISM.	5. Edificialism.
1. The infancy of the race; an age of wildness, penury, spoliation, servitude, ignorance, and selfishness.	1. Huts, caverns, excavations, tents, cabins, &c., &c.; the rudest and simplest dwellings and structures.
2. An age of cupidity, superstition, dogmatism, war, rapine, and the brutal subjugation of females.	2. Sacred piles, altars, and monuments. Examples of the perfection of this stage of architecture in Upper Egypt.
3. An age of despotism, arrogance, perfidy, pride, oppression, physical prowess, and deification.	5. Palaces, towers, sacred edifices, temples, and sanctuaries. Of sacred structures, the Pantheon is an example.
4. An age of autocracy, aristocracy, feudality, democracy, and civilization. Aspiration for freedom.	4. Mansions and cottages; — buildings less for purposes of defence — more for convenience and utility.
5. This will be an age of general industry, female elevation, peace, light, security, and . . . . UNITY.	5. Will combine the vastness, grandeur, utility, simplicity, and beauty, of all previous ages . . . . a UNITY.

3. COMMERCE.	4. LANGUAGE.
1. Nundinantal.	1. Automatical.
2. Demi-Personal.	2. Hieroglyphical.
3. Duplicism.	3. Symbolical.
4. Demi-National.	4. Alphabetical.
5. Reciprocal.	5. Axiomatical.
1. Collection of hunting, fishing, and wearing materials, at fixed times and places for purposes of trade.	1. Configuration of countenance, gesticulation, simple expression, discordant and ambiguous speech.
2. Exchange of metals, implements of war, animals, and other articles for women.	2. Representations on stones, trees, and plates; significant figures, simple letters and sounds.
3. Converting wealth into idols; tithe-paying; appropriations for sacrifices and to kingly ambition.	3. Allegorical structures, typefied ideas, significant carvings, sculpture, statuary, and idols.
4. Restrictions, tariffs, antagonism of capital and labor, and of general interests and productions.	4. Conventional signs, letters, words, conjugations, inflexions, syntax — (grammar).
5. International communication, free trade, universal reciprocity of exchanges . . . . UNITY.	5. Natural grammar, clear rules, spontaneous and unequivocal expression, interior sense . UNITY.

5. SCIENCE.	6. PHILOSOPHY.
1. Simplism.	1. Material.
2. Alchemy.	2. Analytical.
3. Transition.	3. Transition.
4. Chemistry.	4. Synthetical.
5. Compound.	5. Spiritual.
1. Perceptive, observation of surrounding things, superficial application, uses scarcely known.	1. Imaginary causes, fantastic origins, gigantic gods, wild speculations on cosmogony, &c.
2. Superstitious deductions, metal-mania, magic, divination, demonology, astrology.	2. Broken inquiry, imaginary researches, in isible arbitrators, speculations on the formation of the earth.
3. Chimeras, supernaturalism, chronology, much of the imaginary but little of the practical.	3. Experience, data, *a priori*, classifications of elements, geometry, dialectic subtleties, metaphysics.
4. Practico-inductive, knowledge of uses, general practical application, e. g., in inventions, navigation, &c.	4. Development of physical systems, doctrines of chance, fatalism, freedom of the will, astronomy, geology.
5. Science the subject of primary education, applied to all departments; knowledge systemized . . . . UNITY.	5. Knowledge of causes, relations, degrees; definiteness, method, interior investigations, all in . . . . UNITY.

7. THEOLOGY.	8. GOVERNMENT.
1. Fetichism.	1. Nulli-Autonicism.
2. Polytheism.	2. Anarchism.
3. Pantheism.	3. Hierarchism.
4. Dualism.	4. Feudalism.
5. Monotheism.	5. Natural-right-ism.
1. First phase of idolatry, worship of exterior objects in Nature, images, chieftains, &c.; adoration.	1. Individual isolation; invasion, local and temporary power; force, torture; distributive justice unknown.
2. Invisible deities with diverse attributes; rites, ceremonies, sacrifices, fasts, feasts, &c.; expiation.	2. Confusion, perversity, instability; artificial standards; enslaving of the weak and conquered; family orders.
3. Resolution of matter into spirit; supposition that all things are God; superstition, fanaticism.	3. Voluntary choice of chieftains and rules; successful warriors become monarchs; the weak oppressed.
4. Antagonistic deities, good God and evil God (or devil), Church, Pope, Bible, Clergy; sectarianism and prejudice.	4. Hereditary aristocracy; serfdom, allegiance, exclusive elective franchise; monarchy, democracy.
5. No arbitrary deities, ONE Cause, ONE Father, ONE Destiny, ONE family, ONE purpose . . . . UNITY.	5. General consent; qualification, attraction, (equitable and) natural legislation, distributive justice . . . . UNITY.

9. AUTHORITY.	10. ART.
1. Desire and Fear.	1. Lifeless.
2. Strength & Mystery.	2. Simple Imitation.
3. Position and Title.	3. Transition.
4. Doctrine and Wealth.	4. Compound.
5. Nature and Reason.	5. Living.
1. Impulse, inclination; the imaginary will of idols; fire, light; superstitions and impressions.	1. Simple outline; rude and grotesque figures with parts disproportionate and incoherent; colorless, lifeless.
2. Power, arbitrary will of chieftains; sorcery, soothsaying, oracles, demons, imaginary divinities.	2. Rude and imperfect imitation; color deep, coarse, unshaded, and noneffective; statuary rough and uncouth.
3. Prophets, kings, nobles, priests; arbitrary and irrevocable laws based upon selfishness and superstition.	3. Bold, rugged, and attractive; due regard to symmetry and proportions; color simple but effective.
4. Church, pope, bible; established articles of faith; hereditary opulence and grandeur; wealth.	4. Color less effective; greater regard to exactness in delineation; delicate tenderness.
5. Interpretation of Nature; native truth; intuition, Reason, Wisdom, and Righteousness . . . . UNITY.	5. Soft, lively color; graceful, sentimental, spiritual; profoundly effective; influence pure and refining . . . . UNITY.

11. MUSIC.	12. POETRY.
1. Discordant.	1. Perceptism.
2. Exciting.	2. Eratoism.
3. Melodious.	3. Transition.
4. Soothing.	4. Conceptism.
5. Harmonious.	5. Intuitism.
1. Confused, incoherent, clamorous, sonorous, discordant; horns, gongs, drums, &c., mere noise.	1. External, wild, startling; abounding with huge and stupendous fancies; — subjects: genii, hunting, war, &c.
2. Intensely vociferous; simultaneous sounds; imperfect rules and time; approximation to order.	2. Erato-inspired, lyric, eccentric, bold, diffusive; — subjects: gods, heroes, warriors, battles, &c.
3. Periodical beats; invention, variety, melody; orphic strains, chants, praises; harps, flutes, &c.	3. Cantos to God, mythological, tragical, amorous, epic, sublime, nervous, and instructive.
4. Sacred, solemn, martial, penetrating, sentimental, eolian; perfect time, order, and harmony.	4. Embodying mythology, theology, science, philosophy; didactic, descriptive, sacred, effeminate.
5. Symphonious, euphonious, harmonious, lofty, delicate, expressive; exquisite order and time . . . . UNITY.	5. Instructive, elevating, refining; the vehicle of truth, and the promoter of peace, progress, and . . . . UNITY.

13. AMUSEMENTS.	14. IDIOM.
1. Sensual.	1. Sanscrit.
2. Mytho-Tragical.	2. Greek.
3. Gladio-Gymnastic.	3. Hebrew.
4. Melo-Dramatic.	4. Latin.
5. Intellectual.	5. English.
1. In a state of nudity; physical, lascivious, great animality; hunting, fishing, and muscular exploits.	1. Ancient Indian, Chinese, Persian, Sclavonic, Celtic, and Gothic: Sanscrit most prominent.
2. Representations of mythological scenes with tragical terminations; marvellous, exciting.	2. A pure language formed from the materials of the primitive languages, mainly of the Sanscrit.
3. Cruel, destructive, gladiatorial; games, such as running, wrestling, &c. Olympic games.	3. The sacred languages of the Egyptians and Jews, the Bible idiom, and other dialects from the parent stock.
4. Representations of historical events and of human passions, foibles, &c.; musical and instructive.	4. Latin, German, Italian, Spanish, French, English, Swedish, Danish, and other languages now in use.
5. Useful, educational, spiritual; embracing science, art, music, poetry, truth . . . . UNITY.	5. The English perfected, being a compound of other languages; a general and final . . . . UNITY.

15. KINGDOM.

1. Babylonian.

2. Medo-Persian.

3. Grecio-Roman.

4. European.

5. American.

1. Includes the savage aud barbarian ages, developing the monarchical system represented in the Babylonian.

2. Glides from the first into a new reign; the Zoroasterian era; Medes and Persians hold the sway.

3. Kingdoms following Alexander the Great, the era being one of carnage, hostility, and wealth.

4. The Roman empire and subsequent European monarchies, now nearly closed.

5. A general Republic, the stepping-stone to Freedom, Association, Justice, Accord, and . . . . .
. . . . UNITY.

There is nothing more positively certain than that the HARMO-
NIAL AGE will eventually dawn upon this rudimental world. Study
the fundamental principles that stream unchangeably through and
control all existence; for they, far more than I, will utterly convince your understanding and gladden your deepest heart.

What is true of the Individual is equally true of the Race. For
illustration: the first Age—Savageism—is *infancy;* the second
Age—Barbarism—is *adolescence;* the third Age—Patriarchalism—is *virility;* the fourth Age—Civilism—is *manhood;* the
fifth Age—Republicanism—is *maturity;* or, a ripening of the
preceding ages into a state of comparative Wisdom and Harmony.
Meanwhile, you will bear in mind that, as there are infancy and
old age in the same family at the same time, so are there savageism and harmonialism in the same age and in the same Nation.
And again, you will observe that, as extremes meet by the linking
of maturity with childhood, so will the highest harmony of the Race
touch the lowest discord; and thus, by interchange of interest and
sympathies, keep up the progressive rotations, and reproductions,
and similarities, of human experience. In other words: that which
is Old age to a Man is, in reality, but the *infancy* or initiative of a
similar career on a higher plane; even so, that which is Harmony
to the Race is, in reality, but the *savageism* or beginning of a similar historical experience on a grander scale.

Now, in the twenty minutes' vision of which the foregoing Chart
is but an abstract, I beheld the *certainty* of a period of Peace and
Happiness. Not that all nations and all lands will be simultane-
ously harmonized and perfected, but that the best portion of the
Race and the purest soil of the earth will unfold the Kingdom of
Heaven.

Poets are no dreamers! Prophets are no impostors! Seers
are no visionists! Philosophers are not insane! No, no! Poets
all have sung of an "Elysium." Prophets have foretold of a
"New Jerusalem." Seers have seen an "Era of Universal
Unity." Philosophers have ciphered out a "New Atlantis." The

Millennial day, the Utopian period, the reign of Justice, the age of Happiness—all! yes, all—is but one declaration of Father-God through the several inspired offspring of Mother-Nature.

What do I mean? The meaning is, that all conceptions of which the above terms and titles are expressive, have their secondary origin in the human soul—the primary source always being Father-God and Mother-Nature. "Unity" is the last word at the bottom of every column. "Unity" is the name of the Era of Harmony. "Unity" includes the full growth and harmonious action of every passion, desire, or love. "Unity" is the ultimate of God's design and of Nature's desire. Therefore, when accomplished, "Unity" will be the harmony of Man with himself, with his neighbor, with the universe—or, with Father-God and Mother-Nature!

The experience of the Race, recorded in profane and ecclesiastical history, shows that it has passed from stage to stage in regular progression—that men were first savages, then barbarians, next demi-civilized, then civilized, and now are advancing toward general Republicanism. Parallel with the social state of Mankind in each Age, has been the state of philosophy, art, theology, morals, &c. If we know one, we know the other. Appealing to the *authority* of past ages as a rule of faith and practice in the present age, is manifestly doing violence to principles of progress, as well as going counter to all natural teachings and human intuitions. As men look to the indiscretions of youth for instruction, so should Mankind review the experience of former generations, and, by their errors and follies, learn to pursue the path of Truth and Righteousness. The arts, doctrines, theories, &c., of former ages should be religiously preserved, and whatever is good and true in them should be adapted and applied to present use; but to value them above modern improvements, or to dream that a Golden Age has been lost, is to invert the order of progress, and to exalt ignorance and discord above Wisdom and Harmony.

CHAPTER XLVII.

THE FURNISHED ROOM.

"In stillness deep I walk a land
  Where spirit-forms my footsteps greet,
And beauteous thoughts — an angel-band —
  Chant low and sweet."

RETURNING to my boarding-place, I found piles of letters from all degrees and shades of human "wants," to which the writers expected immediate and satisfactory answers. Amid numerous packages, my eyes rested upon a familiar superscription. From that letter I will make a single extract:—

"WALTHAM, MASS., *August*, 1847.

"BROTHER BEST BELOVED!—Light of my path!—My only earthly friend!. . . . . The motive that induced me to purchase this comfortable 'Stone House' was to give thee a refuge—a home of thine own to flee to—when fatigued with toiling in the field of Human Redemption. Rev. O. H. Wellington, my agent, is planning to remove the encumbrances. He will take up the mortgages now resting upon these premises, settle all the bills for furniture, &c.; and then, dearest brother, this is thy home—a place where the son of man can lay his head, and be wholly at rest. May I do this? Will it be wisdom? It is the darling thought of my every hour, to minister unto thy material wants, though I may not in this world be permitted to see thy perishable form. Tell me, my best friend, wilt thou accept this house as thine?

"Thy Spirit-Sister, —— —— ——.""

Immediately on reading the above, I took into consideration her generous proffer, and the propriety of my accepting it. The details of that interior examination I will not chronicle, but the result thereof belongs in justice to the reader. I replied that I must not allow my mind to be trammelled with the cares of property; and consequently, though she would exert herself to pay for the house and give me a clean title, I was compelled in wisdom to decline. But in regard to "our not meeting in this world," I wrote that she might rest assured that we should have the pleasure of a personal interview. This assurance I predicated on the strength of the impression conveyed to me by the vision already related.

Shortly after this I received a letter from the self-appointed missionary. This heroic pioneer was now delivering discourses in Utica. On the 3d of October he preached in Troy, New York, on which occasion, as he says, "I avowed my belief in the Revelations;" and, in the evening, "I preached on Immortality, making use of the great Central Idea in 'Nature's Divine Revelations'—God the Cause, Matter the Effect, Spirit the Ultimate—to show the truth that the interior wisdom of Jesus formerly, *and our living Prophet now*, proved that 'a spirit was in man.'" Then, after candidly reporting a few details of his work, he adds: "I find that it will need mighty and heroic efforts to commence the great revolution. I am determined to 'conquer or die,' but shall need, for the present, to be much advised by your interior wisdom."

Under the swaying impulse of benevolence, I had previously requested this energetic apostle to write me as he went on his way, at the same time promising that I would give him all the counsel possible for me to furnish. But on the perusal of this first important epistle, my heart began to tremble, while my head warmed with the forebodings of fear.

"Can it be possible," said I mentally, "that the poet looks upon me as a Heaven-appointed prophet? And does he proclaim my words as being more divine and authoritative than those of any other person intuitively exalted? Ah, I fear he has been too long a believer in the supernatural, without investigation. He loves religious truth, but he does not discriminate. He is positive and determined, however, and his words will ever be an exponent of his belief, right or wrong. This trait of his mind I particularly like. But what shall I do for him? Just look at the facts! In obedience to his own convictions of duty, he heroically relinquished a large salary, abandoned all his former claims to pecuniary aid, and, like the apostle Paul, has now gone forth, fearlessly and alone, to preach the gospel of ' Nature's Divine Revelations.' But he did not go by my influence, and yet he ' depends upon my interior wisdom.' "

Meditating thus, I felt sad and dubious. But at length I wrote him a cheering reply, sent him a prescription for his health, and suggested the best places to lecture in. And now, dear reader, we will leave the poet to the prosecution of his painful work, and resume the preceding subject.

The deliberate scribe had just returned from a visit to the " Stone House," where he saw and conversed freely with our benefactress. She was extremely disheartened, and even grieved, because I did not accept her proffered gift. It seemed to unsettle and bewilder her mind — to dissipate her fond hopes and darling plans. Mr. Wellington, her agent, was soon to receive the house out of her possession, and she was determined once again to breathe the invigorating air of her native Rhode Island. Only one more request would she now dare venture. This was soon communicated to me, both by the scribe and the following :—

　　　　　　　　　　　　" WALTHAM, MASS., ———, 1847.

. . . . " I submit. Thy wisdom is my reliance. But, my best and only friend, I have one more plan. In the ' Stone House' I have furnished a room and *consecrated* its every article of comfort and luxury to thee. It contains everything requisite for a gentleman. There are pictures on the walls, too, and a collection of choice books. Do not deny me! My disappointment would be past endurance! My health is failing fast, and I feel that my life on earth is short. Allow me to furnish a bedroom and a study for you, wherever you may reside during the ensuing year. Do not refuse, for I fear it would sever the last remaining link that binds me to the things of this world. May I do so?

"Thy Spirit-Sister, —— —— ——."

Her generous appeal was directly to the affections; yet I had the power to silence their promptings. My interior examination of this new request was immediate and satisfactory. I replied in harmony with her wishes, and informed her where I contemplated spending the fall and winter months.

I was now but just commencing my journey up the Mountain of Power. The secret of my safe progress thus far was the Magic Staff. A few weeks of unimportant experiences passed by, between my acceptance of the lady's last benefaction and the incidents about to be related.

"Why, Brother Davis, how glad we are to see your face once more!" This cordial salutation emanated from the naturally warm heart of the editor's amiable wife, on my arrival from Poughkeepsie. Her sunny eyes of cloudless blue beamed with an expression of friendly welcome, and her fair face reflected the attractive alternations of pleasurable emotion. The editor had procured a comfortable house in the fine-appearing Colonnade Row, in Williamsburgh. From the upper windows the occupant might gaze out upon the expanded bay, covered with the gliding agents of commerce; and beyond, upon New York, the innumerable structures whereof oppressed the eye as would the drear prospect of an interminable forest.

"Thank you, Mrs. Brittan," said I; "so am I glad to see you once more."

"What have you been about all this long time?" she asked.

"Oh, at all sorts of things," I replied; "writing out my new chart, answering letters, doctoring sick folks, &c. How's all the children?"

" Healthy and beautiful as ever," said she, clasping with enthu
siasm a blooming baby-boy in her arms ; "they delight me to per
fection !   They 're so sweet, and so bewitchingly mischievous !"

" Have you seen Mrs. Dodge lately ?" I asked.

" Oh, certainly I have.   She 's been doing all kinds of splendid
work for you up-stairs."

" Ah, indeed !   What 's been going on ?"

" Do n't be in too great a hurry, Brother Davis," said she, smiling archly ; "when Mr. B. comes, we 'll all walk up and look in
together."

Now, though I had been the recipient of surprises from my boyhood, still I was not fond of having a delicate secret sprung upon
me, and so I begged to be excused from further waiting.   But
the editor soon entering, up-stairs we went as first proposed.   The
door of my winter retreat was thrown open, and lo ! I beheld with
material eyes a perfect copy of *the pleasantly-furnished room that
was pictured in my vision of the mountain-structure*.   Everything
was in exact accordance with that foreshadowing, save the presence of the strange lady : but, leaning firmly on my Staff, I held
my heart still, and my tongue betrayed nothing of the deep astonishment and gratitude which stirred my nature — astonishment at
the perfect fulfilment of my Guide's pictorial prophecy ; gratitude
that he had inspired the lady to strew my rugged path with violets.

The initial or specimen number of " The Univercœlum" had
already appeared, and matter for the succeeding number was
partly on hand.   The main motive that moved me to board in the
editor's family was the desire I had to bring about a unity of inter
ests in the publishing enterprise.   The first step toward unity of
action was unity of thinking ; and a close proximity of individuals,
whose affections were more or less involved, was the primary consideration with me.   At the same time, I had resolved to exercise
no authority over any person ; and, equally, that I would not submit to be in any degree arrested in my individual pilgrimage.

It required but little insight, however, to discern the error that lurked at the very core of our glorious movement. That seed of disorganization was the lack of capital and talent adequate to sustain the publication. My belief was, that our body should have originated as the *crystal* is formed in the bosom of matter — two particles that are congenial first uniting; and then by their quiet emanations making others congenial, and segregating them as they thus gravitate, until is developed a strong ard beautiful body. Our movement, on the contrary, was begun in the external sphere of common business; and though it was flushed, *to all appearance*, with redeemable promises, yet I foresaw its ultimate dissolution. But my purpose was to write almost every week for the paper, and thus — co-operating with the editor, the scribe, the poet, J. K. Ingalls, Frances H. Green, Rev. W. M. Fernald, and others — try to diffuse some spiritual light o'er the human world.

The painful events to be recorded in the next chapter will not be seen in their true light, unless the reader first imbibe another draught of the troubled waters that foamed and bubbled round about the writer's citadel.

Previous to leaving Poughkeepsie, I received several letters from the poet-missionary. In one of them — dated November 14, 1847 — I found the following :—

"To-day I have rejoiced in spirit. I feel strong. I feel inwardly assured, in spite of apparently unfavorable circumstances, that there is reserved for *this truth* a final and universal triumph. I know not what my fate may be. The future, as far as worldly things are concerned, is dark. It may be that I shall *fall a martyr* to the malignity and prejudice of the age. But be assured of this, that while I am in the form, I will lift my voice continually — crying, 'Reform! for the kingdom of heaven is at hand.' The more they oppose the more do I see the necessity of the work in which we toil. O for spiritual might — to enable me to overcome all things, and stand undaunted in the front rank of the battle!"

The spirit of this poet was truly heroic. His idea of what a reformer should be and do, was congenial to me, and his ambition

to stand in " the front rank" I regarded as laudable and consistent
with his temperament. But he looked for an outward authority.
Alas! I was the standard around which the pioneer's affections
spontaneously rallied, as the following, from the same letter, too
clearly proved:—

"I must have an answer to this immediately. The cause demands it. *I must know to what places I am to go on leaving
Cleveland, Ohio.* Leave all else unnoticed, so that you answer this."

Long and sadly pondered I over that letter. At length I resolved tenderly to disturb his confidence in me as an authority.
" But," soliloquized I, " how can I do it and not be cruel? Fraternal sympathy, giving a bias to my judgment, soon suggested a
plan, however — which, without harming his work, would tend to
cast him upon his own central reason. That plan was — to specify a number of places to lecture in, the most of which could
easily be reached; but others were so unimportant and out of the
way as to give the impression that my vision was unreliable.
This worked like a charm to the end desired. His next letter but
one — dated December 18, 1847 — contained the following welcome sentence: " *The places which you indicated lie, I think, out
of the road, and can not be visited without great expense.*"

Thus the wedge had entered that catalogue of evidences which
had induced the poet unquestioningly to rely upon my intuitional
dictation. And that *logue* was eventually split from end to end,
by virtue of that first little wedge, as ensuing chapters will abundantly show.

Soon after my arrival at the editor's residence, the mild-eyed
and broad-browed scribe returned from a business-tour through
portions of Maine. As he entered my pleasant study, I hailed
him with —

" Welcome back, my dear old scribe! How's your health and
spirits?"

" The fact is, prophet," replied he playfully, " I'm in a pretty
generally considerable state of mental confusion."

" Why so, Brother Fishbough ?" I asked ; " what's happened ?"

The surface of his generous brow gathered up into gloomy ridges, as he answered, still playfully:—

" Why, the fact is, I have had my pate almost be-addled by the diverse transmogrifications incident to my unsuccessful trip and, besides," he seriously added, " I feel many unpleasant conflicts about affairs connected with the book and the paper."

" Well, take a chair, and let's talk over the troubles."

" Yes," said he, looking downcast, " I think there is a crisis near at hand, and I want to counsel a little with you on rudimental matters."

" Very well, scribe," said I cheerily, " let's overhaul these matters."

" ' Double, double toil and trouble,' " said he, smiling sadly — " there's something going wrong somewhere."

— But I will not report that conversation. And yet the reader, in my opinion, has a right to know the secret of the scribe's gloomy forebodings. The " evil spirit" that troubled him was pecuniary embarrassment, brought on by causes strictly local and mundane. The scribe, be it remembered, was my best friend among the band of earnest fellow-laborers. He knew me well — treated my position with deference, but regarded me not as an infallible guide — and concealed nothing. We were each other's spirit-brother. In such a relation I found utter repose. But I believe that he did not detect the *real cause* of his private troubles. They did not originate with Providence, but with improvidence. In this there was no dishonesty, but a sort of necessity. When I separated from Dr. Lyon in the early spring, every source of support was at once closed up, save the capital loaned to publish the book, upon which both the scribe's family and the operator lived till August. Then the sales became the only basis of their income, and so continued up to the time of our conversation, and for months afterward. Consequently, the means for publishing future editions decreased proportionally with the natural decline of the sales.

The operator seemed to know all this, and so did the editor.   But the affectionate scribe appeared subsequently to confound his personal perplexities with something *infernal* in certain imaginary, invisible abettors of the New Movement.

At the time of which I now write, the operator, (a cherished brother of the editor's wife,) with his recent bride, was occupying apartments below mine.   Quietly, he began to ask " if it was n't most time for me to be magnetized again."   This was very unpleasant to me ; but, in order not to wound his feelings, I would simply suggest, in reply, that I did not feel the need of his influence.

At this time, also, the poet was in Ohio — lecturing through much tribulation, selling books for the partners, and obtaining subscribers to " The Univercœlum."   Such was the situation of affairs when the events of the next chapter were inscribed on the tablet of my memory.

CHAPTER XLVIII.

NIGHT AND MORNING.

" Be the thing that God hath made you —
Channel for no borrowed stream.
HE hath lent you mind and conscience;
See you travel in their beam !"

THE furnished apartments — a study and bedroom — were sumptuously decorated. My writing-table was spread with every imaginable article of use and beauty. Between the windows there stood a case of valuable books, which, like the profusion of other objects, were new and quite beyond my needs and wishes.

The existence of those books, however, gave rise to a foolish report that I was a vigilant and toilsome student. " Let me whisper a word in your ear"—said a rosy-faced *litterateur* who once visited my study, to an enemy of clairvoyance—" let me tell you that Davis was writing *medical* articles for the paper, when I saw a *medical* book on his table. There! think what you please. I simply tell you what I saw." But I had a consciousness that these suspicions were baseless, and hence I did neither attempt to hide the books nor to avoid the existence of appearances unfavorable.

Well do I remember the chilly day in bleak December when I walked the floor, and, remarking the exact likeness of my study to the room I saw in my vision, I asked myself: " What was meant by the presence of the lady? Did it mean that she is to visit me here?" A warm breath passed over my face as I queried, and presently I heard the words: "*Look—into—the—history—of —thy—Spirit—Sister.*"

Although my mind was interested in a subject then before me —"The true but unloved Religion"—yet did I turn my whole interior perception in the direction suggested. And once again looked I along the pathway of my benefactress. I saw her birth and babyhood; her life at the boarding-school; her visits with her parents in Washington city; her marriage, to please others, with a gentleman toward whom she felt an unconquerable repugnance; how this repulsion ripened into a positive hatred; her journeyings to Europe for personal freedom; her return; her efforts to endure the false union for relations' sake; her second tour upon the Eastern continent; her sojourn at Berlin, at Paris, and at London; her presence in the midst of fashionable glitter and regal festivities; the death of her parents; her refuge in the endearments and attractive faith of the Catholic Church; her uniform discontent amid all circumstances; her second return to America; her attempt to fix her affections upon some lofty aim in life: her increasing uneasiness; her preparations for Buenos Ayres; her visit to me at No. 252 Spring street; what I there saw for her; the wisdom of our not meeting during the intervening months, viz.: that my mind at this early period of its growth might be kept in that indifferent external state which was necessary to insure success in its difficult interior work; that my mission, including myself, alone occupied her affections; that, as she had no children, and her reasons for a separation were abundant, she should procure a divorce; that it would then be right and just and useful for us to be married; that she would thus be rescued from trials more severe than any consequent upon our marriage; that her income, while it would be of little or no assistance to me individually, would still be sufficient to support her in her own luxurious habits of living; and, finally, that I need not longer concern myself with the local influences and especial wishes of surrounding minds.

How did I see all this? Not by a spiritual communication, dear reader, but by the clairvoyant power of exact investigation. The chequered past was all before me; the circumstances of the present I contemplated; the principal links in the chain of future events I traced and estimated as the astronomer foretells an eclipse.

Ah, now my Poughkeepsie vision began to look like an entire vaticination. Accordingly, I wrote the lady all about my interior investigation. The barrier of distance was now removed; and the next morning she came personally into my presence. She was greatly agitated; and when I reiterated the message from the inner life which my letter had first conveyed to her, she trembled with emotion, and tears gushed forth abundantly from her long-wearied heart.

"Can it be," said she, when her voice once more found utterance, "can it be that we are to be married?"

"Yes," I replied, "I never saw anything more plainly in my life than that."

"In this world, dearest brother?" she asked.

"Yes, in this world, my Spirit-Sister."

"Oh, my heart never dared to hope so far!" she exclaimed with raptured tone. "This is the happiest day of my life! for, I began to fear that I should never see you. But"—she added, as a sudden cloud shadowed her features—"what will the world say?"

"The world has no right to interfere, if you but get a divorce," said I. "That's the first thing for you to do now."

"But I'm so much older than you, and people are so unused to such a disparity of ages—will not this be an objection?"

"No," said I, "nothing is worth noticing but the question of a speedy divorce."

"Yes? Are you sure? Is that all? Will your friends agree to this?"

"My true friends will," I answered. "False friends are of no account."

"Thanks! brother, best beloved, thanks! I will prepare to leave for Bristol next Monday."

"Why do you go to Bristol?" I asked.

"Because a very talented lawyer lives there," she replied; "and evidence can be obtained in the village, to secure my release from a hateful bondage."

Her visit was long and useful. Having seen through her history, I could talk with her of her travels; of what dangers she had encountered at different periods of her life, and how she had escaped them. She seemed beautifully subdued, at times, and then indignant at certain memories. The reader may form some idea of this my benefactress, from a few descriptive sentences:—

She was physically well-proportioned, a little above the medium height, and looked about twenty years older than I. Her countenance, once beautiful, expressed every inward emotion. Strength, suffering, ambition, devotion, childhood, impetuosity — were all depicted in the lines of her expressive face. Feeling, not thought, predominated. Unerringly did I perceive that she was just *the character* to accompany me up the Mountain of Power. In her dark eye there was a look of regal dignity and daring. When angered, few could meet and reciprocate her expression. She was born to rule. Her manner and speech were most gracious and flattering to her particular favorites; but to those whom she did not like, there was that in her flashing eye and imperial deportment which compelled immediate hostility. Her benevolence was impulsive. Nothing was too good for those she loved. To such, her expressions and gifts were profuse and expensive. But for her enemies, there was no punishment too severe.

Seeing all this, I said: "You are governed by love, not by wisdom. Your impulses alone make you ofttimes unhappy, while a calm exercise of wisdom would give you heaven on earth."

"Yes, brother mine — I know you can read me," she answered. "What can you do for me? Will you give me wisdom?"

"I will help you to be quiet," was my response — "I believe I can make your life more useful and happy, else I would not propose this extraordinary marriage."

Thus ended our first interview. Previous to her departure for Bristol, we had two more conversations, and she went away freighted with courage.

A few weeks elapsed ere she completed her arrangements for the legal separation. The business was fixed to come before the next session of the Rhode Island legislature. But her health was much impaired, and she longed for quiet and medical aid. I now took upon myself the responsibility of advising her. Under the circumstances, I deemed it wise to have her near me, until the instituted legal proceedings demanded her presence. I therefore secured of the editor a room on the same floor with my own, and thus opened the way for a temporary sojourn of our mutual benefactress amid the household socialities.

In accordance with this arrangement, but in advance of the time fixed upon, my Spirit-Sister arrived — redolent with enthusiasm. She was justly looked upon as a distinguished guest. Hence her arrival from the boat in the early morning, when "things wasn't in order," was manifestly unpleasant to all save me. She warmly greeted the several inmates, however, promptly took possession of her room with the air of one accustomed to command, and prepared herself to breakfast with the family.

My heart was grateful for this second advent of my endeared friend. Her age and nature were a double barrier to everything but the most respectful reserve between us. My regard for her was as pure and reverential as though she had been a gifted being from that fabled Atlantean Isle —

> ' In the far-off South, where no rude breeze
> E'er sweeps o'er the plain of the halcyon seas,
> Where the airs breathe balm, and the heavens smile
> With a glorious radiance."

She seemed like some queenly abbess, or elder sister, for whom

I cherished a deep and holy affection. Being fatigued with writing for the "Univercœlum," and knowing that she was resolved to disburse with her own means my future boarding-expenses, I gratefully accepted the needed opportunity for leisure, and devoted the fleeting hours to rest and conversation. The day soon passed, and night came o'er the world. Now, I related to her many visions, and instructed her in the principles of spiritual existence. But the retiring hour ere long arrived. The fire in my study-grate glowed warmly. The couch there was rich and large. Her own room was comparatively cold, cheerless, and ordinarily furnished. Her health was quite unsound. Therefore, I counselled her to exchange rooms with me, or else occupy the spacious couch before the study-fire. To the latter suggestion she acceded, whereupon I retired to my adjoining room for the night.

Next morning, ere my esteemed sister had left her quiet resting-place, I heard the servant's knock at the study-door. 'Twas time to rekindle the fires. Noiselessly, and hastily, I passed from my bedroom, behind the couch, to the door, to request the working-woman not to enter just yet, saying that we would soon be prepared to admit her, and then as hastily retreated into my own sleeping-apartment. All this I detail, dear reader, that you may the better comprehend what grew out of it. Furthermore let me add, that for the promotion of our kind benefactress' health and comfort, I induced her to make the same pleasant room, which I could not but consider more hers than mine, her own sacred dormitory for several succeeding nights.

A few mornings after my sister's unexpected arrival, I entered the office of the "Univercœlum," in Broadway, opposite the Park fountain, when the gentlemanly editor said: "Ah, how's your Prophetic Highness?"

This appellation was of course playfully applied—for the editor was one of those who never received my clairvoyant revealments as his standard of belief—much to my gratification and not less to his intellectual credit. Indeed, I have heard him affirm his general acceptation of "Nature's Divine Revelations," because all the leading propositions thereof had previously occupied his own mind. And though the assignment of this reason as the basis of his adoption of the novel truths, seemed to me to be slightly tinged with ideality, still I never questioned the sincerity of his statement.

"Thank you," said I, "since I have stopped writing and examining, I begin to feel better."

There were two or three persons present at the time, and the editor manifested great warmth toward me, but I saw a dark cloud hanging between us. I was startled. "What can this mean?" thought I. And wishing for solitude in which to solve the query, I turned to leave the office; whereupon the editor approached, and cordially asked: "Which way are you going, Brother Davis?"

"I have an appointment at Mr. Freeman's, the artist," said I, "where I expect to meet Mrs. Dodge."

"Wait a moment, till I look over this proof, then I will accompany you."

Very soon we were walking arm in arm, toward the artist's residence. My friend's manner was extremely fraternal, his tones mild as love's own music, but within there lurked an oppressive secret destined for my ear.

"I have to say a word in relation to a certain matter, painful as it is to disturb your spirit, Brother Davis," he at length began; "and I trust it will not alienate your regard for me or any of your valuable friends."

"I think I can hear anything from you, without disturbing my friendship," said I.

"My spirit has been greatly troubled since the morning subsequent to Mrs. D——'s arrival, owing to a painful suspicion that pervades my family against both of you."

"Indeed!" I exclaimed. "Do tell me what it is?"

"The next morning after the lady came," continued he, "when

the servant proceeded to her (Mrs. D——'s) room to make a fire, she found the door unlocked, Mrs. D——'s day-garments suspended on one of the bed-posts, and the bed undisturbed, showing it hadn't been occupied. Then she proceeded to your room, knocked for admission, as it was late, when you came in undress 'o the door, and requested her to wait a while longer."

On hearing this my soul was sorrowful; but, leaning on the Magic Staff, I said: "Well, Brother Brittan, what did all that amount to?"

"Why, the girl came down-stairs in a high state of excitement, frightened and angry, and declared that she knew positively that Mrs. D—— had occupied your room."

"What!" said I, "you do not mean to say that she declared my bedroom to be thus occupied?"

"Yes," answered he, sadly, "but I worked immediately upon her fears. I showed her that she could not be certain—that she was not personally cognizant of any positive circumstances—and that, for so serious a slander, she might be made to suffer even in prison. Yes, Brother Davis, it was only by the utmost energy of opposition that I temporarily silenced our servant's tongue."

"Then," said I, "this suspicion existing in the family against us, explains all those gloomy and acid looks which have been so abundant for a few days past."

"Doubtless," he replied. "I much regret these recent circumstances and events."

"Why didn't you tell me of all this before to-day?" I asked.

"Because you kept yourself away from us—neglecting, at the same time, to bestow any attention on the Bridgeport friends who were our guests — which rendered it necessary for me to wait for a more convenient season."

"Now, Brother Brittan, I will candidly confess that appearances, as you represent them, are against me. But," said I firmly, "*the facts* are wholly in my favor, and that's enough for me to know." Then I gave him a brief sketch of the *real* circumstances, and the *actual* motives which characterized our private movements, just as I have sketched them for thee, dear reader, among the records of preceding pages. But, knowing the editor to be extremely sensitive in regard to the avoidance of evil appearances, I added — " I suppose that I should be more guarded in my conduct for the future."

" For reasons which you may perceive," said he with cordial energy, " I deem it important that your fair fame should remain untarnished."

" It is more important," I replied, " that I act in harmony with my own interior perceptions."

" I trust you will not deem me insincere, Brother Davis," returned he, " when I say that your friends think too much of you not to feel deeply concerned at whatever may injuriously affect your reputation before the world."

" No, Brother Brittan, I believe you 're sincere," said I. " But the friendship of friends is not so important to me as justice and a consciousness of right doing."

" Yes, yes," replied he blandly, " but even where there 's internal purity a man may suffer if outward circumstances and appearances are unfavorable. Perhaps you do not know that my wife has suffered extremely under these painful allegations. Why, she regards you as a model of personal excellence."

" I 'm not insensible to the approbation of my friends," said I. " And in regard to the present affair, I will promise to look the whole matter over, and to act in accordance with what seems to be our mutual welfare."

So saying we entered the artist's room where my honored benefactress was in waiting. Having the Staff to support me, I betrayed nothing of my inward agitation, and soon asked the lady to accompany me to Williamsburgh. During our walk across New York to the Peck Slip ferry, I related to her all that had transpired between the editor and myself. 'T was a most resplendent day without, but a royal darkness pervaded the lady's face as she listened. Emotions of fright, scorn, vengeance, sorrow, were alternated and mingled in her dark eyes. These rapid changes rendered her expressions dramatic and her displeasure tragical. "Restrain your feelings, dear sister," said I, "for all this may redound to our benefit. I will to-night look interiorly at the affair, and determine our future course."

"*Mon Dieu!*" exclaimed she bitterly. "What a conspiracy! What a malignant falsehood! Do not these men and women, your friends, place confidence in *you?* Can they not read you well enough to *know* that you would not thus err?"

"Appearances, dear sister," said I soothingly, "appearances are against us, and from these the world judges, you know."

"'*Honi soit qui mal y pense!*' as the French say," she replied. "These people call themselves 'Reformers' do they?" (A withering satire now predominated.) "They style themselves your 'best friends,' do they? Most noble 'friends!' most noble 're- formers!' most noble 'teachers' of purity! I have seen much of the world," she continued, somewhat subdued, "yet, amid those who make no reformatory pretensions, but who live only like butterflies on the fading flowers of silly fashion, *I never heard any scandal to equal this!*"

"Do n't feel too much disturbed," said I. "We must cherish the spirit of forgiveness, you know, and do good even to those who misconstrue our worthiest deeds."

"I recollect the words of a German countess," she warmly replied: "'I *forgive* in justice to my enemies — I *remember* in justice to myself.'"

Having arrived within a few rods of the editor's residence, we slackened our pace, and I said: "Now let me ask of you, dear sister, to conceal from the family your present severe prejudice. To-night I will seek wisdom, and to-morrow morning will tell you what path we are to tread. If 't is best for you to leave immediately for Bristol, and await there the session of the legislature, or if 't is best for you to remove to some other residence in this vicinity, or, finally, if 't is best for you to board right where you are even under the existing circumstances, I shall presently know and will tell you frankly. Meanwhile, be calm, my sister! for, with this consciousness of innocence dwelling like an angel in each of our hearts, nothing can work us an injury."

"Thanks! dear brother. Thanks!" she submissively replied. "I know *you* will do right. I trust you. I will not, before the family, betray my displeasure. I promise you!"

Directly I proceeded to hold a conference with the kind scribe. I told him all concerning my sad position. He was extremely regretful, but like a true friend, offered me the abiding sympathy of his soul.

CHAPTER XLIX.

FACTS AND FANCIES.

*"Come one, come all, this rock shall fly
From its firm base as soon as I."*

HASTENING into the sweet retirement of my parlor study, and locking the door to prevent intrusion, I passed into interior meditation.

First, I contemplated and estimated the value of my relation to our newspaper; the desires of the editor to maintain an unsullied reputation; the immense pecuniary service that my spirit-sister had been to the cause in which we toiled; the knowledge I had that she was to become my wife after the divorce; that her health was much impaired and required judicious treatment; that I had begun to separate myself from the false position of being *the centre* of a new phase of religious propagandism; that the work of self-extrication was now fully inaugurated; and that, aided by my sister's mental peculiarities, I would ere long reach a sphere of *individuality* which was the first grand end sought by my every guardian angel. Recalling the prophetic words of Swedenborg — spoken on the 7th of March, 1844 — I quoted: "*Obstructions of various kinds will affect thy external life ; but they will tend more fully to expand thy interior being.*" And again: "*Press on thy way, and love only those things tending to truth and wisdom.*" Then I reasoned thus: "Here is a question of external policy, of worldly reputation, of doing that which can only bring me the approbation of persons in the sphere of friendship. Suppose I should yield to this temptation to make friends with the world, then would not 'truth and wisdom' flee in sorrow from my apostate soul? And what would come as my appropriate and only reward? Ah, full well do I know that I should, at best, be oppressed by the weary weight of public adulation. Just this, and nothing more. No," said I, "my benefactress shall remain! She must be respected as my future companion, and I will take the private and public consequences."

This anti-popular conclusion being reached, I sought my honored sister and briefly told her all. She seemed to be satisfied. The tea-bell rang and we seated ourselves with the household group. But her severe prejudice toward the entire family was irrepressible. She *looked* a towering and defiant displeasure. They felt it, and grew pallid with an undefinable uneasiness. Returning to my study, I admonished her to control and overcome her expressions, lest bitter hostility would be speedily excited toward us. That a midnight darkness, from the external sphere, would fall about our feet I was infallibly assured. The only individual in the house, beside my sister-friend, to whom I cared to speak, was the still friendly operator.

Therefore, I forthwith solicited his personal presence. When he entered the study, I said: "A storm-cloud has broken upon our house, doctor, and I wish you to know how it happened."

"I regret it exceedingly," said he, kindly. "Yet I'd like to know all about it."

After repeating the simple facts which led to the compound suspicions, I said: "Another thing, doctor, that induced me to take the liberty of inviting her here as a boarder, was this — that on a certain day (showing him the record in my diary) I interiorly discovered that she is to become my wife."

At this, the doctor's naturally sedate and considerate countenance became still more grave and thoughtful. Very soon, however, he said: "If you would but consent to be magnetized, and while in your superior condition, say that this is right, I think your friends everywhere would be satisfied."

Now, although I had published in the first number of the "Univercœlum" that I could enter the superior state whenever circumstances and my will demanded it, yet did the doctor remain particularly oblivious to the fact, like several other friends who thought they knew all about me; therefore, upon that point, I did not attempt to utter a word of further explanation.

But I resumed: "Now, doctor, there is no need for any trouble here. Let it be understood that the family receive our mutual benefactress as my future companion. The opinion of this world is nothing to me; yet I would neither do evil nor seem to. I need rest and recreation. Hence I do not write articles for the paper now; but I expect soon to resume this labor for the public."

The friendly physician conveyed this information and request to the several members, and thus was established a sort of fictitious harmony for many successive weeks.

Toward the last of March, 1848, after an absence of nearly six months, the poet-missionary returned to New York. His spirit and body were troubled and travel-worn. During a sojourn in Cincinnati, his mind, coming in contact with a vigorous brotherhood of systematic progressives there, became somewhat centralized and morally strengthened. He appeared to have grown up into a spiritual oneness, and to stand out nobly as a child of God. His last letter seemed to me to be full of good news. I was no longer his religious standard. In fact, his mind was so truly individualized and self-centred, that he gave me many definite directions with regard to my own works and ways.

The first night after his arrival he roomed with me. Without reserve, I told him all that had happened. The sighings and wrestlings of his spirit, during those darkly-draperied hours which hung between us and the dawn, made me feel that he was deeply and painfully agitated. He continued to be my avowed friend, however, until the editor's side of my conduct was, on the following day, communicated; and then (much to my private satisfaction) I was completely cast out of a certain circle of spiritual purity!

" 'The Univercœlum' is a fine-looking as well as a fine-reading paper," said I one day, taking up a recent copy, "and the management reflects great credit upon its chief editor, as all must see."

" Undoubtedly the paper would become extremely influential," said a feminine hearer, " if we could only preserve its *purity*."

" Yes!" responded the poet with intense emphasis; " God holds the hearts of men in his hands. God does not, will not, can not, speak through misguided and polluted mediums!"

Thinking that these words might be applied elsewhere, I asked: " Why! do you take our paper to be an impure medium?"

At this the poet's uneasiness became more apparent. Closing his right hand painfully tight, he replied: " Sinful affections, selfishness, materiality, corruption, God can not shine through. A man blinded by passions—a man who yields to his lusts—who loses himself in sensuality—can not be in unity with God!" Saying which, he trembled as if overcome with feelings of unhappiness and horror.

But, leaning and believing firmly upon my Staff, I said: " Yes, that's all true enough; and I am anxious to have all men practise upon so good a principle. But why do you speak so earnestly? Have you met with any such misdirected and corrupted individuals in the state of Ohio?"

" As for Brother Davis," interrupted a visitor, with satire in his tone—" as for him, there's no danger, because he's *so spiritual* and *so careful* about his company."

" True," I replied; " I have always tried to keep good company But I sometimes fail, as I have on *the present* occasion."

At this moment I observed a change thrill through every hearer's heart. Instantly, much fraternal love was converted into fraternal hate. My severe and unqualified retort — the very first I had ever uttered — went straight to the mark! Feeling sad and regretful, I left the room and hastened to my quiet study.

Finding my spirit-sister seated there, I requested her to seek her apartment, that I might thus be left utterly to my own interior meditations. She did so. Whereupon, taking off my glasses for near-sightedness and putting on my clairvoyance for far-sightedness, I looked straight down into the editor's parlor. Thus I could discern the thoughts of each person.

"The case is clear," said the poet with emphasis. "That woman has a positive sphere — is a woman of the world — has ambitions to gratify — is actuated by mixed motives — is dragging Brother Davis down to her own sphere — and we, his brethren, must be equally positive, and rescue him at once!"

"The influence of her mind is extremely positive," observed the doctor. "I think she has partially psychologized him. She has diverted his regard from his best friends, too. I'd like to know what he'd say about it in his superior condition!"

"Yes," interposed the poet, "Brother Davis is a victim! He has lost his purity. His clairvoyance is gone! His letters to me prove it. I put my trust in God."

But no — I will make no further record of the cruel and unjust words that were spoken that night and on subsequent occasions. Ere many days were elapsed I had removed the rich furniture of my rooms to the scribe's not-far-distant residence. My frightened, fatigued, and indignant benefactress, was now about to depart for Bristol, Rhode Island. The scribe's unprejudiced wife welcomed and cheerfully entertained her till she left.

Previous to this event, however, the scribe and I called on the perturbed editor. The poet was already there. We four retired to one of the rooms, when the poet trembled and said:—

"Brother Davis, the occasion demands great plainness of speech. I am a plain, earnest man, and must so express myself. I shall be guilty before God unless I tell you all that is on my mind."

"Certainly," said I, feeling true kindness, "I hope you will speak very plain, Brother Harris."

"Our movement is embarrassed," he nervously continued. "Your friends are troubled in every direction. The news of your corruption has reached Vermont. People talk of it in Troy. It is in every man's mouth everywhere! Articles of exposure are sent to the Tribune, to the Herald, to the Sunday Dispatch. Ruin is upon our path. Before us walk the powers of destruction. We stand in the temple of a dark Night. And we look to you! But you, my brother, are the victim of a strange magnetism!"

"See here," interrupted the scribe, with a determined look, "I think the scandalous reports have not reached so far, by considerable."

At this the editor's eyes flashed with intense excitement. "There is a point," said he, with emphatic energy, "beyond which forbearance ceases to be a virtue."

My heaven-bequeathed Magic Staff was now very strong, and, having a blessed consciousness of private rectitude, my heart was peaceful, and I quietly smiled. The friends did not know that I had investigated the extent of my unpopularity. "Your charges," said I, "are wholly false, and your extravagant story of the widespread excitement is rather poetical. But I am willing to hear any proposition you may have to offer. Only one thing I ask: that Mrs. Dodge be permitted to take her departure in peace."

The next item of importance to me — and to all who may desire to trace my toilsome ascent up the Mountain of Power — was the reception of a fraternal notice from the editor. A meeting of the brethren was to be held at his residence. How thankful was I that our afflicted benefactress had escaped all knowledge of this ecclesiastical trial! She had departed for Bristol.

The scribe and I walked arm-in-arm to the editor's house. The different members of the secret tribunal were seated about the room. The special aim of the session I well enough understood.

It was to induce my return into my former position relative to our social life and public work. As a means for the accomplishment of this object, they were to forge a chain of circumstantial evidences: first, to settle the question of my personal corruption; and, second, to establish the suspicion that my spirit-sister was a misdirected and designing woman. But I had perfect knowledge to the contrary of these allegations, and hence my whole soul was serenely strong, and prepared to receive the criminations without bitterness or strife. There were a few persons present, as I observed, who did not highly appreciate the position assigned them, for they were secretly my steadfast friends. But my open defender was the faithful and conscientious scribe.

Privately, I had resolved to commence the trial—and to say in thirty minutes all I should utter in self-defence. After stating what I considered to be the objects of the conference, I said:—

"It is affirmed that I am the victim of a designing woman. Now, let me read some of our correspondence."

Then I proceeded to read a few extracts from her letters—to show, first, that she did not entertain the least hope of ever seeing me in this sphere, until I gave her permission to visit me in person on a certain day; secondly, to show that she did not think of becoming my wife, till she received the proposition from me to that effect. While reading an extract which indicated that she was actuated by no design—that 'twas her heart alone that held the reins which guided her movements—the editor interrupted:—

"Aha! I didn't know that there was so much love in the affair." Then he added, "I beg leave to suggest that all this reading has no essential bearing on the specific objects of this meeting."

So saying, he arose with firm dignity, and leaned upon his belief, while I leaned upon my Staff. He prefaced his remarks by expressing "the painful regrets he experienced in thus reviving the memory of past circumstances and transactions." And then, with words carefully selected, he made a statement of many facts and many fancies. His affirmations all told against me and mine; and yet I could not feel angry. My soul went out and stood charitably in his mental position. I viewed the case from his stand-point and temperament, and thus made myself realize the naturalness of his inferences. Besides the fear of being publicly condemned for shielding a fancied domestic evil, the editor, naturally kind and confiding with his friends, had become severely exasperated by a long-continued encounter with my sister's unguarded and severe expressions of imperious indignation. Though I frequently softened her prejudices, yet she could not, at times, control her arrogant impulse verbally to burn out all opposition Neither could the thus *burnt* opponent control feelings of wounded pride, nor yet the bitter expressions of consequent personal repugnance. Hence I could not realize the least resistance to the proceedings instituted and the unkind words uttered on the night of that memorable meeting.

At length the poet, who had taken an active part in the transactions of the evening, drew near to me in a more tranquil mood, and said:—

"Come, now, Brother Davis, you are among your brethren; we are your friends, and will not betray you. Tell us, then — have you been led into this criminality as the evidence goes to prove?"

"Why do you ask?" I inquired. "Do you, after all, *doubt* the evidence so ingeniously arrayed here to-night?"

"Oh, no; but we wish you to be candid with us, your brethren, and we will sustain you through it all."

See here, now," interposed the scribe, who as yet had said but little, "I object to Brother Davis giving any answer. In common law, a man is considered *innocent* till proved to be guilty. No man is called upon to testify in such a case, and I counsel Brother Davis to make no response whatever."

This sudden opposition from the considerate scribe shot into the editor's bosom, and his fraternal love seemed to be thereby invert-ed. He seldom indulged himself in the luxury of being entirely mistaken; and the scribe's offence consisted in this open declaration of skepticism regarding his positions. His ideal of a full-grown man seemed to be one who is never obliged essentially to change his propositions. To be unexceptionably consistent was ever his laudable aim. Hence, any direct opposition was a reflection upon his reasoning faculties. Therefore the mild scribe was for weeks afterward made aware of the trespass he had committed Perhaps he has not yet wholly recovered from private wounds inflicted in consequence of his conscientious friendship for me.

About midnight the secret conclave was disbanded, with an understanding on the part of some that I was to "reconsider" my openly-avowed intention to be married. The principal reason assigned for wishing to prevent the union was, their belief in the outrageous scandal that my spirit-sister had lived unworthily.

Next morning my meditations were these: "How cruelly has my cherished friend been misrepresented! But, grant that she has been a misguided woman, as the poet openly and positively declared last night — what then? Should I therefore forsake her? Can the erring be reclaimed by austerity and denunciation? Of late I have heard nothing but insinuations about 'purity' — silly platitudes concerning 'virtue' — poetic dissertations upon 'sensuality' — from persons whose pretended mission is to *reclaim the wanderer!* who profess friendship for the misdirected traveller! who believe in returning good for evil — words of love for words of anger — who erect a high standard for humanity! If my benefactress were the woman whom these men describe, (which I know is false as error itself,) then the more potent the reason why I should unfailingly cause the spiritual sun of fraternal love to shine upon and heal her bruised heart. These men I can not make my guides. They say the world will frown upon and condemn me. Well, the condemnation of the ignorant is all the worldly approbation my soul requires. The poet says the 'Tribune' may publish an exposure of my conduct. Well, if there were daily Tribunes issued on every rod of space between the earth and the sun, and if each number contained an article against me, I should go on in the path I have chosen. What conscience dictates to be done, that will I do, nor turn aside to confer with the powers of this world."

What supported me, dear reader? 'T was the inward conscious ness of right-doing, and my blessed Magic Staff. My course led up the Mountain of Power—not power over men's minds or circumstances, but power over whatsoever was selfish and imperfect in myself—a pilgrimage of psychical benefits eternal.

CHAPTER L.

THE FRATERNAL MARRIAGE.

ABOUT the middle of April, 1848, soon after the memorable midnight meeting, I took my flight from the habitations of men. The beloved scribe accompanied me to the boat, and left upon my heart the seal of indissoluble affection.

Spring was smiling all around. Poughkeepsie seemed beautiful as ever. Heaven was transcendently glorious. The exilement which I had temporarily imposed upon myself, was for the accomplishment of two objects, viz.: to cut off all further attempt to make me "the prophet" of a theologico-philosophic movement, and to prepare my mind for a higher plane of public usefulness. Looking back upon my Williamsburgh brethren, I said: "'Father forgive them, they know not what they do.'" And a dewy shower of angel-blessings fell upon my spirit. O how sweet was my rest! My most lonely hours were beguiled by loving words from lips not seen by mortal man.

I had two valued correspondents—my brother scribe, and my spirit-sister. His letters were freighted with impressions, from without and within; while hers bore decided marks of fear, sorrow, tribulation, fatigue, and pure affection. In one of her written messages she said:—

"You will be surprised, brother best beloved, if I ask you to consider once again the propriety of my present plans. Are you still sure that I shall succeed in my legal proceedings? My anxiety to throw off the hated manacles, is intense! Many, many years have I longed for liberty! Shall I obtain it? Do you know that I will? Tell me — I can bear it — for I can die. . . . . I regret that I have caused you so much trouble. I sometimes fear that I am not suited for you. Is it right? Are you sure that we ought to be married?"

But from week to week I stilled the troubled waters and inspired her with courage, and hope, and power to conquer. Day and night I was tranquil as truth, nay, elevated, supported in purpose, full of light on great questions, and happy. Yet I longed for the presence of some confiding friend; and hence, toward the last of April, I wrote the scribe and requested him to visit me. He came, and our spirits mingled in the pleasures of elevated fraternal converse.

"Brother Fishbough," said I, "there are three cardinal principles by which a true man may infallibly regulate his life — viz.: Self justice, Fraternal justice, and Universal justice."

"Yes," he replied, "these ideas have lately come up before my mind in a new aspect."

"That's good!" exclaimed I. "What did you think about them?"

"It came clearly to my mind," he replied, "that self-justice is the *basis* from which a man may begin to perfect himself in harmony."

"Yes — that's right — go on," said I. "So I saw it when writing that article on 'The True but Unloved Religion.'"

"Self-justice," continued the calm scribe, "teaches me, first, my duties to my own body (to preserve health, &c.); second, my duties to that *other part* of me, my wife and children; and, thirdly, my duties with reference to property, reputation, &c. I feel now, as I never felt before, that *this* SELF-justice is the basis on which rests *all justice* to the neighbor and to the world."

"That's the very principle by which I have tried to regulate my life," I replied. "I have maintained steadily this idea of *justice*, regardless of expediencies, in all my proceedings, and that's why the brethren do not understand my steps."

Next day the scribe departed for New York.   Returning from the wharf, leisurely walking through one of the by-streets of Poughkeepsie, I was suddenly and powerfully pulled back a step or two as by an invisible hand.   At the same instant there shot into the sidewalk before me, to the depth of several inches, *a heavy crowbar !* which had by accident slipped from a workman's grasp upon the roof of a very high building.   'Twas the work of a moment.   My escape was alarmingly narrow ; and as I passed onward my nerves trembled with the shock they had received. But my soul was silent.   This fresh testimony from my guardian spirits filled me with gratitude too deep for words.   I felt that a well-ordered life only could pay for the life preserved.

As I had foreseen, the legislature granted the bill which secured personal freedom to my spirit-sister.   The scribe accompanied me to Boston, and there I met the liberated woman.   And, as I had also foreseen, we were married.   The legal ceremony took place at the scribe's residence, on the 1st of July, 1848.   'Twas not a fashionable wedding, dear reader — not a season of heartless festivities — but an *event* sanctified by a holy purpose.   From the first hour of our acquaintance, I discerned, with my interior understanding, the wisdom of this extraordinary union.   But my reader has seen that " the ways of wisdom" sometimes lead through perilous circumstances, and yet, that to the true and determined traveller, " all her paths are peace."

Returning from a brief tour to Poughkeepsie, I made arrange ments to begin housekeeping next door to the scribe's residence. Knowing that my companion's income consisted of a definite sum semi-annually received, and wishing to keep a memorandum of our current expenses, I purchased a day-book and ledger, and thus commenced a systematic record.   The first entry in my day-book was as follows :—

" Williamsburgh, August 4, 1848.   The earth and the world to

A. J. Davis and companion—Debtor. To a respectable living and competence." Then, to open and balance the account commercially, I charged our firm as follows: "A. J. Davis and companion to the earth and the world—Debtor. To living a life that shall prove the 'kingdom of heaven to be within.' Also, to practising the doctrine which teaches that Self justice is the truest kindness—that Universal justice is the highest expression of true Religion."

The hired dwelling was neither large nor elegantly finished. But within, owing to my companion's oriental taste, the comforts and decorations were original and sumptuous. "Your moderate income," I quietly suggested, "will not cover the bills." But the slightest idea of interference or restraint was to her intensely disagreeable. Her impulses were strong, child-like, extravagant, generous, regal, excitable, undisciplined, and majestic. "Economy" was not to be found in her organization. Her habits of living, compared with mine, were all cast in a large mould. For many years her fortune had been ample and commensurate with her generous outlays, but now, as I had interiorly seen, owing to various financial disbursements, it was barely sufficient to meet her own necessary expenses.

"Well, brother," said she fondly, after the first wave of irritation had swept past, "I will not rebel against your advice. I know your spirit should not be disturbed with these worldly matters."

But even while she spoke there flashed over her countenance a look of sharp regret and severe impatience. Seeing which I said: "Nay, nay, dear sister, do not feel sad nor disappointed. We, you know, should not derive our happiness from externals. Petty cares and trifling incidents, to you and I, should be no more than bubbles on the bosom of some mighty river."

"Yes, yes, brother mine—there! I think I shall never get over calling you 'brother.' Now that we are married the world will not comprehend it. But—O that blessed, pure, holy, beau tiful *correspondence* of ours! Your sweet letters began 'Dear Spirit-Sister,' and I addressed you my 'Brother best beloved. Yes—beautiful! And I fear I never shall learn to exchange that blessed word for anything else. What may we style each other now? Can you give me a name—a new, unearthly name —one that expresses our holy union?"

While she was speaking thus, I distinctly heard the word "*Silona*" whispered near my ear; and I said: "Yes, I will give you the name by which the angels know you."

"Oh, joy, joy!" exclaimed she, "what is it? What do they say? Oh, would that I could look and hear for myself. Tell me, brother mine!"

"A well-known guardian," said I, "has just whispered the word 'Silona.' I do not now know its meaning. But it is your spiritual name. So, after this, before folks I will call you 'Katie,' and 'Silona' when we are beyond the reach of human hearing."

"Oh, beautiful word!" said she, with a subdued and tearful look. "I will not any more be troubled by these materials things. But —what is yours? If you hav'n't a spiritual name to give yourself, I will call you 'My Jackson.' That's what my heart keeps naming you."

At this moment our mutual friend and neighbor, the scribe, entered and desired me to go and look at a chart.

"Mr. Fishbough," said she with an imperial severity, "I'd thank you, sir, to let Mr. Davis remain with me."

This was more irritating than anything I ever before heard addressed to the affectionate scribe. It was not only unexpected and emphatic, but it was *commanding* also, and I dreaded the effect on my friend's heart. But remembering that Katie was my companion up the Mountain of Power, I offered no remark to soften the expression.

Taking my Staff, and excusing myself for a few minutes, I followed the scribe into his study. "What have you to show me, my friend?" was my first inquiry.

" My chart," said he, " that was suggested in a dream of which I told you something."

The faithful scribe — having completed his last important editorial work for me, viz.: the copying off and preparation of my chart, entitled, " The History and Destiny of the Race"— ad just sketched out his own chart at the time of which I now write.

" Your metaphysical mind will work," said I, " and I am glad to see its productions."

" This chart," commenced the scribe with characteristic particularity, " is constructed upon strictly correspondential principles. It shows," said he, pointing to the concentric circles and conspiring sections, " it shows the action of principles that underlie universal progression, education, development, government, &c. As you perceive, it is based upon *your* classification of the Affections, and not only illustrates the structure and progress of all material creations, but distinctly shows the spiral path of human progress which leads from Infancy to the summit of Perfection."

" That's a very interesting chart," said I. But as I examined it more closely, methought I noticed a tendency to complexity or involvement, so to speak, and so I added : " Brother Fishbough, the world, I fear, is hardly prepared to comprehend its principles."

A heavy shade of sadness gathered on his brow as I spoke, and his thoughts, as it seemed to me, reverted to Katie's severe rebuff. Thus was ruffled the placid stream of his friendship, nor did subsequent expressions from her tend at all to smooth the troubled waters. These slight changes and checks in the flow of his sympathies surcharged his heart, and also excited a feeling of resistance. But I did not yield to unhappy emotions. Because I had foreseen the righteousness of the work which this spirit-sister was to accomplish as my private associate. She was destined to isolate me from my best friends, and thus to instruct me in the art of relinquishing external dependencies and overcoming external obstacles in the pathway of spiritual progression.

CHAPTER LI.

THE RECONCILIATION.

"Who blesses others in his daily deeds,
    Will find the healing that his spirit needs;
For every flower in others' pathway strewn,
    Confers its fragrant beauty on our own."

THE influence of "The Univercœlum," under the careful and tasteful management of its chief editor, was daily widening and deepening.   Many who had slept at the gates of light, and those who had entered in thereat, were equally benefited by its spiritual magnetism.   The reports of my troubles had not injured its circulation so much as the fact that I had not written anything for its columns during many weeks.

The editor's physical health was becoming enfeebled from over-mental taxation, but his fine abilities remained firm and every-where acceptable.   His task had been arduous and embarrassing. He ceaselessly yearned for a system of united action, and I knew that in private he was still my friend.   The external proof of this was presented through a letter of his in answer to one of mine soon after I imposed upon myself the discipline of exilement.   It was as follows:—

"NEW YORK, *May* 26, 1848.

"DEAR BROTHER DAVIS: . . . . . . I can hardly suppose that any one has a desire that you should be an exile from your friends, and I am constrained to think that you have misapprehended the wishes of those friends whose devotion has perhaps rendered them unnecessarily solicitous in your behalf. . . . . I grieve that a cloud lingers in the horizon which reflects a shadow on thy spirit, whose appropriate place is in the midst of light which is inaccessible to less-gifted souls. May it pass quickly away, and the fresh joy, which baptized thy spirit when first we met, return and make thy earthly being bright and beautiful again.

" With undiminished affection, I am
" Yours faithfully,   " S. B. B."

Such was the editor's genial expression of undisturbed regard. My marriage called out no opposition. On the contrary, soon afterward — in August — I received a letter from the poet, proposing a reconciliation, as may be seen by the following transcript of the same :—

"NEW YORK, *August,* 1848.

" ESTEEMED FRIEND: Although I have not seen or heard from you for a considerable time, and during that period many unforeseen circumstances have transpired, I feel moved to write to you; and shall do so in a spirit of cordiality and frankness — believing that you will recognise and respond to the spirit that prompts and the feelings that find utterance. . . . . .

" I feel that your inward desire is for Unity. I feel the same desire myself. I wish to behold all who are interested in spiritual progress brought together — to see all errors forgiven, all animosities buried, all roots of bitterness destroyed. You feel and desire the same. . . . . . But the feeling of good-will and the desire for unity are not beneficial unless they find an open expression. Having these feelings, I have felt impelled to express them — thinking it might aid you in considering the position of the Friends of the Cause.

" With feelings of respect for your companion and of regard for yourself.

" I remain yours,   " T. L. H."

" What letter is that, my Jackson?" asked Katie, just as I had read the last sentence.

" It's a very noble and welcome note from Brother Harris," replied I.

" How dare he !" she exclaimed indignantly —" how dare he, after all that's past, write *you* a letter ?"

" He's asking for a reconciliation," said I ; " to bury all animosities, to have all errors forgiv—"

" Heaven knows," interrupted she, " that I am willing to forgive, but I can not *forget* the treachery of your pretended friends !"

" They were not treacherous," said I soothingly ; " they were only anxious to save the nucleus of the movement from blemish. When I place myself in their positions, I do not wonder at their trepidation."

" Well," said she haughtily, " what does he propose ?"

" Nothing directly," I replied. " But I gather from the tenor of his words that the friends would like to have a meeting."

" A meeting !" exclaimed she with dignity. " Would you consent to meet again with those men ?"

" Most gladly," I replied. " And will you not say ' Amen,' Silona ?"

" Oh, yes," returned she, suddenly subdued, " if *you* request it."

" Ah, that's quite worthy of my spirit-sister," said I. " Now, I'll reply to the friends immediately, and fix a meeting to come off in this very house."

The time between this conversation and the meeting of reconciliation was brief. The result was good. There seemed to be peace and good-will pervading the session. But my indignant companion found it difficult to restrain her resentment, as her haughty manner plainly indicated, though she said nothing to mar the interchange of friendly sympathies. The conclusion was — that we, the editors, would sign and publish a brief notice of the reinstatement of our mutual harmony, and that I would thenceforward make the " Univercœlum" the vehicle of my highest intuitions. The principal editor, the poet, the scribe, &c., all voluntarily agreed that I was the proper person to write the notice. On the subsequent morning I wrote the statement, as delicately as I could, and hastened to leave it at the office in time for the next issue. The poet read it over, and said, "It's very scientific." 'Twas published in the number dated September 9, 1848, and read as follows :—

"To our Readers : Last spring there was a development of previously-existing disturbances among editors and contiguous minds immediately connected with the Univercœlum—a *misunderstanding* having for its parent three causes, viz. : a misappreciation of individual motives, a misconception of individual responsibilities, a misarrangement of individual persons in reference to their true positions and spheres of action. This misunderstanding not being speedily removed, ultimated in a voluntary divergence. But *time* has developed the motives of all ; and *circumstances* have modified their respective responsibilities, defined their true positions, united their efforts ; and *experience* has mapped their course in the future. Henceforth they form but one body, tread but one path, labor but for one purpose ; and will endeavor to represent, by their oneness of Soul and combination of Strength, the triumph of the threefold manifestation of the Religious Sentiment viz., Self, Fraternal, and Universal Justice.

"Editors of Univercœlum."

In accordance with my agreement, I recommenced writing and publishing for the world. In consenting to this fraternal reconciliation — which I did with my whole heart — I did not assume any responsibility of leadership, but maintained my chosen post as only *one* among *many*. My path still led up the steep, dark Mountain, and my painful experiences were naturally incidental to my pilgrimage. Hence I did not complain nor lose my essential serenity. And with exceeding joy did I treasure the kindly words, the hearty smiles, the noble sentiments, which produced and sealed that remembered reconciliation.

My soul was now armed for the battle of life. With peaceful words and just principles I had resolved to treat with the world. Panoplied with no coat-of-mail, hidden behind no shield, energized by the force of no passion, fearing neither to live nor to depart, wrapped only in the mantle of universal charity, and accompanied by no visible being save "Silona," I had pledged myself to drink deep of the infinite waters of Truth, to tread with fearless foot the rugged precipices in the distance, and thus solve the problem of Individuality and test the value of independent illumination.

Among the living pictures of memory, there is one of a noble man who served me when I most needed him. Katie's income was considerably less than our expenses. She had loaned money to help on Reform. Her outstanding obligations were equal to the amount thus appropriated. Seeing that we could not meet the bills sent in from various sources, I devoted a whole day to the question of liquidation. At length the air trembled with sweet sounds, wavelets of ethereal music thrilled into my deepest heart, and the same loveful voice of years agone said, " *Write—to —thy—brother.*"

" Do you mean the person of whom I was just thinking?" I asked.

The celestial voice replied: " *He—is—the—friend—to—stand —between—thee—and—the—world.*"

Straightway, while my heart was overflowing with wordless joy, I wrote to the chosen brother, who then resided at Boonton Falls, New Jersey. Only a few days elapsed ere he called at our house. He forthwith examined the accounts, made an estimate of our liabilities, drew checks and gave notes to meet them to the amount of nearly fifteen hundred dollars; advised us to break up house keeping; and, finally, that I might be free from property cares and weekly expenses, he cordially invited us to share with him the joys and freedom of his family group. Beautiful indeed is the providence of the angel-world! The steadfast friendship of this brother, and the many deeds of intelligent kindness that spontaneously issued from the sanctuary of his heart, are among the best pictures which hang on the walls of my memory.

Before moving to the residence of Mr. Green, I wrote out my penetrations concerning pestilential cholera. A published statement of the particulars of what I saw, by voluntary clairvoyance, ir

Paris, in Berlin, and in St. Petersburg — of the number of cholera-patients in each hospital and locality — gave the public an opportunity to judge, on the arrival of the next steamer, of the reliability of my perceptions. The editor of the "New York Sun," noticing this article in the "Univercœlum," copied nearly the whole of it, and appended the following:—

"A communication from a professor of clairvoyance, relating to the causes and cure of the cholera, the origin of the potato-rot, a flying visit of twenty minutes to St. Petersburg, etc., will be found in another column. This communication, made before the arrival of the Hermann, is strongly confirmed in its facts by the news by that steamer, which, it will be seen by a glance at yesterday's Sun, represents the cholera as *declining in Russia* and *increasing in Prussia.* Whatever our readers may think of clairvoyance, there is an amount of common sense in the philosophy of the communication worthy respectful attention. We have not seen the subjects of cholera and potato-rot more earnestly and scientifically treated."

We will now revert once more to the poet of this psychological drama, whose nature was aspiringly spiritual. My impressions, when first he avowed his determination exclusively to preach from "Nature's Divine Revelations," were strictly fulfilled. The ebb was equalled only by the flow. The backward swing of the pendulum was legitimate. During the summer of 1848 he preached for the "Independent Christian Society" at the Broadway Coliseum. He thus perfected the admirable work of centrifugation To show that his separation from me, as a religious authority, was complete, I will introduce a paragraph or two from his pen to the "Univercœlum" of September 30, 1848, as follows:—

"I observe a tendency on the part of certain minds to place implicit reliance on all statements which come from persons in states of mental illumination; to make their words authoritative; to receive their sayings as oracular and infallible; to accept and endorse their statements, without evidence and without investigation. This is visible among the sect of 'Swedenborgians.' Many

among them receive Swedenborg as infallible authority, and en-
slave their minds to his statements.   They carry their blind, idiotic
subserviency so far as to deny their reason and distrust their intuitions, if so b: that they are at variance with the statements contained in their teacher's 'Doctrines of the New Jerusalem,' or
'Memorable Relations of Things seen and heard in Heaven and
Hell.'   No matter how reasonable be an idea, or how great a mass
of evidence sustains it — provided Swedenborg deny it, it is treated
with contemptuous indifference, as unworthy of notice.

"I observe the same tendency among some who have been interested in the various statements put forth by Mr. Davis.   It
pains me to the heart to find men who ridicule the supernaturalists for making the sayings of Moses, or Jonah, or Jude, authoritative and infallible — greater than reason, more reliable than conscience, falling themselves into the same error — believing whatever Mr. Davis alleges, because he utters it — without investigation, without proof — without even asking for proof.   It ought to
be borne in mind that Mr. Davis's book contains errors and contradictions, in the midst of much that is truthful.   It ought to be
remembered that he has made grave mistakes, and at any time is
liable to repeat them.   The very ideas he advocates show conclu-
sively that this slavery of the mind to the assertions of any man
— this voluntary paralysis of reason — this setting up of oracles,
and blind reception of their words — is a foul transgression; and,
history adds, has been the cause of unnumbered misfortunes to the
race.   If I apprehend aright the position of Mr. D., he recoils as
much from this as I do.   Now, while the evil is in its incipient
state, be warned and let it extend no further."

The few active supporters of the "Univercœlum" were now
struggling to keep the publication above the impending and con
centrating storm of pecuniary embarrassment.   But the Fates had
spoken: the paper was destined to be dissolved.   Such was the
disastrous scene enacted before my inner vision a few hours after
the proposition was made to publish it.   Yet, against the laws of
cause and effect, I prayed for its continuance.

The melancholy hours of one dark December day I devoted to
planning a new distribution of existing forces.   The principal ed

itor, as I was well aware, had influence with several liberal and wealthy persons. I therefore suggested that he be delegated to the work of procuring means and subscribers, while the scribe might assume the editorial responsibilities. Thus co-operating, I hoped that the excellent publication might be sustained for a yet longer period.

But the ponderous wheels of Time at length rolled over the office. They utterly crushed and destroyed our winged idol. There was straightway heard a wail of lamentation in many homes — a dirge-like requiem trembled upon the bosom of reformers — a few lingering notes reverberated through "The Spirit of the Age" — distant and familiar faces looked sad and thoughtful; but, anon, the human-world was clashing as before, while the angel-world continued to smile benignly, and to send forth its truths freely and universally.

CHAPTER LII.

THE FATAL GEM.

OUR removal to the residence of Mr. Green, in Boonton, New Jersey, secured to us a blessed relief from worldly cares, and brought to our hearts the luxury of refined and genial and elevated associations. But Silona's health continued to be quite imperfect, and, therefore, after a few months, we went to the South Orange Water-Cure.

Shortly subsequent to our arrival there, in September, 1849, I began to feel the intuitional foreshadowing of the initial volume of an "Encyclopædia" which had been previously promised to the world. As yet, I had not sufficient confidence to go on in so great a work, without some one to review the orthography and grammatical construction of my sentences and paragraphs. Hence I penned a note to the scribe requesting a visit. His aspirations were steadily philanthropic. And I had in mind to propose an associate publishing establishment, including several departments of reformatory work — a sort of Eclectic Institution for the promulgation of the high moral principles forming the basis of the Harmonial Philosophy, and of the several sciences embraced within its boundless sweep.

To my letter the scribe responded in person. Our conversation was long and explicit. But the sweet endearments of a former period did not return. We each vividly remembered the tenderness of our fraternal attachment. But neither felt the upgushing tide of communion that once mingled and blended our private sympathies. The unconscious cause of this effect was my frank and fearless Katie. She did not seem to realize the depth and poignancy of the past trials of the generous scribe. His manly and self-sacrificing words and deeds in our behalf she appeared utterly to forget. He did not personally please her temperament and the extraordinary vivacity of her face mirrored forth her prejudice. Still, she did not object to any reformatory plan I had in contemplation. Nothing could be more certain, however, than this: that she was too sensitive and too aristocratic for my plainly-dressed and plainly-spoken associates, while I was too unpopular and too democratic for the wealthy classes with whom she had mingled during all her previous years. Therefore, each shielded the other from contact with the external world. She was isolating me and I was isolating her: and I rejoiced, while she did not complain, at this grand result. It gave me the perpetual retirement of a Monastery, the seclusion of a mountain home above the sea, and still I dwelt amid the multitude.

One day, as I was walking in the grove near the Water-Cure, a soft breath, as of mingled melodies, floated o'er me, and my Guide said: "*Tell—Silona—that—the—twain—owe—her—nothing.*"

The effect of this message I could not anticipate. The parties were far from being Katie's favorites. But feeling full confidence in my Guide's judgment and counsel, I sought Silona, and said: " Do you feel that your notes against Lyon and Fishbough need ever be paid?"

" No," she replied, " and I would give them up to-day if I thought those men would be the better for it."

" The readiness of her generosity, the absence of all opposition, greatly surprised me. " 'Tis my opinion," said I, " that they are both oppressed by this obligation. Suppose I just enclose them the whole amount of their indebtedness to us. Would you like that, Silona?"

"Anything *you* desire," said she with tenderness. "You are my wisdom."

Glad enough was I to send the brothers, in accordance with the spiritual suggestion, this testimonial of our mutual good-will. The notes returned amounted to two thousand dollars only; as we concluded to retain our right to the English edition. The scribe's delicate response was as follows:—

"DEARLY BELOVED BROTHER:......... Your very kind letter I have read over many times, and feel the utmost embarrassment in attempting to answer it ..... I accept the kind offer which it bears, holding myself responsible to Heaven to see justice done according to the best perceptions of my conscience. If the Revelations should hereafter become profitable in a pecuniary sense, I will not—I must not—allow myself to appropriate the proceeds exclusively to myself.

"Yours in love,   "W. F."

We felt richly rewarded. The money and labor had sent into the world a valuable aid to struggling humanity. 'Twas a work of unadulterated love; the brothers were the wisely-selected agents; and in this view we mutually rejoiced.

My sole object in making this item public is to keep up the chain of *spiritual providences* which distinguishes my individual history. That peculiar modesty which is unfavorable to a free personal confession, pro or con, is a species of delicacy that will not stand the test of clairvoyant penetration. It will not answer at the Day of Judgment—beneath the sun of conscience—ever at its noontide effulgence in the mind of an honest man.

One of the Water-Cure patients, a pedantic and highly-conceited character, returning from his walk one morning, accosted me and said: "Sir, I have been here almost a month, without exchanging a word with you, but my wish has been to propound a few questions if you do not object."

"Oh, no," said I, "when not writing I'm ready to answer all the questions I can."

Accordingly we seated ourselves on a rustic bench, beneath the waving trees, and he began: "I am free to confess, sir, that my mind is decidedly prejudiced against you; yet I am not one of those who will not investigate a new thing. Permit me to ask, sir, if you have ever clairvoyantly looked into the origin of modern religious worship?"

Instantly I knew that he was not wholly sincere; that he only wished to while away an idle hour. "Yes," I replied, "I have examined the subject many times."

"Where did it originate?"

"In the East," said I, "toward the rising sun."

"Why in the East?" he inquired with a show of interest.

"Because of a necessity in human nature there," said I, "before the western hemisphere was populated."

"Do you really believe," he asked, "that you have seen the eastern hemisphere?"

"Yes, sir. My recollection of what I saw is clear as the noon-day sun."

"What have you seen there of interest?"

"The first thing I saw that interested me," I replied, "was disconnected with the subject upon which I was lecturing at the time."

"What was it? Pardon my curiosity; but I'm fond of travellers' stories," said he laughing.

"Nadir Shah's footsteps on Persian lands first attracted my attention," I replied. "The plunderings and cruelties and assassinations and licentious excesses of this Invader were inscribed on the very sands and soils of India."

"Indeed!" was the listener's response. "What became of the tyrant?"

"In a few moments," said I, "while looking over the traditions of the people, I saw that he was at length horribly assassinated by the chiefs of his own band."

"What else did you see?" inquired the patient.

"I perceived," said I, "that the Hindoos had a floating superstition concerning Nadir Shah, which might be imported into this country and applied."

" Ah !" returned he.   " Can you tell me what it was ?"

" It was that the robber carried upon his person a GEM which was certain to bring desolation upon any individual or nation that possessed it.   The people seriously believed that this fabulous gem was a reality, and that it has brought disaster, sorrow, and ruin, upon several kings and dynasties since the days of Nadir Shah, the merciless robber of the Cabul Mountains."

" I have never before heard of this superstition," said he. " But how would you apply it in this country ?"

" I 'll tell you.   Milton's devil carried about with him a splendid Gem which, like the Hindoo diamond, is certain to bring misfortune upon its possessor."

" What do you refer to, sir ?" asked the patient.

" I refer to his *Ambition* to succeed in his undertakings — not because the object in view was good, but because he had too much Pride to be defeated in the prosecution of his selfish aims."

" I can not comprehend the application," said he.

" The fatal Gem," I continued, " is the personal *Pride* that fixes lawyers, physicians, clergymen, and others, in several unjust and discordant relations to humanity.   They are not childlike in the pursuit of Truth.   Respectability is more precious to such persons than Wisdom.   Ambition is the ruling star of their destiny. Society bequeaths this fatal *trait* to its offspring from age to age, and hence the misfortunes and sorrows which rankle in the world's bosom."

The sound of the dinner-bell was now upon the air, and directly our conversation ended.   Occasionally, for months afterward, I wondered what there was in the stranger's temperament or state of mind which elicited the words on " Pride" during our first and last interview.   At length, however, the post brought me a letter from the almost forgotten hydropathic patient, in which I read this sentence :—

"'The fatal Gem,' sir, is no longer in my possession. As a result, my wife and children and neighbors love me better — I love myself better — and I have had much less difficulty in my business relations. Ninety days after our short talk I withdrew a foolish lawsuit — confessed myself wrong for the first time in twenty years — and I now speak to persons to whom, for years, I have been as a thorn and a scourge. If you should ever come into this region, my dear sir, do not fail to give me and my family a call."

Katie's health was rapidly improving. She pursued the treatment and adopted the diet for many weeks. Well do I remember the hour when, immediately after returning from one of her baths, she exclaimed: "Oh, Jackson, how I long to read over once again some of your dear letters to me!"

"Why so, Katie? Am I not as consoling as my letters were?"

"You don't understand me," said she with an anxious look. "You are so taken up with your writing, every day, that I seldom get anything from you about our beautiful union."

"Silona," I responded, "we both realize the purity of our marriage and the pleasure which it brings us."

"Oh, yes," she replied, "but I love to hear you talk about it every day."

"Well, Katie, what would you like to have me say?"

"Oh, tell me whether you think that our union is for eternity. Will it continue for ever? Are you sure — very, very sure — that all marriages are eternal?"

"As far as I can see," said I, "all true marriages are indissoluble."

"My heart is overpowered with happiness at the thought, my Jackson," exclaimed she. "And now tell me once again, do you know — really, truly, surely, positively know — that our marriage is a *true* union?"

"Nothing is more certain, Silona, than the purity of our relation.   But," I added, "remember I said that ' *as far as I can see*' all true marriages are indissoluble."

" Good Heavens !" exclaimed she with a look of queenly dignity and heartfelt alarm — " What do I hear?   Tell me, Jackson ! Do you not *know* that our relation is unalterable ?"

" Nay, Katie, I do not know, but I *believe*, that our union is eternal."

" You really *do believe*, then, that our marriage is to last for ever ! Do you still believe this, my Jackson ?"

" Yes, Silona — I have faith in the perpetuity of our union."

We talked over the blissful advantages of unwavering conjugal ties — how one soul is buoyed up by the confidence and devotion of its kindred soul — and that, amid all the treachery and uncertainty of outward events, there is sweet strength and joyful rest in the consciousness of truly-blended hearts.   And ever after this conversation — whenever the question of marriage was alluded to by others — she would affirm, positively, that " our union was eternal, because I had so declared it ;" and yet, when alone in each other's society, she would sometimes recall my words, and ask : " What did you mean by saying that our marriage was eternal ' *as far as you could see*' ?"

My reply was that " I did not yet know whether a marriage is eternal because it is true and desired, or because of other reasons and principles hidden in the spiritual constitution.   But of one thing I was always certain : that our union was *a true one*, and by virtue of this certainty we had a powerful evidence in favor of its perpetuity."   Her warm heart and imperious mind, however, could endure to be neither contradicted nor checked in their enthusiastic and overwrought expressions.   Hence, believing that she was my true companion, and that I should tenderly shield her temperament from pain, I attempted no explanations nor modifications of her words, but constantly leaned upon my Magic Staff and lived a life harmonious.

CHAPTER LIII.

READINGS AND TEACHINGS.

" I live for those who love me;
  For those who know me true;
For the heaven that smiles above me,
  And awaits my spirit, too :
For the cause that lacks assistance;
For the wrong that needs resistance;
For the future in the distance,
  And the good that I can do."

ANGEL-FACES shone down from skies so deeply pure, and immortal voices shook the inner air so gently, that, though we were travelling up the rugged Mountain, our feet faltered not, and our hearts misgave us never for a single day. The ambrosial bounties of Nature were shed silently along our pathway, and the struggles consequent upon the pilgrimage were more and more softened and subdued and tempered to our capabilities of endurance. And yet, these aids would have been like so many empty shadows and of no avail, had it not been for my own private determination to depend on one ever-present source of strength—the Magic Staff.

Time dropped down, hour by hour, into the ocean of eternity. Sometimes a whole month would drop, while I was interiorly composing chapters for another volume, and, but for the plash it made in the waters of memory, it seems to me that I should have realized no lapse of time. The events of the journey, and not the days consumed, clustered on the vine of life.

Without the scribe's aid, without external help from books, I wrote the first volume of the "Harmonia." This was my principal occupation during the fall and spring of 1849–'50. Soon afterward, obeying a constitutional desire to investigate for myself, I visited the family of Dr. Phelps. Katie's health and spirits, being greatly improved, permitted her to accompany me. The hours spent in that house were golden. The solace of solitude, the comfort of silence, the mysteries of spirit-power, the signs of coming wisdom, all came unto me there.

"What means this shocking disturbance?" asked the venerable gentleman, as a table-fork went sailing through the air, and small pebbles fell upon the strings of the open piano.

"Your positive anxiety to know, doctor," said I, "will but the more excite. Indulge the manifestations—do not fear them—and good only will come."

Sudden sounds and unpleasant surprises, however, became more frequent and numerous. At times the family seemed to be wild and rash in their opposition. But no expression of daring or repugnance could remove the "annoyance" of the dropping proofs. The tread of unseen feet were heard in the upper room; the artistic works of invisible hands were seen; the playful ingenuities of impalpable thinkers were scattered in all directions; the suppliant messages of mysterious beings were written on the walls; but, amid all the puzzling perplexities of the venerable gentleman's family, I was not for one moment disturbed.

"See that!" exclaimed the disconcerted clergyman, when returning with his son, whose dress had been suddenly torn by unseen fingers—"See! is not that a shocking plight? What but powers of evil would perform such deeds of violence?"

"I shall soon write out my answer," I replied. "And with your permission, I will read it to your family." Ere long that promise was fulfilled. The results of that examination were also published, and, in order to avoid repetition, I refer the reader to my pamphlet, entitled, "Philosophy of Spiritual Intercourse."

'T was irresistibly amusing, sometimes, to observe the grimaces of Connecticut Orthodoxy! The pious people of Stratford were impiously perturbed. And many minds there, not troubled with any religion, were irreligiously prejudiced. The clergyman's residence was sanctimoniously scrutinized. There was nothing "evil" about or within, however, except the misapprehension of the spiritual revelation. Now and then a passing inhabitant would stare at the ghostly pillars of the piazza, as if they had recently acquired the power of making "mysterious noises," but no one of the sagacious bystanders could penetrate that realm of intelligent causes which produced corresponding effects so alarmingly unmistakable.

A few weeks subsequent to this we went to Cambridge, Massachusetts. This journey was taken for Katie's benefit. She wished to feel the invigorating breath of the ocean, and we therefore sought a spot to which the salt breezes came. But now my own health began to wane, and at last I was prostrated with a violent attack of Typhoid Fever.

Previous to my illness, for six weeks, I was constantly engaged in writing upon the most stupendous subject that ever incited human thought. My whole mental organization was exercised extremely. That subject was "God, the Ruler of the Universe." The second volume of the "Great Harmonia" contains the result of my labors. This extreme exercise of the spiritual faculties pressed my entire system into the extreme positive state, which inevitably develops the terrible *fever* that caused my exceeding prostration.

In the early stages of my disease, I was daily visited by an allopathic physician of acknowledged skill and ability; but, as my complaint became more positive, his faith in my ultimate restoration to health subsided, and it was generally believed, by those who witnessed my condition, that I should soon become a permanent resident in the Spirit-land. But Mrs. Mettler, of Bridge port, Connecticut—the existence of whose clairvoyant powers I had discovered some years previous—hearing of my condition, came immediately to Cambridge. My case was submitted to her inspection, and her diagnosis of the symptoms was exceedingly accurate. Out of several millions of medicines which exist in the world, her discriminating perceptions selected, for my case, two simple vegetable remedies. Of these a tea was made, and administered according to her directions. Through the agency of this simple tea, the applicability of which to my complaint the wisdom of a clairvoyant only could discover, my fever was subdued.

Combined with the tea, in the removal of this fever, was human magnetism or psychology. I can never forget the morning when the following miracle was wrought upon me: The physician who had seen me but two days previous, gave it as his opinion that I should be obliged to remain in bed six weeks, and abstain from food twenty days longer. I had already sunk so low in physical strength that I could not turn in bed, nor assist myself with my hands. And my food and medicine, for nearly three weeks, with but few exceptions, had been confined to Congress Water, which I drank freely.

Such was my condition when Mrs. Mettler, in accordance with her interior directions while in the clairvoyant state, came to my bedside, and, taking my hand in her own, and gazing a few moments steadily in my eyes, said, " *Now you can raise up in your bed.*" The requisite strength and confidence to do so flowed throughout my system in an instant, and I forthwith raised up with ease. Now she made *passes* down my spine, and over my entire body, and bade me walk from my bed to a chair, which had been prepared for the purpose, about four yards from the bed I was occupying. This I did with astonishing ease; and I rested in my chair that day nearly four hours. Thus I substantially *took up my bed and walked.* For several succeeding mornings about the same hour, I was magnetized by the lady; and in ten days I could drive out and enjoy the sunlight and air.

The harmonizing and tranquillizing influence of this illness upon my body and mind was deep and thorough. My entire system experienced a species of regeneration or purification; and my mind was vastly more free to explore the infinite ramifications of those great and lofty subjects which constitute the vital system of my subsequent volumes.

The next scene opens, not in Trinity college, but in College street, in the city of Hartford. Urged merely by the confluence of external circumstances, and hence without any hidden motive, we became boarders in a family of congenial sympathies. Soon after our arrival, some four or five gentlemen called, and one said: "We welcome you, Mr. Davis, to the land of 'blue laws,' and hope your stay will be long."

"Yes," said another, "we've been struggling against prejudice of all sorts. A little help, now and then, would cheer us."

"What have you been doing?" I asked.

"We've obtained an office in Kellogg's building, and met in it every week for several months. But we can't get many of the outsiders to take part in our investigations."

At this moment I felt the presence of my Guide. Stepping out into the open air, I was enabled to hear the lute-like tones of his voice, and these words: "*This—is—thy—station. Loyal—minds —are—here. Begin—thy—teachings.*"

Hearing these rich sentences, and rejoicing in the thought of beginning a career of oral teachings, I danced and laughed like a young boy. But of what I had heard I related nothing to any living soul. Before the friendly guests departed, however, I assured them of my willingness to attend their meetings.

Accordingly, at the next Wednesday evening's session, I narrated what I had witnessed in Stratford; the absolute facts — bold, bare, bewildering — and nothing more. The philosophy of them I reserved for a future occasion. At length that occasion arrived. My matter, not my manner, was acceptable. Whereupon I evoked the assistance of Silona. Her voice was clear and her pronunciation forcible. She had few equals as a reader — even among professors — especially when her mind sympathized with the author's meaning. Firmly and earnestly, therefore, did she, from week to week, read to the assembly the lectures which I had intuitionally written. 'Twas all new to the dwellers of the Charter Oak city. A few of the boldest intellects became permanently interested.

Ladies of Fashion! look upon that picture. There sat a lady, once a star in the world, dressed in expensive garb 'tis true, but amid unpolished mechanics and ungloved merchants. What did she there? Her voice was lifted — without an emotion of fear — against prejudice and its atrocious crimes. She read the discourses with that vitalizing heartiness which is the result of true devotion. Did she a popular work? Nay! But 'twas strong and sunk deep in the brave souls of living men and women. The truth made them free; and they rendered unto her gratitude. Most piteous devotees of St. Custom are they who dare not follow that lady's emphatic example!

In the early spring of the next year, 1851, I was myself addressing the people. The task weighed heavily upon me, yet, impelled by the hidden law of my soul, I bore up against the pressure and succeeded. Of a high ancestral name I could not boast. Of rank and riches I had none. Of college lore and credentials from the Faculty I was destitute. And yet, I had spiritual access to the best advantages that could accrue from all these — not because of any hereditary or acquired right, but because my INTUITIONS were emancipated from the thraldom of sense. And thus I journeyed up the Mountain of Power. Not from motives of ambition did I pursue this precipitous path, but I walked up for the same reason that water flows down, because I could not help it! If the reader would know what were the subjects of my first oral teachings, he may ascertain by examining the third volume of the " Great Harmonia."

For public services I made no charge. Indeed, so happy was I to render them that I would sooner have paid for the privilege than tax the bounty of those who listened. Our crippled income was still exceeded by current expenses. And as the spring days melted away, one after and into another, I began to think about returning to the hospitalities of the spiritually-appointed brother.

While thus considering one evening, the well-known voice said: "*Be—firm—my—son. Thy—home—is—here.*"

"How glad," thought I, "that I'm no longer a youth! If I were, the words just spoken would in ten minutes seem like a dream. Now, there's no mystery—no ambiguity—nothing to unravel."

At this moment an acquaintance arrived, a generous-looking Hartford publisher, who said: "I think the cottage can be obtained."

"'Tis very beautiful there," replied Katie. "But my Jackson thinks we can not purchase this year."

"Perhaps," said the visitor, "some other arrangements can be made."

"There's no use of planning as I see," she replied. "'T would only result in disappointment."

Nothing more of consequence was uttered that night. While breakfasting next morning, we had another call from the same gentleman.

"I've called early," said he apologetically, "to tell you that Mr. Turnbull is willing to sell his cottage."

"Well, Seymour," I replied, "we can not raise money enough this year. So I guess I'll look about for something cheaper."

"You could pay the rent, I suppose?" inquired he, with a business look.

"Oh, yes!" said Katie, with much vivacity. "We should have plenty for that, and to spare."

The publisher was silent and thoughtful. Presently he departed. When next he came he told us that the cottage was his property for our immediate benefit. Thus did my Guide scan this brother's noble heart, and anticipate the flow of approaching circumstances.

Yes, my home was to be in Hartford. The cottage was agreeably retired, nearly enveloped in trees, and situated on high ground not far from the railroad depot. The frantic voice of that symbol of civilization — "the Iron Horse" — would shake the air within the dwelling, and shout: "Hurrah! for the progressive world!" There was a balcony about the ornamented structure — from which cherries, apricots, and the fragrant magnolia, could be reached — whereon, more than once, I have clairvoyantly examined eternal truths. And when in my ordinary state, too, there were sometimes dreamy lingerings upon that same shaded pavilion, during which my mind would revert to Poughkeepsie, to Hyde-Park, to Union Corners, to Hiram Marshall's house, to Bart Cropsey's stories, to the poverty of my childhood, and, lastly, to my little prayers to "kind Prov'dence," which I could not but utter once again with tenderest reverence.

In December following, in accordance with an impression derived from the perception of a human need, I began a series of argumentative discourses. My attention, in the first place, was arrested by reading the following public notice: "Rev. Dr. Bushnell will commence next Sunday evening a course of lectures on 'the Naturalistic Theories of Religion as opposed to Supernatural Revelation.'"

Moved by a curiosity to *know* the positions he would assume, I became quickly intuitional. I scanned and inhaled the atmosphere of his mind. This perception required but a moment. and yet I could state all his propositions. Being in the presence of brethren I did so, and requested them to attend his lecture that they might ascertain the literal correctness of my report. This occurred in the forenoon of the day on the evening of which his introductory discourse was to be delivered. The friends attended accordingly, and the result was in favor of Intuition. Directly my review commenced and progressed to its completion

Of that peculiar work I will not further chronicle, except to refer to the record published soon afterward, entitled: " The Approaching Crisis." To assure the public, however, that the esteemed clergyman's positions were not misrepresented in that Review, I will add the following testimony obtained at the time, but never before published:—

" We, the undersigned, having had the opportunity and pleasure of listening to Dr. Horace Bushnell's recent lectures on the subject of ' Supernaturalism as opposed to Naturalistic Theories of Religion;' and having, also, with much gratification, listened to the various and successive reviews or ' criticisms' thereupon, written by Andrew J. Davis and delivered by him in this city; do hereby certify, that, to our best knowledge, recollection, and belief, *Mr Davis has rendered Dr. Bushnell's ideas accurately —* ' nothing extenuated or aught set down in malice.'

JAMES S. HOOKER,	Hartford, Ct.		R. K. STODDARD,	Hartford, Ct.	
H. ROBINSON,	"	"	MARY B. STODDARD,	"	"
HIRAM ROGERS,	"	"	W. B. JOHNSON,	"	"
TIMOTHY DRAKE,	"	"	JOHN C. PRATT,	"	"
JOHNSON S. DOW,	"	"	GEORGE WHEELOCK,	"	"
JOSEPH SILAS BROWN,	"	"	EBENEZER CHAMBERLAIN,	"	
ANDREW WELLS FOX,	"	"	SAMUEL D. SMITH,	"	"
H. H. BUCKLAND,	"	"	EPHRAIM PARKHURST,	"	"
J. SEYMOUR BROWN,	"	"	EMELINE A. SMITH,	"	"
ASA ROGERS,	"	"	JANE CUNNINGHAM,	"	"
JAMES B. ABBOTT,	"	"	ROGER CASEMENT,	"	"
FRANKLIN L. BURR,	"	"			

About this time, in the spring of 1853, the Brotherhood procured Union Hall. Our audiences had increased and improved from week to week. The participators were intellectual persons of both sexes. Minds from nearly every form of religious faith came to our meetings and conferences. The chilly blasts of popular prejudice swept through our ranks. Biting frosts of calumny touched the tree of life that we were culturing; but no

external blight could either penetrate or sear the leaves and buds
of promise.

The first lecture I delivered in the more spacious hall, was a
statement of my individual relation to the work of Human Progress. That the reader, also, may fully apprehend the non-sectarian
nature of that "relation," I will here introduce the initial portion
of my discourse :—

MEN AND BRETHREN : If I appeared before you as a member
of some Sanhedrim, as the sworn advocate and avowed propagandist of some new dogma or system, it would then be but
reasonable to expect from me only *onesided* evidences and arguments strictly sectarian. As the publicly-pledged attorney of an
exclusive scheme, it would be one part of my plan to misrepresent
skeptics and expose all antagonists to ridicule and derision. And
perhaps, as a tolerant civilization would not permit me to *burn* an
opponent at the stake as the great Calvin did the good Servetus,
I might contrive a substitute — and roast him in a vast Gehenna
of hard words, fed by igneous adjectives and scorching epithets
altogether terrific and unendurable.

As it is impossible to elicit light from darkness and absurd to
gather figs from thistles, so is it beneath the dictates of Reason to
expect a benign spirit of toleration to emanate from a conscientious
sectarian. He is boldly challenged by each element of his faith
to be consistent. The requirement of a creed is sacredly binding,
and every way imperative. His terrible and implacable motto is —
" *Believe, or be damned !*" Whether the mind has adopted the
Bible or the Koran, or any system which claims supernatural
origin and authority, its reasonings are the same : " If I profess to
be on the Lord's side, my words and actions should correspond ;
and I should feel myself called upon openly to oppose all ideas
and all persons denounced and rejected by his word. My aim is
— ' Be God-like.' Therefore, God's enemies are my enemies,
whomsoever God hates, I hate also ; His friends are my friends
and all condemned by God are condemned by me. When God's
word is assailed and impeached, I should haste to the rescue and
defence ; if the wicked march against Zion, I must gird on my
armor and resist them ; yea. all the years of my life, I must strive

to be God-like — to make His Word my word, His commandments my commandments — and whenever He sends any soul ' by light ning express' to that tropical country called PERDITION, I should feel myself authorized to go and do likewise." Thus reasons the sectarian.

To receive the totality of any one record as the only " Word of God," is equivalent to the total rejection of every other record. Toleration, therefore, is logically impossible. To be a true fol- lower and advocate of any *one* Man, is to do what he does and believe what he believes — rejecting, by the fiat of a conscientious prejudice, all opponents as infidels and enemies of truth. To be liberal and free while a champion of some sectarian scheme, is to be unfaithful and inconsistent. The daily journals contain notices now and then of a party calling themselves " *Liberal Christians,*" than which no paradox was ever more glaring, no solecism more dangerous. They profess to adopt a Book with " Believe, or be damned," as its eternal standard of judgment, and yet paint the blessed word " liberal" over the vestibule leading to their sanctu- ary. Te admit the possibility of the existence of any soul-saving TRUTH in any other religion, is to openly dishonor your creed be- fore all men, and cause them to associate with your professions a catalogue of fatal absurdities.

Occasionally, I have met with liberal and charitable Christians. My spirit said: " Verily, these men are more magnanimous than their creeds." And I have added: " May we not also conclude that the character of the Divine Being is infinitely *better* than the best man's report of it? Whereupon the illuminated air seemed to *throb* throughout with the rushing waves of a deathless song. whose refrain was " Selah !" meaning, " Repeat the question, till all men behold an affirmative answer emblazoned on Nature's every realm !"

The uncharitableness and impatience of supernaturalists exhibit their most repulsive features toward those who are usually termed " skeptics" — as if the soul could *control* its 'onvictions ! Per- haps bible-believers would be more just to disbelievers if they had our philosophy, which teaches that the intellectual faculties are constitutionally skeptical; that he who lives mainly in the front part of his head is of necessity *a doubter.*

The illiberal denunciations and profane anecdotes of *excited* re ·

vival preachers, who act as mental thermometers, indicate the la
tent animosity and intolerance lurking in the atmosphere of the
more dignified and self-possessed. Let a person who intellectually doubts the soul's eternal duration, acknowledge his skepticism to
a professed Christian or Mohammedan, and, in ninety-nine cases
out of every hundred, the reply would be ; " Oh, sir, *you are an
infidel ;* all further convers. between us is useless !"

To be a consistent Christian is to be illiberal. On the other
hand, to be consistently liberal is to be an illegitimate Christian.
Unheeding the philanthropic suggestion that " the whole need not
a physician, but those that are sick," the conceited believer leaves
the disbeliever in a mental state *much worse* than he found him ;
for now the skeptic thinks himself to be in all probability more
right than wrong ; and, remembering his treatment, he justifies
the next thought also — that he is personally conscious of being a
better man than the dogged and bitter believer of churchianity.
And straightway his skepticism, before as unwelcome as disease
and not less painful, is encouraged and prepared for battle. Thus
it happens that unwholesome dissensions arise between those
who, with our philosophy of things, might be the best and happiest of friends.

In truth, the genius of supernaturalism is never ready either
for liberal consideration or dispassionate judgment. It is by
nature *unnatural,* and denies hospitable entertainment to the
opposite statement, even in its mildest form. An opponent must
be repulsed at all events ; because, in brief, it is impossible that
any form of sectarianism should be impartial.

But as I come before you not as a propagandist, not as the
founder or abettor of a new sect, but simply as a free mind,
pledged only to be faithful to an interior principle of undogmatic
Truth, regardless of the form, you may expect from me an unbi-
ased and dispassionate presentation.

Although in the midst of public teaching, yet there ever
streamed through my being the silent principle of personal progress. The rude swell of the wildly careering tempests of outward opposition, the crash of the enemy's thunderbolt, and the
moaning of disturbed theological forests in the dells and lowlands

were all as nothing to the possessor of the Magic Staff. Silona's involuntary repulsion of many of the fond friends who came to the cottage, united to my unyielding determination to be no man's leader, swept our private path completely clean of almost every social allurement.

Our embowered dwelling was expensively as well as cozily furnished. The breezes of the distant fields entered it, healthy conditions prevailed in all that neighborhood, and yet Katie's physical system yearned for the strengthening influence of the ocean air. 'Twas to obtain for her this luxury, that we temporarily left Hartford, and sought the retirement of High Rock cottage. And there it was, away from the turmoil of the wide-spread city below, that I reached the highest peak of the Mountain of Power! 'Twas the end of a long and weary battle. The celestial vision from that commanding elevation, is before the world. It was grander than all that had gone before — a climax to every preceding experience. It occurred on the 7th August, 1852, and is chronicled in my volume, entitled, "The Present Age and Inner Life."

Besides this spiritual benefit, Katie's health and feelings were much improved during those summer months; and, after the vision, my own body rested, while a novel tranquillity pervaded my every inward faculty.

CHAPTER LIV.

IN THE OPEN FIELD.

 ·'I thank thee, Father, that I live;
  Though wailings fill this earth of thine,
  To labor for thy suffering ones
      Is joy divine."

A FEW weeeks after our return to Hartford we set out into the open field of reform toil.   Ere long we reached the city of Cincinnati, Ohio, where I began a course of public teachings.   For three successive evenings the congregation, though small, was composed of capable and critical persons of considerable prominence.   I felt the presence of a cloudy prejudice floating o'er the audience.   Notwithstanding this, however, I freely invited the people to visit me, at the private residence of Mr. A. O. Moore, on days and evenings not devoted to public teaching.   Accordingly this brother's parlor was the scene of many excellent interviews with the friends, and memorable encounters with the foes, of unlimited Progression.

  "The object of my calling," said a maidenly-looking male agent of some religious institution, "is to talk with you about the employment of your talents."

  "Ah, that's very fraternal and good in you," I responded, "and I may be pleased, sir, with your counsel."

  "Looking over the morning papers," he continued, "I see you are advertised to lecture on the ' Causes of Civilization,' and it occurred to me that you are misusing your influence and making yourself unpopular when there's no need for it."

"Indeed!" said I. "Do you know of some better method for me?"

"I think I do," returned he moderately. "That better way is this: for you to adopt the course common among our best clergy."

"What is that?" I inquired.

"Why our intelligent ministers preach the moral principles of the New Testament, and the plan of salvation therein set forth; but they never excite people's prejudices, as you are doing, by disclosing their theological perplexities."

"Do your ministers, then, doubt certain points of doctrine?" I asked.

"Certainly!" replied the honest agent, "but they almost never preach on doctrinal points. And the reason is, that the clergy know how prone the world is to skepticism. So they withhold their doctrinal differences and perhaps *doubts* from their congregations. And knowing that religion of some kind is necessary for men, and believing the gospel precepts to be the best in the world, the clergy husband their influence over people, and confine themselves to what we call practical Christianity."

"Well, friend," said I, "what would you counsel me to do?"

"Why, when I perused the notices this morning," replied he, "it struck me that if you would adopt precisely this course, the church people would turn out in multitudes to hear you lecture. Instead of a few auditors you would have throngs of supporters, and we, the friends of the gospel, could secure a situation for you in one of the best pulpits in this country."

"What good would that do?" I asked.

"Why, sir, you would then be respected as a talented and useful man; and your salary might be, perhaps, *three thousand dollars per annum!*"

The gentleness of his seductive speech was quite pleasant to my ear, but what effect it exerted upon my soul may be gathered

from what followed. "Your suggestions are kindly offered," said
I, "and I thank you for your frankness. But, in regard to the
course you recommend for me I can only reply in the language said
to have been used by the son of Joseph and Mary long ago, when
he received a similar suggestion."

"I do n't get your meaning," said the agent slightly nettled.
"What language do you refer to?"

And I replied: "When the devil of worldliness invited the
Man of Love to stand upon the top of a high mountain, in order
to contemplate the kingdoms of the world and the glory of them
as the promised reward of popular proceedings, he used words
which I now reiterate—'Get thee behind me, Satan.'"

"No, no!" exclaimed the agent, "you misunderstand my motives. My object is to tell you how you may become respected,
and therefore more useful."

"Well, friend," said I rising, "I think you will have to excuse
me now, as I have writing to do and must devote no more time
this morning to the pleasures of conversation."

Subsequently I noticed this person in the audience, but nothing
further of importance occurred between us. The morning following my discourse on the "Causes of Civilization," I took from
the postoffice three anonymous letters of the most scurrilous
character. They purported to emanate from as many different
persons, who, professing to have attended my lectures, stated that
they had been exceedingly shocked at my alleged indelicacy and
profanity. From one of these missives I will quote a single
paragraph.—

..... "When you sat down after your last night's lecture and
covered up your eyes with your hand, I pitied you! For you
was thinking of your drunken sprees, of your flour speculations,
of your licentiousness, and of merchants who have been ruined
by your pretended power to make money. You need n't deny it,
sir, for your former associates can prove it."

My knowledge of Katie's sensitive and imperial temperament

caused me to conceal from her all communications so wholly false and malignant. My safety and strength were in the Magic Staff and the protecting power of Truth. But, though I had before immediately destroyed every such evidence of assassin-like enmity toward me, I retained the letters, on this occasion, for the purpose of an experiment. In one of the three I read this: "I don't believe a d——d word in your professions. I am ready to believe though, and won't sign my name — so if you ain't a d——d humbug you can tell who wrote this."

When alone that day, I psychometrized the writing and found but one person as the author. Toward him my soul felt not the slightest retaliation. Indeed, on seeing into the man's mind, I felt surprised that the letters did not contain language more severe and falsehoods more numerous. By clairvoyance I easily individualized the author, and it so happened that, before I left Cincinnati, he came into a store which I had entered just a moment previous. He believed I did not know that he had written the letters; and so he asked — "How do you like the Queen City of the West, Mr. Davis?"

"My visit has been very pleasant," I replied. "There's only one thing that I object to in the external phases of this city."

"What's that objection, Mr. Davis?"

"The black smoke emitted by the bituminous coal so generally used for fuel," said I. "It soils one's dress in a few hours."

"Humph! How's been your audiences?"

"The last lecture of my course brought out the largest attendance," I replied.

"Can you tell what a man's thinking about?" asked the stranger.

"I can tell what a man's ambition is," I answered.

"Can you tell what's mine?"

"You have three ambitions," said I. "First, to have the best cigars to smoke; second, to own the fastest horse to trot; third, to have your beef-steak on the table at precisely *one* o'clock, P. M."

Hearing this he laughed heartily, and then replied: "You hav'n't lived in old Connecticut so long for nothing. You're good at guessing, like all wooden-nutmeg folks. Say, do you know Barnum?"

"There!" exclaimed I half-mirthfully, yet in earnest, "I've omitted to acknowledge the receipt of your letters, but I will do so now."

"Thunder!" said he with a startled expression, "what letters do you mean?"

At this moment Mr. Moore entered to conduct me to another place, and having no desire to afflict my already regretful-looking opponent by needless exposure, I departed. Thus was the interview abruptly terminated. But my belief was, that the man of *three ambitions* would never again trifle with the sacred powers of clairvoyance.

From Cincinnati we journeyed to Cleveland, Ohio, and there also commenced a social and public work. Nothing occurred of special importance during a stay of ten days in that city, except a circumstance reported by President Mahan—a report involving a question of personal veracity.

The statement of this logical gentleman is, in brief, this: That while delivering a public address in Cleveland, I suddenly stopped, went into one of my favorite states of abstraction, and then "professed to the audience to have a vision" of Horace Mann's lecture on "Woman;" that I then delivered a "spirit-stirring paragraph," which, being ended, was pronounced by a gentleman in the assembly to be *verbatim* from a condensed report published in a recent *New York Tribune.*

The sentiments and expressions of this statement—which may be found at length in President Mahan's book, entitled, "Modern Mysteries Explained and Exposed"—compel me to believe that he founded his charge of "deliberate" imposition on the editorial gossip of a Cleveland paper, which, because of its many insufficient and unscrupulous allegations against Spiritualism and its receivers, deserved, as I then thought, and still think, not to be honored with a single line of rebuke or vindication from parties thus assailed.

But I will now give the reader a correct account of this much misrepresented circumstance. It is true that I was delivering a course of lectures in Cleveland. My subject was one which concerned the sexes equally, being a definition of their relative positions in the order of creation. It is also true that, while in the midst of my subject, I hesitated and remarked, " that it would be interesting to know what a public teacher, like Horace Mann, had to say on the rights of women and the relation of the sexes." The audience, as well as I, knew that Mr. Mann was announced to lecture soon on that subject. Hence there was nothing irrelevant or marvellous in alluding to him, or to what he might teach on that question. It is likewise true that I stood quiet for a few moments, during which I obtained (by *impression*, not by clairvoyance) what I understood to be an abstract of Mr. Mann's views. In a few brief detached sentences, I gave the audience my impresssions, saying: " Such I receive as a correct rendering of his sentiments, but whether right or wrong, those who will hear Mr. Mann's lecture may determine ;" whereupon a gentleman arose and affirmed that he had read substantially the same in the *New York Tribune*. President Mahan says that I was "taken all aback by such an announcement." The truth is just the contrary, for I was gratified; feeling that my impression was more accurate than I expected to get in the excitement of a public assembly.

Thus you see, impartial reader, that I neither made any profession of reading the lecture by " vision," nor attached any importance to the psychological transaction. But the *Cleveland Herald* reported a foolish account of my " pretensions," " attempts," " mistakes," &c. ; and, because I did not bestir myself to correct a bit of newspaper gossip, this dogmatic author considers it a settled fact, implying " deliberate" imposition, and sufficient to overthrow a series of clairvoyant disclosures which pertain to my past history. This attack I value as of no practical consequence, and believe it will be disregarded by every careful reader of President Mahan. His work is a materialistic house, built with timbers hewn by other hands, decorated with

> "Rich windows that exclude the light,
> And passages that lead to nothing."

But the saddest consequence of our western journeyings was the serious disturbance of Katie's physical health. The fitful winds and driveling rains of Lake Erie seemed to develop a hepatic disease which, till then, had been held in check from year to year by diet and medication. Her most painful symptom was a violent and incessant cough.

Turning and yearning homeward, we took cars for Rochester. Here Katie's illness became yet more desolating to her energies. Three whole weeks she suffered. At length we were referred to a physician who greatly assuaged her anguish. Soon she became strong enough to accomplish the journey to the Hartford cottage. And there, while the fresh morning dew lay sparkling on the young turf, and the soft spring air blew blandly through the open door, her body gained strength and her spirit repose.

My first important public work after returning, was the writing of impressions concerning man's ultimate control over the causes of droughts and the fall of rain. These impressions were communicated in a series of letters to the "Hartford Times," and had the effect to bring down a shower of strictures from Professor Vaughn, of Kentucky, who openly charged me with the crime of plagiarism. The appearances were, at the first blush, decidedly against clairvoyance. But if the reader would ascertain *the facts* —which show how utterly untruthful were the professor's imputations—and also learn the laws by which mankind may control the fall of rain, let him peruse my pamphlet, entitled "The Harmonial Man."

By this time I began to realize that the summit of the Mountain was overpassed. Already my face was turned toward the un known valley beyond. Now and then I would hear Amphion strains of melody as if a lyre made of sunbeams were touched by an angel's skilful fingers. At such times, it almost seemed that trees and birds and rocks and streams, and even untamed nations of distant lands, responded to the harmonious music of these celestial Arcadians. Such tokens assured me that the angel world was silently blending with the human, as the sidereal heavens cover the dull earth day and night for ever; and then I longed to have the inexorable supporters of conservatism hear the cadence so melodious. But they would not listen, and I—what could I do? Ah! I must culture patience from year to year, and, leaning on my Magic Staff, toil for the God-like race of a far future.

The next event was the Hartford Bible Convention; a great and significant fact, worthy of remembrance. It indicated the prevalence and strength of Free Thought in the very heart of New England orthodoxy. The convention was continued for four days and nights. There was a large and respectful attendance throughout, of minds liberally disposed.

But the last night, although it closed over a sabbath-day, was a scene of the most uncivil and belligerent confusion. The unfriendly circulated a report, saying, " such was the legitimate effect of doctrines promulgated by those who called the convention." But my attention was alive to every expression of the audience. And I *know* that the frightful noises and rowdyistic tumult did neither originate with nor receive countenance from a single friend of the Harmonial Philosophy.

Shortly previous to this great gathering, there occurred a strange midnight circumstance within our vine-clad home. Our cook and housekeeper had retired. The cottage was still, and sleep was upon all eyelids, save my own; when I heard an unusual sound below. A burglar was entering the dining-room door; his chiselings and pryings came distinctly to my ear. I walked noiselessly down the stairway, and confronted the thief at once. He had accomplished an entrance, and evidently considered himself safe, till I stood between him and the outer-door, with a walking-stick in my right hand. The moon shone obliquely in, and enabled me to see the outline of his face, which was black as that of a genuine negro, though his form and features were those of the European race. At this instant the well-known voice whispered: "*Jackson!—speak—to—him.*"

Fearing no personal injury, I quietly asked: "Have you no food at home?" Receiving no reply, I began to expostulate: "This is unkind, my friend, to visit me as if I were your enemy. Do you not know that I am ever willing to help a poor man?" He made no answer, and I continued: "Do you think that you have done right? Do you treat me like a brother? If you should come here in open day, and tell me truthfully what are your sufferings and needs, I might be enabled to aid you and commend you to the generosity of others."

To all this he made no reply, but darted past me through the open door and fled, I knew not whither. Fortunately, the inmates of the cottage heard nothing of the disturbance, and thus were saved from a midnight fright.

We will now revert to the close of the Bible Convention. The excited gang were pressing and forcing their way through the assembly to the platform. The speakers were in danger. The frenzied opponents meant to refute argument by physical force. But the Magic Staff sustained me, and I sustained Katie, who was now suffering with great consternation.

Taking my arm she clung to my side, and we worked our way down one of the aisles toward the outer-door, closely followed by a strong-armed and broad-breasted man, who was silently and successfully exerting himself to keep back the mob from pressing down against us. Thus we reached the street, amid hoots and yells and imprecations, the herculean stranger still acting as a body-guard. The turbulent forces subsided about a hundred rods from the convention hall, and we were left to ourselves unharmed. The moonlight was faint, yet, as the stranger left us and passed on, I *recognised the outline of that blackened face which I had seen at midnight!* Our protector was the burglar! The thief proved to be our benefactor! Tell me, dear reader—suppose I had withheld kind words, and, instead, dealt heavy blows on the midnight disturber of our private rights; do you believe that he would have so nobly piloted us through that perilous storm of human passion?

Although I was now journeying a little every day toward the valley between Mount Power and Mount Beauty, yet, directly after the Bible Convention, my condition was extremely favorable to clairvoyant and impressional exercises. My lectures on "Physiological Vices and Virtues" were therefore soon perceived and conceived and written out. Ultimately these discourses were published in the first part of the fourth volume of the "Great Harmonia."

But the long summer-days shed down too much tropical influence upon my honored companion. Her fine form slowly gathered the indices of an approaching illness. Weary, worn, and weak, was she; her sleep was curtailed and irregular; and a shadowy paleness overspread her brow and cheek.

Nature always prescribed for her the soothing stimulus of ocean breezes. To secure this remedy we hastened to a settlement, one mile east of Lynn, Massachusetts, known as Swampscot; where we found comfortable accommodations directly fronting the open sea. Maria, her faithful handmaid, was with us. Not long after our arrival, however, Katie's illness increased. And as I had for six years made no medical examinations, for the reason that my mental energies were exercised constantly upon different and higher planes, I found myself under the necessity of procuring the aid of a physician. Dr. B. F. Hatch, accordingly, was called at her request. Under his prescriptions her symptoms abated, and I was rejoiced to find her again able to take the air in an open carriage. The drives on the broad beach, and the exhilaration of the salt breezes, soon exerted a favorable influence.

But one day, being again greatly prostrated and confined to the bed, she grew chill and disheartened, and said:—

"Jackson dear, this body is most worn out I fear. I feel broken down — tired of life — provoked with dragging about this diseased frame."

"Do not despair, Silona," I responded. "Your organization is strong yet, and may continue for many years. When the weather becomes less sultry, and the beautiful days of October arrive, perhaps you may get quite well again."

"Do n't talk to me about getting well," said she with a look of resistance. "I would rather go now, and not have this painful process to go through with again."

"You have been very ill many imes, Silona," I replied. "You have felt the restraint, the slavery, the tedium, of many days and months of sickness; but so good were your natural powers of restoration, that you have again recovered and enjoyed the luxury of health. Now I think you may rely upon your natural vigor, and not be disappointed."

She made no answer. Her speechless lip quivered, her bosom slightly heaved, but all was still in the chamber. Anon, she asked: "Do you fancy, my Jackson, that I fear to go hence? If you do, you are much mistaken with reference to my feelings. Maria!" said she, addressing the maid, "open the trunk and hand me my portfolio. Jackson, raise me up in bed — I wish to write a letter."

When her posture was rendered easy, and the writing implements were on her lap, I took my departure for Boston. Thither I often repaired, where I could select the choicest grapes, sickle pears, peaches, melons, and other fruits, congenial to her appetite. On my return she said: "There, Jackson, when you go out again put that letter in the office. I have written and sealed it," she added, "that no one can say I was under your influence."

The letter was addressed to "Joseph M. Blake, Esq., Bristol,

Rhode Island," the lawyer who had transacted much business for her.

A few days subsequently the above-named gentleman arrived, and consulted with her concerning the method of bequeathing me all her property. In due time the necessary legal papers were made out and signed, and thus was another act of her generous nature perfected. There dwelt in my mind not so much as the shadow of a desire for the possession of her fortune. And one day, when I quietly expressed this fact, she replied: "Oh, I know that! my Jackson. But you'll need all my cherished father left me, and more too, to sustain the work of your life. All I regret is, that I have not a larger portion to leave you."

These events transpired during the hottest days in August, 1853, when Katie's bodily prostration most oppressed her heart. But the cooling and strengthening breezes of September greatly revived her, and, ere long, we returned to Hartford animated with the pleasures of Hope.

CHAPTER LV.

LIFE IN THE COTTAGE.

" How calm and sweet the victories of life,
How terrorless the triumph of the grave !"

My pilgrimage had progressed almost to the lowest dell in the psychical valley. 'Twas, therefore, a period of complete spiritual rest. Hence I wrote but little, did not exert myself to deliver public discourses, and the angel-world seldom breathed its musical messages into my ear. The greater part of each day, on the contrary, was devoted to ministering unto Katie's wants. For, soon after our return, she became again nervously weary and discouragingly prostrated.

Sometime in October, I think, while walking toward the city, I was accosted by an elderly woman, poorly clad, who asked : " Is this Mr. Davis ?"

" Yes," was my reply.   " Do you wish for anything ?"

" I do, sir," said she much agitated.   " Be you a master of the Black Arts ?"

" No !   But why you ask ?"

" 'Cause I'm a dyin' daily — dyin' by inches — 'cause I've been bewitched by an enemy."

" Indeed !   Do you know how it was done, and who did it ?"

" Mercy to me, sir, I don't know nothin' who my enemy is. Some person, unbeknown to me, sent me this ere letter."

So saying she presented me a scrawled note, which read as

follows: "Black cat, wild cat, cat—This is to let you no that ef you do n't quit and clere out of the rume whare you liv' now I will torment you ev'ry day of ev'ry week an ev'ry hour of ev'ry day an ev'ry minnit of ev'ry hour an ev'ry second of ev'ry minnit till you clere out or die.   (Signed)   "†"

After reading the malicious note I folded it up and kept it in my right hand.   The distance to the postoffice was yet considerable, and as my business there was urgent, I invited her to walk thitherward.   "Where do you live?" I asked.

In reply, she informed me that her room was in a tenant house which held several families.

"Has any person in that house ever requested you to move elsewhere?"

"No, sir."

But I felt, from the sphere of the letter, that some one in the tenement begrudged her the hired apartment she was occupying, and that the jealous party had taken this culpable course to frighten the superstitious woman away.

"How do you support yourself?" I asked.

"I go out washing and housecleaning, sir."

"What do you eat and drink?"

"Oh, sir, since bein' bewitched I ain't eat hardly nothin'.   My stomic is gone, and I ain't no appetite for victuals, but jest coffee for six weeks.   Oh, sir, I'm so faint—I know I'm a dyin' by inches—I can't live long so!   Oh, dear!"

Now I had resolved to do this woman good.   I appreciated her weakness of mind, her belief in witchcraft, and her total ignorance of the fact that she was merely *psychologized* by Fear.   Logic, persuasion, philosophy, religion, was none of them the remedy; nothing but a psychological power more positive, applied without explanation, would cure and save her.   Of this I was morally certain.

Having reached the Unitarian church, I stopped and said: "We will now part.   Did you notice that I have carried this note in my right hand?"

" Oh, yes, sir," she replied with a look of mental relief.

" Observe !" said I — taking out my pencil and crossing the fac⸢ of the letter, then breathing on it for a moment, and returning it to her hand — " Observe ! that letter can not now injure you. It is harmless. You must burn it as quick as you get home. Brush the ashes into the stove or fireplace, and think no more about it."

" Mercy to me ! sir — won't them words of the letter bewitch me jest the same ?"

" No, never fear the words," said I. " But I wish to ask you a question. Do you know that your coffee is just the color of Night, when dark influences prevail ?"

" Yes, sir," she answered, " though I never know'd it to hurt me."

But while she spoke a shudder passed over her, as if alarmed at the similarity of complexion between her favorite beverage and a certain cloven-footed celebrity.

" You must n't drink a *black* fluid," said I.

" Mercy to me ! what shall I do then ? If you take away my coffee, sir, I shall die I'm 'fraid. Oh, dear me !"

" Go right home," I replied, " and, as soon as you have burnt the letter, prepare for yourself a roast potato, and eat that with bread and butter. To-morrow morning, besides the potato and bread, you may take a tablespoonful of coffee, and so also for a month to come, but not afterward. And, remember, never tell a human being that I gave you these directions."

She promised me, and departed, apparently full of faith. Little more than a year elapsed ere we met again. 'Twas at evening twilight. Withdrawing to the outer edge of the sidewalk, in North Main street, she whispered : " May the Lord reward you, sir."

" Are you quite well and happy now ?" I asked.

" Never better, sir, in many years — what you told me to do was my cure. Nobody never disturbs my peace no more. Oh, sir, I know'd you was master of the Black Arts !"

"No," said I. "My art is *Nature* not understood. If we should meet again, when I have an hour to spare, you shall know how I drove the witches out of you."

"Oh, thank'ee sir—I 'm obleeged to you—can you jest tell me the name of your Art, sir?"

"Certainly, good woman," said I. "The name of the charm that cured you is *Psychology*."

"Skylolloge!" she exclaimed, "skylolloge!"

"Yes," said I, "Psychology. But do n't impart the word to others."

"Oh, sir—never fear—I 'm too obleeged to you for that."

With these words we parted, and I have never feared any betrayal of the secret.

Prejudice is impudent as idiotic, and merciless as erroneous. Of this my private history is a demonstration. Minds too blunted to feel a truth, and too indolent to examine a principle, are the first to cry "mad-dog!" and to shout "infidel!" Hoots, hisses, and silly exclamations, reached my outer ear almost every day. Sunday-school boys would chalk vulgar words upon our cottage-fence and gateposts. Students of Cicero, Xenophen, Locke, Bacon, and Divinity, would echo in public the ridicule which salaried professors ofttimes whispered in private. And young ladies, too, not overstocked with that charity which thinketh no evil—but imbibing the prejudice of preceptress or minister or parents, all equally misinformed—would nervously ejaculate cunning little epithets and harmless satires with which they sought to check the progress of our Movement. What was all this to me? *Amusement*, and nothing more. In the blue sky I had friends stable as the everlasting mountains!

But suppose I had realized no such support, what then? What remained? An interior consciousness of *right doing*—this, and the Magic Staff. What more was needed? Nothing! The sun that wakened music from the marble breast of Memnon's statue, is but a symbol of that hidden orb which bespangles the path of justice with joys innumerable. And yet, besides this private source of strength, there came unto me certain companionable spirits — congenial, loving, musical, joyful, gifted spirits — redolent with blessings ambrosial and with sympathies sweet as fields of imperishable violets.

"'*Deus illuminatio mea*,'" thought I, when — walking one day through the park of Trinity college — the sportful boys deluged my person with a pail of filthy water from one of the upper windows. "God is my light, the Magic Staff is my support, and there's nothing on earth that is able to hinder." But the freshmen laughed — and so did I — at their fun and folly. "And yet," methought, "how much better if this college would teach *the spirit* of the motto of the Oxford University! Then, instead of artificial minds, the Institution would give to the world *living Men!*"

'T was a fair October day without, the sun shed golden beams upon the earth, but there was suffering within the Cottage. Wearied with her continued prostration, and impatient because of the confinement consequent thereto, Katie said : "Shut out that disagreeable light — close the curtains before both windows — and do n't let me see the sun again !"

Dutiful Maria immediately obeyed. "What so troubles you, Silona?" I asked, going to her bedside. "Do you feel worse to-day?"

"I'm provoked!" replied she despairingly. "I'm tired to death with this incorrigible illness! I get neither better nor worse. It's nothing but a wearisome drag. The day is so tediously long, and the night brings me no rest."

"Your symptoms are better to-day, Silona," said I. "Perhaps, by next week you can resume your carriage-rides, and enjoy the mild air as heretofore."

"Do n't talk about uncertainties," replied she with a sad emphasis. "This old body won't oppress me much longer, I hope."

Maria gently bathed her hands and forehead, and then placed before her the waiter of carefully-prepared delicacies to tempt her waning appetite, but the fatigued sufferer declared that she felt no delight in the taste of anything. At her request the food was removed, and she said: "My Jackson — promise me one thing will you?"

"I think I can promise anything you may ask," said I.

"Promise me," said she, with much energy, "that when my spirit is gone, you will keep the rabble from looking at this old wornout body."

"I hope," said I, "that you will retain the use of your body for many years; but, if you should not long continue in it, who among our friends shall I invite here?"

"None," returned she, with an indignant look. "This weeping over a dead body, after having neglected to treat the living spirit with respect, is supremely ridiculous."

"Why, what do you mean, Katie?" said I, really surprised at the singularity of her request— "who shall I admit, and who exclude?"

"Exclude everybody," said she, with much resolution. "And what is more, I don't want my relatives to be informed of my death, only as others will hear of it; for the lifeless body, when my spirit has flown, will need no expensive paradings and show of mourning."

"Silona," I asked, "do you consider the feelings of human nature on such occasions?"

"Promise me!" said she, suddenly taking my hand — "say that you will promise to fulfil my last request."

"Yes, Katie," was my reply, "I promise. Our views harmonize on these subjects. I will carry out your wishes strictly."

"There's one more thing, my Jackson," she then continued "which you must promise me."

"What is it, Silona?"

"You know," said she, "that I have a perfect *horror* of being buried alive."

"Yes, Katie, I do!" was my fully appreciative response.

"Then," said she, "promise that you will not have the body buried, until you are *positive* that I am wholly and entirely out of it."

"Upon my soul, I promise. As I would not be entombed alive myself, so will I prevent a like misfortune whenever it is within my power to do so."

"Do you promise me, my Jackson? Speak!"

"I do. Solemnly I promise you. On this you may fully rely. But you may yet outlive me on earth; so cheer up, Katie."

"There!" exclaimed she, more subdued and cheerful, "I'm satisfied. Maria dear, bring me the guava jelly, and that given me by Mrs. Cheney; I wish to taste and compare them. But my tongue is so dry, I can scarcely taste at all."

"Shall I turn aside the curtain, Katie," I asked, "that you may see the jellies?"

"Yes, dear," she replied, "the sun is nearly down. The light is more agreeable."

*   *   *   *   *   *

Time rolled silently on, and had wafted three weeks into eternity's ocean, when the spirit of my benefactress was about to soar away. By imperceptible degrees the immortal personality withdrew from sensuous observation. Her sufferings were not from pain, but from total exhaustion. The majestic daring of her eye was displaced by expressions of tenderness and affection. There was, at times, a dawn of glory upon her features, and occasional sounds of the higher harmonies in the tones of her voice. And, at length, when the stillness of evening gathered upon the hills, she passed on to her "home."

In the presence of a few friendly witnesses, the exhausted body was deserted without a struggle — on the eve of the 2d of November, 1853 — and upon its familiar face she had left a smile of rest and satisfaction. Relatives from the Second Sphere came for her while yet she lingered in the form; and when her spirit was completely freed, they conducted it gently to her Father's high pavilion. They made a singular request of me, which I have chronicled in another place; also, in the same work — " The Penetralia' — are records of two remarkable visitations from her disembodied spirit; and, therefore, to avoid repetition, I will but refer my readers to page 165 of the above-named volume.

The comfortable and costly cottage-furniture was ultimately sold; others purchased and occupied the sequestered domicile; and thus the cur. ain rolled down upon that portion of my life.

CHAPTER LVI.

THE DOUBLE SUICIDE.

"When thy struggling heart hath conquered.
When the path lies fair and clear,
When thou art prepared for heaven,
Thou wilt find that heaven is here."

SOON after Silona's spirit had withdrawn from the world of effects, I began indistinctly to hear Eolian preludes to celestial harmonies innumerable. Though the shades of the deep valley enveloped me, and though a mist of tears shrouded my lone heart, yet, at times, did I hear the mystic murmurings of many voices from the unseen Mountain of Beauty. Like the refreshment of April rain, or like the blossoming of immortal thought-flowers in the garden of the soul, seemed the "preamble sweet of charming symphony" which sounded through my being.

The attraction was irresistible! My eyes turned toward the slopes of the future eminence, and my feet kept time to the music that reverberated from its invisible summit. The sacred depth of that Mountain music, dear reader, imparted a cheerful solemnity to my spirit. It sighed like the Hermean dream-sound of the ocean shell; and yet there was also the Amphion charm-power in it, and that harmonious measure which the eternal spheres roll through immensity.

With a waltz of my faculties, I continued my pilgrimage athwart this peaceful plain of contemplation. The spiritually designated brother, Mr. Green, was then a citizen of Hartford

With his accustomed hospitality, he caused me to feel "at home" in his residence.

The reckless opponents of spiritualism had, at this date, reached the third degree of absurdity. They had sounded the trumpet of "Infidelity" until their lungs must have been almost collapsed with sheer exhaustion. But I repelled the charge through public discourses, in which I set forth the Harmonial idea of immortality. I taught that pure Christianity is unadulterated Love, to which our Philosophy is the principle of Wisdom. Hence, that we were not "infidel" to whatsoever is good and true and divine.

Then, the opponents changed their position and denounced spiritualism as the chief cause of "insanity." This charge I also repelled by showing that the origin of lunatic asylums dated further back than 1848, when modern manifestations were first openly inaugurated in this country. Also, I taught that human nature had been *causa non cognita* — that the principles of man's spiritual organization were hidden to the church-people — and, therefore, that the skeptical world and church could not explain spirit intercourse.

Next, there issued forth "the gossip" of church deacons and of the narrow-headed among newspaper editors. They unqualifiedly affirmed — of course without the first iota of evidence — that "Spiritualism is Free-Loveism." The charge of licentiousness was unreservedly made. This seemed to me to be the last degree of malice and absurdity. But although I had not claimed to be a "spiritualist," yet I had frequently professed to be a "lover of wisdom;" consequently, praying to know the exact truth, I accepted the work of examining into the origin, laws, rights, wrongs, &c., of the marriage relation. This, therefore, became the labor of my pilgrimage all the way up the Mountain of Beauty.

"What progress do you make with the marriage question?" asked Mr. Green, who knew that I had consecrated the first half many days to the solution of the problem.

" I find," said I, " that the marriage ordinance is more divine than the world generally believes it to be."

" What's the natural law ?" he inquired.

" Ah, that I have not yet discovered."

" Is there any way," he asked, " by which to decide who's the true companion ?"

" I do not yet know," I replied. " My interior examinations are not completed. But from what I have perceived, I am sure that the public discussion of this relation between the sexes is absolutely necessary."

" Why so ?" he asked.

" Because," said I, " evil offspring result from bad marriages, while from heart-unions the world receives children at once peaceful and beautiful."

" What do you think about divorces ?" he inquired.

" It is my impression," I replied, " that a man and woman who find that they *can not* live peacefully in the marriage relation, should have honor and humanity sufficient to assume the relation of brother and sister."

" But the laws," said he, " would not grant divorce on such considerations."

" Then the laws should be altered," I replied, " so that the general happiness of mankind may be promoted."

This conversation occurred just before I departed on a lecturing tour through a portion of Massachusetts and western New York. My interior penetrations were as yet confined merely to a clairvoyant survey of the " physiological vices and virtues" of both the married and the young ; and, incidental to such a survey, I could not but detect a multitude of atrocious evils growing out of existing marriage relations, which nothing, save divorce, could effectually banish from thousands of homes and hearts.

In compliance with an invitation I proceeded to Boston, and delivered several reform discourses. While there I received calls from many persons, of both sexes, who, as they affirmed were suffering under the painful consequences of false unions But to them all my reply was: " I have not yet completed my examination of the marriage relation. Therefore I am not prepared to offer you anything but my sympathy."

One day I called upon a lady, Mrs. Newton, who was gifted with the power of discerning spiritual things. She had a word and a symbol for every emotion and every thought. Human desires and sympathies would glide into picturesque and fairy embodiments, in obedience to the mandate of her inspired ideality; and at the gentle fiat of her will, the condition and future of a person, *en rapport*, would rise up and pass before her vision like a panorama of uses and intelligible proportions.

Having exchanged a few words of friendly recognition, she seated herself near me and said: " Not through your intellect would I approach you, brother. With that I can become acquainted by reading your writings."

" How, then, do you wish to know me?" I asked, much pleased with the gentleness of her speech.

" Through your social nature," she frankly replied; " and thus I would have you know my blessed husband also."

I assured her that my spirit was ever grateful for any accession of fraternal joys. And for a considerable time we conversed concerning the pleasures and truths of the Spirit Land. At length she exclaimed, " How happy the world would be — how joyful the heart of every one — in the true marriage relation!"

" Yes," I replied, " the miseries of false marriages are blighting and corrupting to all concerned."

" Not long since," said she, " a very refined gentleman called upon me, whose heart was overflowing with both happiness and misery."

" Indeed!" said I. " What was the cause of his conflicting emotions?"

With tones of tenderness she replied: " He is bound, and has been for years, to an uncongenial, unresponsive, unloving person."

"Has he found any one to whom he feels truly attracted?" I asked.

"Oh, yes, brother. While here, his heart was o'erburthened with its immense love for another; one who is ardent, gentle, and congenial."

"Does the uncongenial and unloving wife know of his attachment to that other more responsive heart?" I asked.

"It's a very singular instance, brother," she replied. "His legal wife, as I said, is not affectionate. She seems to have but little idea of those finer sensibilities which, in his nature, call for a delicate and loving response. She must be a worthy woman, however, for she not only knows of his entire and devoted love for another, but consents to it. And she is even willing to *defend* this truer relation because she believes it to be right.

"A very singular case, indeed!" said I. "If it be true that she who is his legal wife agrees to this new relation because she believes it to be an act of justice — if this impression that you received from the mind of the unhappy gentleman be correct — then she must be a noble-minded woman, even if she is not affectionate, and I would like to look at her. In fact, so rare is it for a human soul to choose the path of self-sacrifice from the promptings of a high justice-loving principle, that *I would willingly start this night, and walk five hundred miles to see such a person!*"

The gifted lady now related the substance of a vision, concerning the past and future of her friend, which she had witnessed while he was in her presence. Her child-like descriptions were at once loveful, tearful, prayerful, beautiful, sunny, prophetic, and eulogistic. This charming symbolic scene of the gentleman's golden future in a happier union, as contrasted with the chill and gloom of a loveless past, was written out and printed in a Boston paper. 'T was true poetry in the garb of prose. But the hour soon glided by which I had set apart for pleasant converse with this esteemed sister; and I departed with a dream-like picture

painted on the walls of my memory, to which I have often reverted with the most heartfelt satisfaction.

The public announcement that I was willing to travel and discourse on Reform topics, soon brought more invitations than I could
personally accept. Old Winter had nominally withdrawn his claim
upon the weather, and Spring stood in the portal of March's dreary
temple, yet dark and grim and fitful were the passing days.

"Does the weather affect you?" asked Mr. Tirrell, to whom I
had been that moment introduced.

"Very little, sir," I replied. "With certain precautions I can
bear almost any temperature."

"Will you come to our place and deliver a few lectures?" he
inquired.

"Where do you live?" I asked.

"In Quincy, this state, in the region of the granite quarries."

Arrangements were completed, and, after the lapse of a few
days, I arrived at Mr. Tirrell's house. This was about the 4th of
March, I think, 1854. My lecture was appointed for sabbath
evening. The afternoon of that day was very spring-like, and we
set out on a ramble to the celebrated granite hills.

My liberal-minded conductor, Mr. Tirrell, said: "I think we'll
go through the graveyard. It's but little out of the way."

Accordingly, we entered the enclosure, and soon halted in front
of a smooth marble headstone, to which the friendly conductor
directed my attention. And now I leaned upon the Magic Staff;
for, looking in the direction indicated, I beheld distinctly chiseled
on the face of that inanimate stone, these startling words: "In
memory of John and Hannah Greaves, deluded by the writings
of A. J. Davis."

The story, as it was related to me, lies vaguely in my memory;
but, I think, it ran in substance as follows: A youthful pair, legally married, came from the West. They were at first supposed to
be both young men, because the romancing wife clad herself in

male attire. Their evil spirit was Poverty. The adventure-loving husband, a shoemaker, worked occasionally at his trade but from some cause, he did not earn sufficient to pay their board.

At length, suspicion led to the shocking discovery that the younger of the twain was a female in disguise. As they had roomed together, and the Braintree people did not know that they were legally one, the inhabitants became incensed against them. This, added to the goadings of poverty and the general weakness of their moral faculties, impelled them into a simultaneous suicide. Among some scraps of paper and a few small books, found in the room which the romantic pair had occupied, there was discovered the first volume of the " Great Harmonia." And on looking over its pages there appeared to be some evidence that, previous to committing the dreadful act of self-murder, they had read certain paragraphs in the philosophy of Death. When the inconsiderate and prejudiced father of the young man arrived from the West, and discovered this slight thread of circumstantial evidence, he at once closed his judgment against the perception of *every other* circumstance and inducement for suicide, and caused the gravestone-carver to express the glaring falsehood which I have frankly chronicled.

" Friend Tirrell," said I, " this, then, is the case of suicide which the opponents of spiritualism *harped* upon so furiously about three years ago, is it ?"

" That's the very case," he replied. " But it hasn't amounted to much in this region."

" Why not ?"

" Because," he answered, " everybody in these parts knows that *your* writings had nothing to do with causing their suicide."

" Indeed !" said I. " Is it true that the people, our opponents here, do not endorse that gravestone statement ?"

" Yes," he returned ; " I don't believe that your worst enemy in this village feels in favor of that inscription."

"What, then, do they think of Mr. Greaves, the father of the young man?" I asked.

"All that ever I heard speak of the matter," replied Mr. Tirrell, "agree that the father has made himself ridiculous in this case; because the several private causes which led to the fearful deed are well known to most of our citizens."

But the spirit of meditation came upon me, as I leaned upon the Staff, and silently I thus soliloquized: How wretched the features of that mind which, swayed and enraged by prejudice, could carve on marble the hieroglyphs of error! Suppose I were an enemy of Harmonial Philosophy. Suppose I were a citizen of this state or of some distant city, on a visit of pleasure to this the birthplace of John Quincy Adams and other illustrious personages. To imbibe the sunshine and air, suppose I wander here — stepping noiselessly and reverently between the silent signs of the buried dead. Presently my eyes rest upon that inscription. I inquire of a lingering passer-by the exact import of those plainly-sculptured words. The white features of a self-murdered pair are at once pictured on my thoughts. Stretched and still, shrouded with a heavy shade of moral darkness, cold as the moon, betrayed into their dumb slumber by A. J. Davis! Who is this dangerous person? Where does he live? What does he write? Can it be that such a being is allowed to go at large in a civilized community? My breath comes quick, and I rub my eyes; I step back and consider; I pause and return; I stoop to the soil; I gaze once more, and I hate the man!

But these suppositions are for strangers, not for me. What, then, do I think of this monumental record? Let me tell you. I think that the father of these departed children has published a *falsehood*, which is not only a lasting injury to his own character, but an open insult to a natural right of the living world. That natural right is, to be possessed of Truth. But what an apostate to justice is he who wantonly publishes a baneful fabrication! How reckless to every insignia of an honorable man! Here is one who has knowingly caused even inert matter to impart to the stranger soul a most hurtful delusion; who has attempted to arrest a Truth by a blockade of marble, even as a stone was rolled to the door of the sepulchre by those Jewish apostates who sought to immolate the divine principle of Love. To an angel's mind the inscription reads thus: "The world, deluded by an unjust father." Recently three persons committed suicide in New York. In each instance, the cause was: "disappointment in love." The deserted bodies were decently entombed. But instead of those beautiful words engraved upon the headstone of each, why not present the bystanders with something like this: "Deluded by the author of Love!" Who wrote "love" within the book of human life? Who made the heart? Who enlivens and occupies the universe?

Thus was I meditating, dear reader, when Mr. Tirrell requested me to continue the proposed ramble to the granite works beyond the fields. That evening, notwithstanding the gravestone falsehood concerning the cause of the Double Suicide, the great hall was overflowing with eager and loving listeners; and, on the subsequent morning, I departed with a soul full of gratitude to Father-God and the angel-world.

All the way from New England to central New York, with very few intermissions, I heard music from the Mountain in the distance. Inexpressibly sweet and irresistibly elevating was the melody that rolled down the psychical slopes between me and the eminence of Beauty. Whether in hotels or cars or private dwellings, or even when before and addressing the assembled public, my inward ear caught the celestial anthems of invisible choristers. And once, while standing on the piazza of an Auburn hotel, I heard: "*Thou—art—not—a—lone—wanderer, my—son.*" The voice was that of my honored Guide. 'Twas musical as the song of purling waters; gentle and low and harmonious, like the beating of an angel's deathless heart.

The inhabitants of Auburn, as a general remark, were decidedly hostile to my public discourses; and yet the questions, to which I solicited attention, were of universal import. If a pulpitarian had delivered my lectures, multitudes would have flocked to hear them; but as it was, with nothing popular at my back or in my speech, the attendance was limited.

But to those who came I presented the philosophy of human existence, the value of life, the moral blessings of physical health I taught that the married should avoid every description of blood love indulgence; that the yet unmarried must resist every impulse toward sexual perversion; that tea and coffee, pork and tobacco, alcohol and powder, profane words and indelicacy of every kind, were enemies to the reproductive functions; by and through which department of our common nature the race could be improved and elevated out of organic tendencies to war, cruelty, slavery, private crimes, and disasters of every name and magnitude.

"What's the object of your lectures?" asked a citizen of Auburn.

"To destroy your prison-house yonder by the depot," said I, "to invite the world to Nature's altar."

"What do you mean by Nature's altar?" he inquired.

"Nature's altar," I replied, "is the human spirit."

"I can't comprehend you, sir — upon my word, I can't."

"Well, friend," said I, "the spirit of man is a pocket edition of the great volume of Nature. Men are taught by the church to go *outwardly* after truth and Deity. Therefore the people grope about in the world of effects, in the sensuous sphere, for truth and righteousness and happiness. Such seem to me like an old man who, with his spectacles on, is hunting all over the house to find them."

"Can you tell, sir, in a few words," inquired the impatient citizen, "just exactly what you're driving at in your public lectures?"

"Yes, friend, I can. First: I teach that, by physical temperance *in all things,* the soul is elevated in spirituality. Second that, by obedience to the laws of justice and harmony, the spirit of every man may become radiant with celestial light and perpetual inspiration. By reverencing and obeying the Laws of Nature, as written upon the inner constitution, the human spirit may enjoy a heaven upon earth. To grow up into goodness — to be true, and pure, and divine, and therefore happy — is the birth-right and destiny of every human being. The Christian church says you can attain to purity only through its remedies; but the church has not destroyed war and slavery and licentiousness; though it has wrought, with but little opposition to hinder it, for eighteen hundred years."

At this moment another citizen came up, and said: "Mr. Davis, I saw a gentleman from Rochester yesterday who expressed himself pleased with the prospect of your coming there to lecture."

"That's good," I replied. "I expect to be there day after to-morrow."

"The Rochester gentleman remarked," continued the citizen, "that your counsel would, perhaps, be sought to prevent a divorce by reconciling the now disaffected parties."

"A divorce!" said I. "Did you hear who the parties are?"

"No, the gentleman did not inform me," he replied, "but they are somewhat expected to attend your lectures in Rochester."

CHAPTER LVII.

THE THEOLOGICAL ECLIPSE.

THE next scene in this psychological drama was enacted beneath the roof which has sheltered many a weary traveller. What Palestine is to the Christian, Mecca to the Mohammedan, Rome to the Catholic, Italy to the Artist, such is a hospitable "Home" to the way-worn Reformer. Sweeter than a sylvan scene, more blessed than blossoming youth, dearer than a thousand laurel wreaths, is the Refuge which certain hearts prepare for the Evangelists of the New Dispensation.

I had arrived at Rochester, and was exchanging kindly words with visitors at the Reformer's Refuge, when a Friend asked: "What does thee think of Slavery?"

"If you had asked 'What do you think of Liberty?' I might perhaps reply to your satisfaction."

"It appears to me," said the Friend, "that thee has overlooked the question of Slavery in all thy volumes."

"But have I overlooked the question of Liberty?"

"Perhaps not," was the reply. "But I do not recall any of thy writing even upon Liberty."

"On all proper occasions," I responded, "I have publicly declared that Liberty is not local, but general; that it is not a sentiment, but a principle; that Liberty is an infinite ocean, while our individual aspirations are but the surges thereof."

"Ah, Friend Davis," said the visitor, "thy words upon Liberty do not touch the Southern Slave question."

"Are you quite sure?" I asked. "Let us apply the test. Liberty, as a principle, is not local, but general. A liberty-man is a man of principle. He looketh upon policy, and presseth it beneath his feet. His struggles and sufferings are not designed to subserve isolated interests. His patriotism is boundless as the earth."

"That's all very good, Friend Davis; but thee does not apply it to our national evil."

"I think," said I, "that my view of Liberty is more searching and complete in its application than yours."

"Oh, no, Friend Davis, I feel that thee is mistaken."

"Let us see," said I. "My proposition is, that Liberty is a principle. A principle, you perceive, will have universal application or it will have none. A true liberty-man loves freedom in the United States because he loves it in his own soul. He loves Liberty in Germany and France, in Austria and Poland, in Hungary and Italy, because he loves Liberty as a sacred principle. The struggle is sublime because it is universal. Now let me apply this more closely. That is not Liberty which liberates the intellect, and enslaves the affections; that is not Liberty which emancipates the African from bondage, and refuses freedom to the unhappily married; that is not Liberty which frees the wrongly-married, and withholds from woman the rights of property and citizenship."

"Thy words remind me," interposed Isaac, "that we expect a couple to attend thy lectures."

"A couple!" said I mirthfully, "I hope there will be several of them in the audience."

"I was going to say," he continued, "that the report is that they have concluded to separate."

"Ah, they must be the parties of whom I was told in Auburn." I replied. 'Do you know who they are?"

"They are school-teachers," said Isaac, "living near or in Randolph I believe. They seem to us to be very kind and affectionate to each other, and we feel that thee may say something to settle the trouble between them."

"I shall not meddle with their private affairs," said I. "And yet, if they should ask my opinion of Liberty, you know, from what I have been saying, that my reply would be in favor of the Principle."

During all this time, dear reader, my first source of strength was the clairvoyant flow of my Intuitions: then, ever and anon, I felt the calm baptism of the angel-world; and, in addition to all else, there was the quiet power of the unbending Magic Staff.

One morning, soon after breakfast, Isaac came to me and said in an under tone: "The troubled persons, the school-teachers, have just come. When thee is ready I will give thee an introduction."

We proceeded to the sitting-room, and I was introduced to "Mr. and Mrs. Love." Several others were present at the time, and the conversation became quite chatty and generally distributed. But nothing was said about marriages or divorcements. Two days intervened between this introduction and another call from the teachers. On this occasion the gentleman asked me, in the course of general conversation, one question which I thought might have some bearing on their conjugal troubles.

"Mr. Davis," said he, "I wish to inquire how you would decide to act in a case where expediency was in opposition to what you believed to be a principle of right?"

"A principle contains all there is of value in a policy," I replied. "I would act upon the principle, therefore, and take the public and private consequences."

On hearing this reply the gentleman addressed himself to the lady, his wife, and said: "Do you remember what I said to you in our conversation on a certain subject the other day?" To which the lady, who had been a silent listener from the first, simply bowed her assent.

While on this visit at Rochester, which continued during the few days devoted to the fulfilment of my appointments, I had friendly and familiar conversations with many of both sexes upon topics set forth in my public discourses. But no person broached the subject of domestic unhappiness, save in the general way Although I had met several times with the school-teachers whom report said were in quest of "divorce," yet neither of them had spoken of or hinted at any nuptial disaffection. I had neither heard nor seen anything that indicated in the slightest degree a thought of separation, unless it was the gentleman's single ques tion concerning principle and policy.

"I guess it must be a false alarm," said I mentally, after closing my last lecture; "or else they shrink from speaking for fear that such conversations would annoy me." This latter thought moved me to step to them, while the audience was retiring, and express my willingness to receive letters if they should feel inclined to write me.

While speaking to the few liberal minds of Rochester on "vices and virtues," I felt that there were awakened many silent resolutions to live higher, happier, and more harmonial lives. And I returned to Hartford immensely rich in such reward.

My writing-table, in Mr. Green's residence, was loaded with letters. They were from persons of almost every social and intellectual grade. Some of my unknown correspondents were bristling with the tactics of logical disputation. Others, though less disposed to controvert my cardinal propositions, were equally vigorous in their imperative demands upon my clairvoyance for personal benefits. But there were also letters of a different temper, full of pale and shadowy imaginings, concerning spiritual communications; and yet other epistles, soliciting my services as a teacher of Harmonial principles, glowing with words of universal philanthropy.

Among the letter packages that had arrived during my absence.

was a sort of valedictory epistle from the conscientious scribe, who has performed so important a part in several eventful scenes of this drama. And as his letter contains a clear and candid statement of his ultimate position with regard to me and my work, I think it due both to him and the reader that I insert it entire in this connection :—

WILLIAMSBURGH, *March 16th*, 1854.

MR. A. J. DAVIS :—

DEAR BROTHER : I feel that it is now proper for me to write you and propose a little friendly communion concerning matters pertaining to our own individual spiritual interests, and to the interests of the latter day unfolding.

You doubtless still remember the time when a most warmly sympathizing intimacy existed between you and me — an intimacy which I once believed could never be interrupted or suspended by any untoward human event, or by any promptings originating either in the natural or the spiritual world. That intimacy, so long as it subsisted, was no doubt intended by the Power who overrules all things, for a good and wise purpose, and that purpose I can now see has been accomplished. A few days after a particular event in your career had been consummated (viz.: I think, on the 5th or 6th of July, 1848), and while you were visiting at Poughkeepsie, as I was sitting at my writing-table a distinct impression came to me, to the following effect :—

"There! you have now nothing further to do with Davis. It has ceased to be your duty to stand between him and those who speak against him. Leave him, and let him pursue his own course while you pursue yours."

This impression was so unexpected, and I must say so contrary to my intentions and even desires, as to create no small degree of astonishment in my mind ; and although I could not possibly refer it to any mundane source, I was for a time disposed to doubt its heavenly authority, especially as I did not receive any confirmation of it through *you*, whom I then regarded as far more capable of receiving truthful spiritual impressions than myself. You are aware, however, that external events as well as internal convictions ensued, which were of such a nature as to force us asunder. From that time to the present you and I have been following

divergent paths. Viewing matters upon their externals (to say the least) the set of convictions to which *my* path has led me would appear to be, in some respects, totally different from certain important and prominent points of doctrine set forth and defended in all your published writings.

During the last three years more especially, I have been constantly pained to see what I am forced to regard as the most sacred truths, and on which I believe the salvation of the world depends, ignored, misconceived, misrepresented, and virtually (though of course ignorantly, and, therefore, unintentionally) abused *by* and *through* yourself and a majority of the more prominent spiritual mediums and writers who adopt the essential principles of your philosophy and theology. During this period I have kept comparatively silent, not feeling that the Master whom I desire alone to serve had yet called me into his field. I now, however, feel that it is time to begin to speak forth my convictions to the. public, and with the promptings which are constantly growing stronger and stronger within me, *I dare not* keep silent much longer.

I, indeed, dread the task that is before me. I foresee that the course which conscience and duty will force me to pursue will be the means of sundering the last bond between me and the many friends which I made upon the plane of your theology. Besides it will probably involve me in a struggle in which (aided of course by my invisible Guide) I will have to stand almost single-handed and alone against a host; and I am not a man of war but of peace, as you well know. I would, therefore, that conflict and public discussion, and especially conflict between myself and my friend Davis, could be avoided as much as possible; and to this end I address you this epistle in order to invite you first to a friendly comparison of notes for the purpose of ascertaining how far you and I can possibly *agree*, and not how far we can *differ* Another object I have in view is to respectfully and fraternally solicit on your part a careful reconsideration of certain questions of *vital importance* on which, if I do not misunderstand you, I am either so fortunate or unfortunate as to widely differ from you Upon the result of any epistolary or oral consultation which you may agree to have with me upon these subjects, will depend in my mind the question of how far I am to include my friend Davis as among the supporters of, or dissenters from, those teachings against which I shall probably be interiorly prompted to contend.

Please, then, understand me as making the following concessions to what I apprehend to be your own views:—

1. That there is much bigotry and intolerance in the world which ostensibly rests upon a religious basis, and that this bigotry and intolerance, besides being intrinsically unjust, constitute one of the most formidable obstacles to all true reform, and that we should hence labor to remove them by all fair and honorable means.

2. That neither the Bible nor any other religious book should be implicity accepted upon mere *traditional* authority, or without subjecting it to the scrutiny of our own developed reason, intuition, and elevated and purified moral and religious sense; and hence that the Bible should be (*candidly*) investigated, criticised, and judged of according to its intrinsic merits, which, however, we should be careful to interiorly perceive.

3. That there have been true revelations spiritually given to man, more or less, in all ages and among all nations, and that the relative importance of these must be judged by their subject, character, scope, and, above all things, by the *fruits* which they have been calculated to produce.

On these and many minor points, I suppose you and I would not essentially differ. At the same time I am, after the most serious and patient investigation continued now for several years, inclined to strongly affirm the following propositions among others of less importance:—

1. That the *religious* element is the true, central, and pivotal element of human nature, and should hence always have the supreme government of the whole man. This element, therefore, is, in my judgment, the beginning point of all true, thorough, and radical reform, and if it is ignored, or its behests disregarded, there will be a constant tendency on the part of professed reformers, to presumption, pride, self-deification, and hence to disunity. By the religious element I of course mean the tendency to love, worship, and render filial service to an ever-present God who takes personal cognizance of the conditions, thoughts, and actions of his creatures, who personally hears (or *knows*) and answers the righteous prayers of his servants. Aside from the recogni-

tion of such a God no religion, in my sense of the term, can exist.

2. That while all minds should hold themselves open to true instruction from any and every source, it so happens that the book, or collection of books, called the BIBLE, especially as viewed with due reference to its *interior sense*, contains the highest, the truest, and the most purifying instruction concerning God, his providences, his plans to save man, and his fatherly requirements of human beings, of any other book extant among men, and is, therefore, altogether indispensable as a guide to the reform of ourselves and of the world. Judging it altogether "*by its own merits*," and irrespective of any *traditional* authority, I am compelled to regard it as *precisely* what it claims to be—in all its most essential parts a *divinely* originated production, and in its own sense of the term, the "Word of God." Moreover,—

3. I regard the doctrine of the divine incarnation in the person of Jesus Christ, taught in John's gospel, chapters I. and XIV., and many other places, as not only perfectly philosophical, but as absolutely necessary to restore the junction between God and the ultimates of humanity, which junction had been previously lost in consequence of man's sins. Hence I believe that Jesus Christ is the only "Way, the Truth, and the Life, and that no man (or society of men) can come unto the Father except by him"—that is, by entire self-abnegation, and an unreserved and unconditional surrendry of themselves to him as their exemplar and their moral and spiritual guide.

Do not by this, however, understand me as supposing that the whole infinite *quantity* of the Divine essence was shut up and comprehended in any limited space or form, and thus withdrawn from other parts of the universe. No intelligent person ever yet supposed that. The fact is God dwells in *all* space, and everywhere his interior qualities assume, by correspondence, the form of a man visible to the interior perceptions of the high and pure angels who are sufficiently *en rapport* with him; and the physical body of Jesus Christ was only the temporary clothing in limited space, of that omnipresent spiritual form, for purposes of human redemption.

These propositions, which I firmly believe to be truths, have wrought the most salutary and happifying effects upon my affections and life, as well as upon the affections and lives of millions; and I must say, that, after witnessing the disunity and confusion, and, in some instances, the positive malignity and wilful deceptiveness of spirits to whom you and I both once looked for true guidance, they constitute my only hope for the salvation either of myself or of the world.

Yet, if I have apprehended the meaning of your writings, you have materially differed (as you were free to do, of course) from all three of the propositions last numerically laid down. Perhaps your dissent, after all, might not appear so wide as I have supposed, if I could persuade you to come to a little closer definition; and the hope of eliciting such definition from you, is one inducement which I now have for writing. Please *do*, Brother Davis, seriously and solemnly reconsider these *vitally important* points. Enter deeply into their inner significance — pray, yes, pray *fervently* to *whatever* spiritual power you may recognise as the highest and best above yourself that can still exercise a guardianship over your inner life — to open your soul to a perception of *whatever* of good and truth may be involved in these several propositions and their kindred Christian doctrines; and after duly pondering the matter, write to your old friend the Scribe how the subject appears to you.

Your frank response to the sundry matters specially propounded in this letter, will enable me to speak with more assurance, when I may have occasion to allude to your views in my public writings and speeches, and will thus protect me against the danger of unintentionally misrepresenting you. I feel, however, that the time is fast approaching, if it has not already arrived, for the commencement of the death-struggle between religionism and anti-religionism, Christianism and anti-Christianism, Bibleism and anti-Bibleism, as connected with the modern spiritual unfolding; and if the Truth simply has fair play, it has nothing to fear, on whichsoever side of the question it may lie.

I have already written much more than I intended when I commenced, but am prompted to add the following ere I close : You are aware that there is a very numerous class of people in the world, to whom the idea of humbling themselves, taking up the cross, and unconditionally and unreservedly following the Divine teacher (as the New Testament requires) wheresoever he may lead them, is *extremely distasteful*. If you will reflect candidly for a moment, you will, I think, admit with me, that it is among this class principally that the stronger admirers of your teachings are to be found, and that they admire them because they find (or think they find) in them an excuse or justification of their native reluctance to conform to the gospel principle of humility and an unreserved surrendry of themselves to God. I am prompted to say, in all fraternal kindness, that God requires you not to serve this class of persons by pandering to their self-love, but to serve HIM by advocating his truths and precepts whether men will hear or forbear. Don't you remember that once in your vision you found yourself lying upon an *altar* between two mountains? Oh, get upon that altar, my beloved brother, without one moment's delay! and then, after witnessing the thunders and lightnings, and receiving the rains of heaven (a new class of spiritual influences), you will be refreshed and invigorated, and the *spiritual sun* — the Lord himself — will shine upon you; and then you will be really prepared to assist the great and only true shepherd, JESUS CHRIST, to collect his scattered and disunited sheep together — which, permit me to say, in all kindness, *you never can do*, until you first recognise him as the *only true shepherd*. Brother Davis cultivate the *religious* element of your nature, and then your intellect will perceive these things more clearly.

Please let me hear from you as soon as possible, and believe me, with many prayers for your spiritual welfare,

Affectionately, your brother,   WM. FISHBOUGH.

And thus the curtain rolls down, dear reader, between the esteemed scribe and the rugged position which I occupy before the human world. In this event, however, I see nothing at which to murmur or be surprised. Well do I remember the first impression which was imparted from his spirit to mine, viz., that his intellectual faculties were swayed by his spiritually-affectionate soul; and that whatever religious conviction might once become *fixed* in the depth of his loving heart, *that* would dominant all subsequent reasonings and take precedence in the conduct of his destiny. This total Theological Eclipse of a human mind is no new phenomenon. We have seen it many times before, and so we shall again. But after carefully reading and reflecting upon the worthy Scribe's letter, I made the following reply :—

HARTFORD, *April* 17, 1854.

Mr. WILLIAM FISHBOUGH :—

DEAR BROTHER : Saturday evening I returned, from an ab sence of over nine weeks, and found your favor (of the 16th March) on my writing-table. It is quite needless for me to express here my gratification at the truly fraternal tone of your communication. In regard to its contents, however, I have to remark in brief :—

1. That the *three* " concessions" you make — to views which you apprehend me to entertain — seem, so far as they go, to bring us into fellowship of private thought and public action ;

2. But owing as you say to a most " patient investigation continued now for several years," you have arrived at other and different conclusions which you very clearly and candidly state. With those conclusions I can not at all harmonize. If I should give my reasons for not accepting your propositions, I do not conceive that I should be thereby helping you out of your present situation. It seems to me like a theologic speculation.

In all true kindness, therefore, I decline any presentation of the intuitional discoveries which (simply perforce of their intrinsic character) have led me to conclusions directly opposite to your own. Your religious experiences and conclusions, so far as I can apprehend their basis and bearing, are in strict accordance with orthodox theology ; with the superaddition of your somewhat painful spiritual exercises, during the past three or four years, which give your present convictions the appearance of being an improvement upon the crude speculations of ancient theologians.

Therefore, Brother Fishbough, I do not see how we can do otherwise than fraternally disagree. I have no sympathy with any scheme of salvation which rests upon the teachings of any one book in the bible, or out of it — nor yet on all books combined. On the contrary, I believe in the progressive growth and harmonization of the whole Human Family. This universal growth, so far as I can, I will help to accelerate.

You greatly err, I believe, when you say that the stronger ad

mirers of my teachings are to be found among those to whom the
"idea of taking up the cross is extremely distasteful." You certainly know that the best of Harmonial Philosophers are among
those *who have tried* the old system thoroughly. They can not be
accused of ignorance. Nor have they been reluctant to test experimental religion. But I will not multiply words. If you feel
called to commence a warfare against Nature and Reason, I will
not interpose an objection, unless I feel somewhat more like it
than at present.

In all the fraternal ties, I still remain,   A. J. DAVIS.

My mode of warfare is not ancient. I believe in muscular
energy — of the soul. I practise in the amphitheatre of Wisdom.
When I become a victor, Love crowns me with the amaranth,
and conducts me to a seat beside those nobler than kings. I worship at the shrine of Omnipotence, and the celestial athletæ display their strength before mine eyes. I admire the chivalry of
the knights-templars of Truth, and the most daring of their number ride to my side and guard me. Translate into mental exercises the physical games of Athens and Rome — show me an intellectual Hercules, a poetic Hector, a prophetic Samson, an
Achilles of moral integrity, a Goliath of impartial goodwill, a
Titan of universal benevolence, a mighty Jupiter of self-control, a
God of Harmony, a Universe of Happiness — show me these
celestial athletæ, these imperishable attributes and exercises, these
sovereigns in the empire of immaculate perfection, and I will bow
down and worship them day and night! Lead me to these, and
I will be an idolator! But why write with reservation? Do
you not know me? I am an idolator, I am a worshipper, I am
a praying child of Father-God — and why? Because my vision
calmly rests upon that mighty troop of immutable principles which
perform unerringly in the amphitheatre that spreads over those
immeasurable fields of matter and mind, composing the infinite
domain of Deity.

CHAPTER LVIII.

THE INFINITE CONJUGATION.

'Mysterious, infinite, exhaustless Love!
On earth mysterious, and mysterious still
In heaven! sweet chord, that harmonizes all
The harps of Paradise! the spring, the well,
That fills the bowl and banquet of the sky!"

VERY soon after my return to the Charter-Oak city, I felt
the attractive influences from the summit of Mount Beauty.
Therefore I prepared myself, by abstemiousness of diet and regularity of outdoor exercises, to consummate the pilgrimage. I was
not alone, dear reader, except outwardly. My journey up the
Mountain of Power had strengthened me for the present attempt.
From the awful precipice of the Table mountain, of South Caro-
lina, many have retreated nerveless and appalled. Not so with
me in this psychical work. The dizzy heights of Mount Power,
though presenting the deep abyss of possible degradation below,
had not shaken the fortitude of my soul.

In my public lectures at this period, I taught that indifference
or discontent among the married is mainly traceable to *a cessation*
of those tendernesses and delicate tokens of pure love which led
to the hymeneal altar; and, therefore, as an almost certain remedy for such domestic disaffection, I prescribed the reinstatement
by the married of those *pure devotions* which characterized and
sanctified their attachment previous to the hour of wedlock.

Another part of my teaching was: that to marry a person

whom you can not love, is a crime against the "higher law" of your own soul, the penalty of which is disastrous and inevitable. Also, that all intercourse not prompted by mutual love, is positive adultery ; and that the sanction of priest or passion or statute-law, is no source of justification, and can not render the private vice a public virtue.

Modern statutes, as well as the demon custom of a stupid anti quity, give the husband a legal right to the person of his wife. The consequence is, that, when ordinary politeness and refinement do not prevent, the worn and weary woman is forced into child-bearing, as a result of those adulterous relations which can not but be pronounced "criminal" by the pure-minded in this and the angel-world. Therefore, I taught that, where my prescription for *indifference* would not cure, and where each and every other merciful and conciliatory measure failed to restore the domestic life to its Eden state of nuptial love and gladness, then the parties were in duty bound, as members of a human family whose universal weal they should seek to promote, to obtain personal freedom by legal divorce. Furthermore, to prevent litigious troubles in questions of property, to avoid societary confusion, and to arrest individual abuses of the conjugal attraction, I taught the value of making a mutual open avowal to the state when a marriage relation was to be consummated. And, finally, I taught that the world's business was, not to kindle a bonfire of malicious scandal around every case of divorce, but *to prevent bad marriages ;* and that, to this end, those legal barriers which are deemed expedient for the regulation of individual conduct, should be placed high and strong *between the sexes and the hymeneal altar ;* while the licentious impediments which State and Church have fixed between the Atlar and the Right of the individual to chastity and liberty, should be either reduced or removed.

As the prudential reader might imagine, I was accused of advocating licentiousness and of sanctioning the absurdities of " free love ;" but possessing at once the plain Truth and the Magic

Staff, I did not turn aside to join issue with the ignorance of my assailants. The return wave of these public teachings, however, wafted many letters from both sexes to the safe harbor of my writing-table. One of these contained the following:—

. . . . . I listened to your late lectures in Auburn, and, for the first time, fully realized the cause of my life-long sufferings. Sixteen years ago I married a man almost the exact opposite of myself. Our four children are sickly and ill-mannered. I know, too, that they have been morally injured by our distressing differences of feeling and speech. Sometimes I have left home, taking my youngest child with me, and stayed away for weeks to get a little relief. . . . . . I am compelled to yield to his wishes, contrary to my every inclination and sense of propriety. I sometimes hate and despise even my own body, and feel more willing to die than to live, for I am weak, weary, and despairing. The people say that I must make my husband happy, and obey him as the Scripture saith; but my life is a sacrifice to his passions, and I must have liberty or death.

. . . . . My relatives are all opposed to my making this disaffection public, though they know full well that *I am a martyr to legal sensuality.* . . . . The minister here entirely disapproves of divorce except on Bible ground, and I get no sympathy from any one in this region. . . . . Will you please answer this, Mr. Davis, and tell me whether you think such should be divorced?

With much sorrow and sincere respect, S. A. H.

In reply to the foregoing, which was but a type of many letters from the miserably married, I said that the special righteousness of divorce, as applied to individual cases, I did not feel called upon to consider; that my work was a general one, viz.: to define and promulgate the unalterable laws which, in the economy of Nature, regulate the marriage relation, and to show the justice of divorces under certain domestic circumstances; but that I must leave all to decide for themselves with reference to their own personal demands and surroundings.

On opening another letter among the mass before me, I read the following sentences and sentiments:—

HOLLEY, N. Y., *April*, 1854.

MY KIND FRIEND: You gave me the privilege of writing you, and this morning I feel inclined to do so. May I speak to you freely of my past experiences — of the sorrows as well as the blessings that have attended my existence? It is pleasant and cheering to find a friend who seems so worthy of confidence as you; for, though there may be many such in the wide world, they have seldom crossed my own pathway.

From the hour of my legal union with my friend and brother, but not companion, we both realized that ours was *a false* marriage. Yet we strove to be happy. We endeavored to assimilate to each other and to become entirely congenial. We hid from the world all traces of the fearful chasm which, spite of all our efforts, continually widened between us; and thus we have lived on from year to year, calling each other "husband" and "wife," while our hearts throbbed with agony at the profanation of those holy words.

What wonder then, that I felt gratitude for the fearless utterance of those self-evident truths which constituted the basis of your lectures in Rochester? My heart bleeds with pity when I see the thousands who bow down in anguish beneath the false fetters of society. Oh, if I live, and find the strength within me, I will do *something* toward shaking our selfish law-makers from their posts — unless they will give us statutes that more fully meet the wants of Humanity.

I am happier than formerly because I see a work to do. In the path of active effort, I have discovered a new significance in life. There is a beauty in existence that I did not discern in years gone by; and, gladdened by its light, I feel my sympathies going out toward all the human race. There are those on earth, and I fondly hope in Heaven, whom I gratefully trust, feeling that —

> "Warm from their spirits spreads around
> An atmosphere serene — divine —
> Magnetical, like golden haze,
> Encircling mine."

I intend leaving here the first of May. The West will be my home during the summer — what part or parts I have not yet

determined. Should you answer my desultory letter, please direct
to this place. With much respect, yours fraternally,

MARY F. LOVE.

It was evident that the foregoing emanated from the individual
of whom I was told by the gifted lady in Boston, and to whom I
had been introduced while in Western New York. " This case,"
thought I, " is of long standing, and not a recent disaffection as I
was let to suppose by the whisperings of the people." My reply
was prompt and brief:—

HARTFORD, *April* 18*th,* 1854.

MY DEAR FRIEND : Your letter came to me safely, and I was
pleased with its tone of friendly confidence. Feeling the freedom
of Truth, you could not well do otherwise than speak to me freely
of your past experiences. I comprehend, with a true sympathy,
the sufferings you have realized, and which have been shared
equally by your fraternal, but not conjugal, companion — with
whom, also, my soul deeply and steadily sympathizes.

The world needs great light on the question of true Marriage
and Parentage. How profoundly do I pray that your soul may
be moved in strength to aid in rousing the law-makers of our
century to a full and free and salutary discussion of the wrongs
of present relations between the sexes — and, no less, to a new
estimate of the nature and mission of marriage in its bearing on
human progression, and the right development of our species.

Like many others from whom I receive letters, you write of
unhappiness in your own false relation, and I know, from what I
discovered to be the nature of your " friend and brother," that he
no less experiences the pain arising from a consciousness of the
same cause. In these things you may both open your wounded
hearts to me, in all the simple confidence of little children, and I
will give to each my fraternal sympathy, even though I know
not how to break the unseen fetters which bind you in painful
bondage. Sincerely your friend,   A. J. D.

Mount Beauty sent forth music of the diviner kind. From
the topmost crag, through the dales below, there flowed whole
rivers of melody. Its billowy undulations swept down through

my being, and, as with the lute-like tones of angel-voices, they awakened portions of my sealed-up nature into beauteous and harmonial animation. Thus my higher faculties were excited to the perception of symmetry and proportion. At one breath I could inhale the gospel of the Beautiful.

What I called "Beauty" before, now seemed low and vulgar. Ashamed of what I had admired during previous years, and overcome by a sense of the opening glories of the present, I hid my face and wept. A flower, a blushing cheek, a true word, a simple song, a sweet breath, a clean skin, white teeth, a pure smile, graceful motion, childhood, love, playfulness, innocent expressions of the heart, delicate thoughts of the manly soul, the sacred mission of the woman-nature, the adaptation of Love to Wisdom, the evil of conjugal inharmony, the beauty of the true nuptial relation, the purity of Love's offspring, the deformity of the sin-conceived —such attractions and thoughts occupied my soul as I walked up the broad table-land of Mount Beauty.

From that elevation, dear reader, I viewed the wide world of living men. My vision of the follies of the valleys of life I will not relate in this volume. Immediate individual interests I did not consider; I looked and wrote for the human world. Into the causes of domestic troubles I looked; into the far-off homes of the unhappy; into the habits of the solitary man; into the veiled mysteries and miseries of public women; into the memory of him who broods low and dishonorable thoughts; into the blue eyes of blighted girlhood I looked; into the torpid souls that preach with the lip and practise with the battle-axe of error; into bedroom revelations, from Harlem to Castle-Garden, from river to river, and from shore to shore; whole days I devoted to clairvoyant penetrations into hearts living in cities and country-villages, that beat with a weary weight of unutterable anguish; through long, dark, dreary histories of private domestic suffering I looked; and I said: "Let me not to 'the marriage of true minds admit impd-iments'; but against that sensual love which 'alters when it alteration finds, or bends with the remover to remove,' I will speak with the tone of a trumpet." For, behold the sickly children of sensual progenitors! Behold the insanity of those who were brought forth in iniquity! Behold the idle limbs and silly tongues of those who came from antagonistic parents legally wedded! Behold innocent youth disfigured and overrun by the blotches of hatred and repulsion which some delicate woman has felt toward her drunken and sensual husband! Behold the manifold *deformities* which I saw from the sacred summit of this Mountain! Behold the fiery riot of the animal love of the heated blood — the invisible mob of reproductive essences — rushing, under legal sanction, into the holiest sanctuary of the woman soul! And then behold the consequences — the loss of delicacy — the indifference to truth — the abandonment to the seductions of evil! Behold what I beheld, dear reader — see what I saw — and you will not wonder that I wrote the fourth volume of the "Great Harmonia."

But the Mountain of Beauty — by which I mean a state of mind that enables the individual intuitively to see and comprehend the harmonies of the universe — had its charms also. While meditating upon its broad summit my lips were mute. Because I saw no words that could describe the Beautiful. Suns and clouds, seas and mountains, forests and fields, flowers and pictures, men and angels — these are but the symbols, the types, the mirrors, the shadows, of that divine beauty which my soul felt, but could not express. Then came swiftly gathering thoughts of all that is useful, just, potent, unchangeable — of all that is harmonial and eternal — and my raptured heart exclaimed: "Surely this is the realm of the Beautiful!"

Filled with principles, and animated by the angel-melody that floated upon the soft air, I set myself to investigating the laws of conjugal harmony. In order to solve this problem, I penetrated, as far as I could, the nuptial code of Father-God and Mother-Nature — parts and counterparts; the two halves of one whole heart and head ; soul and body ; sun and earth ; light and heat right and left ; attraction and repulsion ; expansion and contraction ; positive and negative ; male and female ; intellect and love ; MAN and WOMAN!

The infinite conjugalities of the universe I contemplated. The marriage of all elements and forms in things inanimate, I first examined ; then the higher uses of nuptiality, till I comprehended the worth of human love and the sublime laws which make its devotions eternal. In applying the principles of marriage to human beings, I discovered that man's highest dower is the power to eternize a temporal union. Not that all legal relations can be converted into future and permanent blessings, but those marriages only that are begun with a certain compatibility of temperament. Even then disobedience to those laws and disregard of those delicacies by which Love is awakened and nurtured, might cause a good union to dwindle down and at length vanish in a cold and hateful separation for eternity. On these points the reader will, perhaps, get my meaning, by consulting the volume to which I have already alluded.

About this period — in the full-blown summer-time of 1854 — I received a romantic sketch from Silona, of her own life and marriage in the Spirit Land. Her very breath was warm with enthusiasm. Her joy-abounding soul exulted in the deathless love of her new-found and gifted companion! But her poetic and vivid descriptions may be found at length by turning to page 174 of the "Penetralia." Hence there remains to be chronicled only this: that, previous to her marriage with the wise and beautiful "Cyloneos" of the Brotherhood of Morlassia, I had made deep excursions into the very *interior* territories of conjugal science. From my discoveries in reference to temperamental harmonies — that only certain combinations can eternally cling to each other — I had concluded, although the relation between us was temporarily wise and fraternally beneficial, that it could not extend beyond the tomb and be crowned with the Harmonial perpetuity   Therefore her narrative, although it had at first somewhat of sadness in it, did not surprise me.   And as she withdrew from earth, sustained and enraptured by the strong and steadfast love of her real conjugal companion, my heart calmly rejoiced in their happiness, and my lips breathed an affectionate farewell blessing.

CHAPTER LIX.

CAUSE AND EFFECT.

" Grown wiser for the lesson given,
    I fear no longer, for I know
  That where the share is deepest driven,
    The best fruits grow."

A NEW creation was opened by the conjugal revelations of Mount Beauty. I saw that the domestic world waited to be harmonized, but the first need was the perfection of individuals — then, by virtue of internal unity and sympathy, human society would feel the " atmosphere, serene, divine, magnetical," bringing harmony out of existing discords.

Again: I realized that the truest and most favorable state for every human being is that of true marriage; not a housekeeping, social, humdrum, commonplace relation for purposes of physical comfort and personal convenience; but that nuptial *union* which consecrates soul to soul — tender, loving, deep, steady, immutable, divine — like the marriage between Father-God and Mother-Nature. The true woman, therefore, with all the depth of her affection yearns for a congenial home in the sanctuary of man's nature; while the true man, with the strength of Jupiter and the tenderness of a child, seeks to identify his soul's destiny with one embodied in the form of woman. In all this there is nothing but crude poetry to him whose attractions are sensual; but, to the truly spiritual heart, I have but touched the key-note to which its every chord tearfully and gratefully responds.

"And here am I," methought, "without my mate. If there be a woman in the domain of human society with whom I could become eternally united, I would seek her—a soul in which I could at once behold the child of love and the woman of intelligence—a friend, a playmate, a sister, a power unto progression, a noble-minded associate, an eternal companion. And to that soul I would be an equal, a source of strength, lifting her above the valley storm, a Harbinger, her spirit's resting-place, and its safe conductor to higher and fairer spheres of existence."

Thus I was meditating, dear reader, when a shower of genial influences descended upon my head. Opening the door, there came into my study four friends from the Spirit Land; and one, who was my familiar Guide, said:—

"Wouldst thou behold one who might become thy true companion?"

"Kind Guide," said I, "there is in me a power of love which needs a corresponding ministration."

"Hast thou long felt a need so powerful?" he inquired.

"No," I replied. "Ere this I never realized the existence of any such capability to love."

"True love," he answered, "is of God. It fills, comforts, calms, elevates   Dost thou feel these sublime emotions?"

"The love that fills my heart," said I, "is the same that I see between Father-God and Mother-Nature."

"Jackson, my son," said the blessed Guide, "if thou hast a true perception of this, thy tongue can describe to me its laws and its mission."

After thinking a few moments, I replied: "True conjugal love is that which transcends all outward circumstances, and dominates over the changeful impulses consequent upon the trials of days and hours. It is an essential spring to personal development—a necessity in schooling the soul—the best agent in harmonizing character. It brings out the beauties, perfections, enjoyments, of the inmost heart. It reveals each to the other and both to man kind. It is the holiest benediction of Heaven — the divinest ordination of the universe — the crown of life upon the *one* destiny of two immortal beings!"

"Thou dost well appreciate the true conjugal life," said he. "Therefore, as thou knowest the law of temperaments, use thine own clairvoyance to *find* and thine own intuitions to *estimate* thy counterpart. But a few moments since we looked on one with whom thy spirit might form that eternal relation."

"Thanks, kind friends," I replied. "Your words fall upon my heart like blessings. I do not much question your decision. But I, too, would read the hidden record. I desire to *know* as the basis of my confidence and future conduct."

"'Tis well," smilingly responded my celestial visitor, "such has ever been the import of my mountain lessons."

They now began to retire toward the door, when I said: "If either of you know which way I should look to see the person of your choice, please point in that direction."

My graceful and quiet Guide raised his hand and pointed toward the setting sun. Being in clairvoyance I looked, and soon my vision rested on four or five persons walking in an ornamented garden in southern Ohio. There were three ladies; one of whom I instantly recognised as her whose fraternal letter I had recently answered.

"Seest thou, my son?" said the beautiful Guide. "She is the being of our choice. Now proceed with thine analysis." Thus saying the four departed, and I was alone with my interior meditations.

My investigations into the laws of marriage had given me the knowledge that there was no inexorable *destiny* to contend with; that God had not predetermined and foreordained that a certain man must be married to a certain woman in order to secure the eternal marriage; but, on the contrary, I saw that the Divine Code is within the scope of human discovery, and teaches that it is for the twain to decide whether they will be transiently or permanently related. With his knowledge to guide me, I first scanned the immense field of human life — to detect, if possible, among the vast throng of female natures, a soul whose invisible constitution and mental circumstances were alike suited to my own. To this clairvoyant penetration I devoted one hour for five successive days, but without satisfaction. At length, I concluded to examine the lady to whom I was referred by my visitors. I did so, and found that they were not mistaken.

The steps of her baby-feet I traced; the plays and works of her girlhood; her fondness for intellectual pursuits; the innate love of her soul for proportion, melody, and beauty; the native tranquillity of her very affectionate heart; the plighted vows and her fraternal marriage; mutual efforts to be contented and happy; how the existence of their two children exerted a reconciling influence for a time; the subsequent attachment that involuntarily ripened into conjugal love between the legal husband and a more congenial woman; the struggle of her silent soul both to yield assent and to conceal the fact from the observation even of friends most intimate; the final and mutual agreement to a conjugal separation as an affair of honor and justice; the consideration that, inasmuch as neither could possibly love the other as husband and wife should love, their spurious relation should be suspended and legally abolished; that this conclusion became fixed in both minds even before I was told of their singular situation by the Boston lady; and that the unmated heart sometimes bled with the agony of desolation, but was moved with no desire to disturb the harmony of the new relation before her eyes. Now I saw her exposed to and affected by several unrighteous influences; then I beheld her as a teacher of the young, as a friend of the domestic group, as the rejector of uncongenial natures, as a lonely wanderer in the field of public effort. Through many sad and trying scenes I traced her footsteps, up to the hour when my physical eyes first rested upon her at the Reformer's Refuge. And now I detected the reason why the twain did not consult me, viz., because the determination to procure a

divorce, particularly in her mind, was fixed as the hills, and she
sought no one's opinion. I observed, too, that her motive for obtaining a legal separation, was to remove every barrier to his immediate happiness, and not to subserve any selfish ends; I saw
this extraordinary example of self-sacrificing benevolence, this very
unusual reason for seeking a divorce, and I admired the firm and
justice-loving woman. I traced her to Cleveland; saw her pretended friends, her real friends, and the enemies of her peace; each
and everything I penetrated; and then, although she was not yet
divorced, I looked upon the flow cf present circumstances and cast
the horoscope of future events; yea, with the speed of the whirlwind, I unravelled the skein of her most private experiences;
and, finally, I resolved to conceal from her the fact that I detected
a genuine fitness of her soul to mine.

My friend, Mr. Green, having some business which called him
into Ohio, asked me to bear him company. While in the cars
between Buffalo and Cleveland, an elegantly-dressed but shabbily
minded individual, recognising me, advanced and asked: "Can
you tell how the sun looks outside of our atmosphere?"

"I have never personally risen beyond our atmosphere," I replied; "yet, by impression and clairvoyance, I have viewed the
sun from space, and can therefore tell you how it appears."

Taking the cigar from his mouth, and puffing a column of fetid
vapor into the air I was breathing, he said: "I'm posted in astronomy, sir, an' I can tell whether you're right d—n quick, if
you'll answer my questions."

"Well," said I, smiling with a momentary emotion of the ludicrous, "what are your questions?"

"If you know how our sun looks from a distance," he replied
pompously, "tell me."

"From the earth's surface," said I, good-naturedly, "the heavens appear filled with light, as you know by observation. But
should you ascend to the outer rim of our atmosphere and look

toward the sun, you would see a rayless ball of fire, steadfastly burning in a universe of Night. The sun would present no atmosphere, the countless stars would emit no scintillations, and the now azure sky would seem like a black concave immeasurable."

"Fudge!" he exclaimed. "That's all spiritual twaddle, sir All d—n nonsense! What reason can you give for what you've been sayin'?"

"The reasons are very simple," said I, quietly. "Light is equalized on the earth by the operation of two causes. First, the perfect absorption and refraction of the sun's rays by our atmosphere; second, the reflection of light thus diffused by bodies on the earth's surface."

The questioner seemed a little less irritable now: "Some say the air is cold in space: is that so?"

"Yes, sir," said I. "The temperature, at the distance of forty-five miles from the globe, is lower than any cold known to man."

"What! do you mean to say that it's colder up there than at the North Pole?"

"Yes, sir," I answered, "the intense cold in the regions of eternal snow is almost warm weather when compared with the upper air."

"Look a-here now! don't pile up the agony in that 'are horrid way—jest tell the plain truth for once, and see how 'twould sound!"

"The plain truth is more wonderful than fiction," I replied. "Therefore, till that fact is found out, the people choose mythology instead of spirituality, and pictures instead of the realities which daguerreotyped them."

"About this 'ere cold weather up there," he replied—"say, ain't you confoundedly mistaken?"

As he spoke, the superior condition flashed upon me, and, instantly detecting more truth in regard to the cold, I replied: "Chemists can produce a lower temperature than that which prevails within the Arctic circle. They can convert carbonic gas into a solid substance, and quicksilver would become firm as iron yet this intensely freezing temperature, about one hundred and fifty degrees below zero, is warmer by nearly eighty degrees than the cold of the upper realm."

Although the day was extremely sultry, yet the interrogator shivered at the thought; but, still skeptical, he continued: "You ain't stuffin' a feller, are you? If you're telling the truth, then I'd like to know how *the spirits* can come through such a cold region, and not freeze to death. I'd give five dollars to see you get out of *that* difficulty, anyhow!"

" Do you believe in the existence of such beings?" I inquired.

"That ain't neither here nor there; jest let me see you get out of that trap, sir—that's all I ask."

" My answer is very simple," said I. " Spirits, when drawing near to the earth, move in a soft, magnetic, summery river of elements which flows, from the North to the South Pole, a few miles above the earth's surface."

" No, no!" exclaimed he. " You do n't get out in that way."

" Yes I do," said I. " That's one third of the explanation. The next is: that spirits can, by the mere exercise of their *will*, render themselves invulnerable to temperature either high or low. And the last part of the explanation is: that spirits seldom come right down into our midst."

" If what you last said is true," he returned, "then why do mediums say the spirits stand all around folks?"

" Because," said I, "the lower stratum of our atmosphere is a mirror, similar to the surface of a placid lake, into which spirits from far distant elevations can cast a perfect image or likeness of themselves. The reflections of these images are so distinct and positive, like the shadow of one's own body in a looking-glass that inexperienced mediums mistake them for the spirits themselves."

" Humph! Yes, yes!" returned he with more interest and civility. " That looks kind o' reasonable. But I do n't understand how that are can be when tables are moved and voices are heard in a room."

"I have not denied," said I, "that spirits come into our immediate presence. Only this I say, that they do not come so frequently as is supposed by those who act as mediums. Tables and persons can be influenced from an immense distance. Words can be whispered into the soul from beyond the sun! And yet, my friend, it is also true that spirits do come into our homes, and would like to find a welcome in our hearts."

The locomotive whistle was now proclaiming our entrance into the Cleveland dépôt, and the gentleman seriously said: "You have done me good, sir. I like your doctrines, and shall read books in order to examine the subject. I wish you well, sir, and success in your undertakings."

"You have more patience with such a fellow than I should have," remarked Mr. Green, as we walked into the Forest city.

"The Harmonial Philosophy," I replied, "teaches that a man should not be repulsed, even when disagreeable, if there's any chance to do him good. Now I believe that this stranger will yet be a friend of temperance and human reform. At all events, he is much more likely to heed the voice of his better nature than if I had repelled him in the same spirit of pugnacious bitterness which he at first manifested."

The next scene opens in the parlor of a Cleveland friend. Twelve hours had elapsed since our arrival, and many persons had assembled to enjoy a social season. At length the hostess, a lady endowed with a kindly heart and a sincere and active love of truth and justice, withdrew from a group of animated guests, and, seating herself beside me, made some allusion to the singular divorce case. Hearing which I asked if "the merits of this unusual proceeding were known to the community?"

"I guess, not," she replied with a thoughtful look. "People are not prepared to approve of divorces under such circumstances."

"What circumstances do people require?" I asked.

"The world, you know, demands something more than a mere disaffection," said she regretfully. "Most people seem to think that there should be some crime, outrageous abuse, and ill-treatment, to justify a suit for legal separation."

"Is it possible, Carrie," said I, "that human beings can not see a *crime* in brother and sister living as husband and wife? What is more a violation of purity and principle? The fact is, Mrs. Lewis, this case commands my respect. These persons have, as I am informed, spent several years in trying to be contented together. They have failed; and now they are willing to give each other freedom. This is the *first* instance I have known of a pair separating upon a law of mutual good-will and justice. It is a bold and original stand to take, and I trust both parties will have the courage to go through with it as they have begun."

"I hope they will," said she. "But Mr. Love appeared to be rather faint-hearted when he left Mary here, and wanted her to defer the suit awhile. He has, apparently, been very anxious indeed to become divorced whenever I have seen him before, but now, it seems to me, that he begins to dread the disagreeable publicity of a legal separation."

"What does the wife say to that?" I asked.

"She seemed to feel badly to see him so disheartened," replied Carrie; "but said that she was sure he would be far happier when he could marry the one he loves; and that as she also needed freedom for her own peace of mind, she could not feel that it would be right to postpone her painful undertaking."

"On what ground can Mrs. Love apply for a legal separation?" I inquired.

"I hardly know what she will do," said the lady with a look of sympathy. "But I suppose her main charge will be 'desertion.'"

"Suppose a bill should be granted—what plan do the parties then mean to adopt?" I inquired.

"As far as I know," replied the conscientious Carrie, "their plan is the same as it has been, that is, for Mr. Love to get married and take the children, and for Mary to make it her home at his house so as to be with the little ones whenever she is not lecturing or teaching." The gentle lady here relapsed momentarily into a mood of pensive thoughtfulness, and then said: "Jackson, I fear she won't get her liberty."

The conversation now became generally distributed, and other topics soon displaced the subject of our fortuitous interview.

Four days hastened by — during which the spiritually-designated brother and I visited many well-remembered friends in Amherst and Cleveland. 'Twas one of the most beautiful sabbath days of the season — the 24th of September, 1854 — a large portion of which I had devoted to public lecturing. At the conclusion of my discourse I accepted the whole-hearted invitation of a citizen, and proceeded with him toward his considerably-distant but attractive residence. While on the way, he remarked upon the hampering and disagreeable restraints of fashionable ignorance; that most people were loutish and selfish upon a question of justice and liberty; and, among other instances where action was necessary, he adduced the case of Mr. and Mrs. Love as one calculated to elicit words of calumny and vituperation. On hearing which I asked: "Do you know where Mrs. Love is, Friend Sterling, and whether she has yet made application for a legal divorce?"

"She left here some time since," he replied, "and the few Cleveland friends of her cause have heard nothing from her until quite recently."

"Then you do not know how far she has proceeded?" I asked.

"The fact is," said he with a firm and impatient tone, "she's gone on without asking our advice, made application away off in Indiana, and her brother-in-law has written up here for testimony."

"Well, is there anything wrong in that?" I inquired.

"It's all out of the regular course suggested by her Cleveland friends," he replied, "and from the way the whole thing has gone on, I expect she'll find herself defeated and obliged to wait a year or two longer."

"What's her brother-in-law's name?" I asked.

"Charles M. Plumb," he replied. "He acts like an intelligent and enterprising young man, but I think he's been injudicious in this case."

"Is it true," I asked, "that Mrs. Love is persevering in this divorce business *without the counsel and aid of her Cleveland friends?*"

"Yes," he responded somewhat testily. "She can't blame any of us if she should be defeated; which I am almost positive will be the result of their operations."

"Friend Sterling," said I, "this fact makes me both sad and thankful. I am sorry that she is not vigorously sustained in a just cause, and yet I am very glad that she has not depended on the Cleveland friends for counsel."

"Well, it can't be said that I have done anything to hinder her success," he answered. "In fact, I am intending to send her something in the way of pecuniary assistance immediately. But why are you glad, Friend Davis?"

"Because," I replied, "if she should succeed, the prejudiced world can not truthfully accuse my friends nor the friends of spiritualism of being instrumental in causing the separation."

"Yes, that's true! But, Davis, I'm surprised to hear a reformer talk as you do. Public prejudice should be nothing to one who advocates principles of universal justice and liberty."

"For myself," I replied, "I fear nothing, as you know. But in regard to the strength of some professed reformers to bear up against public condemnation, I am unpleasantly doubtful."

"What do you mean?" he asked.

"I mean this: in the sequestered recesses of some retired street, in the protection of a closed parlor, in some out of the way corner of society, I have heard many make noble declarations, avow themselves the friends of woman and the lovers of equal rights, speak enthusiastically in favor of every good word and perfect work ; and then, Brother Sterling, I have traced the private and public conduct of such characters, and with unutterable sorrow have seen those same bold and beautiful talkers play fantastic tricks, and do deeds enough contemptible and diabolical, to make the angels weep."

" True, very true," said he with a deep emphasis and tone of regret. " There are few who can withstand the world's opposition. My experience for years in anti-slavery and other battles has settled that fact in my mind."

At this moment we reached his beautiful suburban home, and were ushered into the midst of those refined hospitalities which had been, on previous occasions, freely and gracefully bestowed on me and mine by the members of his household. Upon the foregoing subject nothing further was said till after breakfast on the subsequent morning, when the gentleman handed me a letter he had received from the parties in question.

" Come," said he, " as I am going to answer that letter to-day, suppose you put in a word of encouragement."

" I don't wish to identify myself with the affair," I replied. " The struggling woman deserved to be sustained, however, and I have occasionally written her a cheering letter, but perhaps I had better not do so now."

" Why, Davis," said the firm and fearless brother, " you're just the man who should sustain individuals in their struggles for liberty Come, make haste ! Let 's have a note in fifteen minutes, for I must go right down street."

It is presumable that the reader appreciates the reason which induced me to decline any participation in this particular case. It will be remembered that, by clairvoyant penetration, I had discovered that a relation might eventually be formed between the then undivorced woman and myself. I had also seen faintly foreshadowed the torrent of false charges which an unscrupulous gang of drawing-room gossippers would develop against both of us Hence, my reservation was more decided and uniform than would have been justifiable under other circumstances. But I consented, however, to write and send the following :—

CLEVELAND, Sept. 25, 1854.

To Mrs. MARY F. LOVE :—

DEAR SISTER : Friend Sterling <i>insists</i> upon my sending you a line with his letter. He thinks " a kind word from me" will cheer you. I have therefore consented to join him in the pleasurable effort to sustain and encourage you in this struggle for civil and mental freedom. Be very firm and hopeful, for the angels Love and Wisdom send you good and true friends to aid you externally ; and they strengthen your purposes also, in the present exertion for Justice and Liberty.

If you do not succeed at this term of the court, you need not despair. A few months more will doubtless accomplish all you desire. Remember that if you fail now, there remain plenty of time and ability to achieve the ends of reciprocal justice.

With an unchangeable regard, your brother,   A. J D.

My friend, William Green, continued his journey into southern Ohio, to visit the celebrated Koon's spirit-room, while I, having a positive engagement to attend a Reform Convention at Peterboro', New York, delayed no longer, but hastened directly toward the proper destination. Of the incidents and blessednesses of that great gathering I will not chronicle. And, yet, I must record the glorious and prophetic fact, that inspired words through many speakers were freely and fearlessly uttered in a white structure called a "church," in the fence-like pews whereof sat noblemen from ploughed fields, liberty-lovers from machine-shops, and auditors from almost every grade of belief and incredulity. Energetic reformers spoke mighty truths on that propitious occasion ; and I did not observe more than twenty in the crowded assembly, but thanked Father-God for the possession of their reason.

While in the homeward-rolling cars, between Albany and Hartford, a stranger, having first ascertained my name, asked, "if I could give him any positive evidences of the soul's eternal individuality?"

"Not to-day," I replied. "My mind does not work at all times."

"I much regret your disinclination to talk," said he, "for I consider your Philosophy the only consistent theory in the world."

The adjoining seat was occupied by an owlish-looking individual, who exhibited a remarkably large and white neckcloth, and still other indications of an evangelical profession. Overhearing the intelligent gentleman's opinion of the Harmonial system, he exclaimed :—

"Away with your vain philosophy, with your much learning, striving to be wise above what is written! Have we not the testimony of an arisen Christ? Have we not the positive declaration of the apostle Paul that man shall live after death? What more do you ask, sir, to convince you of immortality?"

"Be patient with the doubter," said I, addressing the clerical interlocutor, "and do yourself the justice to listen. I have a few sentences to utter touching this very matter."

The pulpitarian looked extremely dignified at me, and I looked extremely imperturbed at him, while the skeptical gentleman looked extremely interested at both of us.

"The rational mind," I began, "will not deny that Man begins life in total ignorance. Not knowing anything absolutely, the surface of the human soul must be a blank book, an unspotted sheet of paper, so to speak, on which the pen of experience has never traced a line of thought. Consequently, viewed in this respect, Man commences a sensuous existence, like the untutored forest brute, *i. e.*, in exclusive devotion to the phenomena of time and space. Therefore the strongest primary element in Man's intellect is a blank skepticism — a sort of disbelief — which, after all, and wisely enough. is the mainspring to all thought and investigation."

"Your talk, sir, don't touch the case in question," sai the dig nified minister.

"Now inasmuch as the law of action and reaction is as distinctly a law of mind as of matter," I continued, "it happens that Man's mind, without any real growth in experience, darts off like a comet from perihelion to aphelion, from skepticism to superstition, from atheism to supernaturalism, swinging like a pendulum from one extreme to the other; and so it happens, also, that they who most firmly believe in ancient revelation are frequently quite *as ignorant* of living truth as those who have no faith at all in the supernatural and miraculous. All argument, in either case, is superfluous."

The skeptic here interrupted: "I can not believe in the soul's immortality, sir, although I much wish to."

"Why can you not believe it?" I inquired.

"Because," he replied, "I behold trees, herbs, brutes, birds, men, all coming into being, living for a season, and disappearing all alike—changing into other forms—leaving behind no trace of a future existence."

"But how do you know," I asked, "but that the spirit of Man, which is so vastly superior to animal mentalities, lives on after death?"

"Oh, I don't know to be sure," he promptly returned; "but this I honestly say, *when I shall see a spirit distinctly organize l,* separate from the physical body, I will believe in the existence of such a being, and not till then."

At this, the clergyman said to the skeptic: "Oh, I'm sorry for you, sir—very sorry! You are a materialist—an infidel! Oh, that you could have my perfect faith!"

"What is your faith?" asked the gentlemanly skeptic.

"My faith, sir—my faith?" vociferated the enthusiastic pulpitarian, "why, I believe in a God, sir! and in a divine revelation, sir—yes, sir—and in resurrection or judgment-day, also, sir—when this mortal shall put on immortality, sir—and each shall be judged according to deeds done in the body."

" On what grounds do you believe all this ?" the skeptic calmly asked.

" On *what* grounds do you ask, sir — on what grounds ? Why, sir, hav'n't we the testimony of Moses and the prophets ; and the positive affirmations of Jesus, sir, and of his inspired apostles ?"

" Yes, indeed, you have," rejoined the skeptic. " But, my Christian friend, let me ask — what proof is all this array of testimony to *my* mind ?"

" Why, sir, your awful disbelief causes me to shudder in every limb," said the clergyman.

" Moses, and Jesus, and the apostles, are entire strangers," replied the skeptic. " I never met them myself, nor any person who has. They may have existed ; may have been honest, or the contrary, I don't know. All history is defective. And, besides, when I shall have revealed to me personally the same evidences of immortality which those men professed to have received, then I too shall probably have reasons for believing that which seems to contradict all the analogies of organic life. A revelation made to *another* is no revelation to me. It is only a ' say-so,' a second-handed article, and can not therefore have the satisfying effect which would result from a direct importation of the positive evidence to my own mind."

The cars reached the principal dépôt, and so the colloquy was terminated. Thus the matter stands between the educational Christian and the intellectual skeptic. They can never " persuade" each other. Why not ? Because both doubt and both believe, although oppositely, from the authority of externals. Neither occupy the philosophic ground of internal principles. The church reposes upon ancient oracles and theological abstractions. Over the future it has thrown a mantle of vaporish sentimentalism. A distressing vagueness, an uncertainty and unreality, it casts upon the soul's destiny. And thus, as it ever will be, too much faith provokes and develops too much doubt

CHAPTER LX.

GOLDEN TOKENS.

MOUNT Beauty was now surmounted. Its topmost acclivity was behind me. There was also a mental release from that unbroken exercise of intuition which had been necessary in solving the conjugal problem ; and while wending my way toward the future valley, I had an inward joy and tranquillity transcending speech. It is true that many trials had sauntered arm in arm across my mountain path, and looked assassin-like upon me : and it is also true that I had walked to the measure of celestial music which enchanted the air and enraptured my spirit. But 'twas the Magic Staff, and not the melody alone, which enabled me to convert every interloping trial and adversary into a minister of personal development.

And my soul was of necessity very still ; for its inward glee of gratitude to Father-God would not flow into words. Hence I could not be interesting in social intercourse. The friends would call upon me, however, and I had no heart to deny them entrance. They wished to express a kindly word, or to ask questions on various subjects. These visitors were all beloved. Yet more attractive were those tokens of exalted wisdom that floated hourly down from regions of thought and philosophy.

Three days did my soul yearn to be away from external sounds and sufferings. This will not appear strange to the reader who keeps in remembrance the impressible power that I possess to feel "another's wo" from a distance of hundreds and even thousands of miles. The compact walls of my abode, in the healthy and beautiful city of Hartford, were no protection. The study and discipline of Mount Beauty had opened my sympathies toward all mankind. The descriptive and questioning letters that came to me daily, from far and near, were not necessary to put my soul *en rapport* with the private sufferings of the earth's inhabitants. Oh, friend, it is not an easy and idle task to be an unselfish worker for selfish and sorrowing multitudes! Human *Intuition*, when *clairvoyant*, knows no space. The sensibilities of the soul may merge into one river, unseen to physical eyes, roll between the rugged mountains of human life, and gather upon its wide margins "impressions" of individual trials on both sides of the Atlantic. These are not idle words, dear reader; I transcribe from the pages of my own life-book. Between breakfast and dinner, during the morning hours of one day only, I have, while in my quiet study, received telegraphic impressions concerning hearts beating hundreds of miles away! To their momentary joys I was utterly insensible at the time, because my mission was to their private sorrows. Intuitionally I became identified with the living world of human beings. My soul yearned to free the slaves I saw— to shelter flying fugitives in all departments of life—fugitives from false theology, from political bondage, from the slavery of licentious domestic alliances, which equally contaminate husband and wife and offspring—and when I beheld these fugitives in every great city and sometimes in rural hamlets, O, how I prayed for power to awaken in each human soul a moral *courage* that would not stop short of universal justice!

One day, while contemplating and sympathizing and praying thus for the human race, the well-known Guide breathed into my ear three words: "*She—is—free!*" Instantly I asked: "Do you mean Mrs. Love? Tell me once again, kind Guide—did I understand you?"

"*She—is—free!*'" replied the gifted being, and his voice I heard no more.

This occurred on Saturday, September 30th, just five days after I sent the note recorded in the last chapter. "Good!" I exclaimed. "The persevering woman has obtained a divorce from bondage. The certified decree will liberate both parties, and each may legally enter upon relations more congenial."

Hearing nothing to confirm my Guide's positive declaration, however, I wrote to the lady for direct information; and her prompt and definite reply showed that her divorce was granted on the very day that my kind guardian apprized me of it, and that, notwithstanding the intervening distance of nearly one thousand miles, I had knowledge of the legal emancipation thirty-six hours before her own far more interested and anxious mind received tidings of the same fact from her faithful attorney!

'Twas a suggestive October day that I devoted to an examination of my immediate future. The great lessons of my Mountain journey were yet fresh, and through them I read the destiny of outward things. "Autumnal tints," said I mentally, "appear on leaf and life. As the river floweth down and mingleth with the mighty ocean, so journeyeth my companionless soul toward the boundless sphere beyond the tomb. But the dull heavy sound of earth falling upon the coffin, the darkness that envelops and the stillness that pervades the cast-off body, can impart no gloom to the spirit of an harmonial pilgrim. What if we do behold clouds between us and the sun, shall we despair? Does not the same eternal orb shine beyond? What if my soul is sad to-day, at the prospect of battles to be fought ere I reach my mate, is there not an era of peace to succeed?"

While I meditated a familiar voice came stealing through the air, and my Guide said: "*What—if—an—autumn—cometh; hath—it—not—a—spring—in—store?*"

And I answered: "To my public mission and its trials I will admit no murmur. No, kind Guide! Let others be sad who believe in the darkness, who breathe the mists of old mythology, but I? no, never, never — Excelsior!"

The reader will not marvel at these transient feelings of sadness, when told that, by means of clairvoyant penetration, I saw that my public teaching in Hartford was finished; that I must conceal from the freed woman the fact of our conjugal fitness, (in order to leave her affections at liberty to fix upon their own object;) and lastly, that I must journey through a maze of bitter prejudices in order to act justly and accomplish the true marriage. All this loomed up before me like a dark autumnal storm. Leaning upon the Magic Staff, however, I wrote my valedictory, and prepared for the open field.

The *Hartford Times* published the farewell address. But owing to the newspaper tirade that succeeded, I sketched an additional valedictory letter in a spirit of criticism. To all of which the conservative and religious press replied by ridicule and satire, fun and *some* wit, calumny and misrepresentation. Just previous to my final departure, a friend asked: " Have you seen the call for a meeting to-morrow night?"

On assuring him that I had not, he remarked that " the friends would expect me to be present."

Next evening I accordingly repaired to the bannered and decorated hall, in which our principles had been taught, and found a large congregation in waiting. The chosen chairman, William Green, jr., arose and read the following:—

Resolved, That we hail the promulgation of the Harmonia. Philosophy as a New era in the world; and, by faith in cause and effect, we prospectively see the day when, through its influence, the discordant powers and principalities of this world will become ONE KINGDOM OF LOVE, WISDOM, AND HARMONY.

Resolved, That as Brother Davis purposes in future to devote a very considerable portion of his time as a teacher by discoursing through the country, we sincerely hope that the public at large may receive into their *life* the principles taught by the Harmonia Philosophy, which, we feel assured, are fully competent to harmo nize this world — which all the religions heretofore existing have proved to be utterly *incapable* of doing.

Resolved, That something *more* than a vote of thanks is due from us to him, for the many invaluable lectures which he has gratuitously enlightened us with during his four years' residence among us; and that we feel a high degree of gratitude; therefore,

Resolved, That as a small expression of our love and gratitude, Brother Davis be requested to accept from us a Watch, bearing an inscription, expressive of our feelings and sentiments as above declared.

Immediately after the foregoing resolutions had been passed, the chairman presented the golden memento for my acceptance. But fancy my bewilderment, dear reader! There I stood before a large and expectant assemblage, with not a word to say — completely confused and intimidated — feeling at once an overpowering emotion of gratitude, and a demand upon my untrained mind for an off-hand address as a thank-offering. Fortunately, I had a few sheets of letter-paper with me, so I managed to ask the audience for permission to retire to the adjoining room. In a moment my soul was full of light and language. And as quickly as thought can travel over a landscape, so rapidly did I sketch in pencil-marks the following words of reply, which I directly read to the yet seated congregation :—

BRETHREN OF THE NEW DISPENSATION: You speak of Gratitude. All gratitude is mine, not yours. From time to time I have discoursed to you, as it were involuntarily, because I could not help it —'t was such a blissful relief to my soul to communicate its irresistible impressions.

Moralists have taught that benefited parties owe a debt of gratitude to their benefactors. Hence the doctrine and popular practice of making perpetual acknowledgments to the supernatural. But nothing can be more absurd. 'T is the benefactor, not the recipient, who enjoys the first good of his acts. He alone feels, and must of necessity feel, the deepest debt of gratitude. Consequently, it is always more blissful to give than to receive

You have, dear friends, frequently permitted me the enjoyment of such bliss, and I am grateful to you for it; but now, as I am about to depart, the natural happiness of the benefactor is yours — *and I am the receiver* — causing me to feel myself unable to express in words the pleasurable emotions awakened by this unexpected transposition.

Your token of friendship is wrought from earth's purest metal — a substance said to be untarnishable. This fact, so externally significant, it not without its moral. I hope that I shall profit by a suggestion so delicately expressed by you.

And you have presented me with a *recorder of Time.* This is a startling thought! It will everywhere remind me of the pulsations of Eternity — of the hours, minutes, and seconds, as they spread their wings and fly from the empire of life into the realm of death. But this reflection can not disturb or sadden us — for we know that, to our inmost principles, *there is no Death;* but Life, unfolding more and more beautifully as we pass along with the flight of time for ever.

This Watch will help my soul to keep its vigils day and night. My spirit is deeply impressed with your beautiful token. In its shining countenance I shall behold the ever-happy, ever-cheering faces of my Harmonial friends in the city of Hartford; and its extended hands will impress me henceforth to remember, with a thrill of unmingled happiness, the famliar grasp of many earnest women and fearless men; who, notwithstanding the oppressiveness of popular prejudices, have stood firmly forth, forming a pioneer phalanx, in favor of the gospel of Nature and Reason.

My soul is joyous, my friends, because you have given me a gift so significant — one, which I shall keep warm with the emanations of my spirit, because everywhere it will be my constant speaking companion — a meter of time; the recorder of each succeeding moment, which I shall be admonished to improve as it passes. It will keep me at my happy work. It will ever sing: "Now's the day, and now's the hour!" That terribly sad poet, Robert Pollok, says: "The angel of God appeared in a statue of fire, blazing, and, lifting up his hand on high, * * swore that Time should be no more."

But, notwithstanding the oath of this apocryphal angel, my conviction remains unshaken that Time is Eternal, or, rather, what we term " Eternity" is composed of Time as drops constitute the ocean.   And, constantly, in all latitudes and under all circum-stances, your gift will serve to remind me of this conviction. inspi-ring me with new efforts for mankind.

Day unto day uttereth speech! We talk of *yesterday, to-day,* and *to-morrow.* What are these but the proper names of ever-receding, ever-present, ever-approaching waves of the ocean of Time? Your token, brethren, is beautifully symbolical of hidden prayer, dwelling within each soul, that I may lose no Time in doing all that I, as an individual brother, can, to break the fetters of ignorance — to teach the philosophy of our existence — to bring man into fellowship with his own Intuitions and Reason — and, through the benign influence of a rational Spiritualism, to do something toward establishing harmonious relations between the Heavens and the Earth!

I said that gratitude was mine, not yours — that you need not express any toward me. But I think your token of friendship will not diminish my indebtedness to you. No, my friends, the uniform kindness and candor with which you have listened to my " impressions" — your increasing confidence in that final disap-pearance of Ignorance and Suffering from the earth — your reli-ance upon the Eternal Religion of Justice and Liberty, based upon the deific laws of universal Nature — the gradual emancipa-tion of your affections from the *despondency* of popular *supersti-tions,* and from the *slavery* of proscriptive *creeds* — the progressive development of your intellectual faculties toward a perception of philosophical principles — your manifest determination to be free, and true to the living God within you — to oppose all you conceive to be Error and Oppression, and to cling steadfastly to whatsoever you apprehend to be Truth and Freedom ; yes, brethren, my rec-ollection of all this, in addition to the abiding fragrance of Friend-ship's flowers, the germs of which we have planted silently in the garden of each other's hearts — will, through all the coming years, augment yet more the debt of permanent gratitude which I have long had the happiness to experience.

As you so touchingly and substantially express your affectionate sentiments, I know not how I can depart without urging upon you to remember, in all places and under all circumstances, the impres-sive words which you have written on the walls of this room, cor responding to the four quarters of the world — " Love" — " Wisdom" — " Harmony" — " Excelsior." May the sound of these words act like Truth's magic upon each heart, saying evermore to all, " Peace, be still!" so that, whether bowed down in affliction or elated with happiness, you may feel yourselves *consecrated* both soul and body, to the immortal Cause of Human Harmony, of which these electric terms are so universally expressive! And let me solicit you always to bear in mind that THIS PLATFORM, on which I now stand, is, while in your possession, *dedicated* to the Rights of Man and Woman — the pulpit of Free Speech and Impartial Discussion! And, whether you remain in this city, or remove to other parts, whether at home or abroad, may you never forget to preach and practise the great Law, written over yon rostrum, viz., " LET NO MAN CALL GOD HIS FATHER WHO CALLS NOT MAN HIS BROTHER!"

The motive that moves me to chronicle the foregoing is, the apology it affords for recording the following witty burlesque; which appeared in the Hartford Courant, a conservative journal, soon after my remarks were published in the *Times*. The travesty is excellent. There is genuine wit in it, though it be limited and transient as the rhetoric twinkle of a comedian's eye:—

PRESENTATION OF THE WATCH.

GULLVILLE, *November 1st,* 1854.

MR. EDITOR: Knowing your willingness to aid the development of the Beauty of Love and the Magnificence of Wisdom, for the good of organized substantial spirits, I am impressed — or rather, I realize an inclination, to send you a notice of a meeting held in this place on Tuesday evening, for the presentation of a gold (plated) watch to Professor Z. J. ROBACK, the discoverer and vender of the celebrated Astrologico-Magnetic Univercœlestia Pill for the cure of all diseases.

The watch was presented in behalf of the members of the Freelove Fraternity, an association composed of Professor Roback's patients and a few agents, journeymen and apprentices to the pill trade. The following resolutions were passed at a previous meeting of the fraternity, and show the occasion of the presentation:—

Resolved, That as Brother Roback purposes in future to devote a very considerable portion of his time to selling his pills in other and less over-stocked markets, we sincerely hope that the public at large may receive this invaluable panacea into their universal stomach — to harmonize the world, in consentient and unisonal subjection to its mild cathartic virtues ; a result which all the pills and purges of the regular practice have proved to be utterly incapable of attaining.

Resolved, That something more than a vote of thanks is due from us to him, for the much invaluable "advice gratis" with which he has, for four years past, enlightened those of us who have purchased his pills ; and that we are very grateful for the same : Therefore,

Resolved, That as a small expression of our love and gratitude, we request Brother Roback to accept from us a Watch, with the following inscription, *Tempus abire,* meaning, " It's time to be going."

After these resolutions had been communicated and the watch presented, in due form, by the chairman, Professor Roback then made the following remarks :—

PROFESSOR ROBACK'S REMARKS.

BRETHREN AND VICTIMS : It is always more blissful to give than to receive — especially pills. You speak of gratitude, because you have received benefits. Speak so no longer, for you thereby recognize and encourage the absurd churchian dogma that man owes gratitude to his Creator and preserver. Our noble philosophy teaches better things — that the benefactor ought to be grateful to the recipient, and that the imaginary obligation for benefits received is cancelled by the mere passive reception of them. I accept your watch. Don't thank me, brethren. You are quite welcome. [Applause : tears from the earnest sisters, and subdued knockings by the attendant spirits.]

Your token of friendship is wrought from two of earth's metals — brass within, and a thin layer of gold without. This fact, so externally significant, is not without its moral. I hope that I shall profit by the hint so delicately expressed by you. It shall be my constant care to maintain the " external significance" which gilding gives to brass

This watch will help me to remember important truths. It will remind me of the eternity of time and matter. It moves, and you have already been taught that "matter and motion are co-eternal principles existing in Nature," and that "matter possesses motion inherently." Therefore, it will move for ever. It will not wear out—because matter is eternal. It will not run down—because motion is eternal. It will grow better and brighter, and more perfect—because the "laws of matter and motion are eternally progressive." Yes, brethren, let us rejoice together at the thought—this little ticking monitor may yet become in some other, purer, more elevated sphere—an eight-day clock! [Applause. Salaam by the great table. Enthusiastic somersets by the benches and chairs.]

My spirit is deeply impressed with your beautiful token. I look upon its dial of brass—and face answereth unto face. Its extended hands turn to every point of the compass, and, at every hour of the day, cry give! Its *hair*-spring suggests a fundamental truth of our philosophy, that the intellect and the spirit are developed in the ratio of the *beard*. Its motion demonstrates the possible attainment of all motion originated by an internal, or self-contained power—a series of revolutions about its own little centre, in a very circumscribed orbit; and this, our philosophy terms progression.

And now, brethren, I am about to go from you for a season. I shall not forget you. The uniform kindness with which you have listened to my "impressions," and swallowed my pills—the favor you have so often received at my hands, of being permitted to minister to my wants—your faithful support in the warfare I have waged against the regular practice—your cheerful rejection of popular prejudices and superstitions, discarding the old-fashioned creeds which recognize a religion, a Bible, and a God, and adopting with me the more sublime belief that the universe has no greater or wiser being than we ourselves are or may become—all these things make our parting sad. But, brethren, the capacity for swallowing is not infinite. In you, I foresee its limit is approaching. Your stomachs no longer crave pills with the ardent longings of their first love. I have "a few more left"—and (while you are whetting your appetites for another course), I go to sell them. One more familiar grasp of these earnest women, one more parting gripe of my fearless patients; and now, brethren and sisters, farewell. [Sobbing. Spirit of Dr. Franklin wipes his spectacles.]

At the conclusion of the professor's remarks, he was presented with an elegant watch-holder of ebony, in the form of a miniature gallows — with the motto (allusive to his astrological researches and investigation of the superior spheres), *Sic itur ad astra.*

QUIZQUIS.

P. S.—For the information of those friends of Professor Roback who were not present on this interesting occasion, I am permitted to state that he will deliver four other farewell addresses, at the same place, at intervals of one week.

My mental and social experiences have been a perfect and repetitious fulfilment of my first vision. Mankind's religious, social, patriotic, and other affections, though naturally pure and disposed to huddle together like sheep, would, regardless of their shepherd whose name is "Truth," run to and fro in the streets and between the mountains of life. At one time the cause of confusion and opposition in the public mind was the alarming cry of "infidelity." Plainly-attired and unpretending Truth, the everlasting shepherd, could do but little toward establishing harmony. Whereupon he would ask me to aid him, and I have done so through lectures and publications. Then peace would appear to reign throughout the flock. Anon, however, the people's prejudices began to ascend silently like the mists of a diseased country; from which great black clouds were formed in the upper air, the contents whereof descended in frightful torrents, with thunders and lightnings; and thus, many times, I have been drenched with the abundance of outward opposition.

The altar was reputation. Reputation is but a brush-heap at best. A few flashes of fire from falsehood's forked tongue would destroy it root and branch. Therefore, to live and labor for "reputation" as most public men do, seemed beneath the moral dignity and true calling of a Man. Hence, although wet and shivering with the storm of outward ignorance and prejudice, I

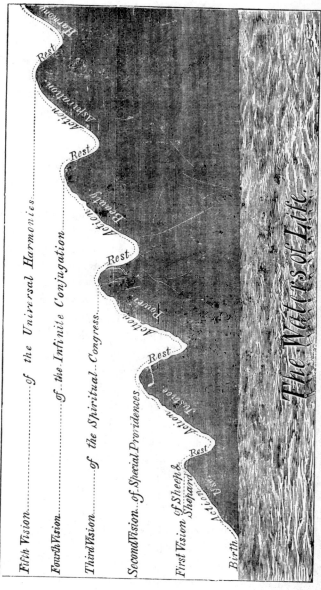

A Symbolic Representation of my Experience.

The Waters of Life.

Fifth Vision............of the Universal Harmonies............
Fourth Vision............of the Infinite Conjugation............
Third Vision............of the Spiritual Congress............
Second Vision...of Special Providences............
First Vision of Sheep & Shepherd............
Birth............

forthwith removed myself from the frail altar, rejected a prostrate position of mind, and tried to stand firmly upon the honest earth my head toward the firmament. Then came fresh accusations and empty causes of alarm — "insanity" — " free-love" — " evil spirits" — "infernal delusion," &c. — at which the flock (*i. c., the* people's prejudiced affections) would take fright and scamper away in every ridiculous direction. The grand old mountains of Justice and Power were too high, however, and the people's judgments, finding neither confinement nor escape, have been forced to yield from time to time to "Truth," the beautiful and eternal shepherd, whose mission I have ever endeavored to proclaim and promulgate throughout the land.

Thus, dear reader, have I been compelled to climb, beginning first with the Mountain of "Use." But every fresh discipline, every new effort, has added more physical strength and spiritual wisdom; and I have not been "depressed" while in the valley nor "elated" when on the highest summit. The artist has engraved a symbolic representation of my individual progression. The reader need not be told that my first chapter, "The Use of Autobiography," is a general explanation, while the succeeding ones reveal the minutiæ of that experience.

The day before I left the Charter Oak city, upon a lecturing tour through New England and portions of the West, an educated and refined gentleman asked "if Modern Spiritualism was not immoral in its tendency?"

"As I accept and teach spiritualism," I replied, "it is more salutary than the church, and more restraining than the state."

"Now, Mr. Davis," said the questioner, "I can't understand why you should say so, when it is well known that you teach the doctrine of free-love."

"Did you ever hear me teach that doctrine?" I asked.

"No, sir," said he, "but the papers report you as advocating it."

"Newspapers are not always the Evangels of truth," I replied. "The popular journalist is a chronicler of what he individually knows and thinks — a mere reflector of the surface facts and fancies of the passing multitude — and can not therefore be counted upon as more than partially correct in his statements."

"That's true, unquestionably," said he. "But if you do not teach free-love, Mr. Davis, I'd like to know what you would call it.'

"Since you ask me in so kind a spirit, sir, I feel free to tell you. The Harmonial doctrines of marriage, which I uncompromisingly advocate by lip and life, are these: That all the treasures of *one* heart's boundless love belong to some other *one* heart which is equally opulent. It is an immutable law that, when two hearts feel truly and wisely drawn into *one* embrace, the parties thus united possess the power to render their union either transient or permanent."

"What! Do you mean, Mr. Davis, that two human souls can build up or demolish for ever a marriage which is at first agreeable to both parties?"

"I do," said I. "At evening's dewy hour, 'when gentle hearts to tenderest thoughts incline,' two youthful natures may mutually breathe declarations of affection's rich excess — each being the beautiful translator of the other's purest heart — and form a union which seems the acme of their dearest hopes; but, when the gray and chilly twilight of a wornout honeymoon creeps upon the legally married pair, they may be lovers no longer, nor civil friends, but positive *enemies* of each other's purity and happiness."

"True, Mr. Davis," interposed the listener. "But what's your remedy? Don't you teach that such better live together without getting married, and separate when they get into a quarrel?"

"No, sir," said I. "On the contrary, I teach that true marriage *is the consecration of one man to one woman;* that there should be no familiarity between the sexes, other than friendship's greetings, unless two hearts are thus reciprocally consecrated and *then not*, until they have openly avowed, in the presence of witnesses, their voluntary conjugal relation."

" But, Mr. Davis, let me suppose a case : here's a woman who has a good husband as the world goes, yet she does not love him, and can not — now, what do you say ?"

" Under such circumstances," said I, " the husband has no right (in the sight of heaven) to insist upon his legal privileges. If he does, it will require long years of self-appointed work in the moral penitentiary, to expiate and efface his spiritual sin. The twain should live in the divine relation of brother and sister. Thus, also, should they live in reference to every other human being."

" But," asked the gentleman, " suppose one of the parties has conceived a conjugal love for another person — what then ?"

" If they have a family," said I, " wisdom might prescribe the continuance of the fraternal relation, for the children's sake."

" But suppose the husband will not consent to maintain the purity of that fraternal relation; and suppose the children suffer under the influence of domestic discord; and suppose the wife and mother finds her health failing daily — what then ?"

" Then," said I, " wisdom would prescribe immediate and unconditional divorcement."

" Now, Mr. Davis, let me put the question in another shape : suppose there are no children ; and suppose the husband and wife both honorably consent to live in the chastity of the fraternal relation ; but suppose one or the other loves somebody else — what then ?"

" In such a case," I answered, " the parties should candidly consider and carefully decide as to what course would best secure their mutual happiness and the good of the world. Be the circumstances as they may, however, wisdom ever proclaims one great consoling truth, viz., that *every innate desire will meet with ultimate gratification.* In other words, if your inmost soul longs for a companion — yearns for a heart of pure love which earth has thus far denied — wait, do not despair, but live a pure life ; for when the trial of death is o'er, and the Spirit-Home is reached you will surely meet with your eternal mate."

" But, Mr. Davis, suppose I have an ardent, enthusiastic, san guine temperament?"

" Then your trial will be more severe," I answered, " and your conquest all the more sublime."

" That's a rather difficult doctrine to practise," said the gentleman.

" But such is my philosophy," said I, " and such is my practice. Many delicate women and robust men have sought my opinion in regard to their own domestic difficulties, and my answering words have been such as these : ' You must await the developments of the coming time. Perhaps your eye hath seen your true companion ; perhaps, not ; but *the soul is no deceiver ;* it yearns for a mate, and there is one who will satisfy those yearnings ; be patient, then ; keep your spirit pure, and your body free from blemish, to receive the sacred treasures of some eternal spirit."

" The report is, Mr. Davis," said the gentleman, " that your people follow the spirits on the marriage question."

" Perhaps there are some believers in Spiritual Intercourse who have gone astray," I responded. " But such have not taken the Harmonial Philosophy as their rule of faith and practice."

" Do you really believe in eternal unions?" asked the gentleman.

" Yes, from the bottom of my soul I do," said I. " When circling years have wrought infinite changes, when the deep seas are dry, when the great earth no longer produces, when all human beings reside in higher worlds, when, in the far-off realms of matter, new systems and universes shall roll into order and proportion — even then the truly married, knowing no indifference and no decay, will love with ever-increasing tenderness and devotion."

" Thank you, Mr. Davis, for this frank statement of your principles. You don't teach free-love, sir — I see that. You put the bars up very high, *too high,* for most mortals. My own opinion is, sir, that the moral tendency of your doctrine is in the direction of more purity than people generally imagine."

For many weeks previous to my departure, and even while on my journey, I was assailed by an extremely novel experience. The reader may be sufficiently sympathetic and imaginative to realize the awkwardness of my position. I had freely expressed my ideal of the true marriage — had frequently pictured the bliss consequent upon a pure union of soul with soul — when, lo, much to my embarrassment, several gentle minds seemed to confound my person with the principle !

Fancy my surprise and mortification. It is true that I had not steeled and panoplied myself with a cold exterior. Simply and naturally I had, when solicited, spoken the truths I saw concerning conjugal science. Little did I think, however, that any un-mated nature would fix upon me as the embodiment of an ideal. The Magic Staff became necessary. Coldness, austerity, rebuff, neglect — contrary to my every inclination — were summoned as a body-guard. It seemed to me that the mistake was not only painful and dangerous, but singularly absurd also ; as if a patient had confounded the physician with his disease, or sought to swallow the bottle instead of the medicine. And yet I could not smile at the spontaneous expression of these divine and central attractions. They indicated the existence of an ungratified need in deeply-loving natures. Yet I could love but ONE, and, oh, how did my soul rejoice to know that *one* to be a resident of earth ! Philosophy had endorsed and established the primary tendency of my attractions to be unchangeably monogamic. And the many delicate letters that came to me from pure and affectionate persons, whose lone hearts separately sought a conjugal refuge in mine, taught me the necessity of soon fixing my own nuptial posi tion before the world.

CHAPTER LXI.

SINGULAR VISITATIONS.

"A day, an hour of virtuous liberty
Is worth a whole eternity of bondage."

THE heavily-freighted train of three months have passed since the conversation last recorded. The now uplifted curtain enables the reader to look once again into the Reformer's Refuge at Rochester, New York. In a comfortably-warmed and usefully-furnished chamber, just above the sitting-room, you may behold the subject of this autobiography.

'Twas midwinter; the 25th of January, 1855. The serenely-cold air, so full of electrical frost, crackled like a silken robe. Very keen and calm and still was the abounding atmosphere. It glittered in the sunlight like an ether from the distillation of diamonds. But sweetly through that quiet chamber breathed the greetings of my revered Guide. 'Twas the voice of love I heard; to which my heart beat musically. My well-known guardian's affection was pure and unearthly—soft and fragrant as blossoms from the tree of Life—ever growing and flowering in the spirit's garden.

"Kind Guide," said my soul, "I have felt through the space that there is a private work for me to do among Mary's relatives in Orleans county."

"Ah, 'tis well!" he replied. "My mission this morning is to strengthen thy purpose."

"My desire is," said I, "to visit her friends to-morrow. My

next appointment to lecture gives me a leisure of two days and nights."

" Go, in *propria persona*," he replied. " You will touch and break the chain that binds thirteen relatives into one *objection* against you as Mary's companion."

" What can they object to?" I asked. " Is she not a legally free woman? Is she not the owner of her own person? Did she not obtain her freedom independent of my counsel and influence?"

" Human prejudice is powerful," replied the Guide. " But God is Love, my son ; are you not a child of God?"

" To that divine Father I absolutely yield all that is immortal in my nature," I replied. " But tell me, can I overcome the prejudices of her family?"

" A battle between private pride and a law of justice must be fought," said he firmly. " Are you not prepared to bear reproach, and to conquer?"

" Good guardian Angel," said I, " the work is a blessed one and I will not wait or weary in it."

Stillness was again there. The celestial visitor had withdrawn from the earth's atmosphere. Therefore I was once more at liberty to mingle with the happy inmates of the Refuge.

'Twas just twenty-nine hours subsequent to the foregoing interview when, in accordance with my own intuitions of right and the words of the affectionate Guide, I took my Magic Staff and the six o'clock train for Holley. The intense frigidity of the air had given way to another fiat of old Winter, now careering wildly and playing fantastically through the open fields, with such toys as wind and hail and snow. " This is a singular night," said I mentally, " to start on a mission so delicate. The prejudiced family will surely be anything but pleasantly impressed with this unceremonious intrusion." But onward rolled the loaded chariots, and ere long I was standing upon the dépôt-platform at Holley.

Fortunately, while on my way from New England to Western

New York, I had stopped at memorable Albany to introduce myself to Mr. Charles M. Plumb, a literary assistant at the legislature then in session, and to express my appreciation of his honorable and prompt and fearless conduct in the aforesaid case of legal separation. During my brief stay, he kindly and cordially asked, "If I would n't have time to call upon Mrs. Plumb, his wife, while on the road from Rochester to the West?" This little fragment of friendly courtesy, dear reader, was the only rational verbal pretext I had for this visitation. Thus armed and equipped, away I went to the hotel, engaged a room for the night, supped upon a few mouthfuls of bread and honey, and then, after several inquiries, reached the habitation of Mr. Chancey Robinson, upon the hill.

Fancy my personal appearance, dear reader, just before I knocked at the stranger's door. My drab over-coat, save its length, was of the Horace Greeley pattern; my large blanket-shawl, save its disposal about my person, was of the latest Broadway fashion; my low-crowned and broad-brimmed hat, save its impious flexibility, was of the George Fox school; my black hair and full beard, save the regularity of their adjustment, were of the Italian banditti cut; lastly, being well-nigh covered with the fast-falling snow, and a stranger coming like a thief in the night, it was not to be wondered at if the Robinson family did look upon and treat me with marked reservation. What a singular visitation! What a presentation to one's future *friends*-in-spirit and *relatives*-in-law! Was it not rashness to accept a work so delicate and unexplainable?

Being admitted, I asked: "Do the parents of Mrs. Plumb reside in this house?"

There was an air of home-comfort about the room; in which were a young woman, a young man, and a neighbor. The young woman, whom I afterward learned was a recently-married daughter, replied: "Yes, sir"—but her manner said: "I wish you would n't ask me another question."

In a few minutes, however, the clouds of discomposure and timidity began to float off. Presently, too, the father came in from his supper; and, discharging at me a volley of sharp, inquisitive looks, he asked: "Who are you?"

"My name is Davis," I replied — leaving a broad margin for the imagination of each to add any *Christian* prefix that would sound most agreeable. "Having seen Mr. Plumb at Albany," I continued, "with whom I was well pleased, I have promised myself the additional pleasure of forming the acquaintance of Mrs. Plumb also, in accordance with his polite request."

At a glance I saw that the father, though physically below the six-foot mark, was considerably taller than most people in mentality. There was a sharp point in the expression of his eye, too, and a rifle-crack in his firm speech, with which I was exceedingly well impressed. Feeling that such a man must have something reformatory in him, I inquired: "What's the news in the Temperance line through this region?"

"Hard work!" said he quickly and determinedly. "We'll fetch 'em though."

"Do the people favor reform in this community?" I asked.

With a firm, self-reliant, half-defiant air, he replied: "Can't do much with folks who live on Rum, Ignorance, and Tobacco."

By this time the matronly wife appeared, dressed for the street, whereupon the man of principle said: "You must excuse us. The family's going to a speaking exhibition at the academy. The hour's arrived. I must go now."

Having no disposition to spend the evening otherwise, I asked permission to accompany the mother, to which she very amiably consented. But being unaccustomed to gallantry, I somehow caused the good woman to tumble out of the front gate into a huge snow-bank. She was not hurt, however, and seemed to enjoy the accident, as well as the ridiculous attempt we each made to apologize to the other.

While at the academy I was much pleased with a student who

delivered a memorized portion of General Warren's celebrated speech. Toward the close of the well-conducted academical exer cises, the same young man, with considerable power of declama- tion, gave a short original address on "Past and Present;" and after the entertainment was concluded, the talented scholar was introduced to me as "Charles J. Robinson." From him, then, I obtained information that Mrs. Plumb, whom he called "Zilpha," was some four miles in the country, spending a short time with a married sister whom he called Mrs. Pettengill. At my request, he promised to pilot me thither on the subsequent morning.

True to his word the young brother called at the hotel. The obliging landlord provided the horse and cutter for a reasonable "consideration;" and, cuddled down 'neath the buffalo robe, away we sped through the driving storm.

'Twas difficult to draw Charlie into conversation. At length, however, notwithstanding the increasing inclemency of the weather, he became moderately familiar and talkative. But the intention of my visit—in such a storm and at such a time—was to him as yet an unsolved riddle. In truth, I could not myself foresee what was to come of it. One thing I did know: that the object re- ceived the entire justification of my conscience—for I was on a mission of peace and good-will to the family of her whom my heart designated as its conjugal companion. How her friends could have become particularly prejudiced against me, was an unexplained query; yet, distinctly as my face felt the smiting snow, so definitely did my soul realize that *something* was going wrong in the distance. To the intrusion of this feeling, the buffalo robe and the driving storm were no impediments.

At Charlie's suggestion, we halted and talked an hour at the house of Mr. Colby Dibble; next, a dinner was cheerfully served up at the residence of Joseph Pratt, Esquire; lastly, we arrived at the home of Mr. D. N. Pettengill, in the retired village of Clarendon. The yet reserved Charlie entered in advance and introduced me to his "sister Eliza."

The moment she caught the sound of my *Christian* name, a rebellious expression gathered upon her naturally fine face, and there was an indignation meeting instantly called among the mental forces. The ample stove shed its heat in abundance, and directly the snow on our garments began to melt. "I'll take off my overcoat, Eliza," said Charlie. "It's too thick for this hot room."

"Yes, Charlie, do," she kindly replied. "I'll hang up *your* coat."

The emphasis of her voice on the word "your," gave me to understand that "my" coat would n't be suspended if I did take it off. And sure enough, after Charlie's over-garment was disposed of in a sisterly manner, she seated herself with a dignity at once resolute and beautiful.

"My coat is also too warm for this heated room," I remarked, "so I'll just put it aside."

"Do as you like, sir," replied she with a look of forced severity.

But as she granted me the liberty, I removed the garb in question, and re-seated myself for further developments. Presently Mrs. Plumb entered with her sister's joyous children, and I was greeted with sincere cordiality. Zilpha, instantly reading the import of Eliza's countenance, apologetically remarked: "My sister is no believer in spiritualism, Mr. Davis."

"I can sympathize with her," said I soothingly, "for I was in the same state of mind about ten years ago."

At this, Eliza bore her fine form yet more proudly, touched her gold-framed glasses, (for like myself she was near-sighted,) and said: "That's not my trouble, sir."

At length I began to fear that my present visit would result in but little benefit, and therefore remarked: "This evening I must be in Rochester — so, Charlie, please get the horse and we'll return to Holley."

"I wish Mr. Davis to remain," said Eliza with much determination. "There are some questions I wish to ask him, then he can go as soon as he likes."

Her prompt speech aroused my hopes of doing some good. "Any woman," thought I, " who is capable of manifesting that amount of frankness and decision, is also capable of being a lasting and valuable friend. Her utter freedom from hypocrisy is admirable; and when her soul becomes fully alive to the principle of Justice, none can be more firmly its advocate. She has evidently much preju dice against me, but when she knows the *whole truth* in regard to this matter, that prejudice will vanish like the morning dew. Hence I am very thankful for this interview."

At this moment a gentleman entered to whom I was forthwith introduced, and from whom I felt the emanation of a hostile sphere The group present seemed at once to resolve themselves involun tarily into a sort of domestic jury, I became the witness on the stand, and the newly-arrived brother, the prosecuting attorney. A fire was kindled in the parlor, the gleeful children were ex- cluded, while we " of a larger growth" assembled there.

" Mr. Davis !" said the brother, " I'm glad you 're here, sir."

" So am I," was my response.

" I've read some of your works, sir," said he, " and I find they tend to infidelity and the destruction of all our institutions."

" Do my works tend to destroy *good* institutions ?" I asked.

Unheeding my direct question, he proceeded : " Your doctrines go against the sabbath — and — what is worse, sir — they break up family ties — uproot marriage relations — and, sir, you must know that your doctrines are immoral and dangerous."

" Will you tell me what books of mine you have read ?" I asked. " For myself I am not acquainted with any volume of mine that teaches such doctrines."

"Oh, I hav'n't read much more than a few extracts in the *Tribune* some years since. But the general drift of your writings is plain enough to be seen."

" Do you denounce upon so litttle evidence ?" I asked.

" We might as well come to the important point," he replied. " That is this : the news got here yesterday that you met our sister, Mrs. Love, in Rochester last winter, and that you then influenced her to reject her husband and take you instead. The report is, that 'the spirits' told you to do this, and that she was induced to believe it."

"That's a very ridiculous and utterly false report," said I. "My friends who know me are aware that I never follow the *dictum* of spirits either on earth or in heaven. But suggestions I am ever ready to receive from any one."

"Please answer me the plain question, Mr. Davis," said he: "Did you, or did you not, tell our sister that she was your spiritual affinity?"

The lawyer-like directness of his question was rather amusing; but, in all sincerity I replied: "No sir. Not even at this date— four months after the divorce—have I informed her of my intention, which is, sir, to honorably ask her to become my companion. But of this intention she is more ignorant than you. I have now told you that which she will know *for the first time* when I write her an epistolary history of this memorable interview."

Now there was silence in the room for the space of half a minute. Then, addressing myself to the dignified and reserved Eliza, I said: "Please put *your* questions now, for I must soon depart."

"No, sir," she replied with a more subdued tone. "Nathan has asked what I wish to know."

Charlie and Zilpha, during all this time, looked mortified and indignant, while another sister, Minerva, and the merchant, Mr. Pettengill, who had been silent listeners, seemed to occupy neutral ground. My soul could not blame the prejudiced relatives, however, because I fully appreciated the origin of their appalling apprehensions. It appeared that their sister, Mary, had procured a divorce without the knowledge of her family; also, that no relative, save Mr. and Mrs. Plumb, was informed, even after the divorce, of all the private reasons which, during years of silent suffering, had been paving the way to this legal separation. Of course the family pride was roused and concentrated—the dread of being persecuted by professional tattlers, and identified with what an undeveloped generation calls "the disgrace of divorce"—this pride, much stronger than the holy principle of justice, originated their mutual distress; and the fear that she would bring still greater reproach on herself and them, by forming another marriage-union, strengthened their impatient opposition. Of all this I would make no record were it not to illustrate two facts—first, that "nothing is easier than to be mistaken;" second, that this generation consents to *cover up and conceal vice by legal and popular liveries.*

"Thank you, Mr. Davis," said the now composed brother; "you have frankly answered my questions, sir, and I trust the future will bring everything straight."

The affectionate and noble-minded Zilpha, who had been a sort of guardian angel to Mary during all her severest trials, now expressed a hope that our next meeting would be under circumstances more favorable to friendship. She had, during the interview, testified directly and positively that I had nothing to do with causing the separation, but, on the contrary, having lived in Mary's family for years, she *knew* that the desire for a divorce took root in the heart of both her husband and herself, long before either of them had met with me.

On the road to Holley, Charlie maintained a gloomy silence, with an occasional expression of regret at what had that day transpired.

'T was almost night when we reached the hotel. Before taking the cars I repaired to the pleasant dwelling on the hill for another interview. It required but little discernment to discover that some members of this family were more or less affected with evangelical theology. It seemed to me that the parents had imbibed rather too much from the turbid channels of Baptist orthodoxy. There was, nevertheless much sturdy intelligence in the

dcmestic group—sufficient, I thought, to insure an ultimate rescue from the entanglements of documentary religion.

A fire was kindled in the parlor-stove, and the parents invited
me into the retired apartment; when the out-spoken father said :
" Well, if you want anything o' me, say it."

" I am here to inform you," I replied, " that your daughter
Mary may become my—"

" Can't listen to any such talk as that, sir !"

" Let the gentleman say what he wants to," interposed the considerate mother.

" Well, go on."

" As I was saying," I continued, leaning upon the Magic Staff,
" she may become my wife."

On hearing this the keen-eyed and resolute gentleman squared
himself in his chair, and, with a remarkable perpendicularity of
deportment, said :—

" My daughter Mary, sir, has a first-rate education. She's
qualified to teach in any public institution. Her relatives are
many, intelligent, and respectable. The first we knew of her
domestic difficulty was after she came home a divorced woman."

" Don't speak quite so loud, Mr. Robinson," said his motherly-
looking companion.

" Well, sir," he continued, with a lower voice but more positive
manner, " I've advised her to keep single; not get married into
another trouble. I won't give my consent to her marrying any
one under several years—and you, NEVER !"

To this my reply was: " I think you do not consider that your
daughter is at liberty to dispose of her own affections."

" My daughter, sir," said he, yet more sternly, " has made
shipwreck of religion and shipwreck of marriage. What she's
coming to, I don't know." He now arose from his chair, and,
planting himself like an indomitable captain of the Invincible Ar-
mada, thus proceeded : " No, sir! she's got my advice, and so
have you. 'T would be the destruction of both, and all concerned

No matter how correct her course has been, if she marries you people will say that her purposes were wrong, and you can't make them believe otherwise. No, sir! I'll never consent to it — NEV-ER!" With the ejection of the last word his hand shot suddenly up, as if to convince me that I was "blown sky-high."

"Mr. Robinson," I quietly responded, "your feelings of father-ly solicitude are all very natural and admirable. But in this pro-posed relation there is nothing wrong. Truth and justice are with us. Hence the speech of the world is as nothing. Your daughter has procured her legal liberty without your aid or mine; and I have a firm belief, sir, that she is equally capable of deciding this question. But you will not doubt the honorable nature of my intentions, at least, when I inform you that I am imparting to you and your family this knowledge of my choice, even before ac-quainting her with the same fact. I have not yet asked her to become my wife; but when again I shall write to her, she will doubtless learn of my honest wishes."

He gave me a quick, surprised glance as I concluded, and then said: "Well, if it's gone no further than that, I'll write to her. I believe I can break it all up."

The half-indignant father now left the room. But the lingering mother, with gentle tones of admonition, said: "I'm afraid the people won't understand it. Mary is one of my best children. She has a very good disposition — steady, home-like — and she never made any trouble."

"Your daughter's private history is familiar to me, Mrs. Rob-inson," said I. "Your praises are all deserved."

"And then," she continued with beautiful tenderness, "there's her two dear little children. What'll become of them I do n't know. Mary says the understanding is that she can have them part of the time. But they are to live with their father, and he has no home for them yet."

"Rest assured," I replied, "that your daughter's best interests, and the happiness of her darling children, shall never be impaired by my influence." So saying I hastened to the dépôt, and soon embarked for Rochester.

On the following morning I was visited, at the Reformer's Refuge by a medium, who asked: "Do you think it right for me *ever* to act contrary to the directions of spirits?"

"Certainly," said I; "whenever reason and conscience tell you to."

"But can not spirits give us light in advance of our own judgment?" he asked.

"Not as a general principle," I replied. "Spirits are eternally human beings. To believe that spirits can overstep the essential boundaries of human Intuition, and impart knowledge superior to what men can obtain by large talent and large industry, is equivalent to a repudiation of the fundamental laws of all development."

"Why, what's the use of spiritualism, then?" he exclaimed.

"Spiritualism is useful as *a living demonstration* of a future existence. It abundantly proves this; but nothing else with certainty."

"Why, Mr. Davis, you astonish me!" exclaimed the gentleman, "Don't *you* follow the advice of spirits?"

"Yes, when I can do so in harmony with my own Intuitions. Spirits have *aided* me many times; but they do not *control* either my person or my reason."

"Then you do acknowledge that spirits can help us?" said he, somewhat comforted.

"Yes," I answered; "with gratitude I acknowledge that *spirits can and do perform kindly offices for those on earth.* I would not discourage any friend from obtaining all the benefit he reasonably can through the aid of spiritual beings. But this benefit can be secured only on the condition that we allow them to become our *teachers, not our masters;* that we accept them as companions, not as gods to be worshipped."

CHAPTER LXII.

THE CONJUGAL MARRIAGE.

"No more alone through the world's wilderness,
Although I trod the paths of high intent,
I journeyed now: no more companionless."

THE next scene opens in another Refuge for Reformers. 'T was located in Harveysburgh, Ohio, and was hallowed by its intelligent proprietors. Earnest and truthful and loving were Valentine and Jane Nicholson and their family of four daughters. The time was February 12, 1855; some three weeks after my visit at Holley. In her journeyings through southern Ohio, for purposes of lecturing, Mary had reached Brother Valentine's home.

On the very eve of my arrival, as good luck would have it, she had an appointment to lecture. To that discourse I listened with critical attention. Her subject was "Temperance;" a common theme treated with uncommon skill. Her thoughts and illustrations were orderly, logical, beautiful, truthful, and broad; while the tones of her voice were firm, far-reaching, humane, and capable of true eloquence. I saw that her nature was at home in the broad fields of Reform. The reader may imagine my happiness on finding such a co-worker. All my visions of her endowments were fully confirmed. Of her personal appearance I need say nothing; as the artist has pictured that in the fore part of this volume.

Returning to the Reformer's Refuge, I said: "Mary, this visit is necessary for you to become acquainted with me. Personally, we are almost total strangers to each other. And yet *you* are no stranger to my spirit, for I have seen you through the distance many times."

"A long way have you journeyed Brother Jackson," she soothingly replied. "Many hours of weary toil have you undergone. How grateful must be a season of rest to such as you !"

During my visit at this fraternal abode I several times assured Mary that I had no claim upon her affections ; that she was at liberty to decide against my proposition of conjugal union ; that my life was one unbroken battle with ignorance and wrongs and sufferings of every shade and magnitude ; and that, should she consent to become my companion, her relatives would frown upon us and the world also for a time.

"Marriage is too sacred a relation to be thoughtlessly formed," said I. "Therefore, Mary, before you decide, ask yourself this one question : ' *Can I, in obedience to my highest attractions and noblest impulses and purest aspirations, yield to Jackson all my affections and confidence for ever?*' I would have you compare me with all others you have seen ; and then, in the retirement of self-questioning, come to a true conclusion. You see, my dear Mary, how tender my soul is of your personal, spiritual, and social liberty. How painful, how unutterably and insupportably dreadful, would be a *second bondage.* If it be possible that any other spirit can exert a *more* attractive and satisfying influence upon you than does my own, then should you cling to that other spirit and return to me no more. The thought is painful — very chilling to the spirit's life-currents — but we will obey the voice of Wisdom."

Thus did we converse long and earnestly upon the beautiful philosophy of the true marriage ; and, just before I departed for Cleveland, my Mary said : "Should the time ever come when I can be a co-worker *with you*, in the holy mission of redeeming the world from its ignorance and sufferings, then will my soul be happy and very grateful."

"But, Mary," said I, "do you not fear that your peace might be disturbed by the prejudices and misrepresentations which our union would elicit?"

"Jackson," said she with an earnest, honest emphasis, "I feel that no reproach would be too bitter for me to bear, no sufferings too great to meet, no labors too severe to perform, if I can but be sure that you are my soul's companion."

"Mary," said I, "you may become my eternal mate, by so desiring and so living through all the years of this life."

And she assured me that such was her soul's central desire and thus would she live — wholly consecrated to my spirit, and thereby to the vast brotherhood of humanity. This was the pledge of that holy union to which my Guide referred on the summit of Mount Beauty. A perceptible chain of spiritual providences had extended from my earliest recollections to this moment, but the perfect *consecration* of this one beloved heart to me and my work was the brightest of all the links composing it. Therefore I departed, to meet my appointments in Ohio and Michigan, with my spirit full of elevated joy.

On the 15th of May, 1855 — three months after the visit just chronicled — I arrived at the rural residence of Joseph Pratt, Esq., in Clarendon, Orleans county. In accordance with the laws of the state of New York, and in harmony also with our mutual perceptions and teachings, Mary and I did openly avow our union in the presence of sixteen friendly witnesses. The intelligent proprietor of the residence, (Mary's brother-in-law,) being a Magistrate, ably conducted the ceremony and placed in my hand his legal certificate.

Previous to this event, I had forwarded a kindly letter of invitation to her parents at Holley. But they did not appear. In fact, several members of her troubled family kept at a "respectable distance"—thereby acknowledging that, for the time being, one question was uppermost: "What will the people say?"

At the conclusion of the brief ceremony, feeling that our true position was not yet fully understood, I said:—

"FRIENDS: To-day your sister Mary, now my companion, will depart for the city of New York. Feeling that you are acquainted with the steps, just and honorable, which have led to this alliance —also that you appreciate the position of the other party, and the total falsity of several newspaper articles in this region—I will utter no words of explanation or comment on these topics. 'Tis of other matters, of vital interest, that I wish to speak.

"Mary's children, as you are aware, were claimed a few days since by their legal protector, and departed from her presence. She bade them farewell, not willingly, but in obedience to Statute-Law. The tyrannical laws of the state of New York—which were instituted by men *for* men—wrest from the mother the right to her own children. These man-made laws patronizingly provide for such dependents as women, infants, apprentices, and idiots; and, politically speaking, all such are considered possessed of "equal rights"—viz.: to obey the fiat of legislative enactments, and to keep away from the ballot-box. Under these circumstances many women would decide to endure every hardship that a false marriage could impose, rather than seek a legal separation which must inevitably deprive them of their cherished offspring. Mary would no doubt have yielded to a similar attraction, had she not felt entire confidence in the honor and generosity of her children's father, and in his assurance that she might freely see and express her love for them during all the future years.

It seems to me, however, that a mother's love is but one sixth of a true woman's heart; and the proportion of time necessary to bring up a family is but a fourth of a woman's proper lifetime. Therefore, when a mother sinks herself in the depths of a repulsive and impure union for her children's sake, she is very liable not only to see her offspring ruined by the moral poison of domestic discord, but to become herself a blighted, useless being. If Mary, then, believes that, while she is no less tender and regardful of her own darlings, her public teachings may eventually benefit the children of a thousand parents, is she not choosing the wiser and better part? The empty question of ' Reputation' we will resign to the future."

Four months rapidly rolled into the returnless Past. But the family changes and reconciliations wrought out during that brief period were many and welcome. Mary's bold and worthy father had written me an invitation, "short and sweet," to bring my "wife" and visit the family. Accordingly we arrived at the Holley-home on the 11th of September, 1855; and, by a few honest words of retrospective import, grim-visaged Prejudice was driven from the parental habitation! Next day, Mary and I and two others rode over to Barre on a brief visit to her children, at the residence of their grandparents. The embarrassment and irritation consequent upon our unexpected call, were painful to all save the possessor of the Magic Staff. But Mary's heart was grateful for a sight of the pets, who were healthy and contented. During the succeeding week we were kindly welcomed to the thriving homes of all the resident relatives; and, in the whole circle, none treated us with more delicate and loving cordiality than sister Eliza.

We will now glide over a few months more, and take an observation of the world's ways to us. Ever and anon letters from unknown correspondents would arrive freighted with inquiries concerning the facts of our marriage. Many such questions I had not time to answer, but have done so in this autobiography. Of course, I was never astonished nor annoyed; because, long before, the plain shadows of these events were cast upon my vision. But— "What can I do," was my query, "for the disturbed faith and friendship of our distant friends?" The answer was: "Publish the facts." This was a most unwelcome task; but I have nearly completed it. One day I received a paper containing the following, said to have been concocted by some *religious* persons in Dundee, New York:

"*Resolved*, That Spiritualism ... removes the barriers to licentiousness and vice, as exemplified in the conduct of Andrew Jackson Davis, *who is now living an adulterous life in the city of Brooklyn with the wife of Mr. Love of Buffalo.*"

The appearance of the foregoing " pious fraud" made me realize how easy it is for the unscrupulous to circulate a falsehood against some reformer whose doctrines they may dislike. But I received a letter from Buffalo not long after which revealed to me the fact that this absurd charge *could be apparently proved against me and mine,* by reference to the record of a legal decision by the Supreme Court of Erie county. The letter was as follows :—

A. J. DAVIS :—SIR : I want to write you, and I will tell you why. I have just seen a decree of the court in Erie county, granting Mr. S. G. Love a divorce on positive testimony. I quote from the decree — " that the defendant is now and has been for some time living in open adultery with the said A. J. Davis, and that the said defendant Mary F. Love now calls herself Mary F. Davis" . . . . . and, sir, the decree of the court further is — " that it shall be lawful for the said plaintiff to marry again as if the defendant was actually dead ; but it *shall not be lawful* for the said defendant to marry again until the said plaintiff is actually dead.'

This letter shocked and saddened us, but its contents were neither surprising nor mysterious. Several months previous to its date, we had received a communication from Mr. Love, which was as follows :—

BUFFALO, *February* 16, 1856.

MY DEAR MARY : Having lately seen several articles in the papers on the subject of Divorces, I took counsel in regard to my own condition. I find that, never having been a resident of the state of Indiana, I am not necessarily free by the conditions of the Divorce granted on your behalf, while I remain a citizen of this state. At least, trouble might arise in regard to it.

Have you objections to my obtaining a divorce from you in this state ? Without opposition, it can be accomplished very quietly. It will be obtained solely for the purpose of avoiding the possibility of trouble to all parties concerned, hereafter. An early reply will be very acceptable.

A letter from the children, a day or two since, reports them quite well and happy. Hastily, but very truly, S. G. ——.

Mary was prompt in her reply, assuring him that we felt not the least objection to the divorce proposed, especially if there was any danger of trouble without one. Accordingly, when the summons was served upon her to appear against him, she received it and offered no resistance either then or ever afterward. In fact, she rejoiced at the thought of removing every impediment to her friend's personal happiness. Giving the subject no further attention, we were proceeding with our public teachings through eastern cities, when the letter already chronicled came freighted with the unwelcome tidings of the *barbarous scandal* which had been legalized and perpetuated by the Supreme Court of Erie county.

At first blush, one might be inclined to blame the originator of this divorce, for obtaining his bill by intentionally *concealing* the priority of Mary's liberation granted in Indiana. But we, on the contrary, attach no blame to any person. Mr. Love was compelled to do as he did by the absurd and inhuman laws of the Empire State; which laws demand an allegation of the commission of the most detestable of crimes, as the only ground of release from an unhallowed union. What is this but a guaranty to vice — an incentive to practices the most revolting?

But, notwithstanding that I had no thought of censure, still this act of legal illegality *forced* me, contrary to my every innate inclination, to take a positive stand on the plane of self-justice. I felt that the prospective influence of this false record must be neutralized; not for my sake nor Mary's, but for that of the Harmonial Philosophy — not for any present personal benefit, but for the future good of the world. Therefore, to prevent a deep and lasting injury which might eventually accrue to the cause of Human Progress by the existence of this glaring but uncontradicted slander, I caused a certified copy of Mary's previous divorce decree to be recorded in the Erie county clerk's office, on the 6th of April, 1857. The poison and its antidote are thus inseparably associated. But be it remembered that such laws as rendered this measure necessary, can not but be *an everlasting shame to the legislature of any state or country.*

But like every other valley cloud this also had " a silver lining."

Our souls were made happy by learning that, shortly subsequent to this legal release of our "friend and brother," he consummated the true conjugal relation which his deeper nature had so long and steadily desired. Thus the children find a safe refuge in the bosom of affection, and are blessed with wise and careful guidance in the path of development. Of this we have abundant assurance, through a noble, beautiful letter recently received from their father's refined and accomplished companion.

The last social act in this psychological drama is now performed. Most of the foregoing clouds passed while I was resting in the valley between Mount Beauty and Mount Aspiration. Mount Aspiration means a mental (or psychical) state, which enables the mind and heart to make absolute and permanent PROGRESS. Even so all the Mountains are symbols of mental states; in which the soul passes from one definite experience to another. From the commanding eminence of Aspiration I wrote the wisest of all my volumes, "The Penetralia." Oh, that I could picture the glory of those "Universal Harmonies" which — while on Mount Aspiration — awakened and strengthened my entire existence!

Mount Harmony, with its overhanging grandeur and stupendous attractions, is before me! And I know that my spirit, accompanied by its mate, will continue to climb. Already I can overhear certain holy words of harmonial Love whispered to Mother-Nature from the deep, deep Wisdom heart of Father-God. The silvery tides of their indissoluble affection set musically through my being. Amid eternal visions my silent soul is perpetually overflowing with reverent love and boundless liberty. But all mental experiences, like Music and the Seasons, progress in ascending circles. Thus the summit of Mount Harmony is but the base of another mountain yet more distant and exalted.

THE END.

Forbidden Love

Elise Hayden

ISBN 978-0-9957203-1-2

Published in 2016 by FeedARead.com Publishing
Copyright © Elise Hayden

FORBIDDEN LOVE

Elise Hayden works full time as a district nurse case manager in Lincolnshire where she lives with her husband. The book was originally inspired by the Police hit song 'Don't Stand So Close To Me,' where she originally came up with the idea for this debut novel. For many years she has dreamt of completing the book, and writing a story that will capture the hearts of the readers. Putting pen to paper she has created this debut novel based in Lincoln, *Forbidden Love,* which is concluded by the sequel *Second Chances.*

Enjoy

ACKNOWLEDGEMENTS

I am indebted to the following people for their help and support:

To my husband Darren; thank you for supporting me through writing this, and allowing me time to do it.

To Jade, for welcoming into the family my imaginary friends, as you called them!

To my mum and Pete, for reading all the drafts and encouraging me to carry on when I nearly gave up.

To Keleigh Carter, for proofreading the book.

To my daughter Jade Kelly and Dave Brumpton for modelling for the cover.

To Gina Naraidoo for all your advice at work about publishing and how it should be done.

To Michael Hall for the photography for the book cover.

To Dave Brumpton and Elpeeko Printers, Lincoln for all your input with the design of the book covers.

To all of the pubs, restaurants, hotels and venues that have been mentioned in the book, some of which have advertised the book on my behalf; these include – Ann Summers, Asda, Brown's Pie Shop, Burton's Menswear London, Claire's Accessories, Costa Coffee, Hotel Noir, Jorvik Viking Centre, KFC, Little Chef, Magna Carta, Nando's, Natureland Seal Sanctuary, New Look, Next, Odeon, Primark, Royal Oak, Royal William, Treble's Bar, Walkabout Bar, Wetherspoon's, Whisby Nature Reserve, The White Hart, W H Smith, Ye Old Cheshire Cheese Inn, Yorkshire Museum.

For Darren, my soul mate,
the man who made my life complete,
my beautiful daughter, Jade,
and my gorgeous granddaughter, Ellie-Mae
xxx

Thank you

To all my friends and family
for supporting my dream;
I love you all xxx

I hope anybody who buys the book enjoys reading it xxx

Chapter One

Helen Mitchell was an ordinary girl with an ordinary life. She lived with her mum, Katherine, in a small town-house on Brant Road, on the outskirts of Lincoln; her sister, Beth, living two streets away with her fiancé, Steve. Helen had been dating David for three years, after meeting him on a bus into town when she was fifteen. It was not love at first sight; in fact, Helen had described David to her friends as 'a bit cocky'. However, she soon began to realise that this was a front he put on for the purpose of impressing his friends. When they were alone, he was a different person, loving and sensitive and, although he was not romantic, Helen knew he cared deeply for her. The relationship had blossomed gradually over the last three years and they were happy together; arguments were few and far between. David worked as a tyre fitter, a job he didn't intend on doing for the rest of his life, but it brought him an income, enabling him to pay rent on his small bedsit on Boultham Park Road. Helen and David had never discussed living together as, although they cared for each other, neither was ready for that kind of commitment. In addition to this, Helen only had a small bursary, as she was halfway through the second year of her nurse training, a career she had wanted to pursue since the age of twelve.

It was three days after her twelfth birthday when Helen and Beth (then fifteen), experienced something no child should ever have to go through… The loss of a parent. Their dad, Richard, only thirty-eight, had a successful career as a solicitor, and they lived happily as a family, enjoying regular holidays. Sundays were always family days; it was the Mitchell house rule. Whether it was a day out at the seaside, or a day at home playing games and watching films, Sundays was their special day. Ironically, it was on a Sunday that Richard had taken his last breath, with his family by his side.

It had all happened so quickly. Richard had displayed no signs of being ill; he looked well, he felt well, and life was as it always had been. One particular morning, he struggled to go to the toilet, and when he eventually succeeded, he noticed some blood; he was not concerned and just put it down to straining. However, when, after a few weeks, the bleeding continued, and his bowel habit fluctuated from constipation to diarrhoea, he decided to see his GP for a check-up. At this point he was still not concerned, as he felt fit and healthy. However, the look on the doctors face when he performed a rectal examination, then requested a two-week referral for further tests, told Richard that something was not quite right. His instincts proved correct as, a month later, he sat stunned in the oncology consultant's office, having received a diagnosis of bowel cancer, with metastatic spread to the liver, kidneys, bladder and lungs. Treatment was not an option; the prognosis was poor. Telling his girls was the hardest thing he had ever had to do in his life.

'I'm so sorry, my darlings, but I have a terrible disease and I'm not going to get better.'

Helen knew she would never forget that moment, the feelings of shock, nausea, hysteria, and anger, all at the same time. She still remembers hearing the scream, then realising that it was coming from her, as her daddy hugged her tightly, and the whole family sobbed for what seemed like an eternity. He promised to fight the disease, but the disease was too advanced for that. Within weeks, her handsome, fit daddy turned into a shadow of his former self, with a skeletal look and shallow eyes, nursed on a special bed in the front room. Nurses came in regularly towards the end, and ensured that Richard was free of pain. Helen would watch in awe as they performed their duties. He had watched Helen sadly open her presents on her birthday, then slipped into a coma that same night. His eyes remained closed for the next three days. Helen and Beth helped their mum wash his hands and face. Finally, he opened his eyes and looked at his girls.

'I love you all so much. Be strong and look after each other,' he said weakly, and that was it. He closed his eyes, and they watched in despair as his chest rose and fell twice, then nothing. He was gone. Thirty-eight years old.

The next few weeks passed in a blur, with the funeral, and visitors, and enough cards for them to open their own shop. Helen and Beth had some time off of school and Katherine stayed with them, taking compassionate leave from her job as a florist. They mourned together, and cried all day, every day, as they looked at photographs and watched family videos, over and over again. However, after a while, they knew that life had to go on and they returned to school, to the delight of their friends. Teachers were very supportive and if they needed time out to cry, it was accepted and understood. They could just leave the room quietly and come back when they felt ready. Helen was due to pick her GCSE options and she confidently told her tutor, Miss Green, that the choices she made would need to enable her to become a nurse, so that she could look after dying people, just like they had for her dad. With the help of careers advisors, that is exactly what she did.

Eventually, despite feeling that they would never smile again, the pain became easier, and when they put on the film 'Shallow Hal' one Sunday, they laughed out loud, and there began the rest of their lives.

Chapter Two

The sun streamed through the window as Helen tiredly stumbled out of bed. She smiled as she opened her curtains and saw the blue skies above; she loved the sunshine. It instantly made her feel happy. It was Friday, and today was the last day of Helens placement on the dermatology clinic. Although she had enjoyed her placement, and had learnt a lot about skin complaints, she was ready to leave. She found clinic work quite boring. She was scheduled to finish at four o'clock, giving her enough time to get home and get ready for a romantic weekend at the coast with David. She hadn't been to Skegness since the death of her father, six years earlier, and was looking forward to the trip. They had booked into a cosy bed and breakfast on the sea front, with a room that had a balcony overlooking the beach. Helen liked to be organized, so she had already packed her bag, just in case she was late leaving work. Whilst shopping with her friends the previous weekend, she had treated herself to a sexy red lace negligee which she planned to surprise David with that night. Thinking about it gave her butterflies, as it had been weeks since they had made love.

Helen spent most of the morning with the consultant, reviewing patients who had been treated with UV therapy for their eczema and was stifling yawns as all of them were given the same advice about lotions and potions. There was no way that she would get a job here when she qualified; she had decided that after the first week. Jo, her mentor, was lovely though. She seemed to love her job and was clearly very knowledgeable about her speciality.

'So how have you enjoyed your time with us?' Jo asked as she happily signed off Helens competencies. Jo had enjoyed having Helen as a student and thought she showed great promise in her abilities. She wrote Helens placement progress with praise and described her as an 'enthusiastic student who is hard working and has been a valuable member of the team.' Helen beamed with pride.

'I've really enjoyed the placement and feel I've learnt a lot,' she replied. Jo smiled.

'Do you think you would come back here at all in the future?'

Helen was honest in her answer, 'I don't think so, Jo. Although I've enjoyed it, I already knew that I wanted to work in palliative care. That is all I've ever wanted to do.'

Jo shook her head. 'I admire you if you do that; it certainly isn't something that I could do. It takes a special kind of person to do that day in, day out.'

'I know,' Helen agreed, 'but that is what I've wanted to do since I was a girl, and I'm part way there so I don't think I'll change my mind now.'

Jo looked at her watch.

'It's two o'clock. Do you want to go now and get ready for your dirty weekend with your gorgeous man?' Jo had met David on a night out a few weeks earlier, and several of the nurses had commented on his good looks. Helen had laughed when they spoke about him on the Monday morning and referred to him as 'dishy Dave'. With his dark brown hair and smouldering brown eyes Helen still found him attractive even after three years together. Her feelings for him were strong and she couldn't imagine ever being with anyone else. However, she had recently confided in her mum that something just was not there. She couldn't explain what it was; she loved being with him, they got on well and laughed all the time. They liked the same music and the same films and shared a particular love for comedy films that made them laugh until their insides hurt. When her mum questioned what was missing Helen had simply answered, 'The spark in the eyes that you and dad had every time you saw each other.'

Helen was grateful of the offer to finish early, and after hugging everyone goodbye and thanking them for a great placement, she skipped happily to her car and drove home. Her mum was still at work when she got in so Helen ran herself a hot bubble bath and helped herself to a sneaky white wine spritzer, in celebration for finishing another placement successfully with good feedback. She loved her training, although she found the assignments a bit tedious, so she tended to leave them until the last minute and then panic until she got her results. Although she was not an academic person, she was achieving modest grades and Katherine was very proud of her daughter.

The hot water was inviting as she lowered herself down into the bath, allowing the bubbles to envelop her skin. Her mobile phone pinged on the windowsill and she stretched up to read the message, taking care not to drop it in the hot water. It was from David;

Can't wait for this weekend with my sexy lady.

Helen chuckled and typed in her reply;

Neither can I lover boy. I'm already home enjoying a bath whilst I wait for my man. Several flirtatious messages passed between them, until he sent one announcing that he, too, was finished and was going home for a quick shower, then would be on his way. At this time, Helen noticed how cool the bath now was, so she climbed out and wrapped herself in the fluffy towel that her mum had put out that morning. She applied her favourite creams and perfumes, ones she knew David loved, and put on the gold diamanté ankle chain that David had given her for her eighteenth birthday a few months earlier. Opening her wardrobe door, she flicked through her clothes, deciding what outfit to wear. She had already decided on her black silk underwear with lace top stockings, as they always made her feel sexy. She opted for a short red and grey tartan skirt which was complemented with a red jumper and grey boots. With her shoulder length blonde hair, red was a colour that suited her and was a particular favourite of David's.

Helen heard the door open downstairs.

'Hello. Are you still here, love?' Her mum shouted.

'Yes mum. Stick the kettle on and I'll come and make us a quick cuppa before David gets here.' She did a last check of her bag to make sure she hadn't forgotten anything before going downstairs.

'Are you all set?' Katherine asked.

'Yep, ready and raring to go,' Helen said excitedly. Despite being together for three years, this was to be their first time going away together. Helen often stopped with David in his bedsit, and he would stop with her if ever Katherine went to spend a weekend with her family. Although Richard had died six years previous, Katherine had never had another relationship, claiming that she 'could never replace her soulmate'. Several people had tried to fix her up with dates, but she wasn't interested, and Helen and Beth seemed not to mind that their mum wasn't replacing their beloved father.

'Are you excited?' She asked her daughter.

'I can't wait! I'm so in need of a break,' Helen replied. Katherine nodded. She knew how hard Helen was working on the course, and felt she deserved a few days away before going back into university the following week. She listened happily as Helen told her all the places she wanted to visit; the sea life museum, the miniature village, the fair, the shops, the beach. She laughed to herself, thinking that they would need a week to fit in all of the plans that Helen had made. Katherine loved her daughters with every beat of her heart, and was so proud of how they had turned out, never having any trouble with their upbringing. When compared to some of her friends and the problems they had had with teenage daughters, she felt privileged to have been blessed with 'her angels' as she called them. Although Beth, now twenty-one, hadn't gone to university like Helen, she had achieved a hair and beauty diploma and enjoyed her job in a busy salon in the town centre. Beth had moved in with her fiancé Steve the previous year, and although as yet there were no plans for a wedding, Katherine was thrilled that they lived so close and the Mitchell ladies continued to have their family Sunday's as often as they could. Obviously Helen wouldn't be there this weekend but Katherine had been invited, and had accepted, Sunday lunch at Beth and Steve's. They were a close family and everybody knew it, and comments were often made that Richard would be looking down proud at his three girls.

A tap at the door interrupted their conversation and in walked David looking casual in a black pair of jeans with a black shirt, which he wore untucked with the top two buttons undone. Katherine welcomed him with a hug; she was very fond of David and secretly hoped that one day her youngest daughter would marry this lovely young man. David was Helen's first boyfriend and although David had had a few short-term relationships, he was only sixteen when he met Helen and she was the first girl he had had a physical relationship with. However, he had respected at the time that Helen was only fifteen and it was not until her sixteenth birthday that they had their first very quick, and very awkward sexual experience in his parents shed. Not very romantic, and neither particularly enjoyed it, but it released a lot of built up tensions that they had had brewing inside due to friends talking sex talk on the school buses, (they went to different schools). Another encounter didn't occur for several weeks after, and this time it was in David's bedroom whilst his parents were at work. The experience was completely different for both of them, and they enjoyed exploring each other's bodies, and over the following two years their relationship had blossomed.

'Are you ready then gorgeous?' David asked Helen with a wink. Her cheeks flushed but she had no idea why.

'As ready as I'll ever be,' she replied, draining the last bit of tea from her mug.

'Well you two have an amazing time,' said Katherine as she handed Helen an envelope.

'What's this?' Helen quizzed, tearing it open.

'A bit of spending money for you both,' Katherine said, at the point that Helen pulled out fifty pounds and gasped.

'Mum I can't accept this,' she said, and David agreed.

'It's too much,' He said.

'This is your first trip on your own. It isn't much, now go on and enjoy yourselves. End of discussion.' She laughed, handing Helen her bag and waving them out of the door. She stood at the door waving until after the car had disappeared from view. Tears welled in her eyes as she remembered her first weekend away with Richard, the weekend she agreed to be his wife and spend a lifetime as Mrs. Mitchell. Or so she had believed!

In just over an hour, Helen and David arrived at the guesthouse. It had been a steady journey with no hold-ups, and they had passed the time talking about their daily events. David felt proud as Helen discussed the feedback she had received from Jo about her placement; he knew how much it meant to her being a nurse. They received a warm welcome from the owner of the guesthouse and were shown to their room, number twenty-two. The honeymoon suite. Helen beamed at David who had booked the break; she had no idea he had booked the best room in the building. They gasped as they entered the room and saw a four-poster bed with burgundy satin draped around it. A tray with champagne and chocolates sat on a table in front of the window. In the bathroom, a Queen Ann bath sat in the middle of the room, and soft robes hung on the bathroom door, embroidered with 'his' and 'hers' on the back.

'Mmm, I know where we will be later,' Helen purred. 'A lovely bath with a glass of bubbly.'

'I can't wait!' David exclaimed, with a pinch of her bum. She squealed with delight and ran to the window. Popping a chocolate into her mouth, she looked out at the view and sighed with content.

'This is perfect. Simply perfect,' she said with a smile. David stood behind her and wrapped his arms around her waist.

'Fancy fish and chips on the sea front?' He asked.

'That sounds perfect. I'm starving!' Helen replied, secretly thankful that they were going to eat.

They walked hand in hand along the seafront. The night was setting in and the air was turning cool, the stars starting to appear in the sky above. Helen loved the sound of the sea. It reminded her of being a child, and it reminded her of her dad and their family trips to the seaside.

'I hope I make my dad proud,' she said sadly. David turned her towards him and kissed her softly on the lips.

'Sweetheart, your dad would be so proud of you he would burst,' he said wiping a tear from her cheek. Helen smiled and squeezed him tight.

'I miss him so much...' she wept, and they held each other in silence until her tears subsided. David knew how much Helen missed her dad and although he had never met him, he felt like he knew him.

After enjoying fish and chips, Helen and David spent all evening in the amusement arcades, playing on the slot machines and competing on the bike racing game. Helen had the most fun that she had had in a long time and at the end of the night she felt the happiest that she had felt in years.

'Shall we go back now?' She asked, after another defeat at bike racing.

'OK, gorgeous,' Dave said, taking her hand and pulling her towards him. 'Let's go and have that bath with our glass of bubbly.' They took a slow stroll back to the guesthouse, hand in hand, not a care in the world.

David stood on the balcony to pop the cork of the champagne bottle, and the cool breeze ruffled his hair. Helen watched him from inside and laughed heartily as the liquid fizzed out of the bottle and David tried to slurp it up, nearly choking in the process.

'Waste not, want not!' He said with the cheeky grin that Helen adored. He poured them both a glass and sat down next to her on the bed.

'Cheers!' They said in unison, clinking their glasses together.

'Here's to a fantastic weekend,' Helen said with a smile.

'And a fantastic future,' David added and kissed her gently on the nose. He looked deep into Helens eyes and she suddenly felt nervous, silently praying he wasn't going to propose. Although she cared deeply for David, she was not ready for marriage - she was only eighteen - and she coughed awkwardly and looked at her glass, closely examining the bubbles. 'Are you OK?' David asked, looking worried.

'Of course,' she replied. 'I just don't want anything to ruin this moment.' David put his glass down then, taking Helen's glass from her he set it down on the table next to his own. He took both of her hands in his and looked lovingly into her eyes.

'Helen darling,' he began. 'I love you with every beat of my heart, and I hope that one day in the future we will commit to each other, but I feel at the moment we are still too young for marriage.' He had guessed what she was thinking and Helen did an exaggerated 'phew' and wiped the back of her hand across her forehead.

David leant forward and kissed her gently on the cheek, then slowly moved down to kiss her neck. Helen gasped as he gently pushed her down onto the bed, his hands roaming underneath her jumper to touch her silky flesh. He kissed her passionately on the lips as she became more and more aroused; she wanted him more now than ever before. Unbuttoning his jeans, she discovered that he was as aroused as she was and she was overcome with desire. Helen pulled David on top of her and, without even undressing fully, they made love frantically. Helen moaned with pleasure as David made her shudder with satisfaction. Afterwards, they held each other in silence, happy and content from their lovemaking.

'Oh my God it's six thirty!' Helen gasped as she awoke, still fully clothed. David woke with a start and laughed, as he hadn't even pulled up his trousers.

'We must have fallen straight to sleep,' he said picking up the untouched glass of champagne.

'I obviously wore you out,' Helen purred seductively, as she teased David with a flash of her lace top stockings that she was still wearing.

'Last night was amazing,' he said, stroking her leg and she nodded in agreement.

'How about that bath now?' She suggested and walked into the bathroom. Turning on the taps Helen picked up a complimentary bottle of bubble bath and tipped it into the running water, sniffing the aroma that it created. It looked so inviting as the bubbles frothed in the water and very quickly the bath was ready. Helen stood in the doorway and performed a seductive striptease for David.

'I am one lucky boy,' he said as her body became exposed.

'Bring the champagne,' said Helen. 'I know its morning but what the Hell. We are on holiday and don't need to drive. Let's make the most of it!'

David eagerly threw off his clothes, picked up the glasses and entered the bathroom where Helen was already waiting in the bath. He looked at her and admired her beauty with her hair scraped up onto the top of her head and her huge saucer-like blue eyes, enveloped with thick lashes. David knew at that moment that he truly loved Helen and wanted to spend the rest of his life with her.

Climbing into the bath, he handed Helen her drink and kissed her gently on the lips before laying back into the warm water and sighing with content. Helen watched him as he lay smiling with his eyes closed, his toned torso visible above the bubbles. She found David incredibly attractive and knew she was the envy of many girls who thought the same. She felt very proud when she was on the arm of the gorgeous David Thomas. Taking a sip of her champagne and, without swallowing the drink, she leaned over and laid on top of David. As he moved towards her for a kiss, she slowly dribbled the champagne from her mouth into his, an action that he found very arousing. She circled his lips with her tongue and felt his lustful desire as he pressed against her body. Bending her legs, she lowered herself onto him and he groaned with pleasure as she made love to him, oblivious to the water swishing over onto the floor. Their bodies slid together in the bubbles, moving in unison until they climaxed together.

'I love you Helen,' David whispered and she kissed him and squeezed him tight.

Whilst eating a hearty, full English breakfast Helen and David made plans for the day. They decided to visit the seal sanctuary first and then walk along the seafront to the miniature village.

'I want a seal,' Helen said as they stood and watched them

being fed. 'Look how cute their little faces are!' She swooned, and David had to admit they were cute, especially the little baby seals, which had apparently been rescued after their mum had been found dead on the sand. They seemed to be thriving now though as they hungrily swallowed the fish that the attendant threw their way. Helen captured every moment with her digital camera.

'Let's go and see the crocodiles' David suggested, and they walked over to the reptile house as he slipped his arm lovingly around her tiny waist. Helen sighed happily and rested her head onto his shoulder. This weekend was perfect and she wanted it to last forever.

'These are not so cute,' she said to David as she eyed up the crocodiles' fang, which was showing despite it having its mouth closed. He laughed and kissed the top of her head.

'You, however, are incredibly cute,' he said, nuzzling her ear. Helen leant forward and kissed him. A long, loving kiss, only stopping when the door opened and a family walked in. Helen blushed as the two small children giggled at the fact that they had just seen a couple kissing.

'Are you hungry?' David asked, after realising it was half past two.

'Not really,' said Helen. 'Are you?' David shook his head.

'No, but I could murder one of those warm doughnuts you get near the seafront'.

'Mmm,' Helen said, licking her lips. 'Let's go and get some.' They decided to walk along the sand and Helen slipped off her sandals, her feet burying into the sand, the warm grains trickling between her toes. The sea breeze was cool and Helen, wearing only a short-sleeved top shivered as it blew against her skin. Seeing her goosebumps, David wrapped his arms around her to keep her warm, encasing her petite frame. Helen smiled in appreciation and snuggled up close to him

'I'm having a lovely time,' she said happily. David stopped

walking and cupped her face in his hands, slowly moving towards her and kissing her full on the lips, touching her tongue with his own. Her heart beat rapidly as she once again became overcome with desire. She wanted to rip her clothes off there and then but knew she couldn't; never before had she felt so aroused. She slipped her hand up the back of his t-shirt and felt his hairs stand on end as she slowly caressed his skin, running her fingers gently down his spine. 'Maybe we should come back here later tonight,' she whispered, and he nodded eagerly in agreement.

The doughnuts were delicious and sweet and they enjoyed them as they occupied their minds with the miniature village. Both were mesmerized at the details of the small town with working trains and funfair. They enjoyed reading about the history and the making of the village and laughed at the different names of the businesses, such as 'Curl up and Dye Hair Dressers'. Although other people were there, David and Helen were oblivious in their own little bubble of contentment. Watching the tiny carousel spinning around, Helen told David about the times her and her father used to go on the carousel, whilst her mum took Beth on the roller-coaster, as Helen had been too small to go on herself.

'Can we go to the fair tonight?' Helen asked, eyes lit up like a child.

'Of course,' David smiled. 'That would be fun, and hopefully you'll be tall enough for the roller-coaster now.' Helen poked him in the ribs. At five foot four, she was average height, but David still teased her about her size, despite the fact that he himself didn't tower above her.

'Small is beautiful,' she said, and twirled like a ballerina.

'It certainly is,' David beamed.

The day passed all too quickly, and was finished off with the planned trip to the fair. Purchasing a wristband each enabled

15

them to spend the next few hours going on as many rides as they wanted. Helen loved the roller-coaster, whilst David preferred the pirate ship, so they enjoyed several goes on each of those. David found it highly amusing when Helen was heaving on the waltzers, especially when the fairground attendant insisted on spinning their cart more than any other. His sides hurt from laughing by the end of the ride and Helen looked a funny shade of green afterwards.

'Never again am I going on that!' She exclaimed, blowing out her cheeks. 'I need a drink now. I can't go on another ride.' They decided to go into a busy pub in the town where there was a karaoke for entertainment. Helen surprised David by getting up and singing 'Into the Groove' by Madonna, for which she received a standing ovation.

'Three years together and I never knew you could sing,' he said, shocked, as she returned to her seat and promptly finished the Bacardi and Coke that sat on the table.

'I have many surprises stuffed up my sleeve,' she winked. 'Another drink?' She asked, shaking her empty glass.

Several drinks later and a further two songs sang perfectly by Helen, they were both feeling slightly tipsy.

'Do you fancy an early night?' Helen whispered into David's ear as she discreetly squeezed his thigh.

'It's half twelve,' he laughed, 'not really an early night but I like where you're coming from...' Hand in hand, they stumbled awkwardly back to the guesthouse, having forgotten their plan of a trip back to the beach.

'Sssshhhh!' Helen hushed loudly, as she herself tripped on the stairs.

'I think someone is a little bit drunk,' David teased, and Helen shook her head in an exaggerated manner, claiming she had only had one or two and was not even merry. That was enough for

David to know she was drunk, as she said that every time she was. He chuckled to himself as she tried to put the key in the bedroom door upside down. After several attempts and refusing to give in, Helen finally managed to open the door, letting out a loud 'yippee!' when she did.

'Sshh people will be asleep,' David said putting his finger over her lips. 'It's nearly two o'clock.' It had taken them an hour and a half to walk less than a mile. Helen took his finger into her mouth and sucked it provocatively whilst giving him a smouldering look. 'Don't go away,' he said, as she flopped onto the bed. He raced into the bathroom after being desperate to go for the last half an hour.

When he returned Helen was laid flat across the top of the bed with her eyes closed.

'Helen,' he said, tapping her foot. Nothing. 'Helen,' he repeated slightly louder and tapping her foot slightly harder. A slight snore made him realise that she was asleep and from past experience, David knew that waking Helen from a drunken sleep was mission impossible. He shook his head and smiled to himself and, patting his manhood, he said, 'down boy your luck is over for today.' After a difficult attempt to undress Helen in her comatose state, he looked in her bag for a nightdress and was pleasantly surprised to find the red negligee, although slightly disappointed that she wouldn't be modelling it this evening. Snuggling up to her from behind, he too quickly fell asleep.

He awoke to the sound of the kettle boiling and opening one eye he saw Helen, looking radiant in her negligee, making them a cup of coffee. As she turned to face him, he wolf-whistled, as her firm breasts were visible through the red lace.

'You are truly stunning Helen. Do you know that?' He said, getting up to give her a kiss.

'Pleased to see me then?' She asked, looking down at his aroused body.

'Am I ever?' David said, taking her in his arms. 'You look absolutely gorgeous. I love you in red.'

'I know you do, that's why I bought it,' she said, wrapping her arms around his neck. His hands and eyes explored her body taking in every ounce of detail. Helen hated her body, but to David she was pure perfection in every way. Seeing her now made him hungry with lust, and Helen knew by the way he kissed her that he wanted her. She took his hand and, feeling very sexy, she led him to the bed and lay down. Slowly and gently, they made love. There was no raw aggressive passion like the previous times that weekend, but it was beautiful, and Helen felt like she was in paradise. 'This has been the best weekend of my life,' she said afterwards. 'Thank you for making it so special.'

'It wouldn't have been so special without you, beautiful,' David replied and kissed her softly on the end of her nose. 'I love you so much,' he said and Helen kissed him softly. It gave him butterflies inside. Although Helen never said it back, David was confident that she did. Helen knew she cared deeply for David, but love was a strong word and a word she didn't know how to use.

A trip around the shops followed by a game of crazy golf drew their weekend to a close. They had to leave in the afternoon, as Helen needed to get her things ready for university the following day. She had three weeks of lectures before her next placement on the elderly medical ward.

They drove home feeling sad that the weekend had come to an end, but also content in the special time that they had shared.

'Let's go away again soon,' Helen said taking his hand.

'Without a doubt,' David smiled.

Chapter Three

Helen felt exhausted when she was awoken by the shrill of the alarm clock at quarter to eight. She groaned and stretched her arms above her head, and then, rubbing her eyes, she threw back the quilt. Helen was not good in the mornings, especially after a weekend of late nights, but she smiled when she thought of the weekend she had just had. Picking up her mobile phone, she texted David good morning before heading off for a shower. The warm water was refreshing against her skin and she soon began to feel more alert.

She arrived at university with only minutes to spare, after getting carried away on the phone to Beth, telling her all about her weekend. Katherine had already left for work by the time Helen had come downstairs. She had left a note for her daughter, giving her instructions on what to do for tea if Helen arrived home before her, which she often did when she was at university. It was good to see all of her friends, and although she loved being on placement, Helen appreciated a few weeks in the classroom to relax and make the most of shorter days. She sat herself down next to Amy and Michelle whom she had got particularly close to during her first year of training.

'So how was it?' Amy asked, nudging her arm and straining to see if there was a ring on her left hand. She was disappointed to discover that David hadn't proposed to Helen whilst they were away. Helen told her friends about her wonderful break by the sea, claiming it to be 'the most romantic weekend of my life'.

'Ahhh,' Michelle gushed. 'Did you get lots of nookie?' Helen blushed and looked away.

'That is none of your business, cheeky!' Although Amy and Michelle openly discussed their sex lives, Helen was not like that, believing it to be a personal act between her and David.

The classroom door opened and silence filled the room, as three of the lecturers entered, one of them being Abigail, Helens personal tutor, whom she met for assignment support and advice. She got on well with Abigail, and had been sad to receive an email confirming rumours that Abigail was leaving at the end of the week to work in another university.

'Good morning all,' Abigail said in her usual chirpy manner. She was acknowledged by a chorus of tired grunts from the fifty-two students who sat in front of her. She turned to her fellow colleagues, Debbie and Bill, and laughed. 'All pleased to be back then!' She smiled, shaking her head. Abigail Turner had been a lecturer at the university for three years, after being a nurse in theatres. Although she loved her job, the offer of promotion had been too good to refuse, but she was still sad to be leaving the group. 'As you all know this is my last week here,' she said sadly. 'However, I'm being replaced by a very experienced lecturer called Marcus Edwards, and he will be here tomorrow to meet you all. Anyone who had myself as a personal tutor will be assigned to Marcus as from tomorrow'.

'Is he fit?' Amy said to the amusement of the other students. Helen rolled her eyes and shook her head.

'I believe he participates in a number of sports, yes.' Abigail winked at Debbie, knowing exactly what Amy had meant.

The morning passed quickly, with discussions about the previous placements, completion of evaluation forms and a brief overview of the lectures that would take place over the next few weeks. As the bell rang for lunch, the students were told that they could take a study afternoon, which, to most people, generally meant an afternoon of shopping or in the pub. There were only four males in the group, Tom, Kev, Adam and Paul, and although Helen knew them, she didn't spend any time with them, and she found it irritating that one of the tutors, Debbie, spent more time with them than the rest of the group. Debbie Saunders was in her late thirties, slim build, black hair, blue eyes and long legs. Her passion was orthopaedic nursing, and all of her lectures focussed around this topic in some way. Helen had often commented to Amy and Michelle that it was unprofessional how Debbie would 'bat her eyelids' at the boys in the group. Although nobody else seemed to notice, Helen observed that in group discussions, Debbie would listen more to them and pay more interest in their stories than anyone else's. For this reason, Helen didn't like Debbie Saunders, but kept her views quietly to herself, as she didn't approve of name-calling.

Amy opted to go home for an afternoon nap, as she had a late night planned with a 'hot date' that evening. Helen and Michelle decided to drive into the town and indulge in a Costa coffee and some window-shopping. Sipping the frothy caramel latte, they chatted about their ideas for the assignment they were due to hand in in a few weeks. Like Helen, Michelle was never proactive when it came to academic work and would wait until the last minute before starting to write. The subject was ethics, and Michelle had chosen to write about abortion, a subject she felt very strongly about.

'I'm going to write about euthanasia,' Helen said, and looked at Michelle for a response.

'Good subject,' Michelle agreed. 'Are you for or against it?' Helen knew she had to tread carefully with this topic, as it had already provoked heated debates in the classroom.

'I'm actually in favour,' Helen stated and quickly added, 'on the condition that the disease is terminal and the symptoms are not controlled.' Michelle nodded and waited silently for Helen to continue. 'My dad was lucky in the sense that he had a peaceful death, but I've seen people who are not so lucky and have died in the most horrendous manner, writhing about in agony despite heavy doses of painkillers.'

Michelle took another sip of coffee and without voicing an opinion on the subject simply said, 'I'll be interested to read that when you have finished'.

After finishing coffee, the girls went into several shops and Helen treated herself to a new white and pink bag that caught her eye, with a matching pair of pumps. She also bought David a jumper that she had seen him eyeing up a few weeks previously. After all he had treated her to the honeymoon suite for their weekend away. She relived the weekend by telling Michelle all about it, and laughed as she told her story of trying to convince David she was not drunk. That was the side of Helen that Michelle found amusing whenever they went out. Helen was known for being absolutely convinced she was sober when she was clearly paralytic. They also talked about Amy's new boyfriend, the fifth since starting the course and each of those at the time being 'the one'. For about a month, until Amy had caught the eye of the next candidate. They loved their friend, but both wished that she would find someone and settle down for a while as they were aware that Amy was getting herself a bit of a reputation. They didn't like this for their friend, who deep down was a lovely, caring girl, but who sadly got badly hurt when she was seventeen and swore that no man will ever hurt her again. Michelle had been in a long distance relationship with a man called Philip for the past seven years, and although she only saw him every other weekend, they spoke on the phone every night, and she was content with the arrangement. Although Michelle was loyal to Phillip, Helen didn't feel he showed the same commitment, after seeing him kissing another girl in a club when they were all out one night. Helen had failed to share this with her friend, fearing it would break her heart, and she eventually convinced herself it was a stupid drunken mistake that he probably truly regrets.

Are you OK?

The text from Katherine read, when Helen checked her phone before suddenly realising that it was gone five.

'Oh my goodness where did the time go?' She exclaimed and after giving Michelle a lift home, she gave her mum an apologetic hug and explained how they had lost track of time. Katherine had invited Beth and Steve for tea and they enjoyed some chicken fajitas and crispy potato wedges, one of Helens favourites.

'Where's David tonight?' Steve asked.

'I have GOT to make a start on this assignment tonight, so I said I'll meet him for a drink about nine thirty,' she replied. 'Do you want to join us?' She asked. 'You too, mum,' she said, not wanting to leave her out.

'Not tonight love. I'm planning a night in front of the TV, catching up on the soaps,' Katherine said, collecting everyone's plates into a pile.

'Me too,' Beth agreed. 'You go if you want, Steve,' she said, kissing her fiancé on the cheek.

'Mmm, a night of gooseberry? No thanks,' he laughed, screwing up his face, imitating a disgusted look. 'We'll all arrange a night out soon though.' Helen topped up all of their glasses with wine and, after helping clear the table, she excused herself and went to her room and turned on the computer. Sitting herself at her desk she clicked onto Google and tapped euthanasia into the search box. There were pages of hits, and grabbing a pen and paper, she started making notes from some of the scholarly articles. She hadn't heard from David much today, so she texted him to make sure he was OK. He responded positively and texted that he couldn't wait to see her later, and would meet her in the pub down in Aubourn at nine thirty.

Tapping her fingers on the desk, Helen looked at the clock on the wall and sighed. It was already nearly eight o'clock, and she felt she was getting nowhere. She clicked onto Facebook and made a status that she was bored doing homework and wanted to see her man. This was quickly followed by a comment from Michelle questioning if she was doing homework or was she actually on Facebook. Helen laughed at the fact that she had been caught out so quickly, and commented back that it was the pot calling the kettle black, before clicking off of her homepage. She picked up a book she had taken out of the library on law and ethics, and started flicking through the pages. She came across a whole section on euthanasia and began to read making notes along the way. This, she felt, was going to be the most interesting assignment she had written, especially as it was such an emotive subject. She was slightly unsure, however, how to structure the work, so she made a mental note to herself to book a tutorial to discuss this. Helen was very pleased with herself when at nine o'clock, she had not only made several pages of notes, but she had also put together an essay plan to help structure her work.

Slipping on a pair of tight white jeans with a dusky pink hooded jumper, Helen complemented her outfit with her new pumps and bag. She scooped her blonde hair up into a high ponytail and accessorized with a pink flower at the side. Helen was lucky to have long, dark eyelashes that most women envied, so she didn't need much makeup, but she finished off her look with a swoop of pink lipstick.

'You always look lovely,' her sister smiled, as she wandered into the room where Beth and Katherine were watching Holby City. Beth looked nothing like her younger sister; she was heavier in build but not overweight. Her hair was short and mousy brown and she had tiny freckles that she hated but Steve loved.

Despite knowing that Helen was the one who received all of the admiring glances, Beth never felt jealous or resentful. Helen was her sister and she loved her and everything about her.

'Thanks Beth,' Helen smiled. 'Where's Steve?'

'Gone home to watch football,' Beth explained, mocking a yawn. 'You know him and his sports.' Helen was grateful that David was not into sports as it was one of her pet hates. 'Grown men getting excited about a bag of air being kicked around a field' as she described it, 'and don't get me on the subject of their wages' was a regular comment she made when it came to footballers' salaries.

The Royal Oak was busy for a Monday evening and, as arranged David sat at their usual table in the corner, with a glass of Bacardi and Coke waiting for her.

'I'll be tipsy,' Helen laughed. 'I've already had two glasses of wine!'

'You tipsy? Never, you don't get drunk.' David laughed, getting up to give her a hug. She breathed in his aroma as she snuggled up against his chest.

'I got you a present,' she said, handing him a bag with the jumper inside. David loved the gift and thanked her with a kiss. He had been wanting that jumper since first spotting it, and was pleased Helen had treated him to it.

'I've missed you today,' he said, taking Helens hand.

'I've missed you too,' she replied truthfully.

'I've got a bit of bad news, though,' David said sadly, looking down at his drink. 'My grandad isn't very well, so I'm going to go over this weekend and spend some time with him. Is that OK with you?'

Helen squeezed his hand tightly; she knew how much David loved his grandad and she also knew the heartbreak of losing someone you love.

'I'm so sorry David, is there anything I can do?' she said

sympathetically and he simply shook his head. Helen was shocked to see a tear in his eye, as David didn't show any emotion in that way. She leant forward and kissed his cheek. 'Shall we go back to yours for a coffee?' She suggested, conscious that he might feel uncomfortable with people around.

'Have you got time? You're at uni tomorrow...' He said, aware that Helen liked to go to bed early during the week.

'David, you are more important,' she said, standing up to leave. That made him smile inside. Helen was so thoughtful; she was definitely going to make a lovely nurse.

Although it had been a warm day, David's bedsit felt cool. It was a small room with a kitchen area in the corner, a double bed, a TV and a two-seater sofa. There was a small bathroom that consisted of a toilet, a small sink and a bath with a shower over it.

'Sorry about the mess,' he said, embarrassed, picking up some dirty clothes and magazines. He hadn't been prepared for Helen coming back, as normally he would tidy up first. Helen flicked on the kettle and ran some water to wash the dirty pots that sat in the sink.

'What's up with your grandad?' She asked softly. David sat on the edge of the bed and explained how his grandad had always been a heavy smoker, and was now suffering from emphysema and required constant oxygen. Helen felt sad; she had nursed a lady with that condition on her first placement, and the memory of it had stayed with her. Watching her gasping for air was a vision she had found difficulty coping with. She hoped David would cope with seeing his grandad like that, but didn't say this, as she didn't want to upset him more than he already was. 'If there is anything I can do, you only need to ask,' she said sympathetically, as she handed him a steaming cup of coffee, which he accepted gratefully.

Helen stayed with David until the early hours, when he gave her a lift home, and she was conscious of the fact that she would struggle to get up in a few hours, but she felt he needed her there. She leant over to kiss him and he cupped his hands around her face.

'Thank you Helen. You are one in a million,' David said, before kissing her gently on the mouth, prising her lips apart with his tongue. They kissed a long, passionate kiss, and they both wished they were still back at the bedsit. Helen felt flushed as she got out of the car and waved him goodbye. She didn't know what was happening to her lately, but she was lusting after David more than ever before. Stumbling into bed, she sighed a content sigh, and then thought sadly about David's grandad. She had never met him, as he lived in Carlisle but she knew David was very fond of him.

As she had suspected, Helen didn't find it easy to get out of bed the following morning, and for the first time since the course began, she was five minutes late. Luckily, as she clumsily clattered into the classroom, students were talking amongst themselves as she made her way to the back of the room where Amy was telling Michelle about her date the night before. No sooner had she sat down than the door opened and Abigail walked in, followed by Bill, Debbie and a tall man with brown hair, wearing beige cords, a striped shirt and a brown jumper.

'This is my replacement, class. I would like to introduce you all to Marcus Edwards.'

'Hello,' the new addition greeted the group with a smile.

'Oh well, not Mr. Universe then,' Amy whispered to Helen, who hadn't even looked up as she tried to find her pen in the bottom of her bag.

Chapter Four

Marcus Edwards probably looked slightly older than his years. At thirty-eight, he had worked as a nurse in A&E and ICU before training to be a district nurse, a job which he enjoyed for ten years. Sadly, a car accident had resulted in a back injury, which didn't cause mobility problems but had affected his ability to do certain aspects of the job. He had therefore trained to teach on the nursing course, and although he missed patient care, he enjoyed being involved in the training of up-and-coming nurses, and thrived on sharing his experiences. He prided himself on being a supportive tutor to his students, and always visited them whilst on placements to ensure there were no problems. He had an open door policy, whereby he could be contacted at any time for help and support. He was excited to start his new career in Lincoln, after the college he previously worked at in Brighton had closed and he had been made redundant. He felt lucky to have been offered the job in another city, and with no commitments in Brighton he had sold his flat, and made enough money to buy a small house near the hospital where the nursing school was based.

He had only moved into his house at the weekend, and other than coming over to view the property, he hadn't explored the city at all, although he was keen to visit the historical attractions, such as the cathedral and castle. Abigail had kindly given him a book on Lincoln, which he had browsed through in between setting up his home and stopping for coffee breaks.

Marcus had never been married and had no children. He had fallen desperately in love at the age of twenty. Her name was Chloe and she was everything to him. She had blonde hair and green eyes and together they seemed the perfect couple. Marcus had proposed and to his delight Chloe had accepted and she had chosen a large emerald ring to 'match her eyes'. The wedding was booked for the following year and life had seemed perfect, until one evening when they were out. Chloe had started to become verbally aggressive to one of Marcus's colleagues Jenny. No one knew why; all Jenny had done was touch Marcus on the arm as she was talking to him and whoosh, Chloe had gone mad. She stood up, swearing at Jenny, calling her a tart amongst other derogatory names and Marcus had ushered her out of the room, apologising, embarrassed and horrified by her performance. Tears followed from Chloe, with exclamations of she didn't know what had got into her, and he loved her so much that Marcus had forgiven her. However, this was the start of the downward spiral, as Chloe's jealous rages became more frequent and more aggressive. The final straw was when she slapped Marcus in front of her family for no reason, other than he was talking to her own sister. Marcus had felt humiliated and embarrassed but most importantly, every ounce of love he had felt for Chloe had gone, and she knew that by the look in his eyes. She didn't argue as he walked out of the house without saying a word, nor did she run out after him; Chloe knew she had blown it.

Marcus had enjoyed several flings over the years but had never met anyone who had made him feel the way he had felt about Chloe and he was in no rush to settle down. He was happy being a bachelor, with no-one telling him what to do.

Marcus sat himself down at the front of the class and told the students about his past career and then sat patiently as one by one all of the students told them their names, knowing full well he would never remember them all. He would start by remembering the names of those he was to be personal tutor to; Tom, Michelle, Tammy, Helen, Katie, Laura, Jodie who liked to be called Jo-Jo and Melissa who liked to be called Mel. He requested that at the end of the day they all stay behind so they could book a tutorial before their next placement so he could get to know them. He had a list of times and dates to choose from, Marcus liked to be organized, and he was pleased to have been given his own private office to arrange how he wanted. He planned to stay behind after work to set it up.

'He seems nice,' Michelle said to Helen, after the brief meeting.

'He does,' Helen agreed as she rummaged in her bag for her car keys. 'Do you want a lift home?' She offered, knowing Michelle would be catching a bus home. At twenty-two, Michelle, was also living at home with her parents, enabling her to do the course without having to worry about rent.

'That would be great thanks,' she said, thankful that she didn't have to get on the bus with all the noisy school children. Michelle hated kids and swore that she would never have any, referring to them as devils' work. Helen had no plans either way; if she did have children, that would be way in the future. All she could think about at the minute was having a long, hot soak in the bath with a glass of wine before spending another evening reading up on euthanasia. She wanted to revise her essay plan, as she had arranged a tutorial for the following day. Helen was keen to start writing about a topic she was actually interested in. David was having a night out with friends from work, so she had the whole evening to herself and she was looking forward to it.

Helen arrived home before her mum, so she decided to surprise her by cooking a meal. She prepared some spaghetti Bolognese, with grated cheese and a side portion of garlic bread. She also found time to make a homemade trifle, which was

Katherine's favourite dessert. She knew her mum would be going out afterwards, as every other Tuesday she went to a reading club with friends, an activity which Helen thought would bore her to tears, but was grateful it got her mum to meet up with friends. Whilst waiting for Katherine to return from home, she went upstairs and logged onto Facebook and typed in a new status.

Tea prepared, wine poured, bath running then on goes my student head!

She scrolled down the newsfeed to see what other people had written;

Amy Templeton is feeling hot!

'Typical Amy,' Helen chuckled to herself.

David Thomas is out tonight... Watch out Lincoln! She commented on that one.

You behave young man, she put, teasing, knowing she could trust David with her life. She cringed at some statuses people had put for all to see, and laughed at some of the others. Helen liked Facebook. For her it was a way of catching up with a lot of her friends but she was careful on anything she put on there, as she had seen a lot of damage caused by Facebook. Her friend Holly had been mortified when pictures of her boyfriend were plastered all over his wall, dancing with another woman when he had said he was at work. For that reason, Helen used it wisely, as a social network and nothing else. She only had a profile picture. All other photographs were safely in their albums and that's where they could stay, excluding pictures put on by others that she had been tagged in.

'Mmm, something smells good,' Katherine shouted upstairs.

'Hey mum, I'm coming down,' Helen said, logging off of the computer and going down to greet her mum, who was putting fresh flowers in a vase.

'Thought I'd brighten the place up,' Katherine smiled, placing the bouquet, beautifully arranged, into the middle of the table. 'What are your plans tonight?' She asked her daughter and Helen told her about her scheduled evening. The spaghetti was cooked to perfection and was greatly enjoyed by both, and Katherine especially loved the trifle. No sooner had they cleared up, it was time for Katherine to go to her reading group and, armed with her book of the week, that she hadn't yet finished, she went, leaving Helen alone with a glass of wine.

Heading up the stairs to run a bath, Helen didn't hear the kitchen door quietly open and David tiptoe inside. She went into the bathroom and turned on the taps, throwing in a bath bomb that began fizzing instantly. She took a sip of her wine, got undressed and put on her robe, as the bath was still only half full. Checking the temperature of the water, she slowed down the cold tap, as she liked her water hotter rather than cooler. Using a makeup wipe she cleaned her face and began looking in the bathroom cabinet for a razor to shave her legs. Suddenly she thought she heard a noise in the bedroom.

'Mum?' She shouted, but received no answer. Helen felt nervous as she slowly opened the bathroom door and peered round it. 'Hello?' She said loudly, as she slowly walked into the hallway and kicked her bedroom door open. She screamed when she saw David lying on her bed, and he guiltily rushed over to her as he saw the fear in her eyes.

'I'm sorry sweetheart, I wanted to surprise you,' he said, wrapping her in his arms.

'You idiot! You scared the life out of me,' she said harshly, her heart still racing. 'I thought you were going out.'

'I am,' he said. 'I just thought I would come and give you a kiss goodnight first.' Helen mellowed instantly. What a sweet gesture. David really was adorable and she smiled as she noticed he was wearing his new jumper.

'You look gorgeous,' she purred, wrapping her arms around his neck.

'Is your bath OK?' He quizzed and laughed as she gasped and ran into the bathroom.

'That was close!' She exclaimed, turning off the taps, the water a few inches from the top. 'Fancy joining me?' She asked in a seductive tone as she tugged open the belt of her robe causing it to fall open, much to David's delight. She swayed her hips as she approached him and pressed her silky, firm body against him. She forcefully pulled up his jumper so that he could feel her pert breasts against his bare skin. He ran his hands across her tummy to her waist and, taking a firm grasp of her buttocks, he pulled her even closer towards him. He moaned as Helen began to undo the zip of his trousers, eager for what was to follow, until the moment was interrupted by the shrill of his mobile phone. Helen pulled away and laughed.

'No, don't stop. Ignore it!' David pleaded, pulling her back towards him.

'It might be important,' she said pulling the phone out of his pocket and handing it to him.

In the heat of the moment he had forgotten that he was supposed to have picked his friend Carl up ten minutes ago for their night out. He made an excuse that he couldn't find his car keys but was just leaving, and pulled a sulking expression as he watched Helen provocatively cover herself in shower gel for the benefit of taunting him even more.

'Have fun,' she teased when he hung up the phone and held her arms outstretched for a hug goodbye.

'I don't want to go now,' David said grumpily. 'I'm going to tell them I have a better offer.' Helen laughed.

'You can't do that,' she scolded. 'You've had this planned since last week so go and enjoy yourself and forget about me here, naked in the bath…' David found Helen so irresistibly sexy and she knew it, and she loved teasing him and making him want her more. He moved towards her and kissed her hard on the lips, not being able to resist one last stroke of her breast, and feeling very frustrated he left to pick up Carl.

Helen had quite a progressive evening and not only did she manage to restructure her essay plan, but she also wrote three pages of her assignment ready for her tutorial the following day. Feeling pleased with herself, she decided on an early night after a mug of cocoa. Sitting at her desk with the steaming frothy chocolate she inhaled the aroma and licked her lips. She loved cocoa before bed. It helped her sleep and after last night, she had some catching up to do. Clicking onto Facebook quickly she chuckled at a picture that was already on of David, balancing a pint of beer on his head. He was always up for a laugh, even when he was not drinking.

Snuggling up in her comfy bed, engulfed by the fluffy duvet, Helen quickly drifted into a deep sleep, and was not even roused by the pings of her phone, or Katherine poking her head around the door to bid her daughter goodnight. When she was awoken by the alarm the following morning, she felt refreshed, and knew she had benefited from the early night. Today she arrived at uni, which was based in the hospital, with half an hour to spare, so she sat in the reception area enjoying a hot cup of coffee. Helen sat watching the people coming in and out of the doors of the hospital, wondering if they were visiting loved ones or ready to begin a day at work. She smiled to herself as she saw Marcus walk through the door, looking like he hadn't slept a wink. He ran his fingers through his dishevelled hair in an attempt to smarten himself up. Helen had predicted right, and he hadn't slept and had spent the night sorting out his house to pass the time.

'Morning, Mr. Edwards,' she greeted him, as he walked past. He seemed startled at first, glancing around until he caught Helen's eye.

'Marcus, please,' he grinned. 'I can't bear all the formalities of Mr. Edwards.' Helen noticed how the corners of his eyes creased when he smiled. Marcus had a kind face, and Helen was glad he was going to be her personal tutor.

'See you in class,' he said, as he made his way down to his office and Helen nodded in response, whilst waving at Amy, who she had just spotted walking through the door.

Marcus enjoyed his teaching sessions that morning and was looking forward to becoming part of the group.

'They seem a great bunch,' he had commented to Bill at lunch.

'Yeah most of them are,' Bill had agreed and they chatted casually in the staff room whilst eating their sandwiches, enquiring about each other in order to establish a rapport.

'Well I better go off to my office; I have an afternoon of tutorials,' Marcus said, getting up and pushing the chair under the table. He had stayed late the previous night setting up his office and was pleased with the results. Files and books neatly displayed on shelves above his desk, which harboured a smart computer and a selection of stationary. There were no photographs on his desk, unlike his colleagues, who had pictures of their partners and children to look at. Instead Marcus had a calendar on the wall, which had a comic strip for each month of the year. He had a leather bound duplicate book, so that he could write down advice for his students to assist with their work, whilst retaining a copy for himself, so he couldn't be accused of not telling them something.

First in was Tom, a likeable lad, who shaved once a week and wore nothing other than baggy jeans and t-shirts. Tom was dating another girl on the course called Laura, who was also in Marcus's tutor group and she walked in shyly behind Tom, dressed also in baggy jeans and a t-shirt.

'We thought we could come in together, because we haven't got a clue what we're doing,' Tom said with a cheeky grin. Marcus laughed and shook his head.

'That's fine,' he said. 'You better get started soon though, it is due in in a few weeks.'

It turned out they both had some good ideas, and with some

additional suggestions from Marcus, they left their tutorial happy, planning on spending the evening together to start their assignments.

Next was Tammy. Marcus, stereotypically, thought that she must be a lesbian, as she had short spiky hair with a blue streak across the top, tattoo's on her arm and a ring through her lip - not your typical image of a nurse. Tammy however, was a grade A student, who always produced good work, and had already finished her assignment on consent, and simply wanted Marcus to scan read it. Marcus was impressed with what he read, and complimented her on her efforts. He discovered that Tammy wanted to work in theatres as a scrub nurse when she qualified, and he secretly thought that would be a good idea, as some patients who were not under anaesthetic could possibly judge her on her appearance. His suspicions about her sexuality were confirmed when Jodie, or Jo-Jo as she reminded him, had the next tutorial and he spotted Tammy squeeze her bum on the way out; of course he pretended not to notice.

Katie didn't turn up, as she had gone home feeling ill, so he had half an hour to kill before his last tutorial with Helen. He had bought himself a kettle for his office, with an assortment of coffees, so that he could make a drink whilst he worked. He flicked the switch and then realised he had forgotten milk; he took his mug through to the staff room to use some from the staff fridge. Returning to his office, he saw Helen waiting outside, her blonde hair tucked behind her ears as she sat reading her notes.

'Come in,' he beckoned, holding the door open for her. 'Would you like a coffee? The kettle has just boiled.' Helen gratefully accepted and waited patiently as he disappeared back to the staffroom for more milk. She looked around the office, impressed at how tidy it was. Abigail's office had never been like this. 'An organized mess,' as she had described it. She noticed that there were no photos of any family, and wondered if he was married or not. She smiled as he re-entered the room, and sat quietly as he poured hot water into the mugs.

'How are you enjoying it?' She asked politely as he handed her her drink.

'I think I'm going to love it here,' Marcus replied enthusiastically. 'Everyone has been so welcoming.'

Marcus observed Helen as she talked through her essay plan. He watched as she bit her lip nervously, keen for his approval. She looked so innocent, with her striking blue eyes surrounded by thick lashes. He hadn't noticed before how beautiful she was. He chastised himself; firstly, she was his student and secondly, he was old enough to be her father. Despite this, though, he couldn't help but imagine what it would be like to kiss those soft delicate lips.

'Are you alright, Marcus?' Helens question interrupted his thoughts.

'Oh yes, sorry,' he stuttered, embarrassed in case she had guessed what he was thinking. 'I find euthanasia a very controversial subject, and I'm looking forward to reading it,' He said, as he made some notes for Helen to take with her. 'If you need any further help or tutorials my door is always open.' He smiled handing back her work. Helen thanked him and got up to leave. As she walked to the door, Marcus examined her from behind, and his eyes were drawn to her slightly tanned legs that looked perfect in the knee length Burberry skirt that she wore. She left without looking back, and Marcus leant back in his chair. Tipping his head back, he sighed and ran both hands through his hair. What was he thinking?!

Chapter Five

Helen worked hard for the rest of the week, spending the afternoons working on her assignment, and seeing David in the evenings. As planned, he was going to drive over to see his Grandad on the Friday evening, whose condition had apparently deteriorated. He called to see Helen before he left, and she waved sadly goodbye to him, knowing how much he was hurting inside. She waved until his car disappeared over the brow of the hill, and stood at the roadside silently, thinking about her dad.

Her thoughts were interrupted by the blast of a horn, and she looked up and smiled when she saw Beth pull up in her ford fiesta, which had butterfly stickers plastered all over it. Beth was smiling excitedly, as they had planned a girl's night out into town, and Helen had agreed to Beth giving her a makeover. The sisters enjoyed each other's company and would try to spend some time together, just the two of them, every few weeks. Although, with all the work Helen had been doing, it had been two months since their last trip to Sheffield for a day of shopping.

Helen helped carry Beth's boxes of makeup into the house.

'I hope you don't need all of this to make me look decent,' she laughed.

'You always look gorgeous,' Beth complimented. Katherine looked up and smiled as her daughters walked into the kitchen, chatting excitedly like a couple of teenagers. She was sat at the kitchen table reading a magazine, whilst enjoying a cup of coffee and a chocolate biscuit. Chocolate was Katherine's downfall. When she lost her husband, she turned to chocolate for comfort, and before long she had spread slightly around the middle. She didn't care though; she was content in her life and had no ambition to look like a super model.

'So where are you two off to tonight?' She asked, dunking her biscuit into her drink. Helen grimaced.

'Urgh! Mum that's disgusting,' she said, screwing up her face. Beth chuckled, as it was a thing she liked to do too. She loved the warm, softened chocolate as it melted away from the biscuit. 'We are going for an Italian then off to a few pubs.'

'But first, it's a makeover for my little sis,' Beth grinned. Katherine looked at the clock.

'Well girls, it's nearly seven, so you'd better crack on,' she said whilst beckoning them out of the room. 'I'll bring you both a nice glass of wine up in a minute,' she promised.

'Have you eaten mum?' Helen quizzed.

'Yes love, I treated myself to fish and chips at lunch time, so I'll probably just grab a sandwich later.' Beth offered for Katherine to go with them for a meal, but she gratefully declined, saying she had plans to have a bath, get in her robe and watch a movie that she had borrowed from Barbara at the book club.

Beth loved her job as a beautician and took great pride in her work. She didn't believe in plastering people in make-up, and often opted for a subtler look. She loved doing Helens hair; it was so silky and smooth. Picking up some curling tongs, she carefully wrapped pieces of hair around it, until delicate curls cascaded around Helens pretty face.

'So, what are you wearing then?' She asked, standing back to admire her handy work.

'My skinny jeans and red blouse with some red killer heels,' Helen smiled, shaking her head so the curls swished around her face. Beth rummaged around in her make-up box and pulled out a bright red lipstick.

'Perfect,' she said, smiling as she covered Helen's full lips with the colourful tone. She continued with a delicate pink eye shadow and a streak of silver glitter, complimented with a sparkling black mascara that showed off Helen's eyes.

'I love it!' Helen exclaimed happily. The door opened and Katherine walked in with two glasses of wine.

'Sorry it took so long, girls. I was chatting to Aunt Lucy on the phone.' She handed each of her girls a glass of sparkling wine, and sat down on the bed watching Beth apply her own make-up.

'How is she?' Helen asked. She hadn't seen her aunt in years, as she had married a pilot and lived overseas.

'She seems fine. Still living the highlife; being pampered, going skiing in the afternoons and being wined and dined,' Katherine said, rolling her eyes. 'Oh how the other half live.'

'Yes mum, but think of when they're older, having never had children. It will be very lonely for them,' Helen said fastening up her blouse and slipping her feet into a pair of shoes, which Katherine was certain she would break her neck in if she attempted to wear them herself. She nodded in agreement and standing up she gave both her daughters a kiss on the head.

'Have fun,' she said and went through to the bathroom to run herself a lovely relaxing bath.

It was nearly nine o'clock before they were sat in the restaurant, tucking into a meal of creamy garlic mushrooms, spaghetti carbonara and a side dish of garlic bread. This was washed down with a bottle of wine that quickly went to their heads.

'I'm stuffed,' Helen said, after they had eaten, leaning back in her chair she and pulling the waistband of her jeans away from her full stomach.

'Me too,' Beth agreed, and they giggled as she covered her mouth and let out a belch that was slightly louder than she had anticipated, much to the disgust of the elderly couple at the next table.

'Come on, let's pay and go into town for a few more drinks and a boogie,' Helen said, getting her purse out of her bag. 'This is my treat for giving me a make-over.' Beth took the purse from Helen and shook her head.

'No way, you're on a measly bursary! I'm paying for this; you can buy the first round.' Helen smiled gratefully and stood up from her chair, stumbling slightly as she did.

'Oops, I think this wine has gone to my head,' she laughed, draining her glass. She took a quick look at her phone and saw some texts from David that he had sent one, two hours earlier saying he had arrived at his grandads, then another text half an hour ago asking if she was OK, as Helen usually replied straight away. She guiltily typed back an apology that she hadn't heard her phone and explained she was out with Beth. David knew she was tipsy because she always spelt things wrong when she'd had a drink. He texted her goodnight and told her to have fun.

Lincoln was heaving with people out for a good time. Beth and Helen walked with their arms linked, commenting on peoples' outfits, especially the young girls with skirts that barely covered their bottoms and crop tops that clung to their bust. It was a warm evening, and there was a happy atmosphere around, people laughing and smiling, which made a change from the last time Helen went into town with Michelle and Amy. That night was full of angry football fans out for a fight because their home team had lost again; another reason Helen hated the sport.

'Let's go in here,' Beth squeaked excitedly, as she heard her favourite dance track blasting from inside, and she steered Helen towards Walkabout, which was brimming with students drinking their alcopops and dancing to the rhythm of the music. Helen stopped to say hello to Tammy and Jo-Jo as Beth disappeared onto the dance floor, waving her arms about and gyrating her hips.

'She's hot, your sister,' Tammy said, winking at Helen as Jo-Jo gave her an annoyed look. Jo-Jo got very jealous if her girlfriend looked at another woman and Tammy enjoyed teasing her for it. Helen bought two vodka and Cokes and took one over to her sister, who was clearly enjoying the attention she was receiving from on-looking men, who were watching her every move. Beth lacked self-confidence and although she would never betray Steve, she enjoyed some male attention to remind her that she was not as frumpy as she thought.

The two sisters danced into the early hours, drinking vodka and Coke and indulging in a few shots. Their heads were spinning as they walked outside into the cool air of the early morning.

'I can't believe it's two o'clock!' Beth slurred, and she kicked off her shoes to carry them; the long hours of dancing had taken their toll.

'Let's go and get a taxi,' Helen suggested. They walked happily down the high street looking in shop windows and laughing hysterically at a provocative PVC outfit in the window of Ann Summers.

'I bet Dave and Steve would like that,' Beth chuckled and Helen agreed making a mental note of the price in her head.

The queue for the taxi was long and Helen groaned. She was tired now, and just wanted to go home and tuck herself in bed. She leant against the railings, folded her arms and rested her head on Beth's shoulder to close her eyes. Her body was starting to ache with exhaustion and her head was spinning from all of the alcohol they had consumed.

'Hello Helen,' a voice interrupted her thoughts, and she opened one eye to see who had spoken. It took a few seconds for her to focus and to realise that it was Marcus. Standing up straight, she flung her arms around her tutor and gave him a drunken hug. He inhaled the smell of her perfume and hoped the dim light would disguise his face flushing. Helen introduced him to Beth and began to tell him all about their evening.

'Now I just want to go home, and look at this queue,' she said, exaggerating a point at all the people lined up along the road. 'What are you doing out at this time anyway?' Helen asked cheekily, giving Marcus the impression she thought he was too old for being in town.

'I've been catching up with some old friends who are over for a wedding tomorrow,' he explained. 'My car is around the corner. If you want, I can give you girls a lift home.' Helen and Beth looked at each other.

'Are you not drunk?' Beth asked in a surprised tone. Marcus laughed and shook his head.

'I don't drink very often,' he explained. 'Only on special occasions, but usually I'm quite happy drinking a diet Coke and watching everyone else make a fool of themselves.'

They accepted his offer gratefully.

'I think I'll go home to Steve, and he can bring me to fetch my car when I get up,' Beth slurred, as she sprawled across the back seat and closed her eyes, promptly snoring silently.

'Do you mind? She only lives a couple of streets away from me,' Helen explained, giving Marcus directions.

Steve was up, waiting for Beth, as he always was when she went out. He liked to make sure she got home safely.

'Come on, sleepy head,' he said, helping his fiancée out of the car and thanking Marcus for bringing her home. 'We'll see you over the weekend Helen.' He closed the door behind him, and Marcus and Helen laughed as Beth stumbled all over the place. Helen yawned and stretched her arms above her head. Her blouse lifted slightly and Marcus caught a glance of her toned stomach. She had a pink diamanté stud sparkling in her belly button.

'So where do you live, Helen?' He asked, quickly diverting his attention from her body. Helen, who was starting to sober up, directed him to her home a few streets along.

'Have you settled in?' She asked, as he pulled up outside her door.

'Just about. It's only a small house, but it's near to work so it suits me fine.' Helen looked at him.

'You live near the hospital? I would never have accepted a lift if I knew you were coming this far out of the way,' she said, moving a stray curl away from her eye.

'It's not a problem,' Marcus said, as he got out the car and opened Helen's door for her. She smiled gratefully, as he steadied her when her heel wobbled on the pavement.

'Would you like a coffee?' She offered, and Marcus looked at his watch.

'It's gone three o'clock,' he said. 'Don't you want to get to bed?'

'I always have a coffee before I go to bed,' she explained. 'Come on, it's the least I can do after you've been so kind.' Marcus accepted and followed her into the house, taking care to be quiet as she unlocked the door.

Helen flicked on the kettle and quietly shut the kitchen door, so as not to wake her mum.

'Do you live with your parents?' Marcus asked.

'Just my mum. My dad died when I was twelve,' she said sadly, and Marcus apologised.

'Tea or coffee?' Helen asked, changing the subject, knowing full well how emotional she got when she'd been drinking.

'Coffee, milk, no sugar, please,' Marcus replied, and pulled out a chair to sit down. Helen didn't notice that he was watching her make the drink. He was mesmerised by her beauty. His heart was beating as he took in every aspect of her body. He wanted to reach out and pull her into his arms. It had been a very long time since Marcus had felt this way about anyone. He was angry with himself for being so stupid and mentally reminded himself that Helen was his student, and in addition to that she was twenty years his junior. Helen sat down next to him and handed him his coffee.

'So, have you had much chance to do any sightseeing yet?' She asked, as she took a sip from her cup.

'Not yet. I was hoping to have a look up near the cathedral tomorrow, perhaps,' he replied.

'It's lovely up that end of the town,' Helen smiled. 'The castle is interesting too, if you get a chance.' They chatted casually about university, and drank another cup of coffee before Marcus got up to leave.

'Well, thank you for the lift,' Helen smiled and leant up to kiss Marcus on the cheek. Marcus coughed and looked down at his shoes. 'I'm sorry,' Helen apologised. 'I shouldn't have done that.' She turned away, embarrassed. Marcus touched her arm and she turned to face him. She hadn't realised quite how handsome he was until now, but then again she was tipsy. At least, that was what she convinced herself.

'Do you have any plans tomorrow?' He asked and Helen shook her head. 'Well I could do with a tour guide to show me around this place.' Helen looked at him and smiled.

'It would be a pleasure. I'll meet you in Costa Coffee at eleven o'clock. Do you know where it is?' She asked.

'I'll find it,' Marcus smiled and turned to leave, closing the door behind him.

Helen sank into her bed and picked up a photo of David from her bedside cabinet. Giving it a kiss, she felt butterflies in her tummy. Should she really be doing this? Would David mind? Well Marcus is old enough to be her father. She was only showing him around the town; what was the harm in that? She held the photograph against her chest and soundly fell asleep.

45

Chapter Six

The sun streamed through the window, hurting Helens' eyes, as Katherine pulled back the curtains and handed her a mug of coffee.

'What time is it?' Helen groaned, feeling like she had only just gone to bed.

'It's just gone ten,' Katherine said. 'I have to pop to Asda to get some shopping. Do you want to come?' Helen remembered that she should be meeting Marcus at eleven, so she declined, saying she was meeting Michelle in town. She climbed out of bed and headed to the bathroom, holding her forehead, which was throbbing from the night before. Taking some paracetamol from the cabinet, she swallowed them down with water and looked at herself in the mirror. Her makeup from the night before was smudged down her face, so she hastily had a wash and brushed her teeth. Seeing the sunshine, she put on a long floral maxi dress and a pair of sandals, and scooped her hair up into a bun. She had no time to do anything else; she was going to be late as it was.

It was nearly quarter past eleven when she walked through the door and Marcus smiled. He had started to think she wasn't coming. She apologised profusely as she sat down opposite him and breathed heavily; she had run from the car park.

'I am so unfit,' she laughed, taking a large gulp of air. Marcus laughed and shook his head.

'Coffee?' He asked, and Helen nodded appreciatively.

'Skinny latte, please,' she smiled as Marcus joined the queue. He was wearing some chinos with a black t-shirt which, although was not tight, showed off his muscled physique. Helen nervously bit on her fingernail as she pulled out her phone and texted David to see how his grandad was. He replied that he was hanging on in there, and told her he would be home about four the following day. She offered him a Sunday roast, knowing her mum wouldn't mind and he accepted the offer with a stream of kisses and a love heart. Helen felt a pang of guilt as Marcus sat in front of her. He brushed his fingers through his hair as he asked Helen if she had a hangover.

'Not at all,' she lied and took a sip of her coffee. She loved Costa Coffee and often went there with Michelle and Amy.

'I hope you don't mind steep hills, because we have one to tackle to get up onto the bail,' Helen said, breaking the silence. Marcus shook his head as he drained off the last of his coffee.

'I run quite regularly, and I like to tackle the odd hill or two,' he said reassuringly.

Within minutes of climbing up what felt like Mount Everest, Helen could feel her chest tighten as she puffed heavily, chastising herself for not putting on comfier shoes, and thinking that she really ought to join a gym or a running club.

'Are you OK?' Marcus asked, looking concerned. 'Do you want to stop for a rest?'

'I'm fine,' Helen lied. 'We are nearly there anyway,' and she smiled, seeing the top of the hill in the distance.

'Fancy an ice-cream?' Marcus said, as they passed a quaint little shop offering homemade luxury ice cream. Helen loved ice cream and readily accepted, choosing a waffle cone with a lemon ice cream that was packed with tiny pieces of meringue. Marcus opted for a Peach Melba and chocolate sauce, and they enjoyed them silently as they walked through the arch heading for the cathedral. Helen enjoyed telling Marcus about the cathedral, and showed him the areas in which 'The Da Vinci Code' had been filmed. Marcus was mesmerised by the beauty of the building, and stood still to look at the detail of the architecture. Helen watched him closely. She watched how his eyes creased in the corners as he smiled; he had lovely eyes, she thought, and she wondered why he had never married, although Marcus had already told her he had simply never met the 'right one'.

After the cathedral, they went into the information centre and whilst Marcus was reading up on the history of the Lincoln imp, Helen was fascinated by a book about the hauntings that supposedly occur in Lincoln. Ghosts and spirits were something that Helen was interested in and, taking a notebook from her bag, she jotted down a number from a poster on the wall advertising ghost walks. David would enjoy that too as it was an interest they both shared.

'Are you in a hurry to get back?' Marcus asked after purchasing a book on the history of the city.

'No, not really. I have no plans for the rest of the day,' Helen answered.

'Would you mind if we went and looked at the castle then?' Marcus smiled, as he looked over to the old building standing proudly in front of him.

'Great idea. I haven't been there since I was a kid; my dad used to bring me all the time,' Helen replied enthusiastically. As they walked through the castle grounds, Helen told Marcus about her dad, and the reasons she had wanted to go into nursing. Marcus also chatted about his career, and how the accident had been the reason he had chosen a career in teaching. Helen was surprised how easily she could talk to Marcus, considering they had only just met. She was pleased they had gotten to know each other, and equally as pleased that he was her personal tutor. Although Helen had liked Abigail, she was pleased that her replacement was so easy to get on with.

Helen looked up at the sky as the sun disappeared behind a stream of grey clouds, and a chilling breeze swept through the air, causing her to shiver. Before she had chance to say anything, the sky clattered with a clap of thunder, and heavy, fat raindrops burst from the sky. Helen squealed and covered her head with her bag, Marcus laughing at her childlike ways.

'Come on let's go in that old bath house,' he suggested, pointing to the nearest building and taking her hand as they ran across the grass for shelter. They laughed as they darted through the door, and Marcus put his hands on his knees and shook the rain from his hair. Helen tried to smooth her dress, feeling conscious that Marcus would be able to see her underwear, as the rain had made the dress almost transparent. She shook her head and laughed.

'Well you have seen me at my worst now,' she said.

'You look beautiful,' Marcus complimented her, as he wiped some rain from under her chin. Their eyes locked for what seemed like an eternity and Helen could feel herself blush. Her heart was beating so hard, she thought she could hear it pounding in her chest. Marcus looked sexy, as the water trickled down his face, like he had just emerged from a shower. Very slowly, and forgetting about the boundaries of teacher and pupil relationships, Marcus lowered his head towards her. He paused, waiting for her to object. Helen could smell his aftershave as she tipped her head back and closed her eyes, waiting for his lips to meet hers. The shrill of Marcus's phone abruptly interrupted the moment and Helen pulled away, flustered, astounded by what she had nearly done. The realisation dawned on her that she had nearly betrayed David and her eyes prickled with tears.

'I have to go,' she cried, ignoring Marcus calling her name as she ran across the wet ground. She ran all the way back to her car, and sitting inside with her head in her hands, she sobbed uncontrollably.

Marcus had walked from his house to meet Helen, and as he trudged home in the rain, he went over and over in his mind what had just happened. What an idiot. He could lose his career over this! He convinced himself that it was a stupid mistake in the heat of the moment, and would apologise to Helen when he saw her in uni the following week.

That night, Katherine could see that Helen was not herself, but her daughter insisted otherwise. After enjoying a meal of homemade shepherd's pie, Helen indulged in a bath and worked on her assignment. She spoke to David, who sounded very down, as his grandad was not making any progress and was now not responding to any of the family.

'I'm sorry Helen, but can we give tea a miss tomorrow? I'm going to phone work and tell them I need to stay here with grandad.' Helen understood and promised him that he could ring her at any time if he needed her. 'I love you Helen,' David said sadly. 'I know you won't say it back, but I just want you to know that I really love you, and one day I know you will love me too.'

Tears glistened in Helen's eyes as he spoke. She adored David; she loved everything about him. She thought he was good looking, funny, kind and sensitive and she told him this all the time. But love was a big word, and it was a word she couldn't use without meaning it. She felt frustrated that she felt this way. Everyone thought they were a great couple, and they were, but deep down Helen knew that something was missing; that sparkle that her mum always talked about when she reminisced about the love of her life.

Aware that her mum was downstairs alone, Helen joined her to watch a late night movie, and they chatted over hot chocolate. Helen never mentioned her day; she didn't want her mum to get the wrong idea, so she changed the subject when asked, and spoke about the family day they had planned the following day, just Katherine, Beth and Helen having a day of chick flicks with bowls of popcorn and fizzy drinks.

As Helen snuggled in bed that night, she wrapped the duvet tight around her and closed her eyes. Her mind wandered to that moment in the bathhouse, and her heart began to race as she closed her eyes and pictured Marcus drawing towards her. She began to cry guiltily, silent tears, as she questioned whether she would have pulled away if his phone hadn't rung. She convinced herself that she would have done and, kissing her picture of David, she turned over and went to sleep.

Meanwhile, Marcus sat on the windowsill in his bedroom, looking out at the few people returning from a night of drinking. He trembled as he thought of Helen. Never in his life had he known anyone so beautiful, and sipping a glass of brandy, something he rarely did, he wished that things could be different. He wished that Helen didn't have a boyfriend, he wished she were not his student, and, most of all, he wished that she were with him right now.

Chapter Seven

It felt like a blink of the eye and it was Monday morning. Helen didn't have to be in class until eleven o'clock, so she went downstairs in her dressing gown and popped some bread in the toaster. Katherine had already left for work, so Helen set to washing the pots from the previous night. She turned her nose up as she sniffed the flowers on the table, which were starting to wilt, and hastily took them outside and threw them in the bin. She chuckled to herself as she thought about a scene from one of the films they had watched the previous day. It had starred Jim Carey, one of her favourite comedy actors, and was about a man with two personalities, called 'Me, Myself and Irene'. The three of them had laughed until their sides hurt and tears streamed down their faces. It had been a great day, which they had finished with a Chinese, as Katherine didn't feel like cooking a roast. Steve had come round to join them for supper, and they had played a few games of thirteen card brag before retiring to bed.

Helen took her toast and a cup of coffee up to her room, and opening her computer, she clicked onto Facebook to see what had been happening over the weekend. Michelle had posted some pictures of herself and Phillip, enjoying a day in Newark. Helen hadn't realised he was coming over that weekend; perhaps he had come as a surprise for Michelle, as he often did. Scrolling down the page she saw that Amy had changed her relationship status from 'in a relationship' to 'it's complicated'.

'Here we go again,' she muttered to herself, through mouthfuls of hot buttered toast. Helen had no idea why Amy couldn't just settle down with someone for a while, instead of moving from one man to another. She texted her and asked if everything was OK, and Amy replied positively, explaining that there had been a bit of a misunderstanding but they had sorted it now. Popping the last piece of toast into her mouth, Helen decided to give David a call before she had a shower. She was scrolling down the names in her phone when it started to ring showing David's name on the display.

'I was literally about to ring you,' she said as she answered the call. David was quiet on the other end. 'Is everything OK?' Helen asked softly, it sounded like he was crying. This upset Helen as she had never seen or heard David cry.

'He's gone,' David said, trying to sound emotionally stronger than he actually felt. Helen's heart lurched as she put her hand to her mouth.

'Oh David, I'm so sorry.' There was little else she could say. All she wanted to do was give him a big hug and take away his pain. The conversation was brief as David was struggling to compose himself, but he promised to ring her later that evening when he got home.

Sitting in the classroom, Helen was relieved that it was Debbie doing the lesson and not Marcus. She still felt ashamed of herself for what had happened, and couldn't endure the embarrassment of facing him this morning. As usual, Debbie waffled on about orthopaedic nursing, explaining about different treatments for a DVT; how some surgeons like patients to wear stockings after surgery and others don't. She watched as Adam and Paul exchanged notes, which she suspected were comments about the revealing top that Debbie was wearing. Helen noted the wedding ring on her left hand, and wondered if her husband was aware of what a flirt he was married to.

'God, she is boring,' Amy said, stifling a yawn and taking out her mobile phone. She started looking through and showing pictures to Michelle and Helen of her weekends antics. Amy had also been in town on the Friday night, and Helen expressed surprise that they hadn't bumped into each other.

'I bumped into that new teacher whilst I was out,' Amy whispered. 'He was out with a bunch of guys. He said hello. He seems a nice old chap,' she commented, as she put her phone away, conscious that Debbie was giving her a look of disapproval. It was not unknown for Debbie to request people to leave if they were not paying attention. Helen shrugged her shoulders, hoping no one would notice her cheeks burning.

'I wouldn't know,' she said awkwardly, writing some notes to avoid any further conversation about Marcus Edwards.

She saw him later in the day, as she stood in the canteen queue waiting to be served. He was over the other side of the room with a few of the other tutors, eating his lunch. Helen turned away, and pretended to herself that she was not having butterflies in her stomach at this moment in time. Paying for her cappuccino, she looked around for Michelle and Amy and was horrified to see them waving her over, sat at a table just feet away from him. Clumsily, she squeezed her way through and sat heavily onto a chair, making sure not to look over in his direction. Out of the corner of her eye, she saw him giving a pretend punch to Bill and laughing at a joke being shared.

'They seem to be having a laugh about something,' Michelle said, turning around on her chair to see. Helen looked over, just at the point that Marcus turned and saw her. He smiled slightly and carried on his conversation, so as not to arouse any suspicion about what he was thinking. He had hardly slept since their encounter, and after a lot of thinking, he had made the wise choice to talk to her, and suggest that they should forget all about it. It was towards the end of the day that the opportunity arose, and he managed to see Helen as she was walking out of the library, clutching a pile of books on ethics and euthanasia.

'It's nice to see you're working hard,' he said, smiling and holding open the door for her. Helen thanked him as she looked around to make sure no one she knew was around.

'Have you got five minutes for a quick chat in my office?' Marcus asked as he awkwardly ran his fingers through his hair.

'Umm…' Helen hesitated, not quite knowing what to say. She was feeling embarrassed and her mouth felt dry, like she hadn't had a drink all day. 'OK,' she mouthed, although no words came out, and she followed him along the corridor into his room. Closing the door behind them, he gestured for her to sit down and flicked on the kettle.

'Coffee?' he smiled but Helen shook her head trying her best to avoid any eye contact. 'I have latte,' he said shaking the box for her to see. She laughed slightly.

'OK, you twisted my arm,' she said, and put the heavy books onto his desk.

'Thank you for Saturday. I really enjoyed myself,' Marcus said with his back to her, as he poured the hot water from the kettle.

'Me too,' Helen said, looking down at her hands as she circled her fingers around each other nervously. He put the drink on the desk and sat down to face her.

'The thing is, Helen…' He paused, searching for the right words to say. 'I should never have thought about kissing you. It was unfair of me, and I hope you don't think I was taking advantage of you.' For the first time Helen looked straight at him with her blue eyes. He trembled as she smiled at him and pushed her hair behind her ear.

'Let's just forget about it,' Helen said, with a sigh of relief and changed the subject to her assignment.

Marcus listened with interest as she talked about her ideas and watched her intently as she drained her mug of coffee. Despite what he had said, he still thought Helen was possibly the most beautiful woman he had ever seen, and as she got up to leave he couldn't resist looking at her amazing figure.

'See you soon,' she said as she closed the door behind her.

'I hope so,' Marcus murmured under his breath.

The waft of fish and chips filled the kitchen as Helen walked through the front door.

'I thought I'd treat us,' Katherine smiled as she put some plates in the oven to warm.

'Mmm my favourite,' Helen said, licking her lips and putting the books onto the kitchen side. 'I'll set the table,' she offered, and Katherine gratefully accepted as she handed her the cutlery. Helen was ready for her tea, as she hadn't eaten anything since her breakfast, and she enjoyed the succulent fish, covered in salt and vinegar. She cleared her plate hungrily, as she sadly told her mum about David's grandad. Katherine felt sorry for David. She thought very highly of him and didn't like to think of him upset.

'What time is he due back?' She asked her daughter, and Helen shrugged her shoulders.

'Just sometime this evening,' she replied, mopping the last few mushy peas up with a slice of bread and butter. Afterwards she rested back in her chair and patted her tummy contentedly. 'That was yummy,' she smiled. 'I'll wash up and then I'll go and get this assignment finished whilst I wait for David to call,' Helen said standing up and clearing away the plates. Katherine put her hand on Helens.

'You get on with your work,' she said. 'I'll do this.' Helen kissed her mum on the cheek and, helping herself to a can of Coke from the fridge, she went upstairs to do her writing. Reading some newspaper cuttings about Diane Pretty, who had died several years ago after fighting for the right to an assisted suicide, Helen made notes and thought this would be an interesting case to discuss.

Typing away on her computer, she wrote page after page, highlighting arguments that were both for and against euthanasia. She felt that this was the best piece of work she had written on the course, and hoped that she would achieve a good grade for her efforts. Glancing at her bedside clock, she saw that it was almost nine and felt anxious that she hadn't heard from David. She checked her phone, which was on the desk next to her, fearing she may have left it on silent since coming in. Checking the screen, there were no messages or missed calls, so she dialled David's number. She felt a gulf of nausea as the phone rang and then clicked onto the answer phone after several rings. She waited a few minutes then tried again. David never failed to answer his phone, and Helen was terrified something was wrong. Had he crashed on the way home? Was he lying in hospital somewhere? She was beside herself with worry, cursing herself for not phoning him sooner. She saved what work she had written as she tried again, only to be greeted by the same message. She stood still, dazed and wondering what she should do, her mind frantically working out how long it should take him to get home. But then, she didn't even know what time he had left. Helen felt bile rise in her throat and her imagination ran wild, picturing all sorts of horrible things that could have happened to him.

She then remembered that her mum had possibly got the phone number of David's parents, as his mum, Rebecca, was also in the same book club as Katherine. Relieved that she had thought of that, she promptly went downstairs to find her mum. Katherine was sat in her robe, curled up on the sofa doing a crossword puzzle in a magazine; she looked up startled as her daughter burst into the room.

'Mum, do you have Carl and Rebecca's number?' Helen asked, the anxiety obvious in her tone of voice.

'I have it somewhere. Is everything OK, love?' Katherine asked, concerned, as she pulled open the drawer where she kept her address book. Helen explained that she hadn't heard from David and she was worried. Katherine reminded Helen that he might just be upset about his grandad.

'I know mum, but he isn't answering his phone either,' Helen exclaimed, her eyes filling with tears. Katherine flicked through her book until she came to the number and handed it to Helen, along with the portable phone. Plonking herself onto the sofa, Helen dialled the number, only to hear an engaged tone. Her heart was palpating now. She needed to know what had happened, if anything.

'Calm down, love' Katherine soothed. 'I'll go and make us a lovely hot cuppa, you just keep trying the number. They are probably telling family about their dad.'

Helen heard Katherine in the kitchen. She heard the flick of the kettle and the cups being taken out of the cupboard, but this was being muffled by the sound of her beating heart, which she could hear as if it was beating in her head. The number continued to be engaged each time she tried, and she held her face in both hands as panic continued to rise inside her. It was now gone ten o'clock.

'Helen can you come through here a minute,' her mum beckoned from the kitchen and Helen obliged. There, stood at the door, was David, unshaven and heavy eyed.

'I left my phone in Carlisle,' he said, as he held out his arms for a hug. Helen ran and threw her arms around him, as he buried his head into her shoulder and sobbed fat, heavy tears. Helen stood silently, allowing him to express his grief, and simply stroked the back of his hair, as Katherine tactfully returned to the front room.

'I'm so sorry about your grandad,' she said sympathetically, knowing the hurt that he must be feeling inside.

'I know we were expecting it but it doesn't make it any easier,' David said sadly, as he blew his nose on the tissue that Helen had handed him. Helen picked up the two cups.

'Come on let's go to my room. You can stay here tonight. I don't think you're in a fit state to go home.' After checking with Katherine that this was OK, she led the way upstairs to her room. Putting the cups down onto her desk, Helen turned and put her arms around David and kissed him tenderly on the lips. 'I'm going to run you a nice hot bubble bath to relax in,' she said, as she brushed her soft lips against his cheek. David held her close and slowly inhaled the smell of her hair. Helen always smelt lovely to him.

The bath was warm and inviting as David lowered himself into it. Helen had lit candles around the room, creating a lovely relaxing atmosphere for him. Tapping on the door, she came in with a small glass of brandy.

'This should help you sleep,' she said, handing it to him. 'Mum has made up Beth's old bed for you,' she winked. Although they had been together three years, Katherine still didn't like them sleeping together whilst she was in the house, and both Helen and David respected her decision. It didn't take Helen long to fall asleep as it had been a long day, and she felt exhausted. However, she woke suddenly to hear the muffled sound of David crying in the next door room. Straining her eyes to look at her bedside clock, she saw it was four am. She wondered if he had slept at all.

Carefully tiptoeing across the landing so as to not wake her mum, Helen gently opened the door to the room where David lay, and quietly closed it behind her. Climbing into the small bed, she cupped herself around his naked body and held him tight until the tears subsided. David turned his head towards her and kissed her softly.

'Thank you for this, Helen,' he said gratefully. 'I didn't think it would hit me as hard as it has.' Helen traced her fingers down his arm and across his chest. She knew he relaxed when she tickled him, and he sighed contented as she circled the hair

59

on his chest around her fingers. He turned to face her and she stroked his face with her soft hands.

'Try and get some sleep,' she whispered softly, as he closed his eyes and rested his cheek against the palm of her hand. The bristle on his chin felt rough on her wrist. She leant forward and kissed him gently on the forehead, with the intention of going back to her own room. David opened his eyes and looked deep into hers, before bending down to kiss her neck. Helen felt a rush of desire as he cupped her breast gently with his hand, feeling her erect nipple through the silky fabric of her nightdress. Using one hand, he held her hands together against the pillow above her head, preventing her from being able to respond. Helen gasped as, using his other hand, David lifted up her nightdress and caressed every inch of her silky flesh, softly and gently. She arched her back as he prised open her legs with his hand and feeling her excitement with his finger he gently stroked her, feeling more and more aroused as she groaned softly.

'Make love to me, 'she pleaded, biting his bottom lip firmly, and as he released her hands, she guided him into her.

They were conscious as the bed started to squeak.

'Come and lie on the floor,' Helen said hungrily, pushing him off of her, not wanting to wake her mum, yet too aroused to stop. David quietly got off of the bed and lay down on the floor as Helen slipped her nightdress over her head. Lowering herself onto him, they smiled at each other at the thought of being heard, but that didn't stop them moving gently together, lustfully fondling each other's bodies. The movements became more forceful, until the electricity bolted through their bodies, David burying his head into the carpet as Helen dug her nails hard into his chest, throwing her head back with pleasure.

They lay together silently, contentedly, and both inwardly smiling at what they had just encountered until Helen, realising it was almost six o'clock, returned quietly to her room.

Chapter Eight

The next few weeks seemed to fly by. Helen went with David to his grandad's funeral, despite never having met him; she wanted to be supportive. As the funeral had taken place on a Friday, they had stayed in Carlisle until the Sunday afternoon, where Helen had met some of David's extended family. Obviously, the funeral itself was very sad and Helen had even shed a tear herself when David's voice cracked as he read a poem during the service. However, the rest of the weekend had proven quite enjoyable, staying with one of David's cousins, Clarissa, who had shown them the sights, and introduced Helen to black Russians, which she swore she would never drink again, after spending most of the night in the bathroom being sick.

Helen had also managed to finish her assignment, resisting any further tutorials in an effort to avoid another awkward moment with Marcus. She had felt happy with the final copy, and both Amy and Michelle had proof read it and given positive feedback. She had handed it in, along with a two-thousand-word report on smoking cessation that she managed to knock up in a weekend, following a visit to the Phoenix Centre in the town that provided a service to help people stop smoking. It was now just a matter of waiting for the results, which she would get whilst on her next placement.

Helen was looking forward to her placement, as she was going to be spending the next six weeks working in the community, with a team based on the outskirts of the town. This was the one area that Helen was confident she would love, as she felt that nursing someone in their own home was much more rewarding than the hustle and bustle of a busy ward. Her mentor was going to be called Charlotte, and she had arranged to meet her in the office the following morning at nine, where she would be shown around and introduced to other members of the team.

David treated Helen to a meal at a small Italian restaurant in the town that night, which overlooked the Brayford. The glassy water looked still in the warm evening, and the lights illuminated the surface. Boats rocked gently in the water; retired couples accommodated some, whilst others were used only at weekends and holidays.

'I would get seasick, living on one of those,' Helen muttered as she took a sip from her wine. David laughed.

'You would get used to it I'm sure,' he said. Gazing out of the window, Helen spotted a familiar figure, sat alone on a bench, looking out over the water. It was Marcus. He was wearing a pair of jeans and a tight-fitting bright yellow t-shirt, and he looked very relaxed, with his arms spread over the back of the bench and his foot resting on his knee.

'Who is that?' David asked, following her gaze, and Helen blushed, conscious that she had been staring.

'Oh, it's just our new tutor,' she stammered, and taking David's hand, she kissed the tips of his fingers, in order to avert the attention back to the present moment. 'Shall we have a stroll back to yours for a coffee? Then I suppose I should be getting back to prepare for tomorrow,' she sighed.

'That sounds like a plan,' David nodded, as he beckoned over the waitress and paid the bill.

Stepping out into the evening hand in hand, Helen breathed in the aroma.

'How is it that food smells lovely when you are hungry, but when you are full it smells horrid?' she said, grimacing.

'I know, I'm stuffed,' David agreed patting his taut stomach. 'Hopefully the walk back will make us feel a bit better'.

'Mmm, I'm ready for a coffee,' Helen sighed and giggled as David nuzzled her neck.

'Only a coffee?' he teased, cheekily pinching her bottom.

'I have an early start,' Helen reminded him. David exaggerated a disappointed look before laughing and winking at her, and Helen laughed happily, knowing full well he would persuade her to change her mind when they got back to his place.

Marcus recognised that laugh; it was the laugh that he thought about every day and dreamt about every night. He turned around, and there she was, looking as beautiful as ever, in a short white dress with white sandals. Her legs looked perfectly tanned against the delicate cotton, and her eyes shone with happiness as she looked at her boyfriend. Marcus felt a stab of jealousy as he watched them together, wishing he could be the one by her side, sharing jokes, laughter and kisses. He could only see the back of David, as he took Helen into his arms to present her with a long, gentle kiss, and afterwards he held her close as she rested her head on his shoulder. It was at this point that Helen saw Marcus looking over, the gentle breeze blowing his hair as he nodded his head slightly and smiled, revealing the slight creases at the side of his eyes that Helen thought was so damn attractive. Their eyes locked for a second and, still embraced in David's arms, she raised her hand slightly to wave and smile back.

'Come on then, let's get you this coffee.' David interrupted the moment, and taking her hand they walked in the direction that Marcus was just standing up to leave himself.

'Hi, Helen' he said pretending that he had only just noticed her.

'Hello, Marcus,' she smiled shyly. 'This is my boyfriend,

David.' The two men shook hands and exchanged a few words, before heading off in their separate directions, Helen aware that Marcus would have turned around to look once more but knowing she couldn't do the same.

'He seems OK,' David said.

'He seems it,' Helen agreed, 'but then I don't really know him, he's only just started with us,' she lied, as they walked along the waterside. David listened as Helen told him about the placement she was about to start, a conversation that lasted the entire walk back to his bedsit much to his amusement; he loved listening to Helen talk.

She kicked off her sandals and put her feet onto the arm of his sofa, as David prepared her a steaming mug of coffee.

'Make yourself at home,' he laughed, and Helen grinned at him cheekily.

'Thanks,' she said, blowing him a kiss.

'I'd rather have a real one of those,' he said, coming towards her. Helen sat up and stretched out her arms.

'Come here then, gorgeous,' she said, giving him several soft pecks on the lips. Resting her head on his shoulder, she sighed with content. She'd had a lovely evening, and felt sad it was coming to an end. She closed her eyes and snuggled in close to him. David had such strong arms, and she felt secure when she was in them. As he kissed her head she held him tightly and then, without any reasoning, she pictured Marcus in her head, visualizing the way he had been looking at her earlier. She pictured the creases of his eyes as he smiled, the soft breeze gently ruffling his hair. Her heart was beating frantically. What the hell was she thinking? He was old enough to be her father, yet there was something about him that made her shudder with desire to taste his lips against hers. She thought back to the moment at the castle where their lips had almost met, and wondered how it would have felt if they had.

Eyes still closed, she felt David's lips gently kiss her nose, and, still thinking of the moment in the castle, she tipped her head back as if she had been transported back to that moment. Keeping her eyes firmly shut so she could keep the image of Marcus in her head, she pulled David towards her and pressed her lips against his, kissing him gently at first, then hungrily, embracing him as she had never done before, exploring every part of his mouth with her tongue. David trembled with desire.

'Oh God Helen, you are so damn sexy,' he groaned, as she nibbled on his ear. The sound of his voice bought Helen back to her senses and she pulled away guiltily, tears prickling her eyes. 'What's up?' David asked, not able to hide the disappointment in his voice. Helen shook her head apologetically.

'I'm sorry, I just got a sudden pain in my head,' she lied, taken aback by the fantasy she had just had.

'Well I know a good cure for a headache,' David purred as he gently pushed her back down onto the sofa. Helen tried to dismiss her previous thoughts and as a tear trickled down her cheek, David made love to her, oblivious to the fact that Helens enthusiasm from a few minutes previous seemed to have dwindled.

Helen enjoyed the first day of her placement, even though they didn't go on any visits. Charlotte had taken Helen to meet some of the doctors at surrounding surgeries, as the team were not attached to a surgery, but were all based in a large office shared by case managers, general nurses and rehabilitation nurses. They all seemed a nice crowd, and Helen had been made to feel welcome from the moment she walked into the building. She was especially pleased to find another student there called Karen, who she recognised from the university. Karen was into the last part of her final management placement, and had her own small caseload of ten patients, with varying complaints. Karen had chatted enthusiastically to Helen over lunch, and explained that she too had done her first community placement with the team, and had been thrilled when she got to return for her final stretch of twelve weeks before qualifying as a nurse. She had secretly told Helen that she was hoping to apply for a job in the team, as one of the nurses was going to be handing in her notice so she could move away to Manchester to live near her boyfriend.

Charlotte had gone through all of the outcomes and action plans that Helen wanted to achieve, and had acknowledged her love for palliative care, stating she would get a lot of experience in this area, as they had several patients who were approaching end of life. Charlotte also said that she would arrange some insight visits for Helen with the Macmillan nurses, and at the hospice inpatient unit, as well as possibly spending a day with the Hospice At Home team. Helen felt very excited for the next few weeks, and hoped that the days wouldn't all go as quick as her first.

Helen was finished earlier than she thought, so she decided to surprise David by going to pick him up from work. As it was only a short distance from his bedsit, he tended to walk most days, if the weather was fine. She pulled up into the car park and caught sight of him changing the tyre of a flashy sports car. He was dressed in a pair of oily overalls that he had taken his arms out of and tied around his waist. His previously white t-shirt was now patterned with oily prints, where he had wiped his hands and Helen chuckled to herself at how dirty he got from changing tyres. Still sitting unnoticed in her car, Helen glanced over to see the owner of the flashy car casting admiring glances David's way. She was a leggy, busty brunette, wearing a skirt so short, Helen could almost see her underwear.

'How can you drive in those?' Helen muttered to herself as she caught sight of the black killer heels that would land Helen straight on her bottom if she even attempted to stand up in them. In the background, two of David's colleagues were eyeing her up, and Helen could literally see them undressing her with their eyes, almost salivating at the vision of this brazen beauty that was clearly aware of her admirers. She sat twiddling her hair around her fingers as she took a sip from the plastic cup of complimentary coffee, still with her eyes fixed on David. Helen smiled as she looked over at David who was oblivious of all of this, as he tightened the last bolts on the wheel, before yet again wiping his hands on his t-shirt.

Helen waited for the brunette to drive away before she got out of her car, feeling frumpy in her light blue tunic and navy trousers that was the standard student nurse uniform. Regardless to how unflattering she felt that she looked, the two lurches still wolf-whistled as she walked towards the building.

'Oi! Eyes off, she's all mine,' David jokingly chastised as he turned to see her. 'This is a pleasant surprise,' he said, kissing her on the cheek, careful not to dirty her clothes. 'You look ravishing,' he murmured quietly in her ear.

'I thought I would give you a lift home. I'm out with Michelle and Amy tonight for tea, so I won't get to see you otherwise'. Helen had forgotten her date with her friends until she had received a text earlier in the day from Amy, saying they were meeting in the restaurant at seven. Looking at his watch, David turned to his colleagues.

'Is it OK if I go now? It's almost five,' he called.

'Yeah, we'll lock up. You go ahead,' said Mike, the older of the two. At twenty-five he still lived with his parents, and never seemed to have a girlfriend. David often wondered if he was gay, but after the way he had been ogling the girl earlier, Helen had her doubts.

Helen had a quick drink with David as she told him about her first day, and the plans she had for the placement. He took her hand and squeezed it gently.

'Are you sure you'll cope looking after people with cancer?' He asked gently. 'You know, after what happened with your dad…' Helen nodded sadly.

'It's dad's death that made me want to do this,' she said. 'I want to be able to make a difference to people, just as the nurses did for us.' David pulled her towards him, and gave her a tight hug.

'I'm so proud of you, Helen Mitchell,' he said and Helen knew that he meant it. She kissed him softly on the cheek.

'I had better go and get ready to meet the girls,' she said, standing up to leave. David stood up to see her out.

'Thanks for the lift,' he said gratefully. 'Say 'hi' to Michelle and Amy for me.' He stayed stood at the door to wave at her as she drove past, then went inside to decide what to do with his evening.

Helen didn't have time for a bath, so she had a quick shower, scooped her hair into a bun and dressed casually in tight fitted jeans and a jumper, complimented by a long silver necklace. Slipping on some grey suede ankle boots, she joined Katherine briefly for a cup of tea, then headed off to the restaurant to meet her friends. They often went to the same one, as there were unlimited soft drinks with a meal, and Monday's was student night where they got two courses for the price of one. Tammy and Jo-Jo were also there. They said hello as they walked past, but didn't have any further conversation, as it seemed apparent that the two were in the middle of some harsh words.

'I don't know why those two stay together. They are always falling out' Amy chuntered as she piled pasta salad onto her plate. Helen and Michelle looked at each other and smiled.

'So how is your love life?' Helen asked her with a grin.

'Don't even go there,' Amy sighed. 'I'm having a break from men for a while. They are all only after one thing, and its 'wham bam, thank you, ma'am.' Michelle raised her eyebrows.

'Well maybe if you didn't give it to them on the first date, they might not all be like that,' she said, winking at her friend.

'Well at least I'm not like you two, stuck with the same guy month after month. How mundane is that?' She patted her open mouth, pretending to yawn.

'Well I wouldn't swap Phillip for the world,' Michelle said, smiling. 'OK, it may be a long distance thing, but it is great when we are together, and we make up for lost time.' By now they were sat at the table with their food.

'Ah, but how do you know what he's doing when you're not around?' Amy taunted, as Helen cast her a glance implying for her to shut up. Michelle paused, fork in mid-air.

'What do you mean by that?' She quizzed. 'Are you saying I shouldn't trust him?' Helen kicked Amy under the table. They'd been together when they had seen Phillip kissing another girl in the club, and had decided between them to say nothing.

'Don't be daft,' Amy laughed. 'I'm winding you up.'

Helen quickly changed the conversation to their placements. They were all in the community; Amy was based in a surgery, and Michelle, like Helen, was in a big team, based in Skegness, which hadn't impressed her. She had to travel quite a way each morning. Amy, being Amy, thought it was going to be boring, but then again she was obsessed with Casualty and Holby City, and dreamed of a job in an A&E department. Michelle, on the other hand, wanted to work in theatres and was looking forward to a placement there after the summer holidays, which was for four weeks following their current placement.

'Shall we pop next door for a quick drink?' Amy suggested. She lived near the town so could enjoy a drink. 'You two can drink and stay at mine if you want' she offered.

'I'll come for a drink, but I can't stay as my uniform is at home,' Helen said, and Michelle was in agreement.

The bar was surprisingly busy for a Monday evening, but then again it was mostly students from the college and university, enjoying the offers that were promoted to them: two for one beers, or pitchers of a cocktail for a fiver. Michelle and Helen opted for soft drinks, and they shook their heads in disbelief as Amy bought a pitcher of blue lagoon to consume all on her own. Popping a single straw into the jug, she asked Helen to take a photo with her phone, and promptly put it on Facebook with the word 'yummy' underneath. Within a minute, she had received three likes and a comment from Mel on the course calling her a piss-head, which four people liked. Amy was renowned, not only for her relationships, but also for her drinking. Not that she was an alcoholic, but she proclaimed that she could drink any man under the table.

'Is that your ex, Steve, over there?' Michelle pointed towards someone playing on the fruit machine, clutching a pint of beer. Amy glanced over to where she was pointing and smiled.

'Mmm, he still looks fit.' She hiccupped, draining her jug, ensuring she sucked every last bit through the straw. 'I think I'll go and say hello.' She winked as Helen and Michelle made their way to the bathroom, laughing as their friend sauntered across the bar.

'She'll feel this in the morning when she gets up for work.' Helen shook her head.

'Knowing Amy she'll phone in sick,' Michelle said. 'She did that last time, and then got in trouble because she had put pictures all over Facebook, like she has tonight.' They stood chatting in the bathroom as they reapplied their lipstick. Michelle told Helen about a two-week holiday to Ibiza she and Phil had planned for the summer. David and Helen weren't going away, as neither could afford it, but they were hoping to have a few days out, and one weekend they were going with Beth, Steve, and Katherine for a picnic in Clumber Park.

'I suppose we better go and find Amy,' Helen said, holding the door open for Michelle. Walking back into the bar, they looked around to the fruit machine, where she had been heading when they went to the toilet. A geeky looking man with big glasses stood watching the wheels spin, until they reached a halt and he punched the air with his fist as coins pumped out, much to the delight of his equally geeky friend.

'Well that is definitely not Steve.' Helen laughed at the excited performance that they were watching.

'Where on Earth is she?' Michelle said, looking around the room. 'I can't see her anywhere.' They stood in the middle of the room looking around for their friend.

'Let's look around there,' Helen suggested, walking towards an area behind the fruit machine, which couldn't be seen from where they stood. As they approached the partitioned area, they stopped dead in their tracks; there, on the large brown leather sofa, Amy was in a passionate clinch with Steve, her legs wrapped around his waist and her hands tugging at his hair. He was almost on top of her, and his hand was slid under her skirt, caressing her thigh, red knickers on show to all.

'Amy!' Helen gasped, as Michelle stood with her mouth open, stunned at what they were doing, an audience around them taking pictures on their phones. One guy was even filming it. Amy looked over to her friends as Steve continued to nuzzle her neck.

'Hey you two, I'll catch up with you later in the week. Steve is going to stop at mine tonight,' she said, with a thumbs up behind her back. The two girls turned away, shaking their heads, and walking out into the cool evening air, they looked at each other and burst out laughing.

'That was a long break then,' Helen said, shaking her head, and they walked together to their cars, discussing Amy and her ever-worsening reputation, before bidding each other goodnight and promising to catch up again soon.

Chapter Nine

Helen was loving her placement, and she couldn't believe she was already half way through. She felt she'd learnt more on this placement than all of her others put together. Charlotte was proving to be an excellent mentor, helped by the fact that she loved having students. She spent an hour each afternoon with Helen, allowing her to reflect on the day, and encouraging her to put her thoughts into writing, as evidence for her portfolio, which all student nurses, as well as qualified nurses, have to produce. Helen was getting to see several patients regularly and was developing her skills with bandaging, injections, and had even performed her first catheterisation. With still three weeks left, Helen had already achieved the majority of the outcomes that were set for the placement. The experience was also enhancing her love for palliative care. She was involved in visiting three elderly patients, two with cancer and one with end-stage heart failure, and luckily she was coping well. She had spent a day with a Macmillan nurse called Trish, who taught her about different medications used in pain control. Unfortunately, Hospice At Home already had a student with them, so couldn't take Helen, but a visit was arranged for the following day at the inpatient unit.

Helen sat happily at the kitchen table, looking around at her family. Katherine had prepared a lovely meal of Hawaiian gammon, spicy wedges and garlic bread and it had been enjoyed by all. Beth and Steve were there, as was David, who Helen hadn't seen for a few days, due to being busy with coursework.

'Is it this week you get your results?' Beth asked her sister. Helen bit her knuckles jokingly. She hated getting assignment results, and always managed to convince herself she would fail.

'Tomorrow,' she replied.

'You will do fine, as you always do,' David reassured her, and squeezed her knee lovingly under the table. The others nodded in agreement.

'She gets her brains from her father, not me,' Katherine said, smiling proudly.

'Goodness, I'm not clever,' Helen gasped. 'It takes a lot of hard work for me to pass, and I never get brilliant grades.' Beth helped herself to another glass of wine and topped up Helens glass.

'At least you pass, and at the end of the day, that's all that matters. You don't need to be academic to be a great nurse,' Beth said.

'Here, here,' David agreed, raising his glass, and they all followed suit and clinked their glasses together.

Several games of cards followed, before Beth and Steve announced that they had to go. Katherine yawned and looked at the clock, agreeing that she was also planning to retire. David helped pack away the cards and ran the tap to rinse the glasses.

'Are you ready for bed, or shall we go for a stroll?' He asked Helen.

'No, I'd like that,' she smiled, as she pushed the chairs back under the table. Kissing Katherine goodnight, they walked out with Beth and Steve and continued to walk with them a while, before cutting through an alley to the park.

Hand in hand, they walked silently, breathing in the scent of the evening air. Stars twinkled in the sky and the moon was bright enough to light up the path, along with the few scattered lampposts. The park seemed deserted, apart from someone in the distance walking his dog.

'Let's sit by the lake,' David suggested, walking towards a bench strategically placed at the water's edge. Helen smiled as she sat down beside him.

'It is nice to see you,' she said. 'I'm sorry I'm so busy at the minute.' David rested his arm across her shoulder.

'It won't be forever,' he said, as he kissed her on the cheek. Helen felt very lucky to have David; he was so understanding and supportive.

They sat for quite a while, sharing occasional kisses but mainly enjoying each other's company, even though a lot of the time was spent sitting in silence, looking at the water, Helens head resting on his shoulder.

'I suppose I had better walk you home.' David interrupted the silence. 'You need to be at the hospice for seven, and its gone eleven now.' He stood up and held out his hand to Helen, who promptly followed. She put her arms around his neck and gently pulled his face towards hers. Standing slightly on tiptoes, she pulled herself close to him and gave him a long, lingering kiss, so intense that they both felt butterflies inside. David wrapped his arms around her waist, and he felt her skin erupt with goose pimples as he traced his finger gently across the flesh of her back.

'I wish we were somewhere else,' she whispered seductively, as she traced his lips with her tongue. She could feel his trousers tightening around his crotch and pressing against her, and she teased him by rubbing the area provocatively. 'How about tomorrow night I stop at yours?' She suggested.

'That sounds like a great idea,' David agreed, allowing his finger to wander below her waistband to feel a satin thong; he suggested she wear something similar the following evening.

Walking back home, they planned an early start, as Helens shift finished at two-thirty and, once a month, David finished at lunchtime on a Friday, which, luckily, was tomorrow. Helen planned to pick up her results then drive to David's, where she would get changed. They decided to go to the cinema to see the new horror film, 'The Pact' that was being advertised and was receiving excellent reviews. They would then pick up a pizza to share back at David's place with a bottle of wine. Neither of them could wait. Kissing goodnight, David didn't come inside, as it was late and she waved as he drove off into the night.

Helen was not tired enough to go to bed so she made herself a cup of hot chocolate, changed into a pair of nylon pyjamas and sat at her desk, logging into Facebook. There were several pictures of Amy and Steve drunk but obviously a couple, although Amy's relationship status still said single. Beth had put a status that she'd had a lovely evening with her family, which Helen liked, before writing a status of her own;

'*Good luck with the assignment results tomorrow, everyone!*'

She continued scrolling through the newsfeed, laughing to herself at the ridiculous things that people write for all and sundry to see, stopping at one particular statement.

'*Tom Boland is now friends with Marcus Edwards*'

Tom was in her class, and although she was friends with him on Facebook, she barely spoke to him when they were in lessons, probably because he was good friends with Adam, and Helen wasn't keen on him. Hovering the curser over the name Marcus Edwards, she clicked on it and a picture appeared on the screen of Marcus, dressed as a cowboy. Helen laughed as she clicked on the 'request friend' box, before rapidly wishing she hadn't.

Sat in his front room, with 'The Kaiser Chiefs' playing in the background, Marcus sat at his computer, chatting via Facebook messenger to an old school friend. Suddenly, the computer pinged to alert him that he had received a friend request. He clicked on the alert, curious as to who it was from, and his stomach lurched when he saw it was Helen. Immediately, he accepted the request and, sitting back in his chair, Marcus wondered if she was alone, debating to himself whether or not to message her.

What are you doing up at this time? He typed, and then hesitated before sending it. He wondered if she would reply, or if she would even get the message, as he resumed his conversation with his friend, who was bidding him goodnight.

Getting up to fetch a drink from the kitchen, Marcus was keen to view Helen's profile and see any pictures she had on there. He poured himself a glass of milk and took a biscuit from the tin. It seemed ages since he had seen Helen, although it had actually only been a few weeks. He had thought about her on more than one occasion. A message alert sounded from the other room, and Marcus rushed in to see if it was from Helen. He smiled to himself as he saw her name.

Nervous about getting assignment results tomorrow, she had replied and Marcus reassured her that she would be fine. After all, he had marked it, so he should know. They chatted for over an hour, before Helen declared that she had an early start and would be up in a few hours to go to work. Marcus couldn't believe it was almost two o'clock in the morning; he would also be up in a few hours. They bid each other goodnight, and Helen said she would possibly see him at uni when she collected her results. Although Marcus didn't say it, he secretly hoped that she would. Before he went to bed, he couldn't resist looking at some of Helen's photographs, just to remind himself how beautiful she was.

The morning came far too soon for Helen, and she found it quite a struggle to get out of bed, depending on a shower and a strong coffee before she felt fully awake. The traffic was quiet, so it didn't take her long to reach the hospice. The weather was warm, and she was looking forward to her day ahead as well as the evening she had planned with David.

Once again, she was made to feel welcome by the other nurses that were there for the early shift, and she sat listening intently at the handover from the night staff. There were only ten patients in the unit at present, all there for symptom control, except a man of only forty, who was very unwell. Brian Thompson had initially been admitted for pain, and the plan had been to review his medication, get his pain under control and then discharge him home to his wife and two sons. Sadly, he had deteriorated over the last two days, and was fast approaching end of life, choosing to stay in the hospice so that his boys wouldn't have to see him die in their home. Helen was allocated to work with Sophie, who had been qualified five years, and had worked at the hospice for the past eighteen months. She loved her job and enthusiastically told Helen about the rewards of working in a hospice. Sophie was going to work in the green bay today, which was occupied by four ladies, as well as side room one where Brian was semi-comatose, being administered drugs through a syringe driver to control his pain. They helped the four ladies get washed and dressed, and Helen was amazed at the strength and determination that the women had, chatting freely about their cancers and treatments they'd had or were having. Helen listened tentatively, asking questions that she felt were appropriate, and listening to their various stories.

'OK, let's go and wash Brian,' Sophie said, when Helen had finished talking. Helen washed her hands at the sink and put on a clean apron. She followed Sophie into the side room, only catching sight of Brian as she reached the edge of the bed. She bit her lip as she stared at him; he was so young, and so thin. She gulped as she saw a photograph on the bedside cabinet of his family, Brian now a shadow of the man in the picture. Helen inhaled deeply, trying to compose herself, and trying desperately not to think of her own father and the pain the family would be going through.

'Are you alright, Helen?' Sophie said soothingly. 'Would you like me to get someone else to help me?' Helen silently shook her head and, picking up the bowl from the cabinet, started to fill it with warm water, checking the temperature with her hand as she wet the flannel. Sophie washed his hands and face and Helen gently patted them dry with the towel, as she admiringly listened to Sophie talk to him; she seemed such a lovely nurse. They changed his pyjama top, carefully threading the syringe driver through the sleeve before checking that the machine was working effectively. By now, Helen had relaxed and was enjoying the moment, doing what she had spent years wanting to do.

Helen sat with Sophie at lunch, apologising about how she had reacted and explaining about her dad. Sophie listened sympathetically, and reassured Helen that it gets easier the longer you do the job, but added that it is still sad, especially with patients that you have gotten to know over a period of time. Sophie admitted that she was struggling with Brian, as she had seen him with his wife and children, and she told Helen honestly that she often chilled with a glass of wine at the end of the day. Their conversation was interrupted with a knock at the door, and the auxiliary nurse, Becky, poked her head around.

'Just to let you know, Sophie, that Dr. White has called in Brian's family. His breathing has become very laboured. She is taking the children to her sisters then she will be here,' she told them solemnly.

'OK, I'm on my way,' Sophie said, putting a half-eaten sandwich back into her lunch box and replacing the lid. 'Stay and finish your lunch,' she told Helen, but Helen shook her head, stating that she would help.

Brian looked very peaceful as his wife, Jessica, lay on the bed beside him, stroking his face and telling him she loved him, as he took his last breath. Afterwards, his wife clung to him and sobbed, and Helen noticed a tear fall onto Sophie's cheek as she said that they would leave her alone with her husband to say her goodbyes. Sadly and silently, Sophie lit a candle on the side; a tribute to a life that has ended, a warm gesture that Helen thought was very touching, and she too shed a few tears to the sound of a bereaved widow expressing her grief. It was a solemn moment in the hospice, with the nurses walking around, silently handing cups of tea to the remaining patients, who sat with magazines, trying to ignore the sound of the crying from the side room, all conscious that soon it would be their own family overcome with grief.

Despite the events of the day, Helen had still enjoyed it, and knew that palliative care was an immensely rewarding part of nursing. She wished that she had arranged more than one day at the hospice, and Sophie suggested that she speak to her mentor about organizing another. She kindly gave her a copy of the dates that she was working so that they could work together again. Helen thanked them all, and bid farewell to the patients she had been involved with, then set off to uni to collect her results.

Helen didn't see anyone from her group when she arrived, and began to wonder if she had gone on the right day. She had forgotten that she had worked an early shift, whilst everyone else would probably work until four or five in the community. Heading towards the office where the envelopes would be placed in a pigeon-hole for her group, Helen felt nauseous with worry, as she always did when she received assignment results. Finding the brown envelope with her name written on the front, she put it into her pocket and walked straight to the toilets to open them alone. Gingerly, she pulled the papers from the envelope with her eyes screwed shut. Scared to look, she glanced down and smiled. The smoking cessation report had been rewarded a C grade, and Helen was pleased with this considering how quickly she had written it. Turning the page, she whooped out loud when she saw that she had been given an A grade for her assignment on euthanasia. Her first A! Helen was over the moon and, grabbing her phone from her bag, she texted David, Katherine and Beth to tell them her good news.

She put the envelope into her bag and walked out of the toilets.

'I guess you opened your results.' Marcus was walking towards her, smiling, and Helen smiled back.

'Thank you so much,' she beamed.

'You did all the hard work, Helen. I just had to mark it,' he complimented. 'Your work on euthanasia was fantastic. It kept me gripped from start to finish, and I mean that.' Helen felt herself blush. 'How is the placement going?' Marcus asked, and she proceeded to tell him all about it. Marcus could tell how enthusiastic Helen was, and he knew that she would make an amazing nurse when she qualified; she had a lovely nature.

'I went to the hospice today,' she told him, and a sadness came over her face.

'Come on, let's get the kettle on,' Marcus said, gently touching her arm and Helen followed him to his office.

The kettle seemed loud as Helen sat in silence trying to compose herself. She couldn't understand what had come over her, but the events of the day suddenly hit her and she thought of her dad.

'Are you OK?' Marcus asking in a soothing voice and, eyes filling with tears, Helen stood up to leave, feeling too embarrassed to cry.

'I have to go,' she began, and her voice cracked. Marcus hastily walked towards her and grabbed both of her arms with his firm hands, turning her towards him as he held her head whilst she sobbed into his shoulder. He pulled a handkerchief out of his pocket and handed it to her.

'Here, it's clean,' he said, as she took it from him gratefully and wiped her tears.

She had stopped crying now, but she didn't pull away just yet. She felt comfort in Marcus's arms. He held her tightly, not wanting her to pull away. They stood holding each other for several minutes, not saying anything and both having their own individual thoughts, both enjoying the moment, both inhaling the scent of the other. Helen could feel her heart thumping. Well, she thought it was her heart but then again, Marcus would have argued that it was his own. He lifted his hand and softly stroked the back of her hair; it felt like silk slipping between his fingers as he tucked some stray strands behind her ear. He then gently touched her cheek with the back of his fingers, and using his thumb, he tilted her head towards him and softly kissed her on her forehead. Helen tingled all over, as he kissed her gently on the tip of her nose.

'We can't,' she protested, as she willingly manoeuvred her lips towards his.

Helen had the softest lips he had ever kissed, it was a very brief kiss, and their lips brushed against each other's for a short moment, paused in the moment they looked at each other, confusion in their eyes, anticipating the next movement. They held each other's gaze for what seemed like an eternity, lips touching slightly, hearts beating rapidly, and arms tightly around each other. It was Helen who pulled away first, putting her fingers to her lips, which were tingling with desire.

'I'm sorry Marcus,' she said, as she rushed out of his office, closing the door behind her. Marcus sat down in his chair. He knew what had just happened was very, very wrong, yet he couldn't help but smile to himself. She had aroused feelings in him that he never thought were possible. Picking up a pen and notebook, he looked at his timetable and began making notes for his next lesson.

Chapter Ten

Tears were flowing down Helen's cheeks as she drove the short distance to David's place, and she felt nothing but shame about what had just happened. She tried to convince herself that nothing had happened, because although their lips had met, they hadn't actually kissed. She found it harder to convince herself that she wouldn't have actually kissed Marcus if he had tried before she pulled away. Parking in the small car park behind David's bedsit, she examined herself in the visor mirror and wiped away the smudged mascara that had smeared underneath her eyes. Reaching into her overnight bag, she pulled out her make-up and reapplied her eyeliner, after dabbing on a few dots of foundation to disguise the fact that she had been upset.

She took a few deep breaths before she knocked on the door, and walked in to see David stood there smiling, with a bottle of champagne, popping the cork as she walked into the room.

'Congratulations, baby! I knew you would do it,' he said, as he tried to catch the bubbles into a glass. Helen could hear the liquid fizzing from where she stood. Gratefully accepting the drink, she swallowed it down in one go, feeling pleasure as it slid down her throat. 'Bad day then?' David laughed, as he poured her another glass whilst kissing her on her cheek.

'No, it's been good,' Helen smiled, throwing her bag onto the sofa. 'I'm looking forward to the film,' she said, as she gave him a tight squeeze. 'Could I have a quick shower first and freshen up?' She asked.

'Of course,' David nodded. 'I'll get you a fresh towel out, and make sure you shout if you need me to rub your back,' he winked.

The bathroom was filled with steam as Helen slid out of her uniform and into the shower. She tipped her head back to wash her hair, the warmth of the water soothing against her skin. She felt slightly tipsy from the champagne and the heat intensified this feeling. She washed her hair, and then lathered soap onto a flannel to wash her body, smiling to herself as she heard the click of the door. She could see the silhouette of David undressing through the glass screen

'You must have read my mind,' she purred, as he climbed into the shower with her.

David gasped as Helen pulled him towards her and kissed him passionately, her pert breasts pressing against his chest. Their hands slipped over each other's bodies, made easy by the lather of the soap. Helen bit into David's shoulder as he grasped her buttocks and lifted her up against the glass screen, slipping inside her as she wrapped her legs around his waist. She reached up to hold onto the shower screen, as it shook with the pressure of her buttocks against it.

'Oh God,' Helen murmured, as she could feel herself quickly reaching the height of pleasure as David thrust inside her frantically, until he groaned loudly and started to shudder as they both climaxed together. They kissed passionately as David released his grip.

'That was amazing,' he said caressing her breasts as he nuzzled her neck.

'Mmm, it was,' Helen agreed. 'And that was only the matinee. I'm sure there will be an evening performance to match,' she said, winking, as she turned off the shower, and David kissed her, smiling at her wonderful plan.

They managed to finish the bottle of champagne as they talked about their day and got ready to go to the cinema, which was only a short walk from where David lived. Buying a large popcorn and drink to share, they opted for seats at the back of the cinema, and they were surprised to see only a handful of people in seats when they walked in. The trailers were already playing as they took their seats and Helen chuckled as David jumped and spilt some popcorn as a loud bang erupted from the screen during the advert for another new horror film ready to be released.

'I think if we come and see that one, I should hold the popcorn,' Helen laughed.

They enjoyed the film and found it very jumpy. Both being horror fans, they often would rent a film, or if they were on offer, they'd buy some ex rentals that were often cheaper than hiring them. Watching them on the television, though, was not quite the same as watching them on the big screen, so once in a while they would treat themselves to the cinema. However, much like tonight, they spent a lot of the time smooching on the back row like a couple of school children.

'I'm starving now,' David said, as the lights came on and the credits started to roll.

'Me too,' said Helen, patting her stomach. 'Let's grab a pizza and go back to yours, maybe watch another film... We haven't got to get up in the morning.'

'Sounds like a plan,' David smiled, putting his arm around her shoulders. 'Plus, I have another bottle of wine in the fridge; not champagne though.' Helen smiled.

'Perfect,' she said.

The pizza house was busier than the cinema had been, and although it was only nine-thirty, there were several people in there already drunk. They joined the queue and watched in amusement as a man of about fifty propped himself up against the wall, whilst unsuccessfully trying to get a fork full of chips and cheese to his mouth. After stabbing himself in the chin, and then his nose, he managed to direct the food into his mouth, burping as he did.

'Urgh, gross!' Helen whispered to David, as she grimaced and turned away to look out of the window. 'Isn't that Mike?' She nodded towards the other side of the road, as David's work mate spotted them and waved. He was dressed smartly and was linking arms with a girl who looked young enough to be at school.

'That's blown your theory of him being gay,' Helen said discreetly as they waved back.

'Oh God, he's coming over.' David rolled his eyes; his friend was crossing the road, dodging the cars with the young girl in tow.

'Now then, buddy,' he said as he shook David's hand. 'Do you two fancy a few drinks?' David looked at Helen, seeing her lack of enthusiasm.

'Maybe another time, mate. We're just grabbing our tea then heading home,' David said.

'OK, bud. No worries,' Mike said, without argument. 'This is Shelly, by the way.' Helen and David greeted her politely, and then bid them farewell as they left.

'She only looks about twelve,' Helen gasped, and David agreed, shaking his head as he walked towards the counter to order their food.

'Let's just eat out of the box,' Helen said as they got back to the bedsit. 'Saves on washing up.' David took the wine from the fridge, and using the glasses they had had their champagne in, he poured them both a drink. Sitting with their feet on the coffee table, they ate their pizza and chatted about the film they had just seen. Helen told David about Amy, who was still seeing Steve, and had texted her the previous day to say that he was the one. David laughed.

'How many times has she said that?' He chuckled.

'That girl has been in love more times than anyone else I know,' Helen agreed, as she took a large gulp of wine. 'I love her to bits, but she is a nightmare,' Helen said, shaking her head as she unbuttoned her jeans. 'I'm stuffed,' she said, releasing the zip before exhaling contentedly. David couldn't help but look at the red satin of her underwear, which was just visible through the open zip, and the silky skin that was revealed above the waist of her jeans.

'What film shall we watch?' Helen said, pulling out the drawer of the coffee table, which housed their small collection of DVD's.

'I don't mind. You pick whilst I nip to the loo and get rid of the rubbish,' David said, as he flattened the pizza boxes down ready to take them to the bin outside. Helen fingered through the cases and pulled out a thriller that they had bought a few weeks ago and not yet watched. Pouring another glass of wine for them both, she rested her head back on the sofa and pulled her phone from her pocket. She clicked onto Facebook to see if there were any amusing, drunken comments. She noticed that she had a message in her inbox and she curiously clicked on it to see who it was from. She gulped as she saw it was from Marcus, her heart racing as she read his words;

I can't stop thinking about you, it is driving me insane ☹. Her hands were shaking as she considered her reply; what the hell should she put to that? Admittedly, she had been thinking about him a lot, but she was with David and David loved her. Despite that, Marcus was her tutor and about twice her age. Helens head was in turmoil, not knowing whether to reply and if she did, what to say? Hearing David flush the chain she decided not to reply, and clicked the delete button to erase the message from her phone. Logging off of Facebook, she proceeded to put the DVD in the player.

'Are you OK sweetheart? You look as white as a ghost,' David commented, concerned as he sat back down beside her.

'I couldn't be better,' she replied, holding out her arms to give her man a tight squeeze. 'I'm having a wonderful evening.' Helen kissed David on the cheek, and closing her eyes, she buried her head into his shoulder, her heart still racing at the words she had just read. She was cursing herself for what had happened earlier. It was a moment of madness. She had been upset, yet she had liked the feel of Marcus's embrace and deep down she knew she had wanted him to kiss her, just to see what it was like. She trembled at the thought, desperately wanting to get the feelings out of her head.

'Let's put the film on then,' she said, pulling away from David and pressing play. She snuggled into him as the film progressed, but she knew she was not concentrating on it, the words of the email going round and round her head. She couldn't stop thinking about him. What on Earth was he doing to her?

Focussing on the television screen, Helen tried to take in what was happening in the film. David was certainly enjoying it and was oblivious to the torment that was going on in his girlfriend's head. Helen sat up and took a sip of her wine, and handing David his glass, she watched him take a drink, eyes still on the screen. She excused herself, and headed to the bathroom, sitting on the toilet and taking her phone out. She clicked back onto Facebook, and going into her friend list she found Marcus Edwards and loaded his profile. Helen thought he looked gorgeous on his picture, but pushing any thoughts to the back of her mind, she clicked on send message and typed;

I'm sorry but I have a boyfriend. Please forget about me. Hovering over the send button, she paused for a while and then, instead of pressing send, she pressed delete; she didn't want him to forget about her. Looking at his photo again, she logged out of Facebook and put the phone back in her pocket.

David was still engrossed in the film when Helen came back into the room. The wine had gone to her head, and she was swaying slightly. Pressing pause on the remote, Helen got his attention as she slowly pulled her jumper over her head and hutched her jeans down, revealing her sexy red lingerie. David grinned as she held his hands, preventing him from removing his own clothes, teasing him with a seductive lap dance. She traced her tongue gently around his ear, and smiled as he groaned quietly. She knew that he was turned on. Helen pictured Marcus as she allowed David's hand to touch her skin; she imagined they were in his office as they had been earlier, but this time she didn't pull away. The thought of Marcus kissing her flesh made Helen feel wild with passion, and pulling down David's jeans only a small amount, she sat on him and made love to him like she never had before.

'Wow! What came over you, you little minx?' David said afterwards. 'That was so God damn sexy.' Helen smiled as she picked up her clothes. She felt terrible that she had imagined that David was Marcus, and had no idea what had come over her. She said nothing as she put on her fluffy pyjamas and snuggled back up to him on the sofa. David sighed contentedly and continued to watch the end of the film as Helen dozed, breathing gently as she rested her head on his shoulder. Stroking her cheek gently, he kissed the top of her head as she fell into a sleep. It was a troubled sleep, as Helen dreamt about David and Marcus dressed as cowboys, having a duel to decide who will have her heart.

Chapter Eleven

It was early when Helen woke up next to David. She couldn't remember actually going to bed, and wondered if he had carried her there. She looked at David, who was snoring gently, with the back of his hand resting against his forehead. Getting out of bed as quietly as she could, she went into the kitchen and flicked on the kettle. Walking over to the window, she looked down at the people walking down the road, whether it was to go to work or into town. She was surprised at how many people were up and about so early. It looked as if it was going to be a warm day and Helen was pleased. She didn't like it when it was cold. She tiptoed into the bathroom to freshen up. Looking in the mirror she thought that she looked tired. She splashed her face with water, and wetting her hands, she brushed her fingers through her hair until it fell tousled around her face. Having no plans for the day, Helen only applied minimal make-up, consisting of mascara and a dusky pink lipstick, which matched exactly the pink on her blouse.

As she poured steaming water into the two cups she had set aside to make coffee, David murmured and stretched his arms above his head.

'What time is it?' He asked, yawning and rubbing his eyes. Helen walked over and handed him his coffee.

'It's only half past eight,' she smiled.

'What are you doing up this early, Helen? It's a Saturday!' He exclaimed. Helen took a sip of her coffee, before answering that she couldn't get back to sleep.

'Do you fancy a walk into town in a bit?' She asked. 'I need to get myself a new notebook. I'm down to the last page now.' David stretched again and sat up in the bed to drink his coffee.

'Anything for you, my lovely,' he said with a grin.

It appeared to be busier than usual in town, and Helen and David seemed to bump into almost everyone they knew, Mike and the twelve year-old, Tammy and Jo-Jo, who were actually holding hands and smiling for a change. Amy and Steve were sat by the Brayford, looking all loved up over a bottle of wine. They invited David and Helen to join them, who politely declined – it was too early for them to start drinking. Amy told Helen that she had seen her sister Beth earlier with 'that fiancé of hers', and commented that they looked like they'd had a row. Amy had never taken to Beth's Steve and Helen had no idea why. She just assumed that there had been some past history with them, but chose not to ask about it.

After enjoying a Costa coffee, they went into a few more shops. David bought himself a T-shirt and treated Helen to some new shorts that she liked, which had an American flag design on one pocket and the union jack on another. The sun was shining brightly, and there was a pleasant atmosphere around the town. Everybody seemed to be smiling and laughing. David felt a tap on his shoulder, and turned around to see his friend Carl.

'Now then, stranger,' Carl said, with a playful punch to the arm. 'When are we having our next night out?' He winked at Helen.

'Well, I'm going in there,' Helen said, pointing to a stationery shop. 'I'll leave you boys to plan.'

There must have been a hundred different notebooks to choose from; fat ones and thin ones, A4 ones and A5 ones.

Helen wanted a pocket sized one, so that she could fit it into her uniform pocket and take notes whilst on placement. She spotted some that were ideal, and although they cost more than she had anticipated, she liked the look of them. There were about half a dozen different designs, and Helen opted for one with a picture of a puppy on it, which she thought was particularly cute. As she looked at the different books and pens, she suddenly had a sense of somebody watching her. She flushed crimson as she looked up and saw Marcus on the other side of the display, his brown eyes looking straight into her own.

'Hi,' he said casually. 'How are you?' Helen felt flustered. She had butterflies in her stomach as she bit her bottom lip.

'I'm really good thanks. How about you?' She replied quietly, diverting her eyes away from his as he walked round towards her.

'I'm better now,' he smiled, reaching for a pen and allowing his little finger to gently brush against her own. 'I need to see you,' he said in a hushed voice so no one could hear. 'I can't stop thinking about you, Helen.' He sounded desperate. Helens stomach lurched as she looked at him.

'I can't, Marcus. I'm sorry,' she said, walking away and shaking her head. Marcus followed her to the checkout, after picking up a book that he didn't even want.

'How about talking on-line tonight, even if it is just for five minutes... Please, Helen?' He pleaded. Just as she was about to answer, David walked into the shop towards them.

'Hey, babe. Carl wants to know if I can go for a few drinks tonight. Do you mind?' He asked.

'You don't have to ask me,' Helen said, as she kissed him on the cheek. 'You go and have a fun night.' She paid for her book, and as she left the shop, she discreetly looked back at Marcus and smiled. He knew that he would be able to talk to her later, or at least he hoped so.

91

After enjoying a pasty from the bakery, Helen and David walked back to his place for a coffee, before Helen drove home. They weren't going to see each other until after the weekend now, as Helen was spending the Sunday with Katherine and Beth, having a DVD day and a takeaway. She didn't have any plans for the evening, and she didn't really want to make any. She planned a chilling night, consisting of a hot bath, a glass of wine and relaxing in front of the TV with her mum. However, on arriving home, she walked into the kitchen to find Beth doing their mum's hair. Katherine smiled as Helen's face lit up upon seeing the shimmering blonde highlights cascading through her newly styled brown hair.

'Mum you look amazing,' she said, shocked at how much younger she looked. 'What's the occasion?' She asked, as Beth stood behind Katherine, grinning as she applied some finishing touches to her work.

'Mum has a date,' Beth answered, before Katherine could open her mouth. Helen was taken aback.

'A date?' She quizzed, and Katherine shook her head adamantly.

'It's not a date. It's just a few drinks with a friend from the book club,' she explained.

'Does this friend have a name?' Helen raised her eyebrows.

'It's George,' Beth answered again, excitedly. 'And it's not just a few drinks. You're going out for a meal.'

'No, I'm going out for tea, there's a difference,' Katherine proclaimed. Her daughters looked at each other and smiled. It had been over six years since their dad had died and Katherine hadn't so much as looked at another man, claiming that 'she would never find another soul mate, so there was no point looking'.

Both Beth and Helen agreed that Katherine looked lovely when she came downstairs, dressed in a simple black dress and some silver sandals. She looked nervous at the prospect of going out with a man, so Beth handed her a glass of wine to calm her nerves.

'It will be fine, mum. I promise,' she reassured her.

'What have you girls got planned?' She asked her daughters, in an attempt to change the subject. Beth told her that she and Steve were going bowling with some friends from work. She invited Helen when she discovered that she had no plans for the evening, but the offer was gratefully declined, with the excuse that she wanted an early night. Helen chose not to mention what Amy had said earlier, as Beth and Steve were obviously alright now.

Waving both her mum and sister off at the same time, Helen went upstairs to run a bath, pouring in a creamy bubble bath that smelt of honey. She went into her bedroom and selected a playlist on her iPod to listen to whilst she had a soak, and pulled out some fleecy pyjamas to wear afterwards. She texted David and wished him a good night in town, cheekily reminding him to behave himself, to which he responded that he only had eyes for her.

Sliding back into the hot, bubbly water, Helen sighed contentedly; she loved relaxing in the bath. Sipping a glass of wine, she listened to a whole playlist of eighteen songs, topping up with hot water when it started to cool. At the point that her fingertips began looking like shrivelled prunes, she decided to get out. It was already gone eight, much to her surprise. Helen put on her pyjamas and a fluffy robe and paddled downstairs in some gorilla shaped slippers that Michelle had bought her for Christmas. Topping up her wine glass, she went into the front room and turned on the television, flicking from one channel to another and finding nothing of interest before turning it back off. She considered phoning Michelle, before remembering that Amy had said Phil was over. She picked up a magazine and sifted through the pages, reading an article on dementia that caught her eye, and laughed at some handy tips that people had written in about.

Eventually, Helen decided to be studious and go upstairs on the computer, to find some articles for some reflection she was doing about Brian. Switching on her computer, she loaded Google Scholar and typed in keywords to find specific research, only to be bamboozled with over two thousand related results.

'I can't be bothered,' she muttered to herself, saving the search before logging off. Looking at the icon for Facebook, she debated to herself whether or not to go on, and then decided she would read up on what everyone had been doing. Looking through the news feed, she shook her head at a photograph of Amy eating a banana, which was strategically held in front of Steve's crotch. The photo had received forty-two likes, mainly from men and a variety of comments of approval, including Steve himself saying;

'*Yes please.*'

David had been tagged in a post with Carl, claiming that they were in Treble's Bar, and Helen smiled, remembering the last time she went in there. She naively hadn't realised the drinks you bought were all trebles, and consequently got very drunk, very quickly, before performing a rendition of 'The Time Warp' on the table-top. The following day had brought the worst hangover she had ever experienced and she had promised to never drink again; the promise lasted approximately ten days.

Realising her wine glass was empty, she decided to fetch the bottle and have what was left. She made herself a sandwich whilst she was downstairs, since she realised she hadn't eaten since lunch. As she was cutting the sandwich into squares, she heard a message alert from upstairs and her heart skipped a beat. She had forgotten about Marcus wanting to talk. Gingerly, she walked back into her room, clutching the plate and the wine bottle, and slowly walked towards the computer. Helen was surprised that she felt so disappointed when she saw that it was Laura, asking how her placement was going. They chatted for a while, before

Laura said her goodbyes. She was working on the Sunday to see how different community nursing was at weekends. Helen bid her farewell, and pouring the last of the wine into her glass, she picked another playlist on her iPod and clicked on the messenger icon to see if anyone else she knew was online.

Marcus sat at his computer, anxiously debating whether to start a conversation. He could see Helen's name in the chat room, but he didn't want to seem pushy. He'd poured himself a brandy and lemonade, which was unlike him, but he wanted some Dutch courage. He couldn't believe the impact that this girl was having on him. He had never done anything like this before, and knew in his heart that nothing could happen; it would put his whole career on the line if he had a relationship with a student. What was he worried about? He wasn't having a relationship with her. Helen had a boyfriend, who she clearly adored plus Marcus was double her age. There was nothing wrong with just talking was there? Draining off his glass he began to type;

Hi. How's it going?

Helen sat back in her chair, debating whether she should reply, consciously aware that her heart was racing. Was she nervous or excited? She didn't know, but there was no harm in saying hello.

I'm not too bad thank you. How are you? Are you finding your way around Lincoln yet?

Marcus smiled to himself.

Not too bad. There's a supermarket down the road, so that suits me fine when I buy my meals for one ☹

Ahhhh, poor old you! Helen playfully replied. *Maybe you'll meet a nice young lady in there; I hear that's where some men go to find a date,* she teased.

No thanks. Once bitten, twice shy.

Oh dear, that doesn't sound good.

I won't bore you with the details, but I would find it very hard to trust a woman enough again to let her into my life. No offence.

95

We are not all like that you know!!! I, in particular, am very trustworthy.

Yes, but, unfortunately, I can't let you into my life, can I? You're already taken ☹

And I'm your student!

Mmm… Good point! Marcus went into the kitchen to pour himself another drink, as Helen sat debating what to write next, if anything. He still beat her to it;

I can't stop thinking about the other day.

Marcus, don't. I was upset and you comforted me. That's all.

Yes, but we shared another moment, just like at the castle.

Please don't, Marcus. I have a boyfriend who loves me so much.

Yes, but do you love him, Helen?

> *I care for him a lot, yes.*

That wasn't what I asked you…

It's none of your business, Marcus!

Would you answer me one question, Helen? Just one.

OK.

If I had kissed you, would you have pulled away?

I did pull away, if you remember!

Yes, eventually.

I'm going now, Marcus. I don't want this discussion.

Helen, please.

What?

If you tell me that you felt NOTHING, I'll never mention it again. But I know you feel the same Helen. I can see it in your eyes.

I'm sorry Marcus. I felt nothing.

Before any more could be said, Helen logged of Facebook, and Marcus sat with his head in his hands. He was unsure about what had just happened, but he was certain that he was right; Helen Mitchell did like him. He just knew it.

Chapter Twelve

'I can't believe this is your last week,' Charlotte said to Helen as they were driving to the first visit of the day. Helen shook her head in mutual disbelief.

'All of my placements have gone by quickly, but this one has by far gone the fastest,' she said.

'Have you enjoyed it?' Her mentor asked, and Helen responded positively, describing it is the best placement that she'd had. When Helen began her nurse training, she had thought that she wanted to work in the community, but this placement had confirmed her desires, and she knew that district nursing was where her heart lay.

Mondays were always busy days in the community, but today seemed busier than normal. One of the nurses had called in sick with a stomach bug, so each member of the team had had to pick up extra visits. In addition to this, there seemed to have been more extra visits than usual come in on the answer machine, and the day was filled with blocked catheters and wet leg dressings. Helen was thrilled to be able to participate in several re-catheterisations, a skill that, prior to this placement, she hadn't managed to obtain. Amy hadn't been fortunate enough to do any yet and Michelle had only been able to do one herself, so Helen felt that she'd acquired a lot of skills in this clinical area.

It was nearly two o'clock when they pulled into the car park to have lunch, and Helen's heart started to beat frantically when she spotted a black fiesta in the car park, which she was sure belonged to Marcus. Why would Marcus be here, though? She was feeling light headed as they approached the main room, where all the nurses sat, and scanning the room with her eyes, she let out a sigh of relief when the only male present was Alex, one of the nurses.

Walking over to one of the unused computers, she pressed the button to turn it on.

'Oh Helen, there you are. Someone's here to see you.' Doreen the team leader, a large lady, waddled through the door, dressed in an oversized green dress with sandals that were scuffed, and toenails that were painted with chipped red nail polish. She had a ruddy complexion, and although the team liked her, behind her back they referred to her as lazy. She often spending days reading emails and pretending to look busy.

'Who?' Helen enquired, although she already knew the answer.

'Your tutor. He's in my office,' Doreen said, holding the door open.

'I wonder what he wants,' Helen said, looking flushed.

'Don't look so worried,' Charlotte said, smiling reassuringly. 'The tutors usually come and see the students on their placements, just to make sure everything's OK.'

Helen stomach fluttered with each step towards the office door. As she stepped inside, Marcus had his head down, reading some notes. As he looked up at her, he smiled and brushed his hair back with his fingers. Helen felt as if her heart was in her mouth as she smiled back, and closed the door behind her. Marcus was wearing some grey trousers, a black shirt, and some highly polished black shoes. As she sat down in front of him, she watched as he adjusted his collar, probably feeling uncomfortable in her presence. He coughed, smiled, and, after what seemed like an eternity, he spoke.

'So, Helen, how are you finding the placement?' Helen struggled to make eye contact as she replied. She couldn't understand the feelings that this man aroused inside her, feelings of such intense desire she felt like her insides were going to burst. She was sat less than three feet from him. She could smell his aftershave; he smelt so good. She wanted to touch his hand, to feel his skin against hers, to feel his arms around her again. To feel his lips against hers… What the hell was going on?

'Are you alright, Helen?' She was suddenly conscious that she hadn't replied… Shit, now she looked like a blithering idiot.

'Erm, sorry I was just a bit dizzy… Yes, the placement is fab. I love it.' She looked at him and smiled. Marcus swallowed hard; he so wished she wouldn't smile at him like that. She was so close to him now that he could smell her perfume. If he stretched out his arms, he could touch her, pull her towards him and kiss her. But she wouldn't want that, because she didn't feel the same way.

Their eyes locked for a brief moment. Marcus coughed again and looked down at his notes, pretending to write something down.

'Have you managed to achieve most of your outcomes?' He asked.

'All of them,' Helen grinned proudly. 'I've been really lucky on this placement, able to learn so much. I'll be so sad to leave next week.' Marcus stopped writing.

'We could look into you coming back here for your management placement, if community nursing is what you would like to do long- term,' he suggested. 'They are usually keen to have management students here. In fact, I believe they have one here at the moment.' Helen nodded.

'Yeah, Karen Green is here. I think she's due to qualify in a couple of weeks. She's been a great help whilst I've been here. I would love to do my management placement here, if that is an option, please.'

Helen told Marcus about her day at the hospice, forgetting that he had already heard that story. He was happy just listening to her talk; he loved the enthusiasm in her voice. Marcus made notes, as Helen told him of the skills that she'd acquired, and as he wrote, Helen studied every detail of him; the creases around his eyes as he smiled, the streaks of grey that were evident in his hair. Helen wondered how old he actually was. Forty, maybe forty-one... Bloody Hell, probably the same age as the guy her mum went on a 'date' with on Saturday. Despite Katherine's insistence it wasn't a date she was glowing when she came home, and it was nice to see her happy again.

After about half an hour, the meeting drew to a close. Helen signed to say that she was happy with everything that they had discussed.

'Well, two weeks break after this placement, and then you're into your final year,' Marcus said, feeling despaired at the thought of not seeing Helen for another fortnight. 'Do you have any plans over the holidays?' Helen stretched her arms above her head and faked a yawn.

'Lie-ins,' she laughed. 'I'm going to be nineteen on Friday, so a few of us are going into town for some drinks and a meal. Then I'm just going to chill for a couple of weeks, ready for the final slog.'

'Nineteen, eh? I remember being that age. It seems so long ago,' Marcus reminisced, as he scooped his papers together. 'Well I hope you have an amazing birthday and get totally spoilt, because you deserve it.'

Helen smiled, and standing up she straightened her dress. She looked at Marcus, then down at her feet and shuffled awkwardly.

'I didn't mean what I said the other night,' she said in a hurried tone, as she turned to leave. As she reached for the handle, Marcus put his hand on the door above her head, preventing her from opening it.

'What do you mean, Helen?' He asked, almost pleading, and

she could feel his breath on the back of her neck.

'When I said that I felt nothing... I didn't mean it, but I'm in a relationship with a lovely guy who really loves me. And you're my tutor.' She turned to face him. 'Marcus, you could lose your job if anything happened between us... It just can't happen... Anyway, it wouldn't work. There's just too much of an age gap.'

Helen looked up at her tutor who was looking torn, hurt, confused, and tormented. So many emotions in one expression; the same as she was feeling herself at that moment in time. She hadn't noticed before how brown his eyes were, like chestnuts, and my God there it was again, that feeling inside her. What the Hell was that? It was like an electric current, tingling every inch of her insides.

'Perhaps,' he said, his voice soft, almost sad, 'if we just had one kiss, then it might release all of the built up tension. Then we could just get on with our lives and get over it.' Helens heart raced with the thought of fulfilling the fantasy that she'd had the past few weeks of finally kissing the man in front of her. Without saying a word, she nodded and closed her eyes, feeling deafened by the sound of her own heartbeat.

Marcus wanted the moment to last forever. He brushed his fingers softly through her hair. He took in every detail of her face, trying to savour the moment and etch it in his memory. He looked down at this image of pure perfection and wished that she could be his, knowing that that would never be the case. His heart beat with desire as he slowly lowered his face towards hers, until their lips met. He cupped her face in his hands and kissed her gently. Helen felt her whole body tingle as she wrapped her arms around Marcus's neck. He was an amazing kisser, and she didn't want this kiss to ever end, so was quite disgruntled when there was a knock at the office door.

'Can I come in?' Charlotte's voice came from outside. Marcus opened the office door with a forced smile.

'We're all done. I'm just leaving,' he said, turning to Helen who was looking flustered and bid her farewell, wished her a happy holiday and said he would see her back in uni in three weeks. And with that, he was gone.

'Everything OK?' Charlotte asked, noticing that Helen looked flushed.

'I'm perfect,' Helen smiled. 'It's just bloody hot in that office without any windows… Right, are we all set for the next lot of visits?'

'You haven't eaten your lunch…' Charlotte said.

'Oh it's OK, I'm not hungry.' Helen had somehow gone off her sandwiches. She had butterflies and her lips were pulsating from that kiss. Far from releasing any tensions, Helen wanted Marcus Edwards more than she had wanted any other man in her life.

As they made their journey to the next patient, a support visit, Helen took her phone from her pocket and saw that she had two messages from David; one asking if she was having a nice day, and another offering a meal at the Royal William after work, which was a pub on the Brayford. Helen instantly felt a pang of guilt at what she had done. She had betrayed David and given in to temptation with her tutor, a man old enough to be her father. Tears prickled her eyes and she felt nauseous. Despite the feelings that she had for Marcus, David was a fantastic person, and she couldn't hurt him for someone she hardly knew. So she texted back and accepted his offer, arranging to meet him at his bedsit at six thirty.

She arrived, wearing a pair of white cut-off jeans and a floral shirt, complimented with some matching pumps. David greeted her with a loving kiss. He hadn't seen her since Saturday and he had missed her. He complimented her on her outfit and offered her a drink before they went into town.

Helen accepted a glass of Coke and happily listened to David's stories of his night out on Saturday, although she had seen some pictures on Facebook.

'I do have something to ask you babe,' David said looking a bit anxious. 'It's fine if you say no, though.' Helen put her drink down, wondering what it was that he was going to ask.

'Go on,' she said expectantly.

'Gaz, one of my old mates from school, is getting married abroad in a few weeks so he's having a stag weekend in Amsterdam the weekend after next, and he's invited me.' David took Helens hand. 'I know what Amsterdam's like so I understand if you don't want me to go, but honestly I wouldn't do anything stupid, and you can trust me one hundred percent.' Helen picked up her glass, and felt herself flush as she thought of what she had done that afternoon.

'Of course you should go and have a fantastic time. Don't be silly, I trust you with my life.' She leant forward and kissed him. David stroked her face and gently pulled her towards him, kissing her full on the lips. Helen screwed her eyes up tight. Why, oh why, did she not get the same feelings she did when Marcus kissed her?

'Are you OK, Helen?' David asked, seeing her expression.

'Oh God, I'm so sorry. I just feel really light headed. I missed my lunch so I haven't eaten all day…'

'Why didn't you say, silly?' said David, draining his glass, and taking her hand, they walked into town.

As it was a warm evening they decided to sit outside by the Brayford, gentle music playing, and the evening sun glistening on the water that was still, like a sheet of glass, rippling only occasionally when a solitary duck swam past. Helen enjoyed a Mexican chicken wrap with curly fries, and a white wine spritzer, whilst David had the curry and a beer offer that was the Monday night special.

'Now then, me old mucker,' came a voice from behind them.

103

Turning around, Helens heart sank as she saw David's work colleague, Mike, with his twelve-year-old looking girlfriend.

'You remember Shelly, don't you?' He said, re-introducing her.

'Of course. How are you?' Helen smiled politely and squeezed David's hand under the table, willing him not to invite them to sit down. It was too late, though, as Mike had already invited himself, and was pulling out the two empty chairs.

'Don't mind if we join you, do you?' David looked at Helen, embarrassed, not knowing how to answer.

'Of course not,' Helen replied, polite as always, albeit begrudgingly, and accepted Mikes offer of a drink. 'So what do you do for a living?' She asked Shelley, and David playfully kicked her under the table. They both expected her to say she was still at school, so they were surprised when she replied that she was a carer in a residential home, and therefore had to be at least seventeen.

'I'm off to the loo,' Helen said, as Mike returned with the drinks. The pub was surprisingly busy for a Monday evening, she thought. There were only two toilets upstairs, and both were occupied, so Helen took out her phone and clicked onto Facebook whilst she waited. Her stomach instantly plummeted as she saw that she had a message in her inbox and hesitated before she opened it; it was from Marcus.

You can't imagine the impact you're having on me. I can't sleep properly. I can't eat properly. All I think about is you. It is driving me crazy. And today... That kiss... What can I say? It blew me away, and my theory of releasing tension backfired totally. I know that we hardly know each other, but I've never felt this way about anyone before. I must sound like a crazy old fool, but I just had to tell you how I feel... I'm going insane with desire for you!

Helen smiled and took a long exhale, as somebody came out of the cubicle. She sat on the toilet and read the message over and over again. Should she reply? Realistically, no she shouldn't. It was wrong, so very, very wrong, but he had written exactly how she was feeling for him. It was insane, totally insane. They didn't know each other practically at all, but every time he was near her, she had feelings she just couldn't explain.

Helen flushed the chain, washed her hands, and read the message one more time, before typing a one-word reply;

Ditto.

She walked down the stairs with her finger hovering over the send button, debating whether to press it or to delete the whole message and forget about it. With a deep breath, she tapped the screen, and swallowed hard as the word sent appeared, before deleting the conversation so David wouldn't see it.

Beep beep. The message alert tone shrilled loudly, at the exact moment that Helen had pressed send, on the table behind the screen. Straining her ears, Helen gulped as she recognised the voices of Bill and Debbi. She stepped around the screen and saw a third person at the table, smiling as he looked at his phone. Marcus.

'Hello everyone,' she said, trying to alleviate any suspicion. 'I thought I heard your voices.' They exchanged a few formalities, before she returned to David and their uninvited guests, who were horrifying poor David with details of their sex life.

'I think we'd better make a move.' Helen came to the rescue. 'I've got an early start in the morning and I've still got some reflection to write up for tomorrow.' She discreetly winked at David. They said their farewells and made a false promise to go out for a meal one day.

'She's hideous' David commented, as they walked back to his bedsit hand in hand. 'Do you know she was actually telling me about a PVC outfit that she was wearing under the dress that she had on. As if I wanted to know that! The brazen hussy.' Helen laughed at David's disgust.

'Well Mike is obviously happy,' she said.

'Only because he's getting his leg over, no doubt,' David muttered, shaking his head. 'I think he would have been better off gay at this rate.' Helen laughed.

'Well, I'm sorry to say that I'm not wearing PVC under my outfit, so try not to be too disappointed.'

David stopped and pulled her towards him.

'You would look gorgeous in a bin bag,' he said, squeezing her bum. 'Do you fancy coming up to mine for a bit?' He winked.

'Oh, I'm sorry gorgeous, but I really do have to do some reflection for tomorrow.' Helen felt a pang of guilt as she saw the look of disappointment in David's face.

'I thought you had finished all your coursework now, until your final year,' he said. Shit. She forgot that she had told him that. She struggled to quickly think up an excuse.

'I have, but this is for one of my outcomes. It's evidence, and Charlotte is going to try and do my final interview tomorrow, as she's off Friday.' It was the first time that Helen had lied to David, but she really didn't want to make love, not today, after what had happened with Marcus. She would feel too guilty. 'Hey, when we go out on Friday for my birthday, I'll wear something extra sexy, and we'll have an amazing night to make up for it. I promise.' David smiled at that thought, and kissing her hard on the lips, he bid her goodnight, waving as she drove off.

David hoped that he didn't have anything to worry about, but he'd thought that Helen was quieter than normal this evening. She hadn't been herself lately. He couldn't quite put his finger on it, but something was different. She never said she loved him, but then again she never had. The last few weeks, though, she had seemed distant, like the sparkle had gone from her eyes. Tonight was the first time she had turned him down in the bedroom too. He was sure she had finished all of her coursework, but if she had evidence to write then that was plausible; she did have a lot of reflection to do. Something was just not right. Like earlier, when she was screwing her eyes up when he was kissing her.

Surely that wasn't because she was dizzy. But then, she still held his hand everywhere. Maybe he was just being paranoid, but she didn't text him as much these days either. That could be because of work, though, and she does text more when she's at college. His thoughts were interrupted by the sound of his phone bleeping.

I will definitely make it up on Friday, sexy xxxxx, David chastised himself for being silly and went inside.

Chapter Thirteen

'Happy birthday!' Katherine opened her daughter's curtains, and sun streamed into the room. Helen pulled the duvet over her head. 'Wakey wakey, rise and shine!' She said, laughing. 'Beth and Steve are downstairs and breakfast is nearly ready. Come on, up you get birthday girl!' Helen yawned and sat up, straining to look at the clock on the wall.

'It's only half past seven!' She exclaimed.

'I know, but we all have jobs to go to, so come on. Up you get,' she said jokingly, tugging the duvet off of her.

Helen pulled on her robe, put on her slippers and trudged downstairs, where she was greeted with a chorus of 'Happy Birthday', followed by a clatter of party poppers. She soon woke up, with the help of a mug of steaming coffee and some delicious bacon and egg muffins, and then she opened her presents. Beth and Steve had bought her a red top from New Look that she had pointed out, and Katherine had bought her a Parker pen, which she was over the moon with. She usually only ever had pens that were given away for free by reps. Helen also received some money and vouchers from family, which she planned to spend on clothes and her night in town later. She was really looking forward to that. She would receive her presents from David and her friends later. David did send her a text though;

To the sexiest woman on Earth: happy birthday! Love you loads, and can't wait for tonight. Grrr xxx

After taking a quick shower and getting into her uniform, Helen had a few minutes to spare, so she logged onto Facebook, and was surprised to have over seventy posts on her wall wishing her a happy birthday. There was also an inbox, and on opening it, she saw it was from Marcus:

Happy Birthday! Have an amazing day. Thinking of you. Enjoy your night out xxxxxxx

She replied with a 'thank you', and added that they would be at the Italian restaurant on Guildhall Street, then in the pubs around town including Walkabout, Varsity, Treble's and Revolutions, just in case he happened to be out at all.

Although Charlotte was not at work today, she surprised Helen by turning up at lunch time with a homemade birthday cake. Other members of the team had also clubbed together and bought in food and a bunch of flowers to have a leaving/birthday party for Helen. She was touched by their kindness. She had thoroughly enjoyed the placement, and was planning to return for her management placement next year. Helen had invited them all to her birthday night out later. Unfortunately, Charlotte was already going to the theatre with her husband, and Alex was on holiday, but Tina and Lizzy were already in town. They said that they would meet up in Walkabout for a drink, as they didn't like to eat before a night of drinking.

Helen was looking forward to going out. Michelle and Amy were going, and Phil had come over as well, which was nice for Michelle. Amy was single, yet again, and Helen had been telling Lizzy, earlier, all about her friend's antics. Lizzy had looked horrified at some of the stories she was hearing, and Helen had reassured her that she was actually a really nice girl. She had no idea what had gone wrong with the latest love of Amy's life, but she was sure there would be a new conquest by the end of the evening.

The door opened.

'Somebody is a very lucky young lady,' came Doreen's voice, from behind the biggest bunch of roses that Helen had ever seen. She blushed, as Doreen had to use both hands to hold them in her direction.

'For me?' She was surprised.

'Well they have your name on them, and it is your birthday,' Doreen smiled, then pulling them back towards her she said, 'unless of course you don't want them? I will happily take them off of you.' She winked. Helen excitedly knelt on the chair, and leaning towards Doreen, she squealed with delight like a young child.

'David has never sent me flowers before. He's bought me them, but never actually had them delivered.' She inhaled the aroma of the flowers. There must have been two dozen roses; red and pink. It must have cost him a fortune. She tore open the envelope and pulled out the card. As she did, her face flushed and her heart skipped a beat; written on it was simply a love heart, a kiss and the letter M.

'What has he written?' Charlotte asked.

'Happy Birthday. All my love, David,' Helen lied, sliding the card back into the envelope and putting it in her pocket. Those familiar butterflies were racing around her stomach again. She couldn't even text him to say thank you, as she didn't have his number, so she would inbox him when she got home.

'Well, they need to get in some water,' Charlotte said. 'If it's OK with Lizzy, I think you should get off early and go get ready for your big night out.' Lizzy agreed, and after saying her goodbyes to everybody, Helen left and went home. She had to use three vases to display her roses, deciding to tell everyone that it was a generous gift from everyone on the placement, as she strategically mixed in their flowers and placed the farewell card alongside. The card from Marcus she tucked inside one of her textbooks, knowing that no one would find it there. Before anybody got home, she logged onto Facebook and sent a thank you message to Marcus, telling him that they were the most beautiful flowers she had ever seen, to which he later replied that she was the most beautiful person he had ever seen.

Helen was still in the bath when David arrived to pick her up, so he sat downstairs, chatting to Katherine about his day. He wolf-whistled as Helen walked in, wearing a short black dress and some red stilettos, her blonde hair hanging loose around her face. She had matched it with bright red lipstick and a red bag. David thought she looked stunning, and he wanted to forget the night out and go straight back to his bedsit. Katherine smiled at her daughter's appearance.

'You look lovely, as always,' she commented.

'Happy birthday, gorgeous,' David said, kissing her cheek and handing her a parcel wrapped in purple shiny paper with pink curly ribbon.

'David, did you wrap this yourself?' Helen asked, surprised.

'Well, with a little help from the wrapping service.' He laughed. Helen gasped as she unwrapped the paper to reveal a beautiful lilac silk jacket.

'Oh David, this is stunning!' She said, putting it on. It fit to perfection. 'I love it!' She threw her arms around him. 'Thank you so much!' She said, kissing him.

'It's my pleasure, beautiful,' he said, kissing the tip of her nose. 'Well I suppose we'd better get going; we're meeting at the restaurant at seven, and it's nearly quarter to now,' David said, tapping his watch. Helen took off her jacket, kissed her mum and they headed to the car.

The car park was quite empty for a Friday evening, and walking through town to the restaurant, it seemed very quiet.

'We probably won't have to queue at the bars much, by the looks of it.' Helen frowned; there wasn't much of an atmosphere when it wasn't busy.

'It's still early. Give it time, babe. It will liven up later; wait and see,' David reassured her, squeezing her hand. Walking past Ann Summers, Helen pointed to a mannequin wearing a red lace bra and panty set.

'That is very similar to what's under my dress tonight,' she whispered, and David became instantly aroused.

'Can we not just go home now?' He asked, nuzzling her ear as she laughed.

They were the last to arrive at the restaurant. Michelle and Phil were sat with Amy, and Beth and Steve sat opposite, with two empty chairs ready for Helen and David.

'Happy birthday,' they cheered as Helen approached, and Helen blushed as other customers turned to look. Michelle handed her a present

'This is from me and Phil,' she said, and Helen delightedly opened the box, revealing a lover pair of diamanté studs. Amy had bought her a voucher for the Odeon, knowing that she and David enjoyed their films, and Helen laughed loudly at the card, which displayed a picture of a huge black penis... Typical Amy!

The restaurant ran a special of two courses for £9.99, so Helen enjoyed some garlic mushrooms, followed by a pizza, although she couldn't eat it all and David had to finish two slices for her. She managed to consume two Bacardi and Cokes, in addition to the two bottles of wine that they all shared, and despite the carbs, by the time they got up to leave, Helen was feeling rather tipsy. David had to steady her a little as she almost lost her balance walking out the door.

'Where shall we go first?' Amy asked, equally as tipsy as Helen.

'Let's go to Treble's,' Phil suggested. 'They have a good deal at this time of night.' Everyone agreed, and they all chatted happily as they headed towards the bar, where a queue had started to form. David wrapped his arms around Helens waist and nuzzled her ear as they waited in the queue, until it was their turn to be let in. Steve was keeping everyone amused with stories of his days at work as a carpet fitter, and the customers that he had to deal with. Today he had met a woman and a man, whom he'd assumed was her husband, until her actual husband came back from work early to pick up some paperwork, and the lover had to wait in the cupboard in the room where Steve was working for over three hours.

'Serves him right,' David said. Helen said nothing.

'Come on in then, you lot,' the bouncer said, beckoning them into the bar and winking at Amy as she walked past, who had undoubtedly winked at him first, or flashed her flirtatious smile. The bar was heaving. The men went to fetch the drinks and the girls headed straight for the dance floor, aware of the admiring glances of the men that circled around it, looking for their prey.

'It's like a cattle market in here,' Michelle commented.

'It always is,' Beth agreed. 'That's why I don't come to town very often; it drives me mad.' Amy was happily swaying her hips to the music, and clearly enjoying the admiring glances from the leering onlookers. 'Clearly we don't all think that way,' Beth said, nodding in her direction. Michelle shook her head.

'She is a bloody law unto herself, that girl. I love her to bits, but she's a little tart.' Amy must have heard the comment, because she turned to Michelle and gave her an evil glare, before storming off to the bar to find the men. 'Whoops. Now I'm in her bad books,' Michelle said, frowning.

'Ignore her, she'll get over it,' Helen said, laughing, and taking Michelle and Beth's hands, she proceeded to spin around to the music until she felt dizzy.

The drink – a treble of course – was enough to make all of them very drunk, and it was only half ten, so they decided to get some fresh air and take a slow walk to Walkabout. As predicted,

Amy had forgotten about Michelle's comment, although she still seemed slightly frosty towards her, linking arms with Helen and Beth, as if trying to make a point. Joining yet another queue, Helen spotted Tina and Lizzy and greeted them, saying that she would catch up with them inside. She turned to give David a kiss. And as she did, she swore she saw Phil pinch Amy on the bum. She looked over David's shoulder, but Phil had his arm around Michelle; she must have imagined it.

There was a happy atmosphere inside, and Helen was enjoying her birthday celebrations. The music was very loud, so she struggled to hear most of the conversation with Lizzy and Tina, but she smiled and nodded anyway. She felt hot in her black dress, and swore that they'd put the heating on despite the warm weather, simply to make you buy more drinks. Although the rest of the group were carrying on drinking, Helen had opted for a glass of diet Coke, as she was starting to feel incredibly drunk and thought she ought to have a break. She stood at the side of the dance floor with Lizzy, watching her friends dance. David was talking to Gaz, who he had bumped into. They were no doubt planning the stag weekend in Amsterdam.

'I take it that's Amy,' Lizzy said, pointing to the dance floor. Helen followed the direction of her gaze and shook her head, promptly following it with a nod.

'How did you guess?' She asked sarcastically, a little bit embarrassed for her friend. Amy was wearing a short white dress, and was gyrating her hips and running her hands down her thighs, her performance being enjoyed by several onlookers, including Phil, much to Helen's disgust. She looked around for Michelle, and was relieved that she seemed oblivious to it. Michelle was talking to Beth, but Helen could see Steve watching Phil intently, and she wondered again if there was any history between Amy and Steve.

Helen felt some arms wrap around her waist, and she turned to see David behind her. Lizzy and Tina bid them farewell, and she faced him, giving him a lingering kiss.

'I'm looking forward to going back to yours later,' she purred in his ear.

'Mmm, me too babe,' he muttered back, squeezing her tight. They turned around to watch their friends dance.

'Where has Amy gone now?' Helen said, at the same moment Michelle came up to them and shouted over the music.

'Have you seen Phil?' Helen gulped and felt nauseous inside. They wouldn't have, would they? As if reading her mind, Michelle then asked 'Where's Amy?' Helen suggested they might be at the bar or in the bathroom, hoping to reassure her friend, but checks of both proved negative. By this time, Steve and Beth had rejoined them.

'Let's go and look outside. They may have just gone out for some fresh air; they are both pretty drunk,' Beth said positively.

The four of them pushed their way through the crowd to the front doors and out onto the high street, where there were lots of people lining the streets, but Phil and Amy were nowhere to be seen. Helen looked both ways, up towards Steep Hill, and down towards the Stonebow, but nothing. She then turned towards the alleyway that ran alongside Walkabout, which led to some other bars.

'They could have gone that way,' she said. They hadn't walked very far when they heard it; a shuffling noise and moan from behind a large wheelie bin, which was propped up against the wall. Michelle was crying as Steve pulled it away. Helen knew what was behind before it was revealed; too drunk and engrossed to even realise they had been caught out, Phil with his trousers down enough to reveal his white arse, and Amy with her legs wrapped around his waist, having sex against the wall.

'You bastard!' Michelle screamed, throwing her bag at the back of his head and dropping to her knees, her head in her hands, sobbing as if her world had ended. Amy and Phil stood in horror.

115

'Babe it wasn't how it looks,' he slurred, yanking up his trousers.

'Save your breath, you tosser,' Dave said, pushing him out the way, as Helen helped her friend to her feet. She turned to Amy with tears streaming down her face.

'You should be ashamed of yourself, you bitch! You're no friend of mine,' Helen spat. Dave had never heard Helen speak like that to anyone, but Amy deserved it. He couldn't believe how the evening had ended.

Dave and Helen took Michelle home in a taxi. She declined going home with them.

'I can't believe they could have done that to her,' Helen said, as they lay in bed later that night, and as they made love, she swore that there was no way she would ever hurt David the way that Phil has hurt Michelle.

Chapter Fourteen

Helen spent a lot of the week with Michelle, who was clearly devastated by what had happened. It was only made worse by the fact that she had suspected that Phil was going to propose that weekend. Both girls felt utterly betrayed by Amy, and couldn't understand how she could stoop so low as to do that to a friend.

'I'm dreading seeing her at uni,' said Michelle, over coffee one day. Helen had agreed, but reassured Michelle that Amy wouldn't be sitting with them anymore. Helen had promptly deleted Amy from Facebook that same night, out of loyalty to Michelle. She had meant it when she said Amy was no friend of hers anymore. They saw her once in New Look, but Amy scurried off in the opposite direction, looking ashamed, much to the relief of Michelle, who didn't want to have to confront her in public.

'I don't want to be responsible for my actions,' she told Helen.

David managed to book the Thursday off as a holiday so they could spend the day together, as this weekend he was going away on the stag weekend. They planned an early start, and Helen was going to stay at David's, so she was meeting him at his. Katherine was still at home after Helen had had her shower, so she spent half an hour with her, sharing a coffee and some toast, and listening about another 'tea' that she'd had with George last night. Helen learnt that George was an accountant, and worked for a company in town. Katherine described him as charming, and a gentleman. Helen smiled. Her mum had a glow in her cheeks; she looked happy, and that made Helen happy, too. She gave her a big hug as she said goodbye.

David was still in his pyjamas when Helen arrived.

'Sorry, my alarm didn't go off,' he apologised. 'Make yourself a coffee, and I'll just jump in the shower,' he said, heading towards the bathroom, kissing her on the way past. 'Excuse my morning breath.' He covered his mouth. Helen threw her overnight bag onto the sofa, flicked on the kettle and made the bed. It was handy being in a bedsit; everything was so compact. Sitting on the sofa, waiting for the kettle to boil, she pulled her phone out of her pocket and flicked onto Facebook. She got butterflies when she saw she had an inbox from Marcus:

I'm missing you so much. Really wish I could see your face. Helen thought back to the scene of her birthday, and feeling nauseous, she pressed delete. She couldn't do that to David. She scrolled down the newsfeed, reading everyone's statuses, but she was conscious that her heart was pumping hard in her chest. She could hear that David was still in the shower, so she went onto her friends list and found Marcus. She flicked through his pictures, admiring his face from so many angles, so many expressions. She could feel herself flush, her heart racing; there were those feelings again. She wanted to be in his arms again, to be near him. She hated the way she felt about him. It was wrong, so very, very wrong, and she knew it.

She jumped as she heard the bathroom door open, and quickly clicked off Facebook, hastily standing up to re-boil the kettle as David entered the room, a towel wrapped around his waist. Water glistening over the taut muscles on his chest, and Helen had to admit that David had an amazing physique.

'That feels better,' he said, removing the towel to rub himself dry, and smiled when Helen wolf-whistled as she walked towards him, holding two mugs of coffee. Just the sight of her, in her blue skater dress and white pumps, sent him crazy. He loved her so much, and as she put the drinks down on the bedside cabinet, he pushed her down onto the bed and kissed her passionately.

'God, I love you, Helen Mitchell,' he said, knowing that she wouldn't say it back, but he got a good enough response. Without removing a single item of her clothing, he pushed her knickers to the side and they made passionate love. It didn't last long, but left them both laying silently for a few minutes, catching their breaths.

By the time they attempted to drink their coffees, they were lukewarm.

'Shall we nip and have a Costa coffee before we go to Whisby?' David suggested, knowing that it was Helens favourite coffee shop. They had their day planned out; a walk around Whisby nature reserve, then they were using the tickets Amy got them to see a new horror film, which was supposed to be based on a true story. They were going to finish off the evening with a takeaway and a bottle of wine back at David's, and neither of them could wait for the day.

'Mmm, yes please!' Helen smiled at the suggestion of coffee, and grabbing her bag, they made their way down to the car.

Helen was surprised how busy it was for a Thursday morning, but as David joined the queue and she took a seat facing the window, she noticed all the parents with children. She suddenly remembered it was the school holidays. Helen loved people watching, and could sit all day watching the world go by. She and David would often play a game where they would pick out people and guess what they did for a living, and see if they came up with the same answers. Looking around the room, she observed all the people of different ages and cultures, all from different backgrounds with different pasts. She wondered how many of them were happy, and how many were sad.

As she looked to the table in the corner, her eyes locked with some familiar brown eyes, slight creases at the side. Eyes that held her gaze for what seemed like an eternity. Her mouth went dry, and her heart started beating frantically, as Marcus smiled and mouthed 'hello'. She smiled back and waved, then looked down shyly, diverting her gaze from his, conscious that the whole of Costa, including David, would be able to see how she was feeling. David hadn't seemed to notice anything as he handed her a gingerbread latte. She sipped it and coughed nervously, desperately wanting to take one more look at Marcus, knowing he was looking at her, but also knowing that she couldn't when David was sat opposite her.

'This is scrummy,' she said, licking her lips, as she put her mug down on the table. 'What have you got?' she asked.

'I've got the hot chocolate,' David said, and she laughed as he wiped away a cream moustache that had formed over his lips.

'I'm really looking forward to the film; it has had some good reviews,' she said, and David nodded in agreement. Helen briefly glanced over towards Marcus. He was still watching her intently, head rested lightly on his hands and a faint smile on his face as he took in her beauty. 'I'm just popping to the loo,' she said to David, and headed to the back of the coffee shop and up the stairs where the toilets were situated.

As she'd hoped, Marcus was waiting outside when she came out of the cubicle.

'Hi,' he said, in a lowered voice, and smiled. 'How are you?' Helen looked over the balcony to make sure no-one was coming up the stairs.

'I'm great thanks. You?' she asked, smiling back, a smile that made Marcus's stomach lurch inside and his legs quiver.

'All the better now I've seen you,' he replied. Helen blushed and looked down at her feet, even more embarrassed that she had blushed.

'I've got to go; David is waiting downstairs,' she said, turning away from him, but before she went down the stairs, she stopped without looking at him.

'Are you doing anything on Saturday night?' She asked quietly.

'No,' Marcus responded eagerly.

'David is away. Maybe we could chat on Facebook again...' Helen suggested, still with her back to him.

'I'll look forward to it,' Marcus replied, and smiled happily as she disappeared down the stairs.

Whisby nature reserve was a popular place for both families and walkers, but David and Helen regularly went to enjoy the scenery. There was a choice of walks of varying distances, colour coded depending on the length of walk you wanted to have. Today they opted for the Willow walk, which was the longest walk, usually taking about an hour and a half to complete. The sun shone, and they walked hand in hand, chatting happily about anything and everything. David was telling Helen about the plans for the stag weekend in Amsterdam.

'You have to go to the red light district,' Helen said. 'Apparently it's a must-see when you're there.' David shook his head.

'I just worry that Carl will try and get Gaz to go in to one of the girls,' he said. Helen looked at him, shocked.

'He's getting married. Surely he wouldn't do anything like that, regardless of what Carl tried to make him do. And Carl should know better.' David shrugged his shoulders.

'Let's hope so. I don't think he would be that stupid.'

They spent some time sat by the lake, watching an elderly couple who sat on fold up chairs, with a flask of coffee and their binoculars, watching the wildlife across the lake. The elderly man turned to them and pointed across the lake to a Kingfisher.

'Look at that magnificent bird with those dazzling colours; electric blue and sunset orange,' he said, smiling. They agreed it was a beautiful species, and after a brief chat with the couple, Helen and David returned to their car and drove back into town to go to the Odeon.

121

Considering it was a new film, the cinema was only half full, so Helen and David positioned themselves on the back row. They both loved 'The Conjuring' and found it quite jumpy in places. It was about paranormal investigators, who worked to help a family whose farmhouse was haunted.

'That was spooky,' Helen said afterwards. 'I'll be scared to go to sleep tonight.' She linked her arm through David's. She wasn't wearing a coat and was feeling chilly now. Sensing she was cold, he wrapped his arms around her to keep her warm.

'What do you fancy for tea, babe?' He asked, squeezing her tightly towards him.

'I don't know, but I'm starving,' she said, rubbing her stomach. 'Let's just grab a KFC or something and take it back to yours,' she suggested, kissing him on the cheek.

The chicken tasted heavenly. David had bought a bottle of wine, which had been chilling in the fridge, and they sat snuggled on the sofa, watching an episode of 'One Foot in the Grave', a DVD box set that David had bought cheap from Asda earlier in the week.

'I can't believe how quick today has gone,' Helen said, licking the grease from her fingers.

'I know, it's flown,' David agreed, shaking his head in disbelief; it didn't seem five minutes since Helen had arrived that morning. 'More wine?' He asked, already pouring it into her glass.

'It looks like that's a yes, then.' She laughed, dropping her last chicken bone into the empty bucket. She picked up her glass and took a large gulp of the wine. 'That is gorgeous,' she said, licking her lips.

'So are you,' David said, taking the glass from her and putting it on the table. He moved towards her and kissed her hard on the lips.

'Are we ready for round two, then?' She purred in a seductive tone. She stood up, and taking his hand, she turned off the television and led him to the bed.

122

'I just have to go to the bathroom,' she said, as David lay down on the bed. She sat on the side of the bath and put her head in her hands. She didn't know what was wrong with her. David was gorgeous, she knew that, and he loved her so much, but she just didn't love him back. There he was, in the next room, waiting for her and she had no feelings of passion for him… She was an utter bitch, because all she could think about was Marcus, and she couldn't help it. She turned on the tap and splashed her face with water; she had to compose herself. David was waiting for her, and it was David she was with. End of story.

'Are you OK, babe?' His concerned voice came from outside the bathroom door.

'I'll be there in a minute. I'm sorry, I've just come over feeling really, really sick,' Helen lied. David opened the door and came inside, to see her sat on the side of the bath. He sat next to her and put his arm around her.

'You do look pale, babe. Come on, let's get you into bed. We can just snuggle up,' he said kindly. Helen felt a pang of guilt as she stood up and followed him back into the room.

David carefully helped her take off her clothes, and gently put on her cream negligee for her. Then, pulling back the duvet, he plumped up the pillow and made sure she was comfy, before climbing in beside her and pulling her into his arms.

'My poor baby,' he said sympathetically, and Helen felt crushed with guilt. David was so warm and gentle, and he deserved her love. She wrapped her arms around him and kissed him softly on the lips.

'Thank you for being so lovely to me,' she said.

'I'll always be like this with you, Helen, because I love you,' he said, kissing her on the nose. Helen looked up at him. He had such a look of sadness in his eyes. She knew that all he wanted was to hear those words back, and it must have been the wine that did it, because without even realising what she was doing she said it;

123

'I love you'.

It was too late. The words had left her mouth, and she couldn't retract them now. What had possessed her to say that? She cared for David, but love… That was another thing entirely. There just wasn't that spark that she used to see in her parent's eyes when they looked at each other. She had never forgotten that look. That was what she wanted to feel, and she didn't with David, no matter how hard she tried, how much she wanted to. It just was not there. But then she noticed something in his eyes… Was that a tear? It is; it's a tear. Oh my God, do those three words mean that much to him?

'I've waited so long for you to say that back to me.' David squeezed her tightly to his chest. 'I think I must be the happiest man alive.' He held her close, and as she eventually listened to him snoring gently, Helen silently wept. She wished and wished that she could wave a magic wand and feel for David the way that he felt about her.

Chapter Fifteen

Helen dropped David off in Hull on the Friday evening, where he met up with seven other stags wearing matching T-shirts, each printed with 'Gaz's Stag Do' on the front, and then a nickname on the back. How original... Helen had chuckled when David had opened his t-shirt, furious to discover that he had been tagged as 'Dirty Dave'.

'How the Hell does that make me look?' He had grumbled, and Helen had told him not to be a spoil sport, but reminded him that he didn't have to live up to his name. The boys also were wearing pink cowboy hats, which David had muttered made them look like knobs, and Helen had to sternly tell him to stop being such a misery guts, before kissing him goodbye and waving him off.

She spent the evening with Beth and Katherine. Steve had gone out, so Beth had cooked them all a lovely meal of steak in pepper sauce, jacket potato and salad, followed by a chocolate cheesecake. They had then decided on a game of Monopoly, which, as usual, Beth was winning. Beth and Katherine were both rather merry, having shared a bottle of wine, but Helen was on the cola, as she was driving.

'So have you heard from that slag, Amy?' Beth asked, moving her counter. She had the boot, and she was stamping it around the board, indicating her anger at Amy.

'No, and I have no intentions of seeing her either,' Helen replied. 'I'll never forgive her for what she did.'

'How's Michelle?' Katherine asked, having been filled in by her daughters at the time.

'She seems OK. I'm having coffee with her in the morning, so I'll see if she's OK then,' Helen replied, taking her turn.

'Has she heard from that creep of a boyfriend?' Beth asked, in an even angrier tone, and Helen shook her head.

'I don't think so, no.'

They didn't stay late, as Katherine was working at the florist in the morning, and then in the evening, she and George were going with Beth and Steve to see Lee Evans in London, and were staying over in a hotel. Helen had winked at Beth when they heard that last part, but Katherine had made it quite clear that she and George were having twin beds. She sternly informed her daughters that they were taking things slowly, before blushing and blaming her flushes on 'the change'.

Michelle needed to get some new trousers, so rather than go into town, they went to the shopping centre on Tritton Road. There was a large Next there, as well as other clothes shops and a Costa. She couldn't find anything she liked in any of the clothes shops, despite there being a wide selection to choose from. After trying on four different pairs in Next, she finally bought the first pair that she had tried on, some white jeans with red roses embroidered around the pockets. She was happy, as she had dropped a dress size, although Helen suspected it was due to the stress of the past week. Not that she was going to mention that to Michelle. Happy with her new size, Michelle also treated herself to a new red top, which perfectly matched the colour of the roses.

'I got a text off Phil yesterday,' Michelle said, not making eye contact as they sat drinking their coffee. 'He wants to meet up for a chat.' Helen paused for a few seconds, convinced that she had misheard, her cup poised halfway to her mouth.

'Please tell me that you told him where to go,' Helen said, placing her cup on the table, almost nervous for Michelle's reply. The way Michelle was biting her lip and scratching her palms with her nails gave Helen the answer she dreaded.

'He deserves a chance to explain himself,' Michelle said, still not making eye contact, and Helen almost choked.

'Are you kidding me, Michelle?' She said in a lowered tone. 'What is there to explain? We caught him red handed, fucking Amy up the wall.' Helen felt furious; how could Michelle even consider giving him a chance to say anything?

'He was drunk,' Michelle said timidly.

'Oh, well that's OK then!' Helen said sarcastically, taking a loud slurp of her coffee. 'Let's forgive Amy as well then, shall we? She was drunk too.' Michelle glared at Helen, but said nothing. 'Michelle you are my best friend, and I love you, but if you forgive him for this you're an idiot,' Helen said, and finishing off her coffee, she stood up from her chair. 'I'm going to go now, because I don't want to fall out with you over this, and if we carry on this conversation, I'm afraid that we will, so I'll see you next week some time.' Without saying another word, she walked to her car, without turning back.

As she was going to be on her own all evening, Helen called into Asda and picked up one of their Indian meals for one; a chicken madras with pilau rice, a mini naan bread and an onion bhaji. She saw Tammy and Jo-Jo in there, and stopped for a brief chat. They'd heard about Amy, and were asking what would happen when they went back to uni. Helen had simply told them that Amy was not her problem. She received a text from David whilst she was in Asda, the first since he had gone, but she had told him not to bother whilst he was with his friends.

Missing you loads xxx

She smiled, and replied that she missed him too and she hoped he was having fun, to which he responded positively. Helen also picked up a magazine to read, although she had already decided she was going to watch one of her favourite films 'The Others' later in the evening, after she had chatted to Marcus; she was looking forward to speaking to him.

The house was empty when she got home, everyone having already left for London. Katherine had left Helen a note telling her that there was a nice bottle of rosé wine in the fridge for her, and said they planned to be home about three the following afternoon. There was a joint of beef to put in the oven about lunchtime and veg in the drawer, if Helen wouldn't mind preparing it. If David was home from Amsterdam in time, he was welcome to come for tea, as the beef was big enough. Helen smiled to herself; her mum's notes were often more like essays.

She went upstairs and put the bath on. It was nearly six already. She was looking forward to a night to herself; it didn't happen very often. Helen poured some bubble bath under the tap, and inhaled the aroma of white musk, one of her favourite smells. She lit the candles that were placed around the bathroom, and going back downstairs, she put her meal into the oven, so that it would be ready for when she got out of the bath. Pouring herself a glass of the wine, she went back upstairs, turned on her computer, and clicked onto Facebook. She laughed. The first thing on her news feed was a bunch of very drunk men, dressed in matching t-shirts and pink cowboy hats, all tucking into chocolate brownies. She wondered if they all knew exactly what was in those chocolate brownies, and if they didn't, what state they all were in now. Helen chuckled as she scrolled through pictures of David's weekend; he looked like he was having fun and, she had to admit, she was actually missing him.

Helen sat reading people's statuses, and paused at one in particular.

Michelle Young does not know what to do. Obviously, several people had commented asking if she was OK, and what was wrong, but Helen knew exactly what that status meant and she commented herself.

'*Do the right thing and the sane thing!*' Her comment was promptly liked by three people who obviously realised the meaning of what was being said. Michelle didn't respond to Helens comment at all, but several more people liked it over the course of the evening.

The bath was warm and inviting, as usual. Helen had put on her favourite playlist, and lay with her eyes closed, encased within the bubbles, her silk pyjamas and dressing gown ready waiting at the side of the bath. She was slowly sipping her wine, wondering if Marcus had remembered that they had planned to chat tonight.

Marcus had thought of nothing else since their encounter at the top of the stairs in Costa. He had actually convinced himself that he was losing the plot, because he was counting down the hours to when he would talk to her. That in itself was ridiculous; they hadn't even set a time. So here he was at half past six on a Saturday night, sat poised in front of his computer, waiting for her name to appear. He hoped she remembered… Of course she would remember; it was her suggestion. Even so, she might have had a better offer. He puffed out his cheeks as he exhaled, and brushed his hand through his hair, deciding it probably was still early. He went into the kitchen to make a coffee.

Helen finished her curry, cleared up, and topped up her wine, heading back up to her room and clicking back onto Facebook. She got butterflies when she saw that Marcus was already on line, and likewise when he saw her name appear at the side; like a bolt of lightning in his chest. His fingers hovered over the keyboard, but she beat him to it;

Hi
Hello. How are you?
Really good. You?

Great, thank you.

That was the formalities over with. He wanted to tell her he missed her, but he didn't want to scare her away.

So what are you up to? He asked.

I've just had a nice soak in the bath, had my tea and now I'm talking to you. What about you?

Not much really. Talking to you is the highlight of my day, he said not able to see Helens smile and her flushed cheeks.

I'm going to watch a film later, Helen said, changing the subject.

What are you going to watch? Marcus asked.

The Others.

What's that about?

Are you joking me? Have you never seen it? Helen asked, amazed.

Nope, is it good? Have you seen it before then?

Loads of times. It's amazing.

It must be, if you've seen it loads of times.

Helen sat back in her chair, debating... No one would know if she...

Look, everyone is out tonight. You are welcome to come and watch it if you want... Unless you have other plans...

Marcus almost jumped off of his chair.

I would love to. I'll be there in twenty minutes. He typed, and logging off, he went upstairs and put on some aftershave, straightened his hair, gargled some mouthwash and was on his way.

Helen couldn't decide if she should get dressed, but she decided to stay in her pyjamas and robe; after all, it was the evening. She did brush her hair, so that it fell loose over her shoulders, and she put on a small amount of mascara and a very pale pink lip-gloss. She also put on some deodorant, and a spray of perfume. She checked her reflection in the mirror. Looking at her fluffy robe, she changed her mind and decided to put on her dress. It was too late, though, as she heard a knock at the door.

'Bugger,' she said, running downstairs and opening the door to reveal Marcus standing there, in a pair of jeans with a white linen shirt. 'Come in,' Helen said, standing to the side to let him pass. 'I was upstairs going to actually get dressed,' she said, looking embarrassed.

'Don't be daft, you're fine as you are,' Marcus said politely. 'In fact, I think you look stunning.' He smiled, and Helens heart beat so hard she was grateful she was wearing her robe, otherwise she was certain Marcus would see it pounding through her clothing.

'What would you like to drink?' She asked. 'I've got some lovely rosé wine open.' She smiled, waving her glass in front of him.

'That would be lovely, but I'm driving,' he said, with a frown.

'Not for a few hours you aren't, and one glass won't harm you,' Helen said, pouring him some, as well as topping up her own glass.

'Cheers,' he said, clinking his glass against hers.

'What shall we drink to?' She asked. Marcus took a sip, and after a while, he smiled.

'Happiness.'

They took a few sips of their wine in silence, both unsure of the next move.

'So what's this film about, then?' Marcus asked, breaking the silence.

'It's a bit of a thriller, with a twist, but I can't say too much without spoiling it,' Helen said. 'Come on let's go and sit down, and I'll put it on.' As if it was a natural thing to do, Helen took Marcus's hand and led him into the front room, to the sofa. Their fingers curled around each others, grasping each other's hands as if their lives depended on it, neither saying anything, acting as if it was normal.

Marcus sat down and watched Helen, as she put the DVD into the player, turned on the television and pressed play. She was conscious that he was watching her, but pretended not to notice. As she walked back to the sofa, she sat next to him and he took her hand. It fit like a glove. He traced the back of her hand with his thumb, and it felt like electricity running up her arm. Using her other hand, she gently stroked his arm, and then rested it gently on top of his other hand. Just being close to him felt amazing. Marcus put his arm around Helen, and she snuggled into him as close as she could, both breathing in the aroma of the other, both overwhelmed with emotion at the intensity of the feelings they were experiencing. They watched the film in silence, moving only to drink their wine.

The film ends with a twist so unexpected that Marcus was stunned, and Helen laughed at his reaction; he actually sat forward on the sofa and held his hands up in amazement, shouting 'no way' at the television.

'I reacted like that the first time I saw it too.' She laughed.

'What an amazing twist,' he said, shaking his head. 'I never saw that one coming.'

'I told you it was good,' Helen said, and laughed again as Marcus continued to shake his head in disbelief. 'More wine?' She asked, picking up his empty glass.

'I really shouldn't,' he said.

'Half a glass then?' Helen pouted. 'You aren't leaving me just yet, are you?' She feigned a sad look. Marcus smiled.

'Oh OK, but just half,' he said. 'It's getting late.' Helen gave him a smile.

'It's Sunday tomorrow; no work, remember?' She said and disappeared into the kitchen to fetch their drinks.

Helen was starting to feel light-headed as she sat back down next to Marcus. She had emptied the bottle herself, other than the glass and a bit he had drunk.

'Are you OK?' he asked, seeing that her eyes were slightly glazed.

'I couldn't be better,' she replied. 'Are you OK?' She asked.

'Sort of,' he said, and Helen sat up, concerned by his response.

'What do you mean, sort of?' She asked.

'Well, I just can't get you out of my head, Helen. If I'm honest, you're driving me insane,' he said, taking both her hands in his. 'I literally think about you all the time; when I'm at home, when I'm in bed. I think about that kiss all the time.' He put his hand to his forehead.

'I do, too,' Helen admitted, and Marcus looked at her as if he had misheard her.

'Really?' He asked. Helen nodded.

'Ever since that day, I've wanted you to kiss me again,' she said, her stomach churning with anticipation.

'Can I kiss you now, Helen?' Marcus asked.

'Yes please,' she said and smiled.

Marcus looked at Helen. Her eyes were so blue they dazzled him. Their eyes were locked, studying each other's faces, as if trying to take in every detail. Marcus traced his fingers across her cheekbone, and down to her soft lips. Cupping his hands underneath her chin, he tipped her head back slightly, and as he brushed his lips against hers, Helen closed her eyes and embraced him. She ran her fingers through his hair, and he groaned quietly as she allowed her hands to explore the naked flesh of his back, beneath the linen shirt.

Marcus felt disappointed when Helen stopped kissing him and stood up, thinking he had done something wrong, but his heart started racing so fast that he thought he might have a heart attack when she pulled open the cord of her dressing gown and let it drop to the floor. As if it wasn't enough that she looked a vision of beauty stood in front of him in a pair of silk pyjamas, Helen then removed her top, to reveal the most stunning breasts that Marcus had ever seen. She came towards him, and slowly unbuttoned his shirt, kissing his chest as she did. Marcus thought he was going to explode. He pushed her gently down onto the sofa and removed his shirt. Helen gasped at his physique; she ran her hands over his chest, then putting them around his neck, she pulled him back towards her and kissed him hungrily. Their kisses were becoming more passionate and intense, and as he pressed against her, she could feel that he wanted her as badly as she wanted him.

Helen tugged at his jeans, as Marcus pulled off her pyjama bottoms, and she was almost desperate as she pulled him towards her, and they both groaned with pleasure as he entered her. As they moved together in unison, Helen experienced sensations that she had never before felt. Marcus kissed her like he never wanted to stop, and Helen didn't want him to ever stop. His kisses sent shockwaves through her body. Every touch was like electricity. Their lovemaking lasted for several hours, until eventually they came together, and for both of them it was like multiple earthquakes vibrating through their bodies, a sensation neither of them had experienced before. They clung to each other in silence for a long time after, sharing gentle kisses, stroking each other's skin, not wanting to pull apart from each other.

'Stay with me tonight,' Helen said after a while.

'What if someone comes home?' Marcus said, tucking her hair behind her ear.

'No one will. Please stay; I want to wake up in your arms,' Helen said, looking up at him.

'There's nothing I'd love more,' he said, smiling.

Helen led him up to her room, and as he lay in her bed, she went to the bathroom. She couldn't believe what was happening. It was that sparkle inside, the one she had always dreamt about. But that was ridiculous; she had only just met Marcus, but by God did he ignite some feelings inside her. Standing in the doorway of her room, she looked over to him and smiled. He smiled back, and wondered how he had managed to be so lucky. He was in the bedroom of this gorgeous girl, who he had fallen head over heels in love with. Not that he would tell her that; he'd frighten her off. Helen walked up to him and sat on the side of the bed, and leaning towards him, she kissed him tenderly on the lips.

Neither of them slept much that night, both wanting to cherish every hour that they had together, not knowing when they would see each other again. Helen talked about David and her turmoil with him. She didn't want to hurt him, and Marcus understood that. They also talked about the implications of Marcus being Helen's tutor; it was a very strict policy within the school of nursing, that a student couldn't enter into a relationship with any member of staff. It was totally forbidden. If they did have a relationship, Marcus would lose his job, and Helen really didn't want to be responsible for that; he was an excellent teacher. There was also the age gap. It was now that Helen discovered Marcus was thirty-eight, exactly double her age. Not that she cared, but what would other people think? He was nearly the same age as her mum. The problem was, as she lay in his arms, she never wanted to let go. She didn't want this moment to ever end. Her eyes prickled with tears as he stroked her hair. Marcus was the one, and she knew it.

'Do you want a coffee?' She asked at seven o'clock. They had agreed he would leave at eight thirty, as David's ferry was due to arrive back in Hull at ten, and Helen had agreed to pick him up. She didn't know how she would be able to face him.

'I would love one, but let me make you one,' Marcus said, kissing her cheek. 'I'll be able to find everything.' Helen smiled, and snuggled back under the duvet. She wolf-whistled as Marcus put on his boxer shorts, and her heart fluttered as she watched him leave the room. Just the sight of him made every part of her body tingle. Her head was pounding slightly, probably from a combination of the wine and lack of sleep, so she went through to the bathroom and took some paracetamol, freshening up while she was in there.

Marcus was waiting in bed with the coffee when she returned to her room.

'We will be able to see each other again, won't we?' He asked, a worried expression on his face. Helen put her arms around him and rested her head on his shoulders. He kissed her neck gently.

'I couldn't bear it if we didn't,' she said softly, and kissed his shoulder. 'We'll just have to be really careful; you can't lose your job over me,' she said. Marcus pushed her gently away from him so he was facing her.

'I don't care about my job, Helen. I care about you.' Helen looked down.

'I know, but I can't hurt David either. It's not fair on him; he's done nothing wrong. I just need time to sort things out with him.' Marcus nodded. He understood totally. 'I only have one more year at uni. We can't blow your career, and we need to be careful.'

They held each other in silence, both having their own separate thoughts, thoughts of how they could be together. Helen pulled away and looked deep into Marcus's eyes, then leant forward and kissed him softly on the lips. She shuddered as he followed the length of her spine with his finger, and arched her back as he reached her coccyx. Helen positioned herself on top of Marcus and lowered herself slowly onto him, smiling as he groaned. She threw her head back in pleasure as he cupped her breasts in his hands and caressed them gently as she made love to him. Again, Helen was overwhelmed with the feelings that were stimulated inside of her, and afterwards, as they lay together, kissing each other, she started to cry.

'What is it, Helen?' Marcus asked, concerned at her tears.

'I don't know, I just feel so overwhelmed by everything,' she said, and burying her head in his chest, she sobbed uncontrollably as Marcus silently held her in is arms.

'I'm so sorry about that,' Helen sniffed afterwards. 'I don't know what came over me.' She laughed, embarrassed. Marcus kissed her and wiped her tears with the back of his hand, a loving gesture that made her heart melt.

'Please don't apologise,' he said. 'If I'm honest, I want to cry at times.' Helen looked at him with a confused expression. Seeing the look in her face, Marcus felt he should tell her the truth. 'The thing is, Helen... God, I hope I don't scare you off by saying this but...' He trailed off, and Helen looked at him, waiting in anticipation.

'Go on,' she said.

'The thing is... I think I'm in love with you, Helen.' Marcus closed his eyes, not wanting to see her expression, scared that she would have a look of disgust; instead, he missed her smile. He did feel her lips meet his and kiss him though.

'I love you too, Marcus, more than you would ever believe.' His heart leapt.

Helen meant it, too. She was absolutely smitten with Marcus. Never in her life had she felt this way, and she was devastated when the time came for him to leave, knowing that she probably wouldn't see him for another week, when they were back at uni. They clung to each other as they said goodbye, and shared several lingering kisses. They exchanged phone numbers; Helen put his number in her phone under the name of Maria so as not to arouse suspicion, and they agreed that he would only text if Helen texted first, just in case she was with David. However, no sooner had he driven away than she did receive a text from him;

I love you more than life itself, and that was the most amazing night of my entire life. Thank you for making me the happiest man alive xxxxx.

137

Helen got butterflies simply reading the message.

I love you, too. So much. I had a FANTASTIC time, can't wait to do it again soon xxxx.

She carefully made sure she deleted the received and sent message. She would need to take care doing that, so she didn't get caught out. The thought of that made her feel nauseous, because the realisation dawned that she had been unfaithful to poor David, and the reality was that she would have an affair with Marcus because she loved him.

As she drove to Hull, Helen spent a lot of the journey thinking about what she should do about David. Should she end the relationship? Even if she did, she couldn't have a relationship with Marcus openly whilst he was her tutor. David loved her so much, and she really did care about him, and she would hate to hurt him. They had been together so long; it must be coming on for four years now. Helen was in turmoil. If she carried on seeing David, it would hurt Marcus, and she did love Marcus. That was certain. But he was so much older than her; would it work out with such a big age gap? She compared notes in her head: David was gorgeous. So was Marcus. They both had good bodies. David was a lovely kisser, but when Marcus kissed her, she never wanted the kiss to end. David was great in bed, but Marcus was absolutely amazing, and he had sent her to heaven and back. Most importantly, she cared about David a lot; he was lovely, kind, caring, affectionate and her family adored him, and he loved her. Marcus, she hardly knew really, but he seemed lovely, kind, caring, affectionate, he loved her, and the spark she had always wanted, the spark her parents shared was there. She has it; she truly loves him. Her family haven't met him yet, but she was sure if they did, they would love him.

David trudged off of the ferry looking worn out, hungover and dishevelled, and as he kissed Helen, she felt a pang of guilt at her betrayal. He talked most of the journey home about their antics. He had been pleased that Carl hadn't pushed Gaz into going with a prostitute, although they had all clubbed together and paid for Paul to go in. Paul was a thirty-five-year-old virgin, who still lived at home and apparently was not even in the room five minutes. The poor bloke had endured jokes about quickies the rest of the weekend.

David sensed something was wrong with Helen, and asked her on several occasions if she was alright. She reassured him that she was fine, but had a bit of a headache. She offered for him to go back for a Sunday roast for tea and he gratefully accepted. As they all sat around the table, both Katherine and Beth also sensed that Helen was not her usual bubbly self, but neither said anything. They all laughed as George repeated his favourite jokes from the Lee Evans show the previous night, where the four of them had apparently laughed so hard that their sides hurt.

'What did you do with yourself?' Beth asked Helen, and she was conscious that she blushed.

'I just had a bath, drank that lovely wine and watched 'The Others'.' she said.

'How many times have you watched that film now?' David laughed.

'I've lost count,' Helen smiled. 'I just love the twist.' Thinking of Marcus's reaction to the end of the film, she felt a heavy feeling inside, wondering what he was doing right now, and wishing that she was with him, wrapped in his arms.

Chapter Sixteen

Amy didn't turn up to uni on the first day back, much to the relief of Michelle and Helen, who took their usual seats in the classroom. The girls hadn't seen each other in the week but they had spoken on the phone. Helen had been pleased to hear that, although Michelle had agreed to meet up with Phil, as soon as she had seen him, memories of that night had come flooding back, and she had decided she couldn't forgive him for what he'd done. Helen had seen Tom and Laura in Brown's pie shop on Friday night, when she went with David, and they said they'd seen Amy and Phil together that evening in the The White Hart, having a drink; Helen opted not to mention it to Michelle.

Helen had seen David a few evenings over the week, and things had drifted back to normal. She had stayed the night on the Friday, and they had made love, and they had gone to Matlock for the day on the Saturday before having tea at David's parent's house. Helen had felt uncomfortable when they spent several conversations focussed on when the two of them were planning to get engaged. David, sensing her discomfort, had attempted to change the subject, stating that they were still young and had their whole lives ahead of them. Recently, David had been thinking about it himself, but he was noticing that Helen seemed to be different towards him. He didn't know why; he just had a feeling that something had changed, but every time he asked, she denied it. Maybe he was just being paranoid because he loved her so much; he knew his world would fall apart if he lost her.

The classroom door opened, and Helen was disappointed to see Debbie and Bill walk in, but no Marcus.

'Good morning everyone, and welcome to your final year,' Debbie said, and everybody cheered. 'This is going to be a tough year, with a lot of work and outcomes to complete, but trust me, in the blink of an eye, you'll be graduating.' She smiled, and Bill nodded beside her. Helen looked at Michelle, and bit her lip nervously.

'Oh my God, I can't imagine being qualified...' She said.

'I can't wait!' Michelle said. Adam, who was sat in front of them, turned around.

'I can't wait to have some proper money for a change!' The girls both laughed and agreed.

They would have three last placements for the year and today was the day they would find out the first two, which would either be A&E, theatre, intensive care, coronary care or respiratory. The final placement would be three months of management, for which Marcus was going to try and arrange for Helen to go back to her community placement, as they had agreed to take her. Helen was pleased to hear that she was going to have a placement on A&E, but not so pleased to find this was followed by a placement on theatres. She envied Michelle, who was going to be on coronary care followed by A&E, and wished that they were on A&E together. They would have had a good laugh, and could have travelled together if they got the same shifts.

They received all of their appropriate documentation throughout the morning, which they looked through over lunch. The afternoon was going to be a two-hour session to discuss the assignment and a presentation, then they could go home.

Back in the classroom for the final stretch of the day, Helen and Michelle were busy discussing where they would go for coffee afterwards, seeing as they were going to finish early. Neither heard the classroom door open, and were oblivious as Marcus stood at the front of the room. He had dreaded this moment; obviously he was desperate to see Helen, but having to act normal was going to be a difficult thing to do. As soon as he saw her, his mouth went dry, so he looked away and casually took a sip of his water.

'Good afternoon, everybody. I hope you had an enjoyable break,' he said, smiling. Helen sat bolt upright and dropped all of her papers, causing everybody to turn around and laugh. 'Are you alright there, Helen?' Marcus asked, feeling sorry for her. She appeared nervous as she picked them all up.

'I'm fine,' she said, smiling and blushing. Michelle leant over to her friend.

'Are you OK?' She whispered.

'Yes, he just made me jump,' Helen stuttered.

'This afternoon, we're going to talk about a presentation that we want you to do. You'll be working groups, which I'll assign you to. Depending on your number, you'll be supported by myself, Bill or Debbie. Groups one and four will be with me, two and five with Bill, three and six with Debbie.' While everyone had been talking, Marcus had already counted around the room and worked it out so that Helen would be in his group. She faintly smiled as he counted around the room, pointing at everybody in turn. 'One, two, three, four, five, six, one, two, three, four, five, six.' He continued until he had included everyone in the group.

There were going to be six separate subjects, and one group would present each of them to each other via a PowerPoint presentation. They also had to create a handout, and they had six weeks to prepare this. Their next placements started in three weeks, so Helen's group decided that they would get theirs done before then. They would have to come in half way through to present it, and decided that, not knowing what shifts each other would have, they didn't want to have to commit to having to work on it whilst on placement. The subject Helen's group had was social isolation, and she was with Kev, Paul, Jo-Jo and Kelly, a girl who had returned from having a baby. They didn't know her very well, but she seemed nice. Paul suggested they went to the library to plan what they would do, as it would be quieter in there and they could sit around a table. Most of the rooms in the school of nursing consisted of chairs with a small table that pulled up from the side of the armrest, big enough only to place a notebook. Paul was a natural leader and often would take the lead in most group discussions; Helen thought to herself that he would quickly become a manager when they qualified.

They spent about an hour in the library, each deciding on an area that they would look into; Helen was going to find some references on how social isolation could lead to depression. She had already seen a report from the world health organisation in an earlier assignment that she wrote, so she would use that reference. Apparently Kelly was a whizz on the computer, so she was going to create the PowerPoint presentation at the end, when everyone had got all the information claiming it would only take her an hour. She used to do them all the time in a previous job, which was in marketing, much to the delight of the rest of the group, who were more than happy to allocate her the task. They each photocopied a few articles from nursing journals, and Helen took out a couple of books on depression, then headed back in search of Michelle.

She was surprised to see that there was only one group left in the classroom; Ally, Tom, Laura and Tammy.

'Have you seen Michelle?' She asked no one in particular. Tom looked up, grinning.

'I think she's gone for a coffee with Adam,' he said, and winked.

'Oh has she now?' Helen smiled. 'I've been stood up then, have I?' She laughed, happy that Michelle would forget about

Phil. 'See you guys tomorrow,' she said, and waved them goodbye. Pulling her phone out of her pocket, she texted her friend to have fun.

Shutting the classroom door behind her, she could see the door to Marcus's office was ajar. Looking around to make sure no one was about, she knocked on it gently.

'Come in,' came his voice from inside, and just the sound of it made her heart hammer inside her chest. She walked in, closing the door behind her. Looking up from his papers, Marcus smiled; he had hoped that she would come. Putting down his pen, he walked towards her and took the books from her hands, placing them on the chair so that he could circle his arms around her waist. He lifted her up and squeezed her close to him.

'Oh my God, I've missed you so much,' he said, kissing her cheek over and over again, before pulling her into a passionate embrace. Her legs wrapped around his waist, and her arms around his neck. Marcus couldn't believe how light Helen was.

'How hard was it today, trying to act normal?' Helen asked.

'I just wanted to keep kissing you,' he said, holding her close to him, savouring every moment. 'When can I see you again?' He asked.

'I don't know,' Helen replied. 'I'll try and sort something soon.' They shared another long kiss, then picking up her books, Marcus opened the door for her. Both were shocked to see Tammy on the other side.

'Oh, sorry Tammy. I didn't know you were waiting. Helen just needed to see me about something,' Marcus said, trying to appear casual.

'No worries,' Tammy said, looking at Marcus then at Helen, before breaking into a grin. Helen started blushing profusely, convinced Tammy had guessed something.

'See you tomorrow, both of you,' she said, and scurried off down the corridor.

Helen was meeting David after work; he was treating her to a meal at a restaurant on the Bail, as a thank you for the roast yesterday. As it was still early, Helen decided to have a look around Next on the way home. She had received a brochure the previous week highlighting some special offers. She treated herself to a white cotton dress, and a white bra and pant set decorated with delicate pink roses, all of which she decided to wear that evening. She also found a pair of novelty socks, which she bought for David, with characters on them from his favourite TV show, The Simpsons. He laughed until he cried when he watched it.

Katherine was already at home when Helen arrived. Apparently the florists shop was quiet, so they had told her to go early, which Katherine was happy to do, as she had a book to finish ready for her book club tomorrow.

'Have you got time for a cuppa?' Her mum asked, pulling out a chair for Helen to sit down. It reminded Helen of when they were children, about to be having a 'talking to', as her dad used to say. She nodded and sat down, curious as to what her mum was going to be saying to her. Katherine flicked on the kettle and sat opposite her daughter.

'Is everything OK with you and David?' She asked, getting straight to the point. 'You know you can talk to me about anything, love.' She put her hand on top of Helen's, which was resting on the table. Helen swallowed hard. She felt almost dizzy, wondering if she dared tell her mum the truth. But she couldn't do it.

'Of course, mum. What makes you ask that?' She asked, trying to look confused. Katherine sighed and shook her head, not convinced.

'I've noticed, Beth and Steve have noticed, and I'm sure poor David must have, too. You just seem distant towards him these days, almost like you don't want him around you sometimes... I don't know, I can't quite put my finger on it.'

Katherine stood up to make the drinks, and Helen could feel herself welling up. She swallowed hard, and looked down at her hands, pushing her nails into her palms and biting her lip, desperate not to cry, but she couldn't stop it happening. Large tears fell onto her cheeks, and Katherine gasped as she turned to see her daughters distress. She put her arms around her child.

'Oh my goodness darling, what is wrong? Please tell me. Please don't cry like this.' Katherine held her daughter until her tears subsided, and then handed her a tissue to blow her nose. 'You look like a panda now,' she said, wiping away the smudged mascara, and Helen laughed. Handing Helen a cup of tea, Katherine pulled her chair next to her and took her hand. 'Come on, sweetheart. Tell me what this is all about. You need to get this off of your chest.'

For the next half an hour, Helen poured her heart out to her mum. She didn't tell her about Marcus, but she talked about David, and how much she liked him, and how much he loved her, but how she knew she didn't love him and she knew she never would. She talked about the sparkle she had seen between Katherine and Richard, and how she wanted to have that sparkle with a man, how she wished she loved David the way that he loved her, how bad she felt that she didn't. Katherine sat and listened to her daughter and her heart bled for her turmoil.

'Do you want to finish with David?' She asked Helen.

'I can't break his heart,' Helen replied sadly.

'But you're breaking your own by staying with him,' Katherine replied, and Helen cried again, not knowing what she should do.

'Please don't say anything to anyone, not even Beth...' She pleaded and Katherine nodded.

'My lips are sealed,' she promised.

'I'd better go and get ready, he's taking me for a meal,' Helen said, with a sad smile, and standing up, she kissed her mum and thanked her for listening. Katherine felt shocked and sad that

Helen felt this way. She thought David was perfect for her, and had hoped they would marry one day, but if Helen didn't love him then there was nothing she could do about that.

Even on a Monday, the restaurant was packed; it was a popular Italian restaurant in Lincoln that was always busy. It was quaint. They sat near a group of loud girls, which made it difficult to hear each other speak.

'How was your first day back?' David asked. Helen told him about the presentation, how Amy hadn't turned up and that Michelle had gone for coffee with Adam.

'You can't hear yourself think in here,' she said, looking across at the table of girls, who were exceptionally loud. It looked like it was some sort of leaving party, although it was strange to be taking place on a Monday. Helen noticed that one of the girls kept looking over at David, and she was sure that he looked at her on a couple of occasions too, and she felt a pang of jealousy. She held her hand across the table for David to take it, to make it clear that they were together, and underneath the table she rubbed the inside of David's leg with her foot, gently reminding him he didn't need to look in another direction.

'How was your day?' She asked.

'Same old, same old,' he said. 'But you won't believe it; Mike and Shelley are moving in together next month. They'll be having a house warming party, apparently, and he asked if we wanted to go.'

'You have got to be kidding me! They hardly know each other,' Helen said. 'And she's a kid,' she added, shaking her head.

'He was asking me when we were planning to get a place together,' David said, and looked at Helen as if waiting for a response.

'I've to finish uni for a start,' she said, and sighed with relief when the waiter came to the rescue with the arrival of their meals. Helen had lasagne and David a pizza. He decided not to

147

continue with that conversation; he could see that Helen was not comfortable with the discussion.

They enjoyed a walk around the Bail after their meal, and had a drink in the Magna Carta. They saw the sign for the ghost walk, and decided to buy some tickets for the following Wednesday.

'We really should book another weekend away again soon,' David said, putting his arm around Helen's waist. 'How about we go somewhere on Saturday night? My treat.' Helen thought about it for a while. It might rekindle something inside of her; they did have a fantastic time in Skegness.

'Where to?' She asked.

'Let me surprise you,' David said, pulling her towards him.

'OK.' She smiled. 'Let's do it.' The chimes of the cathedral chimed ten o'clock. 'Come on, we better make a move,' she said.

'Are you going to come up for a coffee?' David asking expectantly, and gave a pretend growl. Helen had parked at his bedsit on Boultham Park road, and they had driven to the Bail in his car.

'I actually think we should save ourselves for Saturday night, now,' she whispered in his ear, and gently bit his earlobe.

'God you are so damn hot,' he murmured. As soon as he got home, he would be looking on the internet to book a hotel.

Kissing him goodbye, she thanked him for a lovely evening and drove away. She would look forward to Saturday now, and she wondered where he would take her. Helen then thought about Marcus. Maybe she should tell him she couldn't see him anymore; she couldn't go on deceiving David. She would tell Marcus it had to end. She pulled over the car, and took her phone from her bag.

Where do you live? She texted. Marcus must have been waiting for her to text, because he replied instantly.

Greetwell Close. Helen knew where it was. She told him

she was going to see him, so he said the kettle was on. She felt nervous as she was driving to his house, planning in her head how she was going to tell him that it was over. Finding his house, she pulled up outside, and checking her reflection in the mirror, she nervously went to his door.

Marcus opened it before she rang the bell. He had been watching out the window, and waiting for her arrival. He had showered recently and was wearing some cotton pyjama bottoms and a t-shirt, his hair still slightly damp, a few stray strands falling over his eyes. He smiled as he saw Helen, and stood to one side, inviting her into his home. The door led straight into the front room, and Helen was surprised to see how tidy it was, with two comfy looking sofas, a TV on a nice oak cabinet that also had a stereo built in, and in the corner, an oak desk and a computer.

'Latte?' He asked, smiling, after giving her a kiss, and Helen nodded and returned his smile, thinking to herself how handsome he looked, even in a pair of pyjamas. She followed him through to the kitchen.

'This is nice,' she commented, looking around as he prepared the coffee.

'Thanks,' Marcus said. 'To be honest, I've not had to do much myself; it was already decorated quite nicely when I moved in.' The walls were a pastel yellow, and he had a selection of pictures displayed, the old fashioned advertisements for teabags, coffee, Oxo and custard powder, which Helen found quite tasteful. Marcus told her that he had bought them from a shop in the waterside a few weeks ago. 'Would you like gingerbread latte? I have some gingerbread syrup,' he asked, holding up a fancy shaped bottle.

'Mmm, yes please,' Helen said, licking her lips. 'My favourite.' Of course Marcus knew that.

Helen watched him as he stirred the coffee with a miniature whisk in order to make it frothy. He had his back to her, and she was looking at his arms, which looked strong, and masculine, and slightly tanned. His hair was slightly tousled as it was drying, and she could see the slight flecks of grey, emphasized by the dampness. Looking down, she could see the shape of his buttocks. They looked so firm. She thought back to the night they had spent together, and tingled with desire at the memory.

'Here you go, beautiful,' Marcus said, turning and handing her the coffee. Helen took the mug from him and put it on the table.

'Kiss me,' she said, putting her arms around his neck and moving towards him. She knew that she couldn't tell him it was over when she ached with desire for him. The feelings she had for Marcus were so intense; she couldn't let that go, not when he felt the same way about her.

'I love you so much,' he said.

'I love you, too,' she replied, and they shared a passionate embrace.

Marcus lifted Helen slightly, so that she was sat on the kitchen table, then moved her coffee onto the worktop. He kissed her neck gently, and ran his fingers along her thighs, aroused merely by her presence, especially in that dress. Marcus thought she looked stunning.

'Would you like to see my bedroom?' He grinned, as their kisses became more passionate, and Helen nodded, her breaths getting heavier. She desperately wanted him. Leading her upstairs, they were both so turned on that they began removing their own clothes along the way, and they fell onto his bed, suddenly engulfed in a luxurious feather duvet with a satin burgundy cover. Helen trembled with desire as Marcus kissed every inch of her body, before slowly and gently making love to her. He told her he loved her, over and over, again until his body quivered with desire and he groaned in pleasure. Helen arched her back and screamed his name, digging her nails into his back, as she experienced the most sensational orgasm that she had ever had.

'Oh my God! That was incredible. You are amazing. I love you,' Marcus said, shaking, and stroking Helen's hair, who, too, was trembling.

'You're amazing,' she said, kissing him full on the lips. 'I love you so much that I would surely die if I lost you.'

'Helen, you are all I ever think about. I've never felt this way before about anyone. You'll never lose me, not now I've found you,' he reassured her, as she snuggled into him.

'What are we going to do, Marcus?' She asked, burying her head into his chest. Marcus knew what she was implying; if their relationship became common knowledge he would lose his job, without a doubt, and possibly struggle to get another anywhere else. There was a strict code of conduct for student/ tutor relationships. The problem was that he was hooked, totally besotted. He needed to be with Helen, no matter what the consequences.

'What about David?' He asked softly, and Helen sighed. After what seemed like a very long pause, she answered.

'I don't know how I'll do it, but I'll finish with him. I just need a bit of time.' Marcus nodded' he understood that Helen didn't want to hurt David, and in a way Marcus felt guilty himself; he'd seen the way that David looked at Helen, but his heart was bursting with happiness. He had done it; he had won her heart.

'I suppose I'd better go,' Helen said, sitting up and looking over at his bedside clock.

'I wish you could stay,' Marcus said, looking at her naked body.

'So do I, but I told my mum I would be home, and she'll worry. Plus, I have to get all my stuff ready for uni,' Helen said. 'I wouldn't want to upset my teacher.' She straddled him, and leaning down to kiss him, experienced the familiar butterflies.

'You blow my mind, Helen Mitchell,' Marcus said, as she walked across the bedroom picking up her clothes, which had been scattered in a state of passion. She turned back and smiled.

'I know,' she said.

Helen's heart lurched as she put her phone on charge and noticed she had a text from David.

Hotel booked for Saturday night. Not telling you where until the day, but we have got a four poster bed, with champagne and chocolates... I love you xxxx

He had sent it two hours ago, and it was followed by another text half an hour ago asking if she was OK, so she quickly typed a reply saying her phone had somehow clicked onto silent, that she had only just seen the message, and that she couldn't wait. She didn't put 'I love you' back, which David did notice. He had noticed that she'd never said it again, since that one time, and even then, she'd had a drink. This weekend, he planned to have an amazing time and woo her, so that she felt so special, just like when they went to Skegness.

Michelle told Helen about her coffee with Adam, which had led to a meal at Nando's. She apologised profusely for disappearing when they should have been going for coffee, but Helen reassured her that she didn't mind at all. She smiled to herself when Adam walked in with Kev and Paul, and he winked at Michelle as they took their seats a few rows ahead. Michelle blushed, then turned to Helen and giggled like a small child.

'He's so lovely,' she whispered. 'I really like him.'

'Are you seeing him again?' Helen asked.

'He's taking me out on Friday.' Michelle smiled, as she looked over in his direction, but Adam was busy in conversation with his friends. Michelle continued to tell Helen how charming he had been, which Helen found hard to believe; he always seemed a Jack-the-Lad in the classroom, but she was happy that he had bought a smile to her friends face again.

'David is taking me away on Saturday,' she said.

'Ooh, lovely. Where are you going?' Michelle asked.

'A surprise,' Helen said, half smiling, and raising her eyebrow slightly.

'Don't sound too excited,' Michelle said, laughing and shaking her head. 'It's like a magical mystery tour; it'll be fun.'

Marcus and Debbie entered the classroom and bid them a good morning.

'I'm assuming you all know Amy Templeton,' Debbie said. Michelle and Helen looked at each other, wondering why they were being asked that question. The class, equally curious, acknowledged that they did, before Debbie went on to explain that for reasons that Amy had chosen not to disclose, she had decided to take a year out of the course, so wouldn't be returning to the group. Several hushed discussions took place. A few people, including Tammy and Jo-Jo, turned discreetly to look at Michelle. Michelle, conscious of the attention, bit her nail and looked at the wall, as Helen affectionately patted her leg and leant over to whisper to her.

'Don't be embarrassed; she's the one who did the dirty, not you,' she reminded Michelle, who turned to her and smiled. Helen could see that she still felt embarrassed, so she gave Tammy and Jo-Jo a look that encouraged them to turn away.

'OK, OK, let's all stop speculating, and get on with today's lessons,' Marcus said, and the room fell silent. 'Today we're going to discuss ethics, in particular 'do not resuscitate' orders being made without a patient's consent when it is thought to be in their best interests. I want you to split into six groups and discuss it for an hour, and then we'll meet back up and feedback what we all think. Any questions?' Tammy raised her hand. 'Yes, Tammy?' He said.

'Sir, talking of ethics, do you think it would be ethical for a student to be in a relationship with a tutor?' She asked, a menacing grin on her face. Helen felt her face flush and her heart beat harder in her chest. Marcus's expression didn't falter.

'I'm not sure of the relevance of your question, Tammy, but no, it wouldn't be ethical, and I can assure you that it's not the sort of practice that would occur in this university, if that is what you're insinuating,' he said casually.

'Not at all sir, I was just watching a film the other day and that was in the story line. I just wondered what your view on the subject was,' she replied, turning to Helen, winking as she did.

'What's up with her?' Michelle asked, and Helen silently shook her head, unable to answer. Her head was spinning, and she thought that if she opened her mouth to speak, she would be sick.

Tammy was in the same group as Helen, but she didn't say anything else. In fact, she acted as if she had said nothing at all in the classroom. Paul did ask her about motive for asking such a bizarre question when Marcus was talking about resuscitation, but she backed up her story about a movie she had watched, so Helen started to relax a little.

'That was a strange thing for Tammy to come out with back there, wasn't it?' Debbie said to Marcus, as they sat having a coffee in the staff room.

'What was that?' Bill asked who had joined them and Debbie told him of her comment.

'She's an odd girl, that one. Can you remember when she came into school with her hair multi-coloured, and we had to remind her that she was training to be a nurse, not an art teacher.' Bill laughed. Debbie nodded, then told Marcus of the time that they were having a lesson on consent, and she asked a random question about vibrators.

'She just likes to try and shock and embarrass you,' Bill said. Marcus shook his head and smiled.

'It'll take a bit more than that to get to me,' he said, but deep down he breathed a sigh of relief that his colleagues hadn't suspected anything from her stupid remark. The whole situation had made him it clear that they definitely had to be very careful in future.

Chapter Seventeen

Helen told Marcus that David was taking her away for the night, and although he felt torn inside at the thought of them spending the night in a hotel, he knew that there was nothing he could do about it and eventually they would be together indefinitely. Although they had not been able to spend any time together during the week, they had spoken on the phone a couple of times and they had made a decision that they would see each other whenever they could. Until Helen had finished at university, their relationship would remain a secret, otherwise Marcus would lose his career. Although they knew they had just under a year to wait, they had agreed that they would still be together and their love was strong enough to ride this through until they could be together forever. Helen was going to end her relationship with David after their weekend away; both agreeing it was not fair to do it before.

Katherine woke her up bright and early on Saturday morning, as she wanted to have a shower before she went. David was picking her up at ten so they could have a full couple of days. Despite everything that was going on, Helen was actually looking forward to going away and was curious to find out where they were going. Katherine knew where they were going but had sworn to keep it a secret and refused to tell Helen even with the threat of being sent to Coventry.

'I hope this weekend does you both some good,' her Mum said as they sat enjoying a cup of tea together waiting for David's arrival.

Helen smiled and almost felt guilty inside because she knew how much Katherine adored David.

'You never know,' she said as she took a sip of her drink.

'Are you still feeling the same?' her Mum asked with a look in her eyes that suggested that she was hoping for an answer different to what Helen gave her.

'I still don't feel that spark, if that's what you mean?' she replied.

'Some people never get that feeling though, love, some people are in love but don't necessarily feel the spark that you are describing,' Katherine said.

'I know that I have those feelings inside of me though, Mum. They are there, just not with David,' Helen said, instantly wishing that she hadn't.

'What do you mean?' Katherine questioned, her eyes widening.

Helen felt incredibly happy when David walked through the kitchen door just at that moment, saving her from a very awkward situation.

'Morning beautiful. Are we all packed and ready to go?' he asked, kissing Helen on the cheek.

'I am now,' she said as she drained the last dregs of tea from her mug.

'Here, this is for later in the hotel,' Katherine said handing them a bottle of wine.

'Gosh, we will be tiddly,' Helen said. 'We have got champagne as well, didn't you say?'

'And chocolates,' David added.

'You have been spoilt,' Katherine smiled.

Helen smiled back but felt guilty, knowing how hard David was trying to win her affections and all she was doing was working out how to end their relationship.

Two hours later, they arrived at their mystery destination, the Hotel Noir in York. It was a beautiful hotel that had a black and white theme throughout. Their room had a beautiful black wrought iron four-poster bed encased with white cotton drapes and white bed linen. At the end of the bed stood a small, round table with an ice bucket containing a small bottle of champagne, two champagne flutes and a silver plate with a selection of Belgian chocolates. Helen promptly popped one into her mouth.

'This is lovely David,' she said with a mouth full of chocolate and David laughed as some dropped out of her mouth onto her top.

'Shall we start early with a glass of this?' David said, pulling the bottle of wine from Katherine out of the bag.

'Go on then, you've twisted my arm,' said Helen, picking up the champagne flutes and holding them steady for him to pour.

'So, what do you fancy doing this afternoon?' David asked.

'I don't know, I've never been to York,' Helen said. 'Is there a lot to do?'

David pulled out a tour guide that he had bought from WH Smiths and flicked through the pages.

'There is a museum, the York dungeons, a haunted house, the Jorvik Viking Centre, the York minster and the Shambles, which is an old shopping street,' he said. 'I thought that would be plenty to keep us going, although I don't think we will even fit all of that in.'

'I like the sound of the haunted house and the dungeons,' Helen said.

'Me too,' David said. 'Shall we grab a sandwich for lunch and visit those this afternoon?'

Helen nodded and smiled as she put another small amount of wine into both of their glasses.

'We won't get out of the room at this rate.' David laughed sipping his drink.

They found a small coffee shop in the town centre that served thick homemade soup and bread, so they opted for that instead and read through the tour guide as they enjoyed their lunch. There were so many attractions in York; you could spend a week there and still not have enough time to do everything. David wished he had booked them in for the whole weekend but they would make the most of the time that they had.

They went to the haunted house first. Standing outside, they looked at the television screens that had cameras filming inside each room.

'Look at all the orbs,' Helen said, pointing at one of the rooms. 'Do you think it is a camera trick?'

'Well I have read up on this place and it is supposed to be genuinely haunted,' David said.

'Come on then, let's go in,' Helen said excitedly and David smiled.

She looked so pretty when she smiled, he was so lucky to have her and he loved her so much. They walked around the house; there was no tour guide, just a recorded history in each room telling the story of the hauntings that had taken place in the house. Helen linked her arm through David's as they walked through the séance room, described as having the most activity.

'It feels spooky in here,' she said, feeling nervous as she recognised this as the room with the orbs on the television screen.

'I will protect you,' David said, placing an arm around her shoulder. 'Anyway, even if we did see a ghost, it wouldn't hurt you.'

'I know,' she said. 'It's funny because although I want to see one, I think I would be scared stiff if I did.'

As it happened, they reached the end of the tour of the house without feeling a presence. Although they enjoyed the haunted house, they both loved the York dungeon. This involved live actors throughout. It began with a show of the great plague, set in 1551, with an actor playing a plague doctor. It followed on with the recreation of an old York pub and the visitors being told ghost stories. There was a torture chamber where one of the visitors, called Mark, was put in a cage and they demonstrated several different torture devices that were used in the 1500's. Their favourite part of the show, which lasted over an hour, was the judgement of sinners where members of the audience were accused of certain crimes. Helen was picked to stand in the box and she was accused of being a witch, and she was told she had to dance naked in the moonlight as punishment. She blushed and giggled as the acting judge made her dance around in front of everybody. Not wanting to be a bad sport, she obliged and jiggled her body to cheers of hilarity before being shouted to 'Be quiet!' by the angry judge.

'That was brilliant,' Helen said as they left the building. 'I'm having a lovely time.'

David pulled her towards him and kissed her softly on the lips.

'Well, it's five o'clock. Are you hungry yet? Or did you want to go back to the room, freshen up and have a drink first?' David asked her.

'No, I'm still full from my soup, to be honest,' Helen replied. 'Let's have a slow stroll back to the room, then we can crack open that champagne and maybe eat in a couple of hours, unless you are hungry now?'

David shook his head.

'Not really, I'm not ready yet and I like the idea of the champagne first, anyway.' He smiled and offered his hand for her to take.

She did and they walked through the streets of York, looking at the sights and planning the following day's activities.

Arriving back at the hotel, they spoke briefly to the manager who was greeting guests as they came in and welcoming them to the hotel. He asked if they had had a nice day and had recommended the Jorvik Viking Centre, which David said they were visiting the following day. The manager kindly gave them a discount voucher that he had, which offered 50% off the entrance fee.

'That was nice of him,' Helen said as they walked to their room.

'Very,' David agreed as he put the vouchers into his wallet.

'This is a lovely room,' Helen commented as they stepped inside.

'I thought you would like it when I found it on the Internet,' David said, smiling, pleased that he had made the right choice.

Helen traced the post of the bed with her fingers, the wrought iron twisted into a gothic design with a matt finish. There was a high headboard and footboard. Together with the white sheets, it looked chic and classy all in one. The pillows looked nice and plump and so comfortable that Helen couldn't resist laying down on the bed to feel how soft they were.

'Oh my God, David come and put your head on one of these pillows,' she said as her head sunk into it.

Not needing asking twice, David climbed onto the bed beside her and rested his head next to hers.

'This is heaven,' he agreed.

'We won't want to get up in the morning,' she said as David snuggled up to her and pretended to snore.

Helen rested her hand onto his shoulder. He was so sweet and she did so love his company. She just wished she could love him like she loved Marcus; why couldn't life be simple.

'Do you fancy a bath?' David asked suddenly jumping up making her jump.

'OK,' she said. 'Let's have some champagne in the bath, too.'

'Now you stay in here, you are not allowed in the bathroom until I call you in,' David said, picking up his holdall and taking it with him along with the champagne and champagne flutes.

Helen nodded then giggled as David ran back and gave her a kiss before closing the bathroom door behind him.

'I wonder what he is up to?' she thought to herself curiously.

She pulled her phone from her pocket and texted Marcus,

Don't text back, I know this weekend must be hard for you but remember I love you and I am missing you so much xxxxxxxxxx

She was right, Marcus was finding it hard. So hard that when he read the text, he put his head in his hands and cried. He cried because he missed Helen but also he cried because he knew that they could not be together properly and that was all he wanted in the world.

'You can come in now,' came David's voice from the bathroom.

Helen put her phone in her bag and gingerly opened the bathroom door, not quite sure what to expect. David stood naked at the side of the bath holding two glasses of champagne, grinning like a Cheshire cat. The lights were off and the room was illuminated with dozens of candles. Helen could see the water was scattered with rose petals.

'Oh David, this looks beautiful,' she said in a quiet voice.

'Not as beautiful as you,' he replied and he meant it as he looked over towards her and the light from the candles shimmered in her blonde hair.

Her thick lashes enveloped her eyes as she looked down at his creation in the bath, she really was a vision of pure beauty.

Helen took the glass he handed to her and took a long sip of the fizzy fluid. She swallowed hard and her stomach felt like it was doing somersaults as her mind went to Marcus, probably sitting at home reading a text saying how much she loved him and here she was in this atmosphere with another man. Then again, she was with the man that she had been with for years. Marcus knew that and until she plucked up the courage to end the relationship, she had to carry on as normal. She took another sip of her champagne and put down her glass.

'Come on then, let's get in this bath before it gets cold.' She smiled, taking off her clothes.

She dipped her toe in the water and the temperature was perfect so, lowering herself in, she held her hand up to David, inviting him to join her.

'What do you fancy eating tonight?' she asked as she stretched over to get their champagne.

She giggled as David gently tapped her bottom.

'How about an Indian?' he suggested.

'Oooh yes, I like the sound of that.' Helen nodded; Indian food was one of her favourites and she had not had one for weeks.

They talked about what they planned to do the following day and stayed in the bath until it was cool, drinking the entire bottle of champagne. Helen felt slightly tipsy as she wrapped the towel around her and hiccupped. She made her way back through into the bedroom.

'Crikey, I better not have any more to drink or I'll be on my back,' she chuckled and dropped face-down onto the bed burying her head into the pillow.

David walked into the room and smiled at the sight of her sprawled over the bed. He walked towards her and, sitting down beside her, ran his hands over her back and legs. Her skin felt like velvet and Helen shuddered as he moved forward, gently kissing her neck and nuzzling her ear. This was the part of the weekend she had been dreading because of Marcus. She felt now like she was betraying him. She closed her eyes and pictured his face. She imagined that it was his hands gliding up the inside of her leg and it worked. Helen put her arm behind her and put her hand behind David's head as he climbed onto her, tracing his tongue down her back. Drawing her to her knees, he took her from behind, wildly and passionately until he came, grasping her hips so tightly that it made her gasp.

'Sorry about that,' David apologised, sensing that he had hurt Helen, rubbing both her hips in unison. 'I think I got a bit carried away.'

'Don't worry about it, Tiger.' Helen smiled, conscious of the guilty look on his face.

She stretched her arms above her head and yawned.

'Shall we make a move in a minute? I'm getting ready for something to eat now,' she said and David nodded in agreement.

They managed to find a nice Indian restaurant that served a set menu. They had poppadoms and pickles to start, a tray of samosa, pakora and bhaji's followed by a chicken korma and rice with naan bread, and finished off with an Indian ice cream. They both sat back in their chairs after their meal and held their stomachs, which were stretched to capacity.

'That was delicious but I am stuffed,' David said loosening the belt to his jeans.

'Me too,' Helen agreed. 'I don't think I could eat another thing for a week.'

Thankfully, she had opted for a pair of leggings rather than jeans so they stretched with her full stomach. David caught the eye of a waiter and beckoned him for the bill.

'Shall we go for a nice walk and then for a quiet drink somewhere?' he suggested.

'That sounds nice,' Helen smiled, quite fancying the idea of walking off some of the meal.

York was bustling, more so than it had been in the day. They saw at least two hen parties and a stag party, easily identified by the outfits that they paraded about in. One of the hens, dressed as a pink fairy, asked David for a kiss and a photo as part of a challenge.

'Not a proper kiss of course, only a peck.' He looked at Helen for permission and she obligingly stood to one side in approval.

They found the Shambles, which was a historical street of shops and cafés, and decided to revisit the following day as there were some nice shops that they wanted to look at, including a shop that made home-made fudge.

Helen turned her nose up as a young man, obviously unable to hold his drink, started to vomit in one of the shop doorways.

'Oh how lovely,' she commented, looking back over her shoulder instinctively to make sure he was alright.

'The young ones of today,' David said and Helen laughed loudly.

'David, they were about the same age as us,' she said.

'Well I know, but they act a lot younger,' David said laughing himself at what he had said.

He put his arms around Helen and squeezed her tightly against his chest.

'You are so beautiful, Miss Mitchell,' he said kissing the top of her head. 'I love you more than you will ever know.'

Helen said nothing but she leant forward and kissed him softly on the lips.

'You are adorable, David. I don't deserve you,' she said sadly.

'Yes you do, you are the most perfect girlfriend anybody could wish for,' David argued and, overwhelmed with guilt, Helen hugged him tightly, feeling a wave of nausea wash over her body.

After finding one of the quieter pubs for a drink, they returned to the hotel and snuggled in bed to watch *Paranormal Activity* on the movie channel which Helen was surprised to find included in the television package. After making love again, David fell asleep with his head resting against her shoulders. Helen watched his breathing. His lips looked like they were blowing bubbles as he exhaled deeply, not quite snoring but breathing loudly. She looked at his dark hair and his dark eyebrows; not a trace of grey like there was in Marcus's. There were no creases in the sides of his eyes as he smiled, no signs of aging at all. In fact, David was perfect to look at in every way. Helen looked up at the ceiling. She wasn't feeling tired at all at the minute despite it being almost midnight.

She got out of bed and went to the bathroom, then made

herself a cup of tea and sat on the chair on the other side of the room. She took her phone off of charge and logged onto Facebook to read some of the statuses that people had put. She immediately saw that she had an inbox and clicked on it to read it, she smiled when she saw the name Marcus Edwards;

I hope you are having a lovely time, although I wish it was me with you, wherever you are ☹ *I love you xxx*

Helen felt sorry as she wished that too. She typed a reply.

I am in York. It is a lovely city. I have never been before and I hope one day that we can come together, I would love that. I am missing you, please believe that and know that I love you xxxx

Marcus was still awake, unable to sleep himself thinking about Helen being away with David, so he heard the message alert on his phone and he quickly got out of bed and logged onto Facebook. He smiled when he saw that she had replied.

I thought you would be asleep by now xx.

Helen looked over to David to make sure the light of her phone didn't disturb him before replying.

Can't sleep ☹ *my head is in turmoil xx*, she replied in turmoil.

I know how you feel, your text actually made me cry today... what a puff!! Xx.

The thought of Marcus crying made Helens stomach lurch.

Why did you cry? Xx, she asked.

He thought hard before he answered.

Because, I don't know how we can properly be together, yet that is all that I want to do.............. Does that make sense? Xx.

Helen knew exactly what he meant.

Perfect sense xx, she replied then looked over at David as he made a groaning noise.

I am going to have to go, but remember I love you and we will get through this xxx, she typed.

I hope so, I love you, goodnight xxxxxx.

Helen put her phone back on charge and, climbing back into bed beside David, she closed her eyes and wondered what on Earth she was going to do. She so wished she had never met Marcus because, although she loved him so much, if she had never met him, she would not be going through this turmoil and her life would just be normal again. She didn't sleep much that night, and when she did it was fraught with dreams of brawling. She woke up not very refreshed at all.

'I'm just having a quick shower before breakfast,' she said in a groggy voice as she brushed her hair back off of her face.

'Are you alright, sweetheart? You look a bit off colour,' David asked concerned.

'I just had a bit of an unsettled night,' Helen admitted, giving him a reassuring peck on the cheek before heading off to the bathroom.

The cool water against her skin was sufficient to make her feel refreshed and, after washing her hair and brushing her teeth, she put on a simple green cotton dress with a black belt and emerged from the bathroom looking like a different woman.

'Wow, that obviously did the trick.' David smiled as he splashed some aftershave onto his cheeks.

'I feel loads better,' Helen smiled. 'I'm ready for the day ahead now I have woken up.'

Over breakfast they looked at the tour guide and decided to visit the Jorvik Viking Centre, the Shambles and the Yorkshire Museum before heading home. Helen still felt full from her meal the previous night, so only managed to eat some toast and a yoghurt but David enjoyed a full cooked breakfast followed by two slices of toast.

'I don't know where you put it,' Helen commented as he wiped the plate clean with his crust, licking his lips as he popped it into his mouth.

They put their bags into the car and checked out before

leaving to enjoy their day. They managed to find a space at a car park situated near the town centre which was central to all of the places that they planned to visit that day.

First on the list was the Jorvik Viking Centre, which was built on the exact site where archaeologists discovered the Viking city of Jorvik. The museum had recreated, as accurately as possible, the town, including the layout of the houses and the characters including the outfits they wore and the language they spoke. Helen was amazed when they were guided around the tour in a capsule and the smell of cooking was everywhere. They both laughed and held their noses when they came across a Viking on the toilet; the smell was so realistic. After the ride-around tour, they walked through and saw some of the artefacts that the archaeologists had dug up and were able to read up on the history of Jorvik. David found this particularly interesting, as he had always been interested in history and the Viking age at school.

They walked to the Shambles from the Jorvik Viking Centre and enjoyed a milkshake before going to any shops.

'Apparently, there used to be lots of butchers down here and they would all hang their meat outside on hooks,' David said. 'A lot of the shops still have the hooks outside, so the tour guide says.'

Helen leant back on her chair to look up the street.

'I can see one outside that shop there,' she said, pointing to a shop a few doors from where they were sitting. 'I wouldn't want to eat meat that had been hanging outside on a hook all day.'

'Me neither,' David agreed. 'They used to have open-air slaughter houses too.'

Helen pulled a face that made him laugh.

There were some lovely shops, it was a historical street and some shops had period features such as beams and Tudor style qualities inside. Helen bought some fudge, vanilla with raisins, and she also bought some lemon fudge for Katherine, whom

167

she knew was particularly fond of it. There were also some nice jewellers' shops that they looked in the window of and Helen gasped at the prices; nothing below four figures.

'How can they justify those prices?' she said and David agreed but commented that there were some lovely pieces.

He especially pointed out a diamond solitaire ring and Helen grew nervous, wondering why out of all the pieces of jewellery in the window, he had looked at that. He was aware of her reaction so immediately pointed to an emerald necklace that he also commented was nice and Helen appeared to relax. Deep down he felt sad because he was ready to commit himself to Helen but somehow he knew she did not feel the same.

It was three o'clock by the time they had looked around all the shops so they decided they would go and spend a couple of hours in the York museum before heading home. There was a Victorian street that was full of old shops, and they enjoyed a magic lantern show from a man dressed in old fashioned attire. The museum harboured an old prison and Helen's favourite attraction was called Toy Story, which had a selection of old toys from generations passed. David pointed to an old Atari machine.

'My dad had one of those and he still says they are better than today's Play Stations.' He laughed. 'You should see one of the games called *Breakout* or something. It is literally a line with a square ball that you have to break through a wall. It was so basic, and the noise goes beep, beep, beep until it drives you mad.'

Helen laughed as David imitated the sound of the game whilst pulling a face.

The sixties era was David's favourite part of the museum as it had some memorabilia of the Beatles; a particular favourite of his after spending most of his childhood growing up listening to their music. He often had a Beatles CD playing in his car and Helen would tease him and playfully call him 'Grandad'. When he was young, he had also been a fan of Thomas the tank engine, more so when his dad had told him that Ringo Starr from the Beatles was the narrator. He had spent hours of his childhood watching the programme and owned all of them on video, watching them repeatedly until he knew them word for word. He loved the fat controller and had posters of him on his bedroom wall until he had been replaced with pictures of pop stars and the actresses who became his teenage crushes.

'I suppose we ought to make a move in a minute,' Helen said, linking her arm through his as they looked at a display of some sixties musicians.

David nodded and kissed the top of her head. He felt sad that the weekend had drawn to a close so soon. Clutching her hand as they walked to the car he smiled as she rested her head on his shoulder.

'I feel bushed,' she said, yawning.

Before they had even departed York, Helen was asleep and she slept for the whole journey, waking only as David turned off the engine outside her house.

Chapter Eighteen

It was soon the arrival of the next placements, and the first day on accident and emergency was a busy one. The shift started at seven and Helen was introduced to her mentor, Alan. He was a laid back individual with long brown hair, tied back in a ponytail and a swallow tattooed at the base of each thumb. All of the staff dressed in scrubs that rustled as they walked, and Helen pointed out that it was hard to identify from a junior to a senior member of staff as they were all in the same colour. Alan agreed but advised that the job role was identified on their name badges, which all staff had to wear on their shift. Being the devil's advocate Helen stated that if people were dyslexic they would not be able to read this and on the wards the coloured lapels were much easier to identify the different job roles. Alan laughed and commented that Helen was not going to be the sort of student who would just accept an answer without challenging him first, and she agreed. At this point they both mutually decided to themselves that they would get on fine.

Tammy was also on placement with Helen, although the first part of her morning was spent in the resuscitation room dealing with a road traffic accident that had come in at the start of the shift. She emerged from the room looking pale and shaken. She headed straight to the water fountain and took a long drink. Helen went up to her concerned.

'Are you alright, Tammy?' she asked.

Tammy did not look up. She shook her head and composed herself before speaking, her voice cracking as she did so.

'It was a young family in the car: a Mum, dad and two young boys,' she said looking around to make sure nobody was able to hear.

Conscious people were in the nearby cubicles waiting to be seen she lowered her voice and whispered to Helen.

'The dad was driving and it looks like a dog ran into the road, he swerved to miss it and hit a tree.' Tammy wiped away a stray tear as it rolled down her cheek.

Helen was surprised as she had never seen a sensitive side to her colleague before and she put her hand gently on her arm for comfort. Tammy looked towards the resuscitation room as the doors opened and her mentor, Sharon, came out with one of the doctors.

'Poor bloke lost all his family,' Tammy whispered before heading off towards her mentor, leaving Helen to take in the shock of what she had just heard.

Helen glanced towards the doors, conscious that a man's world had been torn apart, knowing that he will spend the rest of his life blaming himself.

'Do you want to come into the plaster room and see me plaster an arm?' Alan interrupted her thoughts and she nodded, following him through the department to find ten year-old Abigail being comforted by her Grandma.

Grandma, whose name was Molly, was upset because she was looking after Abigail and her brother Toby for the week while their parents had gone on their first holiday without them. Helen reassured her that accidents happen and advised her not to become too stressed about it. Abigail soon calmed down when she realised she could have a coloured plaster and opted for a purple one. Helen watched intently as Alan applied the plaster with ease, explaining each step as he went along. He told Helen that he would happily let her have a go during her placement after she had observed a few; fortunately two occurred on that shift. One was an elderly man who fell off his step whilst fetching in his milk, causing a fracture to his wrist. Second was a teenaged boy who fell off his skateboard on the nearby skate park, snapping his radius in two.

It only felt like a couple of hours had passed and it was lunchtime. Helen texted David and told him that she was loving the placement already and she was having a great day. She also texted Marcus and told him the same but added that she missed him and hoped that she would be able to see him soon.

'So, are you married, engaged, living with someone?' Alan asked as he took a bite of his cheese and pickle sandwich.

They sat in the staff area, which was situated at the back of reception. It was a small area with a few comfy chairs and a coffee table with some magazines scattered on it. There were tea and coffee making facilities whereby staff contributed a pound a week but students only had to pay fifty pence. Helen had put three pounds in the tin already to cover the whole placement. She shook her head and pulled a face which made Alan chuckle.

'No, but I have a long-term boyfriend, David. We have been together about four years now,' she said. 'What about you?'

Alan popped the last piece of sandwich into his mouth and chewed it before answering.

'I have been married to Maggie for fifteen years now and we have four children: twin boys, aged thirteen, and two girls, one of which, little Alice, was a surprise last year,' he said smiling proudly.

Helen looked surprised. She had imagined Alan to be a bit of a hippy rather than a family man.

'You don't look old enough to have been married fifteen years,' she said honestly.

'We married quite young.' Alan winked.

Helen checked her phone before going back into the department. David had texted saying he was glad she was having a good day and asked if she minded if he went out with Carl tonight so she replied to go and enjoy himself. She had not had a reply from Marcus but she knew he would be at university in lectures anyway.

The afternoon shift was busy for a Monday afternoon. Poor Tammy experienced another death in the resuscitation room when a seventy-year old man came in following a cardiac arrest in a supermarket whilst shopping with his wife. The trauma of the day had proved a little too much and Sharon allowed Tammy to go home early to write some reflection on her sad experiences from her first day.

Helen was busy. She gave a tetanus injection to a man who had cut his hand on a rusty nail and dressed his wound. She catheterised a woman who had gone into acute urinary retention after developing a urine infection. She did a lot of blood pressures and blood sugar readings; one on a man whose blood sugar had dropped below two so they had to put him onto a glucose drip to prevent him from going into a diabetic coma. Alan talked Helen through doing the drip and allowed her to do it herself with his supervision. She knew that he was going to be an excellent mentor and at the next five minute break she fetched her diary from the locker room to ensure that she had as many shifts with Alan as she could, even if that meant doing some night shifts. She checked her phone whilst she was in the locker room and saw she had a text from Marcus;

Hi beautiful, glad you are enjoying it. It has been weeks since we have had any time together. Could you spare any evening, make an excuse and I could cook for you at mine?

Helen smiled. She did not know Marcus could cook but then again there was a lot she did not know about him. She also knew they could not go out anywhere together so a meal at his would be perfect, especially since David was out tonight.

'I wonder if that is too short notice?' she thought to herself; there was only one way to find out.

I know it is a bit short notice but I am actually free tonight if that is convenient, I would love to see you.

Marcus was sat in his office marking some assignments when her reply came through and he smiled. Of course it was convenient. He would have changed any plans to see her. His heart was aching for her, he felt sick inside because he had not seen her or held her for so long. He *had* seen her in university but it was not the same. He wanted to be able to kiss her, to run his fingers through her hair, to smell her as he held her close to him, to feel the warmth of her against him. He typed his reply.

Cannot wait to see you then, is there anything you do not eat? Tell me a time and I will have your tea waiting for you xx I love you xx.

Helen had butterflies as she read the text. God, she had missed him. After what Tammy had said in the classroom the other week, she had not gone to his office again, and she had not had any opportunity to see him outside of university. They had spoken on the chat room every night until late, apart from the weekend when she had slept at David's and fallen asleep drunk but that was still not the same. She could not wait to be in his arms and feel his lips against hers; she quickly tapped a reply, conscious that she had only popped into the locker room for her diary.

I eat anything other than liver and Brussels sprouts and I finish about half three so I will come to you about six if that's OK, we can make an evening of it because I have missed you and I love you too xxxx

Helen deleted all of the messages then quickly texted Katherine not to make her tea saying she was going to be having tea out with friends.

Returning to the department, she could not find Alan. She discreetly looked behind the curtains of some of the cubicles and in the plaster room but he was not in any of them.

'Have you seen Alan?' she asked Julie, one of the sisters on the department.

Julie Steele had a hard face with a look that made Helen feel slightly intimidated in her presence. She had heard nurses refer to her as 'Marmite' during the shift. 'You either love her or you hate her.'

'She's firm but fair and generally if you get a rollicking you tend to deserve it,' Alan had said.

Julie turned to Helen and looked at her with a stern face.

'Do you not know where he is?' she asked harshly.

Helen thought to herself that was a stupid question as if she did know she wouldn't have asked Julie where he was. She opted not to say that though and get herself off on the wrong foot on her first day.

'No, I went into the locker room to get my diary so I could get my shifts with him and when I came back he was gone,' Helen said.

Julie's face softened slightly.

'He has just taken a patient down to the ward. To be fair, he was going to wait for you but I made him go as it is getting busy back there.' She pointed to the direction of the waiting room.

'Oh, that's OK,' Helen said. 'Is there anything I can do to help whilst I am waiting for him to come back?'

Julie smiled and took a folder from the desk.

'He shouldn't be too long, here is the off-duty. You go and sit in the staff room if you want and copy out his shifts so you know what he is doing. Make yourself a coffee if you like.' Helen took the folder, thanked Julie and smiled, she seemed alright after all.

Julie went in the direction of the back doors where an ambulance crew were arriving with a patient. She thought to herself that Helen Mitchell seemed a good sort, she liked her already. She wasn't too sure about Tammy yet, she seemed a bit cocky, but it was only the first day and Tammy had had a particularly traumatic introduction.

Helen wrote down the shifts that Alan was covering during her placement; luckily he was not on any annual leave as he had been on holiday just before she started. In the first three weeks, she would do a mixture of early and late shifts with two weekends. There was then a week where they were in university for two days, doing their presentations, followed by three days of study. During the last three weeks, she would have to do three night shifts and one weekend but Helen was happy to do this as she had managed to complete the two years of her training without doing any nights. As a student she was not obliged to do them but Helen was happy to as she thought it would be good experience on A&E.

'Now then, trouble, what are you doing hiding away in here?' Alan sniggered as he walked into the room making Helen jump.

'Julie said I could come and copy down your shifts so that I could make sure that I am working with you,' she said shutting the off duty as she had put all of the shifts into her diary. 'OK, boss, what are we up to next?'

'Well I don't know about you but I am going to go home to my family,' he said.

Helen looked at her fob watch and was surprised to see that it had just gone half past three.

'Oh my God, today has flown,' she said.

'Welcome to A&E,' Alan replied. 'Well, if you are mirroring my shifts I will see you for the late shift tomorrow at two o'clock.'

He gave her a wave as he headed off to the locker room. They had a strict policy on A&E that all staff, including students, got changed on arrival and before departure as they were not allowed to wear uniform off of the premises. Helen emerged from the locker room at the same time as Alan and smiled to herself as he was wearing a pair of black drainpipe jeans, a tie dye t-shirt of multiple colours, some purple doc martin boots and numerous leather bracelets. He represented the hippy persona that she had imagined him to have outside of work. She had visions of him climbing into an old Volkswagen camper van and was almost disappointed as she saw him drive off in a Ford Mondeo estate.

Helen drove past David's work on her way home so she drove into the car park to see if he was busy. She could see that he was not in the main depot fitting tyres so she switched off her engine to see if he was in the staff room or in the waiting area. As she walked towards the main reception, she could see the back of David's head as he was leaning on the counter. A girl with dark hair whom she had never seen before was behind the counter taking in his every word and laughing as if he were Lee Evans. She saw Mike in the tyre bay see her and he did a loud pitched whistle twice which made David turn around and see Helen walking to the door. He smiled when he saw her and came outside to greet her.

'Hey gorgeous, to what do I owe this pleasure?' he said and gave her a kiss.

Helen looked over to the window to see the dark haired girl looking in their direction before looking away awkwardly and pretending to look busy.

'Who is she?' she asked, not taking her eyes off of her.

'That's Sukie, our new receptionist,' David said casually.

'When did she start here?' Helen enquired.

'About three weeks ago, I would think,' David said, turning Helens chin gently so that she focused on him and not Sukie.

'You have never mentioned her before,' Helen said narrowing her eyes.

'That's because there is nothing to mention about her,' David smiled and playfully squeezed Helen's nose.

'You two seemed to be getting on very well just then,' Helen commented and David smiled and shook his head.

'She was telling me about how drunk she got at the weekend, and I was just telling her about that time when you got so drunk that you kicked all the milk bottles over just after telling everybody else to be quiet.' Helen laughed remembering the moment several years ago, one of many drunken episodes whereby she had embarrassed herself.

David gave her a tender kiss.

'Look, how about I rearrange things with Carl tonight? I'll treat you to a meal out instead,' he suggested.

Helen gulped. She could not let Marcus down now, he would have planned what to cook.

'No, you go, I have made plans myself now to see Tammy for a couple of drinks,' she said.

'Tammy? I didn't think you liked her,' David sounded surprised.

'I don't really, but she had a really horrendous shift and I ended up agreeing to meet her for a chat. Anyway, I've got to spend the next six weeks on placement with her so I might as well try and get on with her.' She shrugged.

David hugged her.

'Be careful then, don't forget she bats for the other side. Watch she doesn't try it on with you' he laughed, jokingly.

Helen screwed her face up.

'She is in a happy relationship with JoJo and anyway, I don't bat for the other side, as you put it, so even if she did, I would tell her where to go.' Helen gave David a kiss and looked over again to see that Sukie was watching their every move.

She did not feel comfortable with the way she was watching them but she did not have time to discuss it now.

'Have fun tonight and I will speak to you tomorrow,' she said.

David waved until she was out of sight.

Katherine was still at work when Helen got home so she made herself a cup of coffee and had a quick shower and washed her hair. She blow-dried her hair and, following a tip she had seen on YouTube, she used her straighteners to add some ringlets. She was really pleased with the end result and went into Katherine's bedroom to borrow some hairspray to hold the curls in place. She smiled to herself as she saw some lynx deodorant on the dressing table, knowing full well that it must be George's. He must have stopped over at the weekend when she was with David. Helen wouldn't say anything as it would look like she had been prying but she was pleased that her Mum had found happiness again.

She spent at least twenty minutes deciding what clothes to wear. She wanted to look special, as she had not seen Marcus for so long out of university. She picked a pretty, black, lace dress with a red trim and red underwear with shoes to match and a rose-shaped clip pinning back one side of her hair. With a swirl of matching lipstick she admired herself in the mirror and, squirting a spray of her favourite J-Lo Glow perfume, headed downstairs to where she could hear Katherine talking in the kitchen.

Opening the kitchen door, the smell of onions frying filled the air.

'Mmm, what are you cooking?' she asked as she walked into the room.

Beth and Steve were sat at the table while Katherine stood preparing a meal. Steve wolf whistled as Helen walked in and she gave him a twirl.

'Wow sis, you look amazing,' Beth said, feeling slightly frumpy in her jeans and t-shirt.

Steve put his arm around her reassuringly and kissed her on the cheek.

'So do you, gorgeous,' he said, conscious that Beth always felt intimidated by her sister's looks.

Katherine looked over and smiled lovingly at her daughter.

'You do look lovely,' she agreed. 'And in answer to your question, I am making spaghetti Bolognese. These two are keeping me company seeing as you are deserting me.'

'Where are you going anyway, all dolled up?' Steve asked curiously.

'Just out with some friends from university,' Helen said as she pretended to look in her bag for something, conscious that if she made eye contact he would see she was lying.

'Where are you going?' Beth asked.

'Somewhere on the Bail I think, Tammy was going to book it and we were meeting for a drink first.'

She picked up her car keys, gave them all a kiss, bid them goodbye and hurried out the door, stumbling slightly on the way out. Beth and Katherine looked at each other.

'She has been acting really odd, recently. Do you think she is alright?' Beth said.

Katherine shook her head remembering her promise not to disclose their recent conversation.

'I have no idea, maybe try and have a chat with her at some point. She does seem to have something on her mind.'

'I will,' Beth said.

Helen turned into Greetwell Close and pulled up a few doors away from Marcus's house. It was just before six so she texted David to have a good night, checked her reflection in the mirror on the sun visor, then, looking around to ensure nobody was about, she walked to his door. Her heart was pounding as she knocked and she had butterflies as she saw him through the glass, approaching the door to answer it. She had missed him so much.

'Wow,' he said when he saw her. 'You look absolutely amazing.'

Marcus closed the door behind him and pulled Helen into his arms, he circled one of the curls around his fingers and let it drop. It bounced against her cheek. Using his thumb and finger he gently traced every detail of her face, feeling the softness of her skin until he reached her chin which he cupped gently with both hands and lowered his face slowly towards her. Helen closed her eyes and eagerly awaited his lips to meet hers. It seemed like an eternity since she had kissed this man that she loved more than life itself and when the kiss happened it felt like an electric shock cascaded through her body. Marcus held her tightly afterwards and sighed contentedly.

180

'I have missed you so much,' he said kissing the top of her head.

'And I you, like you would not believe,' said Helen, pulling his face towards hers for another kiss.

She loved kissing Marcus and he, feeling the same, would have been quite happy stood there kissing for the entire evening.

'Something smells lovely,' Helen said as they eventually pulled apart.

'It's liver and Brussels,' Marcus joked and Helen shook her head and laughed as she followed him into the kitchen.

She gasped as she saw that Marcus had laid the table with a white lace tablecloth, wine glasses with yellow napkins and silver cutlery, set out as if it were in a restaurant. The lights were dimmed and there were four candles lit on the table and a small vase with a single rose in the centre of the table.

'Marcus, this looks beautiful,' Helen whispered.

He stood behind her and wrapped his arms around her waist admiring his handy work.

'A beautiful setting for my beautiful girl,' he said, gently kissing her earlobe.

He stepped forward and pulled the chair out for her to sit down.

'Madam,' he said, pointing at the seat with his open hand.

Helen giggled as she sat down.

'Why thank you, kind sir,' she said.

Marcus went to the fridge and took out a jug of sparkling liquid with slices of lemon in it; he added some ice cubes from the freezer.

'White wine spritzer?' he offered, removing the napkin from Helen's glass and placing it on her lap.

'I know you are driving so it's two thirds lemonade and a third wine,' he reassured her.

'Sounds and looks lovely,' Helen said, holding up her glass to accept the drink.

'Are you hungry?' Marcus asked.

'Starving,' Helen replied.

The smell of the food was making her salivate.

'It smells lovely,' she said. 'What are we having?'

Marcus was stood over by the cooker, stirring then spooning the starter into a bowl.

'Carrot and coriander soup followed by chicken and mushroom medley, duchesse potatoes and roasted veg, all finished off with a chocolate mousse,' he said smiling.

Helen tasted the soup.

'This is gorgeous. Where did you buy this from?' she asked and Marcus shook his head.

'Nowhere, I made it,' he said. 'I made everything myself; the coriander is out in my garden. I grow all of my own herbs.'

Helen looked at him in shock.

'Are you being serious?' she asked, taking another mouthful.

Marcus laughed.

'Don't sound so surprised. I live on my own so I have to do all my own cooking, I love it,' he said. 'I'll show you the carrot peels if you don't believe me.'

Helen smiled.

'Well I never; Marcus Edwards, the chef.' She smiled and put the last spoonful in her mouth.

'I have to say, that was the nicest soup I have ever tasted,' she said.

Marcus kissed her as he cleared away her dish.

'I'll wash up,' she said.

'No, I'll do it when you have gone,' he replied.

'No you will not, you have done all this cooking,' Helen said, sternly pushing her chair away from the table.

'OK then,' said Marcus. 'We'll do it together after we've eaten the meal as I am about to dish up the main course.'

Helen agreed with that idea.

The following two courses were equally delicious and Helen

enjoyed every mouthful.

'That really was a lovely meal, thank you,' she said afterwards. 'You are a fantastic cook Marcus.'

He smiled and thanked her.

'Do you like cooking?' he asked and Helen thought for a while before she answered.

'This is going to sound really bad but my Mum does most of the cooking at our house, I do the odd pasta dish but I have never cooked anything like you just made. I wouldn't know where to start,' she admitted, embarrassed at her naivety.

'Oh well, I'll have to teach you then, or I'll just do all the cooking,' Marcus said, pouring them both another glass of spritzer.

Helen wondered what he meant by that comment. Was he referring to them living together in the future? Unlike the sheer horror she felt inside when David mentioned moving in together, the thought of living with Marcus excited her. She would love to live with him.

'Penny for your thoughts?' Marcus said, seeing Helen in a daydream.

She blushed slightly, choosing not to say what she had been thinking as he had only said he would teach her to cook, no mention of moving in together.

'Gosh, I was in a world of my own. I don't even know what I was thinking,' she lied and smiled at him across the table.

Helen looked beautiful in the candlelight. Marcus smiled happily and sipped his drink.

'I love you so much,' he said.

'I love you too,' she replied.

Helen could not believe the impact that this older man was having on her. He was overpowering every waking moment, every dream, and the force of her emotions felt heavy on her heart. She craved to be near him, it was almost like an obsession, like a young teenager with a pop idol.

'How are things with David?' Marcus asked and Helen was taken aback, she knew what he was referring to.

The last time she had been there she had promised that she would end her relationship with David after their trip to York. That was several weeks ago. She coughed nervously and looked down and started rubbing the tablecloth between her fingers. She had no excuses, she had not kept her promise to Marcus. She just hadn't found the right moment. Her eyes welled up with tears as she looked up at him.

'I'm still with him,' she said in a lowered voice, almost cracking. 'The thing is, he is such a nice person it is so hard finding the right time and the right words to break his heart.'

Tears spilled onto her cheeks and Marcus rushed over towards her.

'Please don't cry, Helen, it doesn't matter. I will wait forever for you, I love you,' he reassured her as he held her in his arms.

Wrapping her arms around his shoulders, she kissed his neck.

'Please believe me Marcus, it is you I love. I've never felt this way about anyone before, I'm just finding it really hard to finish with him as he never does anything wrong.'

Marcus hated the thought of Helen being with David. He had never been a jealous man but he understood the predicament she was in.

'Just take your time, sweetheart, we will be together soon. Anyway, we have to wait until you finish your course until we can go public so there is no hurry.' Helen shook her head.

'No way, I'll do it soon. It's not fair, in a way I am cheating on you both and I hate it, I hate people who cheat. I'm a total hypocrite!' she said, angry with herself as she thought about her betrayal.

'I don't see it that you are cheating on me so don't think of it like that,' Marcus said. 'Now come on, we are supposed to be having a romantic night together so shall we continue with that?'

184

He held his hand out to Helen. She accepted it and stood up to be embraced by his masculine arms into a tight squeeze.

'Shall we get these pots washed, then?' she said turning to clear the table.

'I really can do it when you have gone home, I don't want to waste our precious time washing up,' Marcus argued.

'It'll take ten minutes between us, come on, chop chop,' Helen insisted, taking the remaining plates over to the sink.

'I'll wash and you can dry and put away,' she said, running the water.

Looking in the cupboard below the sink she found the washing up liquid and a pair of rubber gloves. She smiled to herself as she saw a range of cleaning products neatly arranged in the cupboard with dusters neatly folded at the side. Marcus certainly was not a typical bachelor; another thing she liked about him. David did not possess a duster, or cleaning products for that matter, but then again he was only nineteen.

Helen told Marcus about her first day on A&E as they washed up and he listened with interest. He loved listening to her talk; she had such a soft voice. He laughed as she told him about her instincts about Alan being a hippy and then coming out dressed as he did. She told him about Tammy's bad day and the poor man who lost all of his family. Marcus had had a similar experience himself when he worked on A&E but it had been a woman who lost her husband, mother and six month old baby after crashing her car swerving to miss a rabbit.

'By the end of the placement, you will have seen some really tragic cases but probably some really funny ones too,' he said. 'I remember once a man came in with his penis stuck in the hoover pipe. You can guess what he was trying to do with it. Hopefully Tammy will have written some good reflection about that for her portfolio.'

'I would like to think so but this is Tammy we are talking about,' Helen replied.

185

'I can't comment on that, it wouldn't be professional,' Marcus said honestly and Helen nodded, realising it would not be appropriate to discuss other students.

'Would you like a tea or coffee?' Marcus asked, filling the kettle with water from a water filter.

'I would love a coffee please,' Helen replied and she took two mugs from the mug tree that sat on the kitchen worktop.

She placed them next to the kettle that was already boiling. Marcus gently touched the rose in her hair.

'This is pretty,' he said. 'Your hair looks really pretty tonight.'

He leant forward and kissed her forehead.

'Thank you, I think I got the flower from Claire's Accessories months ago,' she said smiling.

'You really are beautiful, Helen, I can't believe how lucky I am,' he said and pulled her into his arms. 'You don't think the age gap will be a problem for you one day, do you? I mean when you are forty I will be nearly sixty.'

Helen pulled away slightly and looked into his eyes.

'Marcus, I know I am only nineteen but I always used to dream of feeling true love. When I'm with you, the feelings I have inside are like nothing I have ever experienced before. I love you so much, I wouldn't care if you were hundred and ten, I love you and that is all that matters,' Helen said.

Marcus felt as if his heart would burst with happiness. He too had never felt this way about anyone before.

'I want to spend my whole life with you, Helen Mitchell, so hurry up and get this blasted course finished so I can shout it from the rooftops,' he said, picking her up and spinning her around the kitchen as she laughed.

They moved through to the lounge to drink their coffee. Marcus turned off the lights and lit candles around the room. He put on an easy listening CD and turned the sound down low. It was already nine o'clock; they could not believe that the time they spent together passed so quickly.

'This sofa is so comfortable,' Helen said, snuggling into the cushions and resting her head back.

She felt so relaxed and she was having a lovely evening. She wished that it would never have to end and time would just stand still. Marcus picked up her feet, removed her shoes and, placing them on the floor and her feet on his knees, he began to give her a foot massage. He gently massaged the base of her foot and each individual toe. Usually Helen hated anyone touching her feet but this felt like paradise, so relaxing and so sensual that she groaned as he massaged the back of her calves.

'This is so relaxing.' She smiled, closing her eyes.

'Would you like me to give you a proper massage?' Marcus asked and Helen opened her eyes.

'That sounds divine.' she smiled.

'We had better go upstairs, you'll be more comfortable up there,' he said.

They both carried a pair of candles each up to the bedroom and Marcus closed the curtains. He helped Helen remove her dress and gave a sharp intake of breath as her red silk bra and panties were revealed. He could feel himself instantly becoming aroused but tried to ignore the feelings as he had promised her a massage.

'OK, lay on your front on the bed,' he said. 'You look absolutely stunning, by the way.'

Helen thanked him and obeyed his instructions, resting her head on her arms. Marcus kneeled down at the side of her and expertly started to massage the nape of her neck and her shoulders. Finding it difficult to be in the right position he adjusted himself so that he was sat over her bum and Helen smiled as she could feel his erection against her. She sighed contentedly as he ran his hands over her shoulder blades and along her spine, unfastening her bra to allow access to the whole of her back. As he leant forward to kiss the back of her neck, Helen was overcome with desire.

'I want you, Marcus,' she purred. 'Right now.'

He did not need asking twice. Clambering off the bed, Marcus eagerly removed his jeans, t-shirt and boxer shorts as Helen removed what was left of her underwear and lay holding her arms up awaiting her man. Marcus bent down and kissed her stomach, gently pulling her belly bar between his teeth as he caressed between her legs with his fingers. Helen grabbed his hair with both hands and pulled him up towards her locking him into a passionate embrace, and then wrapping her legs around his waist she pushed her feet against his bum forcing him to enter her. He groaned out loud as she bit his lip but it was a groan of pleasure not pain. He had missed her so much. Helen kissed every part of Marcus's flesh that she could physically reach as they made love, she wanted it to last for hours but could feel the vibrations already about to take over her body and, as they did, Marcus too started to shake and groan in pleasure.

'That was fantastic,' Marcus said after several minutes of holding each other in silence.

'It was amazing,' Helen agreed.

'I wish you were staying all night,' Marcus said, sadly stroking her hair.

Helen nodded.

'Me too,' she said, resting her head on his chest.

'Is that your phone ringing?' Marcus said, sitting up in bed and straining to listen for the ringtone as her bag was downstairs.

Helen also sat up just as the phone stopped ringing.

'Oh well, I will look in a bit see to who it was,' she said and lay back down only to hear the phone start ringing again.

She sat up again, concerned. Her mobile hardly ever rang and somebody was obviously trying to get hold of her urgently.

'I'd better go and answer that,' she said getting out of the bed and quickly getting dressed.

Helen ran downstairs and taking her phone from her bag she saw that she had eight missed calls, six from David and two from Katherine. Her heart was beating nervously wondering who she should ring first sensing something was very wrong.

'Is everything alright?' Marcus said, walking into the room and seeing Helen looking visibly pale.

'I don't know,' said Helen as her phone started to ring again; it was David.

Hands shaking, she answered the phone.

'Hello?'

There was noise in the background. She could hear that he was in a bar somewhere.

'Where the hell are you, Helen?' David asked.

He sounded angry, very angry. Helen had never heard him sound angry before with her.

'What do you mean?' she asked nervously.

'You told me you were going out with Tammy tonight, only I've seen Tammy and when I asked where you were and she had no idea what I was talking about.' David's voice was getting more agitated.

Helen looked over at Marcus. Bile rose in her throat and her mouth went dry.

'What's up?' Marcus mouthed silently and Helen shook her head, her eyes filling with tears.

This should not be happening, she didn't know what to say.

'Helen, answer me! Where are you? Why did you lie to me?' David was shouting now.

She heard Carl in the background.

'Calm down, mate, come on, calm down.'

'I can explain David,' Helen said, desperately thinking what to say next.

'Fuck you, Helen, forget it,' he shouted and hung up the phone.

Helen burst into tears and sobbed uncontrollably. Sitting on the sofa, Marcus sat beside her and put his arms around her, suspecting but still not aware of what had just happened. Putting her phone on loudspeaker, she played some voicemails. Six were from David, asking where she was, why she was not answering her phone and who she was with. Two were from Katherine who David had clearly phoned, also asking where she was and asking if she was alright. Marcus had his head in his hands unsure what to suggest.

'OK, ring him back and tell him you are here. Tell him I was working on an assignment with you and the reason you lied was because you are not really allowed to do that and we would both get in trouble.' Marcus lifted her chin and kissed her softly.

He actually was feeling sorry for David but he did not want him to find out about the affair and so hoped he would believe that excuse. Helen tried several times to ring David back but his phone went straight to answerphone each time. After the fourth attempt, she left him a voicemail repeating the story Marcus had suggested she tell. She then texted her Mum telling her she was coming home.

As she walked through the front door, Helen was met by Katherine and Beth who had a glass of wine waiting. Beth had sent Steve home so that they could talk in private.

'Are you having an affair, Helen?' Beth was straight to the point.

Helen looked shocked, she took a large gulp of wine.

'What do you take me for, Beth? Why would you say such a thing?' she asked unable to make eye contact with her sister.

'You've been acting weird for weeks, you've been off towards David and tonight you lied about where you are,' Beth said sternly.

Helen repeated her story about going to Marcus's to work on an assignment.

'So where is your work? And why are you so dressed up?' Beth asked. 'Oh God, Helen, please tell me you are not sleeping with your tutor?'

Katherine was looking at Helen, her eyes showed that she knew the truth. She had worked it out, she had realised the meaning of that conversation that had taken place in this very spot just a few weeks ago. Helen felt her face flush. She swallowed hard and shook her head as she looked at the table.

'Bloody hell, Beth, he's the same age as Mum! Don't be so stupid. He was helping me out, that was all.' Grabbing her glass, she left the room and slammed the door behind her.

As she lay crying into her pillow she heard Beth leave and Katherine come into her room. She sat next to her and stroked the back of her hair.

'He is just a father figure, love, that's all. Don't go and do anything rash,' she said.

Helen did not say anything. She buried her face into the pillow and cried silently. Katherine sat with her in silence for a few minutes then left the room. Helen picked up her phone and texted David

Please believe me. I'm sorry.

After a few minutes her phone pinged with a reply.

OKAY, I will speak to you tomorrow xx.

Sighing a breath of relief, she rolled over and went to sleep, still dressed.

Chapter Nineteen

David turned up at Helen's house in the morning before he started work. He had not slept all night, thinking about things and wanted to talk to Helen rather than ponder all day. Although she had given her reasons for lying, he could not understand why she had not told him the truth. At the end of the day, it wasn't like he was going to go running off to the university and tell them that she was having extra tuition.

Helen was dressed in her dressing gown as she poured him a cup of tea. He could see that she had been crying a lot.

'Should I be worried about anything?' he asked, leaning against the worktop.

He didn't even want to sit at the table. He was overcome with waves of nausea, sensing that Helen was going to deliver him some bad news. She turned to face him and, handing him a mug of tea, she shook her head but said nothing. Helen knew she had the perfect opportunity to end the relationship but she was a coward. She looked into his sad eyes and still could not hurt the man with whom she had shared so many years of her life, despite the fact that she did not love him and she did not want to be with him anymore.

'Why did you lie to me, Helen?' David asked bluntly. 'It wouldn't have mattered if you had told me you were having some help with an assignment but I cannot understand why you lied.'

His voice was cold with a hint of anger still present within it. Helen looked down to the floor, ashamed.

'I don't know, I suppose I just thought I shouldn't tell anyone at all that I was going to my tutor's house so I didn't, just in case you told someone,' she said.

David looked hurt.

'What's up, don't you trust me now?' he said.

'Of course I do, please, David, can we just forget about this? I made a stupid mistake and I'm sorry. Please stop being angry with me, I hate arguments.' Helen started to cry.

'Do you love me, Helen?' David asked without going to comfort her.

'What?' she said, blowing her nose.

'You heard me, I asked if you love me. I tell you often enough but you never say it back,' he said abruptly.

Helen swallowed hard. She could either lie and make him happy or tell the truth and break his heart.

'Love is a really big word, David, I think people just say it for...'

Helen did not get the chance to finish her sentence as David turned and walked out of the house.

Where are you going? She texted as she heard his car pull off at speed.

He did not reply until he had got to work.

You have changed Helen. I love you but I need to be loved back.

I do really care about you David x.

Well I'm not sure that is enough anymore!!

What do you mean? Xx.

Helen waited for a reply from David but none came, she sat looking at the messages and replaying the past few months in her head. She thought about her Mum's words last night and she knew that Marcus was not a father figure. She knew that she loved him with every beat of her heart. She also knew that

David did not deserve to be treated like this, and he deserved to be loved. She typed a message to David.

I think we should have a few weeks break to sort our heads out.

Her heart felt like it was in her mouth as she pressed send and awaited his response, which she received almost instantly.

OKAY, whatever, I will see you around sometime.
Don't be like that!!

Helen did not get another reply from David. He had asked Mike if he could be excused for five minutes to get some fresh air but he returned red eyed, obvious that he had been crying. Mike asked if he was alright and simply got a nod in response so chose not to pry any further although he suspected that it was something to do with Helen.

As soon as she arrived at the department, Tammy headed straight for Helen. She was already at work as she had been on the early shift.

'Well well, what were you up to last night?' she said with a grin on her face. 'Your David was livid when I said you weren't with me, if you had pre-warned me yesterday, I could have thought of an excuse, you daft bat.'

Helen just stood in silence as Alan listened, intrigued.

'Well, spill the beans, what were you up to then?' Tammy continued to probe.

'I was out with an old school friend called Tammy, obviously David thought it was you,' Helen quickly thought up the excuse and Tammy looked disappointed.

'Oh, I thought it was going to be some juicy gossip,' she said sounding deflated and walked off back towards her mentor.

'She is a strange character, isn't she?' Alan said, scratching his head.

Helen nodded.

'Are you OK?' he asked, sensing that she seemed quieter than she had been yesterday.

Helen briefly told him that she had separated from David but said that she would rather not talk about it, otherwise she would cry. He diplomatically changed the subject.

'We are in triage this afternoon so anybody that comes through the main doors, we have to prioritise,' Alan explained.

He showed Helen some admission sheets that were already on the desk waiting to be seen.

'As you see, they have either a red, orange or green spot and that determines where in the pile we put them. Red needs to be seen as soon as possible, so shove them under a doctor's nose, orange within an hour or two, and green less urgent,' he said.

The department was reasonably quiet, which Alan said was sometimes the case on a Tuesday afternoon. He said weekends were usually the busiest as Helen had expected and also Thursday evenings were quite active as some of the bars had cheap student nights. They often had a lot of drunk youngsters or people who had been fighting.

'Unfortunately, you do get a lot of people who do not use the service properly,' Alan said and he went on to tell her stories of people who come in with inappropriate reasons such as period pains and ear aches. 'They are the ones you put as a green and make them wait. They won't be in a hurry to come back then.'

Looking around into the triage room, there were some admission sheets in the box.

'Come on then, kiddo, let's go,' he said.

The first patient through was a fifty year old, Bill, who had been at work on a building site and he had sliced his hand on some broken glass. Unwrapping the tea towel that he had used to cover the wound, Alan shook his head.

'Sorry, mate, but it looks like you are going to need a few stitches in that,' he said. 'Are you up to date with your tetanus injection?'

Luckily he had had an injection earlier in the year when he had gone on holiday so he did not need to have another. Helen checked his blood pressure, pulse and temperature which were all normal then he returned to the waiting room to wait to be called through.

'It shouldn't be too long today, mate,' Alan said sticking an orange sticker onto the sheet.

Next in line was Rebecca. She had slipped down the last two stairs at college and twisted her ankle. Her friend, James, helped her hobble into the room and as Helen checked her observations, Alan examined her swollen foot that had already started to bruise. Rebecca winced in pain as he pressed on certain points so he wrote a brief summary then filled out an x-ray card.

'I think it is a sprain rather than a fracture but we had better get it checked out,' he said handing the card to James. 'Follow the blue line to the x-ray department then bring her back to the waiting room. Make sure you tell reception when you are back so we can take another look.'

Helen held the door open and pointed in the direction of the x-ray.

'That looked painful,' she said and Alan agreed.

'Sometimes a sprain can actually be more painful than a break believe it or not,' he said.

The receptionist put a note with a single name, John, written on it on the triage box.

'What is that?' Helen asked curiously.

'We do a needle exchange service for drug users,' Alan explained. 'It doesn't go through as an admission as it is confidential. Do you want to shout him through?'

Helen opened the door and scanned the waiting room, there were only about ten people in there but she found herself look at the scruffy man with the tattoo on his face.

'John?' she said.

The scruffy man did not even look up, instead a smart man in a suit, carrying a briefcase stood up and walked towards the door. Helen had to make a conscientious effort not to look shocked that such a well-presented individual would be on heroin. He looked so smart and professional. She closed the door behind him and he sat down.

'Alright, mate, have you got your old ones?' Alan said obvious that he knew John already.

John opened his briefcase and took out a small, locked sharps bin which Alan took from him. Pulling out a box from underneath the desk, he took out a bag of syringes and a new sharps bin and handed it to John which he put in his case, shut, bid Helen and Alan goodbye and went.

'Oh my God, out of all the people in the waiting room, he was the last one I expected to stand up,' Helen said still shocked and Alan laughed.

'I know, you will find that drug addicts are not your usual stereotypical portrayal that you would expect to see. We've seen lawyers, bankers and even teachers,' he said.

Helen admitted that she had looked straight at the scruffy looking man and Alan reassured her it was a mistake that they have all made in the past.

There was a lull of about twenty minutes before anybody else came through so Alan showed Helen the admission paperwork, and said that he would be happy for her to do some of the triage assessments when patient's came in. He said he would stand in the background and leave her to it as it would fulfil quite a lot of her outcomes. Helen was happy with this, especially as it was only her second shift; she knew, then, that she would definitely learn a lot on this placement.

Bill came through and Helen was able to see him have his stitches. He needed nine in total and he squeezed Helen's hand until her fingers were white despite having stated that he could not feel a thing. Rebecca's x-ray showed that there were no fractures so she was advised to elevate her foot, use ice to reduce the swelling and take ibuprofen for the pain. Helen gave her an information leaflet on sprains and advised her if possible to take the remainder of the week off from college to rest. Rebecca did not seem alarmed at this, as she needed to catch up on some coursework. She was having some small talk about college life and assignments when she caught sight of Alan waving to catch her attention.

'Sorry I've got to go, good luck with the assignments,' Helen said and went in the direction of her mentor.

'There are some new admissions just come in,' he said. 'Would you like to do these ones?'

Helen nodded enthusiastically, feeling confident that she knew the right questions to ask.

The first person was clearly one of the time-wasters that Alan had warned her about. He was called Eddie and had had a toothache for the past three weeks. When Helen asked why he had not gone to the dentist he said that he did not have a dentist. Helen gently told him that this was not an appropriate use of accident an emergency, she took his blood pressure and told him to wait in the waiting room and advised he may have a long wait sticking a green sticker on his form. Alan laughed.

'You've got the knack of this already,' he said as she shook her head in disbelief.

Elsie was next, an eighty year-old bought in by her daughter after falling off of her toilet and landing on her arm. Helen sent her for an x-ray after putting a sling on but she was sure there was a fracture and Alan agreed.

'Would you refer her to the community nurses for treatment if she needed it?' Helen asked.

'No but we would refer her to the GP who would then refer to the community nurses,' Alan explained.

Another note with the name Lucy was stuck to the box and this time Helen did not look for the obvious candidate, although it was the scruffy looking girl who came to the room with heavy eyes, dirty hair and a Lidl bag carrying her sharps bin. She never said a word as the exchange took place despite Helen trying to make conversation with her.

'Poor girl, she looked so sad behind her eyes,' Helen commented after she had left the room.

'There is usually a sad story behind these drug addicts,' Alan said. 'Often some sort of sexual abuse or violence. It is quite sad but you will find some people judge them yet nobody knows the history behind why they turned to drugs in the first place.'

Helen nodded.

'I suppose it is the same with a lot of alcoholics too.'

'Exactly,' Alan said. 'Part of our code of conduct is to be non-judgemental but you will be amazed in your career how many people are when it comes to drugs and alcohol.'

Helen was amazed at how quick the time went on A&E, and it was quicker than on any other placement. She checked her phone on her break, half expecting a text from David but there was nothing. She did have one from Michelle, inviting her out for a drink later as they had not seen each other since starting placement so she replied saying she was on a late but could meet up the following day. Michelle agreed to this.

I suppose you should know now though I have finished with David today.

Michelle had to read the text twice, convinced she had read it wrong.

What? What happened? Why?

Helen was actually not quite sure the reason that she was going to give to everybody for ending this so-called 'perfect relationship'. She could not tell them she had fallen head over heels in love with her tutor and they had been having a passionate affair because then he would get the sack. She would just have to be honest and tell people that she did not have the same feelings for David as he had for her, and she felt he deserved more than she had to offer, which in a sense was the truth.

I will explain all when I see you tomorrow.

OKAY, I cannot believe it.

Michelle genuinely was in shock. She had always thought Helen and David were so happy together, and expected them to potentially get married after they qualified or at least move in together.

Helen decided not to text Marcus. She would call and tell him on her way home, although she told herself she would not stop as it would be late and her shift would not end until ten. She did send him a text and told him that she loved him and could not wait to see him again, to which he promptly replied as he was in his office.

I was just sat in my office thinking about you, beautiful. I cannot wait to see you either. I love you so much, I miss you so much, and I just think about you every moment that I am awake, I am haunted by your beauty.

Reading his words made Helen's heart beat rapidly in her chest, she was overwhelmed with the power of her emotions. How could one person ignite such intense feelings inside of her in such a short space of time?

'So how are you enjoying A&E so far?' Alan asked her.

Helen put her phone into her pocket and, opening up her lunch box, she took out a peanut butter sandwich.

'I love it,' she said before taking a bite. 'How long have you worked here?'

Alan told her that he had qualified as a nurse five years ago and he had worked on the department ever since. He initially worked twilight shifts, which were six at night until three in the morning, and then he did some bank shifts with addiction, which was a service for people with drug and alcohol addictions. After a couple of years, he took a full time post on the department giving up his job but not his interest in drug and alcohol misuse.

'I suppose I got disheartened when the same people kept coming back after falling off the wagon for the fifth time, or telling us they had not taken drugs and bringing in other people's urine samples to test, thinking we were stupid when they handed them to us cold,' he explained.

Helen listened with interest as Alan told stories of his time working with those with addiction. She was amazed to hear how people sold all of their possessions to buy drugs, how they stole from their families or prostituted themselves to fund their habits. She felt grateful that she had never succumbed to such a dreadful habit; Helen had never even smoked. She tried one puff of a cigarette in the playground when she was about thirteen because all of the other girls were doing it and convinced her it was cool. Helen inhaled the smoke as directed by one of the girls and, after some coughing and spluttering, she was promptly sick. She wondered what on Earth the fuss was about and swore never to touch a cigarette again.

'Well I suppose we had better go and see if we have any candidates to assess,' Alan said, shutting his lunchbox.

Helen popped a grape into her mouth and put her lunch bag on the table, as there were still a few bits of fruit left that she planned to graze on throughout the shift if she had the chance. There seemed to be a few people waiting in the cubicles that had not been there before. Either there had been an influx via the front reception or the back door with the ambulance crew, although neither Helen nor Alan had seen a paramedic who would often come into the staff room for a five minute break.

Elsie had since had her arm put in plaster and Helen was surprised to see her in a cubicle on a stretcher with a worried looking daughter, Hayley, by her side. It appeared that Elsie had fainted after having her plaster fitted, so the doctors had decided to admit her overnight onto EAU for observations. As there was nobody waiting to be triaged, Helen offered to go with the porter to take Elsie down so that she could get into a more comfortable bed. It was only a short walk to EAU but the corridor felt cold so Helen got Elsie an extra blanket to keep her warm.

'You will be OK, they will hopefully just keep you overnight to make sure you don't faint again,' she reassured Elsie.

Helen squeezed her hand and also gave Hayley a reassuring pat on the arm.

'How long are you with us for?' Paul the porter asked as they walked back to the department.

Paul was a friendly looking man with glasses and a broad Scottish accent.

'Six weeks altogether but there is a week break in the middle to go back to university,' Helen said.

Paul seemed to be contemplating what he said next.

'Is Tammy in your group?' he asked cautiously as if not wanting to offend.

'Yes she is,' Helen said wondering what Paul was thinking. 'Why?'

'She is a bit odd,' he replied shaking his head slightly and Helen tried not to laugh.

'In what way?' she asked.

Paul looked at her with a surprised expression.

'You actually have to ask?' he said his eyes widening.

Helen smiled and shrugged her shoulders.

'Tammy is just Tammy to me,' she said diplomatically.

'She came to take a patient to a ward with me earlier and on the way back she asked me if we had ever had anyone in with a vibrator stuck up their arse; no word of a lie she just came straight out with it just like that.'

Helen laughed out loud.

'That is typical of Tammy, she likes to shock people,' she said.

'I hope she doesn't try and shock a patient like that,' Paul said smiling.

Helen was a pretty girl with an infectious laugh; he knew he would enjoy working with her whilst she was on the department.

Helen told Alan what Tammy had said to Paul and he too shook his head in disbelief.

'I have had a couple of people make comment about her, I must admit,' he said. 'She needs to be careful as she could easily be heard on this department as the cubicles are only separated by curtains, and curtains are not soundproof.'

Helen nodded in agreement.

'Shall I have a word with her?' she offered.

'No leave it to Sharon to sort out, don't get involved,' Alan advised and Helen agreed to say nothing.

As with the previous day, the shift hastily came to an end. Helen had received several texts from Beth, Kelly, Katie and Tammy all asking if she was alright as they had seen on Facebook her relationship status had changed from 'in a relationship with David Thomas' to 'single'. She could not believe that he had done that without speaking to her about it. At the end of the day, she had only suggested a break for a few weeks and he had announced a full separation by putting their relationship status as single; how dare he. Helen was going to text him, to ask him what he was playing at but then she realised that by doing that he may think she was regretting her decision so she left it. Slipping on her shoes, she left to see Marcus, hoping that he had not seen Facebook already.

Ringing his doorbell, Marcus took a few minutes to answer as he had been in the bath. He came to the door dressed only in a robe and, after an initial curious expression of who would be visiting so late, his face broke into a smile when he saw Helen stood on his doorstep. Helen squealed as Marcus scooped her up in his arms and carried her into the room kicking the door shut behind him. He gently threw her onto the sofa and laid on top of her, kissing her passionately.

'God, I am so happy to see you. What a lovely surprise,' he said eventually brushing his fingers against her cheeks.

'I can't stay long but I had to come and tell you some news,' Helen said, wrapping her arms around his neck and allowing her fingers to ruffle his wet hair.

Marcus kissed her again softly on the lips.

'Go on then, beautiful, tell me your news,' he said, looking deep into her eyes waiting with interest for her to speak.

Helen paused momentarily, mesmerised by his smouldering eyes and those lips that she yearned for every minute of the day.

'I've finally done it, I left David, I am all yours for good,' she said smiling.

Marcus looked down and did not say anything. Helen could feel her stomach churning inside. What had she done? Had he changed his mind? Did he not want this anymore? She gently put her hand under his chin and tipped his head slightly and, as she did, Marcus looked at her and tears spilled onto his cheeks.

'Helen, I cannot tell you how much this means to me,' he said. 'I love you so much, you truly have made me the happiest man alive.'

Seeing Marcus cry was too much for Helen to bare and she too shed a tear.

'I love you too, so much,' she said.

They held each other close until their tears subsided and then they made love on the sofa, slowly and gently until late into the night.

Helen returned home and the house was in darkness so she assumed Katherine had gone to bed. There was a note on the table saying that there was some steak pie in the fridge if she was peckish and her pack-up was made already. Helen smiled to herself; her Mum really did look after her, even at nineteen years old.

Despite it being gone midnight she did not feel tired so Helen made herself a mug of Horlicks, went to her room and logged onto Facebook to see for herself what David had put. Other than changing the relationship status, Helen was relieved to see that he had not made any comments or references to anything, despite several people making comments to the single status. Helen had numerous posts on her wall asking what had happened and why they were not together anymore but she chose not to respond to any of them. David had changed his profile picture from one of them together in York to one of him and Carl with a pint of beer balancing on their heads. Helen did feel a tinge of sadness as she realised that she would not be seeing him again. After all, they had been together four years, and despite the fact she did not love him, he had been one of her best friends and she would miss him a lot.

Helen clicked onto Marcus's profile and felt the familiar butterflies fluttering around inside as she looked at the pictures of him, she longed for a picture of them together but at the minute it was too risky. She had only just left him and she was missing him already, she texted him to tell him that.

I was lying here thinking just the same thing, wishing you were lying in bed next to me, he replied.

Helen held the phone against her chest as if she were holding Marcus close to her heart.

I love you so much, Helen Mitchell xxxx.

I love you more, Marcus Edwards xxxx.

Not possible!!!! Xxxxx.

I feel our first argument brewing ;) xxxx.

Never, I will just always let you be right xxx.

I love you even more now lol xxxxx.

Come back and get in bed with me, there is a lovely empty space next to me with your name written all over it.

I wish I could but my Mum would wonder where I was in the morning xxx.

One day……. Xxx.

I promise xxx.

Helen looked at the clock and realised it was nearly two in the morning. She bid Marcus goodnight as she was due to start work at seven.

The alarm went off just before six but Helen was already awake. She had had an unsettled night thinking a lot about both Marcus and whether David was hurting badly. The truth was, David had cried himself to sleep, and he felt despaired, not knowing how he would get through the next few weeks. Of course, he knew that he would get over the breakup in time but right now, he was totally devastated like his heart was torn in two. He had told himself that this was a permanent split, he knew that in his heart. He had seen the change in Helen over the past few weeks. She had grown more and more distant, and he had known he was losing her, he just could not understand why; they had always been so happy. David was proud and he was not going to beg her to come back. Carl had told him not to text or ring Helen so he had followed his friend's advice, although every hour he was looking at his phone to see if she had texted him. Helen thought about texting him to see if he was OK but thought it would be rubbing salt in the wounds if she did.

After having a quick shower, she put on some black trousers and a tight fitting red top with black roses. She had planned to meet Michelle in town after work for coffee and a cake. She could hear the kettle boiling as she approached the kitchen door.

'You're up early,' she said as Katherine was pouring a pot of tea.

'I thought I would have a drink with my daughter before work, I feel like I have hardly seen you the last few days.' Her Mum approached her for a hug. 'Is everything alright love? I heard about you and David.'

Katherine put two mugs of tea on the table. Helen sat down.

'Gosh, news does travel around here,' she said taking a sip of her drink. 'I just couldn't live a lie anymore Mum. I know David is a great guy and everybody loved him but I don't and that's the point. He deserves to be loved.'

Katherine took a few sips of her drink then looked at her daughter.

'Is that the only reason, love?' she said softly. 'You know you can tell me anything and I will not say a word.'

Helen looked into her Mum's eyes and thought for a moment, she trusted her Mum totally and it would feel so good to tell somebody about Marcus.

'No, Mum, there is nothing else to say,' she said unable to tell the truth.

'Nothing to do with this tutor of yours?' Katherine asked directly, suspecting Helen was hiding something.

'Marcus is a friend, Mum, nothing else and, more importantly, he is my tutor. He's the same age as you,' Helen quickly drained off her tea and stood up to leave. 'I have to go or I'll be late. I'm meeting Michelle after work but should be back for tea.'

Kissing her Mum on the cheek, she hastily left, loudly closing the door behind her. Katherine knew her daughter too well. Helen flushed just mentioning the name Marcus. Whether there was something going on or not, Helen certainly had feelings for this tutor of hers, that much was glaringly obvious to Katherine.

Today's shift was the quickest of them all. Alan had not come in as one of his children was poorly so Helen worked alongside Nikki in triage again. There was a steady flow of patients all day ranging from cat bites to an anaphylaxis reaction to an antibiotic that had to be treated with IV adrenalin. A young boy, Rory came in with a broken arm after falling over in a PE lesson and Helen was pleased when Nikki allowed her to apply the plaster after she said that she had observed several with Alan on her first shift. Nikki kindly talked her through every stage and ensured that Helen felt confident whilst reassuring little Rory at the same time. She rewarded him with a smiley faced sticker at the end for his bravery. Helen also gave him a sticker for being the first person she had ever put a plaster on, so he was exceptionally happy when he left the department.

Helen got on really well with Nikki, as they were a similar

age. She had only qualified a year ago and came straight to work on A&E. She was engaged to a man called Eduardo, who was Italian, and they lived in a flat in Bracebridge Heath, not far away from the hospital or where Helen lived. They had a small wedding planned in Italy the following year and she excitedly told Helen about it over lunch in the staff canteen. They had booked a small chapel near the beach and the ceremony was going to involve their parents, and close friends only.

'It sounds perfect,' Helen said smiling.

'So, do you have a man in your life?' Nikki asked taking a bite out of her panini. Helen shook her head and began to explain about her recent split from David. Nikki felt sorry. She had been in a similar situation herself prior to meeting Eduardo, whereby she was in a relationship with a man called James. He had proposed to her but she knew she did not love him and ended up leaving him at that point. She knew how awful Helen was feeling and reassured her that she had done the right thing. No matter how bad she felt; she should not go back on her decision.

Helen received similar advice from Michelle as they sat drinking coffee in Costa later. Michelle was in shock at the news as she had no idea that her friend had felt this way.

'Why didn't you say anything to me, Helen? You could have told me how you were feeling rather than keep it all to yourself,' she said.

Helen sighed and looked out of the window at the people passing by. There were people from all walks of life; old, young, smiling, frowning. She wondered what stories they had to tell, whether they were happy or sad, whether they were lonely, coming home from work or going shopping.

'Sometimes in life, Michelle, things just happen. They can hit you like a bolt of lightning and everything just changes,' she said then took a sip of her coffee.

Michelle looked confused and her eyes narrowed, she did not quite understand what Helen was implying by that statement.

'What do you mean?' Helen knew again that she could not tell Michelle about Marcus, more so because of how much she had been hurt by Phil's infidelity and especially because he was a tutor to them both.

'I just mean that all of a sudden it hit me that I didn't love him and I couldn't spend another day of my life deceiving either of us, that's all,' she smiled sadly and Michelle leaned over and squeezed her hand sympathetically.

'I'm so sorry, Helen, I thought you two were the perfect couple,' she said smiling.

'Anyway, enough about me, tell me about you and Adam,' Helen changed the subject and Michelle happily gushed over another mug of hazelnut latte.

She blushed when she said they had spent their first night together at the weekend and it had been perfect. She thought he was the one.

'He's so different to Phil, so attentive to my needs, not like the Adam you see in the classroom in front of his mates,' Michelle said smiling.

Helen was happy to see a sparkle in her friend's eyes.

'Anyway, he is taking me out to dinner tonight so I had better go and make myself look beautiful,' she said and, giving her friend a hug, she skipped happily out of the coffee shop.

Helen sat back in her seat to finish off her drink and continued to watch the world ticking by. She too felt content and she sighed happily as she took a sip of her drink and watched an elderly couple walk past hand in hand.

Chapter Twenty

It was a Sunday Mitchell family day. They had not had one for several weeks for one reason or another and they planned to enjoy it. Helen was now half way through her A&E placement and was due to go back to university tomorrow for her presentations. She then had a few days of study so she planned to work on her next assignment, which she was going to write about resuscitation after a discussion with a doctor who signed a DNAR without discussing it with the patient, even though she had capacity to make the decision herself. Helen did not agree with him doing it and believed that the patient should have been involved in the decision. However, he had disregarded her argument and signed it anyway. Alan supported Helen's views but said that was just how it was sometimes.

The plan for the day was to go for a walk after breakfast, have a game of Yahtzee and watch a couple of films. Then Steve and George were going to come around for a roast dinner and a game of cards. Beth arrived for breakfast at just after half nine and Helen had just come down from her shower. She had a smile on her face as she had seen Marcus the previous night and they had driven to Mablethorpe and taken a walk along the beach. Their time together was still limited but she cherished every moment. She still had that sparkle inside when she saw him or thought about him.

'You look happy,' Beth commented as soon as Helen came into the kitchen.

'I'm just really looking forward to today.' Helen smiled and went over to give her sister a hug.

Beth giggled.

'Ugh get off your hair is all wet.'

Katherine smiled to herself as her two daughters playfully fought together.

'Do you both want an egg?' she asked and they both shouted 'Yes!' in unison.

They chatted happily, over a cooked breakfast, about the past few weeks. Although they had all seen each other, they had not spent any quality time together.

'Have you heard anything from David?' Beth asked whilst they were out walking.

Helen shook her head.

'Not a peep. To be honest, I thought I would have heard something but not a word, no.'

They walked in silence for a few steps then Beth continued.

'Do you think you will ever get back together?'

Helen shook her head.

'No, I don't love him.'

Katherine pointed to some flowers and commented at how pretty the colours were, knowing that Helen did not want to talk about this. Beth understood her meaning. She began telling a story about a woman who had come into the beauty parlour and wanted her hair streaked five different colours but she was about sixty years old. The same woman also had nails like talons that she wanted painting purple with black stars and pink glitter.

'You cannot even say a mid-life crisis, it is more of a pensioner's crisis.' She laughed.

'I think I know her. She comes into the florist's sometimes,' Katherine said. 'Does she wear tight jeans and a hoodie, and if you see her from behind she looks about forty years younger than she is because she has quite a good figure?'

Beth nodded.

'Yep, that's the one! Can you imagine some bloke wolf whistling her and getting the shock of his life when she turned around?' They all laughed at the thought.

They walked through the playing field where a gym once stood but was recently knocked down. A pathway had now been made around the edge of the field. A skate park stood at one end. A dozen or more teenage boys were going up and down the half pipe on either their bikes or their skateboards, watched intently by four young girls sipping Monster energy drinks. Around the edge of the path was a variety of exercise equipment with instructions on different exercise regimes.

'Who is going to come down to the playing field and start doing press ups and sit ups?' Beth said looking at one of the pieces of equipment.

'I thought we could all come down after the film and have a go.' Helen grinned.

'You will be coming on your own then,' Beth said and playfully stuck her tongue out.

They cut back through the estate and headed back home. Katherine put the kettle on.

'Do you want to go and get the Yahtzee out of the games cupboard?' she said to Helen.

The games cupboard was situated in the hallway under the stairs, it was the cupboard where the ironing board, iron, hoover and ironing basket were also kept but Richard had built in some shelves to house the array of board games that the family possessed. Yahtzee had always been a family favourite, in addition to Monopoly and Cluedo but as they had wanted to watch some films they opted for the former, being the quickest of the three.

Initially they planned to have the best of three games, but after they all won a game each they had to play a fourth game which was won by a very clear lead from Katherine who managed to get three Yahtzee's in the game.

'You jammy bugger,' Beth said after her second.

When she rolled her third both Beth and Helen shouted out 'fix' in unison as Katherine shook her head in disbelief. She had never rolled a Yahtzee as far as she could remember for as long as she had ever played the game.

They all cried like babies at the first film, *The Notebook*.

'That is such a sad film,' Helen said blowing her nose. 'It is awful when one half of a couple gets dementia and they do not know who their partner is anymore.'

She told them the story of an elderly couple during her placement in the community. She was unable to mention names due to confidentiality but she said she still thought about them now. The woman had advanced dementia and had no recollection of her husband or their children at all. She would often scream if he went into the bedroom, she would hit him, she was doubly incontinent and, if he did not watch her every move, she would walk out of the house and wonder the streets. When the nurses discussed putting her into a residential setting the husband adamantly refused, stating that she may not remember him but he remembered her and he loved her and when they married he promised to stand by her in sickness and in health and he intended to do just that.

'That is remarkable and commendable,' Katherine said wiping a tear from her eye.

'That is true love for you, although as much as I love Steve I am not sure I could live like that if he didn't even know who I was,' Beth said and Helen nodded.

'I know what you mean' she agreed.

Katherine put the beef joint in the oven to start cooking before they started watching the next film. It was already three o'clock and the men were due to arrive at five thirty.

'How are things going with George then, Mum?' Beth asked

as she changed over the DVD.

Katherine blushed as she answered.

'Very well, I think, he is a lovely man,' she said.

Both Helen and Beth nodded in agreement.

'It is lovely to see you happy again, Mum.' Helen smiled.

'So, have you discussed moving in together or anything?' Beth asked.

'Beth, don't be so nosey,' Helen scolded, although curious to know the answer herself.

Katherine flushed even more furiously and coughed nervously.

'We have mentioned it briefly, we thought we would get Christmas out the way and then talk about it again in the New Year.'

Holding the remote out in front of her she pressed play indicating the end of the discussion. Beth and Helen looked at each other and smiled.

'Kevin Costner is so hot,' Beth said as he appeared onto the screen.

'Nah, he's not my cup of tea,' Helen said.

'Who do you like then?' her sister asked and without thinking twice Helen answered.

'Brad Pitt.'

Beth shrugged her shoulders.

'He is OK, who do you prefer, Mum, Kevin or Brad?'

Katherine shook her head.

'I'm a George Clooney fan myself or Nicholas Cage, now I wouldn't kick him out of bed.'

Beth and Helen looked at each other, shocked.

'Mum, I have never heard you talk like that before!'

Katherine laughed, almost embarrassed herself that she had said it.

'Come on, shall we have a glass of wine?' she said still laughing and getting up from the sofa.

'Yes please,' both girls replied together.

'Shall I pause this?' Helen asked but Katherine shook her head, stating that she had seen it so many times she could recite it line for line.

As she poured the wine in the kitchen, she smiled to herself as she heard Beth and Helen laughing loudly together.

Steve and George arrived within minutes of each other to find Beth and Helen laughing hysterically on the sofa as Katherine was doing a charade for chariots of fire. An empty wine bottle was on the side and a half empty bottle was on the table.

'Well, it looks like you have had a good day,' Steve said leaning over to give Beth a kiss.

'It has been brilliant,' she said happily as Helen shouted out and guessed Katherine's mime.

George gave Katherine a kiss and what looked like a tight, manly hug and Helen felt like she was playing gooseberry so she made an excuse to go to the bathroom. She took her phone from her pocket and texted Marcus.

Hope you are OK, had a lovely night last night wish we could have more times like that xxxxx.

Marcus had actually been thinking about it all day and had spent a lot of the day on the Internet.

Hi beautiful, could you think of a good excuse because I would love for us to go away next Saturday for the night, I have found a lovely hotel in Castleton xxxx.

Helen had butterflies in her stomach at the thought; there was nothing she would love more than to go away for the night with Marcus.

Just book it, I would love it more than anything xxx I love you xxx.

I love you too I cannot wait now and I cannot wait to see you in university tomorrow xxx.

Me too, see you there xxx.

'I thought you had fallen down the loo,' Beth said as Helen walked into the kitchen.

'Sorry about that, I had got a text from Nikki in A&E inviting me along to a Christmas market weekend next week,' she said.

'It's only November,' Beth said.

'They start Turkey and Tinsel theme events in October in some places,' George said to Helen's relief. 'That will be a nice weekend for you then, Helen. I take it you said yes?'

Helen nodded and smiled as she took another sip of her wine.

Helen was thankful that they were eating a roast dinner, as it would absorb some of the alcohol that was making her feel tipsy. Steve told them a story about one of his colleagues, Craig, who had laid a carpet in a woman's house, and there had been a small lump under the carpet when he had finished. Craig had stamped several times on the lump to successfully flatten it out, and as he had taken payment he had overheard the children talking about their missing mouse that had escaped from its cage.

'Oh my God, you mean it was the mouse that he had squashed?' Beth said putting her hand over her mouth as the others looked equally as shocked.

'Well we don't know for definite but we assume so,' Steve said putting a forkful of mashed potato into his mouth.

Helen shook her head.

'Imagine when they go to replace the carpet and they find the remains of poor little Mickey under there,' she said, 'Poor little thing.'

They finished their meal and after clearing up together, they spent the rest of the evening playing cards and drinking more wine. Beth was ready to retire just after nine-thirty so they drew the evening to a close. Katherine and George retired into the lounge to watch some television and Helen bid them goodnight and went up to her room.

She was not quite ready to go to sleep so she sat at her computer and logged onto Facebook, scrolling through and looking at people's statuses. She saw a photo of David, it looked like he was at a party. Helen clicked onto the album to have a look. She could see from the pictures that it was Mike and Shelley's house-warming party and she had to admit that they looked happy together. There were a few pictures with David in them and Helen was pleased to see that he wasn't looking miserable. In fact, in one picture he was stood with his arm around a girl who looked familiar. It was Sukie, the receptionist from David's work. Helen sat back in her chair and huffed, it had not taken them long to pair up! She could see her now, comforting him as soon as Helen had finished with him, she knew that that *bitch* had had her eye on him the first time she saw her. Helen shook her head. What was she thinking? Why shouldn't David be happy with someone else? At the end of the day, it was her who had ended their relationship so she should just be pleased for him, besides she had Marcus and she was happier than ever. She exited Facebook altogether and instead Googled some images of Castleton.

It looks gorgeous; I cannot wait xxx, she texted Marcus after looking at the pictures.

It is lovely; do you like caves? There are four to choose from to go down xxx.

I have never been in one but I will give it a go xxx.

Make sure you take some flat shoes and warm clothes xxxx.

I thought I would go in hot pants and stilettos!! Xxx.

Very funny!! However, very sexy, maybe you could still take those xxx.

Naughty Sir!! Are you ready for our boring presentations tomorrow? Xxx.

Nothing you do can ever be boring, I could sit and listen to you talk all day xxxx.

Maybe, but it's not just me is it? Xxx.

Good point!! Xxx.

I will see you tomorrow, goodnight xxxxxx.

Goodnight, I love you xxxxx.

I love you too xxxxx.

Chapter Twenty-One

The presentations were starting at ten so Helen's group met in the library at nine o'clock to run through it one last time. Kelly had printed some hand-outs so they could see all the slides and establish who was going to talk and when.

'You have made a good job of these, Kelly,' Kev said and she thanked him and blushed slightly.

Helen had a feeling that Kelly had a crush on Kev and wondered if he felt the same way.

'Let's hope we get a good mark for it,' Paul said. 'I bloody hate doing presentations and stuff.'

JoJo sat biting her nails.

'We should be alright, we've got Helen in our group,' she said and everybody looked at her then looked at Helen.

'What is that supposed to mean?' Helen asked with a confused look on her face.

'Well Tammy says that you and Marcus seem to have a very close relationship,' she said.

Helen could feel her face redden.

'Tammy really needs to watch her mouth! I don't know Marcus any more than anyone else in this group does, JoJo, and I am sick of her stupid, petty remarks. They are both unjustified and untrue.'

They all sat quietly for a few minutes nobody knowing what

to say and it was Paul who broke the silence.

'Adam and Michelle seem to be getting on well don't they, Helen? He really is a changed man, he refused a night in town last week to go to the cinema with her.'

Helen smiled.

'I am glad Paul, she deserves some happiness after how that creep treated her'.

He nodded.

'I don't know her that well but she seems a nice girl,' Paul said.

'She is.'

Helen smiled.

'Shall we go and get this over with?' Kelly said.

They all stood up and walked through to the School of Nursing and into the main classroom where their presentations were going to be held. Marcus, Bill and Debbie sat to one side of the classroom holding clipboards. Towards the front were a screen and a power point projector with a laptop to plug in the memory stick. There were six chairs for each group to sit at the front and the rest of the room had chairs placed in order for the rest of the students to sit and watch each presentation.

Helen saw Michelle and went over to say hello, all the while making a conscious effort not to look at Marcus. She was convinced that Tammy and JoJo would be watching her every move. She could see them whispering and looking over in her direction but she told herself she would not react to it. Marcus was talking to Bill and Debbie, discussing between them the agenda for the day. As the presentations were approximately twenty to thirty minutes each, they decided to conduct three before having lunch and conducting the next three. It would make it a longer day but they would be done in one day rather than over two as previously scheduled. Bill put this suggestion forward to the group and everyone was in agreement. They put the numbers of the groups into a bag and the order of presentations were 'neglect', 'anxiety and depression', 'social isolation', 'non-concordance', 'mental capacity act' and 'emotional abuse'.

Helen found watching the presentations interesting and when it was the turn of her own group to present theirs, she did not feel as nervous as she had anticipated. As she presented her part on depression, she used an example from her placement in the community, whereby an elderly widowed lady had stopped going out and ended up on antidepressants purely because she had become socially isolated. Helen ensured that she made eye contact with numerous people in the room, including the tutors and her stomach lurched as she looked at Marcus. He smiled slightly, not obviously for everyone to see, but she could see it in his eyes; a twinkle of pride. Helen held his gaze just for a moment but it was long enough for Debbie Saunders to notice. She looked at Marcus then back at Helen who, by now, was looking back at the students. She looked again at Marcus only to see that he was writing something on his sheet of paper. Maybe she had imagined it but they did have a look about them. It bothered her enough to have a quiet word with Bill at lunch. Bill had told her not to be ludicrous and commented that there were numerous occasions whereby she could have been accused of having a thing for more than one male in the group to which Debbie chose to end the conversation.

'They are all doing really well, aren't they?' Marcus said returning to his seat, oblivious to Debbie's conversation with Bill.

Comparing notes, they all agreed that currently all three groups had scored a substantially high grade. The pattern followed with the following groups and Marcus concluded the day by congratulating everybody on their hard work and efforts.

'Now everyone, we have got two choices for the rest of the week,' he said. 'We can come in and have some lectures to refresh on any subject or you can have the rest of the week to work on your assignments, with us here for tutorials.'

Everybody opted for the latter of the two and all of the tutors agreed to put a timetable for tutorials on the back of their door by the end of the day for students to allocate themselves a slot. Helen planned to spend the following day in the library looking for some references and policies on DNAR so she booked a tutorial with Marcus in the morning. Debbie saw her name on his list and decided that she would make an excuse to go into his office in order to try and catch them out. That was if her suspicions were correct. She liked Marcus and if she did find that she had cause for concern she would try and deal with it rather than take it any further to prevent him losing his job.

Debbie watched from out of sight as Helen knocked on Marcus's door. She was close enough to hear him call her in and, making sure she was not being watched herself, she stood outside his office with her ear pressed against his door. She felt almost disappointed to hear Helen and Marcus discussing an incident on A&E whereby a doctor had signed a do not resuscitate form without the consent of the patient or family. She suddenly felt stupid and chastised herself for misreading the situation.

'Are you alright there Debbie?' Adam asked as he saw his tutor with her ear pressed against the door of her colleague.

'Oh yes, I was just seeing if he had anyone in with him as I needed quick chat, but he has so I will catch up with him later,' she lied and, feeling embarrassed at being caught, she beckoned Adam towards her office.

The truth was, Marcus had gone out for a drink with Bill the previous night. Bill had made a joke about Debbie's comment so Marcus had warned Helen to be on guard and act completely normal which she obligingly did, as they had already agreed to play it cool in university anyway. They did share a kiss before Helen left his office, and she whispered that she would speak to him later before spending the rest of the day in the library doing research.

By Friday, Helen had completed her assignment after working

on it for three full days and, although she felt mentally drained, she was ecstatic that she had completed it so quickly. She had planned to go to the cinema with Beth that night but Beth had come home from work early with a stomach bug. Katherine offered for her to go out with her and George for a meal but she declined not wanting to play gooseberry. She packed her overnight bag ready for her trip away with Marcus. She could hardly contain her excitement. Her stomach fluttered and she had no idea how she would sleep tonight. She felt like a child on Christmas Eve. Helen was going to drive to Marcus's house at nine o'clock and then they were going to leave straight away to ensure that they had two full days together.

She packed a black satin negligee with a matching robe into her bag with a selection of clothes and lingerie regardless of the fact that they were only going for one night. As she selected some makeup and put it into her travel bag, she heard her phone bleep in the bathroom where she had left it on the windowsill, as a warm bath was running. Checking that she had everything in order, she fastened the zip and sighed happily, pulling her nightdress from underneath her pillow and heading towards the bathroom. Turning off the taps, she checked the temperature of the water with her elbow. It was perfect so she started to undress when she remembered her text so she picked up the phone to see it was from Marcus.

Cannot wait for our weekend, I am wishing the evening away xxx.

Me too, my bag is packed and I am just about to have a bath xxxxx.

I thought you were going to the cinema, I didn't expect a reply so soon xxxx.

Beth is poorly! Xxx.

Oh dear☹, I hope she gets better soon xxx.

Stomach bug, she should be OK xxx.

Keep away; I don't want you to get it xxxx.

No chance, nothing is going to spoil this weekend it will be perfect xxx.

I cannot wait☺, I love you so much Helen xxx.

Me neither, I love you too xxxx.

Helen bid Marcus goodnight. Lowering herself into the water, she allowed the bubbles to engulf her body and she slipped underneath the water holding her breath as she did so. She washed her hair and used her favourite body scrub to make her skin nice and soft then afterwards put some scented moisturiser on from head to toe, massaging it gently into her skin. Putting on her nightdress, she went downstairs, made herself a mug of hot chocolate and curled up on the sofa. Helen decided on an early night to ensure that she was refreshed in the morning and departed up to bed at just after ten. Docking her phone to her speakers, she put on a playlist and closed her eyes. She listened to a selection of her favourite songs as she drifted off into a sound sleep.

The alarm woke her at seven, which surprised Helen as she had convinced herself that she would wake early with excitement. She did, however, feel refreshed as she got out of bed and, looking out of the window, smiled, despite the fact that it was November. The sky was bright rather than dreary. Looking in her wardrobe, Helen opted for a pair of jeans and a chunky knitted jumper with a pair of fur lined boots to wear, knowing that they would potentially be going down the cave later. She freshened up in the bathroom, applied her makeup and headed downstairs.

Helen was surprised that the curtains were still drawn downstairs. Normally her Mum would be up by now. Looking by the front door, she saw both Katherine and George's shoes placed neatly side-by-side and she smiled to herself and shook her head as she opened the curtains. She boiled the kettle, debating whether to take them up a cup of tea but deciding against it. She made one just for herself, writing them a note as she sipped her own at the table, saying she would see them sometime Sunday night but it would probably be late.

It was still only eight o'clock but she decided that Marcus would be happy to see her whatever time she got there and, if he was not ready, she would just wait. Grabbing her bag, she locked the door behind her and drove to his house. It would not have mattered if she had arrived an hour earlier, Marcus would have been sat on the sofa waiting for her. He had hardly slept all night, unable to contain his excitement. As soon as he heard Helen's car pull up outside, he opened the front door and stood smiling as he greeted her. She ran towards him as she saw him in the doorway and he scooped her into his arms and kissed her.

'I love you so much. I am so looking forward to this,' he said, holding her close to him.

'So am I. I love you too,' Helen said breathing in the aroma of his aftershave. 'You smell lovely. What aftershave are you wearing?'

'Kouros,' Marcus said. 'My parents bought it me for my birthday last year.'

Helen thought for a moment.

'When is your birthday?' she asked.

'Seventeenth of February,' Marcus replied kissing the top of her head. 'Have you got your bag?'

He picked up his own brown leather cabin bag.

'I will grab it out of my car,' Helen said smiling.

'Well, let's hit the road,' Marcus said pressing the keyring to deactivate the alarm and automatically opening the car.

They stopped on the way to enjoy a breakfast at a Little Chef which Marcus paid for despite Helen offering.

'This weekend is my treat,' he insisted putting his finger on her lips to prevent her objecting in any way.

'You are so lovely to me, Marcus,' she said smiling.

'That's because I love you, Helen, and you make me so happy like you could never imagine,' he said.

Helen could feel the familiar butterflies in her stomach.

'I love you too, Marcus, I truly do,' she said, unsure that she had ever felt this happy before in her life.

As they could not check into the hotel until two, they decided to take a walk around Castleton. Zipping up her coat, Helen looked around her and was taken in by the breath-taking views. There was greenery all around, stone walls, and quaint little cottages and shops. She knew that two days was not going to be enough. She would want to stay for weeks here with Marcus in the tranquil environment. Holding hands, they walked for miles along the pathways and stood by a stream, not moving for nearly an hour, mesmerized by the sound of the rapid water.

'I could stand here all day and listen to this,' Marcus had commented and Helen had agreed, finding the sound so relaxing.

She rested her head on Marcus' shoulder. He put his hand under Helen's chin and pulled her face gently towards his to kiss her softly. His lips against hers made her heart hammer against her chest with desire.

'I wish we were in our room,' she said.

'We could go and see if it's ready yet,' Marcus suggested and Helen nodded eagerly.

Ye Old Cheshire Cheese Inn was situated in the heart of Castleton, and Marcus had booked them into the luxury room with the large four poster bed. There was an en-suite bathroom with fluffy robes and slippers for them to use. As their room was ready, they could check in early and Helen gasped as she saw the magnificent room. Marcus helped her take off her coat and hung it onto the hook at the back of the door with his own.

'Now, would you like a hot drink?' he said pointing to a selection of teas and coffees that were available on the side. 'Or perhaps the special treat in my bag?'

He smiled.

'What is the special treat?' Helen asked curiously and Marcus put his case on the bed.

He pulled out a bottle of Moët and Chandon Champagne and a punnet of strawberries.

'I will call down to room service for an ice bucket and some glasses,' he said, picking up the phone.

The request was answered promptly and a silver ice bucket was delivered to the door with two champagne flutes.

'Mr and Mrs Edwards.' The man nodded as he delivered it.

Helen blushed as Marcus thanked him and gave him a tip.

'Are we booked in under those names?' she asked.

Marcus shook his head.

'As much as I would love for that to be the case, no we aren't I just didn't want to embarrass him and say we were not married,' he said, putting the bottle into the ice.

Helen lay on her front and rested her chin on her hands.

'Would you really?' She smiled, looking up at him through her long eyelashes in a way that made his legs go weak.

'Would I really what?' he asked.

'Love us to be Mr and Mrs Edwards?'

Marcus shook the champagne around in the ice, making sure that the whole bottle was covered.

'Helen, I would marry you tomorrow.'

He sat down on the bed next to her and looked down at her.

'What about you? Would you like to be Mr and Mrs Edwards?'

This time it was different, she did not feel anxious like it had been when David talked about the future. Helen knew she wanted to be with Marcus forever.

'Well, Mr Edwards will find out the answer to that if in the future he asks the appropriate question.'

She smiled. Helen sat up on the bed and felt the bottle.

'This feels cool now, are you going to do the honours?' she said handing him the bottle.

Marcus popped the cork catching the liquid expertly in a glass as it fizzed out of the bottle.

'To us,' he toasted and they clinked their glasses together.

'To us,' Helen repeated and she closed her eyes in pleasure as the smooth drink bubbled in her mouth and fizzed on her tongue. 'That is heaven.'

'I've never had Moët before, I can see what all the fuss is about now.' She took another sip and held it in her mouth to savour the sensation.

'I love it but I don't have it very often,' Marcus said smiling at Helen's reaction. 'You really are so beautiful.'

He still could not believe how lucky he was that this young, beautiful girl was here with him, an aging man, old enough to be her father.

As if able to read his thoughts, Helen leant forward and kissed him.

'Thank you for all of this, Marcus' she said. 'It really is perfect.'

Marcus smiled and brushed her hair behind her ear.

'You are perfect, Helen, perfect in every way and I love you.' He took her glass from her and put both of their drinks on the side.

Pulling her towards him, he squeezed her tightly, brushing her hair with his hands. He loved holding her close to him, having her near him meant everything to him. He shuddered as Helen kissed his neck and ran her fingers gently through his hair.

Slowly she pushed him back onto the bed and sat on his waist. His hands rested by his side unable to move gripped down with her knees. He moaned quietly as she took off her jumper and unfastened her bra letting it fall to reveal her pert breasts. Leaning back, she unzipped his trousers. Marcus was becoming very flushed and his breathing was becoming increasingly erratic before Helen allowed his hands to become free. Almost forcefully but passionately, he tore of his jumper. Helen helped him unbutton her jeans and held onto the bedposts, as he could not get them off fast enough.

Their lovemaking did not last long, they were both so aroused.

They lay silently in each other's arms for a long time before either of them spoke, overwhelmed by what had just happened.

'When my dad was alive, I used to see my Mum and dad together, and hoped that one day I would meet a man and have the feelings that those two had for each other,' Helen said as she lay with her head on Marcus's chest. 'I know I'm only nineteen but I thought I wasn't capable of having those feelings. Then I met you and you totally blew me away.'

Marcus gave her a tight hug and kissed the top of her head.

'I know exactly what you mean. The very first time I saw you in the School of Nursing, my stomach did a back flip and the more I saw you the more my feelings for you grew. I kept trying to fight it but, after that first kiss, that was it, I was head over heels in love.'

Helen leant towards him and kissed him.

'I must be a pretty good kisser then,' she smiled.

'An amazing kisser,' he said moving in for another.

They decided to get up and take a walk back to one of the caves. There were four to choose from and they opted for one that was referred to as the Devil's Arse. Hand in hand, Helen and Marcus walked down the cold, damp steps, listening to the tour guide talk about the bandits who took refuge in the depths of the cave. Inside there were lights and different sections in the cave where concerts were held at Christmas. Sometimes people hired the cave for parties and banquets. There was a demonstration of rope making. Marcus found this particularly interesting and purchased one of the pieces that had been made.

The tour lasted about an hour and afterwards they walked past the cottages and the river that ran alongside them.

'I would love to live somewhere like this,' Marcus said, placing an arm around Helen's shoulder.

'It *is* gorgeous,' she said, looking around at the magnificent views.

'I bet these properties would cost a fortune though' she said

228

and Marcus nodded his head in agreement. 'That would be my dream home.'

Helen pointed to a small white cottage with a thatched roof and shutters at the window. There was trellis with ivy running up the centre of the wall and window boxes in each window, each full of colourful flowers. Helen suspected they could be fake as it was November but it looked very pretty. The cottage was surrounded by a low stone wall with a black iron gate and a cobbled path led to the oak front door that had cast iron hinges and a circular window with stained glass roses. Marcus stopped walking and looked at the property that had caught her eye.

'Well I have to admit, Helen that would be my choice too.' He smiled.

Turning towards her, he put his arms around her waist and kissed the tip of her nose.

'You know, we have so much in common it's spooky really,' he said.

It was starting to get dark and there was a slight chill in the air, Helen pulled the zip of her coat up to her chin and put on her gloves.

'Do you fancy going for something to eat?' Marcus asked, looking at his watch. 'It's half-past six, are you hungry?'

Helen nodded her head.

She was starting to feel peckish with all of the walking that they had done. They took a slow walk back to the hotel as Marcus had already paid for an evening meal, as well as breakfast the following morning. The restaurant was small and friendly with beamed ceilings and a coal fire warming the room. There were only a handful of guests present. They picked a table next to the window so they could admire the scenery. The waiter bought a menu with a great variety to choose from, all home-made. They both chose the same, tomato and basil soup to start followed by a seafood platter. Marcus also ordered a bottle of sparkling rosé wine to enjoy with their meal. Each table had a lit candle and as Helen looked out of the window, Marcus looked at her. The light from the candle shined on her face and shimmered in her hair. Conscious that he was looking at her, Helen turned towards him and smiled slightly.

'Two soups.' The waiter interrupted the moment as he placed the bowls in front of them.

'Oh my God, this is delicious,' said Helen as she took the first taste of the thick, warm, home-made broth.

Tasting it made her realise how hungry she was and Marcus agreed with her. They ate it in silence, enjoying the flavours combined with the warm crusty bread that was served with it. They conversed as they ate their seafood platter. Marcus laughed as Helen took a photograph of hers, after claiming that the shrimps were looking at her. The chef had strategically placed them, shelled, in the centre of the plate, on a bed of salad leaves. Marcus had to admit it did look like they were looking up and posing for the picture. Neither of them could manage a pudding, as they were too full despite the tempting options on the dessert menu. They opted for a Baileys' latte instead. They chatted happily as they sipped their drinks.

Helen asked Marcus about his past and why he had never married. He told her about Chloe, a story he had never shared with another woman before. Helen listened intently, saddened that anyone could treat Marcus in such a way and also shocked that anybody could behave in such a way. She then understood earlier conversations they had had when he had said that he found it difficult to trust women. Helen did not speak a great deal about David as Marcus already knew about him and she had not had any other relationships prior to this. She spoke about her family instead, about Beth and Steve, about her Mum and Dad, and about George and how happy she was that he had come into her Mother's life.

When the waiter collected their empty mugs he replaced them with a liqueur shot and an after eight mint.

'Good grief, I hope these chair legs are strong, otherwise they'll snap with everything I've eaten,' Helen said, picking up the small glass and holding her stomach.

She inhaled sharply as she drank the liqueur, it felt hot as it trickled down her throat making her nose tingle at the same time.

'Wow, that *is* strong,' she said in a croaking voice.

Marcus followed suit and drank his shot, he then held the glass in front of his face examining it as if willing it to refill. Helen laughed.

'I take it you liked that, then?' she said and Marcus nodded.

'Very much so. I could have that again,' he replied as he beckoned over the waiter.

'What is this drink called?' he asked as the waiter approached.

'It is called Eblana, sir,' said the waiter. 'It is a mix of whiskey, coffee, honey, almond and peanut. Did you like it?'

Marcus nodded his head enthusiastically.

'Yes, thank you,' he said.

The waiter turned to Helen.

'And you, madam, did you enjoy it?'

Helen smiled and slightly shrugged her shoulders.

'I didn't mind it but it made me shudder a bit. It was a bit strong for me.'

The waiter laughed as he took their glasses away and thought to himself that Marcus was a very lucky man. He bid them goodnight and looked as they walked hand in hand out of the restaurant. They looked so happy together.

After a short walk around the hotel grounds, Helen and Marcus retired to their room and shared a warm bubble bath. Helen closed her eyes and sighed happily as Marcus washed every part of her body with a sponge, gently kissing her at intervals. She felt so blissfully content.

'I wish this weekend would last forever,' she said as Marcus wrapped his arms around her.

231

'As do I, I hate being apart from you. I feel sick when I know I am not going to see you for days.' Marcus sighed, closing his eyes at the thought.

They held each other in silence thinking and wishing there was a way of being together but knowing it could not happen. Marcus cupped Helen's face in his hands.

'I love you so much,' he said then lowered his face to hers and kissed her, gently at first then more passionately as she scratched her nails down his back.

Helen reached behind her and pulled out the plug and, as the water drained away, Marcus helped her climb out. Throwing a towel over his shoulder, he scooped Helen up into his arms and carried her through into the bedroom. He placed her down next to the bed then laid the towel onto the quilt so that it would not get wet. He then guided her gently to lie down and kissed her from head to toe on every part of her body as she tingled with desire.

The curtains were open and the sky was black. The stars glistened and there was a full moon. An owl was hooting in the distance and the whole setting was perfect as they made love softly, slowly and gently until early hours of the morning. Afterwards, they lay naked on top of the covers and fell to sleep in each other's arms both with a smile on their faces.

Chapter Twenty-Two

They woke early to the sound of someone coughing as they walked past the door. Helen shivered. They were both still laid naked on the towel on top of the bed and neither had woken during the night. Marcus leaned over and pulled the duvet over to cover her.

'Would you like a nice cup of coffee?' he asked kissing her.

She smiled and pulled the duvet tight under her chin to feel the warmth.

'That would be lovely,' she said in a sleepy voice.

Marcus slipped on a robe and filled the kettle. As it was boiling, he looked out of the window, the curtains still open from the previous night. Despite a slight mist to the air, the sun was out and the view was magnificent. Hills and fields stretched for miles with sheep scattered about in all directions and hikers already taking in the morning air. Turning around, he saw an even more magnificent view as Helen lay snuggled under the duvet, dozing silently. He smiled to himself, he felt so happy. He had never imagined, when he made the move over to Lincoln and took that new job as a lecturer in the School of Nursing, that he was going to meet the love of his life.

The kettle clicked and he made them both a drink then, checking the time, was surprised to see that it was already nine o'clock.

'We will have to get up and go down for breakfast after this drink,' he said putting the cups on the side.

She yawned and stretched her arms above her head.

'Good morning Mr Edwards,' she said in a sleepy voice with one eye still closed.

Marcus laughed.

'Good morning, sleepy head,' he said and happily approached her as she held her arms up to him.

'There is a coffee on the side,' he said after giving her a kiss

Thanking him, she sat up to drink it. Marcus sat on the bed next to her after picking up some attraction leaflets from the dressing table. Sipping his coffee, he flicked through them then handed one to Helen.

'This looks like it could be interesting,' he said, handing her a brochure on the local castle.

'The castle is such an impressive monument in Castleton, not just for its rich heritage and the fact that the town was named after the castle, but for the opportunity it gives tourists to witness some breath taking and unique views of the beautiful Castleton landscape,' she read out loud.

They agreed that the castle ruins looked fascinating on the photographs so, after sharing a shower, they went down for breakfast.

The same waiter from the previous night greeted them as they sat at the same table.

'Have you been here all night?' Marcus joked and the waiter smiled, filling their cups with coffee.

'Well someone has to pay off the wife's credit card bills.' He laughed.

He pointed towards a table across the other side of the room.

'It is a self-service breakfast. There is a choice of a full English or continental, just go and help yourselves. Give me a shout if you need more coffee.' Smiling, he walked towards an elderly couple who had taken a seat at a table nearby.

'I wonder if he was being serious,' Helen whispered as they walked towards the breakfast bar.

'What about?' Marcus asked inquisitively.

'About his wife and the credit card bills,' she said.

Marcus shrugged his shoulders.

'I have no idea, I don't like credit cards they are dangerous things to have, and it makes it too easy to get into debt.'

Taking a plate from the counter he started to fill it with bacon, eggs and sausages.

'I had one once, purely to pay the deposit on my car but after I had paid it off I cut it up, I would never have another one.'

Helen placed two croissants on her plate with strawberry jam and a pot of apricot yoghurt. The breakfast was as delicious as the meal the previous evening and Helen made comment that the croissants melted in her mouth. They both felt sad when they packed up their bags, ready to check out of the hotel.

'This has gone far too quick,' Helen said, sitting on the edge of the bed.

Marcus sat down beside her and put his arm around her shoulder.

'I know, but we will do it again soon, I promise,' he said. 'And we have still got today to enjoy.'

Helen smiled and kissed him,

'Come on then, let's go and see these castle ruins.'

It was a steep climb up to the castle, and it reminded Helen of when they went up to Lincoln castle. She was panting but Marcus was acting as if he had not even taken a few steps. She chastised herself again for being so unfit and thought that her New Year's resolution would be to join a gym.

'Are you OK?' Marcus asked.

'I'm fine, just not as fit as my action man.' She laughed. 'You would think that you were nineteen and I was your age really the way I'm acting.'

Marcus laughed.

'I'm not that old,' he said and Helen flushed.

'Oh Marcus, I didn't mean it like that,' she said, embarrassed.

As they approached the castle, Marcus paid, and then they entered through the remains of the gatehouse into the main courtyard. From there, the foundations of the great hall, kitchens and other buildings could be seen. Marcus read the history from the brochure to Helen as they walked around. He explained how the castle was founded between the Norman conquest of 1066 and its first mention in the doomsday survey of 1086 by William Peveril. Peveril inherited his father's estates but in 1155 King Henry II confiscated them. Helen grinned at him.

'You really are being my teacher today, aren't you?' she laughed, wrapping her arms around his waist.

They stood for a long time looking at the views.

'This is magnificent.' Marcus sighed.

From the castle, they could see Hope Valley, Cave dale and all of Castleton and beyond.

'I don't want to have to go home not knowing when I am going to see you next,' he said.

Helen put her head on his shoulder, her eyes filled with tears.

'Don't, Marcus, please. I hate it too, I really do,' she said.

They both stood in silence, each with their own thoughts, thoughts of each other and thoughts of their future together.

'Do you like shopping?' Marcus broke the silence.

Helen laughed.

'You are asking a woman if she likes shopping?'

Marcus shook his head and smiled.

'I suppose it was a silly question,' he said.

'Why do you ask?' Helen asked.

'I just wondered if you fancied going to Sheffield to the shopping centre and having a look around?' he suggested.

Helen nodded enthusiastically.

'I would love to, I haven't been there for ages,' she said. 'Do you not mind shopping?'

Marcus put his arms around her waist.

'I will go anywhere with you, but no, I'm one of those weird men that actually enjoys shopping.' He grinned.

Helen stood on her tiptoes and kissed the tip of his nose.

'Another reason why you are my perfect man.' She smiled and Marcus looked around to ensure nobody was looking then cheekily squeezed her bum.

The journey to the shopping mall took less than an hour but the time passed quickly as they talked about their trip.

'I hope we don't see anyone we know,' Helen said as they drove into the car park suddenly aware that they were actually not that far away from home.

'I come here quite regularly and I've never yet bumped into anyone that I know,' Marcus reassured her. 'Let's go and have a Costa to start with.'

Helen smiled, remembering the first time they had been to Costa when she had shown him around the castle and the cathedral. That was the day they almost shared their first kiss in the bath house.

Sipping her hazelnut latte, Helen looked around at all the people busily getting on with their lives, laden with armfuls of bags from the variety of shops that the centre housed.

'Where do you like to buy your clothes and shoes from?' she asked Marcus, intrigued.

'Usually Next, occasionally Burton's,' he smiled. 'What about you?'

'I am a student on a bursary so it is usually Primark but I sometimes go into New Look. I like it in there,' she said.

'Well you always look lovely, whatever you wear,' Marcus complimented and Helen smiled.

They walked around the shops hand in and hand. Helen, after some debate, insisted on treating Marcus to a tie that caught his attention; grey with a flicker of purple in it. 'A thank you for a perfect weekend,' she had said gratefully. As they walked past Next, Helen looked at the model in the window and gasped.

'Wow, look at that dress,' she said.

The mannequin displayed a long turquoise dress cascaded with sequins that glistened in the light.

'Why don't you go and try it on?' Marcus suggested.

'When would I ever wear it?' Helen asked.

'I do believe you have a graduation to go to next year,' Marcus reminded her.

Helen smiled as she looked at the dress and thought how perfect it would be for her graduation ball. Steering her into the shop, Marcus looked around until he spotted the dress. Picking out a size ten, he handed it to her. She looked at the price tag.

'This is seventy pounds! I can't afford that,' she said in a disappointed tone.

'Just go and try it on, I want to see you in it,' Marcus said pushing it towards her.

She took it from him and headed to the changing rooms to try it on. As she emerged, Marcus gaped. She looked stunning, more stunning than he had ever seen her.

'What do she think?' Helen asked, smoothing her hands over the material; she herself thought it was the most beautiful dress she had ever seen.

'You look beautiful,' Marcus said, feeling almost lost for words. 'It would be perfect for your graduation.'

Helen looked at herself in the mirror that was on the wall.

'I do love it.' She looked again at the price tag. 'I just don't know, it's very expensive.'

Marcus smiled at her.

'I would like to buy it for you,' he said.

Helen shook her head.

'No, I can't let you do that, I'm sorry. You have paid for enough this weekend.' She kissed him on the cheek. 'Thank you anyway for the gesture.'

Helen went to get changed, feeling disappointed that she would not be able to buy the dress as it was lovely. She just could not justify spending that much money on an outfit to probably only wear it once. Sadly, she handed it to the assistant and walked back out to the shop where Marcus was waiting for her. He was smiling and holding a carrier bag with Next written on it.

'You looked too beautiful in the dress not to have it,' he said, giving her the bag.

'Oh my God, Marcus, you shouldn't have done that. I will pay you back, I promise,' Helen said, excitedly throwing her arms around him.

'No you won't, it's a gift,' Marcus insisted.

'You spoil me, Marcus, you really do,' Helen said softly and he kissed her gently on her lips.

'You deserve to be spoilt, Helen. I love you,' he said and she smiled happily.

The shutters of the shops started to come down as they closed early on a Sunday.

'Shall we get something to eat here? This restaurant has some lovely food,' Marcus suggested.

'Are the restaurants not closing too?' Helen asked.

'They tend to stay open until about nine o'clock,' Marcus said.

Helen linked her arm through his. Her stomach was rumbling.

'OK then but this really is my treat and I will not take no for an answer.'

Marcus opened his mouth to speak but Helen promptly covered it with her hand and he gently bit her finger. The waiter led them to a booth on the far side of the restaurant. Marcus ordered the Jack Daniels' salmon and Helen the King prawn crispy noodle salad, and they sat sipping a glass of lemonade when Helen heard her phone ping a text message.

'I wonder who that is,' she said, rummaging in her bag for her mobile.

As she opened the message, her face paled and bile arose in the back of her throat.

'What is it?' Marcus asked seeing the look on her face.

She said nothing and handed him the phone; the message was from her Mum.

Hope you've had a lovely weekend, are you going to bring Marcus in to introduce him to me on your way back home so I can meet him? Xxxxxx.

Marcus looked at Helen.

'Did you tell her about us?'

'No, of course not, I haven't told anyone,' Helen said taking the phone back and re-reading the message.

What are you on about? She typed back, not knowing what else to say.

It took a while to receive the reply, by which time their meal had arrived. Katherine was not very quick at writing text messages.

I am your Mum, Helen. I knew you would not have gone on a weekend away with someone you have only just met and have worked with once. I also just know there is something going on between you two, but you can trust me. I promise I won't say anything. I just want to meet the man who has won your heart.

Helen handed the phone again to Marcus who read the message, he seemed thoughtful for a while as he chewed on a piece of salmon. Turning to Helen, he smiled.

'Let's just go, what have we got to lose.'

Helen looked at him and raised her eyebrows and without saying anything she replied.

OK xxxx.

Helen felt nervous as Marcus pulled up outside of her house. She loved him so much and she wanted her Mum to like him. She was also anxious that nobody else was at home. It was going to feel awkward enough as it was and she knew poor Marcus must have been feeling nervous. However, he was doing a good job of disguising it. Neither of them needed to worry as Katherine welcomed them both with a smile and a hug as they walked through the door and poured them a cup of freshly made tea.

They chatted freely for several hours. Marcus answered all of Katherine's questions honestly. He told her about his nursing career and his accident that led him to going into teaching, and most importantly he told her of his love for her daughter. He said that he knew he was a lot older than Helen, but he hoped that that would not stand in the way of her family accepting him into their lives. Katherine smiled as Marcus was talking. She watched as he held Helen's hand, never letting go for a moment. She embraced the gleam in her daughters eye; a look of pure devotion. Helen was in love and if she was happy, Katherine was happy. She could see what had attracted Helen to him. He was an attractive man, very intellectual, very calming, and Katherine liked him a lot. She understood that their relationship had to be kept secret and promised not to say anything to anybody, not even George or Beth. Although she disagreed with the way they had met, she was not going to start handing out lectures because never before had she seen such happiness in Helen.

Helen sighed happily as they drove back to Marcus's house to pick up her car.

'Your Mum is lovely,' Marcus said.

'I know. I think she really likes you too.' Helen had a smile that almost spread from one side of her face to the other.

'This weekend has just been perfect,' he said as he pulled up outside his front door.

Turning off the engine, he turned to face her. They had already agreed that she could not go inside as she was due back on an early shift in the morning.

'When do you think I will see you again?' he asked, already feeling nauseous with dread knowing that it may be a few days.

'I will try and pop in one day after one of my shifts,' she said experiencing the same feelings inside.

Leaning forward, he kissed her, stroking her face as he did.

'I love you so much,' he said.

'I love you too,' she replied.

Collecting her bags, she walked sadly to her car.

Chapter Twenty-Three

It was a hectic week that went quickly. Helen had two early shifts followed by a couple of days off before going to have a late shift on the Friday evening. She had seen Marcus briefly but not for any length of time. However, they had spoken each evening.

Katherine took the day off on Thursday and they spent the day shopping and chatting before meeting Beth for lunch at the Royal William.

'So how are you, sis?' Beth asked. 'How was your weekend away?'

Helen glanced over at Katherine.

'It was alright actually, considering I have only just met them all. They made me feel really welcome,' she said. 'How was your weekend?'

Beth sat back in her seat and took a mouthful of her drink.

'Well, Steve and I were talking about potentially going on holiday next year and then out of the blue Steve suggested we make it a honeymoon.'

Both Helen and Katherine did a double take. Beth and Steve had been engaged for what seemed like an eternity and whenever marriage had been discussed they had always said they were happy as they were.

'Seriously?' Helen said with a slight excitement in her voice.

Katherine grinned on the other side of the table.

'Well we are thinking about it,' Beth said in a matter of fact sort of way. 'Just don't go buying your hats yet because it probably won't happen, you know what we're like.'

Regardless, Helen jumped off of her chair squealing and hugged Beth.

'Get off, you moron.' Beth and Katherine chucked at Helen's childlike ways.

She shuffled uncomfortably in her seat as she spotted David and Mike walking in. He too spotted them and, after appearing to consider what to do, he walked towards them.

'Hi,' he said.

Helen blushed slightly. It was the first time she had seen David since their breakup.

'Hi,' she said. 'How are you?'

He had had his haircut, it suited him.

'You're looking well,' she told him.

They made polite conversation before he returned to Mike to order his drink.

'Well, that was awkward,' Beth whispered and Helen nodded. 'I think he is going out with this dark haired girl now. I've seen a few pictures of them together on Facebook,'

'That will be Sukie from his work,' Helen said.

'So much for a broken heart! It didn't take him long to replace you did it?' Beth shook her head.

'Beth I really don't care, now can we change the subject please?' Helen said in an agitated voice.

Beth promptly obeyed.

'Why don't you just tell Beth about Marcus? She won't say anything,' Katherine said after they had walked her back to the hairdressers.

'No, Mum, I can't tell anyone! Please don't say anything, you promised!' Helen pleaded, her eyes wide.

'I won't say a word. You can trust me, you know that,'

Katherine reassured her. 'I just know you can trust Beth too and she'll be hurt when she finds out.'

Helen shook her head.

'I'm saying nothing.'

Helen could not resist looking at the photographs Beth had been talking about on the Friday morning. She was right, there were a few of David and Sukie together arm in arm. David did not have a relationship status but, then again, why should she care? She was happy with Marcus and, quite frankly, she was not bothered in the slightest. She was more bothered that she could not have any photographs of her and Marcus together. She hated all the secrecy, the creeping around and looking over their shoulders, making sure they weren't being seen every time she knocked on his door. There was less than a year to go until the end of her course and it could not come around quick enough.

Helen heard her phone bleep with a text message; it was from Michelle.

Hi stranger, do you fancy going for a drink tonight?

Sorry I am on a late shift and don't finish until 10, what about tomorrow night? She replied.

No good for me, Adam is taking me away to York ☺ x.

Very nice, I went there with David. It is lovely, have a lovely time xx.

Next weekend? Michelle suggested.

I'm working Saturday and Sunday, late shifts, but could do the Friday night, Helen offered, suddenly realising the impact of shift work on her social life.

It's a date!! Shall we go into town for some drinks and a dance?

Sounds good to me. Will look forward to that, will ring you nearer the time to arrange. Got to go as starting my shift xx.

OK, see you then xx.

Have a great weekend xxx.

It was an emotional shift. They were in the resuscitation room and within the first five minutes an eighteen year old had been bought in via ambulance. He had overdosed on heroin and had a respiratory followed by cardiac arrest. The paramedics had given him four milligrams of intravenous Narcan by the time that he had arrived in the department. The drug is used to reverse opioid and respiratory depression and can be given two to three minutes apart, two milligrams at a time. The consultant administered a further six milligrams as well as Helen and Alan performing CPR but there was no response at all. The boy, whose name they still did not know, had been found slumped in an alley, the needle still in his arm. The consultant and pronounced his time of death at twenty-three minutes past two.

In addition to the unnamed boy, the crew bought in Andrew, a twenty-seven year old who had suddenly collapsed at work on a nearby farm and had a seizure. He went on to have another in the ambulance, causing him to both bite his tongue and be incontinent of urine. Helen covered him with a blanket to preserve his modesty. Andrew was drowsy and incoherent, and seemed oblivious to the commotion around him. Alan rang him up to an ECG monitor and a consultant inserted a cannula to administer drugs if he had another seizure. The radiographers were prepared to take a CT scan of his brain to see if there had been a bleed.

There was a tap on the door and one of the receptionists poked her head around.

'Andrew's wife is here,' she said.

Helen looked at Zamir, the consultant.

'Can she come in?' she asked.

Zamir nodded and muttered something about getting some history about Andrew. Helen felt embarrassed that she struggled to understand Zamir. He had a strong Indian accent and she would often have to ask him to repeat himself several times. She had never been any good with accents whether it was Irish, Scottish, even Cockney if it was too broad.

It was clear that Andrew's wife, Scarlett, had been crying. Helen gave her a tissue and a cup of water before taking her through to her husband. She blew her nose noisily before asking what was happening with Andrew. Helen explained that at present they were completing investigations to try and establish what had happened. As she led Scarlett through to where he lay, Scarlett lost composure and burst into floods of tears again. Helen put her arm around her to comfort her and, as if she had been waiting for the signal, Scarlett threw her arms around her and sobbed like a small child. Eventually she composed herself to answer Zamir's questions. She had been married to Andrew for six years. They had no children, he had no allergies and he had no pre-existing medical conditions. He had worked on the farm since he was sixteen; it was his parent's farm but, at the moment, his parents were on holiday so Andrew had been working extra hours. Scarlett was adamant that Andrew had never had a seizure before. However, she recalled the last few days in which he had been complaining of a headache. Last night, he had gone to bed early with a headache and blurred vision. She turned to Helen, who was holding her hand.

'Andrew has never had a headache in all the years we have been together,' she said looking worried.

'Do you want to take a look at this Zamir?' One of the radiographers said as he printed off the image.

Andrew was groaning and holding his head.

'Give him a shot of Diamorphine through the line. I've written him up for five milligrams,' Zamir said to Alan who promptly went into the side room to draw up a dose as the consultant put the image onto the screen to view.

Helen watched his face for his reactions and knew from the way that he creased his brow that it was not going to be good news. As the pain relief was being administered, Andrew's body once again started to convulse.

'Please do something! Help him!' Scarlett was becoming

hysterical so Helen led her outside as the others commenced a drip of phenytoin to stop the seizures from recurring.

As the drugs took effect and Alan, with the help of another nurse, changed Andrew out of his wet jeans and into a hospital gown, they called Scarlett back into the room. She sat down next to her husband and held his hand. He was still not readily responding to many prompts, just mumbling 'Yes' and 'No' occasionally when asked questions. Zamir pulled up a chair and sat facing Scarlett. He had worked on the department for several years and was somewhat of an expert at delivering bad news. He delivered it in a calm and compassionate tone, unlike some of the other consultants who were abrupt and straight to the point.

'I'm afraid to say that Andrew has suffered what we call a subarachnoid haemorrhage,' he said gently.

Scarlett blinked back tears, she looked at her husband then back at Zamir.

'What does that mean?' she asked in a quiet voice barely audible above the sound of the machines.

'It is a bleed to the surface of the brain caused by a brain aneurysm that has burst,' Zamir explained.

Scarlett looked confused.

'What is an aneurysm?' she asked.

'It is a bulge in a blood vessel due to a weakness in the vessel wall.' Zamir drew a picture on a piece of paper that was attached to the clipboard he was holding.

Scarlett nodded, appearing to understand.

'Will he be alright?' she asked.

Helen looked at Zamir, also curious to hear his response.

'Only time will tell, I'm afraid,' he said in a grim tone as Scarlett held her head down and once again cried large heavy tears.

Everybody stood in silence allowing her to compose herself. Helen handed her more tissues.

'So what has caused this?' Scarlett asked.

'Does your husband smoke or drink?' Zamir asked and Scarlett shook her head vigorously.

'He gave up smoking five years ago and he only drinks when he goes out with his friends once a month, or Christmas and birthdays.'

Zamir gently placed his hand on her knee.

'Sometimes there is just no explanation for why these things happen, and all we can do now is hope that he recovers.'

Zamir explained that Andrew would need to be transferred that evening to the neuroscience unit at another hospital in Sheffield, which is where the specialist unit was based.

'Do you think he will survive?' Helen asked Alan when they were on their break later that evening.

He shrugged his shoulders.

'I have seen cases like this before and often they end up having a stroke which is either fatal or disabling,' he said. 'But then again I have also seen people make a full recovery, so who knows.'

Helen sighed and rested her head against her hand.

'Poor Scarlett, one minute looking forward to start trying for a family and then boom! It's all wiped out in one fell swoop.'

Alan nodded.

'That's life, I'm afraid. It stinks, and working on this department makes it hit home more than working anywhere else. Like Andrew, he got up this morning as normal, and now his life is hanging by a thread.'

They both sat silently for a few moments, absorbed in their own thoughts.

'Well, this has been a cheerful shift so far.' Helen grinned a tired smile.

Alan nodded and rose to his feet after looking at his watch.

'Come on, kiddo, let's see if I can depress you some more before you go home'.

Walking onto the department, there was some commotion by the back door as an ambulance was reversing in.

'Alan, can you get the resuscitation room ready? We have an infant coming in, cardiac arrest, they are trying to resuscitate her now,' Zamir said with urgency as he approached the ambulance hastily.

Helen felt hot. She did not know how she would cope with a child but she followed Alan's lead. She helped him pull the defibrillator and observations monitors so they were situated next to the trolley where the child would be placed. She froze as the doors burst open and Zamir ran into the room clutching a baby. She recognised the voice of the mother before she entered the room.

'Olivia breathe! Breathe! Please breathe for Mummy?' It was Kelly from her course.

Helen could not move as Kelly ran in, closely followed by what she assumed was her parents. She approached Kelly and placed an arm around her shoulder, moving her away from the table to give Zamir and Alan room to do their jobs. She did not speak, what possibly could she say in this situation? Her head thumped with the sound of her own heartbeat, desperately wishing for the sound of Olivia's cry to fill the room. The sound never came. The only sound to be heard was Kelly's screams as Zamir turned around and shook his head sadly.

'I'm so sorry,' he said gently. 'She's gone.'

The family were given time to spend with Olivia before being taken into a small room to have a cup of tea. Zamir explained that Olivia would need to have a post mortem but the most likely cause of death was sudden infant death syndrome. Kelly was numb. She stared at the wall throughout the duration of the conversation and said nothing. Her cheeks wet with mascara-stained tears.

Helen sipped water from the water fountain. She remembered the day that Tammy had spent in resuscitation and how awful she had felt.

'Are you OK?' Alan asked as he came over to her.

'I think this has got to be the worst day of my whole training,' Helen said. 'I just feel emotionally drained, and I feel awful for Kelly. I just wanted to cry. She's my friend, you know, and she adored her little girl.'

Helen's voice started to crack and Alan gave her a gentle squeeze of the hand.

'Look, it's almost nine o'clock. It has been an emotional day so why don't you get off early,' he suggested and Helen gratefully accepted the offer of an early finish.

Standing in the changing room, she splashed her face with cold water and sat on the bench before getting changed. Putting her head in her hands, she cried the tears that she been holding back for the last hour. She felt like she was not able to stop, sobbing until she could hardly catch her breath. When she managed to dry her eyes, she got changed and took her phone out of her bag, she found Kelly's number and typed a text.

Nothing I can say can ever make things better; just know that I am here if you need me, call me anytime if you need to talk xxx.

She sent it, not expecting a reply but she did receive one almost instantly.

Thank you xx.

Helen then scrolled down to find Marcus's number and pressed dial, not sure if he would be at home. He did not answer straight away and she had been just about to hang up when he did. As soon as she heard his voice she started to cry.

'Helen? Sweetheart, what's wrong?' he asked, instantly worried that she was going to say something bad.

She could not speak at first as she was too upset.

'Are you busy?' she asked after she had composed herself.

'I was only marking some assignments, why did you want to pop for a coffee?' he asked.

Marcus was concerned as Helen sounded so upset.

'Have you got anything stronger? I have had the worst ever shift,' she said.

Marcus tutted.

'That's not good, I have got something stronger of course but aren't you driving?' he said.

'Pour me a glass, I'll be there in a few minutes. One won't hurt me,' she said, hanging up the phone.

A glass of wine was waiting for Helen as soon as she arrived.

'First thing's first, though,' Marcus said after giving her a kiss. 'I have run you a nice bubble bath upstairs so go and relax in that whilst you tell me about your shift.'

Helen sighed happily.

'You are a star,' she said as she picked up her glass and headed upstairs.

She smiled as she entered the bathroom. Marcus had lit candles all around it and the bath was filled to the brim with foaming bubbles. As Helen undressed, she tested the water with her toes and it was the perfect temperature so she lowered herself in. Marcus followed into the bathroom behind her and sat down on the toilet seat.

'Come on then, tell me about your awful day,' he said.

'Are you not joining me?' Helen said in a seductive voice.

'I will do in a few minutes. I want you to relax and unwind first and tell me about your day.'

He handed her, her glass of wine and Helen told him about the events of the day. He was shocked and saddened to hear about Kelly and the loss of her baby. He could not begin to imagine how it must feel to lose a child. He could see that Helen was welling up again and he went over and sat on the edge of the bath.

'You will have days like this, sweetheart, especially if you go into palliative care,' he said taking some bubbles in his hands and using them to massage her shoulders.

'I know, I think it was just harder because it was Kelly,' she said, leaning forward, enabling him to manoeuvre down her back. 'Plus, the guy with the brain haemorrhage, I could not help thinking what I would do if that happened to you. I would just want to die, I'm sure. I just love you so much, I cannot imagine not being with you now.'

Marcus was so happy that Helen felt this was about him.

'It's not going to happen to me darling, I'm immortal. Have you ever seen *Highlander*? Well, that film was about me.'

Helen laughed and splashed him with the water. Marcus leant down and kissed her.

'Shall I come in now then?' he asked and Helen nodded enthusiastically.

Holding his hands up in the air, Marcus slid into the bath fully clothed. Water sploshed over the sides.

'Marcus!' Helen squealed and laughed hysterically. 'You've still got your clothes on!'

Marcus pulled a face.

'So I have.' He smiled. 'But at least it got you laughing.'

Helen took hold of his jumper and pulled him towards her, their lips met and they shared a passionate embrace. Marcus clumsily pulled at his jumper but it was stuck to him. Helen laughed as he slid around the bath in an attempt to shed his clothes.

'Shall we get out? It might be easier,' she said, still laughing.

'So much for trying to be sexy.' Marcus grinned.

'Well I think you would be sexy in a paper bag.' Helen winked. 'But I think these jeans will be an impossible challenge.'

The floor was already drenched and still more water spilled over the edge of the bath.

'Come on, let's get out so we can take them off,' she said and Marcus could not get out the bath quick enough, almost slipping on the wet floor.

He helped Helen as she stepped out, preventing her from slipping herself, then wiping bubbles from her hair, he leant forward and kissed her as she unfastened the button of his jeans.

She laughed as she attempted to pull them down but they were tight as if they had been glued to his legs. Marcus jiggled his bum until they were down as far as they needed to be.

'Let's go and snuggle on the sofa for a bit with our wine,' he said pulling the plug out the bath then, sitting on the edge, he tugged at his jeans until they finally came off. He draped them over the radiator and went through to the bedroom and put on some lounge pants patterned with Spiderman.

'Do you like Spiderman?' Helen asked, intrigued.

'No, my brother brought them for me last Christmas,' he said.

'I never knew you had a brother,' she said, sounding shocked.

'I don't really see him much. Phillip is sort of the black sheep of the family, a bit of a loner. He travels a lot; we see him at Christmas but that's about it,' Marcus said.

They went downstairs and Helen sat on the sofa as Marcus dimmed the lights.

'Shall I put on some music?' he asked.

'Yes, that would be nice,' said Helen. 'I love listening to music.'

'I'll put my iPod on and just shuffle a playlist. First, though, I want to play a song that I listen to a lot, it reminds me of you,' Marcus said as he scrolled through his music library.

Helen smiled as she listened to the words of Paul Weller's 'You do Something to Me'.

'That was so appropriate,' she said as the song ended.

Marcus smiled.

'I heard that when I first met you and it hit a nerve because it was if he had wrote that song about you,' he said.

Helen leant forward and gave him a kiss.

'That could be our special song,' she said.

'I think so,' Marcus smiled.

Helen drank the last of her wine.

'Do you want a coffee now?' Marcus asked.

'Can I have another wine?' Helen said. 'I enjoyed that one.'

Marcus looked at her cautiously.

'You can't drive if you have any more wine.'

She smiled at him.

'Well, if that's the case, could I sleep on your sofa?' She winked.

Marcus grinned and almost ran to the kitchen to get the wine bottle.

'Have you eaten?' he asked.

'I took some sandwiches to work, yes,' Helen replied.

She took her phone from her bag and texted her Mum that she was staying out for the night but would be home in the morning.

'Come on, let's have a picture,' she said. 'Nobody other than me sees my phone, and I want to be able to look at you when I am not with you.'

Putting their heads together, they smiled and Helen took a photo. She took one of them kissing and another of them clinking their wine glasses. She made sure to keep them in a separate folder, just in case anybody did look in her photo album. They listened to music and drank wine into the early hours of the morning. They retired to bed and made love before happily falling asleep in each other's arms, content in the knowledge that they would be waking up together. Neither of them did until gone half-past nine.

Marcus made them a breakfast of scrambled eggs and toast before Helen left him to finish marking the assignments that he had been doing the previous night. She promised to call during the week and he offered to make dinner on Tuesday as she was on an early shift. Helen told Marcus of her plans of a night in town on Friday with Michelle and he said that he could possibly see them as it was Bill's birthday so they were also going to be going into town for a few drinks. They knew that they would need to be casual if they did see each other.

Giving Marcus a kiss goodbye, she slowly opened the door and ensuring the coast was clear she ran out to her car, waving as she pulled out of the street.

255

Chapter Twenty-Four

'Can you believe we only have just over a week left on here,' Tammy said to Helen as they had a coffee break together.

Helen shook her head. The placement on A&E had gone very fast and she had thoroughly enjoyed it, so much so that she had contemplated requesting her management placement there. However, after discussion with Marcus, she decided she wanted to return to the community as previously planned. Tammy, on the other hand, wanted to work in the department when she qualified. The trauma of her first week had long since been forgotten.

'Is JoJo enjoying her placement in theatres?' Helen asked.

JoJo was travelling to Louth hospital each day for her placement and, according to Tammy, was not impressed with the travel.

'No, she hates it. She's bored,' Tammy said. 'She said she prefers her patients to be conscious.'

Helen smiled; she was going there for her next placement after Christmas and was not looking forward to it herself. Paul came into the room.

'Tammy, Mr Jones is ready to go down to the ward now, if you are ready,' he said.

Mr Jones had come in several hours earlier after experiencing some left sided weakness, facial drooping and slurred speech. A scan had shown that he had suffered a stroke and he was being transferred to a ward for further monitoring and assessment. Tammy stood up eagerly.

'See you later Helen,' she said and followed Paul to the bay where an anxious Mr and Mrs Jones were waiting.

Helen washed their cups and went out into the department to look for Alan. He had not come for a break as he had been catheterising a man who did not want anybody else present in the room other than a male doctor. Alan was sat on the desk talking to James, a young registrar that was new to the department and had started a six-month placement at the beginning of the week. James was asking if it was always quiet on a Wednesday evening and Alan explained how one day is never the same as another in A&E.

'Isn't that right, Helen?' he asked as she approached them.

Helen shrugged her shoulders.

'I have been here six weeks; one minute it can be like this and an hour later it can be heaving,' she said.

Today was particularly quiet but yesterday had been exceptionally busy as there had been a road traffic collision towards the end of her shift and she was late leaving. She felt terrible as Marcus was cooking her dinner but luckily nothing was ruined. Having worked in A&E himself, he knew how a nurse could get held up with emergencies so he had prepared a chicken stir fry that he could cook as she arrived.

It was the first time tonight that Helen felt the time drag; she found herself cleaning the store cupboard twice to pass the time. She was looking forward to two days off before working the weekend and was especially looking forward to her night in town with Michelle on Friday. She wondered if she would be celebrating as they were getting the results for their assignments and presentations on Friday as well. Marcus, being the professional that he was, refused to give Helen any hints as to whether she had passed or failed. As she thought about it, her stomach lurched. She hated results day. Helen lacked confidence in her academic abilities and always managed to convince herself that she would fail.

'This must be the tidiest store cupboard in the hospital,' Nikki said, coming in for a needle and syringe.

Helen laughed.

'I haven't seen you for a while,' she said.

'I had some annual leave so Eduardo and I went to Italy to see his family.'

Nikki smiled.

'Did you have a nice time?' Helen asked and Nikki put her hand on her chest over her heart.

'Perfection,' she said. 'I didn't want it to end. Anyway, I'd better go and give this poor man some pain relief.'

She disappeared out of the door. Helen looked at her watch; it was still only eight thirty. She went out to Alan who was now talking to James about football. Sharon came over with Tammy.

'Alan, shall we let these two go early tonight? Seeing as it is so dead,' she said.

'Oooh, I don't know about that.' Alan grinned. 'Go on, off you go kiddo. I'll see you for the late shift on Saturday night. Enjoy your night out on Friday.'

'Where are you going Friday?' Tammy asked as they got changed.

'Michelle and I are going into town for some drinks,' Helen said.

'We'll probably see you there. JoJo and I are going into town with Tom and Laura.'

Tammy smiled.

'Crickey, it'll be a right gathering in town,' Helen said before realising what she had done.

'Why, who else will be there?' Tammy asked curiously.

Helen thought quickly.

'My sister and her fiancé said they might go as well,' she said.

They walked out together and Helen bid Tammy goodnight.

Michelle had been on an early shift and so was finished by three on Friday. Katherine had invited her for tea as Beth was coming to do their hair. They all enjoyed fajitas and a bottle of wine Michelle had provided in thanks. Beth also bought a bottle of wine to celebrate as Helen had got an A for both her assignment and her presentation. The three girls drank the wine upstairs in Helen's bedroom as they listened to music whilst having their hair, nails and make-up done.

'I feel like a movie star,' Michelle said as she looked at herself in the mirror when Beth had finished her makeover.

'Take a picture so I can show Adam, tomorrow,' she said to Helen, handing over phone before posing provocatively.

'How was your weekend in York, by the way?' Helen asked.

Michelle blushed slightly.

'It was amazing,' she said happily. 'Adam told me that he loved me for the first time.'

Helen gasped in delight and rushed over to hug her friend.

'Do you love him?' she asked and Michelle nodded eagerly.

'With all my heart,' she said and Helen hugged her again.

'Oh, Michelle, I'm so happy for you I really am,' she said.

'We just need to find you a prince charming, now,' Michelle said. 'Maybe tonight is the night.'

Helen shook her head vigorously.

'No thanks, I'm happy enough and I want a girly night with my best mate, not a match-making night.' She raised her eyebrows and Michelle saluted.

'Yes ma'am.'

Beth gave them a lift into town, declining their offer to join them for the evening. She had bought a selection of wedding magazines she wanted to browse through whilst Steve was out with some friends from work. They decided to go into Treble's bar first and Michelle bought them both a Bacardi and Coke, which was promptly followed by another. The bar was crowded and the dance floor was completely full. Helen could feel her phone vibrate in her pocket. Focusing on the screen, she saw it was a text from Marcus,

Are you in town? Xxx.

Yes we are in Treble's bar. Where are you? Xxx.

We are in Wetherspoon's at the minute but will be walking down to Walkabout soon xxxx.

We will probably be in there when you get there. Cannot wait to see you, although I'll pretend I'm not bothered xxxx.

Helen smiled as she sent the text.

'What are you smiling at?' Michelle asked.

Helen put her phone back in her pocket, grateful that the room was dark to hide her blushing.

'It was just Beth excited about her wedding.'

'When is she getting married?' Michelle asked.

'Not sure yet but probably next year or the year after.' Helen smiled, finishing her drink.

'Shall we head to Walkabout and have a dance?'

Michelle nodded eagerly and finished her drink.

They both felt tipsy, stepping out into the fresh air and clasping arms to steady each other as they walked towards their next destination. Helen hurried Michelle past the alley that she had caught Phil and Amy in together. As always there was a queue outside Walkabout. They walked past the waiting customers and heard their names called out. They waved as they saw Tammy, JoJo, Tom and Laura, but continued walking without stopping to talk.

It was chilly outside. They huddled together to keep warm, ignoring the wolf-whistles from a passing stag party. It did not take long for the queue to disperse and they stepped inside to the beat of Gotye's 'Somebody that I Used to Know'.

'I love this song.' Helen shouted above the noise. 'Let's go and dance.'

They headed straight for the dance floor and moved

energetically to the sound of the music. They danced to several songs before Helen suggested they get a drink, as she was feeling thirsty.

Tammy was at the bar ordering some shots.

'Now then.' She nodded. 'How did you do in your results?'

Helen told her and Tammy smirked.

'I got a C for my assignment but then again I'm not teacher's pet.'

Helen narrowed her eyes.

'That is not fair, Tammy, I worked hard on my assignment,' she said angrily but deep down wondering if Marcus had been biased.

Picking up her shot glasses from the bar, Tammy winked at Helen.

'I am sure you already know this but Mr Edwards and the others are over the other side of the bar.' She nodded in the direction of the other side of the room.

Helen looked over and saw Marcus, Debbie and Bill laughing. Debbie and Bill were drinking wine and it looked like Marcus was drinking Coke. As if conscious that she was there, Marcus looked over and saw Helen. She quickly looked away and ordered her drinks from the barmaid that noticed her. She took them over to Michelle who was stood on the edge of the dance floor, talking to Tom and Laura.

'Hey look, there's Bill, Debbie and Marcus.' Tom pointed. 'Let's go and say hello.'

Helen felt her stomach churn as they all walked over, subconsciously telling herself to act naturally.

'Hey you three, fancy seeing you folks in a place like this.' Tom laughed cheekily.

Bill chuckled deeply and Marcus laughed. Debbie, on the other hand, did not look impressed.

'Excuse me, young man. I am not *that* old,' she scolded in an offended tone. 'Only joking, Miss.'

Tom put his hands in the air.

'Maybe we can have a dance in a bit.' He winked and Debbie smiled.

Helen rolled her eyes, thinking what a flirt she was. She looked towards Marcus and he smiled at her and she smiled back. He looked very handsome tonight in a pair of black jeans and a black shirt unfastened at the top. She wished that she could go over and kiss him; she hated the secrecy. She had missed him and hadn't seen him since Tuesday. It seemed like an eternity. Michelle put her hand on her elbow.

'Shall we go and dance?' she said.

Helen nodded and bid farewell to the tutors stood in front of her. Debbie watched as she walked away. She regarded Marcus as he watched her walk away, his eyes following her to the dance floor. She saw Helen turn and smile at him and she saw his eyes shine as she did.

'They are a nice bunch of kids,' Bill was saying as Marcus drained his glass.

'Another drink?' he asked and went to the bar.

Debbie moved closer to Bill.

'For fuck's sake, Bill, you must see that there is something going on between those two,' she hissed.

Bill looked at her with a confused expression.

'What two?' he asked.

'Oh my God, Bill, how can you not see it?' Debbie said, amazed.

'See what?' he asked, still unsure of what she was implying.

'Marcus and Helen,' Debbie said in a matter of fact way. 'I think they are having an affair.'

Bill spat out his last mouthful of wine and coughed.

'Please tell me that that is a sick joke,' he said in disbelief.

'No I'm deadly serious,' she said. 'I can't believe that you haven't seen the signs.'

Bill shook his head.

'What bloody signs?' he felt angry.

Although he had not known Marcus long, they had become good friends and he did not like these accusations.

'The way they look at each other for a start,' she said.

'Debbie, he is old enough to be her bloody father,' said Bill.

'Is everything alright?' Marcus asked as he handed them their drinks, conscious of the atmosphere between them.

'Ask her,' Bill said angrily. 'Go on Debbie, why don't you say what you have to say.'

Debbie slammed her drink onto a nearby table and stormed off to the toilets, tears stinging her eyes.

'What's up with her?' Marcus asked Bill curiously.

Bill just shook his head.

'Don't worry about it, mate, she's confused.'

Taking another sip of wine, he changed the subject to a fishing trip he had planned for the following weekend.

'You like Marcus, don't you?' Michelle grinned as they reapplied their lipstick in the ladies toilets later that evening.

Helen could feel her face flush.

'I think he's a good teacher, don't you?' she said desperately trying not to look guilty.

Michelle poked her on the arm.

'You know what I mean Helen.' She smiled. 'I mean you *like* like him, don't you?'

Helen stayed facing the mirror, reapplying the same coat of lipstick over and over in an attempt not to make eye contact.

'Michelle, he could be our dad; he must be twice our age,' she said.

'That doesn't matter, and you still haven't answered my question,' she said poking her again.

Helen shook her head.

'That's because it's a stupid question.'

Michelle grinned and put her arm around her friend.

'If he asked you out, though, would you say yes?'

Helen looked at her friend, shook her head and turned around as the cubicle door behind then opened. Debbie Saunders came out, clearly having been crying.

'Of course she wouldn't say yes. Marcus would lose the career.' She blew her nose and looked at Helen through narrowed eyes. 'Wouldn't you Helen?'

Without waiting for an answer, she stormed out slamming the door behind her. Michelle looked at the closed door, then at Helen, and then burst out laughing.

'I guess she has a soft spot for him herself.' She laughed but Helen just smiled nervously.

First Tammy, then Michelle, now Debbie… people were starting to suspect and it was not good.

She looked at her watch and it was gone midnight.

'I suppose we should be heading off soon as I am working tomorrow,' she said and Michelle nodded.

As they walked back through the bar, they saw Debbie back with Bill and Marcus, now laughing. They chose not to go over and speak after Debbie's outburst. Tammy and JoJo were sharing a kiss on the dance floor and they could not see Tom and Laura so they left without saying goodbye to anybody.

Michelle was quite tipsy in the taxi and was asking the driver all sorts of random questions much to Helen's amusement. She told the poor man three times how much she loved Adam. Helen apologised for her friend's behaviour after she had been dropped off but the driver laughed and reassured her that he had seen far worse over the years.

Helen was feeling quite anxious and had a knot in her stomach. She worried that her relationship to Marcus was going to be exposed if they weren't careful. They needed to come up with another plan; she could *not* risk him losing his job. Taking her phone from her pocket, she sent him a text.

I'm on a late tomorrow, will you be around if I come to see you afterwards… we need to talk xxxxx.

She was asleep when she received the reply.

Of course I'll be around, is everything OK? I love you xxxxx.

Marcus did not sleep at all, his grinding worry becoming more overpowering than the promise of sleep. He breathed a sigh of relief when at just gone eight he received a reply.

I love you too xxxxx.

Chapter Twenty-Five

Helen smiled as she went downstairs to find George sat reading the paper, his glasses perched on the end of his nose. Katherine was in her dressing gown, humming happily as she fried bacon and eggs.

'Morning, love! Just in time for breakfast,' she said as Helen walked into the kitchen.

Helen inhaled the aroma and her mouth watered.

'You cannot beat a cooked breakfast after a night out drinking,' George said, reading her thoughts.

'Am I right in thinking you are at work today?' Katherine asked putting a breakfast in front of her.

Helen thanked her and told her she was doing the late shift.

'That's a shame,' George said. 'I was going to treat us all to a Chinese take-away. What about tomorrow instead?'

Helen frowned and shook her head.

'Another late, I'm afraid,' she said. 'You all have one, it's OK. I don't finish until ten, it's too late to wait'.

Katherine buttered a piece of toast.

'The life of a nurse eh?' she said. 'All these different shifts but it's what you always wanted to do and I'm proud of you.'

Helen smiled.

'Ahh thanks, Mum,' she said.

Helen spent the morning sat in her dressing gown, watching

Saturday morning television with George. She then went shopping to Asda with Katherine whilst George caught up on some reading for Tuesday's book club.

'He is always the last one to read the books.' Katherine laughed. 'In fact, half the time I think he just pretends to have read them and scan reads some of the pages.'

'He is a lovely man,' Helen said.

Katherine smiled, she had a contended look on her face.

'When your dad died, I never thought I would find love again and, although nobody will ever replace your dad, George has filled a void in my life.'

She smiled and Helen smiled too.

They walked around the store, planning meals for the week and buying food appropriately.

'So, how is Marcus?' Katherine asked and Helen sighed.

She explained how she was worried that people were becoming suspicious.

'Why don't you just cool things until you have qualified then, it is only nine months,' Katherine suggested.

Helen looked down at the floor.

'Mum, you don't understand. Not seeing Marcus for a few days kills me, to not see him for nine months would eat me up inside,' she said.

Katherine looked at her daughter.

'You really do love him, don't you?' she said and Helen smiled.

'Like you could never imagine,' she replied.

By the time they had unpacked the shopping, it was time for Helen to go to work. She had received a text from Michelle thanking her for a brilliant night and one from Marcus saying he could not wait to see her later.

The department was bustling when she arrived, far from the relaxed atmosphere of her previous shift. Sister Julie gave a brief handover before rushing off to deal with an emergency as an

267

ambulance arrived at the back door. Alan had called in sick with a chest infection and Nikki was not on duty so Helen was not sure whom she should work with. She looked around at who was on duty and spotted Tracy who she had worked with once before when she first started her placement.

'Is it alright if I tag along with you today? Alan's phoned in poorly,' she said and Tracy agreed stating that they would be in triage.

They walked over to see Pauline in there with a patient, so stood back to wait whilst she finished. Helen turned around to see Tammy walking through the corridor with Paul, pushing an empty trolley back from taking a patient to a ward. She had not realised Tammy was working today and thought to herself that she looked worse for wear. Tammy saw her and walked over.

'You missed all the action last night, after you had gone' she said with a glint in her eye. 'All the tutors were having a right old slanging match over something. Well, Debbie was and she ended up storming off, crying.'

Helen swallowed hard. She felt anxious, wondering what the argument had been over and whether or not it had been anything to do with her.

'I wonder what that was about?' she said, not really knowing what else to say.

'Yes, I wonder!' Tammy winked and walked off laughing.

Paul looked at Helen and Tracy, and shook his head.

'Strange character, isn't she?' he said before heading over to speak to James.

It was a busy shift that went quick and Helen was struggling to concentrate, worried that suspicions were rising. Tammy was making comments all the time now. Was she just being paranoid? She was anxious to see Marcus to find out what had happened in Walkabout the previous night.

Marcus was waiting with a mug of coffee when Helen arrived. He relaxed slightly when she kissed him and held him tightly before sitting down.

'Oh Marcus what are we going to do?' she said picking up her drink.

He could see that her hands were shaking.

'What is it Helen, what's the matter?' he asked.

When she asked what had happened between the three of her tutors he had to tell her the truth.

'Apparently, Debbie told Bill that she thought we were having an affair,' Marcus told her.

Helen put her cup on the table and put her head in her hands.

'How the Hell does she know? We have been so careful,' she said, her voice quivering nervously.

Marcus took her hands from her face and held them in his own.

'I don't know, Bill said it was something about the way we looked at each other. He stuck up for me and told her to stop being such an idiot. Anyway, she ended up leaving in tears. I felt a bit guilty really,' he said.

Tears sprung to Helen's eyes.

'What if she says something to your boss, Marcus?' she said and he put his arms around her.

'Helen, please don't get upset. Bill is on my side and he will stick by me, he hasn't even questioned me. He just told her to shut up because he does not suspect a thing. Please don't worry.'

He sat back on the sofa and pulled her towards him. Helen snuggled into his arms as he wrapped them around her. She felt so secure and content, and she hoped that this would all blow over.

'Do you want to stay tonight?' Marcus asked.

'I would love to but Beth is coming around in the morning. We are going for a walk with Mum around Whisby,' she said. 'I've got three night shifts next week, Wednesday, Thursday and Friday, but I could maybe stay on Saturday if you have no plans.'

Marcus smiled at her.

'None at all, we will have to think about something nice to do. We could celebrate another placement finished, perhaps.'

Helen shook her head.

'I know, I can't believe it,' she said. 'Before I know it, I'll have qualified'.

She sat forward and picked up her mug, drinking the rest of her coffee.

'I had better get going. I feel shattered.' She leant forward and gave Marcus a kiss. 'I might pop and see you after work tomorrow for a quick coffee.'

Marcus grinned cheekily.

'We could squeeze in a quick something else too,' he said with a wink.

Helen smiled and, standing up, she seductively rubbed her hand through his hair.

'Well, that depends on if you're a good boy,' she whispered.

She put on her coat, took her car keys from her bag and kissed Marcus goodbye, looking outside to make sure the coast was clear she walked out towards her car.

'Helen,' Marcus called after her and she turned around.

'I love you so much,' he said, walking towards her.

'I love you too,' she said as he leant forward and kissed her gently.

'Thank you for making me so happy,' he said

'Thank you,' she said and watched him as he turned and went back inside.

'Got to go, my phone's ringing,' he shouted and waved as he shut the door.

Helen, still fumbling trying to unlock the car door and conscious of her mobile ringing, wondered who would be ringing her at this time of night. Sitting in the car and finding her phone, she was surprised to see Beth's name.

'Beth, what is it? Why are you ringing this late?' she answered in a worried tone.

Her heart started pounding as she saw Marcus at the window on the phone, a sickened look on his face as he looked at Helen.

'Are you on Facebook?' Beth asked.

'What? No I've been at work, what are you on about Beth?' Helen was confused.

'Helen, that Tammy bitch has just posted a picture of you and your tutor snogging with a comment saying 'Naughty, naughty, is this allowed?" Helen felt bile rising in the back of her throat as she looked at Marcus.

He had his hand against his forehead, looking across to the other side of the road. Helen followed his gaze and saw Tammy and JoJo sat in a car. When they saw her look at them, they both waved, laughed and drove off. Helen felt faint.

'Helen, are you listening?' she became aware that Beth was obviously talking to her.

'Fucking bitch! The evil bitch!' she screamed, bursting into tears.

She was sobbing so hard that she was struggling to catch her breath.

'Yes but Helen, what the hell were you thinking? I bloody knew it, he is a bloody old man.' Beth was shouting down the phone.

'He is not old, Beth, and I love him. That's all that matters, I love him,' Helen sobbed.

'He is your bloody teacher! There are rules about that sort of thing, Helen, do you realise that? Now it is plastered all over Facebook for all the world to see!' Beth ranted. 'The chances are he will be out of a job on Monday and it serves him right!'

Helen was still crying.

'Please, Beth, stop being so horrible! We love each other, we couldn't help this,' she said.

'How many other students has he had flings with? You are probably one of a long line,' Beth said bitterly.

'Stop it! You don't even know him!' Helen said angrily.

She could not believe this was happening. She looked towards the house. Marcus was still on the phone looking shocked; she wondered who he was talking to.

'I will speak to you in the morning,' Beth said and put down the phone.

Helen sat in her car looking at Marcus, wondering if she should go back to the house. She decided against it and sent him a text instead.

I cannot believe that bitch!! I'm so sorry ☹ I don't know what to say other than I love you and I'm sorry xxxxx

Marcus replied after a while. He had been on the phone to Bill. He had arranged to visit Marcus the following evening to discuss things.

I'm sorry, I had to agree to him coming. I couldn't exactly tell him you were coming around ☹ not sure what will happen now but I will probably get either suspended or sacked. Never forget, though, that I love you and this was not your fault xxx.

Helen cried as she read the text. She never wanted any of this to happen. She hated Tammy for this. How would she face her now? More to the point, how would she face everyone at university?

I understand, I will hopefully see you next week xxx.

She looked at the Facebook post when she got home. Tammy had tagged both Helen and Marcus into it. Helen removed her own tag to remove it from her wall but it had already been viewed and commented on by the majority of people from university. The comments ranged from 'Gross' to 'Cradle-snatcher' to 'What a cute couple!'. Helen's stomach lurched when she saw a comment from David.

'Now it makes sense!!!'

She did not sleep that night.

Chapter Twenty-Six

Bill arrived at Marcus' house, dropped off by his wife Marjorie. He was armed with a bottle of Napoleon brandy, suspecting that something stronger than Marcus' usual glass of Coke might be in order. As Marcus opened the door, Bill was not surprised to see his friend unshaven with dark rings around his eyes.

'Where are your glasses?' he asked.

Marcus pointed to the cupboard in the kitchen.

'Have you eaten yet?'

Marcus shook his head.

'I didn't think you would have. I bought you this.' Bill pulled a chicken and Bacon sandwich out of his bag. 'Now, I know you may not feel like it but I want you to eat this while I tell you a story.'

Bill opened the cardboard packaging and pushed it towards Marcus as they sat down in his living room. Marcus reluctantly took a bite of the sandwich as Bill poured them both a generous brandy.

'Marjorie is picking me up at half ten,' he said.

Marcus took a surprisingly large sip of his Brandy, closing his eyes as the warm fluid trickled down his throat.

'So, what is this story you have to tell me?' Marcus eventually said in a sad voice.

Bill coughed. He had never shared this story before but thought it was important for Marcus to hear.

'I've been married to Marjorie for thirty years now but ten years ago she left me because I had an affair,' Bill said.

Marcus turned and looked at him in surprise.

'Really?' he said.

'Yes, it was stupid really. I was forty at the time and based in Derby. It was the same sort of thing, a student who caught my eye; twenty years old, brunette and gorgeous. She fancied me and I was flattered. We started having an affair, we got found out and I was suspended with no pay. Marjorie left me and, at first, it was perfect.' Bill put his hand on Marcus's arm. 'One day, she said to me "Just think, when I am your age, you'll be like a granddad!" And it was then that it dawned on me that the age gap was just too much.'

Marcus put his head back and rested his hand against his forehead. Bill was surprised to see a tear spill onto his cheek. He wiped it away, embarrassed, and swallowed hard, desperately trying not to let any more tears escape.

'Come on mate, don't get upset,' Bill said, patting his friend on his shoulder. 'Can I give you some advice? Friend to friend.'

Marcus nodded his head but didn't speak, his hand covering his tear filled eyes.

'Block contact with her; block her number and walk away. I know it will be hard but it will be the best thing in the long run because tomorrow, when you walk into work, you'll be clearing your desk,' Bill said gently.

More tears spilled onto his cheek.

'But I love her, mate,' he said, his voice cracking. 'I have never been this happy with anyone before.'

Bill felt sorry for Marcus. He remembered how he had felt when he had been in the same situation.

'I know, mate, but trust me it's for the best.'

Marcus poured himself another glass of brandy and refilled Bill's glass. He drank it in one go, then went over to the computer and turned it on. Logging onto Facebook, he scrolled down his friends list until he found Helen's name. He cringed as he saw the post on his wall of them together. Seeing the word 'Cradle-Snatcher' in the comments only helped Bill make more sense. He paused as the system asked if he was sure he wanted to block Helen. Bill leant over him and clicked the mouse to say yes.

His hands shook as he picked up his phone.

'I just have to send her one more text,' he said to Bill.

I'm sorry Helen, please don't ever forget how much I love you xxxxxxx.

He scrolled through his contacts and finally blocked her number.

On Monday morning, Marcus was called into the office as soon as he arrived. As he had been such a good tutor in the short time that he had been with them, the university had decided against suspending him. Instead, they had opted to transfer him to their sister university in Boston. They requested that he empty his desk and leave immediately. His replacement, Alison Jones, was coming from Boston. She was kind enough to suggest a house-swap to avoid them both having to deal with the daily commute. After a telephone conversation with her, he agreed. Returning home, he packed up his clothes, personal possessions and food from his cupboards.

He wept as he saw the napkins that he used when he had made the meal for Helen that first time. He thought about all the things they had done together and thought that his heart was going to break. How could he live his life without her? He couldn't ring her, he couldn't see her; he couldn't even say goodbye. He wanted nothing more than to drive to her house and sweep her up into his arms. However, he had been warned that any contact would ultimately result in dismissal. Instead, he loaded his car, locked the door and, without looking back, he drove away. Paul Weller's 'You do Something to Me' kicked in on the stereo as soon as his car turned on and tears ran warm, wet lines down his cheeks.

'Oh Helen, I'm sorry,' he breathed.

Helen turned her car into Greetwell Close and pulled up outside Marcus's house. Michelle sat in the passenger seat.

'Shall I wait in the car?' she said gently as Helen turned off the engine.

Michelle was worried about her best friend. She had not eaten for two days. She had not expressed any anger that Helen had not confided in her about her affair. She had not criticised about the age gap, she had not condemned anything; she had simply listened to Helen and been a shoulder for her to cry on. It had been her idea to come and try and talk to Marcus after Helen had desperately tried to contact him. Finding out today that he had been transferred, she knew her friend felt responsible.

Michelle watched from the car as Helen walked towards the house and knocked on the door. She knocked several times before looking through the window. Her stomach knotted as she saw her friend drop to her knees and begin crying as innocently as a small child.

She took off her seatbelt and opened the car door. Without closing it, she ran over to Helen. She looked through the window herself: nobody was home.

'What's up, sweetheart?' she said, crouching down next to her and putting an arm around her.

Helen took a few moments to speak, gulping on her sobs. Both her eyes and her nose were running like faucets. Michelle pulled a tissue from up her sleeve and used it to clean her friend up.

'Tell me, what's wrong?' Michelle asked, standing up again to look through the window.

'It's all gone,' Helen said. 'The pictures, his computer, the CD's.'

She began to cry once more.

'He's gone, Michelle, he's gone! He was my soul mate, the first time I have ever truly loved anyone and now I've lost him.' She blew her nose. 'How can I carry on with my life without him in it?'

Michelle took her friend in her arms and Helen sobbed. She felt so heart-broken that she sensed her whole world was falling apart around her. What was she going to do now?

Helen drove home in silence, unable to even utter a goodbye to her friend as she dropped her off home. Michelle had texted Katherine, warning her of what had happened. Katherine held her arms out to her daughter as she walked through the front door. Helen clung to her mother, barely able to stand or breathe as she sobbed. Katherine too felt tears trickle down her face. She did not know what to say. She stroked her hair and wiped the tears from her face.

'I'm sure it'll be OK, love. If you and Marcus are soul mates, then somehow, you'll find a way to be together.'

Helen wiped the tears from her face.

'I hope so, Mum. I hope so.'